MODERN COOKERY

FOR TEACHING AND THE TRADE

VOLUME II

FIFTH EDITION

THANGAM E. PHILIP

(M.S., F.C.F.A., M.H.C.I., M.R.S.H.)
Principal Emeritus
Institute of Hotel Management,
Catering Technology and Applied Nutrition
Bombay

Orient BlackSwan

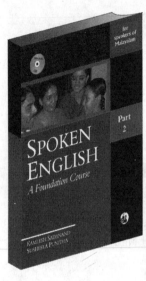
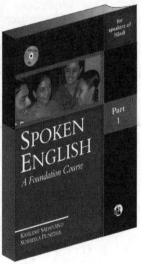

CONTENTS

Advanced Cookery

Hors d'œuvres	3
Potages	18
Oeufs	56
Poisson	75
Entrées and Relevés	98
Volailles	130
Fondues	168
Gibier	171
Légumes et Pâtés Alimentaires	185
Entremets	215
Savouries (Bonnes Bouches)	252

Recipes From Far And Near

France	270
Germany	277
Spain	282
Italy	291
Russia	298
Netherlands	309
Scandinavia	311
Portugal	319
United States of America	322
Greece	329
Turkey	337
China	343
Japan	365
Burma	366
Sri Lanka	369

Indonesia   374
India   376
Chettinad   397
Thailand   421
Romania   422
Nepal   423

Baking And Confectionery

Small Cakes   430
Icing And Fillings   442
Large Cakes   448
Fruit Cakes   463
American Coffee Cakes   477
Pastries   480
Candy   540

Bread Making   553

Sandwiches And Light Savouries   587

Pickles, Preserves, Chutneys And Beverages   623

Sauces   719

Micellaneous   723

Appendix   730

Glossary of Some European Terms in the Book   732

Index   735

FOREWORD TO THE FIRST EDITION

Minister for Food & Agriculture
Govt. of India

A desirable development in India, in recent years, has been the widespread application of science and technology to problems in the fields of food and nutrition. Better methods of processing and cooking can help to increase the effective availability of our food resources. A new kind of education in catering technology and applied nutrition has assumed importance in this context. Four full-fledged institutes of Catering Technology and Applied Nutrition have already been opened in the country. This is a welcome development.

Miss Thangam Philip, Principal of the Institute of Catering Technology and Applied Nutrition, Bombay, has written an exclusive book on cookery. It attempts to introduce new ideas in cookery and bakery and to change the pattern of our dietary. Miss Philip deals with scientific methods of cooking, planning of meals and improvement of the sense of taste and flavour.

I hope that this book will reach a wide and interested public. There is bound to be scope for suitable editions in various Indian languages also.

New Delhi   C. SUBRAMANIAN
5 May 1965

INTRODUCTION

In May 1965, the first edition of the book 'Modern Cookery for Teaching and the Trade' was published. The first volume was reprinted in 1974.

The two volumes have now been revised to update the theory and incorporate many more recipes (traditional and innovative) that the author has standardized to make the book a comprehensive reference book for the hospitality industry and a valuable text book for students training for the hotel and catering industry.

In the ensuing eleven years, the author has been continuously engaged in Food Education and Food Research and the revised volumes are the fruits of her efforts in these fields.

The popularity of the first edition, I am sure will ensure the success of the revised editions.

I wish the author every success in her revised edition of 'Modern Cookery for Teaching and the Trade', and hope she will continue with her work and publish further books in the field of Food.

C. BELFIELD-SMITH
Technical Expert,
Consultant to the United Nations

PREFACE

Modern Cookery for Teaching and the Trade, originally published in 1965, has been one of the most sought after and encyclopaedic books on Cookery published in India. An authentic selection of recipes from all parts of India and an easy-to-follow format have made the book an invaluable tool.

The book was published to meet the need for a standard book on Cooking and Baking for the rapidly expanding Institutes of Hotel Management and Catering Technology, the Food Craft Institutes and Institutes teaching Home Science. My long experience in food education, my love of cookery and my deep appreciation of foods, motivated me to accept this challenge.

The first print of this book soon sold out. The revised edition updated the food science section to incorporate new research findings and also included a comprehensive chapter on Food Commodities, their scientific or botanical names and their vernacular names.

A wide range of recipes—Indian, Western, Basic, Intermediate, Advanced and International as well as Bakery and Confectionery—have been covered. An intimate knowledge of the foods of different parts of India and abroad obtained by extensive travel and stay in the various regions of India and outside is the basis of selection. All the recipes in the book are the product of years of meticulous research and rigorous recipe-testing. The recipes are laid out in easy-to-follow steps and use easily obtainable ingredients. A special feature of presentation is that the ingredients as well as the methods of cooking have been itemized instead of being given in the usual narrative form. Fortification of popular recipes by addition of soya bean flour, multi-purpose foods, peanut flour, peanut butter, Balahar etc. is the theme of the chapter on ancillary foods. Such inputs not only improve the nutritive value of the food, but also increase palatability and sometimes keeping quality. This section has been very carefully selected after much experimental work to meet the needs of the changing times and as a means of providing low-cost, balanced meals.

In this fifth revised edition, the section on Indian Cuisine has been extended to cover several standardized traditional recipes from the rich heritage of our cuisine and several new, innovative recipes.

The increasing popularity of Chettinad food all over the country has prompted me to include a large, comprehensive section of Chettinad recipes in Volume II. Also included for this fifth edition is a section on Chocolate-making. This book, although primarily meant for students and the trade, will appeal to homemakers who wish to improve their repertoire and introduce variety into the daily food of the family. The section on equivalent weights and measures in Volume I allows the user to easily convert metric units like grams and kilograms into spoons and cups. For the sake of convenience, conversions from grams and kilograms to ounces and pounds have also been included.

The accelerated pace of globalization, the increase in tourism in our country and worldwide has brought cultures and nations closer, promoting interest in the cuisines of the different countries of the world. The two revised volumes provide a comprehensive selection of not only the foods from the different regions of India but also standardized recipes of gourmets' favourites found on the menus of great restaurants all around the world and will be an invaluable asset to all hotels interested in serving authentic and high class cuisine. The art of cuisine is, after all, an artistic science if not a scientific art and one in which the homemaker, the hotelier, the caterer and the student can all utilize their creative talents. It is hoped that this comprehensive book on cookery will be a stimulus for promoting this scientific art.

My sincere thanks are once again due to the staff of the Institute of Hotel Management, Catering Technology and Applied Nutrition, Bombay, for their unstinted assistance in the compilation and editing of the earlier editions of this book and for their generosity in making themselves available whenever I have needed their help for this revised edition.

THANGAM E. PHILIP

ADVANCED COOKERY

HORS D'ŒUVRES

1. Allumettes aux Anchois aux Farces de Poisson
2. Artichauts à la Grecque
3. Barquettes
4. Canapés
5. Canapés au Caviar
6. Canapés aux Anchois
7. Canapés aux Crevettes
8. Canapés Danoise
9. Canapés Langue Écarlate
10. Canapés Homard
11. Céleri Bonne Femme
12. Céleri Rave
13. Choux Fleurs
14. Frivolités
15. Harengs Dieppoise
16. Haricots Verts
17. Huîtres
18. Melon Cantaloupe
19. Melon Cocktail
20. Oeufs Farcis et Garnis
21. Olives Farcies
22. Poireaux à la Grecque
23. Poitrines d'Oies Fumées
24. Saumon Fumé
25. Tartelettes de Thon
26. Thon à l'Huile
27. Thon à la Marinette
28. Tomates à la Monégasque
29. Tomates au Naturel
30. Tomates en Quartiers
31. Rôtie à la Lucille
32. Carolines Diverse
33. Cervelle à la Robert
34. Concombres à la Danoise
35. Concombres Farcis
36. Duchesses Nantua
37. Saucisson
38. Pamplemousse
39. Coquetel de Pamplemousse
40. Coquetel de Fruits
41. Coquetel d'Orange
42. Coquetel Florida
43. Compote de Fruits
44. Variantes
45. Les Huîtres
46. Caviar
47. Saumon Fumé
48. Foie gras
49. Pâté de Foie
50. Coquetel de Melon
51. Melon Frappé
52. Jus de Tomate
53. Coquetel de Crabe
54. Crabe en Coquille
55. Sardines à l'Huile
56. Thon
57. Oeufs Mayonnaise
58. Mayonnaise de Crabe; Mayonnaise de Homard; Mayonnaise de crevettes
59. Salade de Pommes de Terre
60. Céleri Bonne Femme (A) Céleri Bonne Femme (B)
61. Salade Russe
62. Salade de Poisson
63. Salade de Viande
64. Salade de Betterave
65. Concombres
66. Salade de Concombres
67. Tomate
68. Salade de Tomate
69. Salade de Tomate et Concombres
70. Celery
71. Salade de Haricots Verts
72. Maïs
73. Radish (Red)
74. Oeufs Farcis
75. Harengs Dieppoise
76. Oeufs Diable (A) Oeufs Diable (B)
77. Poires au Fromage Blanc

I. ALLUMETTES aux ANCHOIS aux FARCES DE POISSON

Rectangles of puff paste masked with fish puree, anchovy, etc. eg. Puff Paste Canapé.

2. ARTICHAUTS à la GRECQUE

Small tender artichokes. Cut the leaves short, parboil for 10 minutes and drain. Finish cooking in marinade of white wine, water, oil, salt, lemon juice, fennel, coriander seeds, peppercorns, thyme, bay leaf. Serve very cold in an hors d'œuvre dish with a little of the cooking liquor.

3. BARQUETTES

Small croustade boats shaped and garnished in an imaginative way, with chicken, vegetables, oysters, fish mayonnaise, etc.

4. CANAPÉS

Toast or pastry cut into various shapes: round, square, rectangular, oval, crescent, star etc.

5. CANAPÉS au CAVIAR

Decorated with butter, centre garnished with fresh caviar.

6. CANAPÉS aux ANCHOIS

Masked and decorated with anchovy butter and a fillet of anchovy.

7. CANAPÉS aux CREVETTES

Masked and decorated with pink shrimp butter, garnished with shrimp tails and a caper in the centre.

8. CANAPÉS DANOISE

Brown bread masked with horseradish butter, garnished with slices of smoked salmon, herring fillets and caviar.

9. CANAPÉS LANGUE ÉCARLATE

Masked with mustard butter, garnished with a slice of star-shaped tongue and a spot of mustard butter in the centre.

10. CANAPÉS HOMARD

Masked with lobster butter, decorated with chopped hard-boiled eggs covered with mayonnaise and a slice of lobster in the middle.

11. CÉLERI BONNE FEMME

Celery, apples and potatoes or celery and apples minced and seasoned with cream mustard sauce.

12. CÉLERI RAVE

Julienne of celeriac seasoned with mustard and cream of vinaigrette with mustard.

13. CHOUX FLEURS

Blanched cauliflower marinaded with oil and vinegar, coated with mustard cream sauce.

14. FRIVOLITÉS

Hors d'œuvres composed of moulded cream, barquettes, tartlets, etc.

15. HARENGS DIEPPOISE

Fresh herrings marinaded in white wine, vinegar, roundels of carrots and onions, thyme, bay leaves, parsley stalks, minced shallots and cooked for 10 minutes. The herrings are allowed to cool in the marinade.

16. HARICOTS VERTS

Parboiled French beans, seasoned while hot with oil and vinegar; chervil and chives added when serving.

17. HUÎTRES

Oysters served in crushed ice with brown bread and butter, lemon quarters or shallot sauce.

18. MELON CANTALOUPE

Served on crushed ice.

19. MELON COCKTAIL

Cantaloup cut into large cubes and sprinkled with sugar. Maraschino, kirsch, cognac or white port is added. Served in glasses, very cold.

20. OEUFS FARCIS et GARNIS

Hard-boiled eggs, garnished to taste.

21. OLIVES FARCIES

Large Spanish olives, stoned and garnished with anchovy butter, salmon, sardines, etc.

22. POIREAUX à la GRECQUE

Leeks cut in short sections, partly cooked in salt water, marinaded with oil and vinegar, scooped and stuffed to taste.

23. POITRINES d'OIES FUMÉES

Smoked goose fillets cut into thin slices.

24. SAUMON FUMÉ

Smoked salmon cut into triangular thin slices and rolled into cones.

25. TARTELETTES de THON

Small croustades garnished with tuna fish puree mixed with mayonnaise sauce. A round of tuna fish is placed on top, surrounded by hard-boiled eggs and chopped parsley.

26. THON à l'HUILE

Tuna in oil.

27. THON à la MARINETTE

Slices of tuna fish, alternated with slices of tomatoes and spring onions, with a border of potatoes, seasoned with oil, vinegar, salt and pepper.

28. TOMATES à la MONÉGASQUE

Small tomatoes, with the tops cut off and flesh scooped out. The inside is stuffed with a mixture of tuna, hard-boiled eggs, onions, parsley and chervil, made to cohere with mayonnaise sauce. Garnished with a sprig of parsley.

29. TOMATES au NATUREL

Small tomatoes, peeled, pressed in a piece of linen and seasoned with oil and vinegar. Garnished with a sprig of parsley on top.

30. TOMATES en QUARTIERS

Tomatoes, peeled and stuffed with fish puree or macedoine of vegetables, made to cohere with mayonnaise and aspic. Placed on ice for a while and cut into regular quarters.

31. ROTIE à la LUCILLE

Oval-shaped toast covered with mustard butter and bordered with a line of finely chopped and very red tongue along the edges. Garnish the middle of each toast with chopped white chicken meat and place a slice of stuffed olive in the centre.

32. CAROLINES DIVERSE

Prepare éclairs with choux paste without sugar. Cool and stuff with pieces of tongue, fowl, game, foie gras etc. Coat thinly with chaud-froid sauce. When sauce has cooled, glaze with a little cold melted jelly using a brush.

33. CERVELLE à la ROBERT

Clean brains of sheep or lamb and cook well in court bouillon. Cool. Cut into thin even slices and place on an hor d'œuvre dish. Rub the remaining brain through a tammy to make a puree. Mix puree with a mustard and cream sauce. Make a fine julienne of celery using only the white part of the celery and add to the puree. Serve with the brain slices.

34. CONCOMBRES à la DANOISE

Cut cucumber in the shape of small cassolettes or barquettes. Blanch and marinate in oil and vinegar. Stuff with a mixture of puree of salmon, mixed with fillets of herring and chopped hard-boiled eggs in equal quantities. Garnish with a little grated horseradish.

35. CONCOMBRES FARCIS

Prepare cucumber as above and stuff with minced meat mixed with mayonnaise or a macedoine of vegetables.

36. DUCHESSES NANTUA

Prepare small éclairs with choux paste without sugar, cool and stuff with crayfish or prawn chopped and mixed with mayonnaise. Coat with cold melted jelly to cover them with a transparent film.

37. SAUCISSON

Salami and a variety of cooked sausages served in thin slices, individually or in an assortment.

38. PAMPLEMOUSSE

Halve grapefruit. Allow half a grapefruit per portion. Loosen segments with a grapefruit knife. Sprinkle a little castor sugar over to neutralize strong acidity: chill. Serve in a coupe with a glace or maraschino cherry in the centre. Serve castor sugar separately.

39. COQUETEL de PAMPLEMOUSSE

Allow half a grapefruit per portion. Peel with a sharp knife to remove all white and yellow skin. Cut into segments and remove all the pips. Arrange segments and juice in a cocktail glass or grapefruit coupe and chill. Garnish with a cherry.

40. COQUETEL de FRUITS

Allow half an orange and half a grapefruit per portion. Prepare segments as for grapefruit cocktail and arrange in a coupe. Chill and serve garnished with a cherry.

41. COQUETEL d'ORANGE

As for grapefruit cocktail but using oranges instead of grapefruit.

42. COQUETEL FLORIDA

Mixture of grapefruit, orange and pineapple segments.

43. COMPOTE de FRUITS

Ingredients	Quantity
Apples	115 gm
Pineapple	115 gm
Grapes (seedless)	115 gm
Cherries (tinned)	115 gm
Lime	½
Sugar	115 gm
Water	300 ml

Method

1. Peel and dice apples and pineapple. 2. Make sugar syrup with water and sugar. Add lime juice. 3. Add apples, pineapple and grapes; when cool add cherries. 4. Arrange neatly in cocktail glasses and chill.

44. VARIANTES

Assortment of blanched artichoke bottoms, French beans, cauliflower, spring onions, pimentos, gherkins etc. marinaded in oil and vinegar, coriander and mustard.

45. LES HUÎTRES

The shells of oysters should be tightly shut to indicate freshness. Oysters should be served very cold. Open carefully with an oyster knife to prevent scratching. Serve in the deep half of the shell to retain the natural liquor of the oyster, placed on a bed of ice. Six oysters are generally served per portion with thin slices of brown bread, butter and lemon.

46. CAVIAR

Caviar is the prepared roe of the sturgeon usually served in its original tin or jar in a timbale of crushed ice. It is served with a glass spoon; 15 to 30 grams is the usual amount in a portion. It is served with toast, butter and lemon.

47. SAUMON FUMÉ

Trim side of salmon to remove dry outer surface. Remove bone with a pair of pliers. Cut into thin triangular slices. Roll into cones and arrange with a curled parsley leaf in the centre.

48. FOIE GRAS

This is a processed delicacy made from goose liver and should served in its original dish or pastry case. If tinned, chill, remove from tin and cut into half-inch slices. Serve on silver flat dish and garnish with chopped aspic jelly.

49. PÂTÉ de FOIE

Ingredients	Quantity
Butter	30 gm
Fat pork	60 gm
Lean pork	60 gm
Liver (Chicken, Lamb or Pig)	115 gm
Onions (chopped)	15 gm
Garlic	flake
Thyme	1 sprig
Parsley	1 sprig
Salt	pepper
Bacon fat	30 gm

Method

1. Cut liver into 2.5 cm pieces. 2. Toss quickly in butter in a frying pan

for a few seconds, along with onions, garlic and herbs. 3. Allow to cool. 4. Pass (along with the pork), twice through a mincer. 5. Season. 6. Line terrine with thin slices of bacon fat. 7. Put the mixture in. 8. Cover with bacon fat. 9. Stand in a tray half-full of water. 10. Cook in a moderate oven for 1 hour. 11. When quite cold cut into 0.75 cm slices and serve on lettuce leaves on a silver flat. 12. Serve with toast.

50. COQUETEL de MELON

Cut melons. Remove seeds. Scoop out with parisienne scoop. Sprinkle over with sugar. Add a dash of lime juice. Arrange in cocktail glasses and chill.

51. MELON FRAPPÉ

Cut marsh melon in half. Remove the pips and cut into thick slices. Cut a piece of skin from the bottom so that the slice can stand up. Serve on crushed ice. Castor sugar and ground ginger are served separately.

52. JUS de TOMATE

Ingredients	Quantity
Tomatoes	450 gm

Method

Use fresh ripe tomatoes. Wash and remove the eyes. Force through a sieve or strainer. Chill and serve in cocktail glasses.

53. COQUETEL de CRABE, HOMARD, CREVETTES

Ingredients	Quantity
Shellfish cocktail sauce	150 ml
Lettuce	½ bunch
Shellfish (prepared0	170 gm

Method

1. Wash, drain and shred lettuce finely. 2. Arrange 2.5 cm deep in cocktail glasses. 3. Add prepared shellfish as follows: (a) Cooked crab (shredded white meat only); (b) Cooked lobster (cut in 0.75 cm dice); (c) Shrimps (shell, remove intestines and wash well; boil in salted water); (d) Prawns (shell, remove intestines. Wash well and boil in salted water. Cut into two pieces if large). 4. Coat with sauce. 5. Decorate with appropriate piece of contents, e.g. prawn on the edge of the glass for prawn cocktail.

SHELLFISH COCKTAIL SAUCE

Ingredients	Quantity
Egg yolk	1
Salt	to taste
Mustard, Pepper	a pinch each
Vinegar	1 dsp
Olive oil	130 ml
Tomato juice	60 ml

Method

1. Make a mayonnaise sauce with egg yolk, seasoning, oil and vinegar. Combine with tomato juice.

54. CRABE en COQUILLE

Allow 225 to 340 gm of unprepared crab per portion. Make sure that the crabs are fresh. Buy live ones wherever possible. Boil in salted water to which a little vinegar and a few peppercorns have been added for 15 minutes. Allow to cool in its own liquor.

Method

1. Remove large claws and sever at the joints. 2. Remove the flexible pincer from the claw. 3. Crack carefully and remove all flesh. 4. Remove flesh from two remaining joints with back of spoon. 5. Carefully remove the soft undershell. 6. Discard the gills and the sac behind the eye. 7. Scrape out all the insides of the shell and pass through a sieve. 8. Season with salt, pepper, Worcester sauce and a little mayonnaise sauce. Thicken with a few fresh breadcrumbs. 9. Trim shell by tapping carefully along the natural line with a rolling pin. 10. Scrub and wash each shell thoroughly. Dry and apply some oil to keep it glossy. 11. Arrange brown meat on either side. Reverse process in the other half of shells. 12. Garnish with parsley, sieved hard-boiled egg yolks, chopped egg whites and sliced olives.

55. SARDINES à l'HUILE

Remove sardines carefully from tin. Arrange neatly in hors d'œuvre dish. Pour a little of the oil on top. Decorate with parsley sprigs and slices of lime.

56. THON

Remove tuna from tin. Shred or cut into cubes and arrange neatly in an hors d'œuvre dish. Garnish with finely chopped chives.

57. ŒUFS MAYONNAISE

Ingredients	Quantity
Hard-boiled eggs	4
Tomatoes	1
Green pepper	1
Mayonnaise sauce	75 ml
Lettuce	1 bunch

Method

1. Cut shelled hard-boiled eggs into halves. 2. Coat rounded side with mayonnaise. 3. Decorate with strips of tomato and green pepper. 4. Arrange on lettuce.

58. MAYONNAISE de CRABE; MAYONNAISE de HOMARD; MAYONNAISE de CREVETTES

Ingredients	Quantity
Crab, Lobster, Shrimp or Prawn	115 gm
Lettuce	1 bunch
Mayonnaise sauce	100 ml
Stuffed olives for decoration	3
Parsley	2 sprigs

Method

1. Cook shellfish as for shellfish cocktail. 2. Shred lettuce finely and arrange in hors d'œuvre dish. 3. Mix mayonnaise and shellfish. 4. Arrange over a bed of lettuce. 5. Decorate with slices of olives and sprigs of parsley.

59. SALADE de POMMES de TERRE

Ingredients	Quantity
Potatoes	225 gm
Mayonnaise sauce	75 ml
Chives	15 gm
Parsley	1 sprig
Vinaigrette	15 ml
Salt and Pepper	to taste

Method

1. Boil potatoes in their jackets till tender. 2. Dice potatoes (0.75 cm) Sprinkle with vinaigrette. 3. Mix with chopped chives. Add mayonnaise and check seasoning. 4. Dress neatly in hors d'œuvre dish. 5. Sprinkle over with chopped parsley.

60. CÉLERI BONNE FEMME (A)

Ingredients	Quantity
Celery (heart)	115 gm
Apples	2
Milk	300 ml
Refined flour	15 gm
Butter	30 gm
Mustard	a pinch
Cream	2 tbsp
Salt and Pepper	to taste

Method

1. Dice celery and boil in salted water. 2. Peel and dice apples. 3. Make white sauce with butter, flour and milk. 4. Add cream and mustard. 5. Add prepared celery and apples. Mix well.

CÉLERI BONNE FEMME (B)

Use equal quantities of julienned (or diced) celery and raw apples tossed in acidulated cream and flavoured with mustard.

61. SALADE RUSSE

Ingredients	Quantity
Potatoes	115 gm
Carrots	115 gm
Turnips	55 gm
Green peas	115 gm
French beans	55 gm
Hard-boiled egg	1
Lettuce	½ bunch
Tomato	1
Mayonnaise sauce	150 ml

Method

1. Peel potatoes, turnips and carrots and boil separately in salted water. 2. Shell peas, string and cut French beans into 0.75 cm pieces and boil till cooked. 3. Mix all the boiled vegetables with mayonnaise sauce. 4. Pile over a bed of lettuce leaves. 5. Decorate with sliced hard-boiled egg and sliced tomato.

62. SALADE de POISSON

Ingredients	Quantity
Cooked fish (free from bone and skin)	115 gm
Cucumber	60 gm

Ingredients	Quantity
Hard-boiled egg	1
Salt, Pepper	to taste
Lettuce	½ bunch
Mayonnaise sauce	75 ml
Parsley	2 sprigs

Method

1. Flake fish. 2. Dice egg and cucumber. 3. Shred lettuce. 4. Mix all ingredients together. 5. Bind with mayonnaise. 6. Arrange in hors d'œuvre dish. 7. Decorate with sprigs of parsley.

63. SALADE de VIANDE

Ingredients	Quantity
Cooked meat (boiled or braised)	225 gm
Tomatoes	60 gm
Chives or Onionss	15 gm
French beans	60 gm
Gherkins (pickled)	30 gm
Parsley	2 sprigs
Lettuce	1 bunch
Vinaigrette	
Vinegar	15 ml
Oil	3 tbsp
Mustard	1 tsp
Salt and Pepper	to taste

Method

1. String and boil beans. Cool and cut into 0.75 cm pieces. 2. Cut meat and gherkins into 0.75 cm cubes. 3. Skin tomatoes. Remove seeds and cut into cubes. Cut chives or onions. 4. Mix all ingredients, check for seasoning. 5. Dress neatly in hors d'œuvre dish. 6. Decorate with lettuce leaves and slices of tomato.

64. SALADE de BETTERAVE

Wash and cook beetroot in a steamer or in gently simmering water, till tender. Cool and peel. Cut into 0.75 cm cubes or thin slices. Serve plain with vinegar or sprinkled over with vinaigrette.

65. CONCOMBRES

Peel the cucumber if desired or cut skin in ridges. Cut into thin slices and arrange neatly in hors d'œuvre dish.

66. SALADE de CONCOMBRES

Ingredients	Quantity
Cucumber	225 gm
Parsley (chopped)	3 sprigs
Vinaigrette	150 ml

Method

1. Peel and slice cucumber. 2. Sprinkle over with vinaigrette and parsley.

67. TOMATE

Wash tomatoes, remove eyes and skin and slice thinly. Arrange in hors d'œuvre dish.

68. SALADE de TOMATE

Ingredients	Quantity
Tomatoes	225 gm
Lettuce	¼ bunch
Onions or Chives (chopped)	5 gm
Vinaigrette	30 ml
Parsley (chopped)	15 gm

Method

1. Peel tomatoes. 2. Slice thinly. 3. Arrange neatly on lettuce leaves.
4. Sprinkle with vinaigrette, onions or chives and parsley.

69. SALADE de TOMATE et CONCOMBRES

Ingredients	Quantity
Cucumbers	115 gm
Tomatoes	225 gm
Vinaigrette	30 ml
Chopped parsley	15 gm

Method

1. Skin and slice tomatoes. 2. Peel and slice cucumbers. 3. Arrange alternate slices in an hors d'oeuvre dish. 4. Sprinkle with vinaigrette and chopped parsley.

70. CELERY

Use only hearts of celery. Wash well. Arrange in a glass tumbler filled with iced water.

71. SALADE de HARICOTS VERTS

Ingredients	Quantity
French beans (cooked)	225 gm
Vinaigrette	30 ml
Salt and Pepper	to taste

Method

Combine all the ingredients and arrange in hors d'œuvre dish.

72. MAÏS

Cook corn on the cob till tender. Remove from cob and mix with a cream sauce.

73. RADISH (RED)

Wash well. Trim stem; slit from top into four or six. Leave in iced water overnight. Drain and arrange in an hors d'œuvre dish.

74. ŒUFS FARCIS

Ingredients	Quantity
Hard-boiled eggs	2
Butter	30 gm
Mayonnaise	150 ml
Salt and Pepper	to taste

Method

1. Shell and halve eggs. 2. Remove yolks and pass through a sieve. 3. Mix with mayonnaise and butter. Add seasoning. 4. Place in a piping bag with a large star nozzle (meringue). 5. Pipe back into egg whites. Arrange neatly.

N.B. For variations add a little tomato ketchup or spinach purée or anchovy essence to egg yolk.

75. HARENGS DIEPPOISE

Ingredients	Quantity
Herrings or Mackerel	2
Carrots	30 gm
Button onions	30 gm
Bay leaf	1
Peppercorns	6
Vinegar	75 ml
Thyme	1 sprig
Salt, Pepper	

Method

1. Clean and scale fish. Remove head and tail. 2. Remove bones and cut into two fillets. 3. Wash well and season with salt and pepper. 4. Roll up with skin outwards. 5. Place in an earthenware dish. 6. Peel and wash carrots and onions. 7. Cut into neat rings. 8. Add to fish with remaining ingredients. Add water if necessary to barely cover fish. 9. Cover with greaseproof paper and cook in a moderate oven for 15 to 20 minutes. 10. Allow to cool. Place in a dish with onions and carrots.

76. ŒUFS DIABLE (A)

Ingredients	Quantity
Hard-boiled eggs	4
Mustard	1 tsp
Salt	to taste
Chilli powder	¼ tsp
Butter	45 gm
Onions (chopped)	15 gm
Tomatoes (blanched)	115 gm

Method

1. Crack eggs and cool in water. 2. Shell and halve lengthwise. 3. Remove yolks and cream well with chilli powder, salt and mustard. 4. Fill back into egg whites. 5. Melt butter. Fry eggs lightly (yolk down) and remove. 6. In the same fat sauté finely chopped onions and blanched tomatoes. 7. Reduce to half and glaze the eggs.

ŒUFS DIABLE (B)

Ingredients	Quantity
Hard-boiled eggs	4
Tomato ketchup	2 tbsp
Worcester sauce	a few drops
Vinegar	2 to 3 drops
Onions (chopped)	15 gm
Chilli powder	½ tsp
Salt	to taste
Butter	30 gm

Method

1. Crack eggs and cool in water. 2. Shell and cut into halves. Sprinkle yolks with chilli powder and salt. 3. Melt butter. Fry eggs, with yolks facing down. Remove eggs. 4. To the same fat add tomato ketchup, finely chopped onion, vinegar and Worcester sauce. 5. Reduce to half and glaze eggs. Serve hot.

77. POIRES au FROMAGE BLANC

Ingredients	Quantity
Pears	6
Cream cheese	170 gm
Milk	30 ml
Walnuts (chopped)	15 gm
Chives (chopped)	1 tsp
Seasoning	to taste
Lettuce	
Tomatoes (80 to 90 gm each)	6
Paprika	a pinch

Method

1. Wash pears thoroughly, cut off the top and core, making sure to hollow the interior of the pear slightly. Cut decorative vertical strips in skins. 2. Place cream cheese in a bowl. Add a little milk and beat until smooth and creamy. 3. Add chopped walnuts and chives, season with salt and pepper to taste. 4. Place pears on cream crackers or in shrimp cocktail glasses on a bed of lettuce and pipe the cream cheese mixture into the pears with a generous swirl on top. 5. Garnish with ¼ tomato or green cocktail onions and dust with paprika. Serve chilled.

POTAGES

1. White Consommé
2. Clarified Consommé
3. Consommé avec Buf
4. Consommé Célestine
5. Consommé à la Julienne
6. Consommé Jacqueline
7. Consommé à la Carmen
8. Consommé à la Jardinière
9. Consommé Royale
10. Consommé Marie Louise
11. Consommé Ambassadrice
12. Consommé à l'Italienne
13. Consommé Brunoise
14. Consommé Vermicelli
15. Consommé Niçoise
16. Consommé Tapioca
17. Consommé Sagou
18. Consommé aux Profiteroles
19. Consommé Alexandra
20. Jellied Crab Consommé
21. Quenelles
22. Consommé Florentine
23. Consommé Grimaldi
24. Consommé Andalouse
25. Consommé Bouquetière
26. Consommé à la Fermiere
27. Consommé à l'Indienne
28. Consommé Parisienne
29. Consommé Réjane
30. Consommé Printanier
31. Consommé Ailerons
32. Consommé Allemande
33. Consommé Anglaise
34. Consommé à la Balzac
35. Consommé Bretonne
36. Consommé Clermont
37. Consommé Orientale
38. Consommé Paysanne

39. Consommé en Tasse
40. Consommé Madrilène (Cold)
41.. Consommé à la Milanaise
42. Consommé Girondine
43. Consommé Montmorency
44. Consommé Vert Pré
45. Crème d'Asperges
46. Crème de Céleri
47. Crème de
    Champignons (A)
    Crème de
    Champignons (B)
48. Crème de Concombres
49. Crème Crécy
50. Crème Dubarry
51. Crème d'Épinards
    (Crème Florentine)
52. Crème de Mais
    (Crème Washington)
53. Crème St. Germain
54. Crème de Volaille (A)
    (Crème à la Reine)
    Crème de Volaille (B)
55. Crème de Volaille Princesse
56. Crème Portugaise
57. Crème de Haricots Blancs
58. Purée de Carottes
59. Purée de Céleri Rave
60. Purée de Lentiles
    (Purée de Conti)
61. Purée de Parmentier
62. Purée de Tomates
    (Purée Portugaise)
63. Purée de Pois aux Croûtons
64. Purée de Pois Frais
    (Purée de Pois Saint
    Germain)
65. Purée de Pois Frais à la
    Menthe
66. Purée Dubarry
67. Potage Ambassadeurs
68. Potage Ciboulette
69. Potage Longchamps
70. Potage Marigny
71. Potage aux Amandes
72. Potage à la Bonne Femme
73. Potage Fausse Tortue
74. Potage à la Hollandaise
75. Potage Ministrone
76. Potage à la Queue de Buf
77. Queue de Buf Lié
78. Velouté aux Concombres
    (Velouté Danoise)
79. Velouté d'Artois
80. Velouté Dame Blanche
81. Velouté Marie Louise
82. Velouté Marie Stuart
83. Soupe aux Gombos au Okra
84. Soupe à l'Oignon à la
    Française
85. Aigo Menager
    (Provençale soup)
86. Soupe Vichyssoise
87. Gulyas Soupe
88. Soupe Cockie Leekie

I. WHITE CONSOMMÉ (4.75 litres)

Ingredients	Quantity
Bone from leg of mutton	1.35 kg
Lean meat	750 gm
Fowl's carcass	750 gm
Carrots	450 gm
Turnips	225 gm
Leeks	115 gm
Onions with a clove	55 gm

Ingredients	Quantity
Salt (gray)	15 gm
Water	6 litre

Method

String the meat together and put it along with the mutton bone (fowl's carcass, salt and water) into a stock pot of suitable size. Place the stock pot on a moderate fire to prevent rapid boiling. Stir from time to time. Under the influence of the heat, the water gradually reaches the interior of the meat where, after having dissolved the liquid portion, it duly combines with it. The liquid portion contains a large proportion of albumen and, as the temperature of the water rises, it coagulates. It also increases in volume, and, by virtue of its lightness escapes from the meat and accumulates on the surface in the form of scum. Carefully remove the scum as it forms, adding a little cold water as the water reaches boiling point. This is done so that a complete expulsion of scum may be effected. The clearness of the consommé largely depends on the manner in which this skimming has been carried out. After all the scum has been removed, add the vegetables, well-chopped. The scum from these is removed as in the previous case and the edge of the stockpot should be carefully wiped to the level of the fluid so as to free it from the deposit which has formed there. The stock pot is then moved to a corner of the fire where it may continue cooking slowly for 4–5 hours. At the end of this time, remove from fire and add 300 ml (½ pt) of cold water. Let it stand for a few minutes to allow the grease to accumulate on the surface of the liquid. Remove the grease carefully before straining the consommé. Strain through a fine strainer or muslin cloth into a wide-mouthed tureen. Cool quickly.

2. CLARIFIED CONSOMMÉ

Ingredients	Quantity
Stock	1.5 litre
Lean meat	85 gm
Egg white and shell	1
Vinegar	optional
Onions	30 gm
Turnip	15 gm
Celery	15 gm
Carrots	30 gm
Salt	to taste
Clove	1
Bay leaf	½
Peppercorns	4
Monosodium glutamate (Ajinomoto)	1 tsp

Method

1. Measure stock, strain and allow to cool. 2. Chop onions, turnips, celery and carrots. Clean the lean meat and mince. 3. Mix chopped vegetables and meat with egg white and crushed egg shell. Add vinegar (if used), cloves, bay leaf, peppercorns and salt. 4. Add the cool stock to the above. 5. Bring to a boil on a fast fire and allow scum to form. 6. As soon as the scum begins to break, lower the fire to the minimum. (The stock should not boil). 7. Allow to simmer for 40–45 minutes. 8. Strain the soup gently through a clean, wet muslin cloth into a clean container. Add ajinomoto. 9. Serve hot, garnished appropriately.

3. CONSOMMÉ avec BŒUF

Ingredients	Quantity
White or brown beef stock	1 litre
Bouquet garni	3 to 4
Peppercorns	
Salt	to taste
Beef (minced or chopped)	225 gm
Egg white	1
Mixed vegetables	115 gm
(Onions, Carrots, Celery, Leeks)	

Method

1. Thoroughly mix beef, salt, egg white and 300 ml of cold stock in a thick-bottomed pan. 2. Peel and wash vegetables. Chop finely. 3. Add to the beef, with the remainder of the stock, the bouquet garni and peppercorns. 4. Place over gentle heat and bring slowly to a boil, stirring occasionally. 5. Allow to boil rapidly for 5 to 10 seconds. 6. Give a final stir. 7. Lower the heat so that the consommé is simmering very gently. 8. Cook for 1½ to 2 hours without stirring. 9. Strain carefully through double muslin. 10. Remove fat by using absorbent paper. 11. Check for seasoning and colour. (The colour should be a delicate amber.) 12. Bring to a boil. 13. Serve in a warm soup tureen.

4. CONSOMMÉ CÉLESTINE

Ingredients	Quantity
Clarified consommé	2 litre
Garnish	
Egg	1
Refined flour	30 gm
Milk	150 ml
Chopped parsley	1 tsp
Grated cheese	1 tsp
Fat for frying	

Method

1. Prepare a pancake batter with above ingredients for garnish.
2. Prepare pancakes. Drain on absorbent paper and cut into very thin
shreds. 3. Place in a soup tureen and pour 2 litres of boiling consommé
over. 4. Serve immediately.

5. CONSOMMÉ à la JULIENNE

Ingredients	Quantity
Clarified consommé	1 litre
Garnish	
Carrots (red part only)	
Turnip	10 gm
Leek (while part only)	15 gm
Celery (heart)	15 gm
Lettuce	

Method

1. Cut vegetables into very thin strips (like matchsticks) about 2.5 cm
long; shred lettuce. 2. Cook all the vegetables (except lettuce) in boiling
salted water until tender. 3. Add to boiling consommé immediately before
serving.

6. CONSOMMÉ JACQUELINE

Ingredients	Quantity
Clarified consommé	1 litre
Garnish	
Carrots	
Peas (shelled)	10 gm
Asparagus	10 gm
Egg yolk	1
Cream	15 ml
Salt and Pepper	to taste

Method

1. With a small spooncutter pick out from the carrots 24 small oval
pellets and cook them in consommé along with shelled peas. 2. Prepare
2 baba moulds of royals (see Method 1 and 2 of recipe No. 9: Consommé
Royale) with egg yolk and cream, salt and pepper. (Here, cream is used
instead of stock.) Cut into cubes. 3. Put the prepared garnish including
asparagus heads into a soup tureen. Pour boiling consommé over and
serve at once.

7. CONSOMMÉ à la CARMEN

Ingredients	Quantity
Consommé	1 litre
Tomatoes	340 gm
Garnish	
Tomato julienne	
Truffle julienne	
Hard-boiled white of egg	1
Boiled rice	1 dsp

Method

1. Add tomato purée from tomatoes to consommé before clearing.
2. Clarify and add tomato julienne, truffle julienne (if available), hard-boiled white of egg and boiled rice. Serve hot.

8. CONSOMMÉ à la JARDINIÈRE

Ingredients	Quantity
Clarified consommé	1 litre
Garnish	
Carrots	20 gm
Turnips	20 gm
Peas	15 gm
Cauliflower sprigs	15 gm

Method

1. Cut carrots into pea-shapes. 2. Cook vegetables in boiling salted water.
3. Add to boiling consommé immediately before serving.

9. CONSOMMÉ ROYALE

Ingredients	Quantity
Clarified consomme	1 litre
Garnish	
Egg yolk	1
Stock	1 tbsp
Salt and Pepper	to taste

Method

1. Beat egg yolk and stock. 2. Season and steam in small greased moulds.
3. Cut into slices and then into fancy shapes. 4. Serve in the consommé.

10. CONSOMMÉ MARIE LOUISE

To 1 litre of Consommé Royale add 115 gm fresh boiled green peas.

11. CONSOMMÉ AMBASSADRICE

Ingredients	Quantity
Clear consommé (Chicken)	1 litre
Garnish	
Royales of tomato purée and peas	
Diced chicken breast	5 gm
Minced mushrooms	15 gm (3)

Method

1. Prepare royals as for Consommé Royale, using purée of tomato and peas instead of stock. 2. Cut royals into cubes. Put into a soup tureen with diced chicken breast and minced mushroom. 3. Pour boiling consommé over them and serve at once.

12. CONSOMMÉ à l'ITALIENNE

Ingredients	Quantity
Clarified consommé	1 litre
Garnish	
One tablespoon shredded Italian paste cooked in boiling salted water	

Method

Put boiled Italian paste in a soup tureen. Pour boiling consommé over. Serve at once.

13. CONSOMMÉ BRUNOISE

Ingredients	Quantity
Clarified consommé	1 litre
Garnish	
Carrots (diced)	1 tbsp
Turnips (diced)	1 tbsp
Onions (diced)	1 tbsp
Celery (diced)	1 tbsp

Method

1. Cook vegetables in boiling salted water. 2. Add to boiling consommé immediately before serving.

14. CONSOMMÉ VERMICELLI

Ingredients	Quantity
Clarified consommé	1 litre
Garnish	
Vermicelli	30 gm

Method

1. Boil vermicelli in salted water till tender. 2. Drain and wash well under a slowly running tap. Drain well. 3. Put into a soup tureen. 4. Pour boiling consommé over and serve immediately.

15. CONSOMMÉ NIÇOISE

To 1 litre of Consommé Vermicelli add a peeled tomato cut into squares. Serve with grated cheese.

16. CONSOMMÉ TAPIOCA

Ingredients	Quantity
Clarified consommé	1 litre
Garnish	
Processed tapioca	30 gm

Method

1. Cook tapioca in boiling salted water till transparent. Pour into a fine strainer and wash under running water. Drain well and add to boiling consommé. Serve at once.

17. CONSOMMÉ SAGOU

As for Consommé Tapioca, using sago instead of tapioca.

18. CONSOMMÉ aux PROFITEROLES

Ingredients	Quantity
Clarified consommé	1 litre
Choux paste	
Butter	55 gm
Water	150 ml
Salt	to taste
Refined flour	115 gm
Eggs	4
Egg (beaten)	1

Method

1. Put water, butter and salt in a pan and bring to a boil. 2. When the liquid boils and rises, remove pan from fire and add flour (all at once) and mix. 3. Return pan to a moderate fire and stir the paste until it ceases to stick to the spoon, and butter oozes out slightly. 4. Remove from fire and add four eggs, one at a time, taking care to see that each egg is mixed thoroughly before the next is added. 5. Put choux paste into a piping bag fitted with plain nozzle of 0.7 cm diameter. Squeeze out the paste on to a tray so as to form balls about the size of a small hazelnut. Brush over with beaten egg and bake in a moderate oven (approximately 5 minutes). Do not remove profiteroles from the oven until they are quite dry. Add to boiling consommé and serve at once.

19. CONSOMMÉ ALEXANDRA

Ingredients	Quantity
Clarified chicken consommé	1 litre
Processed tapioca	1 tbsp
Garnish	
White chicken meat (breast)	1 tbsp
Chicken quenelles	1 tbsp
Lettuce chiffonade	1 tbsp

Method

1. Into a soup tureen put in breast of chicken (julienne), chicken quenelles (grooved and long in shape) and lettuce chiffonade (Remove leaf ribs of lettuce. Wash. Squeeze tightly and shred into fine strips with a sharp knife). 2. Thicken the consommé by adding tapioca, poached and strained through a piece of muslin and very clear. 3. Bring the consommé to a boil, pour over prepared garnish and serve at once.

20. JELLIED CRAB CONSOMMÉ (4 or 5 servings)

Ingredients	Quantity
Consommé (chilled in the refrigerator)	1 litre
White crab meat (tinned, frozen or fresh)	115 gm
Dry sherry	1 tbsp
Salt, Pepper	to taste
Mayonnaise	150 ml
Cream or top of milk (if necessary)	a little
Chopped chives	4

Method

1. Turn consommé into a bowl and mix crab meat, sherry, and a little

salt and pepper through it. 2. Put the soup into 4 or 5 dishes or glasses and leave them to chill in refrigerator. 3. Just before serving, top each helping with a good tablespoonful of mayonnaise, thinned if necessary with cream or top of milk, and sprinkle with chives.

21. QUENELLES

Ingredients	Quantity
Boiled chicken breast	55 gm
Egg	1
Fresh breadcrumbs	30 gm
Nutmeg	a small pinch
Salt	to taste
Pepper	a pinch
Fat	to fry

Method

1. Chop chicken breast and grind it fine. 2. Add beaten egg (whole) gradually. 3. Add seasoning and fresh breadcrumbs. 4. Grind again to a smooth paste. 5. Set aside over ice, or in a cool place for about 10 minutes. 6. Shape into small balls (size of pearls). Heat fat. Fry quenelles.

22. CONSOMMÉ FLORENTINE

Ingredients	Quantity
Clarified chicken consommé	1 litre
Reduced spinach purée	
Cooked tongue	10 gm
Cooked peas	2 tbsp

Garnish

Forcemeat for quenelles (see Quenelle recipe).

Method

1. Prepare ingredients to make quenelles. To a quarter of the forcemeat add finely chopped tongue, and shape into six quenelles. 2. To one half add the reduced spinach purée and shape into twelve quenelles. 3. Shape remaining mixture into six quenelles. 4. Poach or fry quenelles. 5. Put the quenelles and the cooked peas into a soup tureen. Pour boiling consommé over. Serve at once.

23. CONSOMMÉ GRIMALDI

Ingredients	Quantity
Clarified consommé	1 litre
Raw tomato purée	4 tbsp

Ingredients	Quantity
Garnish	
Egg yolks	2
Stock	2 tbsp
Salt and Pepper	to taste
White of celery – cut julienne style	3 tbsp
Butter	10 gm

Method

1. Prepare 2 baba moulds of royale (see recipe 9) with egg yolk, stock and seasoning. Cool and cut into large cubes. 2. Stew celery in butter. Remove grease and cook in a little consommé and tomato purée. 3. Put garnish into a soup tureen. Pour boiling consommé over and serve at once.

24. CONSOMMÉ ANDALOUSE

Ingredients	Quantity
Clarified chicken consommé	1 litre
Cooked ham	1 tbsp
Boiled rice	1 tbsp
Threaded eggs	2 tbsp
Garnish	

Baba mould of royale made with tomato purée.

Method

1. Prepare a baba mould of royale with tomato purée. Dice when cool. 2. Cut ham julienne fashion. 3. Prepare threaded eggs and boil rice. Put all the garnish into a soup tureen. 4. Pour boiling consommé over and serve at once.

Threaded Eggs

Beat 2 eggs in a bowl. Season with salt and pepper. Strain through a sieve.

Into a pan of boiling consommé pour egg through a fine strainer, shifting the strainer in such a way as to let the eggs fall in threads and coagulate. Drain the egg threads very carefully.

25. CONSOMMÉ BOUQUETIÈRE

Ingredients	Quantity
Clarified consommé	1 litre
Garnish	
Carrots	50 gm
Turnip	50 gm

Ingredients	Quantity
French beans	15 gm
Asparagus heads	15 gm
Greenpeas	15 gm

Method

1. Cut carrots and turnip with a tubular cutter. Cut beans into strips 2. Cook all vegetables according to their nature. 3. Put into a soup tureen. Pour boiling consommé (thickened with tapioca poached and strained through fine linen) over garnish and serve immediately.

26. CONSOMMÉ à la FERMIERE

Ingredients	Quantity
Clarified consommé	1 litre
Garnish	
Carrots	30 gm
Turnip	30 gm
Leeks (heads only)	2
Onions	15 gm
Cabbage	50 gm
Butter	45 gm
French flute	

Method

1. Parboil cabbage. Cut roughly in julienne fashion. 2. Mince carrots, turnip, leeks and onions finely. 3. Stew in butter. Remove extra fat. 4. Put garnish into a soup tureen. 5. Pour boiling consommé over. Add a few thin slices of French soup flute (a long crisp roll of bread slightly dried). Serve at once.

27. CONSOMMÉ à l'INDIENNE

Ingredients	Quantity
White consommé	1 litre
Curry powder	1 tbsp
Mince	85 gm
Egg, white and shell	1
Celery, Carrots	30 gm
Vinegar	15 ml
Egg yolks	3
Coconut milk	3 tbsp
Salt	
Pepper	
Boiled rice	4 tbsp

Method

1. Prepare ingredients as given in Recipe 2. 2. Prepare clarified consommé, adding curry powder to consommé during clarification. Clear, strain and set aside. 3. Prepare three baba moulds of royale using coconut milk, egg yolk and seasoning. 4. When quite cold cut into cubes. Put into a soup tureen. 5. Pour boiling consommé over and serve at once. Send boiled rice separately to the table.

28. CONSOMMÉ PARISIENNE

Ingredients	Quantity
Clarified chicken consommé	1 litre
Garnish	
Egg yolks	2
Purée of mixed vegetables	2 tbsp
Salt and Pepper	to taste
Carrots (diced)	1 tbsp
Turnip (diced)	1 tbsp
Peas	1 tbsp
Tender French beans (cut into strips)	1 tbsp
Asparagus heads	1 tbsp

Method

1. Prepare a royale with egg yolks, purée of vegetables and seasoning. When quite cold cut into cubes. 2. Prepare vegetables and cook according to their nature. 3. Put garnish into a soup tureen. 4. Pour boiling consommé over. Serve at once.

29. CONSOMMÉ RÉJANE

Ingredients	Quantity
Clarified white consommé	1 litre
Garnish	
Breast of chicken	50 gm
Leeks (head)	2
Potatoes (julienne)	85 gm

Method

1. Boil consommé. Add breast of chicken, leeks and potato julienne. When potatoes are cooked, remove and serve immediately.

30. CONSOMMÉ PRINTANIER

Ingredients	Quantity
Clarified chicken consommé	1 litre

Ingredients	Quantity
Garnish	
Carrots	1
Turnip	1
Peas	1 tbsp
French beans (strips)	1 tbsp
Asparagus heads	1 tbsp
Lettuce leaves (heart)	15 gm

Method

1. Cut turnip and carrots into roundels, 1.25 cm (½") thick. 2. With a tubular cutter 0.35 cm in diameter, cut these roundels into rods. 3. Cook these rods in consommé and reduce the latter to a glaze. 4. Put carrots and turnips into a soup tureen with boiled peas, beans, asparagus heads and poached lettuce leaves. 5. Pour boiling consommé over the garnish and serve at once.

31. CONSOMMÉ AILERONS

Ingredients	Quantity
Clarified chicken consommé	1 litre
Garnish	
Boiled breast of chicken (julienne)	
Boiled rice	50 gm

Method

1. Put garnish into a soup tureen. 2. Pour boiling consommé over and serve at once.

32. CONSOMMÉ ALLEMANDE

Ingredients	Quantity
Clarified consommé	1.5 litre
Garnish	
Refined flour	115 gm
Milk	40 to 45 ml
Eggs	2
Salt	to taste

Method

1. Mix flour, milk, beaten eggs and seasoning. 2. Let mixture run through a colander into boiling consommé. Boil for 5 minutes. Serve hot.

33. CONSOMMÉ ANGLAISE

Ingredients	Quantity
Clarified chicken consommé	1 litre
Garnish	
Chicken breast	30 gm
Green peas	30 gm

Method

1. Boil and dice chicken breast. Boil peas. 2. Pour boiling consommé over garnish and serve immediately.

34. CONSOMMÉ à la BALZAC

Ingredients	Quantity
Clarified consommé	1 litre
Garnish	
Cooked shrimps (sliced)	30 gm
Cooked green peas	30 gm
Cooked turnips (diced)	30 gm

Method

1. Prepare garnish and put into a soup tureen. 2. Pour boiling consommé over.

35. CONSOMMÉ BRETONNE

Ingredients	Quantity
Clarified consommé	1 litre
Garnish	
Celery (heart)	15 gm
Onions	15 gm
Leek (white part only)	15 gm

Method

1. Cut vegetables in julienne fashion. 2. Put them into boiling consommé till cooked. Serve at once.

36. CONSOMMÉ CLERMONT

Ingredients	Quantity
Clarified consommé	1 litre
Garnish	
Onions rings dipped in batter and fried crisp.	

Method

1. Boil consommé. 2. Add crisply fried onion rings. Serve at once.

37. CONSOMMÉ ORIENTALE

Ingredients	Quantity
Clarified consommé	1 litre
Garnish	
Boiled rice	50 gm
Carrots and Turnips (cut in shape of half moons)	30 gm each

Method

1. Boil vegetables in salted water till tender. 2. Add to boiling consommé with the rice. Serve at once.

38. CONSOMMÉ PAYSANNE

Ingredients	Quantity
Clarified consommé	1 litre
Garnish	
Cabbage leaves	30 gm
Carrots	50 gm
Turnip	30 gm
Leeks	30 gm
Celery leaves	2
Butter	50 gm

Method

1. Cut cabbage into 2.5 cm squares. 2. Slice carrots, turnip, leeks. 3. Stew vegetables in butter. 4. Drain off fat. 5. Pour boiling consommé over garnish and serve at once.

39. CONSOMMÉ en TASSE

This is a basic consommé slightly jellied and served in cups. The basic ingredients should be strong enough to effect jelling. A little gelatine is added if consommé does not jell. For mutton consommé use about 15 gm of gelatine to a litre of clarified consommé. The basic consommé should be well-flavoured.

40. CONSOMMÉ MADRILÈNE (COLD)

This is a basic consommé, well flavoured with tomato, celery and a garnish of neatly diced tomatoes. It is served chilled.

41. CONSOMMÉ à la MILANAISE

Ingredients	Quantity
Chicken consommé	1 litre
Garnish	
Fried macaroni quoits	
Grated Gruyère and Parmesan cheese	45 gm
Macaroni Quoits	
Thick macaroni	60 gm
Béchamel sauce	150 ml
Eggs	2
Breadcrumbs	30 gm
Fat to fry	

Method

1. Cook 60 gm thick macaroni in slightly salted water. 2. As soon as it is cooked, drain, lay on a piece of linen and cut into small rings. 3. Prepare 150 ml béchamel sauce. (See recipe No. 46). Keep it very thick. 4. Mix macaroni rings with sauce. Spread on a dish and leave to cool. 5. Divide into balls, the size of walnuts. 6. Roll and flatten. 7. Dip in egg and breadcrumbs and deep fry. Drain when they become golden brown. 8. Pour boiling consommé over macaroni quoits. Garnish with grated cheese.

42. CONSOMMÉ GIRONDINE

Ingredients	Quantity
Beef consommé	1 litre
Garnish	
Egg yolks	2
Milk or Stock	2 tbsp
Cooked ham (finely chopped)	2 tbsp
Seasoning	to taste
Carrots	100 gm
Butter	10 gm

Method

1. Prepare two baba moulds of royale with egg yolks, stock or milk, chopped ham and seasoning. Cool and dice. 2. Prepare julienne from red part of carrots and stew in butter. Drain off extra fat. 3. Put garnish into a soup tureen. 4. Pour boiling consommé over.

43. CONSOMMÉ MONTMORENCY

Ingredients	Quantity
Chicken consommé	1 litre
Garnish	
Chicken quenelles	18
Processed tapioca	3 tbsp
Asparagus heads (green)	2 tbsp
Boiled rice	2 tbsp

Method

1. Prepare quenelles (see recipe No. 21). 2. Thicken consommé with poached tapioca strained through linen cloth. 3. Put garnish into a soup tureen and pour boiling consommé over.

44. CONSOMMÉ VERT PRÉ

Ingredients	Quantity
Clarified consommé	1 litre
Tapioca	
Garnish	
Cooked asparagus heads (green)	2 tbsp
Cooked peas	1 tbsp
Cooked French beans	1 tbsp
Lettuce	1 tbsp

Method

1. Sprinkle tapioca over boiling consommé. Cook gently for 15 minutes. 2. Into a soup tureen put asparagus heads, peas, French beans cut into lozenges, and poached roundels of lettuce. 3. Pour boiling consommé over garnish. Serve at once.

45. CRÈME d'ASPERGES

Ingredients	For 20
Asparagus	3 tins
Liquor from asparagus tins	2 litre
Refined flour	150 gm
Milk	1.5 litre
Cream	400 ml
Monosodium glutamate	½ pkt
Cornflour	20 gm
Butter	150 gm
Water	to make up 20 portions
Salt	to taste

Method

1. Heat butter. Add flour. Stir till it becomes the consistency of breadcrumbs. 2. Add warm milk gradually to prevent formation of lumps, stirring well. 3. Cook over slow fire till sauce is glossy and cooked. 4. Remove from fire. Cool. 5. Put 100 ml of cream into a bowl. Add a small quantity of sauce to cream, blend well and return the whole to the sauce. 6. Prepare a purée of asparagus. Blend sauce and asparagus purée. Add asparagus liquor. 7. Thicken with blended cornflour. Season with salt and aji-no-moto (Monosodium glutamate). 8. Reheat. Blend in remaining cream and serve hot.

46. CRÈME de CÉLERI

Ingredients	Quantity
Celery	450 gm
Butter	30 gm
Béchamel sauce	650 ml
White consommé	300 ml
Cream	75 ml
Béchamel Sauce	
Refined flour	60 gm
Butter or Margarine	60 gm
Onions stuck with a clove	1
Milk (warm)	650 ml

Method

1. Mince celery, keeping aside heart for garnish. 2. Stew in butter without discolouring. 3. Add béchamel sauce. Cook gently till celery is tender. Pass through a sieve. 4. Add white consommé. Reheat without allowing it to boil. 5. Remove, add cream and add heart of celery cut brunoise (diced small) fashion.

Béchamel Sauce

1. Melt fat in a thick-bottomed pan. 2. Add flour and mix in. 3. Cook for a few minutes over gentle heat without colouring. 4. Gradually add warmed milk and stir till smooth. 5. Add onion with clove stuck on. 6. Simmer for 30 minutes. 7. Remove onion. Strain. 8. Cover with a film of butter to prevent formation of skin.

47. CRÈME de CHAMPIGNONS (A)

Ingredients	Quantity
Butter	60 gm
Chicken stock	1 litre

Ingredients	Quantity
White mushrooms	115 gm
Refined flour	60 gm
Bouquet garni	
Salt and Pepper	to taste
Milk	150 ml
or Cream	75 ml

Method

1. Heat butter, mix in flour. Cook over gentle heat to a sandy texture without colouring. 2. Remove from heat. Cool slightly. 3. Gradually mix in hot stock. 4. Bring to a boil, stirring all the time. 5. Add well-washed, chopped mushrooms, bouquet garni and seasoning. 6. Simmer for 30 to 45 minutes. Skim when necessary. 7. Remove bouquet garni. 8. Pass through sieve and then through medium strainer. 9. Return to a clean pan. Re-boil. Check for seasoning and consistency. Add milk or cream.

CRÈME de CHAMPIGNONS (B)

Ingredients	For 4
Milk	500 ml
Refined flour	50 ml
Butter	50 gm
Mushroom liquor	½ tin
Mushrooms	½ tin (115 gm)
Maggi cube	1
Water	150 ml
Salt and Pepper	to taste
Aji-no-moto (Monosodium glutamate)	¼ tsp

Method

1. Heat water. Add Maggi cube. Dissolve. Set aside. 2. Melt butter. Add flour. Cook over gentle heat to a sandy texture without discolouring. 3. Remove from heat. Cool slightly. 4. Add liquid in which Maggi cube has been dissolved, and mushroom liquor. Blend well. 5. Add milk. Return to fire and simmer for about 30 minutes. 6. Add chopped mushrooms and seasoning. 7. Simmer for another 10 minutes and serve hot.

48. CRÈME de CONCOMBRES

Ingredients	Quantity
Cucumber	1 kg
Butter	85 gm
Refined flour	60 gm
Milk	300 ml

Ingredients	Quantity
White stock	1 litre
Cream	150 ml
Salt and Pepper	to taste
Sugar	a pinch

Method

1. Peel cucumber, cut into pieces and put in salted water. Bring to a boil, and boil for 10 minutes. 2. Melt 30 gm of butter and add cucumber, salt, pepper and sugar. 3. Sauté with lid on pan for 10 minutes. 4. Add stock and boil till cucumber is tender. Pass through a sieve. 5. Prepare a white sauce with remaining butter, flour and milk. 6. Mix purée with sauce. Sieve, stir and boil for a few minutes. 7. Remove from fire. Add cream. Serve hot, garnished with a few pieces of cooked cucumber.

49. CRÈME CRÉCY

Ingredients	For 4
White stock	600 ml
Onions	60 gm
Celery	60 gm
Leeks	60 gm
Leeks	60 gm
Carrots	450 gm
Tomato purée	½ tsp
Salt and Pepper	to taste
Refined flour	15 gm
Butter	15 gm
Milk	600 ml
Rice	15 gm

Method

1. Prepare vegetables. 2. Cook in stock with bouquet garni till tender. Remove bouquet garni. 3. Pass through sieve, 4. Make a white sauce with flour, butter and milk. 5. Add purée to sauce. Add seasoning. 6. Re-heat. Serve hot, garnished with plain boiled rice.

50. CRÈME DUBARRY

Ingredients	Quantity
Cauliflower	450 gm
Onions	60 gm
Leeks	60 gm
Milk	1 litre

Ingredients	Quantity
Refined flour	50 gm
Butter	30 gm
Salt and Pepper	to taste
Cream	75 ml

Method

1. Wash and break cauliflower into flowerets. Keep a few for garnish. 2 Wash and slice leeks. Peel and chop onions. 3. Put cauliflower, leeks and onions into a pan with half the milk. 4. Cook till tender. Pass through a sieve. 5. Prepare a white sauce with flour, butter and remaining milk. 6. Add sauce to purée of vegetables. Add seasoning. Return to heat and bring to a boil. 7. Remove. Add cream gradually. Serve hot, garnished with flowerets of cauliflower boiled in salt water.

51. CRÈME d'ÉPINARDS (CRÈME FLORENTINE)

Ingredients	Quantity
Spinach	450 gm
Béchamel sauce	600 ml
Cream	75 ml
Salt and Pepper	to taste

Béchamel Sauce

Milk	600 ml
Refined flour	60 gm
Onions stuck with a clove	100 gm
Bay leaf	1

Method

1. Wash and shred spinach. Add salt and keep on a gentle fire. When the liquid starts oozing out of the leaves increase heat and cook briskly (with lid off) till done. 2. Remove from fire and pass through a sieve. 3. Prepare béchamel sauce. Add purée of spinach to sauce. 4. Pass through a medium strainer. Re-heat. 5. Remove from fire. Add cream and serve hot.

52. CRÈME de MAIS (CRÈME WASHINGTON)

Ingredients	Quantity
Tender corn	450 gm
Béchamel sauce	600 ml
Cream	75 ml
Stock	50 ml (approx.)
Seasoning	to taste

Ingredients	Quantity
Béchamel Sauce	
Milk	600 ml
Refined four	60 gm
Butter	60 gm
Onions stuck with a clove	1
Bay leaf	1

Method

1. Cook corn in stock till tender. Keep a few grains for garnish. 2. Grind well and pass through a sieve. 3. Add béchamel sauce. Pass through a medium strainer. 4. Re-heat. Remove from fire. Add cream. 5. Serve hot, garnished with a few grains of corn.

53. CRÈME ST. GERMAIN

Ingredients	Quantity
French peas	450 gm
Mint	1 sprig
Onions	30 gm
Water	500 ml
Bouquet garni	
Béchamel sauce	600 ml
Cream	75 ml
Seasoning	to taste

Method

1 Shell and cook peas in salt water with onions, mint and bouquet garni till soft. 2. Remove mint, bouquet garni and onion. 3. Pass through a sieve. 4. Add to béchamel, reboil and simmer for 5 minutes. Check seasoning. 5. Pass through a medium strainer. 6. Return to a clean pan. Re-boil. Skim. Remove from fire and stir in cream.

54. CRÈME de VOLAILLE (A) (CRÈME à la REINE)

Ingredients	Quantity
Strong chicken stock	1 litre
Cornflour	25 gm
Milk	300 ml
Egg yolk	1
Salt	to taste
Breast of chicken	115 gm

Method

1. Make a good strong chicken stock without adding any other seasoning.

Bring the stock to a boil. 2. Stir cornflour to a smooth paste with the milk. Pour boiling stock over blended cornflour. 3. Cook gently on a slow fire in a double boiler for 20 minutes. 4. Beat egg yolk, add a little soup to the yolk after taking soup off fire. 5. Stir egg well to keep it smooth and then add rest of soup.

CRÈME de VOLAILLE (B)

Ingredients	Quantity
Chicken stock	1 litre
Refined flour	6 gm
Onions	30 gm
Leeks	50 gm
Celery	50 gm
Butter or Margarine	60 gm
Bouquet garni	
Salt and Pepper	to taste
Milk or	30 ml
Cream	150 ml
Garnish	
Cooked, diced chicken	30 gm

Method

1. Melt fat. Add peeled, washed and sliced onion, leeks and celery and cook without discolouring with the lid on. 2. Mix in flour and cook to a sandy texture without colouring. 3. Cool slightly. Add hot stock gradually. 4. Bring to a boil, stirring all the time. 5. Add bouquet garni and seasoning. 6. Simmer for about an hour. Skim when necessary. 7. Remove bouquet garni. 8 Pass firmly through a fine strainer. 9. Return to a clean pan. Re-boil and finish with milk or cream. 10. Serve hot with diced cooked chicken.

55. CRÈME de VOLAILLE PRINCESSE

Ingredients	Quantity
Chicken	450 gm
Béchamel Sauce	1 litre
Chicken stock	150-300 ml
Asparagus head	30 gm
Seasoning	to taste
Béchamel Sauce	
Milk	1 litre
Refined flour	60 gm
Butter	60 gm

Ingredients	Quantity
Onions stuck with a clove	1
Bay leaf	1

Method

1. Boil chicken in very little water with seasoning. 2. Bone chicken. Reserve breast for garnish. 3. Make purée of chicken. Mix with béchamel sauce. Add chicken stock if necessary. Pass through a medium strainer. Test for seasoning. 4. Re-heat. Serve hot, garnished with 20 very small slices of chicken breast and asparagus heads.

56. CRÈME PORTUGAISE

Ingredients	Quantity
Butter	60 gm
Bacon	30 gm
Refined flour	60 gm
Tomatoes	450 gm
Stock	1 litre
Milk	300 ml
Carrots	115 gm
Onions	115 gm
Salt and Pepper	to taste
Bouquet garni	
Garnish	
Rice	15 gm

Method

1. Melt butter in thick-bottomed pan. 2. Add chopped bacon, and roughly diced carrots and onions. Brown lightly. Mix in flour and cook to a sandy texture. 4. Add chopped tomatoes and gradually add hot stock. 5. Stir to a boil. 6. Add bouquet garni. Season lightly. 7. Simmer for approximately one hour. Skim when required. 8. Remove bouquet garni and pass through a sieve. 9. Return to clean pan. Add milk. Re-heat. Check for seasoning and serve hot, garnished with boiled rice.

57. CRÈME de HARICOTS BLANCS

Ingredients	Quantity
Haricot beans	115 gm
Carrots	55 gm
Onions stuck with a clove	100 gm
Bouquet garni	
White stock	500 ml
Refined flour	30 gm

Ingredients	Quantity
Butter	30 gm
Milk	600 ml
Cream	75 ml
Seasoning	

Method

1. Soak beans overnight. Cook in stock with carrots, onion and bouquet garni till tender. 2. Pass through a strainer. Add seasoning. 3. Prepare white sauce with flour, butter and milk. 4. Mix purée with sauce. Check for seasoning. 5. Re-heat. Remove, add cream and serve hot.

58. PURÉE de CAROTTES

Ingredients	Quantity
White stock	1.28 litre
Onions	60 gm
Celery	60 gm
Carrots	450 gm
Leeks	60 gm
Tomato purée	½ tsp
Refined flour	30 gm
Butter	60 gm
Bouquet garni	
Salt and Pepper	
Croûtons	
Stale bread (cubed)	30 gm
Fat	60 gm

Method

1. Prepare vegetables. 2. Melt butter. Add vegetables, and stew in butter with a lid on the pan without discolouring till soft. 3. Mix in flour. 4. Add tomato purée. 5. Gradually add hot stock. 6. Stir till it boils. Add bouquet garni and season. 7. Simmer for about an hour, skimming when necessary. 8. Remove bouquet garni and pass firmly through a sieve and then through a medium strainer. 9. Return to a clean pan. Re-boil. Check for seasoning and consistency. 10. Fry stale bread cubes in fat. 11. Serve the soup hot with croûtons.

59. PURÉE de CÉLERI RAVE

Ingredients	Quantity
Celery	450 gm
Butter	30 gm
White consommé	1 litre

Ingredients	Quantity
Potatoes	200 gm
Seasoning	
Garnish (croûtons)	
Stale bread	30 gm
Fat	30 gm

Method

1. Wash and chop celery. 2. Stew in half the batter without discolouring. 3. Add stock and peeled and minced potatoes. 4. Cook till done. Pass through a sieve. Add seasoning. 5. Re-heat gently. Add remaining butter and serve hot, garnished with croûtons.

60. PURÉE de LENTLLES (Purée de Conti)

Ingredients	Quantity
Lentils	225 gm
Lean breast of bacon	60 gm
White consommé	1 litre
Celery	50 gm
Carrots	100 gm
Onions	100 gm
Bouquet garni	
Butter	15 gm
Seasoning	to taste
Garnish (croûtons)	
Bread (cubed)	30 gm
Fat to fry	30 gm

Method

1. Wash and soak lentils in lukewarm consommé for about 2 to 3 hours. 2. Boil in the same liquid. 3. Add diced bacon, carrots, onions, celery and bouquet garni. Cook gently till vegetables are tender. 4. Pass through a strainer. Add seasoning. Check for consistency. 5. Re-heat. Remove from fire. Finish with butter and serve hot with fried croûtons.

61. PURÉE de PARMENTIER

Ingredients	Quantity
Margarine	30 gm
White of leeks	60 gm
White stock	1 litre
Onions	60 gm
Garnish	
Salt and Pepper	to taste

Ingredients	Quantity
Cream (optional)	75 ml
Potatoes	450 gm
Bouquet garni	
Croûtons	
Bread (cubed)	30 gm
Fat to fry	30 gm
Parsley	a few sprigs

Method

1. Melt margarine in a thick-bottomed pan. 2. Add peeled, washed, sliced onions and leeks and cook for a few minutes without colouring, with lid on. 3. Add stock, peeled, washed sliced potatoes and bouquet garni and seasoning. 4. Simmer for approximately 30 minutes. 5. Remove bouquet garni; skim. 6. Pass soup firmly though a sieve and then pass through a medium strainer. 7. Return to a clean pan, re-boil. Check for seasoning and consistency. 8. Remove from heat. Add cream if desired. Serve hot with fried croûtons and chopped parsley.

62. PURÉE de TOMATES (Purée Portugaise)

Ingredients	Quantity
Butter	60 gm
Breast of bacon	30 gm
Carrots	30 gm
Onions	30 gm
Thyme	a pinch
White consommé	1 litre
Bay leaf	
Tomatoes	1 kg
Sugar	a pinch
Rice	7 gm
Salt and Pepper	to taste

Method

1. Heat half the butter. Add diced breast of bacon, minced carrots and onions, thyme and bay leaf. Fry well. 2. Add chopped tomatoes (save a few pieces for garnish), sugar, white consommé and 60 gm rice. 3. Boil remaining rice separately. 4. When tomatoes are cooked pass through a sieve. 5. Re-heat. Remove from fire. Add remaining butter and serve hot garnished with boiled rice and peeled, diced tomatoes.

63. PURÉE de POIS aux CROÛTONS

Ingredients	Quantity
Dried peas	450 gm
Cold water	1 litre
Raw ham	225 gm
Carrots	30 gm
Onions	30 gm
Celery	30 gm
Leeks (green part)	30 gm
Thyme	
Bay leaf	
Sugar	15 gm
Salt	to taste
Butter	15 gm
Garnish (croûtons)	
Bread (diced)	30 gm
Fat to fry	

Method

1. Soak peas in water for a few hours. 2. Add raw ham, boil till tender.
3. Add chopped carrots, onions, celery and leeks, a small bit of thyme,
bay leaf, sugar and salt. Cook gently till vegetables are tender. 4. Pass
through a sieve. Re-heat. 5. Remove from fire. 6. Finish with butter and
serve hot, garnished with fried croûtons.

64. PURÉE de POIS FRAIS (PURÉE de POIS SAINT GERMAIN)

Ingredients	Quantity
Fresh peas	680 gm
White consommé	1 litre
Salt	to taste
Butter	15 gm

Method

1. Shell peas. Cook quickly in boiling consommé till quite tender, with
salt. 2. Pass through a sieve reserving about 2 tablespoons for garnish.
3. Re-heat. Remove from fire. Add butter and serve hot, garnished with
whole peas.

65. PURÉE de POIS FRAIS à la MENTHE

Ingredients	Quantity
Fresh peas	680 gm
White consommé	1 litre

Ingredients	Quantity
Fresh mint	3 sprigs
Salt	to taste
Butter	15 gm

Method

1. Shell peas. Cook quickly in boiling consommé till tender with mint (save a few leaves for garnish) and salt. 2. Pass through a sieve reserving a few peas for garnish. 3. Re-heat. Remove from fire. Finish with butter and serve hot, garnished with whole peas, and chopped mint.

66. PURÉE DUBARRY

Ingredients	Quantity
Cauliflower	450 gm
Milk	1 litre
Potatoes	200 gm
Butter	15 gm
Seasoning	to taste
Garnish	
Bread (diced)	30 gm
Butter	30 gm

Method

1. Boil cauliflower and peeled, minced potatoes in 600 ml of milk. 2. When tender pass through a sieve. Add remaining milk (hot) and butter. Season. 3. Serve hot, garnished with croûtons of bread.

67. POTAGE AMBASSADEURS

Ingredients and method as for Purée de Pois Frais but add 1 tablespoon lettuce chiffonade (see recipe No. 19, Consommé Alexandra) and 2 tablespoons boiled rice for 1 litre of purée.

68. POTAGE CIBOULETTE

Ingredients and method as for Purée de Pois Frais but add 1 tablespoon chopped chives and 2 tablespoons boiled rice.

69. POTAGE LONGCHAMPS

Prepare as for Purée de Pois Frais and add 45 gm of vermicelli poached in consomme and a pinch of chopped mint per litre of soup.

70. POTAGE MARIGNY

Prepare as for Purée de Pois Frais and add as garnish 1 tablespoon of fine French beans cut into lozenges.

71. POTAGE aux AMANDES

Ingredients	Quantity
Almonds or	115 gm
Cashewnuts and	55 gm
Almonds	55 gm
Milk	150 ml
Refined flour	15 gm
White stock	600 ml
Cream	75 ml
Salt and Pepper	to taste
Lime juice	a few drops

Method

1. Blanch, skin, chop and pound almonds with a tablespoon of stock.
2. Stew in milk for about an hour adding a little stock if it becomes dry.
3. Sieve through a strainer. 4. Melt butter, add flour. Blend well. 5. Add almond pulp and stock. 6. Bring to a boil, add seasoning, lime juice and cream.

72. POTAGE à la BONNE FEMME

Ingredients	Quantity
Lettuce leaves	2
Cucumber	115 gm
Butter	15 gm
Stock	590 ml
Egg yolks	2
Cream	75 ml
Salt and Pepper	

Method

1. Shred vegetables and toss in butter until it is absorbed. 2. Add boiling stock and cook for a few minutes. 3. Cool and add egg yolks and cream. Season. 4. Heat without boiling until yolks are cooked and the soup thickened.

73. POTAGE FAUSSE TORTUE

Ingredients	Quantity
Calf's head	½

Ingredients	Quantity
Fat	60 gm
Refined flour	60 gm
tomato puree	30 gm
Onions diced & fried	115 gm
Carrots diced & fried	115 gm
Brown stock	1.8 litre
Bay leaf	1
Peppercorns	6
Salt	to taste
Cayenne pepper	a pinch
Sherry (optional)	2 tbsp (30 ml)

Method

1. Melt fat in a thick-bottomed pan. Mix in flour. 2. Cook slowly to a brown roux. Cool slightly. 3. Mix in tomato puree. 4. Add hot stock gradually. 5. Bring to a boil. 6. Add calf's head and fried, diced carrots and onions. 7. Simmer for 1 to 2 hours. Skim. 8. Add spices. Cook for 10 minutes. 9. Pass soup through a fine strainer. 10. Return to a clean pan. Re-boil. Check for seasoning and consistency. 11. Cut a little of the best part of calf's head into 0.35 cm thick pieces for garnish. 12. Pour boiling soup into a warm tureen. 13. Add sherry and serve immediately.

74. POTAGE à la HOLLANDAISE

Ingredients	Quantity
White stock	600 ml
Butter	30 gm
Refined flour	30 gm
Egg yolk	1
Cream	75 ml
Peas	30 gm
Carrots	30 gm
Cucumber	30 gm
Sugar	a pinch
Salt and Pepper	

Method

1. Cube vegetables to the size of peas and cook in boiling salted water. 2. Melt butter. Add flour. Blend well and add stock. Boil for 10 minutes. 3. Beat egg yolk with cream. 4. Add a little of the hot stock and strain into the pan, stirring constantly. 5. Season and add garnish. 6. Stir till egg is cooked and vegetables are in suspension. 7. Serve immediately.

75. POTAGE MINESTRONE

Ingredients	Quantity
Carrots	100 gm
Tomatoes	100 gm
Turnip	30 gm
Celery	115 gm
Leeks	115 gm
Cabbage	100 gm
Beans	30 gm
Bacon	30 gm
Seasoning	to taste
White consommé	30 gm
Macaroni	30 gm
Rice (boiled)	30 gm
Butter	15 gm
Cheese	30 gm

Method

1. Dice vegetables and sauté them in butter. 2. Add stock, bacon and seasoning to taste. 3. Cook till vegetables are tender. 4. Boil macaroni and rice. Add macaroni, cut into 1.5 cm pieces, and boiled rice to soup. 5. Simmer for a few minutes longer. 6. Remove from fire. Serve piping hot, garnished with grated cheese.

76. POTAGE à la QUEUE de BŒUF

Ingredients	Quantity
Oxtail	1
Butter	60 gm
Refined flour	60 gm
Carrots	55 gm
Turnip	55 gm
Onions	55 gm
Celery	55 gm
Cloves	3
Mace	1 blade
Peppercorns	12
Second stock	2.35 litre
Salt	

Method

1. Cut oxtail into joints and blanch. 2. Strain off water and dry pieces of oxtail. 3. Melt half the butter. Fry oxtail to a good brown colour along with the vegetables, herbs and spices. 4. Strain off superfluous fat. Add stock and salt. Bring to a boil and simmer for four hours. Strain. 5. Melt

remainder of butter. Add flour and fry. 6. Add stock free from fat, bring to a boil, and boil for ten minutes. 7. Strain. Add pieces of meat from tail and very thin pieces of cooked carrots and turnip cut in rounds.

77. QUEUE de BŒUF LIÉ

Ingredients	Quantity
Oxtail	½
Refined flour	60 gm
Fat	60 gm
Carrots	115 gm
Onions	115 gm
Tomato purée	30 gm
Brown stock	1.8 litre
Bouquet garni	
Turnip	30 gm
Seasoning	to taste

Method

1. Cut oxtail into pieces through the natural joints. 2. Quickly fry in hot fat till lightly brown. 3. Add diced onions and carrots and brown well together. 4. Mix in flour and cook to a brown roux over gentle heat or in an oven. 5. Cool slightly. 6. Mix in tomato purée. 7. Gradually add hot stock. 8. Stir to a boil and skim. 9. Add bouquet garni and seasoning. 10. Simmer for 3 to 4 hours. 11. Remove bouquet garni and pieces of oxtail. 12. Pass soup through a fine strainer. 13. Return to a clean pan, re-boil. Check for seasoning and consistency. 14. Garnish with extreme top of tail cut into rounds and diced carrots and turnips cooked in salted water. Serve hot.

78. VELOUTÉ aux CONCOMBRES (VELOUTÉ DANOISE)

Ingredients	Quantity
Cucumber	450 gm
Poultry velouté	600 ml
Butter	30 gm
Seasoning	to taste
Poultry Velouté	
Butter	60 gm
Refined flour	45 gm
Poultry stock	600 ml
Peppercorns	12
Salt	to taste
Parsley stalks	a few
Lime juice	½ tsp
Cream	60 ml

Method

1. Parboil cucumber. Peel, remove seeds and mince. 2. Stew cucumber in half the butter. 3. Prepare a poultry velouté and add stewed cucumber. Add seasoning to taste. 4. Pass through a sieve. 5. Re-heat. Finish with remaining butter, and serve hot.

VELOUTÉ SAUCE

1. Melt butter. Add flour, parsley stalks and peppercorns. Cook for a few minutes without browning. 2. Add stock. Stir till it comes to a boil and boil for another 10 minutes. 3. Season. Add lime juice and cream and strain.

79. VELOUTÉ d'ARTOIS

Ingredients	Quantity
Poultry velouté	600 ml
Butter	15 gm
(See recipe No. 78 Velouté au Concombres)	
Haricot beans	225 gm
White consommé	30 ml
Seasoning	to taste

Method

1. Soak haricot beans overnight. 2. Cook till tender. Pass through a sieve. 3. Prepare poultry velouté. Add purée to sauce. Add consommé and seasoning to taste. 4. Pass through a medium strainer. 5. Re-heat. Finish with butter and serve hot.

80. VELOUTÉ DAME BLANCHE

Ingredients	Quantity
Poultry velouté	1 litre
Sweet almonds	20 gm
Butter	15 gm
Garnish	
Breast of chicken	30 gm
Chicken forcemeat quenelles	12
(see recipe No. 21)	

Method

1. Prepare poultry velouté. 2. Grind almonds (using a little water), to a very smooth paste. 3. Rub through a strong cloth, twisting cloth to aid the process. 4. Add almond milk to velouté. Re-heat. 5. Finish with butter and garnish with diced chicken and quenelles shaped like barley grains.

Poultry Velouté

See recipe No. 78 Velouté aux Concombres, but use 1 litre of stock and 60 gm of flour.

81. VELOUTÉ MARIE LOUISE

Ingredients	Quantity
Poultry velouté	600 ml
(see recipe No. 78 Velouté aux Concombres)	
Pearl barley	60 gm
White consommé	300 ml
Butter	15 gm
Macaroni	10 gm

Method

1. Cook pearl barley in white consommé till done. 2. Pass through a sieve. 3. Prepare poultry velouté. Combine with barley cream. 4. Cook macaroni in salted water. Drain and hold under a running tap. 5. Re-heat soup. Finish with butter. Serve hot, garnished with diced macaroni.

82. VELOUTÉ MARIE STUART

Ingredients	Quantity
Poultry velouté	600 ml
(See recipe No. 78 Velouté aux Concombres)	
White consommé	300 ml
Butter	15 gm
Carrots	30 gm
Pearl barley	60 gm
Peas	15 gm
Turnip	30 gm

Method

1. Cook pearl barley in white consommé till done. 2. Pass through a sieve. 3. Prepare poultry velouté. Combine velouté with barley cream. 4. Cut carrots and turnips brunoise (diced small) fashion, and shell peas. Boil vegetables in salted water. 5. Re-heat soup. Finish with butter. Serve hot, garnished with prepared vegetables.

83. SOUPE aux GOMBOS au OKRA

Ingredients	Quantity
Ladies' fingers	450 gm
Tomatoes	225 gm
Thyme	1 sprig

Ingredients	Quantity
Bay leaf	2 or 3
Onions	30 gm
Parsley	2 sprigs
Capsicum	30 gm
Butter	15 gm
Seasoning	to taste
Vegetable stock	1 litre
Croûtons	
Bread	30 gm
Fat	30 gm

Method

1. Wipe ladies' fingers (or okra) with a damp cloth. 2. Slice and sauté in butter. 3. In a stainless steel or enamel pan put in blanched tomatoes, herbs and stock. 4. Simmer for 10 minutes. 5. Add sautéed ladies' fingers and chopped capsicum (first remove capsicum seeds and wash well). Season to taste and simmer for 30 minutes. 6. Serve hot with fried croûtons.

84. SOUPE à l'OIGNON à la FRANCAISE

Ingredients	Quantity
Onions	450 gm
Butter	30 gm
Brown stock	1.18 litre
Worcester sauce	½ tsp
Salt and Pepper	to taste
Bread (toasted)	55 gm
Cheese	30 gm
Garlic	1 clove

Method

1. Slice onions and brown in butter. 2. Add stock, Worcester sauce, salt and pepper. 3. Simmer till onions are tender. 4. Rub casserole with cut clove of garlic. 5. Pour soup into casserole. 6. Arrage toast on top of soup. 7. Sprinkle with grated cheese and place under grill until cheese melts and browns.

85. AIGO MENAGER (PROVENÇALE SOUP)

Ingredients	Quantity
Chicken stock	1.5 litre
Garlic	6–8 pods
Potatoes	400 gm

Ingredients	Quantity
Saffron	a pinch
Onions	1 large
Tomatoes	350 gm
Mixed herbs – Rosemary, Basil, Allspice,	
Thyme and Tarragon	¼ tsp each
Fresh parsley	½ bunch

Method

1. Slice potatoes and sauté in butter with sliced onion. 2. Add chicken stock and blanched and chopped tomato. 3. Add crushed garlic, herbs and saffron and allow to boil.

86. SOUPE VICHYSSOISE

Ingredients	Quantity
Leeks	450 gm
Butter	55 gm
Onions	55 gm
Chicken stock	1.8 litre
Potatoes	55 gm
Cream	150 ml
Parsley or chopped Chives	10 gm
Seasoning	to taste

Method

1. Cut leeks fine. 2. Mince onions. Stew leeks and onions in butter without browning. 3. Add seasoning, stock and thinly-sliced potatoes. 4. Cook until vegetables are tender. 5. Pass through a sieve. Add more seasoning if necessary. 6. Stir in cream. Reheat. Garnish with chopped parsley or chives and serve grilled or hot.

87. GULYAS SOUPE

Ingredients	Quantity
Beef (diced small)	1 kg
Onions (diced small)	2 large
Hungarina paprika	4 tbsp
Tomato paste	2 tbsp
Flour	2 tbsp
White beef stock	5 litre
Potatoes (diced small)	2 large
Oil	60 ml
Caraway seeds	2 tsp
Salt and Pepper	to taste

Ingredients	Quantity
Marjoram	1 tsp
Bay leaf	2
Garlic	3-4 cloves

Method

1. In a heavy pan brown onions in oil, add paprika, spices, seasoning and meat. Cook for 5 minutes. Add flour. Cook for another 5 minutes. Add tomato paste and stock. Simmer for one and a half hours. Add diced potatoes and cook until potatoes are tender. Check and correct seasoning.

88. SOUPE COCKIE LEEKIE

Ingredients	Quantity
Chicken (small)	1
White stock	1 litre
Bouquet garni	1 litre
Leeks (white part)	225 gm
Butter	30 gm
Seasoning	to taste

Method

1. Gently cook chicken in stock with bouquet garni till tender. Strain. 2. Prepare a julienne of white part of leeks. 3. Stew in butter. Add chicken stock and simmer till cooked. Add seasoning to taste. 4. Bone chicken and cut meat into juliennes. Place in a tureen. 5. Pour boiling soup over garnish. Serve immediately.

ŒUFS

1. Oeufs Bercy
2. Oeufs Chasseur
3. Oeufs Florentine
4. Oeufs au Gratin
5. Oeufs Isoline
6. Oeufs Lully
7. Oeufs Omer Pach
8. Oeufs Parmentier
9. Oeufs Pochés à la Clamart
10. Oeufs Pochés Colbert
11. Oeufs Pochés Maintenon
12. Oeufs Pochés Mirelle
13. Oeufs Pochés Mornay
14. Oeufs Poché d'Orsay
15. Oeufs à la Coque Chimay
16. Oeufs Aurore
17. Croquettes d'œuf
18. Oeufs à la Coque en Rissole
19. Oeufs à la Tripe
20. Oeufs à la Tripe Bourgeoise
21. Oeufs en Cocotte avec Crème
22. Oeufs en Cocotte au Jus
23. Oeufs en Cocotte à`la Reine
24. Oeufs en Cocotte à la Lorraine

25. Oeufs en Cocotte à la
    Maraîchère
26. Oeufs en Cocotte à la Soubise
27. Oeufs Brouillés aux
    Champignons
28. Oeufs Brouillés Chasseur
29. Oeufs Brouillés aux Crevettes
30. Oeufs Brouillés aux Fromage
31. Oeufs Brouillés Grandmère
32. Oeufs Brouillés à la
    Portugaise
33. Oeufs frits à la Bordelaise
34. Oeufs frits à la Portugaise

35. Oeufs frits à la Porvençale
36. Omelette aux Champignons
37. Omelette à la Clamart
38. Omelette aux Epinards
39. Omelette à la Fermière
40. Omelette aux Foies de
    Volaille
41. Omelette à la Lyonnaise
42. Omelette Parmentier
43. Omelette aux Asperges
44. Omelette à la Provençale
45. Omelette aux Rognons

I. ŒUFS BERCY

Ingredients	Quantity
Eggs	4
Butter	30 gm
Salt and Pepper	to taste
Cocktail sausages	4
Tomato sauce	10 ml

Method

1. Melt half the butter in a large frying pan. 2. Break eggs, taking care not to break yolks. 3. Pour into frying pan. Baste with remaining butter and fry till yolks are glossy and whites set. 4. Dish out onto a clean plate. Season. 5. Serve hot, garnished with grilled sausages (placed between egg yolks) and surrounded with threads of tomato sauce.

2. ŒUFS CHASSEUR

Ingredients	Quantity
Eggs	4
Chicken livers	4
Chasseur sauce	1 tbsp
Butter	30 gm
Salt and Pepper	to taste

Method

1. Melt half the butter in a strong frying pan. 2. Break eggs, taking care not to break yolks. 3. Fry eggs, basting well with remaining butter till whites are done and yolk is glossy. 4. Remove and place in a clean dish.

5. Slice chicken livers and sauté in the pan. 6. Garnish eggs on either side with sautéed chicken liver covered with chasseur sauce.

3. ŒUFS FLORENTINE

Ingredients	Quantity
Spinach	225 gm
Butter	30 gm
Eggs	4
Cheese	10 gm
Mornay sauce	100 ml
Salt and Pepper	to taste
Pyrex dishes (small)	4

Method

1. Remove stalks from spinach and wash thoroughly. Drain. 2. Heat butter. Add spinach and salt. Stir well. Cover and cook till spinach is cooked. 3. Spread spinach in 4 small pyrex dishes. 4. Sprinkle over with grated cheese. 5. Break one egg into each dish. 6. Cover with mornay sauce. Place in a hot oven so that the eggs will be cooked and glazed simultaneously.

4. ŒUFS au GRATIN

Ingredients	Quantity
Eggs	4
Mornay sauce	200 ml
Cheese	50 gm
Bread raspings	30 gm
Pyrex dishes (small)	4

Method

1. Put 1 tablespoon very hot mornay sauce into each pyrex dish. 2. Break one egg into each. 3. Cover with mornay sauce and sprinkle with grated cheese mixed with fine raspings. 4. Cook in a quick oven so that eggs and gratin are done simultaneously.

5. ŒUFS ISOLINE

Ingredients	Quantity
Eggs	4
Tomatoes	4 (450 gm)
Garlic	1 flake
Oil	15 ml
Butter	30 ml
Parsley	2 sprigs

Ingredients	Quantity
Breadcrumbs	10 gm
Chicken livers	4
Salt and Pepper	to taste

Method

1. Wash and wipe tomatoes. Halve and press out excess moisture. Season. 2. Heat oil in a frying pan. Place tomatoes cut side down. 3. Turn over when half cooked and sprinkle with finely chopped garlic, parsley and breadcrumbs. 4. Bake in a moderate oven till done. 5. Meanwhile sauté chicken livers and set aside keeping them hot. 6. Melt butter. Fry eggs till whites are set and yolks glossy. 7. Dish out neatly. Place halved tomatoes between eggs. Place chicken liver in centre of each tomato.

6. ŒUFS LULLY

Ingredients	Quantity
Eggs	4
Butter	50 gm
Ham	115 gm
Bread	4 slices
Macaroni	55 gm
Tomatoes	115 gm

Method

1. Boil macaroni. Drain. Hold under running water and set aside. 2. Cut bread with a medium-sized round cutter and fry or toast. 3. Cut ham into rounds with the same cutter and fry. Place over toast. 4. Melt half the butter and fry eggs. 5. Cut them with the same cutter and place over ham. 6. Heat remaining butter. Add chopped tomatoes and stew. Add macaroni and seasoning. 7. Dish out neatly into the middle of a dish. 8. Surround with prepared eggs in the form of a circle and serve hot.

7. ŒUFS OMER PACH

Ingredients	Quantity
Eggs	4
Onions	115 gm
Butter	30 gm
Cheese	50 gm
Pyrex dishes (small)	4

Method

1. Peel and chop onions and stew in butter. 2. Place a fourth of the onion mixture in each pyrex dish. 3. Break an egg into each. 4. Sprinkle over

with grated cheese and cook in a quick oven long enough for a slight gratin to form as soon as the eggs are done.

8. ŒUFS PARMENTIER

Ingredients	Quantity
Potatoes	4 (450-500 gm)
Eggs	4
Salt, Pepper	to taste
Butter	45 gm
Cream	50 ml

Method

1. Parboil potatoes in jackets. 2. Bake in oven till done but before skins break. 3. Cut a piece off the top of each potato. Scoop out centre, mash and mix with salt, pepper and a little butter. 4. Half-fill potatoes with purée. 5. Break an egg into each. Sprinkle over with cream and bake in oven till eggs are done. 6. Replace potato tops and dish out on a napkin.

9. ŒUFS POCHÉS à la CLAMART

Ingredients	Quantity
Eggs (poached)	4
Pastry tartlets	4
Green peas	115 gm
Parsley	1 sprig
Salt	to taste
Sugar	a pinch
Lettuce	15 gm
Onions	30 gm
Butter	15 gm
Cream sauce	30 ml

Method

1. Sauté together peas, finely chopped onion, lettuce, parsley, sugar, butter and salt to taste. 2. Add a little water and cook till peas are tender. Mash. 3. Spread over pastry tartlets. 4. Place one poached egg, trimmed neatly over the prepared tartlet. 5. Cover with cream sauce.

10. ŒUFS POCHÉS COLBERT

Ingredients	Quantity
Eggs (poached)	4
Pastry tartlets	4
Béchamel sauce	50 ml
Parsley butter	30 gm

Ingredients	Quantity
Macédoine of cooked vegetables (**Carrots, Turnips, Peas, Beans**)	115 gm

Method

1. Garnish pastry tartlets with cooked vegetables. Cover with béchamel sauce. 2. Place one poached egg neatly trimmed over each. 3. Serve with slices of parsley butter.

11. ŒUFS POCHÉS MAINTENON

Ingredients	Quantity
Eggs (poached)	4
Pastry tartlets	4
Soubise sauce	30 ml
Mornay sauce	100 ml
Cheese	30 gm
Meat glaze	

Method

1. Reduce soubise sauce till quite thick. 2. Spread over pastry tartlets. Place a poached egg over each. Cover with mornay sauce. 3. Sprinkle with grated cheese. 4. Glaze in a quick oven. Remove. Dish out neatly and surround tartlets with threads of melted meat glaze.

12. ŒUFS POCHÉS MIRELLE

Ingredients	Quantity
Eggs (poached)	4
Pilau favoured with saffron	60 gm
Bread	4 slices
Oil	30 ml
Cream sauce	50 ml
Seasoning	to taste

Method

1. Lightly press pilau rice into 4 buttered tartlet moulds. 2. Cut roundels of bread the size of tartlet mould and fry in oil. 3. Place one poached egg neatly trimmed over each piece of fried bread. Season. 4. Cover with cream sauce. 5. Turn rice out of moulds and arrange rice shapes neatly in a circle on a dish, alternating them with eggs on toast.

13. ŒUFS POCHÉS MORNAY

Ingredients	Quantity
Eggs	4
Mornay sauce	100 ml
Cheese	30 gm
Bread raspings	15 gm
Bread	4 slices
Oil to fry	30 ml
Butter	15 gm

Method

1. Poach eggs. Remove and cover each separately with mornay sauce.
2. Sprinkle over with grated cheese and raspings 3. Trim bread and fry
in hot oil. Remove and place neatly in a fire-proof dish in the form of a
circle. 4. Lift eggs gently and place one on each toast. 5. Sprinkle with
melted butter and set to glaze quickly in very hot oven.

14. ŒUFS POCHÉ d'ORSAY

Ingredients	Quantity
Eggs	4
Bread	4 slices
Butter	30 gm
Chateaubriand sauce	100 ml

Method

1. Poach eggs. Remove and trim. 2. Trim and fry slices of toast in melted
butter. Place poached eggs on toast. 4. Cover with chateaubriand sauce.

15. ŒUFS à la COQUE CHIMAY

Ingredients	Quantity
Eggs	4
Dry Duxelle	30 gm
Mornay sauce	100 ml
Cheese	15 gm
Butter	15 gm

Dry Duxelle

Onions	10 gm
Butter	10 gm
Oil	10 ml
Mushrooms (stalks and parings)	20 gm

Ingredients	Quantity
Salt	to taste
Pepper	a pinch
Nutmeg	a pinch
Parsley	2 to 3 sprigs

Method

1. Hard boil eggs. Shell, cool and cut into two lengthwise. 2. Remove egg yolks, pound into a paste and mix thoroughly with dry duxelle. 3. Fill egg whites with this preparation. 4. Place on a buttered gratin dish. 5. Cover with mornay sauce. Sprinkle with grated cheese. 6. Pour a few drops of melted butter over each and set to glaze in a very hot oven or under a grill.

Dry Duxelle

1. Chop onion and fry slightly in a mixture of oil and butter. 2. Clean mushroom parings and stalks. Dry in a towel to remove excess moisture. 3. Add mushrooms to onion. Stir over a brisk fire till all moisture is completely evaporated. 4. Add seasoning and chopped parsley. Mix well. 5. Transfer to a bowl and cover with a piece of white buttered paper and set aside until needed.

16. ŒUFS AURORE

Ingredients	Quantity
Hard-boiled eggs	4
Dry Duxelle	30 gm
Bechamel sauce	100 ml
Tomato purée	30 ml
Cheese	15 gm
Butter	15 gm

Method

1. Proceed as for recipe No. 15 Oeufs Chimay using béchamel bound with tomato purée instead of mornay. 2. Mask the eggs and sprinkle with grated cheese. 3. Cook under a grill to form a gratin.

17. CROQUETTES d'ŒUF

Ingredients	Quantity
Hard-boiled eggs	6
Mushrooms	115 gm
Thick béchamel sauce	150 ml
Refined flour	15 gm

Ingredients	Quantity
Raw egg (beaten)	1
Breadcrumbs	30 gm
Parsley (fried)	4 sprigs
Fat	to fry
Salt and Pepper	to taste
Cream sauce or Curry sauce	

Method

1. Shell and cut hard-boiled eggs into small cubes (white and yolk). 2. Boil and dice mushrooms and add to eggs. 3. Mix with reduced béchamel sauce and spread to cool. 4. When cold divide into equal portions and shape like eggs on a floured board. 5. Dip in beaten egg and roll in breadcrumbs. 6. Deep fry in hot fat (7 to 8 minutes). 7. Serve immediately garnished with fried parsley. 8. Serve with cream sauce or curry sauce.

18. ŒUFS à la COQUE EN RISSOLE

Ingredients	Quantity
Hard-boiled eggs	6
Mushrooms	115 gm
Béchamel sauce	150 ml
Puff pastry	225 gm
Raw egg (beaten)	1
Breadcrumbs	30 gm
Fat	to fry

Method

1. Prepare eggs and mushrooms as for croquettes. 2. Roll out puff pastry into 0.25 cm thickness. 3. Stamp with round indented cutter (6.50 cm or 2½" diameter). 4. Place one tablespoon of the preparation in the middle of each piece of paste. 5. Moisten slightly all round and make rissoles by folding the outside edges of the paste to form a turn-over taking care to press them well together. 6. Dip in beaten egg and roll in breadcrumbs. 7. Deep fry in hot fat (8 minutes). Drain and serve immediately garnished with fried parsley.

19. ŒUFS à la TRIPE

Ingredients	Quantity
Hard-boiled eggs	6
Onions	225 gm

Ingredients	Quantity
Butter	30 gm
Béchamel sauce	300 ml
Salt and Pepper	to taste

Method

1. Chop onions and stew in butter without discolouring. 2. Add béchamel sauce and seasoning. 3. Cook gently for 10 minutes. 4. Cut eggs into large slices. Add them to the preparation a few minutes before serving. Dish onto a timbale or a pyrex bowl.

20. ŒUFS à la TRIPE BOURGEOISE

Ingredients	Quantity
Hard-boiled eggs	6
Onions	225 gm
Butter	30 gm
Refined flour	15 gm
Milk	600 ml
Salt	to taste
Pepper	a pinch
Nutmeg	a pinch

Method

1. Chop onions. Stew in butter without discolouring. 2. Sprinkle over with flour. Add boiling milk. 3. Add seasoning and cook for 20 minutes. 4. Rub through a fine sieve. 5. Transfer the preparation to a saucepan and heat well. 6. Quarter each egg and arrange neatly in a pyrex dish. 7. Cover with the preparation of onions, which should be very hot. Serve at once.

21. ŒUFS en COCOTTE avec CRÈME

Ingredients	Quantity
Eggs	4
Cocottes	4
Cream	60 ml
Butter	15 gm
Salt and Pepper	to taste

Method

1. Heat cocottes. Put one tablespoon of cream in each. 2. Break an egg into each cocotte. 3. Season and cover with two small lumps of butter. 4. Place cocottes in a saucepan with boiling water which should be

1.25 cm below the brim of the cocottes. 5. Place in moderate oven and cover, leaving sufficient space for steam to escape. 6. The eggs are done when whites are almost set and yolks are glossy. 7. Wipe cocottes and place on a napkin for service.

22. ŒUFS en COCOTTE au JUS

Ingredients	Quantity
Eggs	4
Meat gravy	1 tbsp
Butter	15 gm
Salt and Pepper	to taste
Cocottes	4

Method

1. Butter cocottes. 2. Break an egg into each buttered cocottes. 3. Season and poach as for Oeufs en Cocotte avec Crème. 4. Just before serving, surround egg yolk with a thread of reduced meat gravy.

23. ŒUFS en COCOTTE à la REINE

Ingredients	Quantity
Eggs	4
Cooked chicken	60 gm
Supreme sauce	150 ml
Salt and Pepper	to taste
Cocottes	4

Method

1. Dice chicken. Combine with half the sauce and put a portion in each cocotte. 2. Break an egg over chicken filling. Season. 3. Poach as for Oeufs en Cocotte avec Crème. 4. When set, remove. Pour remaining sauce over eggs and serve at once.

24. ŒUFS en COCOTTE à la LORRAINE

Ingredients	Quantity
Breast of pork	125 gm
Cheese	30 gm
Cream	60 ml
Eggs	4
Salt and Pepper	to taste
Cocottes	4

Method

1. Boil breast of pork in a little water. 2. Dice and sauté lightly. 3. Put a portion of the pork into each cocotte. Cover with a slice of cheese and 1 tablespoon boiling cream. 4. Break an egg over each, season and poach as for Oeufs en Cocotte avec Crème.

25. ŒUFS en COCOTTE à la MARAÎCHÈRE

Ingredients	Quantity
Eggs	4
Spinach	225 gm
Lettuce	100 gm
Butter	30 gm
Salt and Pepper	to taste
Cocottes	4
Parsley	a few sprigs

Method

1. Clean and wash spinach. Dry on a towel. 2. Melt butter and stew spinach. Add sheared lettuce and continue stewing. 3. Put a portion of the spinach preparation into each cocotte. 4. Break an egg over each. Season and poach as for Oeufs en Cocotte avec Crème. Serve hot garnished with a small sprig of parsley placed over egg yolk.

26. ŒUFS en COCOTTE à la SOUBISE

Ingredients	Quantity
Eggs	4
Onions	225 gm
Butter	30 gm
Salt and Pepper	to taste
Meat glaze	15 ml
Cocottes	4

Method

1. Peel and chop onions finely. 2. Melt butter and stew onions without discolouring. Add salt and pepper. 3. Put a portion of onions in each cocotte. 4. Break an egg over each. Season. 5. Poach as for Oeufs en Cocotte avec Crème. 6. When done, surround egg yolks with a thread of melted meat glaze and serve hot.

27. ŒUFS BROUILLÉS aux CHAMPIGNONS

Ingredients	Quantity
Eggs	8
Mushrooms	115 gm
Butter	60 gm
Salt and Pepper	to taste

Method

1. Break eggs into a basin. Season with salt and pepper and whisk thoroughly. 2. Boil and dice mushrooms and add to eggs keeping aside a few for garnish. 3. Melt half the butter in a strong pan. Add eggs and cook over gentle heat stirring continuously till eggs are lightly cooked. 4. Remove from heat and add remaining butter. 5. Serve hot, garnished with slices of mushrooms.

28. ŒUFS BROUILLÉS CHASSEUR

Ingredients	Quantity
Eggs	8
Chicken liver (sautéed)	4
Chasseur sauce	1 tbsp
Salt and Pepper	to taste

Method

1. Prepare scrambled eggs as for Oeufs Brouillés aux Champignons. 2. Dish out. Hollow out middle and fill with sautéed chicken liver. 3. Surround eggs with a thread of chasseur sauce and serve immediately.

29. ŒUFS BROUILLÉS aux CREVETTES

Ingredients	Quantity
Eggs	8
Butter	60 gm
Salt	to taste
Pepper	to taste
Shrimps	30 gm
Shrimp sauce	30 ml

Method

1. Prepare scrambled eggs as for Oeufs Brouillés aux Champignons. 2. Dish out. Place heads of boiled shrimps mixed with shrimp sauce in the middle and surround with threads of shrimp sauce.

30. ŒUFS BROUILLÉS aux FROMAGE

Ingredients	Quantity
Eggs	8
Cheese (2 types if possible)	115 gm
Butter	30 gm
Salt and Pepper	to taste

Method

1. Break eggs into bowl. Add seasoning. Whisk thoroughly. 2. Add grated cheese. 3. Melt half the butter. Add eggs and cook over gentle heat, stirring continuously till eggs are lightly cooked. 4. Remove from fire. Add remaining butter.

31. ŒUFS BROUILLÉS GRANDMÈRE

Ingredients	Quantity
Eggs	8
Butter	60 gm
Bread	2 slices
Parsley	1 sprig
Salt and Pepper	to taste

Method

1. Cut bread into cubes and fry. Remove and keep hot. 2. Prepare scramble eggs as for Oeufs Brouillés aux Champignons. 3. Serve mixed with fried croûtons and garnished with chopped parsley.

32. ŒUFS BROUILLÉS à la PORTUGAISE

Ingredients	Quantity
Eggs	8
Butter	60 gm
Salt and Pepper	to taste
Tomatoes	125 gm
Parsley	a few sprigs
Meat glaze	1 tbsp

Method

1. Chop tomatoes finely. Remove excess moisture. Season and sauté in a little melted butter. 2. Prepare scrambled eggs as for Oeufs Brouillés aux Champignons. 3. Dish out eggs. In the middle, put tomatoes garnished with chopped parsley. Surround with threads of meat glaze.

33. ŒUFS FRITS à la BORDELAISE

Ingredients	Quantity
Eggs	4
Tomatoes	2
Garlic	1 small flake
Oil	10 ml
Parsley	2 sprigs
Breadcrumbs	10 gm
Shallots	2
Mushrooms	30 gm
Salt and Pepper	to taste
Fat to fry eggs	

Method

1. Halve tomatoes and press out excess moisture. Season. 2. Heat oil in a frying pan and place tomatoes cut side down. 3. When half-cooked turn and sprinkle with finely chopped garlic, parsley, shallots and breadcrumbs. 4. Bake tomatoes in a moderate oven till done. 5. Sauté mushrooms and chop fine. 6. Fry eggs. Garnish tomatoes with sautéed mushrooms and place a fried egg on each tomato. Arrange neatly in a dish and serve hot.

34. ŒUFS FRITS à la PORTUGAISE

Ingredients	Quantity
Eggs	4
Tomatoes	3
Pilau	4 tbsp
Butter	15 gm
Salt and Pepper	to taste
Fat to fry eggs	

Method

1. Halve two tomatoes and chop the third. 2. Scoop out centre from halved tomatoes. Season and keep upside down over a rack placed on a plate, to let moisture drain out. 3. After about half an hour fill halves with a tablespoonful each of prepared pilau. Dot with butter and bake. 4. Sauté chopped tomato. 5. Fry eggs. Drain and place over each of baked tomato halves. 6. Arrange in a circle with sautéed tomato in the centre.

35. ŒUFS FRITS à la PROVENÇALE

Ingredients	Quantity
Eggs	4
Tomatoes	2
Garlic	1 flake
Parsley	2 sprigs
Breadcrumbs	10 gm
Eggplant	1
Refined flour	5 gm
Oil	25 ml
Salt and Pepper	to taste
Fat to fry eggs	

Method

1. Wash and halve tomatoes. Press out excess moisture. Season. 2.Heat part of the oil. Place tomatoes cut side down. 3. When half cooked, turn and sprinkle with chopped garlic and parsley and breadcrumbs. 4. Bake in a moderate oven till done. 5. Cut thick roundels of eggplant. 6. Roll in seasoned flour and fry in remaining oil. 7. Fry eggs. Remove and drain. Place tomatoes on roundels of fried eggplant. Place eggs over tomatoes. Arrange neatly and serve at once.

36. OMELETTE aux CHAMPIGNONS

Ingredients	Quantity
Eggs	8
Mushrooms	125 gm
Salt	to taste
Pepper	to taste
Butter	60 gm
Meat glaze	10 ml

Method

1. Mince mushrooms and stew in a little butter. Season and remove. 2. For each omelette break two eggs into a basin. 3. Season with salt and pepper. 4. Beat well with a fork or beater. 5. Heat omelette pan. Wipe with a clean cloth. Add about 10 gm of butter. 6. When butter foams add beaten eggs and cook quickly moving the mixture continuously with a fork. 7. Take to the side of the fire. Add a portion of mushrooms. Roll quickly. 8. Dish out and surround with a thread of meat glaze.

N.B. If button mushrooms are used keep a few whole to garnish each omelette.

37. OMELETTE à la CLAMART

Ingredients	Quantity
Eggs	8
Butter	60 gm
Salt	to taste
Pepper	to taste
Shelled peas	115 gm
Lettuce	30 gm

Method

1. Boil peas. Drain and sauté in a little butter with shredded lettuce.
2. Prepare omelette as for Omelete aux Champignons. Stuff with prepared peas and roll quickly. 3. Dish out neatly. Make an opening lengthwise in the centre and put a thread of peas as garnish.

38. OMELETTE aux EPINARDS

Ingredients	Quantity
Eggs	8
Spinach	450 gm
Cream	100 ml
Salt and Pepper	to taste
Butter	75 gm

Method

1. Clean and wash spinach. Melt 15 gm of butter. 2. Add spinach and salt and let it stew till cooked and dry. 3. Prepare omelettes as for Omelette aux Champignons, but stuff with a portion of spinach bound with cream. 4. Roll. Dish out and serve hot.

39. OMELETTE à la FERMIÈRE

Ingredients	Quantity
Eggs	8
Butter	60 gm
Ham	115 gm
Salt and Pepper	to taste

Method

1. Prepare omelette as for Omelette aux Champignons, but mix diced ham with beaten eggs. (1 tbsp for each omelette). 2. Roll quickly and dish out neatly.

40. OMELETTE aux FOIES de VOLAILLE

Ingredients	Quantity
Eggs	8
Butter	75 gm
Chicken liver	115 gm
Meat glaze	1 tbsp
Parsley	a few sprigs
Salt and Pepper	to taste

Method

1. Clean chicken liver and dice. Season. Sauté in butter. Cohere with meat glaze. 2. Prepare omelette as for Omelette aux Champignons. Stuff with a portion of chicken liver reserving a little for garnish. 3. Roll omelette. Dish out neatly. Make a lengthwise slit in the centre and fill with liver set aside for garnish. Serve hot.

41. OMELETTE à la LYONNAISE

Ingredients	Quantity
Eggs	8
Onions	115 gm
Parsley	a few sprigs
Butter	75 gm
Salt and Pepper	to taste

Method

1. Peel and mince onions. Sauté in 15 gms. of butter. Add seasoning. Keep aside. 2. Prepare omelette as for Omelette aux Champignons, but add sautéed onions to the omelette. 3. Roll quickly and serve hot.

42. OMELETTE PARMENTIER

Ingredients	Quantity
Eggs	8
Butter	75 gm
Parsley	a few sprigs
Potatoes	225 gm
Salt and Pepper	to taste

Method

1. Boil potatoes in their jackets. Peel and dice. Season and sauté in 15 gm melted butter. 2. Prepare omelette as for Omelette aux Champignons using potatoes instead of mushrooms. Add chopped parsley to eggs. 3. Roll quickly and serve hot.

43. OMELETTE aux ASPERGES

Ingredients	Quantity
Eggs	8
Butter	60 gm
Salt and Pepper	to taste
Asparagus	115 gm

Method

1. Blanch and stew asparagus in a little butter. If canned, use as is.
2. Prepare omelette as for Omelette aux Champignons using asparagus instead of mushrooms. 3. Roll quickly and serve hot.

44. OMELETTE à la PROVENÇALE

Ingredients	Quantity
Eggs	8
Tomatoes	4
Garlic	1 flake
Parsley	1 sprig
Oil	15 ml
Salt and Pepper	to taste

Method

1. Wash and cut tomatoes. Remove pips and excess moisture. Dice.
2. Chop garlic and parsley. 3. Heat oil. Add garlic, parsley, tomatoes and seasoning. Cook quickly. 4. Beat eggs as for Omelette aux Champignons.
5. Add a portion of tomatoes to each batch and make omelette. 6. Roll and serve hot.

45. OMELETTE aux ROGNONS

Ingredients	Quantity
Eggs	8
Butter	75 gm
Kidneys	4
Worcester sauce	2 tsp
Meat glaze	2 tbsp
Salt and Pepper	to taste

Method

1. Clean kidneys. Slice and marinate in Worcester sauce. 2. Heat 15 gm butter. Sauté kidneys till cooked. 3. Prepare omelette as for Omelette aux Champignons using a portion of sautéed kidneys instead of mushrooms. Reserve a few for garnish. 4. Roll and dish out. Make lengthwise slit in centre and put in a few pieces of kidneys as garnish.
5. Surround each omelette with a thread of meat glaze.

POISSON

1. Cuts of Fish
2. Saumon Poché
3. Darne de Saumon Poché
4. Saumon Mayonnaise
5. Saumon Grillé
6. Saumon à la Meunière
7. Cadgeree de Saumon
8. Saumon Royale
9. Medallion de Saumon
10. Salade de Saumon
11. Filet de Pomfret ou Sole Mornay
12. Filet de Pomfret Meunière Andalouse
13. Filet de Sole ou Pomfret Dorée
14. Fish Belle Meunière
15. Filet de Pomfret Bretonne
16. Filet de Pomfret ou Sole aux Aubergines
17. Filet de Pomfret ou Sole Meunière à l'Orange
18. Filet de Pomfret ou Sole Dugléré
19. Pomfret ou Sole Grillée
20. Pomfret ou Sole Saint Germain
21. Filet de Pomfret ou Sole Cubat
22. Filet de Pomfret ou Sole Provençale
23. Pomfret ou Sole Dieppoise
24. Pomfret ou Sole Bonne Femme
25. Filet de Pomfret ou Sole Bercy
26. Filet de Pomfret ou Sole Hongroise
27. Filet de Pomfret ou Sole Mexicaine
28. Filet de Pomfret ou Sole Miramar
29. Filet de Pomfret ou Sole Newburg
30. Filet de Pomfret ou Sole Orientale
31. Filet de Pomfret ou Sole en Pilaw à la Levantine
32. Filet de Pomfret ou Sole Pompadour
33. Filet de Pomfret ou Sole Verdi
34. Filet de Pomfret ou Sole Veronique (A)
Filet de Pomfret ou Sole Veronique (B)
35. Filet de Pomfret ou Sole Walewska
36. Filet de Pomfret au Sauce Verte
37. Poisson au Vin Blanc
38. Pomfret Wiesbaden
39. Maquereau Grillé
40. To Cook and Clean Lobster or Langoustes
41. Homard à la Thermidor
42. Homard à la Newburg (A)
Homard à la Newburg (B)
43. Mayonnaise de Homard
44. Salade de Homard
45. Languouste à la Parisienne
46. Salade de Thon
47. Crabe en Coquille

I. CUTS OF FISH

La Darne	a slice of round fish cut on the bone, e.g. Darne de saumon.
Le Tronçon	a slice of flat fish cut on the bone, e.g. Tronçon de pomfret.
Le Filet	a cut of fish free from bone. A round fish yields two fillets and a flat fish four fillets.
Le supreme	a term usually applied to fillets of large fish cut on a slant, e.g. Supême de gol.
Le Délice	a term usually applied to a trimmed and neatly folded fillet of fish, e.g. Délice de sole.
Le Goujon	fillet of fish cut into strips about 7.5 cm long and 0.5 cm thick.
La Paupiette	fillet of fish (generally pomfret or sole) spread with stuffing and rolled.

2. SAUMON POCHÉ

Ingredients	Quantity
Salmon (whole)	1
Court Bouillon	
Water	1 litre
Salt	15 gm
Carrots (sliced)	60 gm
Bay leaf	1
Parsley stalks	2 to 3
Vinegar	75 ml
Peppercorns	6
Onions (sliced)	60 gm
Thyme	1 sprig

Method

1. Prepare court bouillon by simmering all ingredients except salmon, together, for 30 to 40 minutes. Strain and cool. 2. Scrape off scales of salmon, using the back of a knife. 3. Remove gills and clean out heat. 4. Remove intestines and clear blood from backbone. 5. Trim fins. 6. Wash thoroughly using lime and vinegar. 7. Place in a saucepan. Cover with cold court bouillon. 8. Bring to boil slowly, skim and simmer gently.

N.B. Always allow salmon to remain in court bouillon until cold.

3. DARNE de SAUMON POCHÉ

Ingredients

1. **Cut piece of Salmon.**   2. **Court bouillon to cover.**
3. **Hollandaise sauce.**

Method

1. Clean salmon. Wash and place in simmering court bouillon. 2. Simmer gently till cooked (5 to 7 minutes). 3. Drain well. Remove centre bone and serve hot with hollandaise sauce.

4. SAUMON MAYONNAISE

Ingredients	*Quantity*
Salmon (whole) or	1
A cut piece	500 gm (about)
Lettuce	1 bunch
Cucumber	125 gm
Tomatoes	225 gm
Mayonnaise sauce	300 ml
Court bouillon	300 ml

Method

1. Clean and cook salmon in court bouillon as in Saumon Poché for whole fish and as in Darne de Saumon Poché for a cut piece. 2. Cool in court bouillon. 3. If cut piece, remove skin, centre bone and brown surface. Dress neatly on silver flat. 4. Garnish with whole lettuce leaves, sliced tomatoes and sliced cucumber. 5. Spread some mayonnaise on fish and serve remaining sauce in a sauce-boat.

5. SAUMON GRILLÉ

Ingredients	*Quantity*
Salmon	500 gm
Butter	30 gm
Salt	to taste

Method

1. Clean and cut salmon into slices about 2.5 to 3.75 cm (1–1½") thick. 2. Apply salt, sprinkle with melted butter and grill on a rather brisk fire for the first part. 3. Reduce heat and finish grilling. 4. Serve with maitre d'hôtel butter or anchovy butter.

6. SAUMON à la MEUNIÈRE

Ingredients	Quantity
Salmon	500 gm
Refined flour	15 gm
Salt and Pepper	to taste
Clarified butter	60 gm
Lime	1
Parsley	a few sprigs
Fat to fry fish	

Method

1. Clean and cut salmon into thick slices. 2. Dredge with seasoned flour. 3. Heat fat and, when smoking, fry fish, turning over when one side is done and fry other side. 4: Sprinkle a few drops of lime juice and chopped parsley over fish. 5. Just before serving, pour browned butter over which will froth as it touches parsley.

7. CADGEREE de SAUMON

Ingredients	Quantity
Cooked flaked salmon	500 gm
Hard-boiled eggs	4
Pilau (plain)	450 gm
Bechamel Sauce	450 ml
Curry powder	2 tsp
Court bouillon	

Method

1. Boil salmon as in Saumon Poche. 2. Remove skin and bones and flake. 3. Dice hard-boiled eggs. 4. Prepare béchamel sauce and flavour with curry powder. 5. Dish in a hot timbale, putting, salmon, eggs and pilau in alternate layers. Finish with a coating of sauce.

8. SAUMON ROYALE

Ingredients	Quantity
Salmon	1 (about 2.5 kg)
Pastry boats	8
Mayonnaise sauce	300 ml
Hard-boiled eggs	8
Cheese	15 gm
Butter	30 gm
Court bouillon	
Cherry tomatoes	115 gm

Ingredients	Quantity
Cucumber	225 gm
Macédoine of vegetables	450 gm
Prawns	500 gm
Lettuce	1 bunch
Parsley	1 bunch
Red radish	1 bunch
Mustard	

Method

1. Clean, wash, boil and cool salmon as in Saumon Poché. 2. Lay out neatly on a silver flat over a bed of shredded lettuce. 3. Cut cucumber into 5 cm pieces and parboil. Scoop out seeds. Fill with boiled prawns cohered with mayonnaise and garnish with a sprig of parsley on top. 4. Fill pastry boats with macédoine of vegetables mixed with mayonnaise. 5. Shell and cut eggs into halves. Scoop out yolk. Cream with grated cheese, butter and mustard. Pipe centres of yolk. Cream with grated cheese, butter and mustard. Pipe centres of white with prepared mixture. 6. Arrange pastry boats, stuffed eggs and cucumber alternately around the fish. 7. Pipe a pattern over the fish with mayonnaise put into a piping bag with a writing nozzle. 8. Garnish with red radish cut into flowers and cherry tomatoes.

9. MEDALLION de SAUMON

Ingredients	Quantity
Salmon	1 fillet (225 gm)
Mayonnaise sauce or	
White, pink or green chaud-froid sauce	75 ml
Gelatine	5 gm
Aspic jelly	

Method

1. Cut slices 1 cm thick from the fillet. 2. Arrange on a greased tray and poach. 3. Drain and dry in an oven. 4. Cut into ovals or rounds. 5. Coat with mayonnaise thickened with dissolved gelatine or one of the chaud-froid sauces. 6. Decorate as desired and glaze with cold melted aspic jelly. 7. Arrange in a circle on a sliver flat.

10. SALADE de SAUMON

Ingredients	Quantity
Lettuce	1 bunch
Salmon	500 gm
Anchovy fillets	2

Ingredients	Quantity
Court bouillon	
Olives	2
Eggs (hard-boiled)	4
Red radish	1 bunch
French dressing	

Method

1. Clean and cook salmon in court bouillon as for Saumon Poché. 2. Cool in same liquid, then skin, bone and flake. 3. Shred outer leaves of lettuce and arrange at the bottom of a glass bowl. 4. Place flaked salmon over. Decorate with heart of lettuce, anchovy fillets, sliced olives, sliced roundels of hard-boiled egg and radish flowers. 5. Sprinkle over with French dressing.

11. FILET de POMFRET ou SOLE MORNAY

Ingredients	Quantity
Pomfret or Sole	1 (500 gm)
Mornay sauce	300 ml
Fish fumet	
Cheese	30 gm
Butter	15 gm

Method

1. Clean and fillet fish. Skin and wash. 2. Lay the fillets on a buttered dish. Sprinkle some fish fumet over. Add butter. Poach gently. 3. Coat bottom of pyrex pie dish with mornay sauce. 4. Lay prepared fish over. Cover with remaining sauce. Sprinkle with grated cheese. 5. Glaze under a grill.

12. FILET de POMFRET MEUNIÈRE ANDALOUSE

Ingredients	Quantity
Pomfret or Sole	1
Butter (clarified)	50 gm
Lime	1
Parsley	a few sprigs
For Garnish	
Medium tomatoes	2
Eggplant	225 gm
Refined flour	15 gm
Salt and Pepper	to taste
Butter	15 gm

Ingredients	Quantity
Oil	15 ml
Pilau mixed with capsicum	60 gm

Method

1. Clean, fillet and skin fish. Wash and dry. Toss in seasoned flour.
2. Heat half the clarified butter to smoking point in a frying pan. Put in fish. 3. When fish is sufficiently browned on one side, turn over and brown other side. Place in a hot dish. Sprinkle over with lime juice.
4. Garnish with chopped parsley.

Garnish

5. Halve tomatoes, scoop out insides and season. 6. Stuff with pilau and stew in butter. 7. Cut eggplant into thin roundels. Wash, dry and fry in hot oil. Season. 8. Dish out fish. Surround with fried eggplant roundels alternating with stuffed tomatoes. 9. Pour browned butter over fish and serve immediately.

13. FILET de SOLE ou POMFRET DORÉE

Ingredients	Quantity
Pomfret or Sole	2 (500 gm)
Clarified butter	60 gm
Lime	1
Parsley	a few sprigs
Flour	15 gm
Salt and Pepper	to taste
Tomato-flavoured béarnaise	

Method

1. Clean, fillet and skin fish. 2. Wash well. Dry on towel. Coat with seasoned flour. 3. Heat half the butter. Fry fish, turning to brown both sides. 4. Remove, sprinkle a few drops of lime juice and chopped parsley.
5. Just before serving, heat remaining butter till brown; pour over fish. It will froth when it touches the parsley. 6. Serve garnished with slices of lime and tomato-flavoured béarnaise. (see end of recipe 32.)

14. FISH BELLE MEUNIÈRE

Ingredients and method as for Filet de Pomfret Meunière with the addition of 4 grilled mushrooms, 4 slices of tomato and some soft herring roe (passed through flour and shallow fried) all neatly dressed on each fillet.

15. FILET de POMFRET BRETONNE

Preapare as for Filet de Pomfret Meunière but garnish with boiled shrimps and cooked sliced mushrooms.

16. FILET de POMFRET ou SOLE aux AUBERGINES

Ingredients and method as for Filet de Pomfret Meunière but surround with a border of eggplant roundels one cm thick, rolled in seasoned flour and fried in clarified butter. This should be done just before serving otherwise the roundels will lose their crispness.

17. FILET de POMFRET ou SOLE MEUNIÈRE à l'ORANGE

Ingredients and method as for Filet de Pomfret Meunieère but garnish each fillet with a row of segments of orange, peeled and pipped. Pour browned butter over this.

18. FILET de POMFRET ou SOLE DUGLÉRÉ

Ingredients	Quantity
Pomfret or Sole	1 (500 gm)
Onions	45 gm
Tomatoes	225 gm
Parsley	a few sprigs
Salt and Pepper	to taste
Fish stock	60 ml
White vinegar	15 ml
Fish velouté	60 ml
Butter	30 gm
Lime	$\frac{1}{4}$

Method

1. Clean and fillet fish. Wash well. 2. Put fillets in a buttered dish. Add peeled and chopped onions, tomatoes, parsley, salt, pepper, fish stock and white vinegar. 4. Poach gently and dish fillets. 5. Reduce cooking liquor; thicken with fish velouté. Complete with butter and a few drops of lime juice. Cover fish with this sauce.

19. POMFRET ou SOLE GRILLÉE

Ingredients	Quantity
Pomfret or Sole	1
Oil	30 ml
Lime	1
Salt and Pepper	to taste

Method

1. Scale fish. Trim fins. Slit belly. Remove intestines and membranes.
2. Remove gills and eyes but keep head on. 3. Wash well. Make gashes
on fish. Sprinkle with oil and seasoning. Grill fish very gently. 4. Serve
immediately, garnished with slices of lime.

20. POMFRET ou SOLE SAINT GERMAIN

Ingredients	Quantity
Pomfret or	1
Sole	500 gm
Butter	60 gm
Béarnaise sauce	
Fresh breadcrumbs	30 gm
Potatoes	a few

Method

1. Clean fish as for Pomfret Grillée. 2. Dip in melted butter. Cover with
fresh breadcrumbs, patting them down with a flat knife to form a crust.
3. Sprinkle more melted butter. 4. Grill fish gently so that coating
becomes golden. 5. Dish and serve surrounded by fried potatoes shaped
like olives. 6. Send a béarnaise sauce separately to the table.

21. FILET de POMFRET ou SOLE CUBAT

Ingredients	Quantity
Pomfret or	1
Sole	500 gm
Butter	15 gm
Mushrooms	225 gm
Mornay sauce	75 ml
Cheese	15 gm

Method

1. Clean and fillet fish. Skin. 2. Cook mushrooms. Reserve liquid, drain
and mince. 3. Poach fillets in mushroom liquor to which butter has been
added.4. Cover bottom of a pyrex dish with minced mushroom. 5. Lay
poached fish over. Coat with mornay sauce. 6. Sprinkle with cheese and
glaze quickly.

22. FILET de POMFRET ou SOLE PROVENÇALE

Ingredients	Quantity
Pomfret or	1
Sole	500 gm

Ingredients	Quantity
Oil	30 ml
Garlic	2 flakes
Tomatoes (small)	4 (250 gm)
Milk	2 tbsp
Lime juice	1 tsp
Button mushrooms	4
Dry Duxelle	30 gm
Provençale sauce	30 ml
Parsley	a few sprigs
Water	1 cup

Method

1. Clean and fillet fish. 2. Poach fish in milk, water and lime juice combined with oil and a crushed flake of garlic. 3. Drain, reserving liquid, and dish. 4. Coat with provençale sauce combined with reduced cooking liquor. Sprinkle with chopped parsley. 5. Grill mushrooms. Cut tomatoes into halves. Scoop out centre. Stuff with duxelle flavoured with garlic and bake. These should be ready just in time for serving. 6. Surround fish with mushrooms and tomatoes placed alternately and serve at once.

PROVENÇALE SAUCE

Ingredients	Quantity
Tomatoes	225 gm
Oil	15 ml
Garlic	1 flake
Powdered sugar	1 pinch
Salt and Pepper	to taste
Parsley	2 sprigs

Method

1. Peel tomatoes, remove seeds, press and chop roughly. 2. Heat oil. Add tomatoes, pepper, salt, crushed garlic, sugar and chopped parsley. 3. Simmer for 15 minutes over gentle heat.

DRY DUXELLE

Ingredients	Quantity
Onions	10 gm
Oil and Butter	15 gm
Mushrooms (stalks and parings)	30 gm
Salt and Pepper	to taste
Nutmeg	1 pinch
Parsley	a few sprigs

Method

1. Heat oil and butter. 2. Lightly fry minced onion. Add mushroom parings chopped and pressed in a towel to remove extra moisture. 3. Stir over a brisk fire until moisture evaporates completely. Add seasoning and chopped parsley.

23. POMFRET ou SOLE DIEPPOISE

Ingredients	Quantity
Pomfret or	1
Sole	500 gm
Fish fumet	120 ml
Mussels	6
Shrimps	450 gm
White sauce	300 ml

Method

1. Clean pomfret or sole. 2. Poach fish in fish fumet. 3. Drain and dish out. Coat with white sauce. 4. Surround with poached mussels and shrimps.

24. POMFRET ou SOLE BONNE FEMME

Ingredients	Quantity
Pomfret or Sole	1
Shallots	30 gm
Fish fumet	300 ml
Fish velouté	60 ml
Butter	60 gm
Parsley	1 sprig
Mushrooms	45 gm
Salt and Pepper	to taste

Method

1. Grease an aluminium pie dish. 2. Sprinkle finely chopped shallots, chopped parsley, and raw minced mushrooms. 3. Lay prepared pomfret over garnish. Season to taste. 4. Moisten with fish fumet and poach gently, taking care to baste from time to time. 5. When poached, remove fish, and quickly reduce cooking liquor to half. 6. Add fish velouté and finish sauce with butter. 7. Coat fish with this sauce and set to glaze in a very hot oven or under a grill.

25. FILET de POMFRET ou SOLE BERCY

Ingredients	Quantity
Pomfret or Sole	1 (500 gm)

Ingredients	Quantity
Shallots	30 gm
Fish fumet	100 ml
Lime	½
Parsley	a few sprigs
Salt and Pepper	to taste
Butter	15 gm

Method

1. Clean, fillet and skin fish. Wash well. 2. Peel and mince shallots.
3. Put minced shallots into a greased pyrex dish. 4. Place fillets over
shallots. Season to taste. Add fish fumet and butter cut into small pieces.
5. Cook in an oven, basting frequently. Glaze at the last minute. 6. Just
before serving sprinkle over with chopped parsley and lime juice.

26. FILET de POMFRET ou SOLE HONGROISE

Ingredients	Quantity
Pomfret or Sole	1 (500 gm)
Fish fumet	150 ml
Tomatoes	225 gm
Cream	2 tbsp
Lime	½
Onions	30 gm
Paprika	½ tsp
Salt and Pepper	to taste
Butter	15 gm

Method

1. Peel and chop onion. Peel and chop tomatoes. Press and remove excess
moisture. 2. Melt butter. Add chopped onions. Fry lightly without
discolouring. 3. Add paprika, salt and pepper. Moisten with fish fumet.
4. Add tomatoes and cook for 7 to 8 minutes. 5. Lay fillets of fish on a
buttered dish. 6. Pour sauce over and poach fish. 7. Arrange fish on a
dish. Reduce cooking liquor to a stiff consistency. 8. Add cream and lime
juice. Coat fillets with this sauce.

27. FILET de POMFRET ou SOLE MEXICAINE

Ingredients	Quantity
Pomfret or	1
Sole	500 gm
Fish fumet	100 ml

Ingredients	Quantity
Forcemeat	
Fresh breadcrumbs	115 gm
Milk	30 ml
Onions	15 gm
Shallots	15 gm
Mushrooms	30 gm
Parsley	bunch
Garlic	1 flake
Salt and Pepper	to taste
Nutmeg	a pinch
Eggs	2
Butter	15 gm
Garnish	
Tomatoes	115 gm
Button mushrooms	4
Butter	15 gm
Béchamel sauce	30 ml
Capsicum	15 gm

Method

1. Soak fresh breadcrumbs in milk. Press out moisture and put into a bowl. 2. Chop and stew onion and shallots in melted butter without discolouring. 3. Add onion, shallots, minced mushrooms, chopped parsley, garlic, seasoning and beaten eggs to breadcrumbs. Mix thoroughly. 4. Clean, fillet and skin fish. 5. Coat fillets with forcemeat. Roll into a scroll. 6. Lay scrolls on a greased dish. Poach in fish fumet. 7. Grill button mushrooms. Chop and stew half the tomatoes in butter. Make a purée with the rest. 8. Arrange fillets in an oval dish. 9. Coat them with béchamel sauce cohered with tomato purée and diced capsicum. 10. Garnish with grilled mushrooms and stewed tomatoes.

28. FILET de POMFRET ou SOLE MIRAMAR

Ingredients	Quantity
Pomfret or Sole	1
Eggplant	225 gm
Pilau	225 gm
	(made from 100 gm rice)
Butter	60 gm
Salt and Pepper	to taste
Refined flour	15 gm

Method

1. Clean and fillet fish. Wash and cut into slices. 2. Dry. Dip in seasoned flour and fry in butter. 3. Cut roundels of eggplant (one cm thick). Season, dredge and toss in butter, taking care to keep them crisp. 4. Line the sides of a jelly mould with pilau. 5. Mix fish and eggplant. Put mixture into the centre. Cover with rice. Keep hot. 6. Turn out and just before serving sprinkle with melted butter.

29. FILET de POMFRET ou SOLE NEWBURG

Ingredients	Quantity
Lobster	1
Pomfret or Sole	1
Fish fumet	200 ml
Court bouillon	
Butter	30 gm
Cream	600 ml
Egg yolks	2
Salt and Pepper	to taste

Method

1. Cook lobster in court bouillon. 2. Remove the meat and cut into regular slices. Season strongly. 3. Melt butter and sauté slices of lobster on both sides till they acquire a fine red colour. 4. Moisten with Madeira or fish fumet (half) and reduce completely. Add cream mixed with egg yolks. 5. Stir gently on the side of the fire until thick. 6. Clean fillet and skin fish and poach in remaining fish fumet. 7. Arrange fish in an oval dish. Lay a slice of lobster on each fillet. Dice remaining pieces and mix with sauce. 8. Coat fish with sauce.

30. FILET de POMFRET ou SOLE ORIENTALE

Ingredients	Quantity
Pomfret or	1
Sole	500 gm
Lobster	1
Pilau (flavoured with curry powder)	225 gm (made with 100 gm rice)
Fish fumet	200 ml
Butter	30 gm
Cream	600 ml
Egg yolks	2
Curry powder	1 tsp
Salt and Pepper	to taste
Court bouillon	

Method

1. Prepare lobster and sauce as for recipe No. 29, but add curry powder to sauce. 2. Clean, fillet and skin fish. Poach in remaining fish fumet. 3. Dish out fish. 4. Place a slice of lobster on each fillet. 5. Dice remaining lobster and mix with sauce. 6. Pour sauce over fish. Serve accompanied by a mould of pilau flavoured with curry powder.

31. FILET de POMFRET ou SOLE en PILAU à la LEVANTINE

Ingredients	Quantity
Pomfret or Sole	1 (500 gm)
Capsicum	30 gm
Eggplant	1
Butter	60 gm
Pilau (using 100 gm rice)	225 gm
Curry sauce	300 ml
Salt and Pepper	to taste

Method

1. Clean and fillet fish. Skin and cut into cubes. Season and fry in some butter. 2. Add diced capsicum to pilau. 3. Dice eggplant. Season, toss in remaining butter and mix with fish. 4. Mould rice into a border. Put fish cubes and diced eggplant in the centre. Cover with curry sauce, taking care to see that curry sauce does not touch rice. 5. Serve hot with some curry sauce served separately in a sauce boat.

32. FILET de POMFRET ou SOLE POMPADOUR

Ingredients	Quantity
Pomfret or Sole	1
Butter	30 gm
Breadcrumbs	30 gm
Black mushrooms	30 gm
Meat glaze	15 ml
Béarnaise sauce tomatée	30 ml
Château potatoes	450 gm

Method

1. Clean and fillet fish. Season. Dip in melted butter and roll in breadcrumbs patting breadcrumbs well with a flat knife. 2. Grill. 3. Garnish each fillet with a thread of béarnaise sauce tomatée. 4. Dish and surround with château potatoes. Put a cooked mushroom moistened with meat glaze on each fillet.

N.B. To prepare béarnaise sauce tomatée cohere a little, very red tomato purée with béarnaise sauce.

33. FILET de POMFRET ou SOLE VERDI

Ingredients	Quantity
Macaroni	115 gm
Cheese	30 gm
Butter	15 gm
Lobster meat	100 gm
Salt and Pepper	to taste
Black mushrooms	45 gm
Pomfret or	1
Sole	(500 gm)
Fish fumet	200 ml
Mornay sauce	300 ml

Method

1. Boil and drain macaroni. Hold under running water. Set aside.
2. Clean, fillet and skin fish. Wash well. Season. 3. Poach fish in fish
fumet. 4. Melt butter. Toss macaroni in butter. Add grated cheese and
diced lobster meat. 5. Lay macaroni very evenly in a pyrex dish. 6. Place
poached fillets over macaroni. 7. Cover with mornay sauce and set to
glaze quickly under a grill. Serve hot.

34. FILET de POMFRET ou SOLE VERONIQUE (A)

Ingredients	Quantity
Pomfret or	1
Sole	(500 gm)
Egg yolk	1
Butter	60 gm
Lime	¼
Cream	45 ml
Fish stock	75 ml
Fish velouté	300 ml
Salt	to taste
White pepper	a pinch
White seedless grapes	60 gm

Method

1. Clean, fillet and skin fish. Wash well. 2. Butter and season a pyrex
dish. 3. Place fillets of fish. Season. 4. Add fish stock and lime juice.
5. Cover with buttered greaseproof paper. 6. Poach gently in a moderate
oven (5 to 10 minutes). 7. Remove fish and dress neatly on a silver flat.
8. Bring cooking liquor to boil with velouté. 9. Incorporate egg yolk and
pass through a fine strainer. 10. Mix in butter and finally add cream.
11. Coat fillets with sauce. 12. Garnish with blanched and skinned
grapes.

FILET de POMFRET ou SOLE VERONIQUE (B)

Ingredients	Quantity
Pomfret or	1
Sole	(500 gm)
Onions	15 gm
Parsley	a few sprigs
Lime	¼
Butter	45 gm
Grapes	115 gm

Method

1. Clean, fillet and skin fish. 2. Prepare a fish fumet using trimmings of fish, fish bones, minced onion, chopped parsley and lime juice. 3. Strain and use liquid for poaching fillets. Poach gently. 4. Remove fillets onto a pyrex dish. 5. Reduce fumet and finish it with butter. 6. Cover fish with buttered fumet. 7. Glaze under a grill. Garnish with a pyramid of skinned seedless grapes in the centre. 8. Cover dish and serve immediately.

35. FILET de POMFRET ou SOLE WALEWSKA

Ingredients	Quantity
Pomfret or	1
Sole	(500 gm)
Fish fumet	200 ml
Langoustes	2
Butter	30 gm
Black mushrooms	30 gm
Mornay sauce	300 ml

Method

1. Clean, fillet and skin fish. 2. Poach gently in fish fumet. 3. Boil langoustes and remove meat from tails, cutting each tail into two lengthwise. 4. Stew meat in butter along with mushrooms, with the lid on. 5. Put fish into a pyrex dish and surround with langouste meat and mushrooms. 6. Cover with mornay sauce and glaze quickly under a grill.

36. FILET de POMFRET au SAUCE VERTE
(POMFRET FILLET IN GREEN SAUCE)

Ingredients	Quantity
Onions (chopped)	1 (medium)
Pomfret	1
Spinach	3 bunches

Ingredients	Quantity
Court Bouillon	750 ml
Fish carcass	1
Onions (sliced)	30 gm
Vinegar	1 tsp
Lemon juice	½
Grated carrot	10 gm
Peppercorns	4
Salt	a pinch
Water	1 litre
Garlic (crushed)	4–6 pods
Cream	250 ml
Butter	60 gm
Mixed herbs (Rosemary, Basil, Allspice, Thyme and Tarragon)	¼ tsp each
Salt and Pepper	to taste

Method

1. Clean and fillet pomfret. 2. Wash fish carcass thoroughly and put to boil in a litre of water. Add salt, onions, carrot, lemon juice or vinegar and peppercorns. Allow to boil and reduce to ¾ litre. 3. Poach fillets in court bouillon. 4. Boil spinach leaves in salted water. Purée spinach. 5. Melt butter in skillet. Sauté chopped onions and crushed and chopped garlic. Sauté lightly. 6. Add spinach purée and bring to a boil. Add herbs. 7. Allow to simmer. Season with salt and pepper. 8. Stir whipped cream into spinach purée. 9. Grease an entrée dish well. 10. Pour sauce into entrée dish and place fillets on top.

37. POISSON au VIN BLANC

Ingredients	Quantity
Fillets of pomfret	4
Wine	1 cup
Butter	1½ tbsp
Refined flour	1 tbsp
Egg yolk	1
Water	½ cup
Salt and Pepper	to taste
Lime juice	few drops
Finely minced shallots	2 tbsp

Method

1. Clean fillets. Wash well. 2. Put half the shallots at bottom of greaseproof dish. 3. Place fillets on them, season and add remaining shallots. 4. Cover with wine and water. 5. Cook in a moderate oven,

covered with greaseproof paper, for about 20–30 minutes. 6. Take fillets out and keep them warm. 7. Reduce cooking liquor. 8. Add a small piece at a time of "Beurre manié" (flour blended well with butter) using only half the butter. 9. When well blended add rest of butter in small pieces. 10. Pour this sauce over fillets and put dish under the grill for a minute.

38. POMFRET WIESBADEN

Ingredients	Quantity
Fillets of cleaned pomfret	2
Fish stock	100 ml
White wine	30 ml
Butter	30 gm
Refined flour	30 gm
Salt and Pepper	to taste
Dill (suva bhaji)	10 gm

Method

1. Cook cleaned fillets in a mixture of fish stock and white wine on a very slow fire. Mix butter with flour and cook till it forms a smooth paste. Remove cooked fish from stock. Add stock to flour mixture, a little at a time and mix well to form a smooth sauce. Add seasonings and dill. Place fillets in a flat dish and pour sauce over fillets. Grill till lightly browned and serve hot.

39. MAQUEREAU GRILLÉ

Ingredients	Quantity
Mackerels	8 (about 500 gm)
Maître d'hôtel butter	60 gm
Butter	30 gm
Salt and Pepper	to taste
Lime	1

Method

1. Clean mackerels. Slit belly. Remove entrails and black membrane. 2. Cut off head. 3. Make gashes on sides of fish. Season. 4. Sprinkle with melted butter and grill gently, taking care to baste fish with melted butter using a brush. 5. Set mackerels on a round hot dish. Garnish with maître d'hôtel butter and slices of lime.

40. TO COOK AND CLEAN LOBSTER OR LANGOUSTES

Buy live lobsters to ensure freshness. Pick up the lobster behind the head using tongs if desired and plunge it head first into a kettle of boiling salted water (1 litre water, 1 tbsp salt and 75 ml vinegar). Cover and boil for 20 minutes, being careful not to overcook, since overcooking renders the meat tough and stringy. Cool in the same liquid.

Place the lobster on its back and with a sharp pointed knife make a deep cut along the entire length of the body, starting at the mouth. Remove the black coloured intestine which runs from head to tail as well as the 'sac' near the head. Remove the body meat. Break the claws with a mallet and pick the meat from them.

41. HOMARD à la THERMIDOR

Ingredients	Quantity
Lobsters	4
Salad oil	30 ml
Salt and Pepper	to taste
Shallots	30 gm
Cheese	
Parsley	a few sprigs
Cream sauce	900 gm
Mustard	5 gm
Butter	225 gm
Court bouillon	

Method

1. Cut boiled lobsters lengthwise into two. Sprinkle with salad oil, season with salt and pepper and put in an oven and bake, or boil live lobsters in court bouillon. 2. Remove meat from shell and dice. 3. Mix cream sauce, mustard, finely chopped shallots and parsley and the butter. 4. Put lobster meat into sauce. 5. Put back into shells. Sprinkle over with cheese. 6. Bake in an oven till brown. Serve immediately.

Cream Sauce

To 600 ml of béchamel add 300 ml of cream or top of milk.

42. HOMARD à la NEWBURG (A)

Ingredients	Quantity
Lobsters	4
Butter	30 gm
Cream	600 ml
Egg yolks	2
Salt	to taste
Pepper	a pinch

Ingredients	Quantity
Cayenne pepper	a pinch
Court bouillon	

Method

1. Cook lobster in court bouillon. 2. Take out meat and slice. 3. Melt butter. Add lobster slices and seasoning. Sauté till pieces become red on all sides. 4. Mix egg yolks and cream. 5. Stir gently on the side of the fire till thick. Add pieces of lobster. Mix well and serve at once.

HOMARD à la NEWBURG (B)

Ingredients	Quantity
Lobster meat	300 gm (4 lobsters)
Butter	20 gm
Refined flour	15 gm
Cream	300 ml
Egg yolk	1
Cayenne pepper	a pinch
Toast	4 pieces
Paprika	a dash
Salt	to taste

Method

1. Cut meat into cubes and cook in melted butter for 5 minutes. 2. Add flour and bind. 3. Gradually add cream and bring mixture slowly to boiling point. 4. Simmer for 2 to 3 minutes. 5. Add well-beaten egg yolks, salt and cayenne pepper and cook over very low heat for 2 minutes longer. 6. Serve on toast. Sprinkle over with paprika.

43. MAYONNAISE de HOMARD

Ingredients	Quantity
Lobsters	2
Court bouillon	
Salt	to taste
Mayonnaise sauce	150 ml
Garnish	
Anchovy fillets	2
Olives	30 gm
Hard-boiled egg	1
Red radish	2 or 3
Lettuce	1 bunch

Method

1. Boil lobsters in court bouillon. Cool in same liquid. 2. Cut lobster and remove meat from tail, claws etc. Slice meat. 3. Garnish bottom of a salad bowl with chiseled leaves of lettuce (save the heart to put on top). Season lightly. 4. Lay slices of lobster on top. Cover with mayonnaise. 5. Garnish with strips of anchovy fillets, olives, slices of hard-boiled egg, flowers of radish and heart of lettuce.

44. SALADE de HOMARD

Ingredients and method as for Salad de Saumon but substitute lobster for salmon.

45. LANGUOUSTE à la PARISIENNE

Ingredients	Quantity
Langoustes	2
Creamed potatoes	1 kg
Tomatoes	1 kg
Lettuce	1 bunch
Red radish	1 bunch
Hard-boiled eggs	8
Aspic	300 ml
Mayonnaise sauce	300 ml
Court bouillon	

Method

1. Tie each langouste to a board stretching out tail of each to fullest extent. 2. Cook in court bouillon and leave to cool in same liquid. 3. When quite cool, cut a strip of shell from back of head to tail of each langouste using a pair of scissors. The aperture left by the removed shell should be wide enough to allow meat of tail to be removed without breaking tail. 4. Cut a few neat slices and dice remaining meat. 5. Remove meat from carapace (upper part of languouste) and from claws. Dice meat and drub creamy parts through a sieve to make a purée. 6. Prepare a vegetable salad. Add diced meat, purée, melted aspic and mayonnaise. Fill shell with part of the mixture. 7. Stuff a few tomatoes with the remaining mixture and allow to set.

To serve

Dish langoustes on two cushions of creamed potatoes. The cushion should be wedge-shaped so that languoustes may lie at an angle of 45° with their heads raised.

Arrange slices of meat and slices of hard-boiled egg slightly overlapping along the back of langouste beginning at the head with the smaller slices.

Surround langouste with stuffed tomatoes, salad leaves and slices of hard-boiled eggs.

46. SALADE de THON

Ingredients	Quantity
Celery	225 gm
Tuna fish (flaked)	1.5 kg tin
Pineapple	115 gm
Mayonnaise	150 ml
Walnuts	115 gm

Method

Dice pineapple, chop celery and walnut. Mix all ingredients.

47. CRABE en COQUILLE

Ingredients	Quantity
Boiled crab	4
Mayonnaise	55 gm
Fresh breadcrumbs	55 gm
Salt	to taste
Pepper	a pinch
Nutmeg	a pinch
Paprika	a pinch
Parsley	1 tsp
Tomatoes	115 gm
Salad leaves	2 bunches
Lime	1

Method

1. Pull the top shell from body of crab. 2. Scoop out all dark flesh from inside top shell. 3. Discard stomach bag attached to shell below eyes. 4. Discard grayish white 'dead man's fingers'. 5. Pick out white flesh and keep separate from dark meat. 6. Crack claws and small legs and pick out all the meat. 7. Wash and dry shell and smear some oil over to give it a gloss. 8. Season white flesh. 9. Add mayonnaise and breadcrumbs to dark meat. 10. Put meat neatly into shell, garnish with paprika, parsley sprigs and lime butterflies. 11. Serve on a plate surrounded by lettuce leaves and tomato slices. Claws may be used as decoration.

ENTRÉES AND RELEVÉS

1. Châteaubriand
2. Tournedos
3. Tournedos Arlésienne
4. Tournedos Béarnaise
5. Tournedos Bercy
6. Tournedos Chasseur
7. Tournedos Forestière
8. Tournedos à la Mexicaine
9. Tournedos Parmentier
10. Entrecôte Minute (Minute Steaks)
11. Entrecôte (Sirloin Steaks)
12. Stewed Steak and Onions
13. Steak and Kidney Pie
14. Bœuf Wellington
15. Goulash de Bœuf à la Hongroise
16. Escalope de veau
17. Escalope de Veau Napolitaine
18. Wiener Schnitzel (A) Wiener Schnitzel (B)
19. Blanquette de Veau à l'Ancienne
20. Piccate Milanaise
21. Piccatta de Bœuf (Beef Piccatta)
22. Blanquette de Veau aux Céleris
23. Fricadelles
24. Foie de Veau à l'Anglaise
25. Cervelle au Beurre Noir
26. Cervelle au Beurre Noisette
27. Cervelle à la Maréchale
28. Cervelle à la Poulette
29. Gigot d'Agneau Rôti
30. Selle d'Agneau Rôti
31. Gigot de Mouton Braisé
32. Gigot à la Boulangére
33. Gigot à la Soubise
34. Gigot de Mouton Farci à l'Ail au Sauce Herbs
35. Côtelettes d' Agneau àla Réforme
36. Côtelettes d' Agneau à l'Ambassadrice
37. Côtelettes de Mouton à la Villeroi
38. Côtelettes à la Murillo
39. Côtelettes à la Provencale
40. Rognons Sautés Bercy
41. Rognons Sautés Bordelaise
42. Rognons Sautés Hongroise
43. Rognons Sautés Chasseur
44. Rognons Sautés à l'Indienne
45. Rognons à la Brochette
46. Rogons Brochette à l'Espagnole
47. Rognons Sautés à la Turbigo
48. Langue de Mouton Choucroute
49. Salted Ox Tongue
50. Kromeskies
51. Côte de Porc à la Charcutière
52. Côte de Porc à la Flamande
53. Côte de Porc Hongroise
54. Soufflés au Jambon
55. Flan de Jambon Soubise
56. Quiche Lorraine
57. Madras Shepherd's Pie
58. Spinach and Mushroom Quiche
59. Vegetable Quiche
60. Cheese and Bacon Frittata
61. Stuffed Heart

1. CHÂTEAUBRIAND

Ingredients	Quantity
Double fillet steak cut from the head of fillet 3.8 to 10 cm thick	340 gm–910 gm

Method

Trim off all nerves and leave a little fat on steak. Grill or boil to order: rare, medium or well-done. Season and serve immediately.

2. TOURNEDOS

Tournedos are half the size (in weight) of fillet steak, both of which are taken from the middle portion of the fillet. The usual thickness of a tournedo is about 3 cm and it should be cut to a nice round shape. When the meat is not of first quality it should be marinaded first to soften the fibres.

3. TOURNEDOS ARLÉSIENNE

Ingredients	Quantity
Fillet steak	500 gm
Oil	30 ml
Butter	30 gm
Eggplant	225 gm
Tomatoes	225 gm
Onions	115 gm
Salt and Pepper	to taste
Fat to fry eggplant and tomatoes	

Method

1. Cut 4 tournedos each about 3 cm thick and 115 gm in weight. Season. 2. Fry in butter and oil. 3. Dish and surround with fried roundels of eggplant and tomatoes tossed in fat. 4. Place a roundel of fried onion on each tournedo and serve at once.

4. TOURNEDOS BÉARNAISE

Ingredients	Quantity
Fillet steak	500 gm
Bread	4 slices (about 115 gm)
Meat glaze	30 ml
New potatoes	225 gm
Parsley	a few sprigs
Clarified butter	60 gm
Béarnaise sauce	20 ml
Oil/Fat to fry bread	

Method

1. Cut 4 tournedos each 3 cm thick and weighing about 115 gm.
2. Parboil potatoes. Skin and fry in clarified butter keeping them soft.
3. Trim bread to size of tournedos and fry. 4. Grill tournedos and place
each one over fried bread. 5. Dish neatly. Coat with meat glaze and
surround with threads of béarnaise sauce. 6. In the centre arrange
potatoes in a heap and sprinkle over with chopped parsley. Serve
immediately.

5. TOURNEDOS BERCY

Ingredients	Quantity
Fillet steak	500 gm
Meat glaze	30 ml
Bercy butter	
Salt and Pepper	to taste

Method

1. Cut 4 tournedos each 3 cm thick and about 115 gm in weight. Season.
2. Grill and coat with pale meat glaze. 3. Dish them in the form of a
crown and serve bercy butter separately.

BEURRE À BERCY (BERCY BUTTER)

Ingredients	Quantity
Stock	150 ml
Shallots	30 gm
Butter	225 gm
Parsley	a few sprigs
Beef marrow	60 gm
Pepper	a pinch
Lime	½

Method

1. Put chopped shallots and stock into a pan. 2. Reduce to half. 3. Add
butter softened to a cream, chopped parsley and beef marrow poached in
a little salted water and diced. 4. Before butter is completely melted
remove from fire. Add pepper and lime juice. Serve immediately.

6. TOURNEDOS CHASSEUR

Ingredients	Quantity
Fillet steak	500 gm
Chasseur sauce	200 ml
Clarified butter	60 gm
Salt and Pepper	to taste

Method

1. Cut fillet steak into 4 tournedos about 3 cm thick and about 115 gm in weight. Season. 2. Fry in clarified butter. 3. Drain butter away. Add chasseur sauce. 4. Boil for a couple of minutes and pour sauce over tournedos.

7. TOURNEDOS FORESTIÈRE

Ingredients	Quantity
Fillet steak	500 gm
Noodles	115 gm
Potatoes	225 gm
Bread	4 slices
Butter	60 gm
Salt and Pepper	to taste
Oil/Fat to fry bread and tournedos	

Method

1. Cut 4 tournedos each about 3 cm thick and weighing about 115 gm each. Season. 2. Trim bread to size of tournedos and fry. 3. Fry tournedos and place them on crusts of fried bread. Dish neatly. 4. Surround them with alternate heaps of boiled noodles and boiled, diced potatoes both tossed in butter.

8. TOURNEDOS à la MEXICAINE

Ingredients	Quantity
Fillet steak	500 gm
Capsicum	100 gm
Tomatoes	115 gm
Mushrooms	100 gm
Butter	30 gm
Oil	30 ml
Salt and Pepper	to taste

Method

1. Cut 4 tournedos each about 3 cm thick and 115 gm in weight. Season. 2. Cut capsicum into halves Remove seeds and sauté. 3. Grill mushrooms if fresh. Boil and grill if dry. 4. Chop tomatoes. Remove excess moisture and sauté. 5. Fry tournedos. Serve garnished with mushrooms, tomatoes and capsicum.

9. TOURNEDOS PARMENTIER

Ingredients	Quantity
Fillet steak	500 gm
Butter	60 gm

Ingredients	Quantity
Potatoes	225 gm
Parsley	a few sprigs
Salt and Pepper	to taste

Method

1. Cut 4 tournedos each about 3 cm thick and 115 gm in weight. Season.
2. Parboil potatoes. Cut into cubes of about 1.5 cm. Fry in butter but keep soft. 3. Fry tournedos in butter and dish them. 4. Place potatoes in the middle; sprinkle potatoes with chopped parsley.

10. ENTRECÔTE MINUTE (MINUTE STEAKS)

Cut 1.5 cm thick slices from sirloin. Flatten with a cutlet bat dipped in water and make them as thin as possible. Season. Smear with oil on either side and grill to order.

11. ENTRECÔTE (SIRLOIN STEAKS)

Cut 1.5 cm thick slices from sirloin. Smear with oil on both sides and grill to order.

12. STEWED STEAK AND ONIONS

Ingredients	Quantity
Fillet steak	500 gm
Butter	60 gm
Onions	225 gm
Salt and Pepper	to taste

Method

1. Cut steak into about 4 cm rounds. 2. Season and fry in butter on both sides. Remove. Quarter and brown onions and remove. 3. Put fried steaks into a stewpan and add enough stock to cover steaks. Add onions. 4. Cover tightly and cook in an oven for 3 hours. 5. Dish steaks. Surround with onions and braising liquor cleared of all grease and reduced.

13. STEAK AND KIDNEY PIE

Ingredients	Quantity
Fillet steak	500 gm
Mustard	1 tsp
Kidneys	500 gm
Worcester sauce	1 tbsp
Salt and Pepper	to taste

Ingredients	Quantity
Onions	115 gm
Fat	30 gm
Puff pastry (See pg. ??)	225 gm

Method

1. Cut fillet steak into cubes, and marinade in mixture of Worcester sauce, salt, pepper and mustard. 2. Clean and cut kidneys into halves. 3. Heat fat. Brown sliced onions. Add meat and brown. 4. Add kidneys. Sauté for a couple of minutes. 5. Add enough liquid to cover solids. 6. Cook till meat is done and gravy is thick. Cool. 7. Put stew into a pyrex or aluminium pie dish. 8. Cover with rolled out pastry (always roll pastry a little larger than the size required to prevent stretching). Decorate edges. Egg wash. Keep in a cool place as long as possible. 9. Place in a hot oven (450°F, 235°C) for about 15 minutes till paste is set and lightly coloured. Reduce heat to 180°C and bake for another 15 to 20 minutes.

14. BŒUF WELLINGTON

Ingredients	Quantity
Puff pastry	450 gm
Dry duxelle	150 gm
Tenderloin	500 gm
Pâté maison	150 gm
Dry Duxelle	
Chopped mushrooms	90 gm
Butter	30 gm
Chopped onions	30 gm
Chopped shallots	30 gm
Salt	to taste
Pepper	a pinch
Parsley	1 bunch
Nutmeg	a pinch

Method

Sauté mushrooms, onions and shallots in butter. Cook mixture till moisture evaporates completely. Season with salt, pepper, nutmeg and parsley.

TENDERLOIN

Ingredients	Quantity
Undercut	1
Salt	to taste

Ingredients	Quantity
Pepper	a pinch
Oil	50 ml
Worcester sauce	10 ml
Rosemary	2 gm

Method

Clean and trim undercut to about 500 gm and marinate with salt, pepper, Worcester sauce and oil. Sear tenderloin well till it is brown on all sides and place in an oven at 300°F for about 15 minutes till it is three-fourths done.

PÂTÉ MAISON

Ingredients	Quantity
Butter	30 gm
Parsley	1 bunch
Bacon	60 gm
Liver	200 gm
Onions	15 gm
Garlic	12 flakes
Thyme	a pinch
Cinnamon	
Nutmeg	
Mace	
Powdered cardamom	5 gm (tied in a
Bay leaf	muslin cloth)
Rosemary	
Oregano	
Clove	

Method

Clean and chop liver. Sauté chopped onion, garlic and chopped bacon in butter. Add chopped parsley, liver and bouquet garni and cook till liver is cooked and dry. Remove bouquet garni and pass pâté through a mixer to obtain a smooth paste. Season and cool.

Puff Pastry – refer page 504

Method

Roll out puff pastry into a square about 0.5 cm thick. Place duxelle in the centre. then spread pâté maison on it and arrange tenderloin on it. Cover it all around with puff pastry. Seal all the edges using water and turn over and place on a greased baking sheet. Brush with egg wash and bake in an oven at 375°F for about 40 minutes. Slice and serve with madeira sauce.

15. GOULASH de BŒUF à la HONGROISE

Ingredients	Quantity
Shoulder of beef	225 gm
Ribs	225 gm
Fat	30 gm
Onions	115 gm
Salt	to taste
Paprika	15 gm
Potatoes	225 gm
Tomatoes	225 gm

Method

1. Cut meat into even-sized cubes. 2. Peel and chop onions. 3. Heat fat. Fry meat. Add onions and fry. 4. Add salt, paprika, peeled and quartered tomatoes, and a little water. 5. Cover and cook in an oven for about 1½ hours. 6. Add more water (hot) and peeled and quartered potatoes. 7. Continue cooking in the oven till potatoes and meat are tender and gravy is entirely reduced. Serve hot.

16. ESCALOPE de VEAU

Ingredients	Quantity
Cushion of veal	500 gm
Egg	1
Breadcrumbs	60 gm
Seasoned flour	15 gm
Butter	60 gm
Oil	60 ml

Method

1. Trim and remove all sinews from meat. 2. Cut four even slices and beat out till thin. 3 Dip in flour and then in egg and breadcrumbs. Press crumbs firmly on with a palette knife. 4. Heat oil. Place escalopes in shallow hot fat and cook quickly for a few minutes on each side. 5. Serve on an oval flat dish and pour browned butter over. 6. Pipe a thread of meat glaze around.

17. ESCALOPE de VEAU NAPOLITAINE

Ingredients	Quantity
Cushion of veal	500 gm
Egg	4
Breadcrumbs	60 gm
Seasoned flour	15 gm
Oil	60 ml

Ingredients	Quantity
Spaghetti	60 gm
Cheese	10 gm
Tomatoes	60 gm
Tomato sauce	75 ml
Butter	10 gm
Salt and Pepper	to taste

Method

1. Prepare escalopes as for recipe No. 16. 2. Boil and drain spaghetti. 3. Skin tomatoes and remove seeds. Chop roughly. 4. Mix spaghetti with tomato sauce and tomatoes. 5. Serve escalopes on a silver flat dish. Garnish with spaghetti. 6. Serve grated cheese separately.

N.B. Veal escalopes may be cooked plain, in which case they are only slightly flattened.

18. WIENER SCHNITZEL (A)

Ingredients	Quantity
Veal (boned leg or fillet)	500 gm
Fine white breadcrumbs	60 gm
Egg yolk	1
Flour	15 gm
Butter	60 gm
Salt and Pepper	to taste
Lime	1

Method

1. Cut thin slices of veal. 2. Beat till slices are wafer-thin and fibres are broken. 3. Dip slices in flour and then in beaten egg yolk to which salt and pepper have been added. Roll in breadcrumbs. 4. Cook slices in hot butter until golden brown on both sides. 5. Place on a hot dish and serve immediately garnished with slices of lime.

WIENER SCHNITZEL (B)

Ingredients	Quantity
Veal (boned leg or fillet)	500 gm
Lime	1
Butter	115 gm
Anchovy fillets	6
Fine breadcrumbs	60 gm
Egg yolk	1
Seasoned flour	15 gm
Paprika	½ tsp
Stoned olives	4

Method

1. Cut thin slices of veal. 2. Marinade in lime juice for one hour. 3. Roll slices in seasoned flour. 4. Dip first in beaten egg and then in breadcrumbs. 5. Melt half the butter. Add mashed anchovy fillets and paprika. Mix well and keep hot. 6. In remainder of melted butter cook schnitzels until golden brown on both sides. 7. Serve in a hot dish. Pour sauce over and garnish with slices of lime arranged alternately with stoned olives.

19. BLANQUETTE de VEAU à l'ANCIENNE

Ingredients	Quantity
Breast of veal	500 gm
White stock	300 ml
Carrots	55 gm
Onions	115 gm
Clove	1
Leeks	30 gm
Parsley	a few sprigs
Thyme	a pinch
Cream	1½ tbsp (30 ml)
Bay leaf	1
Butter	20 gm
Refined flour	20 gm
Mushrooms (white)	5 (15 gm)
Shallots	15 gm
Egg yolk	1
Lime	1
Salt	to taste

Method

1. Cut meat into even-sized large cubes. 2. Blanch by putting them into boiling water. Strain and cool. 3. Put meat into a saucepan with enough white stock to cover. Add a pinch of salt. Boil and skim. 4. Add carrots, onion stuck with a clove, and a faggot made up of the leeks, parsley stalks, thyme and bay leaf. Set to cook for 1½ hours. 5. Prepare a roux with butter and flour. Moisten with cooking liquor. Add mushroom parings and cook for 15 minutes. Keep aside. 6. Transfer meat into a sauté pan with shallots and mushrooms cooked in stock. Finish the sauce with a liaison of egg yolks, mixed with cream and a few drops of lime juice. 8. Strain over veal and its garnish. Heat without boiling. Serve hot, sprinkled over with chopped parsley.

20. PICCATE MILANAISE

Ingredients	Quantity
Veal cutlets	30 small ones (flattened thin)
Eggs	4
Parmesan cheese	1 cup
Flour	150 gm
Macaroni	500 gm
Julienne of ham, ox tongue, mushrooms	1 cup
Tomato sauce	as desired
Butter/Oil	as desired

Method

1. Trim and flatten veal cutlets. Dip in flour. Mix eggs and parmesan cheese. Dip each cutlet in egg and cheese mixture and fry in a pan till they are a golden brown. Serve on buttered macaroni blended with juliennes of ham, ox tongue and mushrooms. Serve tomato sauce on the side.

21. PICCATTA de BŒUF (BEEF PICCATTA)

Ingredients	Quantity
Tenderloin	500 gm
Eggs	2
Cheese	120 gm
Milk	100 ml
Tomatoes	340 gm
Garlic	10 gm
Seasoned flour	60 gm
Parsley	1 bunch
Butter	250 gm
Spaghetti	200 gm
Onions	120 gm
Milanaise sauce	
Mixed herbs – Rosemary, Basil, Allspice, Thyme and Tarragon	¼ tsp each

Method

1. Clean tenderloin and cut into thin slices. Beat lightly with a steak hammer. 2. Marinade meat in salt, pepper and oil along with mixed herbs. 3. Coat piccattas with seasoned flour. 4. Beat egg lightly, add grated cheese and milk. 5. Put piccattas in egg mixture and sauté in butter till cooked. 6. Drain well. 7. Boil spaghetti in salted water till almost done. 8. Heat butter in frying pan. Sauté chopped onions and garlic. 9. Add blanched and concassed tomatoes. 10. Season with salt,

pepper and mixed herbs. 11. Cook for a few minutes. 12. Toss spaghetti in butter and place in an entrée dish. Arrange piccattas over spaghetti and pour milanaise sauce over. Garnish with chopped parsley.

22. BLANQUETTE de VEAU aux CÉLERIS

Ingredients	Quantity
Breast of veal	500 gm
White stock	300 ml
White of celery	55 gm
Onions	115 gm
Clove	1
Bay leaf	1
Thyme	a pinch
Leeks	1
Butter	20 gm
Refined flour	20 gm
Mushrooms (white)	15 gm
Shallots	15 gm
Egg yolk	1
Cream	1½ tbsp (30 ml)
Lime	¼
Salt	to taste

Method

Same as for recipe No. 19 Blanquette de Veau àl'Ancienne but using celery instead of carrot. Cut celery into 2.5 cm pieces and when cooked, trim and serve with blanquette.

23. FRICADELLES

Ingredients	Quantity
Lean veal	500 gm
Butter	300 gm
Bread	160 gm
Eggs	2
Salt	to taste
Pepper	a pinch
Nutmeg	a pinch
Onions	60 gm
Refined flour	15 gm
Fat	for frying

Method

1. Chop meat fine. Put into a pan with butter also chopped up. 2. Add bread soaked in water and pressed, seasoning, eggs and finely chopped

onions sautéed in butter without discolouring. 3. Divide into portions of about 100 gm each. Roll them into balls on a flour-dusted board and then flatten them out with the flat of a knife. 4. Heat fat and brown on both sides. Drain and complete cooking in an oven.

24. FOIE de VEAU à l'ANGLAISE

Ingredients	Quantity
Liver	500 gm
Salt and Pepper	to taste
Butter	60 gm
Bacon	60 gm
Garnish	
Thin fried onion rings	

Method

1. Cut liver into fairly thin slices each weighing about 75 gm. 2. Season with salt and pepper. 3. Heat butter. Toss liver in hot fat till done. 4. Grill rashers of bacon and serve with liver. 5. Garnish with fried onion rings.

25. CERVELLE au BEURRE NOIR

Ingredients	Quantity
Sheep's brains	8
Butter	115 gm
Parsley	a few sprigs
Vinegar	1 tsp
Salt and Pepper	to taste

Method

1. Clean and slice brains. Season with salt and pepper. 2. Melt butter. Fry brains. Remove on to a hot plate. 3. Add chopped parsley to butter and when well browned pour over brains. 4. Pour vinegar into the frying pan and add to brains. Serve hot.

26. CERVELLE au BEURRE NOISETTE

Ingredients	Quantity
Sheep's brains	8
Butter	115 gm
Lime	½
Parsley	a few sprigs
Salt and Pepper	to taste

Method

1. Clean and slice brains. Season with salt and pepper. 2. Melt butter. Fry brains. Remove on to a hot plate. 3. Pour browned butter over brains. Sprinkle with chopped parsley and a few drops of lime juice. Serve hot.

27. CERVELLE à la MARÉCHALE

Ingredients	Quantity
Sheep's brains	8
Salt and Pepper	to taste
Egg	1
Breadcrumbs (very fine)	30 gm
Butter	115 gm
Black mushrooms	30 gm
Asparagus heads	3o gm

Method

1. Clean and cut brains into regular slices. Dip in egg and breadcrumbs and fry in clarified butter. 3. Boil and grill mushrooms (if dry) or grill (if fresh). 4. Dish brains in the form of a circle and place a mushroom on each. 5. Garnish the centre with asparagus heads (boiled and cohered with butter).

28. CERVELLE à la POULETTE

Ingredients	Quantity
Sheep's brains	8
Allemande sauce	300 ml
Mushroom liquor	3 tbsp
Butter	30 gm
Lime	¼
Parsley	3 sprigs
White mushrooms	85 gm
Salt and Pepper	to taste

Method

1. Clean, boil and slice brains. 2. Boil allemande sauce. Add mushroom liquor. 3. Remove to side of fire. Add butter, a few drops of lime juice and chopped parsley. 4. Add cooked white mushrooms. 5. Add the brains. Check for seasoning and serve at once.

29. GIGOT d'AGNEAU RÔTI

Ingredients	Quantity
Leg of mutton	1

Ingredients	Quantity
Salt	to taste
Pepper	to taste
Fat	for roasting

Method

1. Remove pelvic bone. 2. Trim knuckle clearing about 4 cm of bone.
3. Trim off excess fat. Season with salt. 4. Place on a trivet in a roasting
tray. 5. Put a little fat on top. Keep in a hot oven 232.2°C (450°F). Cook
for 15 to 20 minutes basting frequently. 6. Reduce heat to 190.5°C
(375°F) and continue cooking till done, basting frequently. 7. Cool for 15
to 20 minutes. Holding the bone, carve with a sharp knife at an angle of
45°. 8. Take off each slice as it is cut and turn from side to side as the
slice gets wider.

30. SELLE d'AGNEAU RÔTI

Ingredients	Quantity
Saddle of mutton	1
Salt and Pepper	to taste
Fat	for roasting

Method

1. Skin and remove kidney. 2. Trim excess fat and sinew. 3. Cut off flaps
leaving about 15 cm on either side so as to meet in the middle. 4. Remove
pelvic bone, tie with a string. 5. Season with salt. 6. Place on a trivet
and roast as for Gigot d'Agneau Rôti. 7. Cool and carve.

31. GIGOT de MOUTON BRAISÉ

Ingredients	Quantity
Leg of mutton	1
Salt and Pepper	to taste
Stock	600 ml
Carrots	225 gm
Turnips	225 gm
Fat	30 gm

Method

1. Suppress pelvic bone and trim knuckle. Season. 2. Brown leg in oven.
3. Peel and cut carrots into roundels and peel and dice turnips. Saute.
4. Lay vegetables in a large strong pan. 5. Place browned leg on
vegetables. 6. Add enough stock to just cover joint. 7. Put lid on and cook
gently at 165°C (325°F) in oven till done. (Allow about 45 minutes per ½ kg
of meat). 8. Transfer leg to a tray. 9. Strain braising liquor and clear it

of all grease. Reduce to half. 10. Sprinkle meat with a few tablespoons of reduced gravy and glaze in oven. 11. Serve with remaining braising liquor and a puree of potatoes, turnips, haricot beans or cauliflower.

32. GIGOT à la BOULANGÉRE

Ingredients	Quantity
Leg of mutton	1
Potatoes	1 kg
Onions	500 gm
Salt and Pepper	to taste
Fat	to roast

Method

1. Remove pelvic bone and trim knuckle. Season. 2. Melt fat in a baking tray. 3. Place leg of mutton in fat and brown. Cook for about 15 to 20 minutes at 235°C (450°F) basting frequently. 4. Reduce temperature to 190°C (375°F) and continue cooking till nearly done. 5. Parboil potatoes and cut into roundels about 1.5 cm thick. 6. Slice onions and toss in a little butter. 7. When meat is nearly done set onions and potatoes round joint. 8. Sprinkle garnish with fat off the joint. 9. Complete cooking and serve with garnish.

33. GIGOT à la SOUBISE

Ingredients	Quantity
Leg of mutton	1
Fatty bacon	115 gm
Carrots	115 gm
Onions	115 gm
Parsley	a few sprigs
Bay leaf	1
Vinegar	60 ml
Mustard	¼ tsp
Salt and Pepper	to taste
Fat	60 gm
Onions	1 kg
Rice	225 gm
Butter	15 gm

Method

1. Remove pelvic bone and trim knuckle of leg of mutton leaving about 4 cm of clean bone. 2. Prepare a marinade with vinegar, fried roundels of carrots and onions, crushed garlic, bay leaf, chopped parsley, salt,

pepper and mustard. 3. Place bacon and leg of mutton in marinade and let it steep in for one hour. 4. Drain meat on a sieve for half an hour and dry. 5. Heat fat in a large and heavy pan. 6. When sufficiently hot put in leg of mutton and brown on all sides. 7. Remove leg and lard with bacon strips. 8. Put vegetables from marinade into the pan. 9. Place leg on vegetables. Add sufficient brown stock to barely cover joint. 10. Cover the pan. Bring to a boil and then place in a moderate oven (165°C or 325°F) and cook gently. 11. When two-thirds done transfer leg to another vessel. 12. Strain braising liquor over, add onions and rice. 13. Gently complete the cooking of the joint with onions and rice. 14. When done place leg in a baking tray and glaze it in the oven. 15. Quickly rub onions and rice through a fine sieve. 16. Set the leg of mutton in a flat dish. Put a frill on the bone. 17. Heat soubise sauce. Finish with butter and serve this sauce separately.

34. GIGOT de MOUTON FARCI à l'AIL au SAUCE HERBES

Leg of mutton stuffed with garlic served with herb sauce on a bed of rice.

Ingredients	Quantity
Leg of lamb or	1
Leg of mutton	(1.5 kg)
Garlic	15–18 pods
Rice	200 gm
Butter	200 gm
Salt and Pepper	to taste
Oil	50 ml
Mixed herbs – (Rosemary, Basil, Allspice, Thyme and Tarragon)	1/4 tsp each
Fresh breadcrumbs	made from 6–8 slices

Method

1. Remove thigh bone from leg. 2. Smear with oil, salt and pepper. 3. Clean garlic flakes and insert into flesh. 4. Place in roasting tray, basting occasionally until done. 5. Boil rice, drain and toss in melted butter. 6. Place in an entrée dish. When meat is cool, slice thickly and arrange over rice. 7. Heat butter in pan. Add breadcrumbs, seasoning and herbs. Mix well and pour over slices of meat.

35. CÔTELETTES d' AGNEAU à la RÉFORME

Ingredients	Quantity
Best end neck of mutton	8 cutlets
Ham	30 gm

Ingredients	Quantity
Egg	1
Breadcrumbs	30 gm
Fat	30 gm
Garnish	
Carrots	115 gm
Mushrooms	30 gm
Egg	1
Gherkins (pickled)	30 gm
Réforme sauce	300 ml
Espagnole Sauce (300 ml)	
Butter	30 gm
Bacon	30 gm
Carrots	15 gm
Mushrooms	225 gm
Tomatoes	115 gm
Onions	30 gm
Refined flour	30 gm
Stock	300 ml
Bouquet garni	
Sherry (optional)	75 ml
Salt	to taste
Réforme Sauce	
Wine vinegar	150 ml
Redcurrant jelly	1 dsp
Peppercorns (crushed)	12
Espagnole sauce	300 ml
Salt	to taste

Method

1. Trim and prepare cutlets. 2. Coat with egg and breadcrumbs mixed with chopped ham. 3. Fry in shallow fat. 4. Serve garnished with boiled and sautéd strips of carrot, sautéed mushrooms, hard-boiled strips of egg and strips of pickled gherkin. 5. Pour réforme sauce over mutton.

SAUCE (ESPAGNOLE AND RÉFORME)

1. Cut vegetables and bacon into small pieces and fry lightly in butter. 2. Add flour and cook very slowly till golden brown. 3. Add stock, blanched and mashed tomatoes and bouquet garni. Simmer for 30 minutes. 4. Strain. Re-heat. Add sherry if desired. 5. Reduce vinegar and peppercorns to one tablespoon, add the above espagnole sauce and redcurrant jelly. Boil and strain.

36. CÔTELETTES d' AGNEAU à l'AMBASSADRICE

Ingredients	Quantity
Best end neck of lamb	8 cutlets
Butter	30 gm
Shallots	5 gm
Mushrooms (white)	15 gm
Refined flour	30 gm
Parsley	a few sprigs
Stock	75 ml
Egg yolk	1
Seasoning	to taste
Lime	¼
Mutton marrow	30 gm
Fat	for frying
Ambassadrice sauce	

Garnish

Spaghetti	55 gm
Butter	15 gm
Chopped parsley	3 tbsp

Ambassadrice Sauce:

Espagnole sauce	150 ml
Redcurrant jelly	1 dsp
Sultanas	60 gm
Lime juice	1 tsp
Sugar	
Cayenne pepper	a pinch
Salt	a pinch

Method

1. Boil cutlets. Leave till cold. 2. Prepare farce as follows: Melt butter. Add chopped shallots and mushrooms. 3. Cook slightly. Add flour and blend well. 4. Add stock and boil up. 5. Stir in yolk carefully. Add lime juice, chopped parsley and seasoning. 6. Cook without boiling. Add blanched, chopped marrow. Pour on to a plate and cool. 7. Mask cutlets with farce. Coat twice with egg and breadcrumbs. 8. Fry in deep fat. Dish and pour sauce round. 9. Garnish with boiled spaghetti, tossed in melted butter and sprinkled over with chopped parsley.

SAUCE

1. Prepare espagnole sauce as in previous recipe. 2. Add redcurrant jelly, sugar, cayenne pepper, salt and lemon juice. 3. Boil well together. Add blanched sultanas and use as desired.

37. CÔTELETTES de MOUTON à la VILLEROI

Ingredients	Quantity
Best end neck of mutton	8 cutlets
Seasoning	
Butter	30 gm
Dripping	30 gm
Allemande sauce	150 ml
Cream cracker biscuits	2
Egg	1
Breadcrumbs (dried)	30 gm
Fat	for frying
Garnish	
Fried parsley	
Cucumber sauce	
Allemande Sauce	
Milk	150 ml
Carrots	15 gm
Celery	a small piece
Bay leaf	¼
Refined flour	12 gm
Butter	15 gm
Peppercorns	3
Salt	to taste
Egg yolk	1
Butter	10 gm
Salt and Pepper	a pinch each
Nutmeg	
Cream	½ tbsp
Lime juice	a few drops

Method

1. Prepare cutlets. Season and sauté for 5 minutes, browning both sides well, or braise whole. 2. Press between two dishes till cold. 3. Trim. Spread Allemande sauce thickly on both sides. 4. Dip in crushed biscuits and allow to dry. 5. Coat with egg and breadcrumbs twice. 6. Fry in deep fat. 7. Serve garnished with fried parsley and accompanied by cucumber sauce (see Vol. I)

ALLEMANDE SAUCE

1. Prepare béchamel (see Vol. I). Whisk in egg yolk. Season. Cook without boiling. 2. Remove from fire. Cool slightly and add cream. 3. Whisk in butter. Add lime juice. Strain if necessary.

38. CÔTELETTES à la MURILLO

Ingredients	Quantity
Best end neck of mutton	8 cutlets
Butter	60 gm
Mushrooms (fresh)	60 gm
Béchamel sauce	75 ml
Cheese	30 gm
Capsicum	60 gm
Tomatoes	115 gm

Method

1. Prepare cutlets. 2. Fry in clarified butter. Garnish one side with sautéed mushrooms cohered with reduced béchamel sauce. 3. Set cutlets on a tray, sprinkle with grated cheese and a few drops of melted butter. 4. Glaze in a very hot oven. 5. Dish cutlets in the form of a crown. 6. Fix a frill on each and surround with sliced capsicum and tomatoes sautéed in butter and mixed.

39. CÔTELETTES à la PROVENCALE

Ingredients	Quantity
Best end neck of mutton	8 cutlets
Béchamel sauce	300 ml
Egg yolks	3
Salt and Pepper	to taste
Garlic	flake
Mushrooms	30 gm
Olives	15 gm
Butter	60 gm

Method

1. Prepare and fry cutlets in clarified butter. 2.Grill mushrooms. Poach stoned olives. 3. Reduce béchamel sauce to half, add crushed garlic and egg yolks. 4. Spread this mixture on one side of each cutlet. 5. Set cutlets on a tray. Sprinkle with melted butter and place in a quick oven to glaze garnish and complete the cooking. 6. Dish in the form of circle. Place a grilled mushroom in the centre of each cutlet, and an olive on each mushroom.

40. ROGNONS SAUTÉS BERCY

Ingredients	Quantity
Sheep's kidneys	16 (about 1 kg)
Shallots	30 gm
Stock	300 ml

Ingredients	Quantity
Lime juice	½ lime
Butter	100 gm
Parsley	a few sprigs
Marinade	
Vinegar	15 ml
Salt	to taste
Pepper	a pinch
Mustard	¼ tsp

Method

1. Cut kidneys into halves lengthwise. 2. Remove membrane and fat. Wash. 3. Marinade in vinegar mixed with seasoning. 4. Chop shallots. 5. Melt half the butter. Add kidneys. Sauté and remove. 6. Add chopped shallots and sauté without discolouring. Add stock and lime juice. Reduce to half. 7. Add kidneys and remaining butter cut into small pieces. 8. Remove pan to side of fire and shake pan till butter melts. 9. Sprinkle with chopped parsley and serve hot.

41. ROGNONS SAUTÉS BORDELAISE

Ingredients	Quantity
Sheep's kidneys	16 (about 1 kg)
Mushrooms	85 gm
Butter	30 gm
Worcester sauce	30 ml
Bordelaise sauce	200 ml
Lime	½
Marrow	115 gm
Salt and Pepper	to taste
Mignoette	to taste
Bay leaf	1
Thyme	1 sprig
Butter	30 gm
Bordelaise sauce	
Shallots	50 gm
Stock	600 ml

Method

1. Cut kidneys into two. Remove membranes and fat and wash well. 2. Marinade in Worcester sauce. 3. Heat butter and sauté kidneys. Remove. 4. Sauté mushrooms. 5. Prepare sauce. Add kidneys and mushrooms to boiling hot sauce. 6. Garnish with chopped parsley and serve hot.

BORDELAISE SAUCE

1. Chop shallots and put in a pan with stock, bay leaf, thyme, salt and pepper. Bring to a boil. 2. Reduce to a quarter. 3. Add lime juice and diced marrow which has been poached in boiling salted water. 4. Finish with butter.

42. ROGNONS SAUTÉS HONGROISE

Ingredients	Quantity
Sheep's kidneys	16 (about 1 kg)
Salt and Pepper	to taste
Butter	115 gm
Onions	115 gm
Paprika	5 gm
Cream	115 gm
Velouté sauce	300 ml
Parsley	a few sprigs

Method

1. Cut kidneys into halves. Remove membranes and fat. Wash well. Season. 2. Sauté kidneys in melted butter. Remove. 3. Add chopped onions and fry. Add paprika and moisten with cream. 4. Cook and reduce to half. 5. Add velouté sauce. Boil for a few minutes. 6. Strain through a fine sieve. 7. Re-heat sauce. Add kidneys. Bring to a boil and serve hot in a timbale garnished with chopped parsley.

43. ROGNONS SAUTÉS CHASSEUR

Ingredients	Quantity
Sheep's kidneys	16 (about 1 kg)
Butter	100 gm
Parsley	a few sprigs
Chasseur Sauce	
Mushrooms	15 gm
Butter	15 gm
Salad oil	15 ml
Shallots	10 gm
Stock	300 ml
Tomato sauce	100 ml

Method

1. Peel and mince mushrooms. 2. Heat butter and oil. 3. Add mushrooms and fry till slightly browned. 4. Add minced shallots and sauté. Remove excess fat. 5. Add stock. Boil and reduce to half. 6. Add tomato juice. Boil for 5 minutes more. 7. Prepare kidneys. Season and sauté in butter. Add kidneys to sauce. Cook for a couple of minutes. 8. Serve hot.

44. ROGNONS SAUTÉS à l'INDIENNE

Ingredients	Quantity
Sheep's kidneys	16 (about 1 kg)
Onions	115 gm
Velouté sauce	300 ml
Pulao rice	115 gm
Stock	230 ml
Butter	115 gm
Curry powder	15 gm
Salt	to taste

Method

1. Prepare rice and keep hot. 2. Cut kidneys into halves lengthwise. 3. Remove membranes and fat. Wash well and season. 4. Sauté kidneys in butter. Remove. 5. Add chopped onions and fry. Add curry powder and fry for a few minutes longer. 6. Moisten with velouté. Cook for a few minutes and strain through a fine sieve. 7. Put kidneys into sauce. Bring to a boil. Serve hot in a timbale. 8. Serve rice, which should also be hot, separately.

45. ROGNONS à la BROCHETTE

Ingredients	Quantity
Sheep's kidneys	16 (about 1 kg)
Oil	15 ml
Vinegar	15 ml
Salt and Pepper	to taste
Mustard	½ tsp
Maître d'hotel butter	60 gm
Lime	½
Parsley butter	10 gm

Method

1. Cut kidneys into halves without separating them. 2. Marinade for half an hour in a mixture of oil, vinegar and seasoning. 3. Thread 2 to 4 on a skewer and grill them. 4. Remove from skewer and place on a hot dish. 5. Put a piece of softened maître d'hôtel butter in cavity of each kidney.

46. ROGONS BROCHETTE à l'ESPAGNOLE

Ingredients	Quantity
Sheep's kidneys	16 (1 kg)
Flour	
Oil	15 ml
Vinegar	15 ml
Salt and Pepper	to taste

Ingredients	Quantity
Mustard	½ tsp
Tomatoes (small)	500 gm
Onions	115 gm
Oil to fry	30 ml
Maître d'ôhotel butter	

Method

1. Prepare kidneys as for recipe No. 45 Rognons à la Brochette. 2. Cut tomatoes into halves. Season and grill. 3. Cut onions into rings. Season, dredge with flour and fry in oil till crisp. 4. Garnish each tomato half with a piece of maître d'hôtel butter. 5. Set a kidney on each tomato and surround with a border of crisply fried onion rings.

47. ROGNONS SAUTÉS à la TURBIGO

Ingredients	Quantity
Sheep's kidneys	8 (½ kg)
Demi glace	300 ml
Butter or Fat	60 gm
Button mushrooms	115 gm
Chipolatas (small sausages)	8

Method

1. Skin, halve kidneys, remove sinews and cut halves into 3 to 4 pieces. 2. Fry quickly in a frying pan for approximately 4 to 5 minutes. 3. Add to finished sauce. Serve with button mushrooms cooked in a little fat and grilled or fried chipolatas.

48. LANGUE de MOUTON CHOUCROUTE

Ingredients	Quantity
Sheep's tongue	500 gm
Butter	50 gm
Onions	30 gm
Espagnole sauce	150 ml
Potatoes	225 gm
Pickled red cabbage	225 gm
Salt and Pepper	to taste

Method

1. Blanch tongue. Remove membrane, windpipe and bone. 2. Cook in stock. Slice into two halves and braise in butter. Add espagnole sauce and cook. 3. Dish out in a timbale with pickled cabbage and purée of potatoes.

49. SALTED OX TONGUE

Ingredients	Quantity
Ox tongue	1
Saltpetre	40 gm
Cooking salt	40 gm
Cloves	5 gm

Method

1. Soak full tongue in a vessel with saltpetre and cooking salt for 3–10 days. Turn over midway. 2. Put tongue and liquid extract into a vessel with a tight-fitting lid. Bring to a boil and then simmer for 6-7 hours, or pressure cook for one hour. 3. When cooked plunge into hot water to remove extra salt on surface. 4. Put on a wooden board and trim and scrape tongue to remove fur. 5. To preserve, sun dry tongue. The dried tongue will have to be boiled again for ½ hour before being used.

50. KROMESKIES

Ingredients	Quantity
Minced cooked chicken	450 gm
Ham	150 gm
Mushrooms	115 gm
White sauce	300 ml
Bacon	225 gm
Parsley	a few sprigs
Batter	
Refined flour	115 gm
Salt	a pinch
Fresh yeast	15 gm
or Dry yeast	7 gm
Sugar	a pinch
Milk	150 ml
Eggs	1

Method

1. Cream yeast and sugar. Add warmed milk. 2 Pour on to beaten egg and strain into centre of sifted flour. 3. Mix well and allow to rise for one hour. 4. Mix chicken, chopped ham and mushrooms with white sauce. 5. Season and form into small cork shapes. 6. Wrap in thin strips of bacon. 7. Dip in batter and fry in hot fat till golden brown. 8. Drain and garnish with fried parsley. Serve tomato sauce separately.

51. CÔTE de PORC à la CHARCUTIERE

Ingredients	Quantity
Pork chops	500 gm
Butter	100 gm
Potatoes	450 gm
Milk	60 ml
Fine breadcrumbs	15 gm
Seasoning	to taste
Charcutière Sauce	
Onions	30 gm
Butter	30 gm
Stock	300 ml
Demi glace	300 ml
Mustard	a pinch
Powdered sugar	a pinch
Lime	1
Gherkins	55 gm

Method

1. Season cutlets. Dip in melted butter. 2. Sprinkle over with breadcrumbs. 3. Grill gently, basting from time to time. 4. Dish in a circle. Pour charcutière sauce over and serve a timbale of creamed potatoes separately.

CHARCUTIÈRE SAUCE

1. Sauté chopped onion in butter without browning. 2. Add stock and demi glace. Reduce to half. 3. Add mustard, sugar and lime juice. Mix well. Add chopped gherkins.

52. CÔTE de PORC à la FLAMANDE

Ingredients	Quantity
Pork chops	500 gm
Butter	55 gm
Seasoning	to taste
Cooking apples	500 gm

Method

1. Season chops and fry them on both sides in butter till half done. 2. Peel and slice apples and arrange them in a pyrex dish. 3. Place cutlets over apple slices. Sprinkle with fat. 4. Cover and complete the cooking in an oven (about 10 to 15 minutes). 5. Serve as is.

53. CÔTE de PORC HONGROISE

Ingredients	Quantity
Pork chops	500 gm
Onions	115 gm
Tomatoes	225 gm
Butter	55 gm
Paprika	5-10 gm
Salt and Pepper	to taste
Mustard	a pinch

Method

1. Trim, season, and fry chops. Remove. 2. Fry chopped onions in same fat. 3. Add paprika and peeled and crushed tomatoes. 4. Add pork and enough stock to cover. 5. Cook gently till pork becomes tender.

N.B. The loin can be roasted instead of being cooked in stock. After scoring and marking, roast till meat is cooked and rind crisp. Take out. Cut out chops separately, and put into sauce.

54. SOUFFLÉS au JAMBON

Ingredients	Quantity
Cooked ham	450 gm
Bèchamel sauce	200 ml
Egg yolks	4
Egg whites	6
Cheese (grated)	85 gm

Method

1. Pound ham fine. Add 3 tablespoons of cold béchamel sauce, one spoon at a time. 2. Rub through a fine sieve. 3. Boil remaining béchamel sauce and add to purée. 4. Add egg yolks and grated cheese and fold in stiffly beaten whites. 5. Pour into a soufflé mould surrounded by a band of buttered paper. 6. Place in a pan of boiling water and put in a moderate oven (175°C or 350°F). Cook till done (about 20 to 25 minutes). Serve immediately.

55. FLAN de JAMBON SOUBISE

Ingredients	Quantity
Pastry	
Refined flour	150 gm
Salt	a pinch
Butter	70 gm
Milk to mix	2 tbsp

Ingredients	Quantity
Filling	
Refined flour	15 gm
Butter	15 gm
Onions	15 gm
Seasoning	to taste
Lean ham	55 gm
Eggs (hard-boiled)	2
Milk	150 ml
Cheese	30 gm

Method

1. Make pastry as for shortcrust, using milk to form a richer pastry.
2. Line a deep flan tin about 18 cm in diameter. Prick centre. Bake blind at 200°C (400°C) for 25 minutes. 3. Mince onion and sauté in very little butter without discolouring. 4. Prepare white sauce with flour, butter and milk. 5. Add cooked onion. 6. Slice hard-boiled eggs and dice ham. 7. Put in layers into the pastry covering each layer with white sauce. 8. Sprinkle with cheese and bake at 190°C (375°F) till cheese melts.

56. QUICHE LORRAINE

Ingredients	Quantity
Pastry	
Refined flour	150 gm
Salt	a pinch
Butter	70 gm
Milk to mix	2 tbsp
Filling	
Spring onions	6
or Onions	115 gm
Butter	15 gm
Lean bacon	85 gm
Milk	150 ml
Dairy cream (optional)	3 tbsp
Eggs	2 large or 3 small
Salt and Pepper	to taste
Cheese	55 gm

Method

1. Make pastry in the usual way using milk instead of water to make a richer pastry. 2. Line a deep flan tin about 18 cm in diameter. 3. Leave for half an hour. 4. Trim spring onions, removing outside leaves. Cut into 1.5 cm lengths. 5. Melt butter. Add onions and sauté without browning.

6. Cut rind off bacon and dice. Fry bacon with onions just till bacon is cooked. 7. Break eggs into a bowl and beat well. Add milk and cream. 8. Stir in fried onions, bacon and grated cheese. 9. Season with salt and pepper. 10. Pour into lined flan tin and bake at 205°C (400°F) for 25 minutes. Reduce heat to 195°C (380°F) and bake for 15 minutes more. 11. Remove flan on to a hot plate. Serve at once. 12. If flan is to be served cold, then garnish with sliced hard-boiled eggs and spring onions.

57. MADRAS SHEPHERD'S PIE

Ingredients	For 4	For 100
Minced mutton (cooked)	500 gm	12.5 kg
Onions (finely chopped)	115 gm	2.8 kg
Potatoes	140 gm	3.6 kg
Grated cheese	50 gm	1.35 kg
Curry powder	1 tsp	60 gm
Salt	to taste	80–100 gm
Pepper	a pinch	15 gm
Fat	10 gm	200 gm
Stock to moisten		

Method

1. Melt fat. 2. Fat curry powder. Add chopped onions. Cover and cook for two to three minutes. 3. Mix in meat. Season. Moisten with stock. 4. Mash potatoes with cheese, salt and pepper. 5. Put meat into greased pie dishes. 6. Cover with potatoes. Brush over with melted fat and bake till golden brown.

58. SPINACH AND MUSHROOM QUICHE

Ingredients	Quantity
For Pastry	
Flour	120 gm
Butter	70 gm
Salt	½ tsp
Cold water to mix	
Filling	
Milk	150 m.
Eggs	2
Spring onions with greens (finely chopped)	½ bunch
Spinach	2 bunches
Mushrooms (sliced)	6
Garlic	3 flakes

Ingredients	Quantity
Capsicum (finely chopped)	30 gm
Salt and Pepper	to taste

Method

1. Sieve flour and salt in a clean bowl. 2. Cut frozen butter and rub into flour to resemble cornmeal or fine breadcrumbs. 3. Add cold water gradually and mix with a palette knife to a stiff dough. 4. Let dough rest for 5 minutes in refrigerator. 5. Roll gently on floured surface to 0.5 cm thickness and line a 17.5 cm flan tin with the pastry. 6. Bake blind at 400°F (205°C) for about 8 minutes. 7. Cool and turn out pastry shell on a baking sheet and brush inside with egg wash. 8. Pour in filling and bake at 400°F (205°C) for 25 minutes till filling is firm and top surface golden brown.

Method (For Filling)

1. Sauté finely chopped garlic, sliced mushrooms, parboiled and chopped spinach, chopped capsicum and spring onions with greens in butter. 2. Season and cool. 3. Beat eggs with milk. Add grated cheese. 4. Pour into pastry shell.

59. VEGETABLE QUICHE

Ingredients	Quantity
For Pastry	
Flour	120 gm
Butter	70 gm
Salt	½ tsp
Cold water to mix	
For Filling	
Spring onions	4
Cabbage	100 gm
Carrots	45 gm
French beans	45 gm
Fresh green peas	30 gm
Capsicum	30 gm
Celery stalks	2
Eggs	2
Milk	150 ml
Cheese	30 gm
Butter	30 gm
Salt	10 gm
Pepper	a pinch

Method (For Pastry)

1. Sieve flour and salt in a clean bowl. 2. Cut frozen butter and rub into flour to resemble cornmeal or fine breadcrumbs. 3. Add cold water gradually and mix with a palette knife to a stiff dough. 4. Let dough rest for 5 minutes in refrigerator. 5. Roll gently on floured surface to 0.5 cm thickness and line flan tin with pastry. 6. Bake blind at 205°C for about 8 minutes. 7. Cool and turn out pastry shell on a baking sheet and brush inside with egg wash. 8. Pour in filling and bake at 205°C for 25 minutes till filling is firm and the top surface golden brown.

Method (For Filling)

1. Shell and boil peas, grate carrots and finely chop spring onions with greens, cabbage, French beans, capsicum and celery. 2.Sauté cut vegetables in butter. Season. 3. Cool filling and add to beaten egg and milk mixture. Add grated cheese. Pour into pastry shell.

60. CHEESE AND BACON FRITTATA

Ingredients	Quantity
Eggs	6
Milk	1 cup
Green onion (minced)	1
Butter or	
Margarine (melted)	2 tbsp
Salt	½ tsp
Pepper	⅛ tsp
Shredded cheese	15 gm
Cooked bacon (crumbled)	60 gm (½ can)

Method

1. Preheat oven to 400°F. Grease 27 cm round au gratin pan or 23 by 23 cm baking pan. 2. In medium bowl, with wire whisk or hand beater, beat eggs, milk, green onion, butter or margarine, salt and pepper until well blended. 3. Pour mixture into baking pan. Sprinkle cheese and bacon evenly over top. 4. Bake 20 minutes or until set and golden brown. Makes 4 main dish servings.

61. STUFFED HEART

Ingredients	Quantity
Sheep's hearts	4
Forcemeat stuffing	55 gm
Fat for basting	55 gm
Seasoning	to taste

Method

1. Using kitchen scissors, trim hearts and remove tubes and membranes. Soak for half an hour. 2. Drain hearts and fill cavities with forcemeat stuffing, pushing it well down. 3. Using fine string and a trussing needle, tie tops of hearts together to secure stuffing. 4. Boil till half-cooked. 5. Remove and roll in seasoned flour and bake at 190°C (375°F) till done, basting frequently. Cooking time approximately 2 hrs.

VOLAILLES

1. Volaille
2. Cuts of Chicken
3. Poulet Rôti
4. Poulet Rôti au Lard
5. Poulet Rôti à l'Anglaise
6. Poulet Rôti Farci aux Fines Herbs
7. Poulet Grillé
8. Poulet Grillé Diable
9. Poulet Sauté
10. Poulet Sauté Chasseur
11. Poulet Sauté aux Champignons
12. Poulet Sauté à l'Egyptienne
13. Poulet Sauté à l'Espagnole
14. Poulet Sauté à la Fermière
15. Poulet Sauté Forestière
16. Poulet Sauté Gabrielle
17. Poulet Sauté Hongroise
18. Poulet Sauté à l'Indienne
19. Poulet Sauté Lyonnaise
20. Poulet Sauté Marengo
21. Poulet Sauté Maryland
22. Poulet Sauté Marseillaise
23. Poulet Sauté Mexicaine
24. Poulet Sauté Mireille
25. Poulet Sauté Parmentier
26. Poulet Sauté Portugaise
27. Poulet Sauté Cacciatore
28. Coq Au Vin
29. Poêling
30. Poularde Andalouse
31. Poularde au Céleri
32. Poularde Chipolata
33. Poularde Demidoff
34. Poularde Diva
35. Poularde Edouard VII
36. Poularde en Estouffade
37. Poularde à la Fermière
38. Poularde à la Grecque
39. Poularde à l'Indienne
40. Poularde Mireille
41. Poularde au Riz
42. Poularde Stanley
43. Poularde Polignac
44. Poulet Poché au Riz (Sauce Suprême)
45. Fricassee de Volaille
46. Poulet en Casserole
47. Goulash de Poulet (A) Goulash de Poulet (B)
48. Poulet en Casserole Campanini avec Nouilles
49. Suprême de Volaille à la Kiev
50. Poulet à le Rex
51. Capilotade de Volaille
52. Frittos de Volaille
53. Mayonnaise de Volaille
54. Vol-Au-Vent de Volaille
55. Chaudfroid de Poulet
56. Galantine de Poulet
57. Ballotines de Volaille Printanière

58.	Poulet de Grains à la Bergère	63.	Caneton aux Olives
59.	Poulet de Grains à la Limousine	64.	Caneton Braisé à l'Orange
		65.	Caneton aux Petits Pois
60.	Canard Rôti à l'Anglaise	66.	Oie Rôtie
61.	Caneton Poêle à la Menthe	67.	Dinde Rôtie
62.	Caneton Braisé aux Navets		

I. VOLAILLE

Chickens

Poussin	4 to 6 weeks old. Uses—roasting and grilling.
Poulet de Grain	A young fattened bird 3 to 4 months old. Uses—roasting, grilling, en casserole.
Poulet Reine	Fully grown, tender, prime bird. Uses—roasting, grilling, sauté, en casserole, supreêmes, pies.
Poularde	Large fully grown prime bird. Uses—roasting, boiling, en casserole, galantine.
Chapon	A castrated or caponized cock bird specially fed and fattened. Uses—roasting.
Poule	An old hen. Uses—stock and soups.

2. CUTS OF CHICKEN

	English	*French*
1.	Wing	Aile
2.	Breast	Blanc
3.	Leg	Cuisse
	(a) Thigh	(a) Gras de cuisse
	(b) Drumstick	(b) Pilon de cuisse
4.	Winglet	Aileron
5.	Carcass	Carcasse

Suprême: This is the wing and half the breast of a chicken. The trimmed wing bone is attached.

Cutting for Sauté, Fricassée, Pies, etc.

1. Remove feet at the first joint. 2. Remove legs from carcass. 3. Cut each leg into two at joint. 4. Remove wishbone. Remove winglets and trim. 5. Remove wings carefully, leaving two equal portions on breast. 6. Remove breast and cut into two. 7. Trim carcass and cut into three pieces.

Preparation for Grilling:

1. Remove wish-bone. 2. Cut off claws at first joint. 3. Place bird on its back. 4. Insert a large knife through neck-end and out of vent. 5. Cut through backbone. 6. Open out. 7. Remove back and rib bones. 8. Flatten slightly with a bat if necessary.

Cutting of Cooked Chicken (Roasted or Boiled) 4 Portions:

1. Remove legs and cut in two (drumstick and thigh). 2. Remove wings. 3. Separate breast from carcass and divide into two. 4. Serve a drumstick with a wing and a thigh with a breast.

3. POULET RÔTI

Ingredients	Quantity
Chicken	1 (about 1.5 kg)
Salt and Pepper	to taste
Fat	60 gm
Accompaniments	
Bread sauce	150 ml
Potato wafers (game chips)	30 gm
Watercress	
Brown gravy	150 ml

Method

1. Season cleaned chicken inside and out with salt and fine pepper. 2. Place on a trivet in a roasting tin. 3. Cover with melted fat. 4. Cook in an oven 175°C– 190°C approx. (350°–375°F) or gas mark 5 to 6 for about 1 to 1½ hours, basting frequently. 5. To test if cooked pierce with fork between drumstick and thigh and hold over a plate. The juice coming out should show no signs of blood. 6. Prepare roast gravy with stock and sediment from roasting tin. 7. Serve on a flat silver dish with watercress at back of bird and potato wafers in front. 8. Roast gravy and bread sauce are served separately.

N.B. Always remove trussing string from bird before serving. Bird may be wrapped in aluminium foil and roasted after initial browning. This helps keep the bird moist.

4. POULET RÔTI au LARD

Ingredients and method as for Poulet Rôti with the addition of 4 (four) grilled rashers of streaky bacon either in rolls or left as is.

5. POULET RÔTI à l'ANGLAISE

Ingredients	Quantity
Chicken	1 (about 1.5 kg)
Salt and Pepper	to taste
Fat	30 gm

Stuffing	
Onions (chopped)	30 gm
Breadcrumbs (fresh)	60 gm
Thyme	a pinch
Margarine	60 gm
Chicken liver	
Parsley (chopped)	
Salt and Pepper	a pinch

Accompaniments	
Potato wafers	30 gm
Watercress (optional)	
Bread sauce	150 ml
Brown gravy	150 ml

Method

1. Prepare chicken as for Poulet Rôti but stuff before trussing.

Stuffing

1. Sauté onion in melted margarine without discolouring. 2. Add seasoning, herbs and breadcrumbs. 3. Add chopped liver. Check for seasoning.

6. POULET RÔTI FARCI aux FINES HERBS

Ingredients	Quantity
Chicken	1
Butter	120 gm
Mixed herbs–Rosemary, Basil, Allspice,	¼ tsp each
Thyme and Tarragon	
Parsley	1 bunch
Garlic	10–12 pods

Method

1. Clean and trim chicken. 2. Cream butter. Add mixed herbs and crushed garlic and parsley. 3. Apply this mixture between skin and flesh of bird (around breast area). 4. Secure legs in place. 5. Pan roast bird until light brown on all sides. 6. Put into roasting tin. Baste with oil and roast until meat is tender. 7. When cooked, joint chicken and arrange neatly in an entrée dish.

7. POULET GRILLÉ

Ingredients	Quantity
Chicken (young)	1
Garnish	
Streaky bacon	4 rashers
Salt and Pepper	to taste
Fat	60 gm
Tomatoes	225 gm
Mushrooms	60 gm
Watercress	

Method

1. Season chicken prepared for grilling, with salt and pepper. 2. Brush with melted fat, and place on pre-heated greased grill bars or on a flat baking tray under a salamander. 3. Brush frequently with melted fat during cooking and allow 15 to 20 minutes for each side. 4. Test to see if cooked by piercing drumstick with a skewer or trussing needle; there should be no signs of blood. 5. Serve on a silver flat garnished with watercress, grilled bacon, tomatoes and mushrooms. 6. A suitable sauce such as devilled sauce may be served as an accompaniment.

N.B. Marinate Indian chicken in a marinade of Worcester sauce, mustard, pepper and raw papaya, before grilling.

8. POULET GRILLÉ DIABLE

Ingredients and method as for Poulet Grillé but approximately 5 minutes before each side of chicken is cooked, brush liberally with the following mixture. Sprinkle with white breadcrumbs (about 30 gm) and complete grilling.

DEVIL MIXTURE

Ingredients	Quantity
Mustard	1 tsp
Worcester sauce	1 tsp
Cayenne pepper	½ tsp
Vinegar and Water	2 tbsp

Method

Combine all ingredients and use.

9. POULET SAUTÉ

Ingredients	Quantity
Chicken (young)	1 (about 1.5 kg)
Jus-lie	300 ml
Butter	60 gm
Salt and Pepper	to taste
Parsley	a few sprigs
Jus-lié	
Chicken bones	115 gm
Chicken giblets	
Celery	15 gm
Onions	30 gm
Carrots	30 gm
Bay leaf	¼
Thyme	a small sprig
Tomato purée	5 ml
Arrowroot or Cornflour	10 gm
Stock	300 ml
Mushroom trimmings	

Method

1. Joint chicken as for all sautés. 2. Put butter in a sauté pan over a fairly hot fire. 3. Season chicken and place in the sauté pan (in the following order): drumsticks, thighs, carcass, wings, winglets and breast. 4. Cook to a golden brown on both sides. 5. Cover with a lid and cook in the oven till done. 6. Dress neatly in an entrée dish. 7. Drain off fat from sauté pan. 8. Return to heat and add jus-lié. 9. Simmer for 3 to 4 minutes. Correct seasoning and skim. 10. Pass through a fine strainer onto chicken. 11. Sprinkle with chopped parsley and serve hot.

JUS-LIÉ

1. Chop chicken bones and brown in a little fat. 2. Add chopped giblets and finely chopped carrot, onion, celery, bay leaf and thyme. Brown well. 3. Mix in tomato purée and stock. 4. Simmer for 2 hours. 5. Dilute arrowroot or cornflour in a little cold water. 6. Pour into boiling stock, stirring continuously until it re-boils. 7. Simmer for 10 to 15 minutes. 8. Correct seasoning. 9. Pass through a fine strainer.

N.B. In all cases of sauté chicken, if chicken is not young and tender boil first before following recipe.

10. POULET SAUTÉ CHASSEUR

Ingredients	Quantity
Chicken (young)	1 (about 1.5 kg)
Button mushrooms	115 gm
Jus-lié	300 ml
Butter	60 gm
Tomatoes	225 gm
Shallots (chopped)	15 gm
Parsley	a few sprigs

Method

1. Proceed as for Poulet Sauté upto stage 6. 2. Add shallots to sauté pan. 3. Add washed, sliced mushrooms, cover with a lid and cook gently for 3 to 4 minutes without discolouring. 4. Drain off fat. 5. Add jus-lié (see recipe in Poulet Sauté) and blanched and pipped tomatoes. 6. Simmer for 5 minutes, check for seasoning. 7. Pour over chicken. 8. Sprinkle with chopped parsley and serve hot.

11. POULET SAUTÉ aux CHAMPIGNONS

Ingredients	Quantity
Chicken (young)	1 (about 1.5 kg)
Jus-lié	300 ml
Shallots	15 gm
Butter	60 gm
Button mushrooms	115 gm
Salt and Pepper	to taste
Parsley	a few sprigs

Method

1. Proceed as for Poulet Sauté upto stage 6. 2. Add chopped shallots and mushrooms to fat and cook gently without discolouring. 3. Drain extra fat. 4. Add jus-lié (see recipe in Poulet Sauté). 5. Simmer for 5 minutes. Check for seasoning. 6. Pour over pieces of chicken. 7. Sprinkle with chopped parsley.

12. POULET SAUTÉ à l'EGYPTIENNE

Ingredients	Quantity
Chicken (young)	1 (about 1.5. kg)
Ham (raw)	175 gm
Tomatoes	225 gm
Oil	60 ml

Ingredients	Quantity
Onions	100 gm
Mushrooms	60 gm
Chicken stock	20 ml
Salt and Pepper	to taste

Method

1. Clean and joint chicken as for sautés. 2. Sauté pieces of chicken in oil till light brown. Remove. 3. Toss, in the same oil, sliced onions and mushrooms. 4. Add diced ham. Sauté and remove. 5. Set pieces of chicken in an earthenware or pyrex dish, alternating them with onions, mushrooms and ham. 6. Cover with thick slices of tomatoes. 7. Cover earthenware dish with a tight-fitting lid and complete the cooking in an oven (about 20 minutes). 8. Just before serving, sprinkle with a tablespoonful of chicken stock.

13. POULET SAUTÉ à l'ESPAGNOLE

Ingredients	Quantity
Chicken (young)	1 (about 1.5 kg)
Oil	60 ml
Pilau rice	225 gm
Capsicum	125 gm
Peas	100 gm
Sausages	60 gm
Garnish	
Cherry tomatoes	225 gm

Method

1. Prepare plain pilau using chicken stock. 2. When cooked add diced and sautéd capsicum, boiled peas and sliced sausages. 3. Joint chicken. Season sauté in oil. Remove excess oil and add prepared rice to chicken. 4. Cover pan and cook gently in an oven for 10 to 20 minutes. 5. Dish chicken and rice and surround with grilled tomatoes.

14. POULET SAUTÉ à la FERMIÈRE

Ingredients	Quantity
Chicken (young)	1 (about 1.35 kg)
Salt	to taste
Sugar	a pinch
Carrots (red part)	85 gm

Ingredients	Quantity
Butter	60 gm
Turnips	100 gm
Celery	60 gm
Onions	60 gm
Ham	75 gm
Chicken stock	5 tbsp (75 ml)

Method

1. Clean and joint chicken as for sautés. Season. 2. Sauté pieces of chicken in butter. Remove. 3. Add sliced carrots, turnips, celery and onions. 4. Add a pinch of salt and sugar and let it stew in butter. 5. Put chicken, vegetables and diced ham into an earthenware dish. 6. Cover and complete the cooking in an oven, sprinkling a little chicken stock if necessary. 7. Just before serving, sprinkle with remaining stock.

15. POULET SAUTÉ FORESTIÈRE

Ingredients	Quantity
Chicken (young)	1 (about 1.5 kg)
Butter	125 gm
Shallots	60 gm
Mushrooms	60 gm
Stock	300 ml
Bacon	60 gm
Parsley	a few sprigs
Salt and Pepper	to taste
Potatoes	225 gm

Method

1. Clean chicken. Wash well. 2. Season and marinate in a marinade of Worcester sauce, mustard, salt and pepper. Let it stand for half an hour. 3. Sauté chicken in butter. Sprinkle with chopped shallots and mushrooms. 4. Add stock and stew in an oven till tender and gravy is reduced. 5. Parboil potatoes. Peel, dice and sauté in butter. 6. Grill or fry bacon. 7. Dish out chicken with garnish. 8. Surround with heaps of potatoes and place a rectangle of bacon between each heap. 9. Sprinkle chicken with chopped parsley.

16. POULET SAUTÉ GABRIELLE

Ingredients	Quantity
Chicken (young)	1 (about 1.5 kg)
Mushroom liquor	75 ml

Ingredients	Quantity
Béchamel sauce	50 ml
Cream	3 tbsp
Butter	75 gm
Puff pastry	115 gm
Salt and Pepper	to taste

Method

1. Clean and boil chicken, using very little liquid. 2. Melt 30 gm of butter. 3. Sauté chicken without discolouring. Remove. 4. Swill pan with the mushroom liquor. Add béchamel sauce and cream. Reduce. 5. Finish with remaining butter. 6. Pour sauce over chicken. 7. Surround with small leaves of puff pastry baked white.

17. POULET SAUTÉ HONGROISE

Ingredients	Quantity
Chicken (young)	1 (about 1.5 kg)
Butter	60 gm
Onions	60 gm
Paprika	5 gm
Tomatoes	500 gm
Cream	75 ml
Salt and Pepper	to taste
Pilau rice	225 gm

Method

1. Clean and season chicken. Marinate if necessary or parboil. 2. Sauté chicken in butter without discolouring along with chopped onions and paprika. 3. When onions are slightly coloured add peeled and sliced tomatoes leaving one tomato aside for rice. 4. Cover and cook gently till chicken is done. 5. Prepare a plain pilau rice. Combine with remaining tomato chopped roughly and sautéed in butter (concassed). 6. Make a border with rice. Set chicken in the centre. 7. Add cream to tomatoes in the pan. Reduce. 8. Rub through a sieve. Re-heat and pour over chicken.

18. POULET SAUTÉ à l'INDIENNE

Ingredients	Quantity
Chicken	1
Onions	115 gm
Chicken veloute	200 ml
Coconut	½

Ingredients	Quantity
Curry powder	1 tsp
Oil	30 ml
Pilau rice	225 gm
Salt and Pepper	to taste

Method

1. Joint chicken as for sautés. 2. Season and fry in oil with sliced onions and curry powder. 3. Swill with about 1 cup of coconut milk. 4. Add chicken veloute and simmer gently till chicken is cooked and sauce reduced to half. 5. Prepare plain pilau using chicken stock. 6. Serve chicken in an entrée dish. Serve rice separately.

19. POULET SAUTÉ LYONNAISE

Ingredients	Quantity
Chicken (young)	1 (about 1.5 kg)
Butter	60 gm
Onions	340 gm
Jus-lie	75 ml
Parsley	a few sprigs
Salt and Pepper	to taste

Method

1. Clean and season chicken. 2. Saute in butter. When half-cooked add finely sliced onions. Cover and cook till chicken is tender. 3. Dish out chicken. Add jus-lie (see Poulet Saute) and bring to boil. 4. Pour liquor and onions over chicken. Sprinkle with a pinch of chopped parsley.

20. POULET SAUTÉ MARENGO

Ingredients	Quantity
Chicken (young)	1 (about 1.5 kg)
Olive oil	110 ml
Mushrooms	50 gm
Bread	4 slices
Butter	30 gm
Garlic	1 flake
Shallots	30 gm
Jus-lié	300 ml
Tomatoes	225 gm
Eggs	4
Crayfish	225 gm

Ingredients	Quantity
Parsley	a few sprigs
Salt and Pepper	to taste

Method

1. Joint chicken. Season with salt and pepper. 2. Heat oil. Add pieces of chicken. When browned add chopped shallots and garlic. Remove extra oil. 3. Add jus-lié (see Poulet Sauté), chopped tomatoes and sliced mushrooms. 4. Put into a casserole dish. Cover and cook in an oven till chicken is tender. 5. Dish chicken onto a silver flat. Cover with sauce. 6. Surround with heart-shaped croûtons fried in butter, fried eggs and crayfish cooked in a court bouillon. 7. Sprinkle over with chopped parsley.

21. POULET SAUTÉ MARYLAND

Ingredients	Quantity
Spring chicken	1 (1 kg)
Refined flour	15 gm
Eggs	2
Breadcrumbs	100 gm
Cooking bananas	225 gm
Parsley	½ bunch
Corn-on-the-cob	225 gm
Bacon	50 gm
Clarified butter	150 ml
Seasoning	to taste

Method

1. Cut chicken. Season. 2. Roll first in flour and then in egg and breadcrumbs. 3. Fry in hot clarified butter till brown. 4. Remove rind of bacon and fry till crisp. 5. Fry slices of bananas. Sauté boiled corn. 6. Set fried chicken in the centre of a silver flat. Surround with fried bacon, fried bananas and small heaps of corn. Garnish over with chopped parsley.

N.B. If the chicken is inclined to be tough, boil. Cut into joints. Skin. Dip in melted butter and then in egg and breadcrumbs before frying.

22. POULET SAUTÉ MARSEILLAISE

Ingredients	Quantity
Chicken (young)	1 (about 1.5 kg)
Salad oil	60 ml
Garlic	2 flakes
Capsicum	125 gm
Tomatoes	125 gm

Ingredients	Quantity
Chicken stock	150 ml
Lime	1
Salt and Pepper	to taste

Method

1. Clean and joint chicken. Season. 2. Sauté chicken in oil. When it is half cooked add crushed garlic, diced capsicum (with seeds removed) and quartered tomatoes. 3. Cover and cook gently for a few minutes. 4. Add stock and lime juice. Continue simmering till chicken is tender. Check for seasoning. 5. Dish chicken, cover with garnish and sprinkle over with a pinch of chopped parsley.

23. POULET SAUTÉ MEXICAINE

Ingredients	Quantity
Chicken (young)	1 (about 1.5 kg)
Oil	60 ml
Stock	150 ml
Tomatoes	225 gm
Capsicum	225 gm
Mushrooms	60 gm
Butter	30 gm
Salt and Pepper	to taste

Method

1. Clean and joint chicken. Season. 2. Heat oil. Sauté pieces of chicken. 3. Add stock and one tomato chopped up. Cover and cook gently till chicken is tender. Check for seasoning. 4. Dish chicken. Pour sauce over. Surround with grilled capsicum halves (seeds removed) and mushrooms. Garnish with remaining tomato chopped and tossed in hot butter.

24. POULET SAUTÉ MIREILLE

Ingredients	Quantity
Chicken (young)	1 (about 1.5 kg)
Oil	60 ml
Onions	115 gm
Tomatoes	450 gm
Capsicum	125 gm
Garlic	1 flake
Pilau rice	225 gm
Saffron	a pinch

Method

1. Clean and season chicken. 2. Sauté in hot oil. When half-cooked add chopped onions, tomatoes and capsicum (seeds removed). Cook gently till chicken is tender. 3. When nearly done add crushed garlic. 4. Cook for 10 minutes more. Dish chicken. 5. Reduce liquid to half and strain over chicken. 6. Serve a timbale of plain pilau cooked in chicken stock and flavoured with saffron.

25. POULET SAUTÉ PARMENTIER

Ingredients	Quantity
Chicken (young)	1 (about 1.5 kg)
Parsley	a few sprigs
Jus-lié	300 ml
Potatoes	225 gm
Butter	60 gm
Salt and Pepper	

Method

1. Clean and joint chicken. Season. 2. Sauté in butter. 3. Add parboiled diced potatoes. 4. Cover and complete the cooking in an oven, sprinkling over with a little stock, if necessary. 5. Dish chicken and garnish. Add jus-lié (see Poulet Sauté) to pan. Bring to a boil and strain over chicken. 6. Sprinkle with chopped parsley.

26. POULET SAUTÉ PORTUGAISE

Ingredients	Quantity
Chicken (young)	1 (about 1.5 kg)
Tomatoes	450 gm
Mushrooms	60 gm
Butter	30 gm
Oil	30 ml
Garlic	1 flake
Onions	60 gm
Pilau rice	225 gm
Salt and Pepper	to taste
Parsley	a few sprigs

Method

1. Clean, season and boil chicken in just enough stock to cover. 2. Remove and joint chicken. 3. Sauté in heated butter and oil. 4. Remove chicken. Drain off extra fat. Add crushed garlic, chopped onions, 1 tomato peeled and chopped, sliced mushrooms, and chopped parsley. 5. Reduce liquid

and pour over chicken. 6. Prepare a plain pilau with chicken stock and rice. 7. Cut tomatoes into halves. Scoop out centre. Apply salt and keep upside down to remove moisture. 8. Surround chicken with tomato halves stuffed with rice.

27. POULET SAUTÉ CACCIATORE (8 portions)

Ingredients	Quantity
Hot fat or Salad oil	6 tbsp
Ready to cook broiler-fryers (cut up)	2
Onions (minced)	1 cup
Capsicum (minced)	¾ cup
Garlic (minced)	4 flakes
Tomatoes	1–2½ cans (3½ cups)
Tomato sauce	225 gm
Chianti wine	½ cup
Salt	3¾ tsp
Pepper	½ tsp
Allspice	½ tsp
Bay leaves	2
Dried thyme leaf	½ tsp
Cayenne pepper	a pinch

Method

1. In hot fat or salad oil in a large skillet, sauté broiler-fryers until golden on all sides. 2. Add minced onions, capsicum, garlic; brown lightly. 3. Add tomatoes, tomato sauce, Chianti, salt, pepper, allspice, bay leaves, dried thyme leaf, cayenne pepper. Simmer uncovered for 30 to 40 minutes or until chicken is fork-tender. 4. Pour sauce over chicken.

28. COQ AU VIN

Ingredients	Quantity
Chicken	1
Mushrooms	50 gm
Small onions	50 gm
Fatty rashers of bacon	4
Butter	30 gm
Butter & Oil mixed	3 dsp
Refined flour	1 tbsp
Black pepper	to taste
Salt	to taste
Garlic	3 flakes

Ingredients	Quantity
Chicken stock	
Tomatoes	225 gm
Wine	1 cup

Method

1. Slice mushrooms and fat rashers and fry them with small onions in butter until they are lightly browned. 2. Joint chicken and fry gently in olive oil. 3. Add mushrooms, onions and bacon pieces to chicken. Mix. 4. Strain all fat into a saucepan, mix a tablespoon of flour with fat and stir till brown. 5. Add chicken stock and blanched tomatoes. 6. Put in chicken, mushrooms, onions, bacon, chopped garlic, salt and black pepper. 7. Add 1 cup of red wine. 8. Stir well, bring to a boil, cover and simmer on top of stove or in a deep casserole in an oven for 1 hour.

29. POÊLING

Ingredients	Quantity
Chicken or	1
Butchers' meat	1 joint
Butter	115 gm
Salt and Pepper	to taste
Matignon	
Carrots	115 gm
Onions	225 gm
Celery	60 gm
Raw lean ham	30 gm
Thyme	1 sprig
Bay leaf	½

Method

1. Mince carrots, onions and celery. Chop ham. 2. Place raw matignon in a deep and thick-bottomed pan. 3. Place well seasoned chicken or meat on this bed. 4. Sprinkle generously with melted butter. 5. Cover and cook in a moderate oven (175°C or about 305°F) gently. 6. When the meat or poultry is cooked, remove cover, and let meat acquire a good brown colour. 7. Dish meat or poultry. Add about 300 ml of stock to vegetables and boil for 10 minutes. 8. Strain through muslin. Remove grease and send to the table in a sauceboat to be served with the poultry.

30. POULARDE ANDALOUSE

Ingredients	Quantity
Chicken	1 (about 1.5 kg)
Butter	115 gm

Ingredients	Quantity
Carrots	115 gm
Onions	225 gm
Celery	60 gm
Raw lean ham	30 gm
Thyme	1 sprig
Bay leaf	½
Salt and Pepper	to taste
Stock	300 ml
Tomatoes	115 gm
Capsicum	450 gm
Eggplant	115 gm
Refined flour	10 gm
Pilau rice	115 gm

Method

1. Clean and poêl chicken (see previous recipe). 2. Add peeled and chopped tomatoes to half the stock. Reduce to half. 3. Use remaining stock to prepare poêling liquor. 4. Prepare a plain pilau with rice and chicken stock. 5. Parboil capsicum. Cut into halves. Remove seeds. Sauté in a little butter and stuff with prepared rice. 6. Slice eggplant into roundels. Dredge with flour and season. Fry in butter. 7. Dish chicken. Cover with poêling liquor combined with tomatéd half glaze. 8. Surround with stuffed capsicums and fried eggplant roundels alternating.

31. POULARDE au CÉLERI

Ingredients	Quantity
Chicken	1
Butter	115 gm
Salt and Pepper	to taste
Strong chicken stock	300 ml
Matignon	
Carrots	115 gm
Onions	225 gm
Celery	60 gm
Raw lean ham	30 gm
Thyme	1 sprig
Bay leaf	½
Braised Celery	
Celery (white only)	225 gm
Pork rind	15 gm
Bacon	30 gm
Carrots	125 gm

Ingredients	Quantity
Onions	125 gm
Bay leaf	
Thyme	
Stock	
Salt	

Method

1. Poêl chicken (see poêling) basting towards close of the operation with a little stock. 2. Cut white part of celery, into pieces about 15 cm long. Parboil for 15 minutes. Cool. 3. Garnish bottom of a saucepan with blanched pork rind, sliced carrots and onions, and seasoning. Cover the sides with bacon. 4. Leave celery on this bed and allow to 'sweat' in the oven for 10 minutes with the lid on. 5. Moisten with white stock and cook gently. 6. Remove celery. Cut into 8 cm pieces. 7. Dish chicken. Surround with braised celery. 8. Serve poêling liquor separately.

32. POULARDE CHIPOLATA

Ingredients	Quantity
Chicken	1
Salt and Pepper	to taste
Stock	300 ml
Matignon	
Butter	115 gm
Carrots	115 gm
Onions	225 gm
Celery	60 gm
Raw lean ham	30 gm
Thyme	1 sprig
Bay leaf	½
Garnish	
Small onions	60 gm
Chipolata sausages	115 gm
Bacon	60 gm
Baby carrots (glazed)	60 gm

Method

1. Poêl chicken. (see Poêling) 2. Prepare poêling liquor. 3. Boil and glaze onions and carrots. 4. Fry sausages and bacon. 5. Place chicken in a pyrex dish. Add garnish and poêling liquor. 6. Simmer in an oven for 10 minutes before serving.

33. POULARDE DEMIDOFF

Ingredients	Quantity
Chicken	1
Butter	125 gm
Salt and Pepper	to taste
Bay leaf	½
Stock	150 ml
Carrots	125 gm
Onions	225 gm
Celery	60 gm
Raw lean ham	30 gm
Thyme	1 sprig
Garnish	
Carrots	225 gm
Turnips	150 gm
Small onions	150 gm
Celery	150 gm
Butter	60 gm

Method

1. Poêl chicken (see recipe for Poêling). 2. Cut carrots and turnips into grooved crescents. Cut celery into roundels. Stew all vegetables in butter. 3. When chicken is three-fourths done remove and place in a pyrex dish. Surround with prepared garnish. Cover and complete the cooking in an oven. 4. Add prepared poêling liquor cleared of all grease. Serve hot.

34. POULARDE DIVA

Ingredients	Quantity
Chicken	1
Pilau rice	55 gm
Stock	110 ml
Suprême Sauce	
Clear poultry stock	450 ml
Mushroom liquor	75 ml
Poultry velouté	300 ml
Cream	150 ml
Butter	30 gm
Paprika	a pinch

Ingredients	Quantity
Garnish	
Button mushrooms	60 gm
Cream	75 ml

Method

1. Cook rice in stock till three-fourths done. 2. Clean and season chicken. Stuff with rice and poach in chicken stock till tender. 3. Prepare sauce which should be perfectly white, smooth and delicate. 4. Boil poultry stock and mushroom liquor and reduce to two thirds. 5. Add poultry velouté. Reduce on an open fire, stirring all the time. Add paprika. 6.Add half the cream gradually. 7. When sauce reaches the desired consistency remove from fire and pass through a sieve. 8. Add remaining cream and butter. 9. Stir well and keep covered till used. 10. Dish chicken. Cover with sauce. 11. Serve a garnish of boiled mushrooms cohered with cream.

35. POULARDE EDOUARD VII

Ingredients	Quantity
Chicken	1 (about 1.5 kg)
Pilau rice	55 gm
Curry Sauce	
Butter	15 gm
Onions	85 gm
Parsley	a few sprigs
Celery	30 gm
Thyme	1 sprig
Bay leaf	½
Mace	a pinch
Refined flour	15 gm
Curry powder	1 tsp
Stock	150 ml
Coconut milk	75 ml
Red capsicum	55 gm
Garnish	
Cucumber	225 gm
Cream	50 ml

Method

1. Cook rice in chicken stock till three-fourths done. 2. Clean chicken. Stuff with rice and poach chicken without discolouring. 3. Prepare curry sauce. Brown minced onions, parsley and celery in butter. 4. Add bay leaf, thyme and mace. 5. Sprinkle flour and curry powder over. 6. Cook

for a few minutes without allowing it to brown. 7. Add stock and bring to a boil and cook gently for about half an hour. 8. Add coconut milk and simmer for 15 minutes more. 9. Dish chicken when done. Coat with curry sauce cohered with diced capsicum. 10. Peel and boil cucumber. Cut into cubes and serve with cream separately.

36. POULARDE en ESTOUFFADE

Ingredients	Quantity
Chicken	1
Salt and Pepper	to taste
Ham (cooked)	115 gm
Carrots	225 gm
Onions	115 gm
Celery	115 gm
Butter	15 gm
Stock	200 ml
For Poêling	
Butter	115 gm
Carrots	115 gm
Onions	225 gm
Celery	60 gm
Raw lean ham	30 gm
Thyme	1 sprig
Bay leaf	½

Method

1. Poêl chicken (see recipe for Poêling) till nearly done. 2. Line the bottom of a casserole dish with slices of ham. 3. Sauté slices of carrot, celery and onions. 4. Place chicken and sautéed vegetables over ham. Season to taste. 5. Reduce stock to half and pour over chicken. 6. Cover. Seal lid with a thread of paste. 7. Complete the cooking in a hot oven (about 45 minutes).

37. POULARDE à la FERMIÈRE

Ingredients and method as for Poularde en Estpiffade but instead of lining the casserole with ham, dice ham and add to garnish together with 115 gm of peas and 115 gm of French beans cut diagonally.

38. POULARDE à la GRECQUE

Ingredients	Quantity
Chicken	1 (about 1.5 kg)

Ingredients	Quantity
Pilaff	
Pilau rice	115 gm
Red capsicum	55 gm
Chicken stock	200–250 ml
Butter	30 gm
Onions	55 gm
Fat sausages	55 gm
Lettuce	55 gm
Peas	115 gm
Sauce	
Strong chicken stock	300 ml
Arrowroot	15 gm

Method

1. Boil rice in chicken stock till three-fourths done. 2. Chop onions and fry in butter. Cut sausages into small pieces. 2. Roughly chop lettuce. Boil peas with mint and dice capsicum. 3. Mix above ingredients with rice. 4. Clean chicken. Stuff with prepared rice. Poach till tender. 5. Dish and coat with very strong reduced chicken stock, thickened with arrowroot.

39. POULARDE à l'INDIENNE

Ingredients	Quantity
Chicken	1 (about 1.5 kg)
Pilau rice	115 gm
Curry sauce	200 ml

Method

1. Clean and poach chicken. 2. Boil rice. 3. Dish chicken. Coat with curry sauce (see Sauces, Vol. I and serve hot with timbale of rice served separately.

40. POULARDE MIREILLE

Ingredients	Quantity
Chicken	1
Salt and Pepper	to taste
Carrots	115 gm
Onions	225 gm
Celery	60 gm
Raw lean ham	30 gm
Thyme	1 sprig
Bay leaf	½

Ingredients	Quantity
Garnish	
Rice	115 gm
Stock	220–250 ml
For Poêling	
Butter	115 gm
Saffron	a pinch
Tomatoes	115 gm
Olives	30 gm
Butter	15 gm
Shortcrust Pastry	
Refined four	55 gm
Butter	30 gm
Baking powder	a pinch
Salt	a pinch

Method

1. Poêl chicken (see Poêling). 2. Boil rice. Flavour with saffron. 3. Prepare shortcrust pastry tartlets. 4. Peel and chop tomatoes. Remove excess moisture. Toss in butter. Season. 5. Garnish Pastry crust with prepared tomatoes. 6. Dish chicken. Surround with small moulds of rice alternating with garnished pastry tartlets. Set a stoned olive on each tartlet.

41. POULARDE au RIZ

Ingredients	Quantity
Chicken	1
Allemande sauce (see p. ??)	200 ml
Pilau rice	115 gm
Salt and Pepper	to taste

Method

1. Clean, season and poach chicken. Keep hot. 2. Cook rice in poaching liquor. 3. Dish chicken. Coat with allemande sauce. 4. Surround with rice moulded in small buttered timbales and serve hot.

42. POULARDE STANLEY

Ingredients	Quantity
Chicken	1
Velouté sauce	300 ml
Pilau rice	55 gm
Chicken stock	100 ml
Onions	225 gm

Ingredients	Quantity
Curry powder	10 gm
Fresh cream	300 ml
Black mushrooms	55 gm
Fat	30 gm
Salt and Pepper	to taste

Method

1. Prepare pilao rice in chicken stock till three-fourths done. 2. Clean, season and stuff chicken with rice and mushrooms. 3. Poach chicken, adding sliced onions and curry powder to poaching liquor. 4. When tender remove chicken. 5. Rub cooking liquor through a sieve. 6. Mix with velouté sauce and reduce to a stiff consistency. 7. Rub again through a sieve. Add fresh cream. 8. Coat chicken and serve immediately.

43. POULARDE POLIGNAC

Ingredients	Quantity
Chicken	1 (1 kg)
Fat	1 tbsp
Suprême sauce	1 litre
Mushrooms	
Stock	60 ml

Method

1. Clean and joint chicken. Fry lightly. 2. Poach in stock till tender. Simmer in supreme sauce. 3. Blend with mushrooms just before serving. 4. Garnish with mushrooms and serve hot.

Supreme Sauce

1. To one litre clear poultry stock, add 1 cup (150 ml) mushroom liquor. 2. Reduce to 2/3. Add 600 ml poultry velouté. Simmer to reduce, stirring continuously. 3. Add 1 cup (150 ml) fresh cream — blending carefully.

44. POULET POCHÉ au RIZ (SAUCE SUPRÊME)

Ingredients	8 portions
Chicken (boiling fowl)	1 (about 2 kg)
Onions	60 gm
Rice	
Onions	60 gm
Butter	60 gm
Rice	225 gm
Chicken stock	500–600 gm
Carrots	60 gm

Ingredients	8 portions
Peppercorns	a few
Bouquet garni	
Sauce	
Margarine	85 gm
Refined flour	85 gm
Chicken stock	1 litre
Lime juice	a few drops
Cream	30 ml

Method

1. In a pan put just enough water to cover chicken. 2. Add salt and bring water to a boil. Add chicken. Allow to boil for 5 minutes. 3. Reduce heat. Add sliced onions, carrots, peppercorns and bouquet garni. Simmer till chicken is tender. 4. Prepare rice. Melt butter. Add onions. Brown and remove. Add rice. Fry for 3 to 4 minutes. 5. Add stock and salt and cook till rice is done and all liquid has evaporated. 6. Prepare a velouté sauce using cooking liquor. Check for seasoning. Pass through a strainer. 7. Finish with cream. 8. Cut chicken into portions. Place in the centre of a flat dish. Surround with a border of rice garnished with fried onions. 9. Pour hot sauce over chicken and serve immediately.

45. FRICASSEE de VOLAILLE

Ingredients	8 portions
Chicken (boiling)	1 (2–2.5 kg)
Salt	to taste
Peppercorns	a few
Butter	30 gm
Onions	115 gm
Sauce	
Butter	30 gm
Refined flour	20 gm
Chicken liquor	600 ml
White pepper	a pinch
Cloves	1
Carrots	225 gm
Bouquet garni (Parsley, Thyme, Celery, Bay leaf)	
Cooked button mushrooms	60 gm
Cream	30 ml
Bread croûtons	60 gm

Method

1. Clean chicken. Season. Keep giblets aside. 2. Bring to a boil just enough water to cover chicken. 3. Add salt. Add chicken. Boil for 5

minutes. Reduce heat and simmer till chicken is half-done. 4. Remove and cut into neat joints. 5. Cut up carcass and fry without browning in a little butter in a stewpan. 6. Add 1 litre of stock, cleaned giblets, onion peeled and stuck with a clove, scraped and sliced carrots and the bouquet garni. 7. Boil, skim and add pieces of chicken and more salt if necessary. 8. Cook till chicken is nearly done. 9. Melt butter in another pan. Add flour and cook without discolouring. 10. Gradually add 600 ml of strained cooking liquor. 11. Stir over fire till it boils. Add pepper and nutmeg. 12. Transfer pieces of chicken to this sauce and cook gently for 20 minutes. Check for seasoning. 13. Add mushrooms and cream. Re-heat without boiling. 14. Dish neatly in a hot dish. Garnish with croutons of bread.

N.B. An egg yolk can be added to sauce along with cream.

46. POULET en CASSEROLE

Ingredients	Quantity
Chicken	1 (about 1.3 kg)
Butter	60 gm
Onions	115 gm
Bouquet garni	
Garnish	
Tomatoes	225 gm
Mushrooms	60 gm
Green peas	115 gm
Stock	300 ml
Bacon	60 gm
Carrots	115 gm
Sauce	
Espagnole sauce	300 ml (see Sauces in Vol. I)
Meat glaze	1 tbsp
Sherry (optional)	1 tbsp
Seasoning	

Method

1. Clean chicken and season. 2. Melt butter in a large pan. 3. Add sliced onions, carrots, mushroom stalks and bacon. Fry for a few minutes. Remove. 4. Add chicken and fry, browning breast first. 5. Pour off fat. 6. Arrange vegetables under chicken. Add stock. 7. Cover with lid and place casserole at 190°C (approx. 375°F). 8. Baste frequently and if necessary add more stock. 9. When chicken is tender cut into joints and keep in a warm casserole. 10. Strain gravy. Remove fat from top. Add

espagnole sauce, glaze and sherry. Reduce slightly. Pour over chicken.
11. Garnish with cooked halves of tomatoes, mushrooms and peas.

N.B. Pigeon casserole may be cooked in a similar way but, when dishing,
cut birds into halves.

47. GOULASH de POULET (A)

Ingredients	Quantity
Chicken	1
Onions	115 gm
Tomatoes	450 gm
Butter	30 gm
Paprika	15 gm
Parsley	few sprigs
Salt and Pepper	to taste
Garnish	
Spaghetti	225 gm
Salt	to taste
Butter	15 gm

Method

1. Clean and cut chicken as for sautés. 2. Chop onions and add with
chicken pieces to melted butter. Brown evenly. 3. Add salt, pepper and
paprika. 4. Skin and slice tomatoes. Lay them on top of meat and onions.
5. Cover tightly and cook very gently till chicken is tender. 6. Serve in
a flat dish surrounded by spaghetti boiled in salted water and tossed in
butter.

GOULASH de POULET (Chicken Goulash) (B)

Ingredients	Quantity
Chicken	1
Onions	2
Fat	2 tbsp
Capsicums	2
or Paprika	2 tsp
Stock	500 ml
Tomato purée	2 tbsp
Chopped parsley	2 tbsp (optional)

Method

1. Chop onions and fry with parsley in fat in a thick-bottomed saucepan.
2. Add jointed chicken and quartered capsicums with seeds removed or
paprika. 3. Add salt and chicken stock. 4. Put lid on and allow to simmer
very slowly until tender. 5. Add tomato purée and cook for another 10

minutes. 6. Remove pieces of chicken from pan and place in a very hot dish. 7. Pour liquid over and serve surrounded with boiled and buttered noodles.

48. POULET en CASSEROLE CAMPANINI avec NOUILLES

Ingredients	Quantity
Chicken	1
Suprême sauce:	
Butter	15 gm
Refined flour	15 gm
White pepper	to taste
Cream	30 gm
Chicken stock	500 ml
Salt	to taste
Ham	60 gm
Mushrooms	30 gm
Margarine	15 gm
Noodles	115 gm
Cheese	30 gm

Method

1. Wash chicken, place in a large pan and cover with cold water. 2. Simmer till chicken is tender. Cool. Remove chicken and reserve broth. 3. Bone chicken and slice. 4. Melt butter in a saucepan. Stir in flour. Blend well and cook for 5 minutes. 5. Gradually add chicken broth, stirring constantly until smooth. 6. Add cream while stirring with wire whip. 7. Bring mixture to a boil. Reduce heat and cook slowly for 15 minutes, stirring frequently. 8. Add salt and pepper. 9. Strain and keep hot. 10. Sauté mushrooms and ham in margarine. 11. Meanwhile cook noodles in boiling salted water until tender. Do not overcook. Drain thoroughly. 12. Combine mushrooms, ham and cooked noodles. 13. In individual greased casseroles place a bed of noodle mixture. 14. Add a portion of sliced chicken. 15. Cover with supreme sauce. 16. Sprinkle grated cheese over. 17. Put in an oven at 175°C (approx. 350°F) until cheese is melted and golden brown. 18. Serve piping hot.

N.B. If noodles are not to be used at once, rinse in cold water. Drain and refrigerate. When ready to use, put into boiling water. Drain quickly and add sautéed mushrooms and ham.

Noodles:

Ingredients	Quantity
Refined flour	170 gm
Egg yolks	1

Ingredients	Quantity
Salt	a pinch
Salad oil	1 tbsp
Water	to mix

Method

1. Sieve flour and salt into a basin. 2. Make a well in centre and gently mix in lightly beaten egg yolk and oil. 3. Add water and knead to a smooth dough and set aside for 10-15 minutes. 4. Dust flour on a marble slab and roll out dough very thin. Cut into fine strips with a noodle cutter or a sharp knife. 5. Meanwhile keep enough water for boiling in a large enough pan. Add a pinch of salt. 6. Put in noodles and boil till cooked. While boiling noodles, separate with a fork to prevent them from forming into a lump. 7. Drain noodles and hold under a running tap. 8. Toss quickly in melted butter.

49. SUPRÊME de VOLAILLE à la KIEV

Ingredients	6 portions
Chicken breasts	of 3
and wings	chickens
Chilled butter	115 gm
Salt and Pepper	to taste
Fresh mint	3 sprigs
Refined flour	50 gm
Eggs (lightly beaten)	2
Breadcrumbs	50 gm
Fat or Oil to fry	

Method

1. Halve chicken breasts removing skin but leaving main wing bone attached. 2. Place chicken breasts between pieces of dampened wax paper. 3. Pound until thin with a steak hammer or a rolling pin. 4. Place a ball of chilled butter in centre of each breast. 5. Sprinkle with salt, pepper and ground mint. 6. Roll up, letting wing bone protrude. 7. Dredge each roll lightly with flour. Dip in beaten eggs and then in breadcrumbs, taking care to see that the roll is completely sealed. 8. Place in freezer for at least one hour. 9. Fry in deep fat for two or three minutes. 10. Bake at 175°C (approx. 350°F) for 30 minutes. Serve hot.

50. POULET à le REX

Ingredients	Quantity
Chicken	1
Velouté sauce	300 ml
Mushrooms	115 gm

Ingredients	Quantity
Cream	55 gm
Capsicum	55 gm
Egg yolks	2
Parsley	a few sprigs
Salt and Pepper	to taste
Bread slices	160 gm
Fat	60 gm

Method

1. Poach chicken in stock. Cool. 2. Skin and dice. 3. Chop mushrooms and capsicum. Sauté in a little butter. Add velouté sauce. 4. Finish with cream and egg yolks. Check for seasoning. 5. Add diced chicken. Fry slices of bread. Place portions of chicken mixture on fried bread and serve immediately garnished with chopped parsley.

N.B. Hot buttered toast could be used instead of fried bread. If dried mushrooms are used, boil first.

51. CAPILOTADE de VOLAILLE

Ingredients	Quantity
Leftover pieces of chicken	225 gm
Italian sauce	300 ml
Mushrooms	60 gm
Parsley	a few sprigs
Italian Sauce	
Onions	10 gm
Oil	10 ml
Butter	10 gm
Mushroom stalks	30 gm
Salt and Pepper	to taste
Nutmeg	a pinch
Parsley	a few sprigs
Ham	30 gm
Tomato purée	300 ml

Method

1. Heat butter and oil. Add minced onion and fry slightly. 2. Add chopped and pressed mushroom stalks. 3. Stir over a brisk fire till moisture evaporates. 4. Season with salt, pepper and nutmeg. Add chopped ham and tomato purée. 5. Boil for 10 minutes. 6. Combine with cooked mushrooms and thin slices of cold, leftover pieces of chicken. 7. Dish on to a hot plate garnished with chopped parsley and surrounded with boiled spaghetti.

52. FRITTOS de VOLAILLE ·

Ingredients	Quantity
Chicken	115 gm
Cashewnuts	15 gm
Choux paste:	
Butter	20 gm
Water	50 ml
Egg	1
Refined flour	40 gm
Salt	to taste

Method

1. Mix chopped chicken, nuts and choux paste. Deep fry in spoonfuls. Drain on paper and serve piping hot.

Choux paste:

1. Put butter and water into a thick pan and bring to a boil. 2. Remove from fire and add sieved flour all at once. 3. Return to fire and cook stirring all the time until mixture leaves sides of pan. (It should be quite thick.) Remove and cool slightly. 4. Beat eggs and gradually add to mixture beating all the time. The mixture should have a smooth soft consistency but be firm enough to pipe.

53. MAYONNAISE de VOLAILLE

Ingredients	Quantity
Chicken	1 (about 1.3 kg)
Salt	to taste
Peppercorns	a few
Sauce	
Egg yolk	1
Mustard	1 tsp
Sugar	1 pinch
Salt	to taste
White pepper	a pinch
Salad oil	130 ml
Vinegar	1 tbsp
Lime	½
Garnish	
Lettuce	1 bunch
Olives	30 gm
Hard-boiled eggs	2
Cherry tomatoes	30 gm

Method

1. Boil chicken with salt and peppercorns. Allow to cool in same liquid. 2. Remove skin and cut into small cubes. 3. Prepare mayonnaise sauce. (See Sauces in Vol. I). 4. Garnish the bottom of a salad bowl with chopped lettuce (reserve lettuce heart for decoration). 5. Season with a little salt and a few drops of vinegar. 6. Arrange pieces of chicken over lettuce. 7. Cover with mayonnaise sauce. 8. Smooth and decorate with olives, quartered hard-boiled eggs, cherry tomatoes and lettuce hearts.

54. VOL-AU-VENT de VOLAILLE

Ingredients	8 portions
Chicken (boiling)	1 (about 2 kg)
Chicken velouté	600 ml
Cream	75 ml
Puff pastry	45 gm

Method

1. Prepare puff pastry using 450 gm of flour (see Puff Pastry recipe). 2. Roll out sufficiently to cut out 8 rounds 7.5 cm (3" approx.) in diameter. 3. Turn upside down on a lightly greased, dampened baking sheet. 4. Using a smaller plain cutter, make incisions half way through each, leaving approximately 0.7 cm (¼") border. 5. Egg wash and bake in a hot oven (15–20 minutes). 6. When cool remove lids carefully. Empty out raw pastry from centre. 7. Cook chicken as for boiling. Cool. 8. Remove all skin and bones. Cut into neat pieces. 9. Prepare a velouté sauce using cooking liquor. 10. Check for seasoning and pass through a fine strainer. Finish with cream. 11. Mix chicken with sauce. Dry pastry in oven for a few minutes. 12. Fill warm pastry with prepared mixture to overflowing. 13. Set on a silver flat. Put the lid on. Garnish each pastry with a sprig of parsley and serve hot.

55. CHAUDFROID de POULET

Ingredients	Quantity
Chicken	1
Stock	as required
Carrots	100 gm
Celery	50 gm
Onions	50 gm
Peppercorns	a few
Bay leaf	1
Parsley	a sprig
Butter	30 gm

Ingredients	Quantity
Refined flour	150 ml
Milk	1 cup
Salt	to taste
Gelatine	15 gm
Aspic jelly	300 ml
Cream	4 tbsp

Method

1. Boil chicken in stock along with prepared vegetables, bay leaf, peppercorns and parsley. Remove when tender. Leave to cool. 2. Prepare a white sauce with flour, butter, milk and the same quantity of strained stock in which chicken was boiled. Season well and allow to cool. 3. Dissolve gelatine in half the aspic jelly and mix with cooled sauce. Whip in cream. Mix well. 4. When chaudfroid sauce is thick enough for coating, skin chicken and quickly coat with sauce. Leave in a cool place to set firmly. 5. When remaining aspic is nearly setting, coat chicken again with aspic and leave to set. 6. Garnish with vegetables in aspic or tartlets filled with Russian salad or chipolata sausages on sticks. 7. The chicken can be decorated with vegetables cut in fancy shapes and dipped in aspic to form a design. When decorations are set, apply a coat of aspic to keep decorations in place.

56. GALANTINE de POULET

Ingredients	Quantity
Chicken	1 (about 2-2.5 kg)
Sausage meat	450 gm
Ham	125 gm
Pistachio nuts	15 gm
Eggs (hard-boiled)	2
Stock	600 ml
Salt	to taste
Peppercorns	a few
Onions	1
Garnish	
Meat glaze	
Chopped aspic jelly	

Method

1. Clean chicken. Wash. Do not remove skin. 2 Cut off head. Slit down the back. Open up. 3. Remove bones by pressing and using a knife. 4. Beat chicken with steak hammer. 5. Season chicken. Spread with half the sausage meat, then strips of ham and pistachio nuts. 6. Place

hard-boiled eggs down centre and cover with remainder of sausage meat. 7. Roll tightly. Tie firmly in a muslin cloth. 8. Put into boiling stock to which peppercorns and one sliced onion have been added. 9. Boil for 10 minutes and then simmer for about 40 to 45 minutes. 10. When cooked, take out chicken and hang to remove excess moisture. 11. Strain stock. Reduce till thick enough to form a glaze. 12. Take out chicken from muslin. Brush over with glaze and leave in a refrigerator to cool. 13. Serve in slices with cubes of aspic jelly and salad.

57. BALLOTINES de VOLAILLE PRINTANIÈRE

Ingredients	Quantity
Chicken legs	4
Carrots	225 gm
Green peas	225 gm
French beans	225 gm
New potatoes	450 gm
Refined flour	30 gm
Butter	40 gm
Spinach (chopped)	170 gm
Tarragon	a pinch
Chicken stock	600 ml
Wine	30 ml

Method

1. Remove skin from chicken leg carefully to avoid tearing skin. Leave knuckle and approximately 2 cm of hock bone (feet) attached to skin to de-nerve the leg. De-bone leg and with flesh of leg make a forcemeat along with 100 gms. of chopped spinach. Refill skin with forcemeat, sew up opening and shape like chicken leg. Poach chicken in chicken stock to which a little white wine is added. Add all the vegetables and cook. Separately melt butter, add flour and cook for one minute, add reduced cooking liquor. Whisk well to make a lump-free sauce and boil well to sauce consistency. Finish sauce with leftover spinach and tarragon. Coat chicken with sauce and arrange vegetables around.

N.B. Ballotines may be made from whole small chickens or legs of chicken. In the case of whole chickens bone chicken as for galantine but leave skin on flesh.

58. POULET de GRAINS à la BERGÈRE

Ingredients	Quantity
Spring chicken (fattened, 3 to 4 months old)	1
Breast of pork	125 gm

Ingredients	Quantity
Mushrooms	125 gm
Onions	125 gm
Butter	125 gm
Parsley	a few sprigs
Stock	50 ml
Salt and Pepper	to taste
Sauce	
Butter	125 gm
Refined flour	10 gm
Garnish	
Potatoes	225 gm
Fat	125 gm

Method

1. Clean chicken and season. 2. Cut pork into cubes and fry, in half the butter. Remove. Fry mushrooms. Remove. Add chopped onions and fry without discolouring. 3. Stuff chicken with onions, half the mushrooms and parsley. 4. Fry chicken in remaining butter till brown. 5. Surround with fried pork cubes and remaining mushrooms. Swill with stock. 6. Cover and cook in an oven till chicken is done. 7. Set on a round dish. Thicken cooking liquor with flour beaten up with butter. Season to taste. Pour over chicken. 8. Surround with pork and mushrooms and a border of freshly-fried straw potatoes.

59. POULET de GRAINS à la LIMOUSINE

Ingredients	Quantity
Spring chicken (fattened, 3 to 4 months old)	
Sausage meat	225 gm
Mushrooms	60 gm
Butter	50 gm
Breast of bacon (blanched)	60 gm
Jus-lié	150 ml
Salt and Pepper	to taste

Method

1. Clean chicken. Season. 2. Stuff with sausage meat, combined with mushrooms fried in a little butter. 3. Put chicken in a casserole dish with remaining butter and rectangles of bacon. Cook gently in an oven till done. Sprinkle with a little stock if necessary. 4. Just before serving add 2 to 3 tablespoons of jus-lié

60. CANARD RÔTI à l'ANGLAISE

Ingredients	Quantity
Duck	1
Brown stock	300 ml
Fat	60 gm
Apple sauce	150 ml

Stuffing (Sage and Onions):

Margarine	60 gm
White breadcrumbs	60 gm
Chopped parsley	
Chopped duck liver	
Onions (chopped)	115 gm
Powdered sage	½ tsp
Salt and Pepper	to taste

Method

1. Clean duck. Season inside and out with salt. 2. Prepare stuffing. Gently cook onions in margarine without discolouring. 3. Add herbs and seasoning. 4. Mix in breadcrumbs and liver. 5. Stuff duck with prepared stuffing. 6. Place duck on its side in a roasting tin. 7. Cover with fat. 8. Place in a fairly hot oven for about 30 to 40 minutes. 9. Turn it over and cook for another 30 to 40 minutes. 10. Baste frequently. 11. Serve on a silver flat. 12. Accompany with a sauceboat of apple sauce and a sauceboat of gravy made from sediment in the roasting tin with brown stock.

N.B. Brush duck over with honey to get a good brown colour and a crisp skin.

61. CANETON POÊLE à la MENTHE

Ingredients	Quantity
Duckling	1 (1.5–2 kg)
Mint	a few sprigs
Butter	115 gm
Salt and Pepper	to taste
Jus-lié	75 ml
Lime juice	a few drops

For Poêling

Butter	115 gm
Carrots	115 gm
Onions	225 gm
Celery	60 gm
Raw lean ham	30 gm

Ingredients	Quantity
Thyme	1 sprig
Bay leaf	½

Method

1. Clean duckling. Stuff with 30 gm butter combined with a little chopped mint. 2. Poêl (see Poêling) duckling. 3. Dish out. Swill pan with jus-lié and a few drops of lime juice. Re-heat. 4. Strain and add a pinch of chopped mint. Pour sauce over duckling.

62. CANETON BRAISÉ aux NAVETS

Ingredients	Quantity
Duckling	1 (about 1.5–2 kg)
Butter	60 gm
Brown stock	400 ml
Espagnole sauce	400 ml
Turnips	450 gm
Powdered sugar	a pinch
Small onions	20 (about 500 gm)
Salt and Pepper	to taste

Method

1. Clean duckling. Season 2. Brown in butter. Remove. Drain off fat. 3. Swill pan with brown stock and espagnole sauce. 4. Return duck to sauce and braise gently. 5. Cut turnips into olive shapes. Peel onions. 6. Heat remaining butter. Sauté onions. Remove. Add turnips and a pinch of sugar. Sauté and glaze a nice brown. 7. When duckling is half done transfer to a casserole dish with turnips and onions. 8. Strain sauce over the whole and complete the cooking in an oven. 9. Dish with garnish of turnips and onions arranged around bird.

63. CANETON aux OLIVES

Ingredients and method as for Caneton Braisé aux Navets. A few minutes before serving add 225 gm stoned and blanched olives. Glaze duckling at the last minute and dish it surrounded with olives, turnips and onions and accompanied by sauce.

64. CANETON BRAISÉ à l'ORANGE

Ingredients	Quantity
Duckling 1 (about 1.5–2 kg)	
Butter	30 gm
Brown stock	300 ml

Ingredients	Quantity
Espagnole sauce	300 ml
Oranges	4
Lime	½
Salt and Pepper	to taste

Method

1. Clean duckling. Season. Brown in butter. Remove. 2. Drain off fat. Swill pan with brown stock and espagnole sauce. Add duckling and braise till duckling is done and gravy is quite thick. 3. Clear sauce of grease. Reduce to a stiff consistency and rub through a sieve. 4. Add juice of two oranges and half lime and a julienne of the yellow part only of orange rind. Re-heat but do not boil. 5. Glaze duckling with sauce. Dish and surround with segments of orange, skinned and pipped. 6. Serve remaining sauce separately.

65. CANETON aux PETITS POIS

Ingredients	Quantity
Duckling	1 (about 1.5–2 kg)
Butter	60 gm
Breast of pork	170 gm
Small onions	15 (340 gm)
Meat glaze	300 ml
Fresh peas	1 kg
Faggot	1
Salt and Pepper	to taste

Method

1. Clean duckling and season. 2. Cut pork into cubes and peel onions. 3. Heat butter. Brown pork and onions. Remove. 4. Add duckling and brown. 5. When duckling is well-coloured remove fat. 6. Swill with meat glaze. Add peas, faggot, pork cubes and onions. 7. Cover and cook in a moderate oven till done. 8. Dish duckling and garnish. Remove faggot from sauce and reduce. 9. Cover duckling with reduced sauce.

66. OIE RÔTIE

Roast goose using the same method as for Roast Duck.

67. DINDE RÔTIE

Turkeys are usually stuffed at the breast with a mixture of pork sausage meat and chestnuts in the proportion of 500 gm of the former to 225 gm of the latter. The chestnuts are poêled and cooked in a little stock till tender. Forcemeat stuffing similar to that given for roast chicken may also be used. The method of roasting is the same as for chicken.

Roast turkey is served accompanied by roast gravy, bread sauce, grilled chipolatas and watercress; cranberry sauce is usually served with turkey in America.

FONDUES

Fondue is a dish for entertaining a few friends who can eat literally from the same pot—not for a large group. The best fondue is made in an earthenware vessel and never allowed to boil.

1. Swiss Cheese Fondue
2. Baked Cheese Fondue
3. Fondue without Wine
4. Fondue Bourguignonne
5. Tuna & Chilli Fondue

I. SWISS CHEESE FONDUE

Swiss cheese fondue is a famous Swiss dish made of melted cheese. The cheese mixture is heated in a special fondue dish which is kept hot on the table by a spirit lamp. Diners have long forks with which they spear a piece of bread, dip it in the fondue and eat. Swiss cheese should be used to give a true flavour, though others are frequently used outside Switzerland.

Ingredients	Quantity
Crusty French bread	1 loaf
Garlic	1 clove
Swiss cheese (shredded)	250 gm
Light dry white wine	1 cup
Flour or	1½ tbsp
Cornflour or	1½ tsp
Potato flour	1½ tsp
Salt	¼ tsp
Brandy or	
Light rum	2 tbsp

Method

Cut bread into bite-size pieces taking care that each piece has a bit of crust. In the fondue dish heat garlic with wine till air bubbles appear. Remove garlic. Mix cheese with flour and salt and add to wine slowly stirring with a wooden spoon until fully melted. Stir until mixture bubbles. Stir in brandy or rum.

Have each guest spear his piece of bread with a fork. Dip into fondue and stir until bread is coated. Remove on to another fork and eat immediately. If fondue becomes too thick stir in a little more warm wine.

N.B. I suggest using steamed cauliflower or celery sticks as an alternative along with French bread cubes. This will provide interesting variety.

2. BAKED CHEESE FONDUE

Ingredients	Quantity
Milk (scalded)	1 cup
Soft bread crumbs	1 cup
Cheese (cut into pieces)	120 gm
Butter	1 tbsp
Salt	to taste
Chili powder	a dash
Eggs	3

Method

1. Mix breadcrumbs, cheese, butter and seasoning to scalded milk in the top of a double boiler. 2. Remove from stove. Stir in unbeaten egg yolks. 3. Whisk egg whites stiff. Fold cheese mixture gently into egg whites. 4. Pour mixture into a buttered baking dish. 5. Bake at 325°F (162°C) until firm in the centre (about 35 minutes). Serve immediately.

3. FONDUE WITHOUT WINE

Ingredients	Quantity
Egg yolks	8
Grated cheese	2 cups (250 gm)
Butter	10 tbsp (200 gm)
Light cream	½ cup
Salt and Pepper	to taste
Grated nutmeg	

Method

1. In a chafing dish, mix egg yolks and cheese with a dash of salt, pepper and nutmeg to taste. 2. Place over very low heat and stirring constantly add butter bit by bit. 3. When mixture thickens add cream and stir until well blended. 4. Keep warm over low flame. Do not allow to cook further. 5. Eat just like cheese fondue with French bread.

4. FONDUE BOURGUIGNONNE

This is a cheeseless fondue and a meal in itself individually cooked and flavoured in a festive and friendly setting with everyone seated around the cooking pot dunking cubes of steak and discussing the relative merits of rare and well-done meat and preferences for sauces and condiments. Per person allow 150 gm of undercut, refined groundnut oil, assortment of condiments and sauces. The meat is cut into bite-size pieces about 2.5 cm square and heaped on a platter or a wooden board. Oil is heated in a fondue dish till it reaches smoke point. Each guest spears one piece of steak and holds it in the boiling oil until done to his taste. Use forks with wooden handles. The steak is then dunked into one or more of the following sauces and popped whole into the mouth.

Sauces: Tartare sauce, mustard sauce, mayonnaise, béarnaise sauce, tomato sauce with finely minced onion and capsicum and any chutney such as tomato chutney or date chutney etc.

Accompaniments: Pickled onions, sour gherkins.

5. TUNA & CHILLI FONDUE

Ingredients	6 servings
Tuna	1 can (200 gm – approx. 7 ounces)
Minced celery	½ cup
Minced onion	2 tbsp
Green chillies (without seeds)	¼ cup
Mayonnaise	¼ cup
Salt	to taste
Grated cheese	2 cups
Eggs (beaten)	3
Milk	1 cup
Cream	¼ cup
Tabasco sauce	a dash
Bread	12 slices
Chili powder	a dash

Method

1. Combine tuna, celery, onion, green chillies, mayonnaise, chilli powder and salt. Spread on 6 slices of bread and make sandwiches. 2. Cut each sandwich into quarters and arrange in a square baking dish, sprinkling cheese between layers and on top. 3. Combine beaten eggs, milk, cream, Tabasco sauce and salt if desired. 4. Pour over bread. 5. Bake in slow oven 300°F (149°C) for 50 minutes or until set and browned.

GIBIER

1. Game
2. Venison
3. Poultry and Game Birds
4. Game Birds
5. Grouse (sautéed
6. Partridge (boiled with celery sauce)
7. Partridge (braised)
8. Partridge (roast)
9. Salmis of Pheasant
10. How to Pot Roast
11. Roast Grouse
12. Roast Quail (for 4)
13. Roast Snipe
14. Simple Roast Wild Duck
15. Braised Wild Duck
16. Venison
17. Roast Haunch of Venison
18. Grilled Venison Steaks
19. Hunter's Steak (for 2)
20. Quail
21. Game Hot-Pot (for 4)
22. Pickled Game
23. Times to allow for cooking Poultry and Game by various methods

I. GAME

To Keep Game: Most game is hung before cooking as the flesh is usually dry, tough and tasteless when eaten fresh. All water birds however should be eaten as fresh as possible, because their flesh is oily and soon becomes rancid. Most game is kept until putrefaction has commenced, it being thought that the flavour is thereby developed. The time it may be kept depends upon

(1) the taste of those who are to eat it;
(2) the weather;
(3) the kind of bird and the age of the bird;
(4) if it has been well-shot.

Taking everything into consideration, it is impossible to lay down any precise rules. In damp, muggy weather, even if the temperature is not very high, game will keep for very little time, but in clear windy weather, even if it is not very cold, it will keep for many days. *It should always be kept in the fur or feathers, and should not be drawn. Birds should be hung up by the neck in a current of air.* It may sometimes be necessary to pluck; truss and half cook them, in which state they will keep a few days longer. Old birds may always be kept longer than young ones, and they also need longer cooking. A bruised and badly shot bird, however should not be hung for long. When the tail feathers can be pulled out easily, the bird is ready for cooking.

Selection: The flesh should be firm and plump and not discoloured; blue patches denote that a bird has hung too long. Game should always be heavy for its size. Partridges at the beginning of the season can always be distinguished by the shape of the long feathers in the wing; in an old bird they are round at the end like the letter 'U'; in a young one they are pointed like a 'V'.

The size of the spur, the smoothness of the legs and the tenderness of the pinion are the best guides in choosing a pheasant. If the birds are in good condition the breast is thick and firm; if lean, the breast feels thin and soft.

Hanging Rabbits, Hares and Venison

Rabbits: Should be cooked as fresh as possible, and not be hung longer than one day. Paunch (disembowel) when killed and skin and clean just before using.

Hares: Should be well hung, and not be paunched, cleaned or skinned until ready for use. Hang by the legs (tied together), and tie a small tin cup over the muzzle to catch the blood that drips from it. (This blood is used for thickening the gravy or soup cooked with it). A hare should be hung for six or seven days.

Venison: Sprinkle a coating of pepper or ginger over the venison to preserve it, and hang when the weather permits for two weeks or longer. Wash free of the pepper or ginger before cooking.

Times for Hanging Birds

Wild Duck, Widgeon, Moorhen and Teal (water-fowl) should not be hung longer than one day.

Plover, Snipe and sometimes *Quail* are cooked undrawn and should not be hung for longer than four or five days.

Grouse: Five to fourteen days. Pluck two or three days after hanging.

Pheasant: Seven to fourteen days.

Partridge: Five to fourteen days.

To keep game from tainting: In cold frosty weather, game may be hung for 2 or 3 weeks in an ordinary larder without becoming tainted, but when the atmosphere is warm and damp, great care should be taken to hang it in a well-ventilated place, preferably where there is a current of air. The feathers are a great protection from flies but it is advisable to apply a good sprinkling of pepper, which usually serves to keep these pests away.

To remove taint: As soon as there is the slightest evidence of taint, remove the feathers and draw the birds, and wash them in water with plenty of salt and a little vinegar. If badly tainted repeat process 2 or 3 times and then rinse in fresh water. Dry thoroughly before cooking. Put some fresh powdered charcoal tied in muslin inside the crop before cooking to remove any tainted flavour.

Remove the charcoal before serving: All game birds excepting snipe could be washed in scalding hot water to which some charcoal has been added before dressing.

According to Morell, feathered game should be hung up by its feet and unemptied for 3 days and no more. Woodcocks and snipes which require more mellowing can be hung for 4 days–all game is at its best roasted plain and accompanied by its own gravy prepared from its offal and swilling of the roasting tray, and a bottle of red Burgundy.

All game should be labeled with the date of the shoot before being hung. Put a clove of garlic and pepper in the place where it was shot and three or four bruised peppercorns in the mouth–tough game can be soaked for a while in milk or curd for 10 minutes before cooking or it could be marinaded. Young game birds for roasting should show the following points: (Older birds may be used for salmis, soups, and other made-up dishes).

1. Plumage soft, with feathers not well-developed.
2. Wings pliable with long quills.
3. Lower beak brittle
4. Legs smooth.

Fresh birds will show the following signs:

1. Plumage light, fluffy and well coloured.
2. Eyes prominent.
3. No unpleasant smell.

Points which show that the animal, (Rabbit and Hare) is young.

1. Claws sharp, smooth and pointed.
2. Ears soft and easily torn.
3. Teeth white.
4. Narrow cleft in upper lip.

2. VENISON

Buck venison is in season from June to the end of September, and doe venison from November to February. The flesh is dark and lean and should be firm and springy to the touch. The fat is white and firm.

3. POULTRY AND GAME BIRDS

Plucking: Take care not to tear the skin, especially when plucking game birds. Hold the bird firmly with the left hand and pluck with the right.

Pluck out small handfuls at a time, starting from under one wing, then continue plucking until one side is completely clear. Remove all the pin feathers with a knife.

Preparation before cooking: With snipe and woodcock the head is left on, but the eyes are removed. The long beak is run through the bird to act as a skewer. A few strips of beef steak are often put into a pheasant before trussing.

1. The birds are not washed. When drawn, wipe the inside carefully with a damp cloth.
2. Place a small piece of butter mixed with a little pepper inside the bird before cooking. For a medium-sized bird, use half an ounce of butter.
3. Place a rasher of bacon over the breast before roasting and wrap in greased paper.
4. Baste often.
5. Remove the bacon and paper a few minutes before cooking is completed and dredge with flour. Continue cooking until the breast is well-browned.

Marinade for game: A specially good marinade for game is made by stewing 2 peeled, sliced onions, 2 tablespoons salad oil, 2 sprigs of parsley, 1 glass port wine, 1 pint water, 2 sliced carrots, 3 bay leaves, 1 tablespoon vinegar, and pepper and salt to taste. Marinate for half an hour.

Gravy: Wash and chop the giblets—put into a pan with a small onion peeled and sliced, a pinch of salt, a pint of stock, one small blade mace and a few grains of cayenne. Simmer for 1 hour and then strain. Melt 15 gm butter in a pan, stir in 15 gm flour; then gradually stir in the strained stock. Thin with wine to taste. For wild fowl add a few drops of lime juice just before serving.

4. GAME BIRDS

Wild Duck: Wild duck can be prepared and cooked in the same way as ordinary duck.

Doves: Pluck, singe and draw the birds, season with salt and pepper, and roast them in a pan or before a clear fire. Doves are also tasty when curried.

Pea Fowl: Prepare and cook in the same way as turkey.

Wild Fowl: Prepare and cook in the same way as ordinary fowl, but the flesh of wild fowl is tough and requires boiling unless the bird is young.

Grilled Snipe: Snipe, though generally liked high, is preferred fresh by some people. Pluck the snipe carefully as the skin is very tender, but do not draw them. The head, too, is kept on. Skin and use the beak for trussing the bird instead of a skewer. Rub well with butter, season with pepper and salt, and grill according to directions given for grilling. The time will depend upon preference, underdone or well cooked–from 15 to 20 minutes. Serve hot with pieces of fresh lime. Make a good gravy and serve it separately.

Roast Teal: Pluck and draw the teal, wash it in warm water and dry it in a cloth. Cut off the feet and wings at the first joint and truss it for roasting. Season the bird with salt and pepper, inside and outside, and rub it over with dripping. Place it in a baking tin, pour a little cold water and bake in a moderately hot oven, basting frequently until it is cooked. When it is ready lift it onto a dish, remove the trussing string and pour the gravy round the bird.

Another Method—Place the teal in a stewpan, pour in a little cold water and allow to cook slowly until the bird is tender. The bird should be turned once or twice during the process. Then lift it out of the pan and fry to a nice brown dipping or brown it in an oven.

To Make the Gravy—Pour away the fat from the baking tin, retaining the brown sediment, to which add a small quantity of boiling water' or stock and a seasoning of salt and pepper. Cook for 2 or 3 minutes.

An acid accompaniment should be handed with roast teal, such as orange salad, apple or tomato sauce or guava jelly.

5. GROUSE (sautéed, Vincent style)

Ingredients	Quantity
Grouse	1
Cooking or	
Port wine or	
Cider or Stout	150 ml
Salt and Pepper	to taste
Redcurrant or	
any dark jelly	1 tsp
Brown sauce	295 ml
Orange rind (chopped)	1 tsp

Purée of chestnuts, or if out of season, other suitable vegetables such as peas, carrots and parsnips or stewed red cabbage.

Time: 20-30 minutes. Temperature: low.

Method

Put chestnuts in a baking tin in an oven until shells and underskin can be removed. Alternatively, prepare any other vegetable you have chosen.

Prepare grouse and cut into four pieces. Season with salt and pepper. Put fat into sauté pan, make it hot, then put in pieces of grouse. Fry them gently over a high flame. When done, take out and drain fat from pan. Stir in wine or stout and redcurrant jelly, boil to reduce. Then stir in brown sauce. Reduce again, and stir in grated rind of half an orange or orange essence. Put pieces of grouse into this sauce, and simmer gently for about twenty minutes.

Put shelled and skinned chestnuts into a saucepan with enough stock or water to just cover and simmer until they are quite soft. Rub through a sieve and heat up purée with a little butter. Alternatively, finish prepared vegetables. Arrange a border of chestnut or vegetable purée on a serving dish. Put pieces of grouse in the centre. Pour sauce over and serve. (Serves 4).

6. PARTRIDGE (boiled with celery sauce)

Ingredients	Quantity
Partridge	1
Onions	1
Clove	1
Carrots	1
Head of celery	1
Stock or Water	590 ml
Cooking fat	
Margarine or	
Dripping	55 gm
Salt and Pepper	to taste
Refined flour	55 gm
Cream or Milk	150 ml

Time: About 40 minutes. Temperature: low.

Method

Prepare partridge. Peel onion and stick with clove. Scrape carrot and cut into small pieces. Clean celery and cut into small pieces. Put stock or water into stewpan with onion stuck with clove, carrot and celery, adding seasoning of necessary. Warm, then put in partridge; bring to a boil and simmer until bird is cooked. When it is done, dish on a hot plate, and keep hot. Pass liquid through a sieve, rubbing through as much of vegetables as possible. Make up to 590 ml if some liquid has evaporated. Melt fat in a pan and stir in flour. Add sieved sauce by degrees and stir until it boils. Simmer for four to five minutes, then add cream or milk. Add salt and pepper to taste. Pour sauce over partridge, or serve separately. (Serves 4–6).

7. PARTRIDGE (braised)

Ingredients	Quantity
Partridge	1
Onions	1
Carrots	1
Rashers of bacon,	4
or a handful of bacon rinds	
Bouquet garni	1
or Mixed herbs	
Peppercorns	6
Cooking fat or	
Margarine	30 gm
Refined flour	30 gm (about)
Stock or Water	200 ml
Worcester sauce	1 dsp.
Port wine, other wine, or	1 wine glassful
Cider (optional)	
Anchovy essence (optional)	1 tsp
Salt and Pepper	to taste
Cream or Top milk (optional)	4 tbsp

Time: About 40 minutes. Temperature: low.

Method

Prepare partridge and cut into joints. Peel onion, scrape carrot and cut into slices. Put two rashers of bacon (or half the rinds) along bottom of stewpan. Put in vegetables, peppercorns, bouquet garni or mixed herbs, and pieces of partridge. Cover with rest of bacon (or rinds). Add stock or water. Put on lid and braise for thirty minutes. Take out the partridge pieces and rashers and keep them hot. Remove bacon rinds. Strain liquor from pan. Now add Worcester sauce, wine, anchovy essence, salt and pepper.

Melt a little fat in a saucepan, and stir in as much flour as it will take. Cook for a minute or two and then gradually add enough of the liquor or make a smooth sauce. Stir, and cook for four to five minutes. Then add cream or top milk. Pour this sauce over partridge, garnish with cooked rashers of bacon, if any. (Serves 5–6).

8. PARTRIDGE (roast)

Ingredients

Partridge
Bread sauce (see Gravies & Sauces)
Slices of toast

Ingredients

A slice of bacon
Brown gravy
Fried breadcrumbs
Butter or Clarified dripping for basting

Method

Pluck, draw and truss in the same manner as for roast chicken. Cover breast with a slice of fat bacon, and roast in a moderate oven for about 30 minutes, basting frequently. A few minutes before serving remove bacon, dredge lightly with flour, and baste well to give bird a nice pale brown look. Dish on toast, and serve gravy, breadcrumbs and bread sauce separately.

Time: To roast, about 30 minutes.

9. SALMIS OF PHEASANT

Salmis is a special preparation applicable to all winged game; but as pheasant salmis is especially popular, the recipe is given below:

Semi-roast bird for 10 minutes, cut it into 4–6 pieces; 2 breasts, winglets and legs. Keep these hot while sauce is prepared. Chop up 3 shallots and sauté in butter; place in pheasant's carcass, with trimmings and chopped liver, neck, heart and giblets; add some tomato pulp or purée; moisten with stock or roasting gravy, a few drops of red wine or port; season, add a bouquet garni, bring to a boil and reduce.

Arrange portions of pheasant in an earthenware service dish, then strain off the reduction on to them, adding a piece of butter; test seasoning; garnish with cooked button mushrooms and onions; cover dish and place it in an oven for 10 minutes. Serve very hot with heart-shaped butter-fried croûtons of bread—1 per person.

Madeira may be added instead of red or port wine; sliced mushrooms can be substituted for button variety, and chopped truffle may also be included.

10. HOW TO POT ROAST

To pot roast is to cook meat or poultry in a little fat in a saucepan with the lid on. A heavy saucepan a tight-fitting lid is necessary. Pot roasting is a useful method for small joints and birds when an oven is not available. The following points should be noted:

Wipe the joint or bird and, if necessary, tie it into a neat shape with a piece of tape.

Choose a saucepan into which the joint or bird fits comfortably.

Melt enough fat to cover the bottom of the saucepan well, and make it very hot.

Now put in the joint or bird and brown it well on all sides.

Reduce the heat and cook slowly until the meat is quite tender. If the joint or bird is lean, baste occasionally. A few onions, etc., may be cooked around the joint or bird, if desired, to improve the flavour.

II. ROAST GROUSE

Ingredients	Quantity
Grouse (young)	1 brace
Salt and Pepper	to taste
Butter	55 gm
Bacon fat	
Lemon juice	1 tsp

Method

1. Prepare birds. Put a spoonful of clear bacon fat or a pat of butter inside each. Sprinkle insides with salt, pepper and lemon juice. Livers and hearts should be left inside. Truss. Either brush birds with melted butter, after dusting with salt and pepper, or wrap, in old Scottish fashion, first in fatty bacon, then in greaseproof paper. Place in roasting pan on a trivet, breast downwards, and roast for 25 minutes. Remove paper and bacon, baste with butter or bacon fat, and cook till brown. If cooked without paper, baste frequently with melted butter or bacon fat while cooking. When ready, remove from pan, untruss, and serve each on a piece of buttered toast in a hot dish. Garnish with watercress. Some cooks place the toast in the bottom of the tin under the birds for a few minutes before serving. Others pour the gravy over the toast before arranging the birds. Many Scottish cooks boil the livers, then pound them in a mortar with butter and season with salt and cayenne. The paste is spread on toast which is placed on the trivet under the birds 5 minutes before they are served. Garnish with watercress, and fried mushrooms, if desired.

Accompaniments: Bread sauce, gravy, fried breadcrumbs, potato straws or crisps.

12. ROAST QUAIL

Ingredients	4 portions
Quail	4
Bacon, raw fat	4 slices

Ingredients	4 portions
Butter	2 tbsp
Toast	4 slices

Method

Remove livers from birds. Chop, place in a saucepan with butter and simmer for 5 minutes. Cut some slits in rashers of bacon and tie a rasher over breast of each bird. Place birds on a trivet in a baking tin. Roast in a quick oven for 12 to 20 minutes. While cooking, pound livers, mix with 4 teaspoons warm glaze and spread on hot trimmed toast. When birds are cooked, remove bacon, brush breasts with warm glaze. Untruss and arrange each bird on a piece of toast. Garnish with watercress.

Accompaniments: Gravy, fried breadcrumbs, watercress salad.

13. ROAST SNIPE

Prepare and truss birds, scalding and skinning feet, and removing toe joints and gizzard before trussing. Either place birds on pieces of toast after brushing with oiled butter and covering breasts with bacon, or brush with melted bacon fat and roast, either in a baking tin in a fairly hot oven or in front of fire. The birds can also be run through with a skewer and roasted for 15 minutes, basting frequently with melted butter. When breasts are covered with bacon fat, allow nearly 20 minutes for roasting, for they need about 5 minutes to finish cooking after bacon is removed. Dredge with flour, baste well, and brown. No matter how you roast them, place some toast buttered on both sides, under the birds to catch the trail when cooking. Serve untrussed birds on toast. Pour a little brown gravy, or butter gravy, over them. Allow 1 piece of toast for each bird. Garnish with watercress and cut lemon.

Accompaniments: Bread sauce, fried crumbs, potato straws, brown gravy, watercress salad.

14. SIMPLE ROAST WILD DUCK

Ingredients	Quantity
Wild ducks	2
Butter	55 gm
Onions (small)	2

Method

Scald feet and truss. Sprinkle inside of birds with salt and pepper and put half the butter in each. Sometimes birds can be placed in a hot oven for 5 minutes without basting with butter. Spread butter over them instead of putting it inside if desired. Roast for 20 to 25 minutes, basting frequently. Just before serving dredge with flour and baste. Serve like teal. If bird is liked well-cooked, 25 to 35 minutes will be needed.

Accompaniments: Orange and watercress or orange and mint salad, wine gravy, potato straws. Garnish with watercress.

15. BRAISED WILD DUCK

Season duck with ground pepper and salt. Place in a casserole lined with chopped bacon, 15 gm butter, 1 cup sliced onions, 1 cup diced carrots, crushed herbs, and seasoning to taste. Cook in a hot oven till brown, then reduce heat, drain off any fat and add 300 ml brown sauce and 150 ml of rich stock or giblet gravy. Cover and cook for 20 minutes, then add a glass of red wine or port and juice of one lemon. Remove bird and joint. Boil up sauce sharply and pour sauce with vegetables over joints, arranged in a hot dish. 115 gm chopped fried mushrooms can be added if desired.

16. VENISON

In venison from a buck, the haunch and liver and kidneys are best, neck is second, then comes saddle, then shoulder and civet. In the case of roe deer venison, the saddle is better than the haunches. Venison from red deer is the best and fallow deer venison comes next. Venison from all these should hang for 2 to 3 weeks. To prevent it becoming fly-blown, rub immediately after skinning with flour mixed with powdered ginger and pepper. Dress the furrow of the backbone well with pepper. It is best to wrap venison in butter muslin before hanging up in the larder, but you must inspect it every day and give it a fresh coating of flour and ginger when necessary.

17. ROAST HAUNCH OF VENISON

Trim, wash if necessary and wipe. Brush with melted butter. Sprinkle with salt and pepper. Make a paste of flour and water. Knead till rather tough, then roll out a piece large enough to cover roast. Roll round, and bake in a moderately hot oven for 3 to 4 hours according to size of joint. You will need anything from 680 gm to 1 kg of flour for paste. When cooked, chip off paste and return joint to a very hot oven to brown. Serve with gravy flavoured with port and redcurrant jelly.

Accompaniments: Redcurrant jelly, sauce or brown gravy, baked potatoes.

18. GRILLED VENISON STEAKS

Ingredients	Quantity
Loin steaks	6
Redcurrant jelly	2 tbsp
Butter	30 gm
Mushrooms	350 gm

Method

Cut steaks shaped like mutton chops. Spread with melted butter. Grill, turning often, for about 25 minutes as venison takes longer to cook than steak. When ready, sprinkle with salt and pepper. Melt butter in a saucepan, add jelly and when piping hot pour over steaks arranged in a circle on a hot dish. Pile up 350 gm mushrooms, peeled and fried, in the middle. Serve with potato chips. Lemon butter can be substituted for redcurrant jelly.

19. HUNTER'S STEAK

Ingredients	For 2
Game	225 gm
Pork	115 gm
Egg (slightly beaten)	1
Onions (minced)	1 tsp
Breadcrumbs (fresh)	1 tbsp

Method

Put meat through a mincer three times. Stir in onion, salt, pepper and paprika to taste, breadcrumbs and egg to moisten. Shape into cakes, about 3 cm thick. Fry for 3 minutes on each side in a little hot fat. Serve each on a round of fried bread, with grilled tomato rounds and maître d'hôtel butter on top.

20. QUAIL

Ingredients	Quantity
Quail	8
Flour	30 gm
Butter	115 gm
Onions	5
Ginger (green)	4 tbsp
Lemon (juice of)	1
Stock	590 ml
Garlic	6
Pepper (black)	2 tsp
Cloves	4

Ingredients	Quantity
Saffron	
Salt	to taste

Method

Split birds down the back. Wash well and prick all over with a sharp fork. Rub flour into birds. Wash them again.

Heat butter, brown onions, sliced thin, and pounded ginger. Add birds, close the lid and give them one shake.

Cook stock with 1 tablespoon butter, pounded garlic, pepper and cloves.

When birds are well-browned, pour the above stock and cook till liquid is almost dry. Mix saffron with lemon juice and salt and add to casserole, frying and drying it over medium heat. When birds begin to glaze, serve them piping hot.

21. GAME HOT-POT

Ingredients	For 4
Partridge,	1 or 2 birds
Pheasant,	depending
or Grouse	on size
Onions	1
Dripping Kidneys	2
Egg	1
Turnip	1 small
Bacon (very thin)	115 gm
Tomato purée	1 tbsp
Bay leaves	2
Cooking sherry (optional)	2 tbsp
Refined flour (seasoned)	1 tbsp
Carrots	2
Stock	
Parsley (chopped)	
Paprika	

Method

Dissect birds carefully with a sharp knife. Chop onion and fry until golden brown. Take skin and any fat off kidneys and cut into pieces. Lightly beat egg. Season well. Dip portions of bird and kidney into egg, then roll in seasoned flour. Fry on both sides until well-browned. Dice carrots and turnip. Take rind of bacon and make rashers into small rolls. (These can be fixed by putting a clove through the roll or tying it with a piece of string, removed before serving). Pour tomato juice over pieces of game, add sherry and bay leaves. Cover contents of pan with stock or water. Allow to simmer for 7 minutes. Stir in carrots and turnip. Transfer contents of pan to a casserole. Cook for 1–1½ hours at 190°C (approx. 375°F). Have casserole almost covered while birds are being cooked; otherwise the contents will get dry. Before serving, add paprika and a little chopped parsley.

22. PICKLED GAME

This recipe need not always be used for game. Even good mutton makes excellent pickle, if made ahead and kept.

Step 1. Cut meat into large chunks. Prick all over. Rub well with salt and turmeric (haldi). Spread on flat thali in layers. Cover with another thali. Place weight on top. Leave it like this for a day. If pickle is made during a shooting party in the forest for some reason, the meat pieces are strung on thread and hung out to dry in the hot sun as you would clothes.

Step 2. Masala for Pickle

Ingredients	For about 500 gm of meat
Red chillies	6
Turnmeric (Haldi)	1 tsp
Cumin (Jeera)	1 tsp
Grated ginger	2 tsp
Mustard seeds	2 tsp
Chopped garlic	4 tsp

Method

Wash meat from Step 1 in vinegar and wipe dry. Pack into a jar in alternate layers of meat and masalas. Pour in enough vinegar to cover completely. Screw the top on. Keep shaking the jar every day for the first few days in order to distribute the vinegar. The pickle will be ready for use in a week. At time of use, heat some oil and fry some of the meat adding some of the gravy.

23. TIMES TO ALLOW FOR COOKING POULTRY AND GAME BY VARIOUS METHODS

Name	How cooked	Size or Quantity	Time	
			h.	m.
Duck (wild)	Roast	Medium	0	25
Grouse	Roast	Medium	0	30
Hare	Jugged	Medium	3	30
Hare	Roast	Large	1	55
Partridge	Roast	Medium	0	30

Name	How cooked	Size or Quantity	Time h.	m.
Pheasant	Roast	Large	0	50
Larks	Baked	1 doz.	0	15
Pigeon	Grilled	Medium	0	15
Pigeon	Stewed	Medium	0	30
Rabbit	Boiled	Medium	0	40
Rabbit	Roast	Large	0	50
Quail	Roast	Medium	0	25
Snipe	Roast	Medium	0	20
Teal	Roast	Medium	0	12
Venison	Roast	Large	4	30
Haunch	Roast	Small	3	00
Woodcock	Roast	Medium	0	25

LÉGUMES ET PÂTÉS ALIMENTAIRES

1. Cuts of Vegetables
2. Artichauts en Branche
3. Topinambours à la Crème
4. Asperges
5. Aubergines à l'Egyptienne
6. Aubergines Frites
7. Aubergines à la Provençale
8. Aubergines à la Turque
9. Broccoli
10. Carottes au Beurre ou Glacées
11. Carottes à la Crème
12. Céleri Braisé
13. Champignons Grillés
14. Choux Braisé
15. Chou-fleur à la Crème
16. Chou-fleur au Gratin
17. Chou-fleur à la Milanaise
18. Chou-fleur à la Polonaise
19. Chou-fleur
20. Choux de Bruxelles à l'Anglaise
21. Choux de Bruxelles Sautés
22. Choux de Bruxelles Beurre
23. Courge
24. Courge Farcie
25. Courge Provençale
26. Concombres à la Crème
27. Épinards en Branches
28. Épinards à la Crème
29. Épinards en Purée
30. Épinards au Gratin
31. Haricots Blancs
32. Maïs
33. Oignons Sautés
34. Oignons Frits à la Française
35. Oignons Braisés
36. Petits Pois à la Française
37. Petits Pois à la Flamande
38. Pimentos Farcis
39. Poireaux Braisés
40. Macédoine de Légumes
41. Pouding de Maïs
42. Pommes Persillées
43. Pommes Allumettes
44. Pommes de Terre Anna
45. Pommes Bataille
46. Pommes Boulangère
47. Pommes Brioche
48. Pommes Château
49. Pommes Chips
50. Pommes Croquettes

51. Croquettes de Pommes de Terre à la Dauphine
52. Pommes Fondantes
53. Pommes Gaufrettes
54. Gratin de Pommes de Terre à la Dauphinoise
55. Pommes de Terre Lorette
56. Pommes de Terre à la Maître d'Hôtel
57. Pommes de Terre Marquise
58. Pommes de Terre à la Menthe
59. Pommes de Terre Noisette
60. Pommes de Terre Parisienne
61. Pommes Pailles
62. Pommes de Terre Robert
63. Pommes de Terre à la Saint Florentine
64. Pommes de Terre Soufflés
65. Soufflé de Pommes de Terre
66. Pommes Chateâu
67. Ravioli Paste (For 8)
68. Canneloni
69. Ravioli à l'Italienne
70. Macaroni à l'Italienne
71. Macaroni à la Napolitaine
72. Spaghetti Tetrazzini Armanda
73. Spaghetti à la Créole
74. Gnocchi (Dumpling)
75. Gnocchi Romane (For 4)
76. Spaghetti avec Sauce Barbaque
77. Spaghetti avec Sauce Champignons et Fromage
78. Nouilles Vertes

I. CUTS OF VEGETABLES

Julienne (strips)

1. Cut vegetables into 4 cm lengths. 2. Cut lengths into thin slices. 3. Cut slices into thin strips.

Brunoise (small dice)

1. Cut vegetables into conveniently-sized lengths. 2. Cut lengths into 1.5 mm. slices. 3. Cut slices into 1.5 mm. strips. 4. Cut strips into 1.5 mm. squares.

Macédoine (0.7 cm dice)

1. Cut vegetables into convenient lengths. 2. Cut lengths into 7 mm. slices. 3. Cut slices into 7 mm. strips. 4. Cut strips into 7 mm. squares.

Jardinière (batons)

1. Cut vegetables into 2 cm lengths. 2. Cut lengths into 3.5 mm. slices. 3. Cut slices into batons 3.5 mm. × 3.5 mm. × 2 mm.

Paysanne

There are at least four accepted methods of cutting paysanne. In order to cut economically, the shape of the vegetable should decide which method to choose. All are thinly cut.

a. 15 mm. triangles. b. 15 mm. squares. c. 15 mm. diameter rounds. d. 15 mm. diameter rough-sided rounds.

2. ARTICHAUTS en BRANCHE

Ingredients	For 4
Globe artichokes	4
Lime	1
Salt	to taste

Accompaniment

Hollandaise sauce

Method

1. Cut stems of artichokes close to leaves. 2. Cut off approximately 2.5 cm across the tops of leaves. 3. Trim remaining leaves with scissors or small knife. 4. Place a slice of lime at bottom of each artichoke. 5. Secure with string. 6. Simmer in gently boiling salted water until bottom is tender (approximately 20–30 minutes). 7. Refresh under running water until cold. 8. Remove centre of artichoke carefully. 9. Scrape off the furry inside and leave clean. 10. Replace by placing in a pan of boiling salted water for about 3–4 minutes. 11. Drain and serve on a serviette on a flat silver dish accompanied by hollandaise sauce. They may also be served cold, e.g. Artichauts en Branche Sauce Vinaigrette.

3. TOPINAMBOURS à la CRÈME

Ingredients	Quantity
Jerusalem artichokes	500 gm
Salt	to taste
Cream sauce	300 ml

Method

1. Wash and peel artichokes and rewash. 2. Cut to an even size. 3. Barely cover with water, add salt and simmer till tender. 4. Drain well and add 300 ml of cream sauce. 5. Serve in a vegetable dish.

4. ASPERGES

Allow 6–8 good-sized pieces per portion. An average bundle will yield 3–4 portions.

1. Using back of small knife, carefully remove tips of leaves. 2. Scrape stem, either with blade of small knife or a peeler. 3. Wash well. 4. Tie into bundles of approximately 12 heads. 5. Cut off excess stem. 6. Cook in boiling salted water for approximately 15 minutes. 7. Test if cooked by gently pressing green part of stem, which should be tender. 8. Lift carefully out of water and dress neatly on a serviette in a silver flat dish. Remove string. Serve a suitable sauce separately, e.g. hollandaise or melted butter.

Asparagus is usually served as a separate course. It may also be served cold, in which case it should be immediately refreshed when cooked in order to retain its green colour. Serve with vinaigrette or mayonnaise.

5. AUBERGINES à l'EGYPTIENNE

Ingredients	Quantity
Aubergines (eggplant)	500 gm
Tomatoes	115 gm
Onions	55 gm
Minced meat (cooked)	115 gm
Oil	60 ml
Parsley	a few sprigs
Salt	to taste

Method

1. Wash and cut aubergines lengthwise into two. 2. Cisel the middle to enable quick cooking. Season. 3. Fry in oil till done. 4. Drain. Remove pulp and place shells in a buttered gratin dish. 5. Chop withdrawn pulp. Add chopped onions sautéed in a little oil and cooked minced mutton. Season to taste. 6. Fill eggplant shells with this mixture. 7. Sprinkle with a few drops of oil and cook in an oven at 190°C (about 375°F) for about 15 minutes. 8. Remove and set a slice of tomato, seasoned and tossed in oil, on each eggplant. Sprinkle with chopped parsley and serve.

6. AUBERGINES FRITES

Ingredients	Quantity
Aubergines (eggplant)	225 gm
Oil	60 ml
Refined flour	15 gm
Salt and Pepper	to taste

Method

1. Cut aubergines into thin roundels. 2. Season and dredge. 3. Fry in smoking oil. Serve at once to be eaten crisp. If they are not served immediately they soften and lose quality.

7. AUBERGINES à la PROVENÇALE

Ingredients	Quantity
Aubergines (eggplant)	500 gm
Tomatoes	225 gm

Ingredients	Quantity
Garlic	5 gm
Raspings	30 gm
Oil	60 ml
Salt and Pepper	to taste

Method

1. Wash and cut aubergines into two lengthwise. 2. Cisel centre to facilitate cooking. 3. Fry in hot oil. Drain. 4. Remove pulp and place shells in a buttered gratin dish. 5. Chop up withdrawn pulp. 6. Chop tomatoes roughly. Sauté in oil with chopped garlic. 7. Mix tomatoes with aubergine pulp. Season. 8. Fill shells with this mixture. Sprinkle over with raspings and a few drops of oil. 9. Grill. Serve hot with a border of tomato sauce.

8. AUBERGINES à la TURQUE

Ingredients	Quantity
Aubergines	500 gm
Batter	
Refined flour	60 gm
Flour	15 gm
Egg yolk	1
Salt and Pepper	to taste
Oil	to fry
Cheese	30 gm
Milk	150 ml
Egg	½

Method

1. Peel aubergines and cut them each lengthwise into thin slices. 2. Season, dredge and fry slices in oil. 3. Make a mixture of raw egg yolk and grated cheese. 4. Pair slices of aubergines and join them together using egg yolk mixture. 5. Prepare batter in usual way. 6. When about to serve dip slices in batter and deep fry. Drain and serve hot.

9. BROCCOLI

Cook and serve like cauliflower.

10. CAROTTES au BEURRE ou GLACÉES

Ingredients	Quantity
Carrots	450 gm
Butter	30 gm

Ingredients	Quantity
Salt	to taste
Sugar	a pinch
Parsley	a few sprigs

Method

1. Peel and wash carrots. 2. Cut into neat even pieces, or into barrel shapes. 3. Place in a pan with salt, sugar and butter and barely cover with water. 4. Cover with buttered paper and allow to boil steadily to allow moisture to evaporate. 5. When moisture has evaporated test to see if carrots are cooked. If not, add more water and continue cooking. 6. Toss carrots over fierce heat for one to two minutes in order to glaze them. 7. Serve quickly, sprinkled with chopped parsley.

11. CAROTTES à la CRÈME

Ingredients	Quantity
Carrots	450 gm
Butter	15 gm
Salt and Pepper	to taste
Béchamel sauce (thin)	300 ml

Method

1. Prepare and cook carrots as for recipe No. 10 above. 2. Mix with sauce, check for seasoning and serve immediately in a vegetable dish.

12. CÉLERI BRAISÉ

Ingredients	Quantity
Celery	2 heads
Carrots (sliced)	115 gm
Onions (sliced)	115 gm
Bacon fat	60 gm
Crusts of bread	2
Salt and Pepper	to taste
Bouquet garni	
White stock	300 ml

Method

1. Trim celery heads and root, cutting off any outside discoloured stalks and cutting heads to approximately 15 cm lengths. 2. Wash well under running cold water. 3. Place in pan of boiling water. Simmer for approximately 10 minutes until limp. 4. Refresh and rewash. 5. Place sliced vegetables in a sauté pan or casserole. 6. Add bouquet garni, barely

cover with stock, season with salt and pepper. 8. Add bacon fat, crusts of bread, cover with buttered greaseproof paper and a tight lid and cook gently in a moderate oven for 2–3 hours. 9. Remove celery from pan, drain well and dress neatly in a vegetable dish. 10. Add cooking liquor to an equal amount of jus-lié or demi-glacé, reduce and correct seasoning and consistency. 11. Mask celery and finish with chopped parsley.

13. CHAMPIGNONS GRILLÉS

Ingredients	Quantity
Mushrooms	225 gm
Butter	60 gm
Salt and Pepper	to taste

Method

1. Peel, remove stalks and wash well. 2. Place on a tray and season with salt and pepper. 3. Brush with melted fat and grill on both sides for about 3 to 4 minutes. 4. Serve hot.

14. CHOUX BRAISÉ

Ingredients	Quantity
Cabbage	500 gm
Bacon	60 gm
Carrots	115 gm
Onions	115 gm
Garlic	1 clove
Butter	30 gm
Stock	400 ml
Salt and Pepper	to taste

Method

1. Quarter cabbage. Parboil and cool. 2. Separate leaves. 3. Season with salt and pepper. 4. Put into a pan with slices of bacon, a carrot cut into quarters, an onion stuck with a clove or garlic, butter and stock. 5. Boil and then braise gently for about 2 hours.

15. CHOU-FLEUR à la CRÈME

Ingredients	Quantity
Cauliflower	500 gm
Salt	to taste
Cream sauce	300 ml

Method

1. Cut cauliflower into bunches. 2. Remove small leaves which are attached and cook in boiling salted water. 3. Thoroughly drain and set in a pyrex dish. Cover with cream sauce and serve immediately.

16. CHOU-FLEUR au GRATIN

Ingredients	Quantity
Cauliflower	500 gm
Salt	to taste
Sauce	
Milk	300 ml
Butter	20 gm
Refined flour	30 gm
Cheese	30 gm
Egg yolk	1

Method

1. Wash and boil cauliflower flowerets in salted boiling water. Drain. 2. Prepare white sauce with flour, butter and milk (half milk and half cauliflower liquor may be used instead of all milk). 3. Add half the grated cheese and egg yolk beaten well and mixed first with a little hot sauce. Season to taste. 4. Place cauliflower in a buttered pyrex dish. 5. Cover with prepared sauce. 6. Sprinkle with remaining cheese and bake in an oven or under a grill till light brown. Serve hot.

17. CHOU-FLEUR à la MILANAISE

Ingredients	Quantity
Cauliflower	500 gm
Cheese	30 gm
Butter	30 gm
Salt	to taste

Method

1. Wash cauliflower. Remove outer leaves but keep tender ones. 2. Cut off stalk of cauliflower and cut into 4 from bottom but do not cut through. 3. Boil in salted boiling water till tender. 4. Set in a pyrex dish sprinkled over with a little cheese. 5. Sprinkle remaining cheese on cauliflower. 6. Dot with half the butter and place under a grill till cheese is melted. 7. Remove and sprinkle with nut brown butter. Serve immediately.

18. CHOU-FLEUR à la POLONAISE

Ingredients	Quantity
Cauliflower	500 gm
Hard-boiled eggs	1
Parsley	a few sprigs
Butter	45 gm
Breadcrumbs (white)	10 gm
Salt	to taste

Method

1. Wash cauliflower. Remove coarse outer leaves but keep tender ones.
2. Cut off stalk and slit into 4 from bottom without separating. 3. Boil
in salted boiling water till tender. 4. Drain thoroughly and set in a
buttered pyrex dish. 5. Sprinkle with chopped hard-boiled egg and
chopped parsley. 6. Just before serving, heat butter, fry breadcrumbs and
pour butter over cauliflower.

19. CHOU-FLEUR

Cauliflower can be boiled in salted water and served with melted butter,
hollandaise sauce or one of the prepared butters.

20. CHOUX de BRUXELLES à l'ANGLAISE

Ingredients	Quantity
Brussel sprouts	500 gm
Salt	to taste

Method

1. Wash brussel sprouts. Cook in boiling salted water. Drain and serve
at once.

21. CHOUX de BRUXELLES SAUTÉS

Ingredients	Quantity
Brussel sprouts	500 gm
Salt	to taste
Butter	30 gm

Method

1. Wash brussel sprouts. Cook in boiling salted water. 2. Drain. 3. Heat
butter. Put in boiled brussel sprouts and toss till they are nicely frizzled.
4. Dish and sprinkle with chopped parsley.

22. CHOUX de BRUXELLES au BEURRE

Ingredients	Quantity
Brussel sprouts	500 gm
Salt and Pepper	to taste
Butter	60 gm

Method

1. Wash brussel sprouts. Cook in boiling salted water but keep them somewhat firm. 2. Drain. Put into a sauté pan. Season with salt and pepper. 3. Add butter cut into small pieces. Cover and stew in an oven 15 minutes.

23. COURGE

Ingredients	Quantity
Baby vegetable marrow	500 gm
Salt	to taste

Method

1. Peel marrow with a small knife. 2. Cut into half lengthwise. 3. Remove seeds. 4. Cut into even pieces about 5 cm square. 5. Cook in boiling salted water. 6. Drain well and serve in a vegetable dish.

24. COURGE FARCIE

Ingredients	Quantity
Baby vegetable marrow	500 gm
Rice	50 gm
Sausage meat	115 gm
Salt and Pepper	to taste

Method

1. Peel marrow and cut in half lengthwise. 2. Remove seeds. 3. Prepare a stuffing of boiled rice mixed with pieces of sausage meat and seasoned with salt and pepper. 4. Season marrow and add stuffing. 5. Replace two halves. Tie together. 6. Place in a casserole dish. Barely cover with stock and cook gently in an oven for about 1 hour.

N.B. Rice may be mixed with sautéed mushrooms and tomatoes.

25. COURGE PROVENÇALE

Ingredients	Quantity
Vegetable marrow	500 gm
Onions (chopped)	60 gm

Ingredients	Quantity
Garlic (chopped)	1 flake
Oil	60 ml
Tomatoes	450 gm
Chopped parsley	1 tbsp
Salt and Pepper	to taste

Method

1. Peel marrow, remove seeds and cut into 2.5 cm square pieces. 2. Cook onions and garlic in oil in a sauteuse for 2-3 minutes without colouring. 3. Add marrow, season with salt and pepper. 4. Add tomate concassée (roughly chopped tomato). 5. Cover with a lid, cook gently in an oven or on side of stove until tender, approximately 1 hour. 6. Sprinkle with chopped parsley and serve in a vegetable dish.

26. CONCOMBRES à la CRÈME

Ingredients	Quantity
Cucumber	500 gm
Butter	30 gm
Cream	55 ml
Béchamel sauce	100 ml
Salt	

Method

1. Peel and cut cucumber to shapes resembling olives. 2. Parboil and drain. 3. Cook in butter. Moisten with cream and bring to a boil. 4. Add béchamel sauce. Bring to a boil and serve.

27. ÉPINARDS en BRANCHES

Ingredients	Quantity
Spinach	1 kg
Salt	to taste
Pepper	a pinch
Butter	60 gm

Method

1. Remove stems. 2. Wash very carefully in plenty of water several times if necessary. 3. Cook in boiling salted water until tender for approximately 5 minutes. 4. Refresh under cold water, squeeze dry into a ball. 5. When it is time to serve, place into a pan containing butter, loosen with a fork and re-heat quickly without colouring, season with salt and mill pepper. 6. Serve in a vegetable dish.

28. ÉPINARDS à la CRÈME

Ingredients	Quantity
Spinach	1 kg
Butter	60 gm
Béchamel sauce	300 ml
Salt and Pepper	to taste

Method

1. Cook spinach as for recipe No. 27, Épinards en Branches. 2. Dry over a fierce fire with butter. 3. Add béchamel sauce and serve hot.

29. ÉPINARDS en PURÉE

Ingredients	Quantity
Spinach	1 kg
Butter	60 gm
Salt and Pepper	to taste

Method

1. Cook, refresh and drain spinach as for recipe No. 27, Épinards en Branches. 2. Pass through a sieve or mincer. 3. Re-heat in butter, mix with wooden spoon, correct seasoning. 4. Serve in a dome shape in a vegetable dish and flute or scroll with a palette knife.

30. ÉPINARDS au GRATIN

Ingredients	Quantity
Spinach	1 kg
Butter	85 gm
Cheese	85 gm

Method

1. Prepare spinach as for recipe No. 27, Épinards en Branches. 2. After refreshing, dry over a very hot flame with butter. 3. Place on a buttered gratin dish. 4. Sprinkle with cheese and place under grill to form a gratin.

31. HARICOTS BLANCS

Ingredients	Quantity
Haricot beans	225 gm
Onions	60 gm
Carrots	60 gm
Bacon	60 gm
Bouquet garni	

Method

1. Wash and soak beans overnight. 2. Boil in the same water till tender. Skim if necessary. 3. Add sliced carrots, onions and chopped bacon. 4. Continue simmering till tender.

32. MAÏS

Ingredients	Quantity
Corn-on-the-cob (young and fresh)	4
Salt	to taste
Butter	60 gm

Method

1. Trim stem. 2. Cook in boiling salted water until corn is tender. 3. Remove outer leaves and fibres. 4. Serve on a napkin on a sliver flat with a sauceboat of melted butter.

33. OIGNONS SAUTÉS

Ingredients	Quantity
Onions	500 gm
Fat	60 gm
Salt and Pepper	to taste

Method

1. Peel and cut onions into halves. 2. Slice finely. 3. Heat fat. Cook slowly, turning frequently till nicely browned and crisp. 4. Season with salt and pepper and serve hot.

34. OIGNONS FRITS à la FRANÇAISE

Ingredients	Quantity
Onions	500 gm
Fat	115 gm
Milk	30 ml
Refined flour	15 gm
Salt and Pepper	to taste

Method

1. Peel and wash onions. 2. Cut into 3.5 mm. thick slices, against the grain. 3. Separate into rings. 4. Pass through milk and seasoned flour. 5. Shake off surplus. 6. Deep fry in hot fat. 7. Drain well and season with salt. 8. Serve on a dish paper in a vegetable dish.

35. OIGNONS BRAISÉS

Ingredients	Quantity
Medium-sized onions	1 kg
Salt	to taste
Bouquet garni	
Jus-lié	150 ml
Chopped parsley	

Method

1. Peel, wash and cook onions in boiling salted water for half an hour. 2. Drain and place in an oven-proof casserole. 3. Add bouquet garni, half-covered with stock and a lid and braise gently in an oven till tender. 4. Drain well and dress neatly in a vegetable dish. 5. Reduce cooking liquor with an equal amount of jus-lié or demi-glacé. Correct seasoning and consistency. Mask onions and sprinkle with chopped parsley.

36. PETITS POIS à la FRANÇAISE

Ingredients	Quantity
Peas (in the pod)	1 kg
Lettuce	1 small bunch
Castor sugar	tsp
Refined flour	10 gm
Spring onions	12
Butter	30 gm
Salt	to taste

Method

1. Shell and wash peas and place in a sauteuse. 2. Peel and wash onions, shred lettuce and add to peas with 15 gm butter, salt and sugar. 3. Barely cover with water. Cover with a lid and cook steadily, preferably in an oven, until tender. 4. Correct seasoning. 5. Mix remaining 15 gm of butter with flour and shake into boiling peas until thoroughly mixed. 6. Serve in a vegetable dish.

N.B. When using frozen peas allow onions to almost cook before adding peas.

37. PETITS POIS à la FLAMANDE

Ingredients	Quantity
Peas (in the pod)	1 kg
Carrots	450 gm
Butter	60 gm

Ingredients	Quantity
Mint	one sprig
Salt	1 tsp
Castor sugar	tsp

Method

1. Shell and wash peas. 2. Cook in boiling salted water with a sprig of mint until tender (15–20 minutes). 3. Drain. 4. Slice and cook carrots as for glazed carrots. 5. Melt butter and toss both vegetables together. Serve hot.

38. PIMENTOS FARCIS

Ingredients	Quantity
Capsicums	500 gm
Pilau rice	55 gm
Stock	150 ml
Ham	30 gm
Tomatoes	115 gm
Butter	30 gm
Salt	to taste

Method

1. Cut a slice off stem end of capsicums. Remove seeds. Wash well. Drain and sprinkle with salt. 2. Prepare a plain pilau using rice and part of the stock. 3. Add chopped ham and chopped tomatoes to rice. Season. 4. Stuff capsicums with prepared filling. 5. Cover with stem end. 6. Cook in a moderate oven basting frequently with melted butter and stock.

N.B. Grated cheese can be used instead of ham.

39. POIREAUX BRAISÉS

Ingredients	Quantity
Leeks	1 kg
Carrots (sliced)	115 gm
Onions (sliced)	115 gm
Bacon	60 gm
Bouquet garni	
White stock	300 ml
Salt and Pepper	to taste

Method

1. Cut roots from leeks, remove any discoloured outside leaves and trim green ones. 2. Cut through lengthwise and wash well under running water. 3. Tie into a neat bundle. 4. Place in boiling salted water for

approximately 10 minutes. 5. Refresh and rewash. 6. Place sliced vegetables in a sauté pan and place leeks over. 7. Add bouquet garni. Barely cover with stock. Season with salt and pepper. 8. Add bacon strips. Cover with buttered paper and a tight lid and cook gently in a moderate oven for about 1 hour. 9. Remove leeks from pan. Drain well, and dress neatly in a vegetable dish. 10. Add cooking liquor to an equal amount of jus-lié. Check for seasoning. 11. Pour over leeks.

40. MACÉDOINE de LÉGUMES

Ingredients	Quantity
Carrots	115 gm
Turnips	60 gm
Peas (shelled)	60 gm
French beans	60 gm
Salt	to taste
Butter	15 gm

Method

1. Peel and wash carrots and turnips. 2. Dice into batons. 3. Cook separately in salted water. 4. Refresh. 5. Top and tail beans. 6. Cut into 7 mm. pieces, cook and refresh. 7. Cook peas and refresh. 8. Mix vegetables together and when required reheat in hot salted water. 9. Drain well, serve in a vegetable dish, brush with melted butter.

41. POUDING de MAÏS (CORN PUDDING)

Ingredients	Quantity
Milk	3 cups
Butter or	
Margarine	3 tbsp
Eggs	5
Hot water	
Sugar	2 tsp
Pepper	½ tsp
Whole-kernel corn	1 can
(well-drained)	(500 gm)
Salt	2¼ tsp

Method

About one and a half hours before serving:

1. In a 1-litre saucepan over low heat, heat milk and butter or margarine until tiny bubbles form at edge and butter melts. 2. Meanwhile, in a 2-litre casserole beat eggs, salt, sugar and pepper with a wire whisk or fork until well mixed, and stir in corn. Slowly add milk

mixture to egg mixture, beating constantly with wire whisk. 3. Place casserole in 33 cm by 23 cm baking pan; fill pan with hot water to come halfway up side of casserole. 4. Bake in 325°F. oven for 1 hour or until knife inserted in centre comes out clean. Makes 8 accompaniment servings.

42. POMMES PERSILLÉES

Ingredients	For 4
Potatoes (even-sized)	500 gm
Salt	to taste
Butter	30 gm
Parsley	a few sprigs

Method

1. Wash, peel and again wash potatoes. 2. Cut or turn into even-sized pieces allowing 2 to 3 pieces per portion. 3. Cook carefully in salted water (about 20 to 30 minutes). 4. Drain well. Brush liberally with melted butter and sprinkle with chopped parsley.

43. POMMES ALLUMETTES

Ingredients	Quantity
Potatoes	500 gm
Salt	to taste
Fat	to deep fry

Method

1. Wash potatoes, peel and rewash. 2. Trim on all sides to give straight edges. 3. Cut into slices 5 cm × 0.5 cm 4. Cut the slices into straws 5 cm × 0.5 cm 0.5 cm 5. Wash well and dry in a cloth. 6. Fry in hot deep fat till golden brown and crisp. 7. Season with salt, serve on a dish paper in a vegetable dish.

44. POMMES de TERRE ANNA

Ingredients	Quantity
Potatoes	500 gm
Butter	60 gm
Salt and Pepper	to taste

Method

1. Peel, wash and cut potatoes into cylinder shapes. 2. Slice into thin roundels. Parboil. 3. Place one layer (they may overlap) of potatoes in a well buttered pyrex dish. 4. Season. Spread a layer of butter. 5. Repeat process till all potatoes are used. 6. Cover dish and cook in a moderate

oven for about 30 minutes. 7. Turn the whole over to equalize colouring. 8. Turn over into a saucepan to drain off excess butter. Serve hot.

45. POMMES BATAILLE

Ingredients	Quantity
Potatoes	500 gm
Salt	to taste
Fat to deep fry (deep frying)	

Method

1. Select large, even-sized potatoes. 2. Wash, peel and rewash. 3. Cut into 1.5 cm slices. 4. Cut slices into 1.5 cm strips. 5. Cut strips into 1.5 cm dice. 6. Wash well and dry in a cloth. 7. Cook in a frying basket without colouring in moderately hot fat. 8. Drain and place on kitchen paper in trays till required. 9. When required place in a frying basket and cook in hot fat till crisp and golden. 10. Drain well. Season with salt. 11. Serve hot.

46. POMMES BOULANGÈRE

Ingredients	Quantity
Potatoes	500 gm
White stock	300 ml
Onions	115 gm
Butter or	
Margarine	60 gm
Salt and Pepper	to taste
Chopped parsley	

Method

1. Cut potatoes into 1.5 mm. slices. Keep best slices for top. 2. Peel, halve and finely slice onions. 3. Mix onions and potatoes and season with salt and pepper. 4. Place in a well-buttered shallow earthenware dish or roasting tin. 5. Barely cover with stock. 6. Neatly arrange overlapping slices of potato on top. 7. Add a few knobs of butter. 8. Place in a hot oven for approximately 20 minutes until lightly coloured. 9. Reduce heat and allow to cook steadily, pressing down firmly from time to time with a flat-bottomed pan or fish slice. 10. When ready all the stock should have been cooked into the potatoes. Allow 1 hour over-all cooking time. 11. Serve in a vegetable dish, finish with chopped parsley. If cooked in an earthenware dish, clean the edges with a cloth dipped in salt, place on a silver flat and serve.

47. POMMES BRIOCHE

Ingredients	Quantity
Potatoes	500 gm
Salt and Pepper	to taste
Egg yolks	2
Butter	30 gm

Method

1. Wash, peel and rewash potatoes. 2. Cover with salted cold water.
3. Bring to a boil. Reduce heat and simmer till cooked. 4. Drain off water.
Cover and return to low heat to dry out. 5. Pass through a potato masher.
6. Add 1½ egg yolks and stir in vigorously with a wooden spoon. 7. Mix
in butter. 8. Check for seasoning. 9. Shape into 2.5 cm diameter balls.
Place a half cm diameter ball on top of each. (The top ball should be
pierced through with a knife). Place the brioches on a lightly greased
baking sheet. 10. Place in a hot oven for 2 to 3 minutes in order to
slightly harden the edges 11. Remove from oven and brush over with
remaining yolk beaten with a little water. 12. Brown lightly in oven.

48. POMMES CHÂTEAU

Ingredients	Quantity
Small even-sized potatoes	500 gm
Salt	to taste
Fat	60 gm

Method

1. Wash, peel and cut potatoes into barrel shaped pieces 5 cm long, end
diameter 2 cm and centre diameter 3.5 cm 2. Parboil in salted water.
Drain. 3. Melt fat in a roasting tin. Add potatoes and brown on all sides.
4. Season with salt and cook in a hot oven turning over after about 30
minutes. 5. Cook to a golden brown. Drain on absorbent paper and serve
hot.

49. POMMES CHIPS

Ingredients	Quantity
Potatoes	500 gm
Salt	to taste
Fat	for deep frying

Method

1. Wash, peel and rewash potatoes. 2. Cut with a potato slicer into thin
slices. 3. Wash well and dry in a cloth. 4. Cook in hot deep fat until golden
brown and crisp. 5. Drain well on absorbent paper. Season with salt.

50. POMMES CROQUETTES

Ingredients	Quantity
Potatoes	500 gm
Salt and Pepper	to taste
Egg yolks	2
Butter	30 gm
Refined flour	15 gm
Breadcrumbs	15 gm
Fat	for deep frying

Method

1. Prepare potatoes as for recipe No. 47, Pommes Brioche. 2. Mould into cylinders. 3. Roll in flour. Brush with egg beaten with a little water. Roll in breadcrumbs. 4. Deep fry in hot deep fat till golden brown. 5. Drain on absorbent paper and serve hot.

51. CROQUETTES de POMMES de TERRE à la DAUPHINE

Ingredients	Quantity
Potatoes	500 gm
Salt and Pepper, Nutmeg	a pinch each
Butter	30 gm
Egg yolks	2
Breadcrumbs	
Fat	to deep fry
Egg	1
Choux Paste	
Butter	60 gm
Water	150 ml
Salt	to taste
Refined flour	115 gm
Eggs	3

Method

1. Prepare potatoes as for recipe No. 47, Pommes Brioche, seasoning with salt, pepper and nutmeg and adding 2 egg yolks. 2. Prepare choux pastry. Put water, salt and butter in a pan and bring to a boil. 3. When liquor boils and rises remove saucepan from fire and add flour. Mix. 4. Return to a moderate fire and cook till paste ceases to stick to the spoon and butter begins to ooze out. 5. Remove from fire. Add eggs one at a time taking care to mix each egg thoroughly before adding the next. 6. Add potato mixture to choux paste. 7. Shape into croquettes. Coat with egg and breadcrumbs and deep fry. 8. Drain on absorbent paper and serve hot.

52. POMMES FONDANTES

Ingredients	Quantity
Small even-sized potatoes	500 gm
Butter	60 gm
White stock	300 ml
Salt and Pepper	to taste

Method

1. Peel and cut potatoes into shape of olives. 2. Brush with melted butter.
3. Place in a pyrex dish. 4. Half cover with white stock. Season with salt
and pepper. 5. Cook in a hot oven brushing potatoes frequently with
melted butter. 6. When cooked, stock should have been completely
absorbed by potatoes. 7. Serve hot, brushed over with melted butter.

53. POMMES GAUFRETTES

Ingredients	Quantity
Potatoes	500 gm
Salt	to taste
Fat	for deep drying

Method

1. Wash, peel and again wash potatoes. 2. Using a corrugated potato
slicer cut slices, giving a half turn in each cut to get the impression of a
trellis pattern. 3. Wash well and dry in a cloth. 4. Cook in deep fat until
golden brown and crisp. 5. Drain well and season with salt.

54. GRATIN de POMMES de TERRE à la DAUPHINOISE

Ingredients	Quantity
Potatoes	500 gm
Salt and Pepper and	a pinch
Nutmeg	each
Egg	1
Milk	400 ml
Cheese	60 gm
Garlic	1 flake
Butter	30 gm

Method

1. Wash and parboil potatoes in their jackets. 2. Peel and slice. 3. Put
into a basin with salt, pepper, nutmeg, finely chopped garlic, beaten egg,
boiled milk and grated cheese. Mix well. 4. Pour this mixture into a pyrex
dish. 5. Dot with butter and cook in a moderate oven for 40 to 45
minutes.

55. POMMES de TERRE LORETTE

Ingredients and method as for recipe No. 51, Croquette de Pommes de Terre à la Dauphine but add 30 gm of grated cheese to mixture, shape like crescents and treat them à l'anglaise. Plunge into deep fat for about 6 minutes before serving. Drain on absorbent paper and serve hot.

56. POMMES de TERRE à la MAÎTRE d'HÔTEL

Ingredients	Quantity
Potatoes	500 gm
Onions	115 gm
Bacon	30 gm
Milk	150 ml

Method

1. Wash and parboil potatoes. 2. Peel and cut into roundels while still hot. 3. Place in a casserole dish with chopped onions and bacon. Season to taste. 4. Cover with boiling milk. 5. Cook covered in a moderate oven till milk is completely reduced.

57. POMMES de TERRE MARQUISE

Ingredients	Quantity
Potatoes	500 gm
Salt and Pepper	to taste
Egg yolks	2
Tomato purée (reduced)	50 ml

Method

1. Prepare potatoes as for recipe No. 47, Pommes Brioche. 2. Add tomato puree. Mix well. 3. Through a piping bag fitted with a grooved nozzle pipe rosettes. 4. Set them in a hot oven for two to three minutes. Remove and brush over with beaten egg. 5. Return to oven and cook till light brown (about 5 minutes)

58. POMMES de TERRE à la MENTHE

Ingredients	Quantity
New Potatoes	500 gm
Mint	a few sprigs
Salt	to taste

Method

1. Wash, peel and again wash potatoes. 2. Put into salted water with a few sprigs of mint. Bring to a boil. Reduce heat and cook till done (about

20 minutes). 3. Drain well. Serve in a vegetable dish and set a mint leaf on each potato.

59. POMMES de TERRE NOISETTE

Ingredients	Quantity
Potatoes	500 gm
Butter	60 gm
Salt	to taste

Method

1. Wash and peel potatoes. Cut with a spoon cutter into even balls. 2. Cook in salted water. Drain. 3. Fry in butter till golden brown.

60. POMMES de TERRE PARISIENNE

Ingredients and method as for Pommes de Terre Noisette but after cooking roll in melted meat glaze and sprinkle with chopped parsley.

61. POMMES PAILLES

Ingredients	Quantity
Potatoes	500 gm
Salt	to taste
Fat	for deep frying

Method

1. Wash, peel and rewash potatoes. 2. Cut into fine julienne strips. 3. Wash well and drain in a cloth. 4. Deep fry until golden brown and crisp. 5. Drain well on absorbent paper and season with salt. This type of fried potato is used as a garnish.

62. POMMES de TERRE ROBERT

Ingredients	Quantity
Potatoes	500 gm
Butter	30 gm
Eggs	3
Chives (chopped)	15 gm
Salt and Pepper	to taste
Refined flour	1 tsp
Fat	30 gm

Method

1. Select good-sized potatoes. Scrub well. 2. Make a 1.5 mm. incision round each potato. 3. Place potatoes on a bed of salt in a tray in a hot

oven and cook for about 1 hour, turning over after 30 minutes. 4. When cooked remove. Cut into halves. Remove the centres with a spoon into a basin. 5. Add butter, salt, pepper, beaten eggs and chopped chives. Mix well. 6. Divide into even portions. Mould into 2.5 cm thick round cakes. Flour lightly. 7. Shallow fry on both sides in very hot fat. 8. Serve hot.

N.B. If potatoes are difficult to cook, parboil in jackets before making incision and baking.

63. POMMES de TERRE à la SAINT FLORENTINE

Ingredients and method as for recipe No. 50, Pommes Croquettes but add 60 gm of chopped ham to the mixture. Roll into rectangular shaped portions. Deep fry in hot fat. Drain on absorbent paper and serve hot.

64. POMMES de TERRE SOUFFLÉS

Ingredients	Quantity
Large potatoes	500 gm
Fat	for deep frying (2 lots)
Salt	to taste

Method

1. Wash, peel and again wash potatoes. 2. Trim into squares and carefully cut into 3.5 mm. thick slices. 3. Wash in ice-cold water. Dry thoroughly. 4. Put into moderately hot fat, and heat fat gradually until potatoes are cooked. This will be causes when they rise to the surface of the frying fat. 5. Drain in a frying basket and at once immerse in fresh, hotter fat. This final immersion effects the puffing which results from sudden contact with intense heat. 6. Remove and dry on a stretched piece of cloth. Salt moderately.

65. SOUFFLÉ de POMMES de TERRE

Ingredients	Quantity
Potatoes	500 gm
Butter	30 gm
Warm milk	75 ml
Salt and Pepper	to taste
Eggs	3

Method

1. Wash, peel and rewash potatoes. 2. Cook in salted water till done. 3. Drain off water. Place lid on and return potatoes to low heat to dry them out. 4. Pass through a masher. 5. Add butter and mix with a wooden spoon. 6. Gradually add warm milk, stirring continuously until

they are soft and creamy. 7. Check for seasoning. 8. Add egg yolks one at a time, mixing well. 9. Fold in stiffly beaten egg whites. 10. Set in a buttered soufflé pyrex dish and bake at 190°C (about 375°F) for about 15 to 20 minutes.

66. POMMES CHATEÂU

Ingredients	Quantity
Potatoes	450 gm
Fat or Clarified butter	to fry
Salt	to taste
Parsley	2 sprigs

Method

1. Peel and cut potatoes into the shape of large olives. 2. Parboil in salted water. Drain. 3. Heat fat and fry to a golden brown colour. 4. Sprinkle with chopped parsley. Serve hot.

67. RAVIOLI PASTE

Ravioli are small envelopes of a noodle-type paste filled with a variety of stuffings, e.g. beef, chicken, veal, spinach, etc.

Ingredients	For 8
Refined flour	225 gm
Salt	to taste
Olive oil	45 ml
Water	100 ml
Cheese	60 gm
Egg yolk	½
Tomato sauce	30 ml
Filling	
Cooked meat	225 gm
(Beef, Chicken or Veal)	
Spinach	450 gm
Onions	60 gm
Garlic	1 flake
Salt and Pepper	to taste
Fat	15 gm
Demi-glace	a little to bind

Method

1. Sieve flour and salt. 2. Make a well. 3. Add liquid. 4. Knead to a smooth dough. 5. Leave for at least half an hour in a cool place. 6. Roll

out to a very thin oblong 30 cm × 45 cm 7. Cut in half and egg wash (brush over with egg beaten up with a little water). 8. Place stuffing in a piping bag with a large plain tube. 9. Pipe out filling in small amounts about the size of the cherry approximately 3.5 cm apart on to one half of paste. 10. Carefully cover with other half of paste. Seal, taking care to avoid air pockets. 11. Mark each lot with a plain cutter. 12. Cut in between each line of filling, down and across with a serrated pastry wheel. 13. Separate and arrange on a well-floured tray. 14. Poach in gently boiling salted water for approximately 10 minutes. 15. Drain well. 16. Place in pyrex serving dish. 17. Cover with tomato sauce. Sprinkle over with grated cheese. 18. Brown under a grill. Serve hot.

Filling

1. Mince meat. 2. Cook and mince spinach. 3. Sauté onions in fat without discolouring. 4. Season and add a little demi-glacé to bind mixture if necessary but keep mixture firm.

68. CANNELONI

These are poached rolls of ravioli paste filled with a variety of stuffings as for Ravioli.

Paste and filling as for Ravioli.

Method

1. Roll out paste as for ravioli. 2. Cut into squares approximately 6 cm × 6 cm 3. Cook in gently boiling water for approximately 10 minutes. Refresh in cold water. 4. Drain well and lay out singlly. 5. Pipe out filling across each. 6. Roll up like a sausage roll. 7. Place in a pyrex dish. 8. Add tomato sauce. Sprinkle over with grated cheese. 9. Brown under a grill or in a quick oven.

69. RAVIOLI à l'ITALIENNE

Ingredients	Quantity
Dough	
Refined flour	115 gm
Egg	1
Milk	a little
Salt	a pinch
Stuffing	
Grated cheese	30 gm
Nutmeg	a pinch
Salt and Pepper	to taste

Ingredients	Quantity
Minced mutton (cooked) or	
Minced left-over chicken or	60 gm
Minced vegetable	

Method

1. Sift flour. Add egg and milk and prepare a very soft dough. 2. Mix all the ingredients for the stuffing and cook for a while. 3. Roll out half the dough into a thin rectangle. 4. Place spoonfuls of mixture at a distance of one cm 5. Roll out other half of dough and cover mixture. Seal taking care to avoid air pockets. 6. Mark each lot with a plain cutter. 7. Cut in between each line of filling down, and across with a serrated pastry wheel. 8. Separate and put into boiling water. 9. Simmer for 5 minutes. Serve with tomato sauce.

70. MACARONI à l'ITALIENNE

Ingredients	Quantity
Macaroni	225 gm
Butter	60 gm
Cheese	60 gm
Salt	
Pepper	a pinch
Nutmeg	

Method

1. Cook macaroni in boiling salted water till tender. 2. Drain in a colander. 3. Toss in melted butter. Season. 4. Dish out and sprinkle over with grated cheese.

71. MACARONI à la NAPOLITAINE

Ingredients	Quantity
Macaroni	225 gm
Tomatoes	225 gm
Carrots	30 gm
Onions	30 gm
Cheese	115 gm
Butter	55 gm
Salt and Pepper	to taste

Method

1. Melt 15 gm butter. Add minced onions and brown. 2. Add sliced carrots and tomatoes. Add salt and pepper. Cook until thick. Pass through a sieve. 3. Cook macaroni in boiling salted water till tender. Drain in a

colander and rinse under cold water. 4. Grate cheese. 5. In a pyrex bowl put a layer of cheese. 6. Cover with tomato mixture. 7. Place macaroni over. Sprinkle with remaining cheese and dot with butter. 8. Place under a grill till cheese melts. Serve hot.

72. SPAGHETTI TETRAZZINI ARMANDO

Ingredients	Quantity
Chicken (left over pieces)	500 gm
Sauce	
Butter	30 gm
Refined flour	30 gm
Chicken stock	600 ml
Cream	150 ml
Ham	30 gm
Mushrooms	30 gm
Butter	30 gm
Paprika	tsp
Spaghetti	115 gm
Cheese	15 gm

Method

1. Melt butter in a saucepan. Add flour and stir until smooth. Cook for 4 minutes. 2. Gradually add hot broth and milk stirring with wire whip until smooth. Season to taste. 3. Add cream. Bring to a boil. Reduce heat and cook slowly for about 10 minutes stirring frequently. 4. In another pan melt butter. Add mushrooms and sauté. 5. Add pieces of chicken (boned) and ham cut into thin long strips. 6. Add sauce and paprika. 7. Meanwhile cook spaghetti in boiling water for about 10 to 12 minutes. 8. Drain in a colander and rinse in cold water. 9. Sauté in melted butter till hot. 10. Arrange a border of spaghetti in a pyrex dish. 11. Fill centre with chicken mixture. 12. Sprinkle with cheese. Dot with butter and bake at 200°C (about 400°F) till cheese is delicately browned.

73. SPAGHETTI à la CRÉOLE

Ingredients	Quantity
Tomatoes	115 gm
Butter	15 gm
Onions	30 gm
Refined flour	15 gm
Cheese	30 gm
Minced meat	225 gm
Spaghetti	225 gm
Salt	to taste

Method

1. Cook tomatoes and press through a sieve. 2. Mince onions. Sauté in butter. 3. Add flour. Blend well. 4. Add hot tomatoes stirring constantly. Cook 5 to 7 minutes. 5. Brown minced meat and add to tomato mixture. Simmer. 6. Meanwhile cook spaghetti in boiling salted water until tender. Drain well. 7. Add cooked spaghetti to tomato-meat mixture. 8. Stir in salt. Serve piping hot.

74. GNOCCHI (dumpling)

Ingredients	Quantity
Potatoes	1.8 kg
Refined flour	1.2 kg
Salt	to taste

Method

1. Boil and dice potatoes. 2. Gradually add flour. 3. Knead into a smooth manageable dough (if necessary add a little more flour). 4. Roll dough into long rope-like strips about 2 cm thick. Cut into 2 cm pieces. 5. Dip in flour and with the prong of a fork make a dented design in each piece. 6. Boil in 8 litres of rapidly boiling salted water for about 10 minutes. Drain. 7. Place in a large plate. Sprinkle with grated cheese. 8. Serve with tomato sauce.

75. GNOCCHI ROMANE

Ingredients	For 4
Milk	600 ml
Butter	30 gm
Grated cheese	30 gm
Egg yolk	1
Salt	to taste
Pepper	a pinch
Semolina	115 gm
Nutmeg	a pinch

Method

1. Boil milk in a thick-bottomed pan. 2. Sprinkle in semolina stirring continuously. 3. Stir to a boil. 4. Season. Simmer 5 to 10 minutes till cooked. 5. Remove from heat. 6. Mix in egg yolk, and half the cheese and butter. 7. Pour onto a greased tray 1.5 cm deep. 8. When cold cut into rounds with a 5 cm round cutter. 9. Neatly arrange rounds in a pyrex dish. 10. Sprinkle with remaining melted butter and grated cheese. 11. Lightly brown in a quick oven. 12. Serve with a thread of tomato sauce round the gnocchi.

76. SPAGHETTI avec SAUCE BARBAQUE

Ingredients	For 4
Spaghetti	225 gm
Butter	30 gm
Oil	50 gm
Onions	30 gm
Soft brown sugar	55 gm
Paprika	½ tsp
Worcester sauce	15 ml
Cornflour	15 gm
Tomatoes	450 gm
Water	590 ml
Chopped ham	55 gm
Vinegar	10 ml
Tabasco sauce	a little
Stuffed olives	15 gm
Cheese	30 gm

Method

1. Cook spaghetti (in long pieces) in boiling salted water till tender. Drain in colander and rinse in cold water. Set aside. 2. Heat oil in a saucepan. 3. Add chopped onions and cook for a few minutes without browning. 4. Stir in cornflour and mix well. 5. Add tomatoes (peeled and sliced), water and ham and simmer for 10–15 minutes. 6. Add remaining ingredients except olives and cheese and cook for a few minutes more. 7. Stir in sliced stuffed olives. 8. Toss spaghetti in melted butter. 9. Put spaghetti into a serving dish. Pour sauce over and sprinkle with grated cheese.

77. SPAGHETTI avec SAUCE CHAMPIGNONS et FROMAGE

Ingredients	Quantity
Mushrooms	225 gm
Onions	55 gm
Butter	10 gm
Milk	75 ml
Salt	to taste
Refined flour	15 gm
Tomato sauce	50 ml
Cheddar cheese	115 gm
Spaghetti	225 gm

Method

1. Wash mushrooms and chop into large pieces. 2. Peel and mince onions. 3. Sauté onions. Add mushrooms, milk and seasoning. Cover pan and

simmer for 10 minutes. 4. Make a paste with flour, a little cold milk and tomato sauce. 5. Stir into mushroom mixture, bring to a boil and simmer for a few minutes. 6. Remove from fire. Add cheese and stir well. 7. Cook spaghetti (in long pieces) in boiling salted water till tender. 8. Drain, return to pan and add butter. 9. Turn on to a hot dish and pour mushroom sauce. Garnish with sprigs of parsley.

78. NOUILLES VERTES

Ingredients	Quantity
Spinach	1 bunch (200 gm)
Flour	150 gm (about 1½ cups)
Egg	1
Salad oil	1 tsp
Salt	to taste

Method

1. Remove roots and wash spinach well. 2. Cook in an open pan without water till tender. 3. Remove and grind well or put through a purée machine. 4. Add spinach, salad oil, egg and salt to sifted flour. Knead well. 5. Keep aside for 10 minutes. 6. Roll out paper-thin. 7. Cut into long strips about 8–10 cm wide and about 20 cm long. 8. Cook in boiling salted water.

ENTREMETS

1. Gelée à la Mandarine
2. Pains de Fruits
3. Tangerine Chartreuse
4. Mock Cream
5. Charlotte Russe
6. Variation of Charlotte Russe
7. Charlotte d'Orange
8. Mousse aux Fruits
9. Mousse au Citron
10. Soufflé à la Milanaise
11. Soufflé au Chocolat Praline
12. Bavarois à la Crème
13. Bavarois Diplomate
14. Pouding Diplomate
15. Crème Mosaique
16. Crème Garibaldi
17. Pouding d'Ananas
18. Bavarois aux Fruits
19. Mangue Bavarois (A) (tinned mangoes) Mangue Bavarois (B)
20. Ananas Royale
21. Macédoine de Fruits
22. Papaya avec Noix et Crème
23. Gâteau de Pêches
24. Gâteau d'Abricot
25. Gâteau à la Florentine
26. Gâteau d'Ananas
27. Gâteau de Chocolat
28. Poires à la Florentine
29. Poires à la Portugaise
30. Poires Condé
31. Mangue Cardinal
32. Pommes à la Royale

33. Tangerine au Blancmange
34. Vanilla Glacé
35. Pêche Melba
36. Coupe Jacques
37. Banana Chocolate Sundae
38. Omelette Surprise (Baked Alaska)
39. Trifle Alaska
40. Baba au Rhum
41. Pouding Mousseline
42. Pouding Cabinet
43. Pouding Saxon
44. Lemon Soufflé
45. Soufflé à l'Indienne
46. Pouding à la Viennoise
47. Pouding Soufflé au Chocolat
48. Soufflé d'Ananas (A)
    Soufflé d'Ananas (B)
49. Soufflé aux Lichis
50. Soufflé au Chocolat (A)
    Soufflé au Chocolat (B)
51. Soufflé au Caramel
52. Bavarois d'Abricot
53. Crème Brûlée
54. Pommes Charlotte
55. Pommes Bonne Femme
56. Pâté de Pommes
57. Flan d'Ananas
58. Crêpes Georgette
59. Beignets d'Ananas à la Favorite
60. Rum Savarin
61. Pouding de Noël (A)
    Pouding de Noël (B)

I. GELÉE À LA MANDARINE

Ingredients	Quantity
Water	600 ml
Orange juice	150 ml
Sugar	170 gm
Cinnamon	1.5 cm stick
Cloves	2
Rind of orange	
Gelatine	45 gm
Eggs (whites and shells)	2

Method

1. Whisk all ingredients together till nearly boiling. 2. Boil up three times. 3. Strain through a scalded piece of muslin and set in a refrigerator.

For plain jelly: 45 gm gelatine. For fruit in jelly: 55 gm gelatine. For lining moulds: 60 gm gelatine.

N.B. For Gelée au Citron use lemon juice instead of orange juice.

2. PAINS de FRUITS

Ingredients	Quantity
Mango pulp	450 gm
Crystal jelly	55 gm
Gelatine	20 gm

Ingredients	Quantity
Egg white	1
Water	250-300 ml

Method

1. Dissolve jelly (it should be of same flavour as fruit used) in water.
2. Heat it till it becomes clear and completely dissolved. 3. Coat inside
of a litre jelly mould with a little salad oil. 4. Coat the mould with jelly.
Insert another mould and weight down with ice cubes. 5. Leave to set in
a refrigerator. 6. Dissolve gelatine in a little warm water and add to
mango pulp. 7. Beat egg white stiff and fold it into mango mixture.
8. Remove jelly mould from refrigerator. Take out ice cubes. 9. Remove
inner mould gently (a little warm water may be poured in to facilitate
easy removal). 10. Pour mango pulp into the centre. Allow to set.

3. TANGERINE CHARTREUSE

Ingredients	Quantity
Orange jelly	300 ml (½ pt.)
Tangerines	8
Davis gelatine	25 gm
Tangerine juice	150 ml
Evaporated milk	300 ml
Castor sugar	60 gm
Lemon juice	1 tsp for flavouring
Chopped jelly (green)	
Mock cream	for decoration
Glacé cherries	

Method

1. Put a layer of jelly in the bottom of a 15 cm (about 6") cake tin.
2. Allow it to set. 3. Peel fruit. Divide into segments. Remove skin. 4. Dip
each piece into liquid jelly and decorate the bottom of the mould. 5. Let
this too set firmly. Then cover with another layer of jelly and leave this
to set. 6. Dissolve gelatine in warm fruit juice and let it cool. 7. Whip
evaporated milk until quite stiff. 8. Add sugar, a few drops of lemon juice
and dissolved gelatine. 9. Continue whipping until mixture is nearly set.
10. Pour into prepared tin and allow to set firmly. 11. Turn out into a
dish and decorate with chopped jelly, mock cream and glace cherries.

4. MOCK CREAM

Ingredients	Quantity
Butter	60 gm
Powdered sugar	45 gm

Ingredients	Quantity
Cornflour	15 gm
Milk	150 ml

Method

1. Cream butter and sugar. 2. Mix cornflour with a little cold milk to form a smooth paste. 3. Heat milk on a low flame. Pour over cornflour paste, stirring all the time. 5. Return to fire. Stir until thick. 5. Remove from fire and allow to cool. 6. Gradually add cornflour mixture to creamed butter and sugar, beating all the time.

5. CHARLOTTE RUSSE

Ingredients	Quantity
Sponge fingers (use fatless sponge)	115 gm
Cream	150 ml
Custard	150 ml
Gelatine	15 gm
Water	75 ml
Sherry or	2 tbsp
Vanilla	1 tsp
Sugar	30 gm
Lemon jelly crystals	55 gm

Decoration

Cherries and Angelica

Method

1. Dissolve jelly in 300 ml hot water. 2. Pour a little into a soufflé tin. Leave to set. 3. Decorate with cherries and angelica dipped in jelly. Allow to set. 4. Pour another thin layer of jelly and allow to set. 5. Line the tin with sponge fingers pressing well together. 6. Dissolve gelatine in 75 ml of water. 7. Half-whip cream and add custard. 8. Lightly fold in sugar and essence and finally gelatine. 9. When on point of setting pour into prepared mould. 10. Set, trim edges of sponge fingers level with cream. 11. Turn out and arrange chopped jelly around.

6. VARIATION OF CHARLOTTE RUSSE

1. Add 115 gm of diced glacé pineapple to above mixture and omit sherry. 2. Add 60 gm of preserved ginger to above filling and add a teaspoon of ginger to milk when preparing custard. 3. Prepare filling as for recipe No. 10, Soufflé Milanaise.

7. CHARLOTTE d'ORANGE

Ingredients	Quantity
Sponge fingers	115 gm
Lemon jelly	300 ml
Cherries	15 gm
Filling	
Orange juice	of 1 orange
Egg (large)	1
Lemon	½
Orange	1
Angelica	15 gm
Castor sugar	30 gm
Gelatine	10 gm
Cream	150 ml
Water	30 ml

Method

1. Prepare mould as for recipe No. 5, Charlotte Russe using skinned and pipped orange segments, cherries and angelica for decoration. 2. Beat egg yolk, sugar, orange and lemon juice and chopped orange rind, in a bowl over hot water till frothy. 3. Remove from heat and whisk till cold. 4. Add gelatine dissolved in water. Keep whisking. 5. Fold in lightly whisked cream and lastly egg white stiffly beaten. 6. Pour into prepared tin. Continue as for Charlotte Russe.

8. MOUSSE aux FRUITS

Ingredients	Quantity
Milk	600 ml
Sugar	115 gm
Gelatine	25 gm
Eggs	3
Rum or	1 tbsp
Vanilla essence	1 tsp
Cold water	2 tbsp
Blancmange	
Milk	600 ml
Cornflour	45 gm
Sugar	60 gm
Cocoa	10 gm
Mock Cream	
Butter	60 gm
Powdered sugar	45 gm

Ingredients	Quantity
Cornflour	15 gm
Milk	75 ml
Fruits	
Peaches	1 tin
Cherries	115 gm
Angelica	30 gm

Method

1. Cream egg yolks and sugar to a light fluffy cream. 2. Heat milk. Add to cream. 3. Simmer to custard consistency. 4. Add gelatine dissolved in warm water. Mix well and remove. Add essence and green colouring. 5. Cool on ice. 6. Beat egg whites till stiff. Fold in, mixing well. 7. Put into a wet ring or horseshoe mould and set in the refrigerator. 8. Prepare a fairly thick chocolate blancmange. 9. Put over pudding after the latter has thus been set. Return to refrigerator. 10. To assemble pudding, turn over on to a large dish. Surround with fruit. 11. Decorate with mock cream, cherries and angelica.

Mock Cream

1. Cream butter and sugar. 2. Heat milk on a low flame. 3. Add cornflour and stir well till very thick. Remove from heat and cool. 4. Add cornflour mixture gradually to butter cream, beating all the time.

9. MOUSSE au CITRON

Ingredients	Quantity
Lime	1
Rind of lime	
Water	150 ml
Gelatine	10–15 gm
Eggs	2
Sugar	60 gm

Method

1. Put grated rind, lime juice, egg yolks and sugar into a basin. 2. Whisk over hot water till thick and frothy. 3. Remove from heat and whisk till cold. 4. Add gelatine dissolved in water. Continue whisking. 5. Fold in stiffly beaten egg white and mould when on point of setting.

10. SOUFFLÉ à la MILANAISE

Ingredients	Quantity
Castor sugar	250 gm
Eggs (large)	3

Ingredients	Quantity
Gelatine	15 gm
Limes (small)	3
Cream	300 ml
Water	75 ml

Decoration

Glucose biscuits
Chopped pistachio nuts

Method

1. Whisk egg yolks, sugar rind and juice of lime in a bowl over a pan of boiling water till thick and creamy. 2. Allow to become quite cold. Whip cream and fold in lightly. 3. Add gelatine dissolved in warm water. Mix well. 4. Fold in stiffly beaten whites. When on point of setting pour into a prepared soufflé case. 5. Set in a refrigerator. 6. Turn out on a silver dish over a paper doyley and decorate with chopped nuts and sieved biscuit crumbs.

11. SOUFFLÉ au CHOCOLAT PRALINE

Ingredients	Quantity
Chocolate or	45 gm
Cocoa	30 gm
Milk	75 ml
Eggs	3
Castor sugar/Sugar	100 gm
Vanilla	a few drops
Cream	150 ml
French almond rock (pounded)	60 gm
Gelatine	10–15 gm
Water	20 ml

Decoration

Chopped pistachio nuts
Whipped cream

Method

1. Boil milk and chocolate/cocoa together and allow to cool. 2. Whisk egg yolks and sugar together over hot water till thick. 3. Allow to get quite cold, while whisking occasionally. 4. Add chocolate, half-whipped cream, powdered almond rock and vanilla essence. 5. Dissolve gelatine in warm water. Cool and strain into mixture. 6. Fold in stiffly beaten egg whites. 7. Cool on ice. When on the point of setting pour into wet mould. 8. When set, turn out and decorate with chopped pistachio nuts and whipped cream.

12. BAVAROIS à la CRÈME

Ingredients	Quantity
Egg yolks	2
Sugar	55 gm
Milk	300 ml
Cream	300 ml
Powdered sugar	30 gm
Gelatine	20 gm
Vanilla	1 tsp

Method

1. Cream sugar and egg yolks. 2. Add boiling milk. Mix well. Add vanilla.
3. Return to fire and cook custard till thick. Remove from fire and add
gelatine dissolved in a little water. Mix well. 4. Cool on ice. Whip cream
with powdered sugar and add to mixture. 5. Pour into a wet mould. Set
in a refrigerator. 6. Just before serving, turn out and decorate with
cherries.

13. BAVAROIS DIPLOMATE

Ingredients	For 8
Milk	300 ml
Cream	300 ml
Egg yolks	4
Gelatine	20 gm
Sugar	120 gm
Water	15 ml
Chocolate	10 gm
Strawberry essence	a few drops
Vanilla	1 tsp
Pink colour	

Method

1. Cream egg yolks and sugar. 2. Add boiling milk. Put in a double boiler
and cook till custard thickens (it should coat the back of a wooden spoon).
3. Add gelatine dissolved in a tablespoon of warm water. Mix well.
4. Allow to cool. Add whipped cream. 5. Divide into 3 portions. Flavor
one with vanilla, and another with strawberry essence and pink colour.
6. Blend chocolate with a little cold milk. Cook for a few minutes and
add to third portion of mixture. 7. Mask an oiled jelly mould with the
vanilla-flavoured cream. Set another jelly mould into first one and fill
with ice cubes and keep in a refrigerator. 8. When cream has set remove
ice cubes from the centre one and gently remove inner mould. 9. Fill
centre with alternate layers of strawberry and chocolate cream. 10. Leave
to set. Turn out when about to serve.

14. POUDING DIPLOMATE

Ingredients	Quantity
Milk	300 ml
Egg yolks	2
Cream	300 ml
Castor sugar	120 gm
Vanilla	1 tsp
Gelatine	20 gm
Powdered sugar	15 gm
Glucose biscuits	30 gm
Currants	10 gm
Raisins (seedless)	10 gm
Cherries glace	10 gm
Angelica	10 gm
Apricot jam	30 gm

Method

1. Cream sugar and egg yolks. 2. Add boiling milk. Stir well. 3. Dissolve gelatine in a tablespoon of warm water. 4. Add to mixture and cook on a slow fire. Do not let it boil. 5. When custard begins to get thick (it should coat the spoon) remove and add vanilla. 6. Cool on ice. Add whipped cream mixed with powdered sugar. 7. Decorate the bottom of an oiled mould with cherries and angelica. 8. Fill up mould with alternate layers of cream mixture and biscuits soaked in fruit juice. 9. On each layer of biscuits sprinkle some currants and raisins swelled in tepid water. Here and there set a teaspoonful of apricot jam. 10. Set in a refrigerator and turn out just before serving.

15. CRÈME MOSAIQUE

Ingredients	Quantity
Milk	300 ml
Cream	300 ml
Eggs	2
Vanilla	
Coffee essence	10 ml
Strawberry essence	
Almond essence	
Pink and green colour	
Lemon jelly	150 ml

Method

1. Melt jelly and mask a plain jelly mould. Leave to set. 2. Cream egg yolks and sugar. Add boiling milk. Put into a double boiler and cook till thick. 3. Allow to cool. Add cream and gelatine dissolved in a tablespoon

of warm water. 4. Divide into 2 portions. Flavour one with vanilla. 5. Divide second into 3 portions. Flavour the first with coffee, the second with strawberry essence and pink colour, and the third with almond essence and green colour. 6. Set on three plates and when cold, cut into cubes and decorate bottom and sides of mould in which the jelly has been set, to form a mosaic pattern (pieces may be dipped in jelly to help in arranging them firmly). Set for a few minutes in a refrigerator. 7. Remove and fill with vanilla cream. 8. Set in refrigerator, turn out and garnish with chopped jelly.

16. CRÈME GARIBALDI

Ingredients	Quantity
Clear Jelly	
Gelatine	30 gm
Water	1 litre
Cinnamon	1 stick
Cloves	2-3
Cardamoms	3-4
Egg whites and shells	2
Lime	1
Sugar	85 gm
Cream	
Milk	500 ml
Egg yolks	2
Sugar	85 gm
Gelatine	30 gm
Cream (optional)	120 ml
Almonds	45 gm
Pistachios	45 gm
Cochineal	few drops
Cocoa	2 tsp
Vanilla	½ tsp
Almond essence	a few drops
Rapberry essence	a few drops

Method

1. Soak gelatine in water for half an hour. 2. Add cloves, cinnamon, cardamom, washed shells and whites of eggs and sugar. 3. Bring to a boil. Boil up three times. Add lime juice and when jelly is clear strain through muslin.

Cream

1. Boil and grind almonds and pistachios separately. 2. Cream egg yolks

and sugar. 3. Pour boiling milk over. Return to fire and cook to a thick custard. 4. Dissolve gelatine in a tablespoon of warm water and add to custard. Mix well. Remove from fire. Cool and add cream. 5. Divide into four portions. Flavour one with almond essence and ground almonds, the second with pistachios and add green colour, the third with raspberry essence and colour with cochineal for a pale pink colour. Blend cocoa in a tablespoon of cold milk and add to fourth portion. 6. Set the above in layers, chilling in refrigerator after each layer is added. 7. Cut into fancy shapes. Set half the jelly in a crystal bowl. 8. Place prepared cream over set jelly. 9. Pour remaining jelly over and set in refrigerator.

17. POUDING d'ANANAS

Ingredients	Quantity
Egg yolks	2
Sugar	120 gm
Milk	300 ml
Cream	300 ml
Gelatine	20 gm
Powdered sugar	30 gm
Pineapple (tinned)	225 gm

Method

1. Cream egg yolks and sugar. Add boiling milk. 2. Cook till custard is thick (it should coat the back of a wooden spoon). 3. Remove. Add gelatine dissolved in a tablespoon of warm water. Mix well. 4. Cool on ice. Add cream whipped with powdered sugar. 5. Line a ring mould with diced pineapple. 6. Pour prepared mixture into mould. Leave to set. 7. Turn out. Decorate with half slices of remaining pineapple. Set a small bowl containing flowers in the centre.

18. BAVAROIS aux FRUITS

Ingredients	Quantity
Mango purée	455 gm
Cream	750 ml
Water	590 ml
Gelatine	30 gm
Sugar	55–85 gm
Lime	1
Cherries (canned)	115 gm

Method

1. Prepare syrup with sugar and water (30° saccharometer). 2. Mix with mango purée. Add lime juice and gelatine dissolved in a little warm

water. 3. Add 600 ml whipped cream. 4. Mix well together, put into a wet mould and set in a refrigerator. 5. Turn out when set. 6. Decorate with whipped cream and cherries.

N.B. Peaches, apricots and strawberries can be substituted for mangoes.

19. MANGUE BAVAROIS (A) (tinned mangoes)

Ingredients	Quantity
Tinned mangoes (alphonso)	300 gm
Syrup	300 ml
Gelatine	20 gm
Cream	300 ml
Lime	1

Method

1. Make purée with mangoes. 2. Mix with slightly warmed syrup. 3. Add gelatine dissolved in a little warm water, and whipped cream. Mix well. 4. Put into a wet mould and set in a refrigerator.

MANGUE BAVAROIS (B)

Ingredients	Quantity
Mango purée	300 ml
Milk	150 ml
Egg	1
Sugar	90 gm
Gelatine	20 gm
Cream	300 ml

Method

1. Separate yolk and white of egg. 2. Mix yolk, sugar and milk. Cook till it reaches coating consistency. 3. Dissolve gelatine in 30 ml water and add to custard. 4. Warm mango purée and mix with custard. 5. Cool down mixture. 6. Add whipped cream and beaten egg white. 7. Set in a greased jelly mould in a refrigerator. 8. Present demoulded pudding with whipped cream and mango slices.

20. ANANAS ROYALE

Ingredients	Quantity
Fresh pineapple	1 (about 500 gm)
Peaches (canned)	225 gm
Sugar	55 gm

Ingredients	Quantity
Lime	1
Strawberries or	
Cherries	115 gm
Water	50 ml
Cream	150 ml

Method

1. Slice a piece off the top of fresh pineapple. 2. Scoop out pineapple flesh from inside leaving a shell 1.5 cm (2) thick. 3. Remove core and dice pineapple flesh. 4. Prepare sugar syrup. Flavour with lime juice. 5. Add prepared fruit. Mix with a few pieces of peaches and cherries or strawberries. 6. Fill shell. Put the lid on and set in the centre of a glass plate. 7. Surround with slices of peaches alternating with strawberries. 8. Serve a sauceboat of fresh cream separately.

21. MACÉDOINE DE FRUITS

Ingredients	Quantity
Papaya	115 gm
Mango	115 gm
Banana	1
Lime	1
Oranges	100 gm
Apple	1
Dried apricots	50 gm
Sugar	60 gm
Cream	150 ml

Method

1. Soak apricots overnight. Stew in same liquid. 2. Peel and dice fruits. 3. Prepare sugar syrup. Add lime juice. Chill and pour over fruit. Add chopped, stewed apricots and the nuts from their kernels. 4. Chill. Set in individual glasses and top with whipped cream.

22. PAPAYA avec NOIX et CRÈME

Ingredients	Quantity
Papaya	1
Cream	50 ml
Walnuts	
Cashewnuts	60 gm
Lime	1
Powdered sugar	10 gm

Method

1. Cut papaya in halves. Remove seeds. 2. Sprinkle with lime juice and powdered sugar. 3. Decorate with whipped cream and chopped nuts. 4. Keep in refrigerator till ready to serve.

23. GÂTEAU de PÊCHES

Ingredients	Quantity
Genoise pastry	
Castor sugar	60 gm
Eggs	2
Refined flour	45 gm
Decoration	
Whipped cream	150 ml
Butter	45 gm
Apricot jam	60 gm
Peaches	1 tin
Pistachio nuts	30 gm

Method

1. Line and grease a ring mould. 2. Whisk eggs and sugar over hot water till quite thick and frothy. 3. Remove from heat and whisk till cool. 4. Lightly fold in half the sifted flour and half the butter which has been previously clarified. 5. Add remainder in the same way. 6. Pour into prepared tin and bake at 190°C (about 375°F) for about 20 minutes. 7. Cool. Turn out. Brush with apricot jam. Pour some syrup from tinned peaches over and let it soak through. 8. Place in the centre of a dish. Arrange peaches in the centre and around border. 9. Pipe cream into the centre and on the border between peaches. Decorate with nuts. 10. Add a little red colour to remaining juice and pour around. Serve immediately.

24. GÂTEAU d'ABRICOT

Ingredients	Quantity
Genoise pastry	(see Gâteau de Pêches)
Savoy biscuits	115 gm
Sugar	60 gm
Eggs	2
Vanilla essence	1 tsp
Refined flour	45 gm
Apricot jam	1 tbsp

Ingredients	Quantity
Filling	
Apricots	1 tin
Whipped cream	150 ml
Castor sugar	1 tbsp
Vanilla essence	1 tsp
Wafer biscuits	60 gm
Decoration	
Ribbon (white)	¾ metre
Chopped pistachio nuts	30 gm

Method

1. Prepare genoise pastry as for previous recipe but bake in a round tin 11 cm (about 4½″) in diameter. 2. To prepare savoy biscuits, cream egg yolk and sugar till light and fluffy. Add vanilla essence. 3. Stir in sifted flour lightly. 4. Beat egg whites stiff and fold in. Put into a piping bag with a plain meringue nozzle (0.7 cm or ½″). 5. Pipe into 5 cm long strips onto a floured baking sheet. Sprinkle with powdered sugar. 6. Jerk a few drops of water on the biscuits with the help of a wet brush. 7. Bake at 170°C (about 350°F) till done. Cool. 8. Brush sides of genoise pastry with sieved jam. Place in a silver dish. 9. Stand savoy biscuits around it. Tie with a ribbon to keep it in place. 10. Cut apricots into four, reserving a few for decoration. 11. Mix cream with sugar, vanilla essence and fruit juice. 12. Mix half the cream with crushed biscuits and cut fruits. 13. Put into prepared case. 14. Pipe remaining cream on top and decorate with pieces of apricot and pistachio nuts.

25. GÂTEAU à la FLORENTINE

Ingredients	Quantity
Sponge cake (round)	1
Sherry	1 tbsp
Whipped cream	200 ml
Ripe mangoes	2
Cherries	a few
Fruit juice	1 cup
Mixed fruit jam	
Meringues (oval shaped)	about 20

Method

1. Place sponge cake on a round plate. 2. Cut into halves horizontally. Spread a layer of jam on bottom half. Put top half over it. 3. Pour fruit juice mixed with sherry over cake. 4. Peel and slice mangoes. Spread a layer of cream on sponge cake and over this, place mango slices. 5. Stick

meringues around the edges using a little cream. 6. Finish off by decorating with remaining whipped cream and cherries. 7. Also serve cream separately.

26. GÂTEAU d'ANANAS

Ingredients	Quantity
Refined flour	60 gm
Eggs	2
Butter	60 gm
Granulated sugar	60 gm
Jam	50 gm
Pineapple	1 small tin (450 gm)
Fresh cream	200 gm
Cocktail cherries	4

Method

1. Line and grease a 15 cm (6") cake tin (mould). 2. Whisk eggs and sugar over hot water till quite thick and frothy. 3. Remove from heat and lightly fold in half the butter which has been previously melted. 4. Add flour and remaining butter in the same way. 5. Pour into prepared cake mould and bake at 190°C (about 375°F) for about 20 minutes. Cool. 6. Turn out and slice horizontally into two parts. 7. Soak both layers with some pineapple syrup from tin. 8. Spread jam, some whipped fresh cream, tidbits of 3 slices of pineapple over bottom layer. 9. Cover with top layer and decorate sides and top with fresh cream and pineapple rings and cocktail cherries.

N.B. A dash of lime and a tbsp of white rum can be added to pineapple juice before soaking cake.

27. GÂTEAU de CHOCOLAT (10 portions)

Ingredients	Quantity
For Fatless Sponge	
Flour	70 gm
Grain sugar	90 gm
Eggs	3
Cocoa powder	20 gm
For the Gâteau	
Fresh cream	300 gm
Jam	30 gm
Grain sugar	100 gm (for syrup)
Cadbury chocolate (medium size)	1
Cashewnuts	50 gm
Rum	50 ml

Method (for Chocolate Fatless Sponge)

1. Beat eggs and grain sugar over hot water until light and fluffy. 2. Add flour sieved with cocoa powder and fold in lightly; put into a prepared cake tin. 3. Bake at 205°C (400°F) for 7–10 minutes till done. 4. Keep on a cooling rack for cooling.

Preparations

1. Cut cake into two layers and soak in sugar syrup with rum. Apply jam over bottom half. 2. Whip fresh cream and sandwich layers of cake. 3. Cover cake with the remaining fresh cream. 4. Decorate sides with chopped cashewnuts. 5. Sprinkle grated chocolate on top and keep in a refrigerator till it is served.

N.B. To prepare cake tin, grease and line with greaseproof paper.

28. POIRES à la FLORENTINE

Ingredients	Quantity
Pears	450 gm
Sugar	115 gm
Milk	300 ml
Semolina	45 gm
Castor sugar	115 gm
Cream	30 ml
Apricot jam	60 gm
Cherries	30 gm
Angelica	15 gm
Lime (rind)	½
Water	115 ml
Cloves	

Method

1. Peel and cut pears into halves. 2. Put into a pan with sugar, water, cloves and lime rind. 3. Cook till pears are soft. 4. Drain fruit on a sieve. Reduce sugar syrup to half. 5. Boil milk. Stir in sieved semolina. Add castor sugar and cook till it becomes thick and creamy. Remove. 6. Add vanilla and cream to this mixture. 7. Spread mixture into a circle in a dish and set on ice. 8. Add apricot jam to reduced sugar syrup and strain. 9. Arrange pears over semolina base. 10. Decorate with angelica and cherries. 11. Chill and serve with apricot sauce.

29. POIRES à la PORTUGAISE

Ingredients	Quantity
Pears (tinned)	6
Cream	250 ml

Ingredients	Quantity
Castor sugar	15 gm
Lemon jelly	250 ml
Gelatine	5 gm
Red colour	
Vanilla essence	
Decoration	
Chopped jelly	12
Angelica leaves	12
Cloves	6

Method

1. Dissolve gelatine in 150 ml jelly. Add to 150 ml cream; colour and flavour. 2. Drain and trim pears. 3. Coat with cream and jelly when at point of setting. 4. Leave till firm. Coat with liquid jelly and decorate with a clove and two angelica leaves. 5. Whip remaining cream with castor sugar. Mix with pear trimmings and remaining jelly. 6. Put in paper cases and set a pear on each.

30. POIRES CONDÉ

Ingredients	For 4
Milk	600 ml
Rice	60 gm
Sugar	60 gm
Pears	2
Glacé cherries	2
Vanilla essence	2 to 3 drops
Apricot glaze	150 ml
Angelica	15 gm

Method

1. Boil rice till mixture is thick. 2. Cook rice in milk, sweeten and flavour. 2. Allow to cool. 3. Peel, core and halve pears and poach them carefully; leave to cool. 4. Dress rice either in a glass bowl or on a silver flat dish. 5. Drain pears and neatly arrange them on top. 6. Coat with apricot glaze. 7. Decorate with angelica and cherries.

N.B. Many other fruits may be prepared as a Condé, e.g. banana, pineapple, peach.

31. MANGUE CARDINAL

Ingredients	Quantity
Mangoes	2

Ingredients	Quantity
Jam (Raspberry)	50 gm
Sugar	50 gm
Almonds	50 gm
Vanilla	

Method

1. Peel and slice mangoes. 2. Poach in vanilla-flavoured syrup. 3. Cool and chill. 4. Dish in a glass dish. 5. Cover with sieved raspberry jam and sprinkle with chopped almonds.

32. POMMES à la ROYALE

Ingredients	Quantity
Apples	4
Sugar	115 gm
Cornflour	30 gm
Milk	600 ml
Vanilla	2 tsp
Redcurrant jelly	60 ml
Pineapple jelly	

Method

1. Peel and core apples. 2. Cook in vanilla-flavoured syrup till tender (use half the sugar). 3. Prepare a blancmange with cornflour, sugar and milk. Flavour with vanilla. 4. Set blancmange and set an apple on each. 5. Coat with redcurrant jelly. 6. Arrange in a circle in a round plate and garnish centre with chopped jelly.

33. TANGERINE au BLANCMANGE

Ingredients	Quantity
Oranges	4
Milk	600 ml
Cornflour	30 gm
Sugar	55 gm
Orange essence	a few drops

Method

1. Peel orange, separate segments, skin and pips. 2. Dip segments in a little sugar syrup and decorate the bottom of a jelly mould. 3. Prepare a blancmange with cornflour, milk and remaining sugar. Flavour with orange essence. 4. Pour into prepared mould. Chill and turn out.

34. VANILLA GLACÉ

Ingredients	Quantity
Milk	600 ml
Eggs	2
Sugar	115–130 gm
Salt	a pinch
Gelatine	½ tsp
Vanilla	½ tsp
Cream	75 ml

Method

1. Make a fairly thick custard with egg yolks, sugar, salt and milk, (it should coat the back of a spoon). 2. Add vanilla. Cool slightly. Add gelatine dissolved in a little warm water. Mix well. 3. Cool on ice. 4. Add stiffly beaten egg whites and mix well. 5. Set in refrigerator. When well set take out. 6. Beat well with a rotary beater to almost double its volume, adding cream gradually. 7. Return to freezer. Set and use when required.

N.B. Flavours such as chocolate, coffee, raspberry, etc. can be used instead of vanilla.

35. PÊCHE MELBA

Ingredients	Quantity
Peaches	2
Vanilla ice-cream	150 ml
Melba sauce	150 ml

Method

1. If fresh peaches are used dip in boiling water for a few seconds and then in cold water. Peel and halve. 2. Dress fruit on a portion of ice-cream in an ice-cream cup. 3. Coat with melba sauce. This can be decorated with whipped cream.

MELBA SAUCE

Ingredients	Quantity
Raspberry jam	115 gm
Water	30 ml

Method

Boil ingredients together and pass through a strainer.

N.B. Pears, bananas, mangoes, etc. can be used instead of peaches if desired.

36. COUPE JACQUES

Ingredients	Quantity
Ice-cream	(see vanilla glacé)
Fruit salad	(fresh or canned)
Whipped cream	
Melba sauce	(see Pêche Melba)
Blanched almonds	
Canned cherries	

Method

1. Chop and brown almonds lightly under a grill or in an oven. 2. Arrange fruit in individual glasses. 3. Place a scoop of ice-cream on top. 4. Top with a little melba sauce, nuts, cream and cherries.

37. BANANA CHOCOLATE SUNDAE

Ingredients	Quantity
Ice-cream	(see vanilla glacé)
(Prepare half with strawberry essence	
and colour pink)	
Bananas	
Whipped cream	
Glacé cherries	
Chocolate sauce	

Method

1. Fill individual glasses with vanilla and strawberry ice-cream and sliced bananas. 2. Top with chocolate sauce, whipped cream and cherries.

CHOCOLATE SAUCE

Ingredients	Quantity
Butter	30 gm
Cocoa	30 gm
Vanilla essence	½ tsp
Sugar	60 gm
Water	2 tbsp

Method

1. Put all ingredients into a saucepan and heat gently until cocoa is completely dissolved. Do not boil or sauce will lose its shine.

38. OMELETTE SURPRISE (Baked Alaska)

Ingredients	Quantity
Ice-cream	
Evaporated milk	300 ml

Ingredients	Quantity
Castor sugar	3 tbsp
Davis gelatine	½ tsp
Strawberry essence	½ tsp
Pink colouring	
Cherries	1 small tin
Cream	30 ml
Genoise sponge cake	1 (using 2 eggs)
Egg whites	2
Castor sugar	115 gm
Cherries and Angelica	

Method

1. Set refrigerator at coldest. 2. Mix milk, sugar and essence. 3. Dissolve gelatin in 1 tablespoon of water over heat and stir into milk while still hot. 4. Place in a refrigerator until ice crystals form. 5. Pour into a chilled mixing bowl and beat until stiff. Halve and stone cherries. 6. Fold into stiff mixture. Colour pink. Freeze quickly at a low temperature. 7. Bake sponge cake in a flan tin. Cool. Beat egg whites stiff. 8. Add 1 dessertspoon of sugar. Whisk until stiff. 9. Fold in remaining sugar. 10. Pile ice-cream into flan case. 11. Coat with meringue completely enclosing the ice-cream. Decorate with cherries and angelica. 12. Bake quickly in a hot oven at 230°C (approx. 450°F) until meringue is lightly browned (about 3–4 minutes). Serve immediately.

39. TRIFLE ALASKA

Ingredients	Quantity
Fatless sponge cake with 3 eggs	1
Jam	60 gm
Fruit juice or	
Fruit juice and Sherry	295 ml
Castor sugar	170 gm
Angelica	
Pineapple	1 tin (½ kg)
Custard	450 ml
Bananas	2
Oranges	2
Decoration	
Egg whites	3
Walnuts	
Cherries	

Method

1. Spread jam over cake and cut into small pieces. Put into a pyrex pie dish. 2. Pour fruit juice over and let it soak well. 3. Cover cake with fruit (sliced bananas, chopped pineapple and segments of orange with skin and pips removed); save 2 slices of pineapple for the top. 4. Pour custard over cake and fruit and leave in a refrigerator till quite set. 5. Whip egg whites stiff. Add sugar gradually and whip until dry and standing in peaks. 6. Cover trifle with meringue. Put remaining meringue into forcing bag with rose tube and pipe a firm border around. 7. Put in a very hot oven at 290°C (or approx. 550°F) for 1½ to 2 minutes. 8. Quickly decorate with remaining fruit and nuts.

40. BABA au RHUM

Ingredients	Quantity
Refined flour	115 gm
Yeast (dry)	5 gm
Castor sugar	¼ tsp
Salt	¼ tsp
Milk	75 ml
Eggs (large)	2
Butter	75 gm
Currants	45 gm
Rum syrup	
Water	300 ml
Sugar	225 gm
Rum or	1 tbsp
Rum essence	1 tsp

Method

1. Mix yeast, sugar and slightly warmed milk. 2. Sift flour into a basin. Make a well in centre and pour in yeast and milk. 3. Cover with a little flour from sides of basin and put in a warm place to sponge for about half an hour. 4. Beat in eggs one at a time and melted butter. 5. Grease baba moulds and sprinkle with currants. 6. Half-fill with prepared mixture. Leave in a warm place until mixture nearly fills mould. 7. Bake in a hot oven till firm. 8. Turn out and dip each in rum syrup till fairly soaked. Drain on racks placed on a plate to hold the drip. Baste with remaining syrup.

RUM SYRUP

Boil sugar and water and reduce to syrup consistency. Add rum to taste.

41. POUDING MOUSSELINE

Ingredients	Quantity
Butter	30 gm
Castor sugar	30 gm
Eggs	3
Refined flour	30 gm
Vanilla essence	
Lemon rind	½ tsp
Mousseline sauce	
Egg yolks	2
Cream	75 ml
Castor sugar	15 gm
Egg white	1
Glacé cherries	15 gm

Method

1. Cream butter and sugar. 2. Add well-beaten egg yolks, gradually, beating all the time. 3. Gently stir in flour. Add grated lemon rind and a few drops of vanilla essence. 4. Beat egg whites stiff and fold into mixture. 5. Pour into a well-buttered mould and cover with buttered paper. 6. Steam very slowly for 1–1½ hours. 7. When just set turn out carefully on to a hot dish. 8. Pour mousseline sauce around and serve at once.

MOUSSELINE SAUCE

1. Put egg yolks, cream and castor sugar into a pan. 2. Whisk well. Add egg white and whisk till frothy. 3. Place in a double boiler and whisk till hot. 4. Add chopped cherries.

42. POUDING CABINET

Ingredients	Quantity
Sponge cake (Genoise or butter sponge)	225 gm
Biscuits (glucose)	115 gm
Castor sugar	30 gm
Eggs	2
Milk	300 ml
Vanilla	a few drops
Cherries and	
Angelica	

Method

1. Grease a soufflé mould and line its base with greased paper.
2. Decorate base with cherries and angelica. 3. Fill mould three-fourths

ful with broken-up sponge cake and biscuits. 4. Bring milk to almost boiling point and pour on to beaten egg and sugar. 5. Strain over cake. 6. Cover with greased paper and steam slowly for one hour until firm. 7. Turn out carefully and serve with jam sauce.

43. POUDING SAXON

Ingredients	Quantity
Butter	115 gm
Powdered sugar	115 gm
Refined flour (sifted)	115 gm
Milk	400 ml
Eggs	5

Method

1. Cream together butter and sugar till light and fluffy. 2. Add sifted flour and mix in boiling milk. 3. Cook this mixture over a fierce fire, stirring all the time till it ceases to stick to spoon. 4. Take off fire. Add beaten egg yolks gradually, mixing well. 5. Beat egg whites stiff and fold in. 6. Pour into a well-buttered mould and steam for about 1–1½ hours. 7. Serve with a sabayon sauce (see Sauces in Vol. I).

44. LEMON SOUFFLÉ

Ingredients and method as for Pouding Saxon but flavour with lemon rind and serve with a custard sauce flavoured with lemon rind.

45. SOUFFLÉ à l'INDIENNE

Ingredients and method as for Pouding Saxon but add 15 gm powdered ginger and 115 gm crystallized ginger cut into dice. Serve accompanied by a custard sauce flavoured with ginger powder.

46. POUDING à la VIENNOISE

Ingredients	Quantity
Bread	75 gm
Castor sugar	45 gm
Candied peel	30 gm
Eggs	2
Milk	300 ml
Loaf sugar	30 gm
Sultanas	45 gm
Lime rind	1 tsp
Cream	75 ml
Sherry (optional) or	75 ml
Vanilla essence	1 tsp

Method

1. Shred candied peel and mix in a basin with diced bread, castor sugar, lime rind and cleaned sultanas. 2. Put loaf sugar into a thick aluminium pan with a tablespoon of water. Dissolve slowly and boil till a rich brown. 3. Add milk and stir till caramel is dissolved. 4. Pour on to beaten eggs and strain on to bread. 5. Leave to soak for half an hour. 6. Add cream and sherry or vanilla essence. 7. Pour into a well-greased mould and steam for 1 hour. Turn out and serve with sherry or custard sauce.

47. POUDING SOUFFLÉ au CHOCOLAT

Ingredients	Quantity
Milk	300 ml
Butter	60 gm
Refined flour	60 gm
Chocolate	85 gm
Castor sugar	60 gm
Eggs	3
Vanilla	

Method

1. Put milk into a saucepan with butter. 2. When it boils stir in sifted flour and work vigorously over the fire till it becomes in a smooth paste. 3. Let it cool a little. Then work in chocolate previously melted in an oven, sugar and egg yolks. 4. Add vanilla essence (about ½ tsp) and fold in stiffly beaten egg whites. 5. Pour mixture and bake at 190°C (about 375°F) for about 45 minutes. 6. Turn out on to a hot dish and serve with hot custard sauce.

48. SOUFFLÉ d'ANANAS (A)

Ingredients	Quantity
Butter	30 gm
Refined flour	45 gm
Milk	150 ml
Egg yolks	3
Egg whites	4
Pineapple essence	a few drops
Sauce	
Pineapple syrup	150 ml
Sugar	30 gm
Pineapple	30 gm
Sherry or Rum	75 ml

Ingredients	Quantity
Loaf sugar	85 gm
Water	150 ml
Red colour	

Method

1. Melt butter in a large pan. Add flour and mix well. 2. Add milk and cook till mixture is thick and leaves sides of pan. 3. Cool slightly. Add sugar and diced pineapple. 4. Beat in well-beaten yolks gradually, whisking all the time. 5. Beat egg whites stiff and fold into mixture. 6. Pour into prepared tin and steam slowly for 45 minutes. 7. Prepare sauce. Boil syrup with sugar. Add sherry or rum and red colour. Add diced pineapple.

SOUFFLÉ à l'ANANAS (B)

Ingredients	Quantity
Pineapple	1 tin
Pineola or	
Tinned pineapple juice	2 bottles
Gelatine	6 tsp
Cashewnuts	100 gm
Dates	100 gm
Cream	½ cup
Cherries and	for
Angelica	garnishing

Method

1. Remove syrup from tinned pineapple. 2. Mix syrup with pineola or tinned pineapple juice. 3. Dissolve gelatine in 1 cup warm water. Add gradually to mixture. Chill well. 4. Beat over ice with a rotary beater till light and frothy (like egg white). 5. Fold in cream, pineapple slices chopped into small pieces (save one for garnishing), nuts coarsely powdered, and finely chopped dates. 6. Pour into an attractive mould. Set. 7. When set, decorate with pineapple slice with a cherry in the centre and angelica.

N.B. To prepare a Mango Soufflé, use a tin of mangoes instead of pineapple, and Mangola instead of pineapple juice.

49. SOUFFLÉ aux LICHIS

Ingredients	Quantity
Lychees	310 gm tin (11 oz. approx.)

Ingredients	Quantity
Gelatine	15 gm
Castor sugar	60 gm
Evaporated milk	200 ml
Chopped nuts	
Angelica	
Cherries	

Method

1. Tie a band of greaseproof paper around the outside of a 12 oz. (15 cm (5 or 6 inch) soufflé dish, so that it comes 5 cm (2 inches) above top of dish. 2. Drain and chop lychees, reserving a few pieces for decoration. 3. Heat syrup drained from fruit and dissolve gelatine and sugar in it. 4. Chill milk. Whisk until thick. Whisk in syrup mixture. 5. When almost set, fold in chopped fruit and pour into prepared soufflé dish. 6. When set, remove paper and decorate sides with chopped nuts. 7. Decorate top with angelica, glace cherries and pieces of lychees.

50. SOUFFLÉ au CHOCOLAT (A)

Ingredients	Quantity
Chocolate	115 gm
Butter	30 gm
Refined flour	25 gm
Egg yolks	3
Egg whites	4
Milk	150 ml
Vanilla	1 tsp
Castor sugar	1 tsp

Method

1. Break up chocolate roughly and boil in milk. Cool. 2. Melt butter. Add flour and cook for a few seconds. 3. Add chocolate and milk and cook till thickened, beating well to make smooth. 4. Cool slightly and beat in egg yolks one at a time. 5. Add vanilla and sugar. 6. Fold in stiffly-beaten egg whites and pour into a well-greased tin. 7. Cover with greased paper and steam very gently till firm. (about 45 minutes). 8. Turn out and pour custard or sherry sauce around. Serve immediately.

SOUFFLÉ au CHOCOLAT (B)

Ingredients	Quantity
Powdered gelatine	15 gm
Water	3 tbsp

Ingredients	Quantity
Cocoa powder	60 gm
Instant coffee powder	1 tbsp
Eggs	3
Milk	400 ml
Castor sugar	115 gm
Thick cream	2 tbsp

A straight-sided soufflé dish that can hold a litre of liquid will be required.

For the Decoration

Ingredients	Quantity
Chopped walnuts	60 gm
Thick cream	4 tbsp

Method

1. First prepare soufflé dish. Cut a double strip of greaseproof paper, long enough to go around the dish and overlap slightly, and wide enough to come 4 cm (about 1½") above dish. Wrap this collar tightly round outside of dish and tie it in position with a piece of thin string. 2. Put gelatine into a small pan with water and leave it on one side to soak and soften. 3. Put cocoa and coffee powder into a larger saucepan with cold milk, and stir over very gentle heat until coffee and cocoa blend smoothly with milk. 4. Bring mixture to a boil and watch it carefully lest it boil over. Simmer for one minute. Let it cool slightly. 5. Separate egg yolks from whites and put yolks into a mixing bowl with castor sugar. Beat them really well together with a wooden spoon until they are well blended. 6. Gradually stir in hot chocolate-flavoured milk. 7. Strain mixture back into pan and stir with a wooden spoon over very gentle heat until it almost comes to the boil and will lightly coat back of spoon. It must not be allowed to boil or mixture will curdle. 8. This operation can be done in a double saucepan, if available, when it is less likely to cook too quickly. Keep resulting custard aside until it is cool. 9. Dissolve gelatine and water over very gentle heat, then stir into custard. 10. Whip cream lightly and stir it into mixture. 11. Whip egg whites until they are stiff. 12. Take pan containing soufflé mixture and stand it in a tray or roasting tin surrounded by ice cubes. This speeds cooling though mixture must be stirred continually so that it does not set around the edges of the pan more quickly than in the centre. 13. As soon as mixture begins to thicken and set, fold in stiffly beaten egg whites. 14. Turn mixture immediately into prepared soufflé dish to be held in place by paper collar. 15. Leave

soufflé to set for 1½ hours. 16. It can be left overnight but the texture is much better if it is used the same day.

To Decorate the Soufflé

1. Untie string and gradually peel off paper from around soufflé, holding a knife behind paper and against edge of soufflé. 2. Whip cream very lightly so that it will just hold its shape and spread a little around edge of soufflé, this helps nuts stick to edge. 3. Fill a forcing bag with a medium star nozzle attached with rest of the cream, and pipe it in a trellis over top of soufflé. 4. Put nuts onto a piece of greaseproof paper, form them into a ring and stand the soufflé in the middle. Lift nuts on to side of soufflé with a palette knife. The soufflé is now ready to serve.

51. SOUFFLÉ au CARAMEL

Ingredients	Quantity
Sugar	150 gm
Almonds	25 gm
Cashewnuts	25 gm
Butter	15 gm
Eggs	3
Milk	450 ml
Vanilla	a few drops
Gelatine	22 gm
Cream	300 ml
Tinned cherries for decorating	300 gm

Method

1. Cream egg yolks and 100 gm sugar together. 2. Bring milk to boiling point and add gradually to mixture and heat over boiling water (double boiler) for a few seconds. 3. Remove from fire and cool. 4. Add melted gelatine and few drops of vanilla essence. 5. Strain and place on ice and bring to nearly setting point. 6. Lightly, fold in stiffly beaten egg whites. Add crushed caramel toffee. 7. Put in round glass dish and set in refrigerator. When nearly set, line greaseproof paper around edges of dish. 8. Put in more mixture and set again. When set, remove paper, apply crushed caramel toffee to open side and pipe top with whipped cream and decorate with cherries.

CARAMEL TOFFEE

1. Caramelise rest of sugar without burning. 2. Add chopped nuts and put on a greased plate.

52. BAVAROIS d'ABRICOT

Ingredients	Quantity
Dried apricots	150 gm
Cold water	3 tbsp
Gelatine (powdered)	22 gm
Sugar	115 gm
Lemon juice	a few drops
Milk	300 ml
Eggs (separated)	2
Cream	150 ml

Method

1. Put apricots in a saucepan and just cover with boiling water. 2. Cover with a lid and leave to soak for 2 hours, then simmer over gentle heat for 25 minutes until tender. 3. Keep pan covered while doing this and simmer very gently; if the water is allowed to evaporate too quickly the apricots may burn. 4. Check pan occasionally and add more water if necessary. 5. Meanwhile measure 3 tablespoons of cold water into a small basin and sprinkle gelatine on it. Set aside to soak. 6. When apricots are soft, draw pan off heat and stir in 60 gm of sugar. 7. Then pass apricots and juices in pan through a sieve to make a purée. 8. Discard any pieces of skin left in sieve. 9. Return apricots to saucepan and add soaked gelatine. Stir over very low heat just long enough to dissolve gelatine. 10. Measure milk into a saucepan and bring to almost boiling. 11. Blend egg yolks and remaining sugar in a basin, stir in hot milk and blend well. 12. Return mixture to pan and stir over low heat for 1–2 minutes, but do not allow to boil. 13. Combine fruit purée and egg mixture and set aside in a large mixing basin until cold. 14. When it begins to thicken, first fold in lightly whipped cream and then stiffly beaten egg whites. 15. Pour into a serving dish and chill until set firm. Turn out and serve with fresh cream.

53. CREME BRÛLÉE

Ingredients	Quantity
Fresh cream	300 ml
Milk	300 ml
Eggs	4
Sugar	100 gm
Icing sugar	30 gm
Vanilla essence	a few drops

Method

Dissolve sugar in milk and add whisked eggs. Return to stove to cook slowly. Add fresh cream and essence. Cook in a hot water bath in an oven till custard sets. Sprinkle icing sugar on top and glaze under a grill.

54. POMMES CHARLOTTE

Ingredients	Quantity
Bread	225 gm
Apples	450 gm
Butter	60 gm
Powdered sugar	60 gm
Lime rind	a small piece
Cinnamon	1 stick
Apricots (dry)	30 gm

Method

1. Cut one or two slices of bread into heart-shaped croutons. 2. Cut remaining bread into fingers. 3. Melt 15 gm butter. Dip bread in butter. 4. Arrange heart-shaped croutons in the centre of a well-buttered jelly mould. 5. Arrange fingers around the sides very chose together so as to completely line mould. 6. Soak apricots overnight. Stew and reduce to pulp. 7. Peel and slice apples and stew in butter with cinnamon, lime rind and powdered sugar. When apples are cooked and reduced to a thick puree, remove cinnamon and lemon rind and add apricot puree. 8. Fill mould with this mixture, shaping it like a dome above mould as it settles during cooking. 9. Bake at 170°C (about 350°F) for 30 minutes.

55. POMMES BONNE FEMME

Ingredients	Quantity
Medium-sized apples	4
Brown sugar	55 gm
Crystallized ginger	30 gm
Butter	15 gm
Water	35-45 ml

Method

1. Wash apples. Remove centre with a corer and make a cut round middle of each apple. 2. Put apples in a heat-proof dish. Fill holes with sugar and chopped ginger. 3. Place a small piece of butter on each apple and pour water around them. 4. Bake in a moderately hot oven at 250°C (about 400°F) about 45 minutes, until apples are quite tender.

N.B. Fillings for apples baked in this way may be varied to suit different tastes; golden syrup, honey or white sugar can be used instead of brown sugar and chopped dates, stoned raisins, sultanas, marmalade, currants, mincemeat, chopped walnuts, or almonds, can also be included. With sweet fillings such as dates a little lemon juice can be added.

56. PÂTÉ de POMMES

Ingredients	Quantity
Shortcrust pastry	225 gm
Cloves	4
Cooking apples	4 (500 gm)
Sugar	60 gm

Method

1. Poach apples with skin in a little sugar syrup till half-done. 2. Take out. Remove skin and core. 3. Roll out pastry 3.5 mm. thick into a square. 4. Cut into 4 even squares. 5. Dampen edges. 6. Place a cored apple in centre of each square. Pierce apple with a clove. 7. Fill centre with sugar. 8. Fold over pastry to seal completely, without breaking pastry. 9. Roll out trimmings of pastry. Cut into fancy shapes and place one over each apple. 10. Brush over with beaten egg and place on a lightly greased baking sheet. 11. Bake at 190°C (about 375°F) for about 30 minutes. 12. Serve on a silver dish with a sauceboat of custard.

57. FLAN d'ANANAS

Ingredients	Quantity
Pastry	
Refined flour	115 gm
Butter	85 gm
Egg yolk	1
Castor sugar	1 tsp
Salt	a pinch
Confectioners Custard	
Milk	150 ml
Sugar	15 gm
Refined flour	30 gm
Egg	1
Vanilla	a few drops
Tinned pineapple	1 tin
Meringues	
Egg whites	2
Castor sugar	85 gm

Method

1. Mix flour and salt. Rub in fat. Add sugar. 2. Mix with egg yolk and a little water to form a stiff paste, mixing well. 3. Roll out slightly bigger than flan tin. 4. Line greased flan tin. Trim. Prick base and fill with paper and dried peas. 5. Bake till edge is golden brown. Remove peas and allow pastry to crisp off. 6. Prepare custard. Whisk eggs and sugar till fairly thick. 7. Whisk in flour and then hot milk. 8. Boil well, whisking all the time. Flavour with vanilla. 9. When pastry is ready fill with pineapple slices. Pour custard over. 10. Bake for 15 minutes at 175°C (about 350°F). 11. Cover with meringue mixture piped on top. 12. Dredge with castor sugar. Decorate with pieces of pineapple and return to a cool oven for 20 minutes to set meringue.

58. CRÊPES GEORGETTE

Ingredients	*Quantity*
Flour	55 gm
Salt	a pinch
Milk	150 ml
Egg	1
Castor sugar	15 gm
Butter	30 gm
Pineapple (diced)	250 gm
Sugar	30 gm
Lime	1

Method

1. Sift flour with a pinch of salt. Add castor sugar. 2. Make a well in centre. Add egg. 3. Working gradually from sides make a smooth paste. 4. Add milk and stir well to form a smooth batter. Set aside for half an hour. 5. Dice pineapple. Sprinkle with sugar and lime juice. 6. Heat an omelette pan. Add a teaspoonful of butter. As butter melts pour a spoonful of batter to cover bottom of pan. 7. Fry quickly. Loosen with a knife or by shaking pan. 8. Fill with prepared diced pineapple and turn over. 9. Serve hot on a dish lined with a paper doyley. If desired sprinkle with powdered sugar.

59. BEIGNETS d'ANANAS à la FAVORITE

Ingredients	*Quantity*
Pineapple	225 gm
Sugar	30 gm
Lime	1
Franzipan Cream	
Sugar	55 gm

Ingredients	Quantity
Milk	300 ml
Eggs	3
Butter	10 gm
Pistachio nuts	15 gm
Batter	
Refined flour	30 gm
Milk	150 ml
Sugar	15 gm
Egg	1

Method

1. Slice pineapple. Sprinkle over with sugar and lime juice and allow to macerate for 30 minutes. 2. Prepare franzipan cream. Mix sugar, flour and eggs in a pan. 3. Add boiling milk, stirring briskly. Add a pinch of salt and cook on a medium fire, stirring all the time. Let it boil for a few minutes. 4. Pour into a bowl. Add butter and chopped pistachio nuts and mix well. Spread 2.5 cm thick on a buttered tray and leave to cool. Butter surface slightly. 5. Prepare batter as for pancakes, keeping it thin. 6. Coat pineapple slices with cream and allow to cool completely. 7. When ready to serve dip in batter and deep fry. 8. Drain and sprinkle with icing sugar. Serve hot.

60. RUM SAVARIN

Ingredients	Quantity
Refined flour	250 gm (2 cups)
Yeast	15 gm
Castor sugar	2 tsp
Milk and	150 ml
Water	(about ½ cup)
Butter	100 gm
Eggs	2
For glaze and filling:	
Fruit cocktail (mixed)	a large tin
Rum	2 tbsp
Apricot jam	2 tbsp
Shredded almonds (browned)	60 gm
Diamonds of angelica	8

Method

1. Sift flour and salt and into a warm mixing bowl. Put dried yeast and castor sugar into a basin. 2. Heat milk and pour on yeast. Leave yeast in a warm place to dissolve. 3. Beat eggs well and add to flour with yeast

and mix thoroughly. The mixture should have the consistency of a thick batter. Beat well and keep aside to rise. It should rise to double its original bulk. 4. Cream butter and beat into yeast mixture. Put into a greased ring mould to prove. 5. Bake in a moderate oven at 230°C (or about 450°F). Turn savarin on to a plate. Soak with fruit juice and rum. Spike sides with almonds. Brush jam over surface of ring. Fill centre with fruit and decorate with diamonds of angelica. Serve with cream.

61. POUDING de NOËL (A)

Ingredients	Quantity
Cashewnuts	115 gm
Cleaned sultanas	250 gm
Demerara sugar	250 gm
White breadcrumbs	250 gm
Salt	¼ tsp
Cleaned currants	250 gm
Large raisins (stoned & chopped)	250 gm
Chopped peel	115 gm
Refined flour	25 gm
Ground cinnamon	1 tsp
Ground nutmeg	1 tsp
Finely grated rind	1 lemon
Prepared shredded suet or Margarine	115 gm
Mixed spice	1 tsp
Eggs	3
Stout & Cider	30 ml
or Rum	1 wine glass

Method

1. A Christmas pudding takes two days to make. On the first day mix dry ingredients, on the second, prepare the basin and steam pudding. 2. First blanch almonds by pouring boiling water over them and leaving them to stand for a few minutes, when the skins will slip off easily. Skin almonds and chop them fairly finely. 3. Mix sultanas, currants, chopped raisins and chopped peel in a large mixing bowl. Stir in chopped almonds, sugar breadcrumbs, lemon rind and suet. 4. Sift flour, salt and spices together. Beat eggs and add stout. Add flour and egg mixture to other ingredients and mix them all really well together. 5. Next day, brush basin with melted fat and put mixture into it. Cover basin with doubled, greased greaseproof paper, pleated across the top to allow pudding to

rise, and tie it firmly with a string. 6. Steam large pudding for at least 8 hours, or smaller ones for 6 hours. When pudding is cold, cover it with fresh greaseproof paper and store in a cool dry place until Christmas. 7. On Christmas Day reheat pudding by steaming it in exactly the same way for at least two hours. Turn it onto a plate and decorate with holly.

POUDING de NOËL (B)

Ingredients	Quantity
Suet or Hard fat	500 gm
Fresh breadcrumbs	300 gm (5½ cups)
Refined flour	300 gm
(sifted)	(2⅓ cups)
Raisins (stoned)	150 gm
Currants	150 gm
Sultanas	150 gm
Cashewnuts (chopped)	150 gm (1 cup)
Brown sugar	250 gm (1½ cups)
Grated rind	½ lime
Orange juice	of 1 orange
Candied citron	125 gm
Candied orange peel	125 gm
Stoned prunes	150 gm
or dates	(½ cup)
Peeled & grated	250 gm
cooking apples	(2 cups)
Eggs	4
Rum	4 cups
Mixed spices	3 tbsp
(Cinnamon, Nutmeg, Ginger)	
Salt	10 gm (1⅔ tsp)

Method

1. Prepare ingredients. If suet is used, remove skin and fibre. Sprinkle with a little flour. Chop fine. 2. Chop all other ingredients after stoning. If dates are used, mince well after stoning. 3. Mix together all ingredients except eggs and rum. Stir well. 4. Add a quarter of the rum. Keep in an enamel basin in a cool place covered with a piece of muslin, and stir mixture every day, adding a few tbsp of rum each time. (This mixture can be kept for a fortnight or more). 5. When needed, stir mixture well to ensure perfect blending. 6. If mixture is too thick, add a little milk or stout. 7. Add beaten eggs. Put into greased and floured pudding bowls. 8. Cover with greaseproof paper and steam for at least 6 hours. If

desired, pudding can be steamed for 4 hours the previous day and 2–2½ hours on the day it is needed.

To serve:

Remove pudding from steamer. Let it stand for a few minutes. Turn out pudding. Sprinkle it with granulated sugar. Heat rum. Pour over pudding and set it alight when ready to serve. Serve with rum flavoured zabaglione or brandy butter or rum butter.

SAVOURIES (BONNES BOUCHES)

1. Anges à Cheval	13. Sardines en Croûtes
2. Croûte Baron	14. Canapé Laitances
3. Diables à Cheval	15. Laitances Méphisto
4. Sardines à la Diable	16. Canapé Quo Vadis
5. Rognons à la Diable (A)	17. Canapé Diane
Rognons à la Diable (B)	18. Tartelettes au Fromage
6. Rognons Norvegienne	19. Biscuits à la Duchesse
7. Canapé Charlemagne	20. Biscuits au Fromage
8. Bouchée Indienne	21. Crèmes Beatrice
9. Barquettes de Crevettes	22. Scrambled Egg Crêpes
10. Croque Monsieur	23. Waffles
11. Canapé Yorkaise	24. Beignets de Fromage
12. Croûte Radjah	25. Soufflé au Fromage

I. ANGES a CHEVAL

Ingredients	Quantity
Oysters	8
(live, removed from shell)	
Toast	2 slices (40 gm)
Cayenne pepper	a pinch
Streaky bacon	4 rashers
Butter	15 gm

Method

1. Wrap each raw oyster in half a rasher of thin streaky bacon. 2. Place on a skewer and then on a baking tray. 3. Grill gently on both sides for a few minutes. 4. Sprinkle with cayenne. 5. Cut trimmed buttered toast into 4 neat rectangles. Place two oysters on each and serve.

2. CROÛTE BARON

Ingredients	Quantity
Mushrooms (button)	60 gm
Toast	2 slices (40 gm)
Beef marrow	60 gm
Butter	15 gm
Streaky bacon	4 rashers
Toast	2 slices
Cayenne pepper	a pinch

Method

1. Peel and wash mushrooms. Brush over with a little fat. Season.
2. Place in a baking tray and grill gently on both sides for a few minutes.
3. Grill bacon on both sides. 4. Cut marrow into 1.5 cm thick slices and poach in salted stock. Remove and drain. 5. Cut and trim buttered toast into 4 neat rectangles. 6. Arrange mushrooms, bacon and marrow on toast. 7. Sprinkle with cayenne pepper and serve.

3. DIABLES à CHEVAL

Ingredients	Quantity
Prunes	8
Butter	15 gm
Chutney	60 gm
(Mango or Date or Apricot)	
Streaky bacon	4 rashers
Toast	2 slices
Cayenne pepper	a pinch

Method

1. Soak prunes overnight. Drain and stone. 2. Stuff with chutney. 3. Wrap each prune in half a rasher of bacon. 4. Skewer and place on a baking sheet and grill on both sides. 5. Cut buttered toast into 4 neat rectangles. Place two prunes on each. Sprinkle with cayenne and serve.

4. SARDINES à la DIABLE

Ingredients	Quantity
Fresh sardines	8
Mustard	to taste
Cayenne pepper	to taste
Egg	1
Breadcrumbs	
Fat	to fry
Bread	2 slices

Method

1. Skin and bone sardines. 2. Coat with mustard and cayenne. 3. Dip in egg, coat with breadcrumbs and deep fry. 4. Place on fingers of fried bread. Serve at once.

5. ROGNONS à la DIABLE (A)

Ingredients	Quantity
Sheep's kidneys	4
Butter	15 gm
Worcester sauce	1 tsp
Mustard	1 tbsp
Vinegar	1 tbsp
Salt and Pepper	to taste
Toast	2 slices

Method

1. Remove skin and gristle from kidneys and thread on skewers. 2. Season with salt and pepper. Brush with fat and grill till half done. 3. Prepare a paste with mustard, vinegar and Worcester sauce and apply liberally on both sides of the kidneys. 4. Grill for another 2 minutes on each side. 5. Serve on trimmed buttered rectangles of toast.

ROGNONS à la DIABLE (B)

Ingredients	Quantity
Sheep's kidneys	4
Toast	2 slices
Butter	60 gm
Salt and Pepper	to taste
Diable sauce	150 ml (see Sauces in Vol. I)

Method

1. Prepare kidneys as for sauté. 2. Season and fry quickly in 45 gm of butter. 3. Drain and add to boiling devilled sauce. 4. Mix and serve on buttered rectangles of toast.

6. ROGNONS NORVEGIENNE

Ingredients	Quantity
Sheep's kidneys	2
Butter	15 gm
Olive (chopped)	1
Gherkin (chopped)	1

Ingredients	Quantity
Salt	to taste
Cayenne pepper	to taste
Chopped parsley	1 tsp
Thin bacon rashers	4
Egg	1
Breadcrumbs	
Fat	to fry
Garnish	
Fried parsley	

Method

1. Cut up kidneys and sauté in butter. 2. Add chopped olive, gherkin, seasoning and parsley. Mix well. 3. Spread on a plate to cool. 4. Cut bacon 5 cm long and roll around a teaspoon of kidney mixture. 5. Coat with egg and breadcrumbs. Deep fry in fat. Garnish with fried parsley.

7. CANAPE CHARLEMAGNE

Ingredients	Quantity
Prawns (shelled and boiled)	115 gm
Curry sauce	150 ml (see Sauces in Vol. I)
Toast	2 slices
Butter	15 gm

Method

1. Boil curry sauce. Add shrimps or prawns and simmer for 2–3 minutes.
2. Dress on round pieces of buttered toast and serve.

8. BOUCHÉE INDIENNE

Ingredients	Quantity
Puff pastry cases	4
Prawns (shelled and boiled)	115 gm
Curry sauce	150 ml
Date chutney	15 gm

Method

1. Boil curry sauce. Add prawns. Simmer for 2–3 minutes. 2. Warm bouchées through in a moderate oven. 3. Fill bouchées. Put a little chutney on each. Replace lid and serve.

9. BARQUETTES de CREVETTES

Ingredients	Quantity
Pastry boats made with 60 gm of shortcrust pastry	
Garnish	
Chopped parsley	
Filling	
Prawns (shelled and boiled)	100 gm
Mayonnaise sauce	75 ml
Red radish	6
Cayenne pepper	to taste

Method

1. Prepare 12 small boat-shaped pastry cases. Bake and cool. 2. Chop prawns and add to mayonnaise. 3. Fill pastry boats with prepared filling. 4. Garnish with chopped parsley, slices of red radish and cayenne pepper.

10. CROQUE MONSIEUR

Ingredients	Quantity
Cooked ham	4 slices
Toast	8 slices
Cheese	8 slices
Clarified butter	60 gm

Method

1. Put each slice of ham between 2 slices of cheese and then between 2 slices of lightly buttered toast. 2. Cut out with a round cutter, gently fry on both sides in clarified butter and serve.

11. CANAPÉ YORKAISE

Ingredients	Quantity
Cooked ham	115 gm
Toast	2 slices (40 gm)
Béchamel sauce	300 ml
Butter	15 gm

Method

1. Cut eight neat diamonds of ham for decoration. 2. Neatly dice remaining ham and bind with boiling béchamel. 3. Simmer for 2–3 minutes. Season with cayenne. 4. Dress on round buttered toast. Place two diamonds of ham on each toast and serve.

12. CROÛTE RADJAH

Ingredients	Quantity
Chopped cooked ham	115 gm
Mango chutney	30 gm
Butter	15 gm
Curry sauce	150 ml
Toast	2 slices

Method

1. Simmer ham in curry sauce for 2–3 minutes. 2. Dress on buttered rectangles or rounds of toast. Put a little chutney on each and serve.

13. SARDINES en CROÛTES

Ingredients	Quantity
Tinned sardines	4
Bread	2 slices
Clarified butter	60 gm
Cayenne pepper	a pinch

Method

1. Cut bread into fingers. Fry in clarified butter. 2. Put a sardine on each slice. Sprinkle with cayenne.

14. CANAPÉ LAITANCES

Ingredients	Quantity
Soft roe	6
Seasoned flour	10 gm
Butter	15 gm
Toast	2 slices
Cayenne pepper	a pinch

Method

1. Pass roe through seasoned flour. 2. Shake off surplus flour and grill or shallow fry on both sides. 3. Dress on rectangles of buttered toast and serve.

15. LAITANCES MÉPHISTO

Ingredients	Quantity
Herring roe or	
Soft roe	170 gm
Shortcrust pastry boats	4
Devilled sauce	150 ml

Method

1. Cook roe as for Canapé Laitances. 2. Warm pastry boats in an oven.
3. Mix roe with devilled sauce and fill pastry boats.

16. CANAPÉ QUO VADIS

Ingredients	Quantity
Mushrooms	85 gm
Soft roe	85 gm
Toast	2 slices
Butter	15 gm
Salt	

Method

1. Peel and wash mushrooms. Place on a baking tray. Season with salt.
2. Brush with melted fat and gently grill on both sides. 3. Dip soft roe
in seasoned flour. Remove surplus and grill or shallow fry on both sides.
4. Dress neatly on rectangles of buttered toast. Sprinkle with cayenne
and serve.

17. CANAPÉ DIANE

Ingredients	Quantity
Chicken livers	4
Butter	15 gm
Stready bacon	4 rashers
Toast	2 slices
Cayenne pepper	a pinch

Method

1. Roll each half liver in half a rasher of thin bacon. 2. Place on a skewer
and then on a baking tray. 3. Grill gently on both sides for a few minutes.
4. Sprinkle with cayenne pepper. 5. Cut trimmed buttered toast into four
rectangles, place two livers on each and serve.

18. TARTELETTES au FROMAGE

Ingredients	Quantity
Rough puff pastry	115 gm
Filling	
White sauce	150 ml
Cayenne pepper	a pinch
Salt	to taste
Grated cheese	60 gm
Eggs	2

Method

1. Line pastry tins with pastry. 2. Mix cheese, white sauce, egg yolks and seasoning. 3. Add stiffly whisked egg whites. 4. Fill tins and bake in a quick oven for 20 minutes.

19. BISCUITS à la DUCHESSE

Ingredients	Quantity
Cooked chicken	30 gm
Thick white sauce	1 tsp
Garnish	
Red radish slices or Watercress	
Cream	1 dsp.
Butter	10 gm
Cayenne pepper	to taste
Salt	to taste
Cheese biscuits	6

Method

1. Mince chicken and mix with sauce, butter and seasoning. Add cream.
2. Using a meringue nozzle pipe large stars of mixture onto biscuits.
3. Decorate with red radish slices or with watercress.

20. BISCUITS au FROMAGE

Ingredients	Quantity
Cheese pastry Cream	75 ml
Grated cheese	1 tsp
Heart of celery (finely chopped)	1 tsp
Red radish or watercress	

Method

1. Cut rounds of pastry 3 cm diameter. Prick well and bake. 2. Half whisk cream and mix with celery, cheese and seasoning. 3. Pipe onto cooled biscuits. Garnish with watercress or slices of red radish.

21. CRÈMES BEATRICE

Ingredients	Quantity
Eggs	2
Grated cheese	30 gm
Cream	2 tbsp

Coating

**Egg and
Breadcrumbs**

Garnish

Fried parsley

Method

1. Beat eggs slightly. Add cheese, cream and seasoning. 2. Fill 6 small greased bouchée moulds. 3. Place in a tin containing a little water in a moderate oven till set. 4. Turn out. When cold, coat with egg and breadcrumbs. Fry in deep fat. 5. Serve garnished with fried parsley.

22. SCRAMBLED EGG CRÊPES

Ingredients	For 11
Eggs	3
Milk	30 ml
Butter	10 gm
Salt	to taste
For Sauce	
Refined flour	60 gm
Butter	60 gm
Milk	300 ml
Pepper	2 gm
Salt	to taste
Cheese	100 gm

Method

1. In a bowl, combine eggs, milk and salt. 2. In 25 cm frying pan, scramble egg mixture in butter till just set. 3. Put about 1 dsp. cooked egg in centre of each crepe. 4. Fold ends over. Place, seam side down, in 30 cm × 18 cm × 5 cm baking dish.

Sauce

1. In a saucepan, melt butter. Blend in flour, salt and pepper. 2. Add milk. Cook and stir till thickened and bubbly. 3. Stir in cheese. Pour over crepes. Bake covered at 190°C (375°F) for 20–25 minutes.

For Crêpes

Ingredients	Quantity
Refined flour	150 gm
Milk	100 ml
Water	100 ml

Ingredients	Quantity
Egg	1
Salt	to taste
Butter	for cooking

Method

1. Put salt and flour into a bowl and pour in milk stirring all the while.
2. Add beaten egg and water. Beat well and let it stand for 15 minutes.
3. Melt a little butter in an omelette pan. When it is very hot, add a spoonful of batter and turn pan from side to side so that batter spreads very thinly and evenly over pan. 4. When bottom is done, turn pancake and brown on the other side.

23. WAFFLES

Ingredients	Quantity
Flour	110 gm
Butter	2 tsp
Baking powder	1 level tsp
Egg	1
Milk	½–1 cup
Salt	to taste
Sugar	optional
Butter	1 tsp

Method

1. Sieve flour and baking powder into a bowl. 2. Separate egg whites and yolks. Beat together egg yolks and milk. Add salt and sugar if used. 3. Pour over flour and blend well to form a smooth batter. Add stiffly beaten egg white and melted butter. 4. our over pre-heated and buttered waffle iron. Bake for 2 minutes or till steam no longer escapes from side. 5. Serve hot buttered with honey/palm treacle (pani)/golden syrup or chicken or meat curry.

24. BEIGNETS de FROMAGE

Ingredients	Quantity
Water	150 ml
Eggs	2
Refined flour	75 gm
Grated cheese	60 gm
Margarine	60 gm
Cayenne pepper	to taste
Salt	to taste

Method

1. Bring water and margarine to a boil in a thick-bottomed pan.
2. Remove from heat. Add flour and mix with a wooden spoon. 3. Return to gentle heat and mix well until mixture leaves sides of pan. 4. Remove from heat. Allow to cool slightly. 5. Gradually add eggs, beating well. 6. Add cheese and seasoning. 7. Using a spoon, scoop out mixture in walnut-sized portions. 8. Place in deep hot fat and allow to cook with minimum handling for approximately 10 minutes. 9. Drain and serve on a silver flat on paper. 10. Sprinkle with grated parmesan cheese.

25. SOUFFLÉ au FROMAGE

Ingredients	Quantity
Butter	30 gm
Milk	150 ml
Egg whites	4
Refined flour	20 gm
Egg yolks	3
Grated cheese	60 gm
Cayenne pepper	a pinch
Salt	to taste

Method

1. Melt butter in a thick-bottomed pan. 2. Add flour and mix with a wooden spoon. 3. Cook for a few seconds without colouring. 4. Gradually add cold milk and mix to a smooth sauce. 5. Simmer for a few minutes. 6. Add one egg yolk. Mix in quickly and immediately remove from heat. 7. When cool, add remaining egg yolks. Season with salt, pepper and cheese. 8. Place egg whites with a pinch of salt in a scrupulously clean bowl and whisk until stiff. 9. Add one-eighth of the whites to mixture and mix well. 10. Gradually fold in remaining egg whites. Mix lightly. 11. Pour into a buttered soufflé mould and bake in a hot oven for approximately 15–20 minutes. 12. Remove from oven. Place on a round flat silver dish and serve immediately.

RECIPES FROM FAR AND NEAR

FRANCE

1. Tomates aux Crevettes
2. Oeufs Farcis aux Sardines
3. Croutes au Jambon à la Ménagère
4. Petite Marmite
5. Bouillabaisse
6. Oeufs Noyés
7. Oeufs à la Mimosa
8. Oeufs à la Bretonne
9. Maquereau au beurre Noir
10. Saumon à la Bretonne
11. Homard à la Diable
12. Gigot Rôti à l'Ail
13. Rôti de Porc à ma Façon
14. Poulet àla Navaressa
15. Poulet à la Provençale
16. Crêpes Suzette

GERMANY

1. Kartoffel Suppe
2. Makrel in Ragoût
3. Fisch in Pikanter Sauce
4. Fish Balls with Spinach
5. Konigsberger Klops
6. Stuben Kuecken
7. Blumenkohl Salat
8. Affelsinenbiscuitort Ungefult
9. Apfelstrudel

SPAIN

1. Escudella Catalina
2. Gazpacho (A) Gazpacho (B)
3. Pastel de Tortillas Especial
4. Tortillas
5. Salmon à la Alicantina
6. Sardinas Fritas
7. Camarones Fritos
8. Pelota
9. Chuletas de Tocino con Salsa de Tomate
10. Chuletas de Cordero Vilareal
11. Spanish Rice
12. Spanish Rice Omelette
13. Paella à la Valencina
14. Arroz Estilo Barcelones
15. Pato Alcaparrada
16. Alcachofas de Jerusalem al Gratin
17. Berenjenas Salteadas
18. Churros
19. Chocolate Creams

ITALY

1. Chicken Tartlets
2. Chicken Liver Tartlets
3. Haricot Bean Soup
4. Zuppa Paradiso
5. Zuppa Pavese
6. Noodles with Tuna Sauce
7. Spaghetti with Meat Balls
8. Prawn Risotto
9. Chicken Risotto
10. Pizza
11. Chicken as served in Rome
12. Amaretti
13. Osso Bucco
14. Potato Croquettes
15. Zabaglione

U.S.S.R.

1. Caviar with Eggs
2. Forshmak
3. Studen
4. Cucumber with Smetana
5. Caucasian Salad
6. Pokhlyobka
7. Lazy Shchy
8. Armenian Soup
9. Baked Fish in Sour Cream Sauce
10. Stuffed Fish
11. Crab in Egg Sauce
12. Beef Stroganoff
13. Stuffed Meat Loaf
14. Chakhokhbily
15. Caucasian Shashlik
16. Ham Pasties
17. French Beans with Mushrooms
18. Apple Kissel
19. Malakoff Cake
20. Apple Soufflé

NETHERLANDS

1. Spinazie Soep
2. Vischkoekjes
3. Hutspot
4. Gestoofde Komkommers
5. Flensjes

SCANDINAVIA

1. Mackerel for the Smorgasbord
2. Grapefruit with Shrimps
3. Meat Balls for Smorgasbord
4. Alesondigas
5. White Coleslaw
6. Chicken Salad
7. Lamb and Vegetable Soup
8. Spring Soup
9. Fish Fillets with Mushrooms and Vegetables
10. Baked Fish
11. Kaldolmar
12. Finare Lammragu
13. Roasted Spare Ribs
14. Danish Parsley Chicken
15. Chocolate Chiffon Pudding
16. Norwegian Biscuits

PORTUGAL

1. Ovos Duros a Portuguesa
2. Lobster a Portuguesa
3. Chicken a Portuguesa
4. Tomatoes with Sardine Stuffing
5. Pudim de Noses
6. Fio de Ovos
7. Saurbraten

UNITED STATES OF AMERICA

1. Tomato Juice Cocktail
2. Ginger Fruit Cocktail
3. Strawberry Cocktail
4. Chicken Gumbo Soup (A)
   Chicken Gumbo Soup (B)
5. Prawn/Shrimp Gumbo
6. Okra Soup
7. Devilled Crab

8. Lobster à la King
9. Prawn/Shrimp Créole
10. New Orleans Shrimp
11. Tuna Puffs
12. Fried Chicken

13. Boston Baked Beans
14. Red Pumpkin
15. Waldorf Salad
16. Apple Crisp
17. Carrot Pudding

GREECE

1. Soupa Avgolemono
2. Psarosoupa
3. Psari Plaku
4. Lamb Kebab
5. Moussaka à la Grecque
6. Greek Béchamel
7. Aubergine Sauce
8. Youvarlakia with Avgo Lemono Sauce

9. Chicken Pilaff
10. Aubergines with Peppers
11. Ladies' Fingers with Aubergines
12. Tzaziki
13. Cabbage Dolmas
14. Potato Kephtides
15. Honey Puffs
16. Baklava

TURKEY

1. Wedding Soup
2. Turquoise
3. Baked Fish
4. Shish Kebab
5. Braised Kebab

6. Meat with Okra
7. Dolmas
8. Chicken à la Ture
9. Pumpkin Dessert
10. Turkish Coffee

CHINA

1. Sweet Corn and Chicken Soup
2. Fresh Corn Egg Flower Soup
3. Chicken Clear Soup
4. Asparagus Chicken Soup
5. Chicken Noodle Soup
6. Chicken And Mushroom Soup
7. Vegetable Egg Cream Soup
8. Egg Drop Spinach Soup
9. Hot and Sour Soup
10. Wontons
11. Wonton Soup
12. Egg Fu Yong
13. Brinjal in Garlic Sauce
14. Vegetable Chow Chow
15. Prawns in Garlic Sauce
16. Fried Prawns

17. Mandarin Fish
18. Sweet and Sour Fish
19. Sweet and Sour Prawns
20. Sweet and Sour Pork (A)
    Sweet and Sour Pork (B)
    Sweet and Sour Pork (C)
21. Pork Fritters
22. Deep Fried Spring Chicken
23. Chicken in Garlic Sauce
24. Sweet and Sour Chicken
25. Chicken Chili
26. Chicken Shreds with Chili
27. Chicken Pineapple
28. Fried Chicken
29. Broiled Chicken
30. Hakka Noodles
31. Chow Mein

32. Chinese Noodles
33. Stewed Noodles
34. Chop Suey
35. American Chop Suey
36. Chinese Vegetables
37. Vegetable Fried Rice
38. Chinese Fried Rice
39. Garlic Spare Ribs

JAPAN

1. Tamago Suimono
2. Tempura
3. Suki Yaki

BURMA

1. Chicken Kauswey
2. Balachaung
3. Moh Kya Lapphed
4. Tamarind Lethoka
5. Lathok

SRI LANKA

1. Idde Appung
2. Polmallung
3. Seeni Sambal
4. Kirihoti
5. Mulugutawnny
6. Moju
7. Ceylon Chicken Curry
8. Prawn Badun
9. Kalu Dodol

INDONESIA

1. Ajam Dalam Kelapa
2. Tahitian Chicken Saute
3. Adobo
4. Ajap Djahe

INDIA

1. Yakhni Shorba
2. Tomato Shorba
3. Smoked Pomfret (A)
   Smoked Pomfret (B)
4. Vegetable Jalfraizi
5. Panir Makhani
6. Palak Panir
7. Makhani Dal
8. Kaleji/Kapura
9. Gurda
10. Boti Kabab
11. Reshmi Kabab
12. Tangri Kabab (A)
    Tangri Kabab (B)
13. Chicken Malai Kabab
14. Kadai Ghosht
15. Achar Ghosht
16. Burani
17. Chicken Moghlai
18. Chicken Afghani
19. Chicken Zaibunissa
20. Chicken Shahjahani
21. Chicken Curry Kashmiri
22. Afghani Chicken Khorma
23. Galinha Cafrel
24. Chicken Cafrel
25. Chicken Jaipuri
26. Tandoori Chicken
27. Chicken Tikka
28. Charga

29. Spicy Chicken Saute
30. Chicken Farcha
31. Ranchers Fried Chicken

32 Fried Chicken
33. Muslim Biryani
34. Chicken Biryani

CHETTINAD

1. Nandu Masala
2. Yeera Masala
3. Karuvepellai Yera
4. Porcha Meen Fried Fish
5. Meen Varuval (Fish Fried) Chettinad
6. Meen Kozhambu (Chettinad)
7. Chicken Pepper Fry
8. Chicken Chettinad
9. Koli Porchathu
10. Chicken Pepper Fry
11. Koli Rasama
12. Kola Urunda Kolambu
13. Kari Kolambu
14. Uppu Curry
15. Kari Podimas
16. Samba Saadam
17. Kathrikai Ketti Kozhambu Brinjal Curry
18. Katrikai Kara Kozhumbu
19. Kathrikai Avial
20. Cauliflower Pal Kootu
21. Kaikari Perattal

22. Mushroom Kootu
23. Parangikka Pulicurry
24. Manthakkali Keera
25. Kothorakka Karamani Pachadi
26. Gundu Porial
27. Kizhangu Karvadu Varuval
28. Senai Poriyal
29. Kalan Melagu
30. Paruppu Urundal Kozhambu
31. Vendakai More Kozhumbu
32. Vendakai Mandi
33. Panagam
34. Idly
35. Idiyappam
36. Dosai
37. Appam
38. Kadhambam Chutney
39. Thengai Chutney
40. Tomato Chutney
41. Kothamali Chutney
42. Pal Kozhukattai

THAILAND

1. Tom Yom

2. Momo

ROMANIA

1. Poulet Sauté Roumain

2. Poulet Sauté Princess

NEPAL

1. Jogi Bhath

FRANCE

1. TOMATES aux CREVETTES (TOMATOES WITH SHRIMPS)

Ingredients	Quantity
Tomatoes (large)	4
Mayonnaise sauce	300 ml
Shelled shrimps or Prawns	225 gm
Lettuce leaves	4

Method

1. Cut tops off tomatoes. 2. Empty with a spoon. Season tomato shells with salt and stand them for a few minutes to drain. 3. Cook shrimps in salted water. Drain and when cold mix with mayonnaise. 4. Stuff tomatoes with mixture and serve each on a lettuce leaf.

2. ŒUFS FARCIS aux SARDINES (EGGS WITH SARDINE STUFFING)

Ingredients	Quantity
Eggs (hard-boiled)	6
Sardines (tinned)	7
Gherkin	1
Butter	3 tbsp
Bread slices	6 rectangles
Salt and Pepper	to taste

Method

1. Shell eggs and cut off tops at one end, just enough to uncover yolks.
2. Scoop out yolks with a small spoon taking care not to break whites.
3. Mash yolks. Cream butter and add mashed yolks. 4. Bone sardines. Pass through a sieve. Add to egg mixture. Season to taste and cream well. 5. Stuff eggs with mixture. 6. Trim bread. Spread with remaining mixture and place eggs cut side down on bread. 7. Decorate with slices of gherkins.

3. CROÛTES au JAMBON à la MÉNAGÈRE

Ingredients	Quantity
Bread	6 slices
Ham (cooked)	115 gm
Butter	30 gm
Refined flour	10 gm
Milk (boiling)	150 ml
Egg whites (beaten)	2
Salt and Pepper	to taste

Method

1. Remove crusts from bread slices and cut into two triangles each.
2. Mince lean ham. 3. Heat butter. Stir in flour and cook, stirring gently for two or three minutes. 4. Add boiling milk and prepare a thick white sauce. Season with salt and pepper. 5. Reduce by half, stirring all the while. 6. Add finely chopped ham and stiffly beaten egg whites. 7. Spread mixture on pieces of bread and deep fry in hot fat for about 6 minutes. Serve hot.

4. PETITE MARMITE

Ingredients	For 8–10
Boiling fowl	1
Water	3 litre
Carrots	340 gm
Onions	340 gm
Celery	1 stick
Veal bones	2
Leeks	2
Turnips	115 gm
Cabbage	225 gm
Thyme	1 sprig
Bay leaf	½
Cloves	2
Salt and Pepper	to taste
Grated cheese	
Toasted bread	

Method

1. Put fowl and veal bones into a saucepan with water, thyme, bay leaf, onions stuck with cloves, salt and pepper. 2. Bring to a boil and simmer for 12 minutes. 3. Remove fowl. Cool and remove fat on top. Strain. 4. Dice some of white meat of fowl. 5. Chop all vegetables (except cabbage) and put them with diced chicken into soup. 6. Simmer till vegetables are tender. 7. Chop and boil cabbage separately and add to soup. 8. Warm 10 earthenware tureens. Fill them with soup, chopped vegetables and chicken. 9. Serve with tiny pieces of toast and grated cheese.

5. BOUILLABAISSE (PROVENÇALE FISH SOUP)

Ingredients	Quantity
Lobster	1
Turbot	115 gm
Brill	115 gm
Saffron	½ tsp

Ingredients	Quantity
Onions	250 gm
Tomatoes	340 gm
Whiting	115 gm
Eel	115 gm
Crab	115 gm
Bream	225 gm
Olive oil	150 ml
Garlic	4 flakes
Thyme	a pinch
Bay leaf	½
Parsley	1 sprig
Toasted bread	8 pieces

Method

1. Boil lobster and remove from shell. 2. Clean fish. Bone and cut into 5 cm. long pieces. 3. Crush garlic and place in a sauce pan, with finely chopped onions, and tomatoes skinned and quartered. 4. Add olive oil and all spices. 5. Add fish. 6. Cover with boiling water and boil on a very hot fire for 10 minutes. 7. Place pieces of toast in 8 soup plates and cover with fish, making sure that each plate has a full variety of fish. 8. Pour soup over fish and serve at once.

N.B. An Indian version can be prepared with a variety of white fish in place of French variety.

6. OEUFS NOYÉS

Ingredients	Quantity
Water	2.5 litre
Onions (small)	200 gm
Leeks (white part only)	4
Garlic	1 flake
Eggs	4
Bread	4 slices
Thyme	a pinch
Salt and Pepper	to taste
Saffron	a pinch
Olive oil	1 tbsp

Method

1. Chop up onions and leeks and put them in cold water. 2. Add well-crushed garlic, thyme, salt and pepper. 3. Put lid on pan and boil for 20 minutes. 4. Put in a pinch of saffron and olive oil and boil for another 5 minutes. 5. Carefully break each egg into this soup and let it poach, removing each when it is done. Keep warm. 6. Fry each piece of

bread crisply brown in olive oil. 7. Warm 4 deep, wide soup plates. Place a piece of bread in each, an egg on each piece of bread and pour soup over.

7. OEUFS à la MIMOSA

Ingredients	Quantity
Eggs (hard-boiled)	6
Mayonnaise sauce	300 ml
Parsley (chopped)	1 dsp

Method

1. Cut hard-boiled eggs in half lengthwise. 2. Place them cut-side down on a serving dish. 3. Pour over them 1 cup of mayonnaise sauce highly seasoned and less solid than usual (add a little water to dilute). 4. Sprinkle chopped parsley over and serve.

8. OEUFS à la BRETONNE

Ingredients	Quantity
Eggs	4
Potatoes (medium-sized)	8 (about 450 gm)
Shallots (chopped)	1 tbsp
Grated cheese	30 gm
Salt and Pepper	

Method

1. Peel potatoes. Boil in salted water. 2. Hard-boil eggs. Plunge into cold water. Remove, shell immediately and keep warm. 3. Make fairly thick béchamel sauce. Add shallots and a good helping of salt and pepper. 4. Quarter well-cooked but firm potatoes. 5. Butter a fireproof dish. 6. Lay potatoes at bottom alternating with eggs cut lengthwise in two. 7. Pour béchamel sauce over eggs and potatoes and sprinkle with grated cheese. 8. Place in a medium oven for 10 minutes till cheese melts. Remove and serve hot.

9. MAQUEREAU au BEURRE NOIR

Ingredients	Quantity
Mackerels	2
Capers	1 tbsp
Grated cheese	1 tbsp
Potatoes (boiled)	
Black butter sauce	
Butter	60 gm
Vinegar	1 tbsp

Method

1. Simmer cleaned fish in salted water for 40 minutes. 2. Drain and remove backbone. Place in a hot dish. 3. Sprinkle with capers and grated cheese. 4. Cover with black butter sauce and serve with boiled potatoes.

Black butter Sauce

1. Melt butter and cook until it becomes brown (not black) and pour over fish. 2. Swirl pan with vinegar. Reduce to half and pour over butter.

10. SAUMON à la BRETONNE

Ingredients	For 6
Fresh salmon	1 kg
Mushrooms	6
Butter	60 gm
Lime	½
Parsley	a few sprigs
Salt and Pepper	to taste

Method

1. Clean and cut salmon into small cubes. 2. Slice unpeeled mushrooms lengthwise. 3. Heat half the butter. Put in salmon, mushrooms and seasoning and fry till half done. 4. Place pan in a hot oven to finish cooking. 5. Brown remaining butter. Remove from fire. Add chopped parsley and juice of half-lime. 6. Pour over cooked salmon and mushrooms and serve.

11. HOMARD à la DIABLE

Ingredients	Quantity
Lobster	1
Egg yolks	2
Mustard	1 tsp
Lime	1
Parsley	a few sprigs
Butter	115 gm
Egg (hard-boiled)	1
Salt and Pepper, and Cayenne	to taste

Method

1. Cook lobster in boiling salted water. 2. Remove from shell and cut into 2.5 cm. pieces. Keep hot. 3. Melt butter over hot water. Add chopped parsley and lime juice, salt, pepper and cayenne. 4. Thicken with egg yolks. 5. Put mustard into a bowl. Add sauce slowly, stirring all the time till it has a smooth creamy texture. Keep it warm. 6. Place lobster pieces

in a hot serving dish. Cover with sauce and decorate with slices of lemon and hard-boiled egg. Serve hot.

12. GIGOT RÔTI à l'AIL (LEG OF LAMB WITH GARLIC)

Ingredients	Quantity
Leg of lamb	1 (about 1.3 kg)
Butter	115 gm
Salt and Pepper	to taste
Garlic	2 flakes
Boiling water	300 ml

Method

1. Insert garlic flakes near the bone in leg of lamb. 2. Place leg in a roasting dish. Season with salt and pepper and cover with butter. 3. Cook for 30 minutes at 205°C (about 400°F), basting frequently. Remove. 4. Remove grease from baking tin. 5. Add water. Boil for a few minutes, scraping bottom of pan with a wooden spoon. 6. Pour this liquid into a sauceboat and serve with leg of lamb.

13. RÔTI de PORC à ma FAÇON

Ingredients	Quantity
Loin of pork	1.35 kg
Apples	1 kg
Butter	90 gm
Prunes	450 gm
Salt and Pepper	to taste

Method

1. Soak prunes overnight. Drain. Cover in cold water and bring to a boil. 2. Continue boiling for 7 minutes. 3. Peel apples and slice finely. Place in a saucepan with 60 gm of butter and cook gently for 1 hour, taking care that apples do not stick or burn. 4. Press through a sieve and keep warm. 5. Season and roast loin of pork for 1½ hours in a moderate oven with 30 gm butter. 6. Slice cooked pork. Place in an entrée dish. 7. Surround with prunes and serve apple sauce separately.

14. POULET à la NAVARESSA

Ingredients	Quantity
Young chicken	1
Ham	115 gm
Stock	600 ml
Carrots	340 gm
Leeks	2

Ingredients	Quantity
Butter	115 gm
Lime	½
Refined flour	1 tbsp
Onions	250 gm
Mint	½ bunch
Salt and Pepper	to taste
Bouqut grani	
Boiled rice	

Method

1. Chop mint and mix well with half the butter. 2. Clean chicken and stuff with mint butter. 3. Cover breast of chicken with more butter and roast for 20 minutes. 4. Place chicken in a casserole. Surround with chopped onions, carrots, leeks and ham. 5. Add bouquet garni. Season with salt and pepper. 6. Cover with stock. Add lime juice. Gently simmer in an oven for 45 minutes. 7. Mix flour with fat at bottom of roasting tin. When flour colours a little, add some liquid from casserole, stirring well. 8. Boil for a few minutes and return mixture to casserole. Stir well and simmer a little longer. 9. Place chicken in a hot dish. Surround with vegetables, ham and sauce. 10. Serve with boiled rice.

15. POULET à la PROVENÇALE (CHICKEN WITH GARLIC)

Ingredients	Quantity
Chicken	1
Garlic	5 flakes
Shallot	1
Breadcrumbs	115 gm
Milk	75 ml
Stock	75 ml
Olive oil	45 ml
Butter	60 gm
Salt and Pepper	to taste
Parsley	a few sprigs

Method

1. Clean chicken and keep liver aside. Put 3 flakes of garlic inside chicken. Season. 2. Spread butter over breast and bake in a moderately hot oven for about 35 minutes. 3. Mix chopped chicken liver, chopped shallot and garlic, milk, breadcrumbs, parsley, salt, 1 tablespoon olive oil and stock. 4. Stuff chicken with this mixture. 5. Heat remaining oil and fry chicken gently for about 15–20 minutes, turning frequently. 4. Serve with a salad.

16. CRÊPES SUZETTE

Ingredients	Quantity (16 pancakes)
Refined flour	170 gm
Eggs	2
Salt	a pinch
Milk	300 ml
Water	150 ml (approx.)
Orange juice	½ orange
Olive oil	1 dsp
Butter for cooking	

Sauce	
Orange juice	1 orange
Sugar	1 tbsp
Cointreau	1½ tbsp
Lime	¼

Method

1. Put salt and flour into a bowl and pour in milk, stirring all the while. 2. Add beaten eggs, water, orange juice and olive oil. 3. Beat well and leave to stand for 15 minutes. 4. Melt a little butter in an omelette pan. 5. When it is very hot add a spoonful of batter and turn pan from side to side so that batter spreads very thinly and evenly over the pan. 6. When bottom is done, turn pancake and brown other side. 7. Fold pancake into four. Place in a warm, fairly deep dish and cover with a napkin. 8. Continue until batter is all used up. 9. Prepare sauce by boiling orange juice and lime juice with sugar till sugar is dissolved. 10. Add Cointreau. 11. Pour this sauce over pancake. Light with a match and carry flaming to table.

GERMANY

1. KARTOFFEL SUPPE (CREAM OF POTATO SOUP)

Ingredients	Quantity
Mashed potatoes	2 cups
White sauce (thin)	3 cups (750 ml)
Salt	to taste
Pepper	a pinch
Nutmeg	a pinch
Parsley	a few sprigs
Onions	1
Butter	30 gm

Method

1. Season white sauce. Add mashed potatoes. Pass through a sieve. 2. Mix well. Cook over hot water for 10 minutes. 3. Serve hot, garnished with chopped parsley and onion rings dredged and fried in butter.

2. MAKREL in RAGOÛT (MACKEREL STEW)

Ingredients	Quantity
Mackerels (large)	4
Onions	225 gm
Water	300 ml
Gingerbread cakes	2 (small)
Vinegar	150 ml
Syrup	1 tbsp
Lime slices	a few
Chopped parsley	a few sprigs
Salt	to taste

Method

1. Peel onions and slice very thinly. Simmer in salted water till tender. 2. Put well-cleaned and gutted fish into a casserole. Pour onion with liquid over. 3. Cook in a hot oven for 20 minutes. 4. Crumble gingerbread into vinegar and syrup. 5. Take out fish. Remove backbones. 6. Pour gingerbread mixture into a large dish. 7. Arrange mackerels over mixture. Decorate with thin slices of lemon and chopped parsley. 8. Serve hot.

3. FISCH in PIKANTER SAUCE (FISH WITH PIQUANT SAUCE)

Ingredients	Quantity
Fresh haddock	1 kg
Butter	60 gm
Refined flour	15 gm
Small mushrooms	115 gm
Chopped parsley	½ tbsp
Minced onions	2 tbsp
Capers	1 tbsp
Lime	½
Mustard	½ tsp
Meat extract	½ tsp
Water	150 ml
Salt and Pepper	150 ml

Method

1. Cut haddock into medium-sized pieces. Rub with salt, coat with parsley and set aside for 30 minutes. 2. Mix butter, flour and mustard

to a stiff paste. 3. Stir in meat extract, water, lime juice and pepper and add to paste. 4. Pour a little of this sauce into a casserole. 5. Lay fish and sliced mushrooms in sauce. 6. Sprinkle with onions and capers. 7. Cover with rest of sauce. 8. Place a piece of buttered paper over casserole and put on the lid. 9. Stand casserole in a large pan of boiling water and cook for 30–35 minutes.

4. FISH BALLS WITH SPINACH

Ingredients	Quantity
Fish	500 gm
Bread	15 gm
Refined flour	10 gm
Egg	1
Onions	15 gm
Milk	30 ml
Spinach	500 gm
Anchovies	a few fillets
Breadcrumbs	20 gm
Salt and Pepper and Nutmeg	to taste
Butter	30 gm
Fat	to fry

Method

1. Boil fish in bouillon. 2. Bone and skin. Mix with bread soaked in milk and squeezed. 3. Add finely chopped onions sautéed in a little butter. 4. Season with salt, pepper and nutmeg. 5. Shape into rissoles. Dip in flour, then in egg and breadcrumbs and deep fry. 6. Drain on absorbent paper and serve garnished with chopped spinach cooked in butter to which some chopped anchovy has been added.

5. KONIGSBERGER KLOPS

Ingredients	Quantity
Meat	500 gm
Bread	2 slices (soaked in milk)
Onions	1
Eggs	2
Anchovy essence	1 tbsp
Salt and Pepper	to taste
Fat	to fry
Sauce	
Butter	30 gm
Refined flour	15 gm
Stock	300 ml

Ingredients	Quantity
Anchovies	2 or 3
Capers	1 tsp
Mustard	1 tsp
Sugar	1 tsp
Lemon	2–3 slices
Egg yolks	2
Salt and Pepper	to taste

Method

1. Mince meat. Add bread soaked in milk and squeezed out, finely chopped onion, anchovy essence, salt, pepper and eggs. Mix well. 2. Shape into balls 7.5 cm. (about 3") in diameter and fry lightly in fat. 3. Prepare sauce. Melt butter. Mix with flour and cook slightly. 4. Add stock gradually, stirring all the time. 5. Add chopped anchovies, capers, mustard, pepper, salt and slices of lemon. 6. Cook for 10 minutes and pour over klops. 7. Cover saucepan and simmer for 2 minutes. 8. Just before serving add 2 egg yolks mixed with a little melted butter.

6. STUBEN KUECKEN

Ingredients	Quantity
Spring Chickens	2
Milk	250 ml
Bread	115 gm
Turnips	115 gm
Eggs	4
Bacon	60 gm
Butter	115 gm
Salt and Pepper	to taste

Method

1. Clean and truss chicken. 2. Remove liver. Chop and mix with bread soaked in milk, finely chopped turnips, 2 whole eggs and 2 yolks. 3. Season with salt and pepper. 4. Cook mixture to a light brown in butter and stuff chicken with it. 5. Place a piece of bacon over each bird. Tie with a string and roast for about 25 minutes at 175°C (about 350°F), basting frequently.

7. BLUMENKOHL SALAT (CAULIFLOWER SALAD)

The cauliflower should be boiled in salted water, but should be quite firm. Drain thoroughly, and divide in clusters. Put into salad bowl with a few prawns, chopped parsley, oil, vinegar, salt and white pepper, and cover with a mayonnaise dressing.

8. AFFELSINENBISCUITORT UNGEFULT (ORANGE CAKE)

Ingredients	Quantity
Sugar	85 gm
Eggs	4
Orange juice	1 orange
Castor sugar	10 gm
Rum	2 tbsp
Orange peel	
Refined flour	85 gm
Butter	60 gm
Icing	
Icing sugar	115 gm
Orange juice	

Method

1. Cream 3 egg yolks and sugar till light and fluffy. 2. Add 1 whole egg, orange juice, castor sugar well rubbed with orange peel and rum. Beat thoroughly. 3. Fold in flour and warmed butter. 4. Add stiffly beaten whites of 3 eggs. 5. Pour into a buttered tin and cook at 175°C (about 350°F) for 30 to 40 minutes. When cold, coat with icing.

Icing

Add warm orange juice gradually to icing sugar and keep on beating. When thick pour over cake.

9. APFELSTRUDEL (APPLE STRUDEL)

Strudel dough

Ingredients	Quantity
Refined flour	225 gm
Egg	1
Melted butter	1 tbsp
Lukewarm water	140 ml
Salt	a pinch

Method

1. Sieve flour onto a board. 2. Beat egg well. Mix egg, water and melted butter. 3. Make a well in flour. Pour in egg and butter mixture and add salt. 4. Stir gently so that flour falls down from sides into well. (It will be sticky at first). 5. Knead with floured hands. Rub sticky dough off hands and flour again. 6. Knead until dough becomes smooth and elastic.

7. Toss once or twice. 8. Stretch once and knead again. 9. Leave it covered in a warm place for about 1 hour. 10. Cover table with a linen cloth. Dust with flour. Put dough in the middle and stretch by hand. 11. Place filling while dough is still on cloth. Do not fill right to the edge. 12. Roll by lifting cloth. Pinch edges together and seal contents.

N.B. Strudel dough is rather like a noodle dough and should not be rolled out on a board in the usual way. It should be stretched by hand on a clean floured linen cloth. Strudel always has a filling such as apples, cheese, chocolate, cherries, etc. The filling must be ready before the dough is stretched. The stretched dough should always be paper thin when ready. As you pull and one part gets thin enough leave it and work on another section. The dough should be of an even thickness when stretched out.

Filling

Ingredients	Quantity
Apples	3
Raisins (seedless)	115 gm
Walnuts (chopped)	115 gm
Sugar	170 gm
Grated lime rind	½ lime
Melted butter	115 gm
Icing sugar	for dusting

Method

1. Core and peel apples. Slice very thin. 2. Mix with all the other ingredients and spread thickly over stretched strudel dough (keep aside a little melted butter). Do not fill right to edges. 3. Pour some melted butter on top. 4. With the help of linen cloth roll strudel. 5. Pinch ends together. Brush edge with a wet brush and seal well. 6. Place sealed side down on a baking sheet. 7. Brush top with the melted butter. 8. Bake for 45 minutes in a moderate oven; when cold dust with icing sugar.

SPAIN

I. ESCUDELLA CATALINA

Ingredients	Quantity
Potatoes	115 gm
Rice	115 gm
Vermicelli	60 gm
Turnip	1
Celery	1 stalk

Ingredients	Quantity
Garlic	1 flake
Bacon	30 gm
Onions	60 gm
Carrots	115 gm
Stock (chicken)	600 ml
Salt and Pepper	to taste
Cooked chicken	60 gm

Method

1. Peel and dice vegetables. Put them into a pan with stock and seasoning. Boil for 30 minutes. 2. Add finely chopped bacon, diced chicken, rice and vermicelli. Cook for another 20 minutes. 3. Check for seasoning and serve hot.

2. GAZPACHO (A)

Ingredients	Quantity
Garlic (peeled)	2 flakes
Ripe tomatoes (cut into eighths)	4
Capsicum (seeded, soaked and sliced)	½
Cucumber (cleaned and chopped – slice 6 pieces for garnish)	1
Onions (peeled and sliced)	½
Salt and Pepper	to taste
Oil	2 tbsp
White wine	1 tbsp
Iced water	½ cup

Method

1. Keep slices of cucumber, a few diced capsicum and 1 tbsp concassed tomato aside. Put rest of ingredients into a blender and purée well. 2. Chill thoroughly and serve garnished in bowls. 3. If desired serve with a salad of chopped cucumber, chopped spring onions, chopped capsicum and tomatoes.

GAZPACHO (B)

Ingredients	For 6–7
Ripe red tomatoes	1 kg
Cucumber	½
Capsicum	1
Spring onions	3
Cooking oil	1 tbsp
Wine vinegar	1 tbsp

Ingredients	For 6–7
Red pepper (if available)	1
Cold water	1 glass (300 ml)
Garlic	2 flakes
Salt and Pepper	to taste
Hard-boiled egg	1

Method

1. Chop tomatoes roughly; then put them through a sieve. 2. Dice cucumber very fine. 3. Cut red pepper and capsicum in half, wash out all seeds, then dice red pepper and finely shred capsicum. 4. Slice spring onions into fine rings. 5. Stir all the vegetables into the tomato puree and add oil, vinegar and cold water to make the consistency of a thick soup. 6. Peel outer skin of garlic flake, slice and sprinkle with salt, then crush to a smooth cream under blade of heavy knife. 7. Stir it thoroughly into mixture. 8. Season Gazpacho with salt and freshly ground black pepper. Chill thoroughly. 9. Just before serving, chop the white and sieve the yolk of the hard-boiled egg, and use a little of each to garnish each helping.

3. PASTEL de TORTILLAS ESPECIAL

Ingredients	Quantity
Eggs	8
Mushrooms	115 gm
Shrimps (cooked)	115 gm
Potatoes (cooked)	225 gm
Salt and Pepper	to taste
Peas and Carrots (cooked)	115 gm
Onions	1
Fat or Oil	for frying
Tomato sauce (fresh)	50 ml

Method

1. Dice mushrooms, shrimps, potatoes and mixed vegetables separately. 2. Beat 2 eggs till light and frothy. Add a little minced onion and salt and pepper. 3. Grease an omelette pan and pour mixture in. 4. Sprinkle with a little of each of the diced ingredients. 5. When one side is set turn over and cook other side. 6. Lift out and place on a round plate. 7. Repeat process using 2 eggs each time. 8. Stack omelettes one on top of another. Garnish each with tomato sauce. 9. Cut like a cake and serve.

4. TORTILLAS

Ingredients	Quantity
Cornmeal	2 cups
Refined flour	½ cup

Ingredients	Quantity
Warm water	
Salt	1 tsp

Method

1. Prepare a stiff dough with cornmeal, flour, salt and warm water.
2. Roll dough into small balls. 3. Place one ball at a time on wax paper
or a moist napkin, cover with wax paper and press with a board or palm
of hand until you have a wafer thin cake. 4. Bake on hot, slightly greased
griddle for 2–3 minutes. 5. Turn and brown other side. Keep warm
between layers of cloth.

5. SALMON à la ALICANTINA

Ingredients	Quantity
Fresh salmon	500 gm
Lime	1
Red peppers	2
Onions	1
Olive oil	150 ml
Salt and Pepper	to taste
Parsley	a sprig

Method

1. Clean salmon. Cut into thick slices. 2. Wash and dry. Soak for 2–3
hours in sauce made of 150 ml of olive oil, juice of 1 lime, sliced onion,
salt and pepper, chopped red peppers and a sprig of parsley. 3. 20
minutes before serving take out salmon slices, dry and grill till tender.
4. Garnish with slices of lemon and serve with hollandaise sauce.

6. SARDINAS FRITAS (FRESH FRIED SARDINES)

Ingredients	Quantity
Fresh sardines	24
Refined flour	15 gm
Oil or Fat	for frying
Lime	1
Parsley	

Method

1. Clean sardines and remove heads. Dry well and salt. 2. Dip into flour
and deep fry. 3. Drain well and serve with slices of lemon and garnished
with parsley.

7. **CAMARONES FRITOS** (FRIED PRAWNS)

Ingredients	Quantity
Large prawns	500 gm
Egg	1
Breadcrumbs	3 tbsp
Refined flour	3 tbsp
Oil	for frying
Salt and Pepper	to taste

Method

1. Shell prawns. Remove intestines and wash well. 2 Dry and dip in seasoned flour and then in beaten eggs and breadcrumbs. 3. Heat oil and fry prawns golden brown. 4. Serve with boiled potatoes and mayonnaise.

8. **PELOTA**

Ingredients	Quantity
Mutton	225 gm
Tomato (large)	1
Garlic	1 flake
Pistachios	30 gm
Bread	60 gm
Milk	30 ml
Egg	1
Pepper	to taste
Garnish	
Eggs	2
Tomato	1

Method

1. Mince meat. Chop tomatoes. Soak bread in milk. 2. Mix all ingredients together. Fill into a greased mould. 3. Keep mould in a tray of hot water and cook in an oven till set. 4. Turn out. Surround with timbales of rice, fried eggs and grilled tomatoes.

9. **CHULETAS de TOCINO con SALSA de TOMATE** (PORK CHOPS WITH TOMATO SAUCE)

Ingredients	Quantity
Pork chops	4
Refined flour	60 gm
Tomato purée (thick)	115 ml
Oil	85 ml
Garlic	1 flake
Salt and Pepper	to taste

Method

1. Remove most of the fat from meat and pound gently with the back of a wooden spoon or knife. 2. Season with salt and pepper. Dip both sides in flour. Rub with garlic clove. 3. Heat oil in a frying pan. Brown meat until tender. Keep hot while making sauce. 4. Mix tomato purée with 150 ml boiling water. 5. Drain off half the fat from pan and pour tomato purée into pan. Mix well. 6. Serve sauce separately.

10. CHULETAS de CORDERO VILAREAL (LAMB CHOPS)

Ingredients	Quantity
Lamb chops	10
Stock	2 tbsp
Bacon	4 rashers
Onions	250 gm
Potatoes	500 gm
Salt and Pepper	to taste
Oil	for frying

Method

1. Wash chops. Flatten with the back of a spoon. 2. Season and fry over quick fire till brown on both sides. 3. In another pan fry bacon. When brown fry sliced onions with a sprig of herbs. 4. Pour this together with chops into a casserole. 5. Put lid on firmly and bake in a medium oven. 6. When almost ready add sliced parboiled potatoes. 7. When these are tender serve very hot.

N.B. If necessary add a little stock.

11. SPANISH RICE

Ingredients	Quantity
Onions (choppped fine)	2
Bacon (chopped fine)	2 slices
Tomatoes (concassed)	8 medium
Table rice	300 gm raw
	600 gm cooked
Capsicum (deseeded, washed and chopped fine)	optional

Method

1. Heat large frying pan. Add 1 tsp oil. 2. When hot, add bacon and onions. Brown. 3. Add deseeded chopped capsicum. 4. Add tomatoes and boiled, cooled rice. Add salt to taste. 5. Serve hot with meat curry.

12. SPANISH RICE OMELETTE

Ingredients	For 6
Omelette:	
Eggs (beaten)	6 (270 gm)
Milk	115 ml
Salt	½ tsp
Pepper	a pinch
Butter or	10 gm
Margarine	(1 tbsp)
Cheese	75 gm
Rice filling:	
Butter or Margarine	30 gm
Garlic (crushed)	2 flakes
Tomato purée	2 cups (450 ml)
Onions	75 gm
Capsicum	75 gm
Bay leaves	a few
Sugar	5 gm
Salt	1 tsp
Pepper	a pinch
Cinnamon (powdered)	a pinch
Ripe olives	25 gm
Cooked rice	750 gm (raw weight 250 gm)

Method (Omelette)

1. Beat eggs well. Add milk, salt and pepper. 2. Melt butter in a 10 inch (25.5 cm.) frying pan (skillet). 3. Add egg mixture and cook over medium heat. 4. As the eggs begin to set draw edges towards centre with a spatula, tilting pan to allow uncooked eggs to flow on to bottom. 5. When eggs have set, spoon half the rice filling over eggs and arrange cheese slices on top. 6. Place under grill till cheese has melts. 7. Cut wedges and serve with a portion of remaining rice.

Method (Rice filling)

1. Melt butter in a saucepan. Add finely chopped onions, capsicum and crushed garlic. 2. Sauté until tender. 3. Stir in tomato purée, seasoning and sliced olives. 4. Simmer for about 15 minutes. Stir in cooked rice.

13. PAELLA à la VALENCINA

Ingredients	Quantity
Young chicken	1
Lobster (cooked)	1
Green peas	500 gm

Ingredients	Quantity
Saffron	a large pinch
French beans	450 gm
Rice	1 kg
Bacon	30 gm
Onions	115 gm
Garlic	3 flakes
Oil	for frying
Stock	2 litre
Bay leaf	1

Method

1. Heat oil. Fry chopped garlic and onions. 2. Add chicken jointed into 8 pieces. Sauté till golden. 3. Add rice. Fry for a couple of minutes. 4. Add stock and then beans, peas and cooked lobster cut into 2.5 cm. (1") pieces. 5. Season with salt, pepper, bay leaf and a pinch of saffron. 6. Cover and cook as for pilau.

N.B. The secret of paella is to serve it immediately, before the rice gets too dry.

14. ARROZ ESTILO BARCELONES (RICE BARCELONA STYLE)

Ingredients	Quantity
Margarine	225 gm
Onions	115 gm
Ham	115 gm
Tomatoes	225 gm
Nutmeg	a pinch
Rice	225 gm
Shelled peas	115 gm
Chopped parsley	
Salt and Pepper	to taste
Stock	600 ml

Method

1. Melt margarine in a large saucepan. 2. Fry chopped onions till golden. 3. Add ham and sliced tomatoes. 4. Put in rice and fry till it changes colour. 5. Add boiling stock. Boil rapidly for 7 minutes. 6. When liquid is almost absorbed, add boiled peas. 7. Season and finish cooking in a moderate oven for about 10 minutes.

15. PATO ALCAPARRADA (DUCK WITH CAPER SAUCE)

Ingredients	Quantity
Duck	1
Onions	250 gm

Ingredients	Quantity
Butter	115 gm
Stoned olives	
Stoned raisins	85 gm
Capers	30 gm
Blanched almonds	60 gm
Tomatoes	450 gm

Method

1. Clean and wash duck well. Boil with 1 onion and salt. 2. Remove, joint and bone. 3. Melt butter in a pan. Add remaining chopped onions and peeled tomatoes. 4. When done add pieces of duck and simmer. 5. Add almonds, capers, stoned olives and stoned raisins. 6. Add sufficient hot stock from duck to just cover. 7. Simmer till most of the stock has evaporated and what remains is thick. Serve hot.

16. ALCACHOFAS de JERUSALEM al GRATIN

Ingredients	Quantity
Jerusalem artichokes	500 gm
Melted butter	60 gm
Béchamel sauce	300 ml
Breadcrumbs (fresh)	170 gm
Mushrooms	115 gm
Salt and Pepper	to taste

Method

1. Peel and boil artichokes in salted water. Drain. 2. Cool and dice. 3. Butter a baking dish. Place artichokes in it. 4. Mix sautéed mushrooms with sauce. 5. Pour sauce over artichokes. 6. Fry breadcrumbs in butter till golden. 7. Sprinkle over sauce. 8. Place in a moderate oven for 3–5 minutes.

17. BERENJENAS SALTEADAS (AUBERGINES SAUTÉS)

Ingredients	Quantity
Oil	150 ml
Onions	115 gm
Eggplants	1 kg
Stock	1 tbsp
Tomatoes	250 gm
Salt and Pepper	to taste

Method

1. Fry chopped onions. 2. When golden brown add eggplants sliced into large roundels. 3. Simmer for 5 minutes. Add stock and blanched and pulped tomatoes. 4. Season and cover. Simmer slowly till done.

18. CHURROS (FRIED BATTER)

Ingredients	Quantity
Water	75 ml
Refined flour	225 gm
Butter	30 gm
Salt	a pinch
Eggs	2
Sugar	15 gm
Lime rind	1 tsp
Fat or Oil	for frying
Icing sugar	

Method

1. Put water into a large pan. When warm add butter, a pinch of salt and sugar. 2. Stir and when it comes to a boil carefully add flour, stirring all the time with a wooden spoon to a smooth batter. 3. Remove from fire and beat in eggs. Stir till smooth. 4. Heat oil till it smokes. Force mixture through a piping bag into hot oil and deep fry till golden. 5. Cut churros with scissors into sticks. Drain. 6. Sprinkle with icing sugar and eat hot or cold.

19. CHOCOLATE CREAMS

Ingredients	Quantity
Sugar	225 gm
Water	150 ml
Egg yolks	6
Plain chocolate	115 gm

Method

1. Melt sugar in water. 2. Boil to a thick syrup. 3. Cool and add to beaten egg yolks. 4. Pour into small, greased, fire-proof dishes and bake in a slow oven until set (about 45 minutes). 5. Cool. Turn out. Pour melted chocolate over. Serve chilled.

ITALY

I. CHICKEN TARTLETS

Into 300 ml rich béchamel sauce, mix two tablespoons grated cheese and 150 gm cooked chicken, cut into small pieces. Mix a few chopped, cooked mushrooms and a slice of chopped ham. Mix well together and fill tartlets.

2. CHICKEN LIVER TARTLETS

Same as above but using fried chicken liver instead of cooked chicken.
Omit ham but garnish with pieces of crisply fried bacon.

3. HARICOT BEAN SOUP

Ingredients	Quantity
Haricot beans	225 gm
Garlic	1 flake
Water	1.8 litre
Olive oil	1 tbsp
Chopped parsley	4 heaped tbsp
Salt and Pepper	to taste

Method

1. Soak beans overnight. 2. Drain, cover with water. Bring to a boil and
cook slowly for at least 3 hours. 3. Heat olive oil. Add crushed garlic and
parsley and cook for 5 minutes. 4. Pass beans through a sieve along with
water in which they were cooked. 5. Return to saucepan and stir in garlic
mixture. 6. Serve hot with croûtons of fried bread along with a dish of
grated cheese.

4. ZUPPA PARADISO

Ingredients	Quantity
Strong stock	2 litre
Fresh breadcrumbs	4 tbsp
Eggs	4
Grated cheese	4 tbsp
Salt	
Pepper	to taste
Nutmeg	

Method

1. Beat egg whites till stiff. 2. Add beaten yolks and beat till well
blended. 3. Add cheese and breadcrumbs. 4. Bring stock to a boil, add
seasoning, and slowly add mixture a spoonful at a time. Boil 5–8 minutes
and serve.

5. ZUPPA PAVESE (CHICKEN SOUP WITH POACHED EGGS)

Ingredients	Quantity
Butter or	60 gm
Margarine	(4 tbsp or about ¼ cup)
Bread slices (1.5 cm. thick)	4
Chicken stock (fresh or tinned)	750 ml (4¼ cups)

Ingredients	Quantity
Eggs	4
Freshly grated	20 gm
Cheese	(1¾ tbsp)

Method

1. In a heavy 20 to 25 cm (8" to 10") frying pan, melt butter over moderately low heat and cook bread in it, turning frequently for 4–5 minutes, or until slices are golden brown on both sides. 2. Place a slice of bread in each of 4 individual soup bowls. 3. Bring chicken stock to a simmer in a small saucepan, and let it simmer slowly while you prepare eggs. 4. Bring 5 cm (2") of water to a simmer in a frying pan. 5. Break one egg at a time into a saucer. Holding dish as close to the water as possible, slide egg into pan. 6. Gently lift white over yolk with a wooden spoon. 7. Try to keep eggs separate. 8. Poach eggs for 3–5 minutes depending on how firm you want them. Then remove them from water with a slotted spoon (zara) and place an egg on top of the fried bread in each soup bowl. 9. Sprinkle eggs with grated cheese and pour stock around it. Serve soup at once.

6. NOODLES WITH TUNA SAUCE

Ingredients	Quantity
Noodle dough	
Egg	1
Flour	100 gm
Oil	2 ml
Salt	2 gm
Sauce	
Tuna	1 tin
Tomatoes	200 gm
Onions	115 gm
Oil	50 ml
Salt and Pepper	to taste

Method (Noodles)

1. Mix all ingredients. 2. Make into a stiff dough. 3. Roll dough as thin as possible and cut into a thin strips. 4. Boil water with salt and oil. 5. Add noodles and cook till tender.

Sauce

1. Chop onions, sauté in oil. 2. Add blanched and concassed tomatoes and a little water. 3. When tomatoes are soft, add flaked tuna, salt and pepper. 4. Cook mixture to a sauce consistency and mix with noodles. Serve hot.

7. SPAGHETTI WITH MEAT BALLS

Ingredients	Quantity
Spaghetti	450 gm
Onions	100 gm
Garlic	2 flakes
Meat Balls:	
Lean meat	450 gm
White bread	60 gm
Onions	100 gm
Tomatoes	450 gm
Brown sugar	1 tbsp
Parsley (chopped)	1 tbsp
Cheese	85 gm
Salt and Pepper	to taste

Method

1. Soak bread in water. 2. Squeeze dry and mash with fork. 3. Add finely chopped onions, chopped parsley, minced meat, grated cheese and seasoning. 4. Beat eggs lightly and combine with mixture. 5. Shape into small balls (12) and fry in hot fat. Drain on absorbent paper and set aside.

Sauce

1. Heat oil in a heavy pan. 2. Add chopped onions and crushed garlic and cook till golden. 3. Add blanched and pipped tomatoes, sugar, thyme, salt and pepper. 4. Lower heat. Cover and cook slowly for one hour. 5. Add meat balls and cook gently for another 3 minutes. 6. Boil spaghetti in boiling salted water. Drain and dish into a hot plate. 7. Pour sauce with meat balls over spaghetti. 8. Serve a bowl of grated cheese separately.

8. PRAWN RISOTTO

Ingredients	Quantity
Prawns (large)	1 kg
Butter	115 gm
Onions	100 gm
Rice (pilau)	225 gm
Grated cheese	115 gm
Stock	2 litre
Salt and Pepper	to taste

Method

1. Melt 60 gm butter. Add chopped onions and cook till it starts to change colour. 2. Add washed and drained rice and fry for a couple of minutes.

3. Add stock a little at a time and cook rice. 4. Melt 30 gm butter and add boiled prawns. Sauté. 5. Add to rice. Add 60 gm melted butter and grated cheese. Mix well. Check for seasoning.

9. CHICKEN RISOTTO

Ingredients	Quantity
Cooked chicken (diced)	450 gm
Onions	115 gm
Garlic	1 flake
Mushrooms	115 gm
Chicken stock	750 ml
Butter	30 gm
Rice	340 gm
Tomatoes	250 gm
Carrots	115 gm
Celery	1 stalk
Lean ham	30 gm
White wine (if available)	150 ml

Method

1. Heat butter. Sauté chopped onions, garlic, celery and chopped carrots. 2. After 5 minutes add chopped mushrooms and tomatoes (peeled and cut into small pieces). 3. Allow to cook for a few minutes. 4. Stir in diced chicken, chopped ham and wine. 5. Increase heat so that dish cooks fast for a couple of minutes. 6. Add seasoning. Stir in stock. 7. Cover pan and allow to cook slowly for 30 minutes. 8. Add rice and cook using more chicken stock if necessary for cooking rice. 9. Finally stir in grated parmesan cheese and a generous amount of butter.

10. PIZZA

Ingredients	Quantity
Refined flour	115 gm
Dry yeast	7 gm
Tomatoes	450 gm
Cheese	85 gm
Anchovy fillets	6
Olive oil	1 tbsp
Salt	to taste
Water	
Basil	

Method

1. Put flour into a bowl. Add a pinch of salt. 2. Mix yeast with a little warm water. Keep aside to prove. 3. Put yeast into flour and mix well.

4. Add enough warm water (about 150 ml) to make a stiff dough. 5. Knead thoroughly until dough becomes elastic. 6. Put in a warm place covered with a cloth until it has doubled in size. 7. Roll dough out onto a floured board (7 mm. or ¼" thick) and leave to rise. 8. Peel tomatoes and chop. Cut cheese into thin slices. Halve anchovies. 9. Put pizza dough on to a baking tin. 10. Cover with tomatoes. Sprinkle with basil and a little olive oil and bake in a hot oven for 25 minutes. 11. Lay cheese over top and arrange anchovies in a criss-cross pattern. Bake for another 15 minutes.

II. CHICKEN as SERVED in ROME

Ingredients	Quantity
Boiling chicken (medium-sized)	1
Olive oil	4 tbsp
Leek (sliced)	1
Thyme	1 pinch
Tomato purée	1 tbsp
Refined flour	60 gm
Cloves	4
Chopped parsley	
Stock	600 ml
Macaroni	115 gm
Salt and Pepper	to taste

Method

1. Clean chicken. Season. 2. Heat oil in a large pan. Add prepared chicken, sliced leek, cloves, and herbs. Allow chicken to brown on all sides. (This should be done very slowly). 3. Pour off half the oil. Add stock, tomato purée and flour mixed with a little stock. 4. Cover and simmer gently, stirring now and then, till chicken is tender (1½–2 hours). 5. Meanwhile cook and drain macaroni. 6. When chicken is cooked remove it from sauce and keep hot. 7. Add macaroni to sauce. Mix well and serve around chicken as a garnish.

12. AMARETTI

Ingredients	Quantity
Sugar	225 gm
Egg whites	4
Almonds (blanched)	115 gm

Method

1. Chop and pulverize almonds. Mix thoroughly with half the sugar.
2. Beat egg whites until very stiff. Add remaining sugar and beat again.

3. Add almond mixture. Mix thoroughly. 4. Shape into balls of about 5 cm diameter. 5. Place on greased baking sheet about 2–5 cm away from each other. 6. Bake in a moderate oven till light brown.

13. OSSO BUCCO

Ingredients	Quantity
Shin of veal	1 kg
Salt and Pepper	to taste
Butter	60 gm
Onions (skinned and finely chopped)	1 (medium-sized)
Stock (made from a bouillon cube)	500 ml
Tomatoes (peeled and chopped)	225 gm
Carrots (peeled and thinly sliced)	1
Celery (scrubbed and thinly sliced)	1 stalk
Dry white wine	150 ml
Refined flour	1 tbsp
Dried rosemary	a pinch
Chopped parsley (to garnish)	1 tbsp
Garlic (skinned and finely chopped)	1 flake
Grated rind of ½ lemon	

Method

1. Cut veal into 5 cm (2") pieces. Season with salt and pepper. 2. Melt butter, brown veal all over and remove from pan. If necessary, add a little more butter and dry onion, carrot and celery until they are golden brown.3. Drain off any excess fat, return meat to pan and add wine. Cover and simmer gently for 20 minutes. 4. Blend flour with a little stock to a smooth cream, add remaining stock and add to meat. Add tomatoes and rosemary, cover tightly and continue to simmer for a further 1½ hours or until meat is tender. 5. Arrange in a deep serving dish and sprinkle with a mixture of parsley, garlic and lemon rind. Serve with risotto and a dressed green salad.

14. POTATO CROQUETTES

Ingredients	Quantity
Potatoes	1 kg
Cheese	60 gm
Eggs	2
Salt and Pepper, Nutmeg	to taste
Breadcrumbs	100 gm
Oil	for frying

Method

1. Cook potatoes in boiling salted water. Sieve them and beat in grated

cheese and 1 egg. Season with pepper and nutmeg. 2. When mixture is cool, shape into balls. Roll in egg and breadcrumbs and fry quickly. Drain. Serve hot.

15. ZABAGLIONE

Ingredients	Quantity
Egg yolks	2
Castor sugar	2 tbsp
Marsala wine or Sherry	2 tbsp

Method

1. Beat together egg yolks and sugar until they are pale and creamy. 2. Slowly add Marsala. 3. Place mixture over hot water in a double-boiler and stir slowly until it thickens, taking care not to overcook, otherwise it will curdle. 4. Serve immediately in warmed sherbet glasses. Serve Zabaglione hot.

RUSSIA

I. CAVIAR WITH EGGS

Ingredients	Quantity
Eggs	4
Salt and Pepper	to taste
Caviar	60 gm
Cucumber	1
Lime juice	½ tbsp
Mayonnaise sauce	1–2 tbsp

Method

1. Hard boil eggs and plunge into cold water. When cold, shell. 2. Slice off a piece from narrow end. 3. Remove yolks carefully with a spoon. 4. Fill whites with caviar and sprinkle with lime juice. 5. Wash cucumber but do not peel. Cut into thin slices. 6. Arrange around stuffed eggs. 7. Rub yolks through a sieve; blend with mayonnaise. Add salt and pepper to taste. 8. Cover each egg with the dressing.

2. FORSHMAK

Ingredients	Quantity
Cooked chicken	500 gm
Mashed potatoes	225 gm
Salted herring (filleted)	1

Ingredients	Quantity
Sour cream	300 ml
Eggs	2
Onions	115 gm
Butter	2 tbsp
Breadcrumbs	1 tbsp
Tomato sauce	
Salt and Pepper	to taste

Method

1. Mince chicken meat and herring together. 2. Combine with beaten eggs, sour cream and mashed potatoes. 3. Chop onions and fry in half the butter. 4. Add to mince mixture, along with remaining butter, salt and pepper. 5. Pass through mincer once more. 6. Butter a baking dish, put in mixture, sprinkle with breadcrumbs and bake in a moderate oven for 30 minutes. 7. Serve with tomato sauce.

3. STUDEN (CALF'S FOOT JELLY)

Ingredients	Quantity
Calf's feet	4
Eggs	4–6
Carrots	2
Onions	250 gm
Bay leaves	2–3
Parsley	3–4 sprigs
Lemon	1
Peppercorns	6
Salt	to taste
Water	4.8 litre
Beetroot and Horseradish sauce	

Method

1. Singe and scald calf's feet. 2. Split them lengthwise, separate bones from meat and chop into several sections. 3. Put meat and bones into a saucepan with water about 5 to 7 cm above solids. 4. Add carrots, onions, bay leaves, parsley, peppercorns and 1 teaspoon salt. 5. Simmer covered with lid for 2½–3 hours. 6. Strain. Skim off fat, remove all the meat and chop it. 7. Put bones back into stock, add lemon juice and more seasoning if required and continue cooking till only about a litre of liquid remains. 8. Mix with meat and pour into moulds. 9. Hard boil and slice eggs and place in jelly before it is set. 10. When ready, stand mould in hot water for a few minutes. Turn out and serve with beetroot and horseradish sauce.

BEETROOT AND HORSERADISH SAUCE

Ingredients	Quantity
White radish	225 gm
Cooked beetroot	115 gm
Butter	2 tbsp
Dry mustard	1 tsp
Vinegar	150 ml
Stock	600 ml
Refined flour	3 tbsp
Sugar	1 tsp
Salt	1 tsp

Method

1. Melt butter. Blend with flour. 2. Dilute with stock and bring to a boil.
3. Add grated horseradish, mustard, vinegar, sugar and salt and simmer
for 10 minutes stirring constantly. 4. Add grated beetroot and heat for
another 5 minutes.

This sauce can be served with calf's foot jelly, aspic dishes, roast pork,
cold beef and cold fish.

4. CUCUMBER WITH SMETANA

Ingredients	Quantity
Cucumber	1
Sour cream	150 ml
Lime juice	1 tsp
Salt and Pepper	to taste

Method

1. Peel cucumber. Slice thin. Sprinkle with salt and leave for about
1 hour. 2. Strain off liquid. 3. Mix sour cream with lime juice and pour
over cucumber slices. Serve chilled.

5. CAUCASIAN SALAD

Ingredients	Quantity
Potatoes	340 gm
Peas	225 gm
Sweet apples	2
Sour cream	150 ml
Cold meat (lamb)	115 gm
Cucumber	1
Eggs	2
Mayonnaise sauce	2 tbsp
Salt and Pepper	to taste

Method

1. Cook potatoes, carrots and peas separately and leave to cool. 2. Dice peeled cucumber, potatoes, carrots, and peeled, cored apples and put into a large salad bowl with peas. 3. Make a stiff, firm omelette with 2 eggs and let it cool. 4. Cut meat into small cubes and omelette into small strips and put into a salad bowl. 5. Make a dressing with a mixture of mayonnaise, sour cream, salt and pepper and pour over salad. Mix well. 6. Serve chilled.

6. POKHLYOBKA (RUSSIAN COUNTRY SOUP)

Ingredients	Quantity
Dried mushrooms	115 gm
Sour cream	2 tbsp
Refined flour	½ tbsp
Pearl barley	2 tbsp
Onions	250 gm
Leeks	2
Carrots	225 gm
Potatoes	225 gm
Butter	2 tbsp
Peppercorns	4
Bay leaves	2
Water	2.4 litre
Salt	1 tsp
Parsley	a few sprigs

Method

1. Soak mushrooms in 500 ml of water for at least 2 hours. 2. Chop onions and fry lightly in butter. 3. Slice leeks and carrots. Add to onions. 4. Fry together for a few minutes and then put into a large saucepan. 5. Add remaining water and the water in which mushrooms were soaked. 6. Slice mushrooms, dice potatoes and put into saucepan along with bay leaves, peppercorns, pearl barley and salt. 7. Cover and simmer, stirring occasionally until mushrooms, potatoes and pearl barley are tender. 8. Thicken soup with a mixture of flour and sour cream, about 5 minutes before removing from stove. 9. Serve hot, sprinkled with chopped parsley.

7. LAZY SHCHY

Ingredients	Quantity
Beef	450 gm
Cabbage	450 gm
Turnip	1
Celery	1 stalk

Ingredients	Quantity
Carrots	1
Onions	115 gm
Tomatoes	225 gm
Butter	1 tbsp
Peppercorns	6
Bay leaf	1
Water	2.4 litre
Salt	1 tsp
Parsley	a few sprigs

Method

1. Into a large pan, put beef cut into cubes, water, peppercorns, bay leaf, salt and sliced carrots, celery, turnip and onions. 2. Cover and simmer for 2 hours. 3. Strain stock into saucepan and bring to a boil. 4. Wash cabbage and cut into large sections. 5. Plunge into boiling stock. 6. Add skinned, sliced tomatoes. 7. Put lid on and simmer for another 10 minutes. 8. Brown flour in butter, pour in a cup of warm stock. 9. Mix well and blend with soup. 10. Simmer for a another 15 minutes. Serve sprinkled with chopped parsley.

8. ARMENIAN SOUP

Ingredients	Quantity
Beef	450 gm
Rice	115 gm
Refined flour	1 tbsp
Butter	1 tbsp
Onions	115 gm
Eggs	2
Water	1.5 litre
Bay leaf	1
Thyme	1 sprig
Salt and Pepper	to taste
Parsley	

Method

1. Wash meat and cut into fairly small pieces. 2. Put into a saucepan with cold water and a teaspoon of salt. Bring to a boil. 3. Cover and simmer for 1 hour, removing scum when it appears. 4. Strain soup and return pieces of meat to it together with washed rice. 5. Add chopped onions fried lightly in butter, a sprig of thyme, a bay leaf and salt and pepper to taste. 6. Cook gently for 30 minutes, occasionally stirring rice. 7. Remove soup from stove. Add 2 egg yolks beaten in a little stock and mix well. The soup should be very thick. 8. Serve with pieces of meat and chopped parsley.

9. BAKED FISH in SOUR CREAM SAUCE

Ingredients	Quantity
Fish	1 kg
Sour cream sauce	300 ml
Eggs (hard-boiled)	2
Refined flour	2 tbsp
Potatoes	680 gm
White mushrooms	225 gm
Butter	115 gm
Salt and Pepper	to taste

Method

1. Clean and skin fish, cut into 4 portions. 2. Cover with flour and fry on both sides for a few minutes in 60 gm butter. 3. Put into a buttered oven dish and lay slices of half an egg on each portion. 4. Slice mushrooms. Fry lightly in 60 gm butter and pile over eggs. 5. Parboil potatoes. Peel and slice. Fry in remaining butter till golden brown and put around fish. 6. Sprinkle all over with salt and pepper. 7. Pour sour cream sauce over fish. 8. Cover all ingredients with grated cheese and bake in a moderate oven for 20 minutes.

SOUR CREAM SAUCE

Ingredients	Quantity
Sour cream	150 ml
Butter	2 tbsp
Refined flour	1 tbsp
Stock	150 ml
Salt	to taste

Method

1. Melt butter. 2. Blend with flour and gradually dilute with warmed meat or vegetable stock. 3. Add sour cream and salt to taste. Mix well and simmer gently for 5–10 minutes. 4. Serve with liver rissoles, roast game, vegetables or fish.

10. STUFFED FISH

Ingredients	Quantity
Fish	1 kg (about)
Bread	225 gm
Onions	450 gm
Beetroot	2
Oil	1 tbsp
Carrots	3

Ingredients	Quantity
Sugar	1 tbsp
Eggs	2
Milk	300 ml
Salt and Pepper	to taste

Method

1. Clean fish. Slit belly and remove entrails. Wash well. 2. Soak bread in milk, squeeze dry. Mince with onions. 3. Add raw eggs, sugar, olive oil, pepper and salt. Mix well. 4. Stuff fish. 5. Take a large pan. Put a layer of peeled and sliced beetroot, carrots and well-washed skinned onions. 6. Lay fish over vegetables. Cover with remaining vegetables. 7. Add sufficient water to cover. Put lid on pan and simmer gently for 1½–2 hours. 8. Take care that fish does not burn and if necessary add a little water from time to time. 9. Serve in liquid in which fish is cooked.

II. CRAB in EGG SAUCE

Ingredients	Quantity
Boiled crab	1.35 kg
White wine	150 ml
Vegetable stock	300 ml
Salt and Pepper	to taste
Egg sauce	300 ml
Green salad	

Method

1. Remove crab meat from shell and cut into pieces. 2. Put into a saucepan. Pour in enough wine and stock to cover crab meat. 3. Season with salt and freshly ground pepper. 4. Cover and cook for 10 minutes. 5. Drain off liquid and use for making sauce. 6. Serve crab with egg sauce and green salad.

EGG SAUCE

Ingredients	Quantity
Butter	4 tbsp
Hard-boiled eggs	2
Hot fish stock	3 tbsp
Refined flour	450 gm
Salt	½ tsp
Pepper	a pinch
Lime	½

Method

1. Melt butter in a saucepan. Add flour. 2. Cook gently for 1 minute

without allowing flour to brown. 3. Add hot stock drop by drop into flour
and butter mixture (if no stock add water). 4. Stir gently all the time.
5. Add salt, pepper and the lime juice.

12. BEEF STROGANOFF

Ingredients	Quantity
Fillet of beef	680 gm
Onions (small)	1–2
Mushrooms	115 gm
Butter	85 gm
Tomato purée (optional)	1 tbsp
Sour cream	300 ml
Refined flour	1 dsp
Salt	1 tsp
Pepper	a pinch
Mustard seeds	a pinch

Method

1. Cut meat into thin strips about 5 cm long and sprinkle with salt and
pepper. 2. Chop onions very fine and fry in hot butter until golden.
3. Wash, peel and slice mushrooms and add to onions. 4. Add meat and
fry for 5 minutes. 5. Blend sour cream (reserve a little to add later) with
tomato purée, flour and mustard. Mix well. 6. Pour into pan. 7. Stir
contents of pan. Cover and simmer gently for about 10 minutes or until
meat is tender. 8. Add a little more sour cream just before completion of
cooking.

13. STUFFED MEAT LOAF

Ingredients	Quantity
Minced meat	450 gm
Egg	1
Onions	115 gm
Rice	115 gm
Butter	2 tbsp
Breadcrumbs	60 gm
Salt and Pepper	to taste

Method

1. Boil rice in salted water till tender, and strain. 2. Hard boil egg. Chop
and mix with rice. 3. Chop onions and fry lightly in butter. 4. Soak
breadcrumbs in 150 ml of water. Squeeze out moisture. 5. Mix minced
meat, breadcrumbs and fried onions together. Add salt and pepper.
6. Lay mixture flat on a dish. 7. Pile rice and egg mixture in centre and

push meat mixture up over it, covering it completely, in a pyramid shape. 8. Dot with butter and bake in moderate oven for about 45 minutes. Serve with tomato sauce.

14. CHAKHOKHBILY (CAUCASIAN CHICKEN DISH)

Ingredients	Quantity
Chicken	1 (about 1 kg)
Tomato purée	2 tbsp
Vinegar	1 tbsp
Stock	150 ml
Tomatoes	225 gm
Onions	225 gm
Oil	2–3 tbsp
Bay leaf	1
Lime	1
Salt and Pepper	to taste
Parsley	

Method

1. Divide chicken into 4 portions and put into a saucepan with hot oil. 2. Brown lightly. Then add chopped onions, bay leaf, tomato purée, vinegar, stock, salt and pepper. 3. Cover and simmer gently for 1½ hours. 4. 15 minutes before completion of cooking, skin tomatoes, cut into quarters and add to chicken. 5. Serve with slices of lime and garnish with parsley.

15. CAUCASIAN SHASHLIK

Ingredients	Quantity
Leg of lamb (boned)	½ (about 500 gm)
Bacon	225 gm
Butter	60 gm
Salt and Pepper	to taste

Method

1. Cut meat into 2.5 cm (1") cubes. Melt half the butter and brown meat cubes on all sides. 2. Cut bacon into slightly smaller cubes. Put alternate cubes of bacon and meat onto 4 skewers. 3. Season with salt and pepper. Brush with melted butter. 4. Cook under a hot grill, turning skewers from time to time so that meat is cooked evenly on all sides. 5. Serve with plain boiled rice.

N.B. If lamb is not tender after browning, simmer gently till tender, in just enough stock to cook dry.

16. HAM PASTIES

Ingredients	Quantity
Refined flour	225 gm
Eggs	2
Egg yolks	2
Salt	to taste
Cooked ham or Pork (chopped)	100 gm
Brown sauce	
Butter	50 gm
Parsley	
Lemon juice	

Method

1. Mix flour with eggs and egg yolks until a stiff paste is formed. Leave for 2 hours. 2. Roll out and cut into small rounds. Fill with meat mixed with a little sauce, lemon juice and about 15 gm butter and parsley. 3. Pincn edges together. Cook in boiling salted water for 20 minutes. Serve with melted butter mixed with lemon juice and chopped parsley.

17. FRENCH BEANS WITH MUSHROOMS

Ingredients	Quantity
French beans	680 gm
Mushrooms	225 gm
Butter	2 tbsp
Sour cream	150 ml
Water	150 ml
Salt	to taste
Parsley	

Method

1. Wash and slice beans. Put into boiling salted water. Cook till tender. 2. Wash and slice mushrooms. Fry lightly in butter. Sprinkle with salt. 3. Add 2 tbsp of water in which beans were cooked and simmer for 5 minutes. 4. Add beans. Stir in sour cream and heat for another few minutes. Serve sprinkled with chopped parsley.

18. APPLE KISSEL

Ingredients	Quantity
Apples	1 kg
Sugar	115 gm
Lime	$\frac{1}{2}$
Potato flour	2 tbsp
Water	900 ml
Nutmeg	

Method

1. Core and peel apples. Slice them and stew in water until soft. 2. Pass apples through a sieve and put into a saucepan with the juice of half a lime, a little grated nutmeg and peel of half-lime. 3. Blend flour with a little water. Add to apple purée. 4. Bring to a boil and simmer for 5 minutes stirring constantly. 5. Remove lemon peel, pour kissel into a wet mould and leave to cool.

19. MALAKOFF CAKE

Ingredients	Quantity
Butter	170 gm
Almonds	170 gm
Sugar	170 gm
Egg yolks	2
Double cream	300 ml
Almonds	170 gm
Milk and Rum (mixed)	150 ml
I sponge cake made with sugar, eggs and flour but no fat	

Method

1. Chop almonds very fine and roast them by putting a little sugar in a frying pan and tossing almonds in it until they are slightly brown. 2. Cream butter and sugar and beat in almonds, rum and egg yolks. 3. Cut cake into 3 flat sections, soak each in a mixture of rum and milk. 4. Put a layer of cake followed by a layer of filling into a cake tin of the same size. 5. Repeat these layers and cover with a final layer of cake. 6. Leave in a very cold place for 12 hours. 7. Turn out before serving and cover with whipped cream.

20. APPLE SOUFFLE

Ingredients	Quantity
Cooking apples (large)	4
Egg	1
Sugar	115 gm

Method

1. Peel and slice apples, cook with a little water and sugar until tender. 2. Sieve, cook again until very thick. Mix in egg yolk and fold in stiffly beaten egg white. 3. Put into a greased soufflé dish, cook in a hot oven for 15 minutes.

HOLLAND

1. SPINAZIE SOEP (SPINACH SOUP)

Ingredients	Quantity
Spinach	450 gm
Butter	60 gm
Cream	150 ml
Cornflour	30 gm
Nutmeg	a pinch
Salt and Pepper	to taste

Method

1. Cook spinach in a little salted water until tender. 2. Pass through a sieve. 3. Melt butter. Cook flour in it for one minute. 4. Gradually add spinach purée and some hot milk if necessary. 5. Season with salt, pepper and nutmeg. 6. Stir in cream just before serving. Serve with croûtons of fried bread.

2. VISCHKOEKJES (FISH CAKES)

Ingredients	Quantity
Cooked fish	170 gm
Egg	1
Milk	60 ml
Butter	75 gm
Breadcrumbs (fresh)	60 gm
Chopped parsley	¼ tsp
Salt and Pepper	to taste
Nutmeg	a pinch

Method

1. Flake fish. Mix well with other ingredients. 2. Shape into rissoles or flat cakes. Fry in butter.

3. HUTSPOT (HOTCHPOTCH)

Ingredients	Quantity
Chicken	1
Old carrots	1.30 kg
Potatoes	1.30 kg
Fat	60 gm
Onions	300 gm
Water	900 ml
Salt	to taste

Method

1. Wash chicken and put into warm salted water. 2. Bring to a boil and simmer for 2 hours. 3. Peel carrots. Mince very fine and add to stock after 2 hours. 4. After half an hour add peeled potatoes and chopped onions and simmer for another 30 minutes or till all vegetables are very tender. Add more water if necessary but when cooked fully water must have completely evaporated. 5. Remove chicken. Cut into joints and put in a hot dish. 6. Mash all vegetables with a wooden spoon and surround meat with vegetables.

4. GESTOOFDE KOMKOMMERS

Ingredients	Quantity
Cucumber	450 gm
Butter	30 gm
Refined flour	15 gm
Vinegar	30 ml
Salt	to taste

Method

1. Peel cucumber. Cut into four lengthwise. Remove seeds. 2. Cut into thin strips 9 cm (about 3½″) long. 3. Boil in salted water for 10 minutes. Drain but keep cucumber liquor. 4. Melt butter in a pan. Put in cucumber. Sprinkle with flour. Mix well without browning. 5. Gradually add about 170 ml cucumber liquor and vinegar. Simmer for 10 minutes.

5. FLENSJES

Ingredients	Quantity
Refined flour	115 gm
Milk	300 ml
Eggs	2
Salt	a pinch
Butter	45 gm
Lime	1
Brown sugar or Jam	60 gm

Method

1. Separate whites and yolks of eggs. 2. Beat yolks. Add milk and a pinch of sugar and salt. 3. Stir in sieved flour. 4. Beat whites stiff and fold into mixture. 5. Spread a spoonful of mixture in a frying pan and cook as for pancakes. 6. Spread with jam or sprinkle with brown sugar. Roll in fancy shapes. Serve hot with slices of lime.

SCANDINAVIA

I. MACKEREL FOR THE SMORGASBORD

Ingredients	Quantity
Mackerel	1 kg
Salt	1 tbsp
Mayonnaise sauce	5 tbsp
Vinegar	2 tbsp
Peppercorns	10
Lime	¼
Onions	1
Lettuce	1 bunch
Small new potatoes	
Whipped cream	5 tbsp
Chopped parsley	2 tbsp
Chopped chives	2 tbsp
Hard-boiled eggs	2
Tomatoes	2

Method

1. Clean mackerel and place in a pan with sufficient water to cover. 2. Add salt, vinegar, peppercorns, lemon juice and sliced onion. 3. Bring to a boil and simmer for about 15 minutes, when meat should come free from bone. 4. Let it cool in stock overnight. 5. Just before serving fillet and skin mackerel. 6. Arrange some lettuce leaves on a serving dish and place filleted mackerel on top. 7. Mix mayonnaise and cream and spread over mackerel. 8. Mix chopped parsley and chives and sprinkle on top. 9. Quarter eggs and tomatoes and arrange neatly around fish. 10. Serve on smorgasbord with boiled small new potatoes.

2. GRAPEFRUIT WITH SHRIMPS

Ingredients	Quantity
Grapefruit	2
Shelled cooked shrimps	115 gm
Tomatoes	115 gm
Mayonnaise	4 tsp
Castor sugar	3 tsp
Salt	to taste

Method

1. Cut grapefruit in half and divide into segments, leaving them in the skin. 2. Sprinkle very lightly with castor sugar. 3. Put a helping of shrimps on each half grapefruit. 4. Sprinkle with a little salt and cover with mayonnaise. 5. Decorate with a slice of tomato and serve chilled.

3. MEAT BALLS FOR SMORGASBORD

Ingredients	Quantity
Minced beef	450 gm
Butter	30 gm
Chopped onions	3 tbsp
Breadcrumbs (fresh)	4 tbsp
Water	150 ml
Salt	2 tsp
Pepper	¼ tsp
Cream	60 ml
Fat	for frying

Method

1. Put breadcrumbs into a large mixing bowl. 2. Add cream and water. 3. Let it stand to swell. 4. Fry finely chopped onions in butter until golden brown and add to bowl. 5. Mix in meat, stirring very well until smooth and creamy in texture. 6. Stir in seasoning. 7. Form mixture into small round balls 2 cm (about ¾″) in diameter and fry in fat until evenly brown. 8. Serve cold on smorgasbord.

4. ALESONDIGAS (MEAT BALLS)

Ingredients	Quantity
Balls:	
Minced beef (raw)	500 gm
Soft bread (soaked in milk)	2 tbsp
Chopped parsley	1 tbsp
Grated cheese	2 tbsp
Chopped cooked onion	1
Eggs	2 small
Nutmeg, Salt and Pepper	a pinch
Sauce:	
Oil	1 tbsp
Chopped onion	1
Tomato puree	2 tbsp
Beef stock	300 ml
Chopped carrots	2
Nutmeg	a pinch
Salt and Pepper	to taste

Noodles

1. Sauté chopped onion in oil and divide into 2 parts 2. Put minced meat into bowl. Add bread, cheese and half-cooked onion. 3. Blend with egg. Make into balls and roll in flour. 4. Add stock to remainder of onions in

stew pan, along with tomato puree, chopped carrots and seasoning. 5. Drop meat balls in carefully. Cover and cook on low heat for about 40 minutes.

N.B. It is essential to cook slowly, or meat balls will break.

5. WHITE COLESLAW

Ingredients	Quantity
White cabbage	
Oil	
Vinegar	
Chopped parsley	
Chopped chives	
Salt and Pepper	

Noodles

1. Remove coarse leaves and stalk from cabbage. 2. Shred it fine. Make salad dressing with 3 parts oil to 1 part vinegar. 3. Season to taste with salt and pepper. 4. Mix cabbage well with generous amount of dressing. 5. Let it stand for 2 hours. 6. Sprinkle with equal amounts of chopped chives and parsley and serve.

6. CHICKEN SALAD

Ingredients	Quantity
Cold diced chicken	340 gm
Hard-boiled eggs	3
Vinegar	1 tbsp
Grated horse radish sauce	1 tbsp
Whipped cream	5 tbsp
Chopped parsley	
Salt and Pepper	

Noodles

1. Mash 3 hard-boiled eggs and mix in horseradish and vinegar. 2. Stir in whipped cream. Mix in diced chicken. 3. Season to taste with salt and pepper. 4. Put in salad bowl and sprinkle parsley or top.

7. LAMB AND VEGETABLE SOUP

Ingredients	Quantity
Neck of lamb	1 kg
Water	1.8 litre
Salt	1 tbsp
Carrots	1
Bay leaf	1
Butter	60 gm
Peppercorns	6

Ingredients	Quantity
Celery	1 stalk
Leek	1
Shelled peas	225 gm
Refined flour	2 tbsp
Chopped parsley	

Method

1. Put water and spices into a soup pot and bring to a boil. 2. Cut meat into convenient pieces and brown in butter. 3. Pick out meat and place in boiling water, leaving butter in frying pan. 4. Allow meat to simmer for about 2 hours. 5. In the meantime, clean root vegetables and cut into 1.5 cm cubes. 6. Brown them in remaining butter. Sprinkle flour on top and brown, stirring when necessary. 7. Take 300 ml stock and add to vegetables. Cover and simmer in frying pan for 30 minutes. 8. When meat is tender, remove from soup. Remove bones and cut in smaller pieces. 9. Skim off excess fat from soup. Add meat and vegetables with their stock and parsley. 10. Bring to a boil. Season to taste and serve.

8. SPRING SOUP

Ingredients	Quantity
Carrots (young)	450 gm
Leeks	2
Radish	1 bunch
Spinach	170 gm
Refined flour	2½ tbsp
Butter	60 gm
Water	1.5 litre
Egg yolks	2
Cream	6 tbsp
Salt and Pepper	to taste

Method

1. Wash carrots, leeks, spinach and radishes. 2. Melt butter in a saucepan. Add sliced leeks and carrots. 3. Season with salt and pepper and simmer for 5 minutes. 4. Add water and bring to a boil. Simmer for 10 minutes. 5. Add chopped spinach and sliced radishes. 6. Mix flour in a little cold water and add while stirring. 7. Simmer until carrots are soft. Remove from heat, stir in yolks mixed with cream. 8. Serve immediately with little cheese sandwiches, plain or toasted.

9. FISH FILLETS WITH MUSHROOMS AND VEGETABLES

Ingredients	Quantity
Fish fillets	1 kg
Fish stock	450 ml

Ingredients	Quantity
Mushrooms	115 gm
Leeks	3 tbsp
Carrots	6 tbsp
Egg yolks	2
Butter	100 gm
Refined flour	45 gm
Evaporated milk	300 ml
Cream	2 tbsp
Tomatoes	2
Salt and Pepper	to taste

Method

1. Soak fish in cold salted water for 10 minutes (3 tbsp salt to 1 litre of water). 2. Make fish stock from fish scraps and strain. 3. Slice mushrooms and fry in 75 gm of butter together with leeks and carrots. Season with salt and pepper and add 3 tbsp fish stock. 4. Cover and allow to simmer until vegetables are soft. 5. Remove fish from cold water and poach in fish stock for 5 to 10 minutes. 6. Melt remaining butter in a saucepan and stir in flour. 7. Add 300 ml of fish stock gradually while stirring, letting sauce thicken before adding more stock. 8. Stir in evaporated milk. Season to taste and allow to simmer for a few minutes. 9. Mix egg yolks and cream together and add to sauce while stirring vigorously. 10. Add vegetable mixture to sauce. 11. Place fish fillets on hot serving dish and pour sauce on top. 12. Garnish with quartered tomatoes and serve with boiled potatoes.

10. BAKED FISH

Ingredients	Quantity
Pomfret	1
Boiled rice	2 heaped tbsp
Prunes	6
Salt	a pinch
Margarine	60 gm
Milk	1 cup

Method

1. Clean and scale fish. Remove entrails by making a small slit near belly. 2. Wash well and season. 3. Mix rice and chopped prunes. Add salt and stuff fish with mixture. 4. Sew up opening. 5. Place fish on a baking dish. Dot with margarine and pour milk over. 6. Bake in a moderate oven for 45 minutes.

11. KALDOLMAR

Ingredients	Quantity
Cabbage	1
Rice	60 gm
Minced beef	225 gm
Egg	1
Salt and Pepper	to taste
Butter	115 gm
Stock	600 ml
Top of milk	1 cup

Method

1. Remove outer and coarse leaves of cabbage. 2. Separate remaining leaves carefully, keeping them whole. 3. Dip each leaf in boiling water for a couple of minutes and lay on a cloth to drain. 4. Boil rice and when cooked, mix with minced raw beef and egg. Season with salt and pepper. 5. Lay a spoonful of this mixture on each cabbage leaf. 6. Roll leaf and tie around carefully like a small parcel. 7. Melt butter in a deep frying pan and brown dolmar on both sides. 8. Pour in boiling stock. Cover and cook very gently for an hour shaking pan now and then. 9. Take dolmars out carefully. Remove strings and lay on a hot dish. 10. Pour milk into frying pan. Mix well with stock. 11. Strain and pour around the dolmar.

12. FINARE LAMMRAGU (FINE LAMB STEW)

Ingredients	Quantity
Shoulder of lamb (boned)	1 kg
Celery	1 stick
Bay leaves	2
Dripping	1 tbsp
Flour	3 tbsp
Garlic	3 flakes
Water	450 ml
Bouillon cubes	2
Shelled peas	115 gm
Tomatoes	225 gm
Small onions	450 gm
Carrots (new)	225 gm
Potatoes (new)	225 gm
Chopped parsley	1 tbsp
Salt and Pepper	to taste

Method

1. Cut meat into 2.5 cm (1") cubes and roll in seasoned flour. 2. Melt dripping in a large cast-iron pot. 3. Add meat and brown on all sides.

4. Dissolve bouillon cubes in boiling water and add meat along with chopped garlic, tomato paste, bay leaves and celery. 5. Bring to a boil. Cover and simmer for 30 minutes. 6. Clean and slice carrots. Peel onions. Peel potatoes. 7. Add these vegetables to meat, stirring to mix with meat and stock. 8. Cover and continue to simmer for another 40 minutes or till meat and vegetables are tender. 9. Sprinkle with parsley and serve.

13. ROASTED SPARE RIBS

Ingredients	Quantity
Spare ribs	1.8 kg
Salt	to taste
Pepper	½ tsp
Prunes	20
Ginger (powder)	½ tsp
Sour apples	4
Bouillon cube	1
Water	450 ml

Method

1. Crack bones in spare ribs. 2. Rub with mixture of salt, ginger and pepper. 3. Place spare ribs on a grill in an oven pan and bake in a moderate oven for 45 minutes. 4. Remove spare ribs and pour off fat. 5. Peel, core and slice apples. 6. Wash prunes in warm water. Halve and remove stones. 7. Spread apples and prunes in bottom of oven pan and place spare ribs on top with inner side up. 8. Dissolve bouillon cubes in water and pour over meat. 9. Replace in oven and bake for another 30 minutes. 10. Turn ribs and turn oven up to moderately hot. 11. Bake for another 20 minutes when space ribs should be nicely brown. 12. Remove meat. Cut into portions and place on a hot serving dish. 13. Drain fruit and arrange around meat. 14. Strain dripping into sauce boat and serve with red cabbage.

14. DANISH PARSLEY CHICKEN

Ingredients	Quantity
Spring chicken	2 (about 700 gm each)
Refined flour	15 gm
Bacon	115 gm
Parsley	4 springs
Butter	225 gm
Stock	600 ml
Cream	2 tbsp
Salt and Pepper	to taste

Method

1. Clean and rub outside of chickens with salt and pepper. 2. Remove stalks from parsley but do not chop. 3. Mix parsley with half the butter and stuff chickens. 4. Melt remaining butter in a heavy pan. 5. Brown chickens well in butter, starting with breasts (about 10 minutes). 6. When browned all over place chickens on their backs and add heated stock. 7. Cover tightly and simmer for 1½ hours. 8. Remove chickens to a hot dish. Garnish with crisply fried bacon rolls. 9. Strain the stock. Add flour mixed with cream and a little browning for colour. Simmer for a few minutes and serve with chickens.

15. CHOCOLATE CHIFFON PUDDING

Ingredients	Quantity
Cocoa	5 tbsp
Instant coffee	1 tsp
Gelatine	3 tbsp
Cold water	3 tbsp
Eggs	2
Sugar	100 gm
Milk	300 ml
Cream	300 ml
Vanilla essence	1 tsp
Almonds or	
Chopped nuts	

Method

1. Soften gelatine in cold water. 2. Beat egg yolks and sugar until light and creamy. 3. Stir in cocoa and milk. 4. Pour into a saucepan and bring to a boil while stirring. 5. Add coffee, gelatine and vanilla. Remove from fire. 6. Cool until it begins to set. Beat egg whites stiff and fold in. 7. Whip cream and stir in, saving a little for garnish. 8. Rinse mould in cold water and pour in mixture; chill until set. turn out onto a cold serving dish and decorate with nuts and almonds.

16. NORWEGIAN BISCUITS

Ingredients	Quantity
Butter	45 gm
Castor sugar	45 gm
Top of milk	1 tbsp
Egg yolk	1
Refined flour	85 gm
Baking powder	¼ tsp

Method

1. Cream butter and sugar till light and creamy. 2. Stir in top of milk and beaten egg yolk gradually. 3. Stir in flour sieved with baking powder. 4. Put into a piping bag with a large plain nozzle and pipe into 'S' shapes. 5. Bake in a moderate oven till golden brown.

PORTUGAL

1. OVOS DUROS a PORTUGUESA
(PORTUGUESE HARD-BOILED EGGS)

Ingredients	Quantity
Hard-boiled eggs	4
Olive oil	3 tbsp
Garlic	1 flake
Tomatoes (large)	2 (about 250 gm)
Onions	115 gm
Salt and Pepper	to taste

Method

1. Cut tomatoes in half. Scoop out inside. 2. Sprinkle with salt and pepper and fry for a few minutes in a tablespoon of oil. 3. Place a shelled hard-boiled egg in each tomato half. 4. Chop onions fine and fry until golden brown in a tablespoon of oil. 5. Add tomato pulp, crushed garlic, salt and pepper and remaining oil and simmer gently for 10 minutes. 6. Pour over eggs. Serve as a hot hors d'oeuvre.

2. LOBSTER a PORTUGUESA

Ingredients	Quantity
Lobsters	2
Butter	85 gm
Tomatoes	1 kg
Onions	115 gm
Refined flour	1 tbsp
Brandy	2 tbsp
Garlic	4 flakes
Salt and Pepper	to taste
Boiled rice	

Noodles

1. Boil lobsters in a court bouillon. 2. Cool in same liquid. 3. Cut into two lengthwise and remove meat from shell. Cut into slices and put into a pan. 4. Chop onions and fry lightly in butter. 5. Skin and chop tomatoes. Add to onions and cook until soft. 6. Add crushed garlic,

sprinkle with salt, pepper and flour. 7. Mix well and simmer for a few minutes. 8. Pass sauce through a sieve and stir in brandy. 9. Pour over lobster meat. Cover and simmer for 5 minutes. 10. Remove from heat and leave until next day. 11. Before serving heat up lobsters in a saucepan and serve with boiled rice.

3. CHICKEN a PORTUGUESA

Ingredients	Quantity
Chicken	1
Tomatoes	225 gm
Button mushrooms	60 gm
Onions	1
Garlic	2 flakes
Olive oil	3 tbsp
Salt and Pepper	to taste
Water	
Cooked rice	

Noodles

1. Clean and joint chicken into 8 portions. 2. Fry in oil until slightly brown. 3. Chop onion and fry until golden. 4. Add quartered tomatoes, crushed garlic, sliced mushrooms, salt, pepper and 2 tablespoons water. Fry for a few minutes. 5. Put into a large pan with chicken. Cover with a lid and simmer gently for 1 hour. 6. Serve with boiled rice.

4. TOMATOES WITH SARDINE STUFFING

Ingredients	Quantity
Tomatoes	4
Sardines	1 small tin
Hard-boiled eggs	2
Mayonnaise	
Salt and Pepper	to taste

Noodles

1. Cut a thin slice off top of each tomato, scoop out and sprinkle insides with salt and pepper. 2. Drain contents of a tin of boneless sardines, dice sardines, chop eggs and stir in well with some mayonnaise. 3. Fill tomatoes with mixture, put back top slices of tomatoes, and serve as an hors d'œuvre.

5. PUDIM de NOSES

Ingredients	Quantity
Shelled walnuts	225 gm
Castor sugar	225 gm
Mixed spices	¼ tsp

Ingredients	Quantity
Butter	
Eggs	6

Method

1. Crush nuts and mix with spices. 2. Beat egg yolks and sugar and add nuts and mix well. 3. Whisk three egg whites and fold into mixture. 4. Pour into a buttered mould till it is three fourths full. 5. Cover with greaseproof paper and place in a saucepan of water to steam for about 1 hour. 6. Keep water simmering until pudding is set. 7. When ready turn out of mould and leave to cool. Serve with whipped cream.

6. FIO de OVOS

Ingredients	Quantity
Sugar	200 gm
Citric acid	½ tsp
Water	1 cup
Eggs	8

Prepare a sugar syrup of one string consistency (separate whites from yolks)

Method

1. Beat 2 egg whites till stiff. Add 1 tbsp sugar and vanilla essence gradually. 2. Put into a jelly mould. Steam in a pan of water kept off boiling. Break up yolk. Pass through a jelly cloth. 3. Add colouring. Make a hole in a clean, empty can. Put egg mixture in. Keep sugar syrup over low fire. 4. Pass egg mixture through hole into sugar syrup in long threads. As they cook, remove onto a plate and sprinkle with cold water. 5. Place steamed egg white over a base of coconut and sugar. Cover with threaded eggs. Decorate with cherries and nuts.

7. SAURBRATEN

Ingredients	Quantity
Beef	1.8 kg
Instant meat	1 pkt.
marinade	(4–5 oz.)
Medium onion (sliced)	1
Bay leaves	2
Pickling spices	1 tsp
Fat	2 tbsp
Flour	2 tbsp

Method

Stir ⅓ cup crushed ginger and 1 tsp sugar into gravy pan. Heat till boiling stirring constantly. Boil. Stir for 1 minute.

Pickling spice

Ingredients

Cloves
Bay leaf (small piece)
Red chilli skin
Cinnamon
Peppercorn
Mace
Sesame seeds/Mustard seeds

Marinade

Salt, sugar, modified food starch, spices, garlic, caramel colour, tricalcium phosphate, extractives of garlic, partially hydrogenated vegetable oil and papain.

Sweet & sour

Combine sugar, powdered cornstarch, soya sauce, tomato powder, onion powder, green pepper, salt, paprika extract, garlic powder, yeast extract, monosodium glutamate and flavours.

AMERICA

I. TOMATO JUICE COCKTAIL

Ingredients	Quantity
Tomato juice (strained)	1 cup
Onions (finely chopped)	1 tsp
Lemon juice	1 tbsp
Wine vinegar	1 tbsp
Celery (finely chopped)	½ tsp
Bay leaf	1
Sugar	1 tsp

Method

1. Mix all ingredients thoroughly and let mixture stand for 2 hours in a cool place. 2. Strain through a cloth. Pour into small glasses and serve well iced.

2. GINGER FRUIT COCKTAIL

Ingredients	Quantity
Peaches	2 (cut into cubes)
Pineapple	60 gm (cut into cubes)
Orange	1 (remove skin and chop)
Strawberries	a few

Ingredients	Quantity
Preserved ginger	15 gm (chopped)
Lemon juice	2 tsp
Castor sugar	15 gm
Ginger ale	

Method

1. Mix fruit and sprinkle with a little sugar and lemon juice. 2. Put mixed fruit cocktail in tall glasses. 3. Pour iced ginger ale over it and garnish with chopped ginger.

3. STRAWBERRY COCKTAIL

Cut strawberries into half. Mix with chopped pineapple, Sprinkle with sugar and lime juice and serve iced in cocktail glasses.

4. CHICKEN GUMBO SOUP (A)

Ingredients	Quantity
Onions	115 gm
Fat	60 gm
Ladies fingers	225 gm
Chicken stock	1 litre
Cooked chicken (without bones)	225 gm
Salt	2 tsp
Pepper	a pinch
Capsicum	$\frac{1}{2}$

Method

1. Chop onions fine. Shred chicken meat, thin slice ladies fingers, remove seeds from green pepper and chop fine. 2. Melt fat. Fry onions. Add ladies fingers and sauté. 3. Add remaining ingredients and bring gradually to boiling point. 4. Simmer for 1 minute. Add water if necessary to maintain volume.

CHICKEN GUMBO SOUP (B)

Ingredients	Quantity
Chicken stock	1 litre
Capsicum (remove seeds, wash well and chop)	1
Ladies fingers	115 gm
Onions	100 gm
Tomatoes	225 gm
Chicken (diced and cooked)	60 gm
Raw rice	20 gm
Butter	20 gm
Refined flour	20 gm
Salt and Pepper	to taste

Method

1. Bring stock to a boil. Reduce heat, add rice and simmer for about 20 minutes. 2. Melt butter. Sauté chopped onions. Stir in flour. 3. Add blanched and puréed tomatoes, ladies fingers cut into rounds and chopped capsicum to stock and simmer. 4. Add some stock gradually to blended flour mixture, beating with a whisk. 5. Return to soup, stirring constantly until thick. Add chicken and simmer for another 10 minutes.

5. PRAWN/SHRIMP GUMBO

Ingredients	For 6
Prawns or	
Shrimps	500 gm
Fat	⅓ cup
Green onions with tops (sliced)	⅔ cup
Salt and Pepper	to taste
Garlic (finely chopped)	3 flakes
Ladies fingers (sliced)	2 cups
Tomato purée (red)	1 cup
Bay leaves	2
Hot water	2 cups
Tabasco	6 drops
Cooked rice	1½ cups

Method

1. Melt fat. Sauté ladies fingers for about 10 minutes. Add onions, garlic, salt, pepper and prawns. 2. Cook for about 5 minutes. Add water, tomato purée and bay leaves. 3. Cover and simmer for 20 minutes. Remove bay leaves. Add Tabasco. 4. Put ¼ cup rice in each of 6 soup bowls. 5. Fill with gumbo.

6. OKRA SOUP

Ingredients	Quantity
Ladies fingers	1 kg
Parsley	3 sprigs
Onions	250 gm
Tomatoes	750 gm
Butter	30 gm
Thyme	2 sprigs
Bay leaf	1
Capsicum	1
Water	3 litre
Salt and Pepper	to taste

Method

1. Wash ladies fingers. Slice thin. 2. Chop onions and tomatoes. 3. Melt butter. Add onions and fry. Add ladies fingers and toss lightly. 4. Add tomatoes and herbs. Simmer for 10 minutes. 5. Add seasoning, hot water and finely chopped capsicum (remove seeds). Simmer for 1½ hours. 6. Serve with croûtons of fried bread.

7. DEVILLED CRAB

Ingredients	Quantity
Crab	1 large or 4 small
Cream	300 ml
Butter	15 gm
Refined flour	15 gm
Hard-boiled egg yolks	2
Chopped parsley	1 tbsp
Grated nutmeg	a pinch
Salt and Pepper	to taste
Cayenne pepper	¼ tsp
Fresh egg yolk	½
Breadcrumbs	15 gm

Method

1. Boil crab in shell. 2. Break shell and remove crab meat. 3. Put cream into a saucepan. Add thickening made with flour and butter. 4. Bring to a boil and remove from fire. 5. Stir in crab meat, finely chopped egg yolks, parsley and seasoning. 6. Put mixture back into crab shells which must be well-cleaned. 7. Brush over with a little egg yolk. Sprinkle with breadcrumbs and bake in a quick oven.

8. LOBSTER à la KING

Ingredients	Quantity
Medium white sauce	300 ml
Lobster meat	225 gm
Pimento (minced)	2 tsp
Hard-boiled egg (chopped)	1
Capsicum (minced)	2 tsp
Bread	6 slices
Fat	for frying

Method

1. Add lobster, capsicum, pimento and egg to white sauce. Mix gently. 2. Re-heat and serve on crustades of fried bread.

9. PRAWN/SHRIMP CRÉOLE

Ingredients	Quantity
Shelled, deveined prawns/shrimps	500 gm
Fat	⅓ cup
Chopped green pepper	½ cup
Salt and Pepper	to taste
Bay leaves	2
Refined flour	¼ cup
Hot water	1 cup
Green onions and tops (chopped)	½ cup
Garlic (finely chopped)	4 flakes
Chopped parsley	½ cup
Thyme (crushed)	½ tsp
Cayenne pepper	a pinch
Tomato purée	225 gm
Lime	1
Rice (cooked)	2 cups
Rice (uncooked)	½ cup

Method

1. Melt fat. Blend in flour. Brown, stirring constantly. 2. Add water gradually and cook until thick, stirring constantly. 3. Add remaining ingredients except cooked rice. 4. Cover and simmer till prawns are cooked (about 20 minutes). 5. Remove bay leaves. Check for seasoning. 6. Make a border of rice on a dish and put prepared créole in the centre.

10. NEW ORLEANS SHRIMP

Ingredients	Quantity
Fresh shrimps	1 kg
Onions (sliced)	1
Garlic	1 flake
Bay leaf	1
Celery	2 sticks
Salt	1 tsp
Mustard	2 tbsp
Paprika	¼ tsp
Oil	6 tbsp
Garlic (crushed with salt)	1 flake
Lemon juice	3 tbsp
Marinade:	
Celery (finely chopped)	½ cup
Spring onion (finely chopped)	1
Chives (chopped)	1 tbsp

Ingredients	Quantity
Horseradish	5 tbsp
Cayenne pepper	
Lemon	½

Method

1. Simmer onion, garlic, bay leaf and celery in 1 litre of salted water with a pinch of cayenne pepper for 15 minutes. Add lemon juice. 2. Shell and clean shrimps. Cook shrimps in marinade for 15 minutes and allow them to cool in the pan. 3. Leave shrimps in marinade for about 6 hours. 4. Drain shrimps and serve cold with brown bread and butter.

11. TUNA PUFFS

Ingredients	For 48 puffs
Tuna fish (drained and finely chopped)	1 can
Onions (finely chopped)	1 medium
Butter	4 tbsp
Refined flour	3 tbsp
Milk	1 cup
Salt	¼ tsp
Pepper	⅛ tsp
Refined flour	½ cup
Water	½ cup
Salt	a dash
Egg whites (stiffly beaten)	2

Method

1. Sauté onion in a tablespoon of butter. Make a thick cream sauce with 3 tablespoons of butter, 3 tablespoons of flour and milk. 2. Add tuna fish, onion, salt and pepper. Chill for several hours. 3. Make a batter with ½ cup flour and about ⅓ cup water with consistency of thin pancake batter. 4. Add salt and fold in 2 beaten egg whites. Form balls about the size of large marbles out of tuna mixture and roll balls in batter. 5. Fry for a few seconds in very hot fat. Drain. If tuna puffs are not fried for too long, they can be made several hours in advance and re-heated in a 205°C (about 400°F) oven for about 10 minutes when ready to serve. They must be served hot.

12. FRIED CHICKEN

Ingredients	Quantity
Young chicken	1
Seasoned flour	15 gm
Fat	60 gm

Method

1. Clean and joint chicken. Roll in seasoned flour. 2. Melt fat. Brown chicken, turning when necessary. 3. Add a little water. Cover and cook slowly for 35–40 minutes. (This can be done in an oven). 4. Serve with brown sauce made of the fat in the pan and milk. Season to taste.

13. BOSTON BAKED BEANS

Ingredients	Quantity
Haricot beans	225 gm
Salt pork	225 gm
Salt	to taste
Mustard	1 tsp
Molasses	1 tbsp
Sugar	1 tbsp

Method

1. Wash and soak beans overnight. Drain. 2. Cover with cold water and bring to boiling point. 3. Cook slowly until tender. 4. Drain and save cooking liquid. 5. Fill beanpot half full and put pork into pan. Score pork rind. 6. Place remaining beans in pot and cover them with mustard, salt and molasses dissolved in hot water. 7. Add enough cooking liquor to cover beans. 8. Cover and bake for 8 or more hours at 135°C (275°F). 9. Replenish liquid as needed. Draw pork to surface during last hour of baking. 10. Remove cover, to brown beans and pork.

14. RED PUMPKIN

1. Wash pumpkin and cut into pieces. 2. Peel and cut into 2.5 cm cubes. 3. Cook for 20–30 minutes. (More flavour is retained it pumpkin is cooked until water is evaporates and pumpkin is quite dry). 4. Mash or run through a sieve. Serve buttered.

15. WALDORF SALAD

Ingredients	Quantity
Celery (chopped)	1 head
Bananas (sliced)	2
Salt and Pepper	to taste
Apples (peeled and sliced)	3
Mayonnaise	
Walnuts (chopped)	100 gm

Method

1. Mix all ingredients together. Season with salt and pepper. 2. Serve extra mayonnaise separately.

16. APPLE CRISP

Ingredients	Quantity
Butter	150 gm
Brown sugar	200 gm
Salt	a pinch
Refined flour	75 gm
Apples	4
Water	1 tbsp
Cinnamon or	½ tsp
Lemon juice	1 tsp

Method

1. Mix butter, sugar, salt and flour till crumbly. 2. Peel, core and slice apples. Place in an oiled baking dish. 3. Add water and cinnamon or lemon juice. 4. Cover with flour mixture. 5. Bake at 190°C (about 375°F) until apples are tender (about 1 hour). 6. Serve with thin cream.

17. CARROT PUDDING

Ingredients	Quantity
Fat	115 gm
Brown sugar	200 gm
Carrots	225 gm
Refined flour	150 gm
Salt	1 tsp
Cinnamon	1 tsp
Apple	1
Raisins (seeded)	200 gm
Allspice	½ tsp
Nutmeg	½ tsp
Baking powder	2 tsp

Method

1. Cream fat and sugar. 2. Add grated carrots, chopped apples and seeded raisins. 3. Sift remaining dry ingredients together. Add to fat mixture. Mix well. 4. Pour into a large oiled mould filling it two-thirds full. Steam for 3 hours.

GREECE

1. SOUPA AVGOLEMONO (CHICKEN, EGG AND LEMON SOUP)

Ingredients	Quantity
Chicken stock	1 litre
Eggs	2

Ingredients	Quantity
Lime	½
Rice	60 gm
Salt and Pepper	to taste

Method

1. Bring stock to a boil. Throw in rice. 2. Simmer for 20 minutes. 3. Beat eggs with lemon juice. Add a little boiling broth to eggs, spoon by spoon, stirring all the time. 4. Add this to rest of broth and stir for a few minutes over a very slow fire.

2. PSAROSOUPA (GREEK FISH SOUP)

Ingredients	Quantity
White fish	1 kg
Cod's head	1
Leek (chopped)	1
Onions (chopped)	1
White wine	150 ml
Parsley (chopped)	2 tbsp
Celery	4 sticks
Garlic	1 flake
Tomato purée	3 tbsp
Lemon peel	1 tsp
Salt and Pepper	to taste

Method

1. Clean white fish and cod's head. Peel and slice vegetables. Crush garlic. 2. Put the fish, cod's head, onion, leek, garlic and celery into a large pan. Season with salt and pepper. 3. Cover with cold water, bring to boil and simmer until fish is soft. 4. When cooked, lift out fish carefully. 5. Cool. Remove bones and break into large pieces. 6. Simmer stock for another 20 minutes. Strain and return to pan. 7. Mix flour and milk into a smooth paste. 8. Add tomato purée and white wine. Mix well. 9. Add this to fish stock. Simmer and stir till it thickens. 10. Carefully put cooked fish back into soup. 11. Add the herbs. 12. Serve with toast, one large piece of fish in each plate.

3. PSARI PLAKU (BAKED FISH)

Ingredients	Quantity
Red mullets	4
Onions	225 gm
Tomatoes	225 gm
Garlic	2 flakes

Ingredients	Quantity
Black olives	12
Olive oil	150 ml
White wine	2 tbsp
Salt and Pepper	to taste

Method

1. Clean fish but leave head and tail on. 2. Rub inside and out with a little salt. 3. Lay on a baking dish greased with olive oil. 4. Chop onions fine, and fry in hot oil until golden brown. 5. Add skinned and quartered tomatoes, crushed garlic, salt and pepper. 6. Fry lightly for a few minutes. Add white wine and cook gently for 5 minutes. 7. Pour mixture over fish. 8. Put into a medium oven and bake for 20 to 25 minutes. 9. Stone olives and place around fish in oven about 5 minutes before cooking ends.

4. LAMB KEBAB

Ingredients	Quantity
Leg of lamb	1 kg
Tomatoes	250 gm
Capsicums	115 gm
Lime juice	1 lime
Salt and Pepper	to taste
Skewers	

Method

1. Cut meat from leg of lamb into squares of about 2.5 cm and moisten with lemon juice. Set aside for 2–3 hours. 2. Deseed capsicum and cut into squares. 3. Slice tomatoes. 4. Thread meat, pepper and tomatoes alternately on to skewers. 5. Sprinkle with salt and pepper. 6. Grill under fierce heat and turn until all sides are cooked. 7. Serve with rice.

5. MOUSSAKA à la GRECQUE

Ingredients	Quantity
Brinjals	1 kg
Minced beef	½ kg
Onions	100 gm
Béchamel sauce	100 gm
Parsley	a few sprigs
Red tomatoes	250 gm
Refined oil	150 ml
Salt and Pepper	to taste

Method

1. Slice brinjals lengthwise about 3 cms. thick. 2. Apply a little salt over each piece and keep aside. 3. Heat a little water in a frying pan. Chop onions and put them into water to cook partially. 4. Allow water to evaporate and then add oil and sauté to a light brown colour. 5. Add minced meat and continue sautéing for 5 minutes. 6. Add blanched and concassed tomatoes, salt, pepper, and chopped parsley and cook for 1 minute more and keep aside. 7. Squeeze out water from brinjal and shallow fry them till light brown. 8. Arrange fried slices of brinjal in a pyrex dish. Spread minced meat mixture on top. 9. Cover with béchamel sauce and bake till golden brown on top.

6. GREEK BÉCHAMEL

Ingredients	Quantity
Eggs	2
Milk	½ litre
Flour	30 gm
Butter	30 gm
Salt and Pepper	to taste
Nutmeg	a pinch

Method

1. Prepare a white roux with flour and butter. 2. Add milk, whisk it till lump free and boil. 3. Cool slightly. 4. Beat eggs lightly and add to white sauce a little at a time. 5. Adjust seasoning after adding of nutmeg powder.

7. AUBERGINE SAUCE

Ingredients	Quantity
Seedless brinjal	1 (200 gm)
Egg yolk	1
Garlic	2 cloves
Olive oil	30 ml
Lime	1
Salt and Pepper	to taste

Method

1. Bake brinjal in a moderate hot oven till very soft. 2. Then peel and chop it. 3. Add chopped garlic, lime juice and egg yolk. 4. Put into blender with a little olive oil. 5. Blend to a smooth consistency, adjust seasoning and serve immediately.

8. YOUVARLAKIA WITH AVGO LEMONO SAUCE

Ingredients	Quantity
Minced beef	1 kg
Eggs	2
Pulao rice	50 gm
Onions	115 gm
Salt and Pepper	to taste
Parsley	3 bunches
Butter	100 gm

For the sauce	
Egg yolks	3
Flour	5 gm
Milk	150 ml
Lemons	2
Hot stock	20 ml

Method

1. To minced meat, add two whole eggs, rice, finely chopped onions, salt and pepper. 2. Shape mixture into lime-sized balls. 3. Chop parsley fine and roll mince balls in it. 4. Melt butter in a pan with 500 ml water. 5. When water starts simmering, arrange meat balls in pan. 6. Cover and cook for 30 minutes.

Sauce

1. Separate egg yolks into a bowl. Add lime juice gradually and stir in well. 2. Separately thicken 150 ml milk with 5 gm flour; pour into egg and lemon mixture gradually. 3. When meat balls are cooked, spoon out a little of the hot stock from pot and mix with sauce, a little at a time. 4. Pour back egg and lemon sauce onto meat balls and cook on a slow fire till mixture simmers gently. 5. Remove and keep aside for a while before serving.

9. CHICKEN PILAFF

Ingredients	Quantity
Cooked chicken	225 gm
Rice	225 gm
Onions (chopped)	100 gm
Butter	60 gm
Chicken stock	1–2 litre
Tomatoes	250 gm
Walnuts (chopped)	60 gm
Thyme	1 tsp
Salt and Pepper	to taste

Method

1. Cut chicken into strips. Fry strips with onions in butter in a large pan until brown. 2. Add salt, pepper and chopped thyme. 3. Add rice. Stir well for 5 minutes to prevent sticking. 4. Pour in stock, peeled and chopped tomatoes and chopped walnuts. 5. Cover pan with a clean cloth and simmer gently till all liquid is absorbed and the rice is soft. 6. With a fork stir everything together. 7. Leave covered in a warm place for 20 minutes and serve.

10. AUBERGINES WITH PEPPERS

Ingredients	Quantity
Eggplants	4
Capsicums	4
Yoghurt (curd)	225 gm
Tomatoes	250 gm
Olive oil	120 ml
Salt and Pepper	to taste

Method

1. Cut eggplants into slices. Salt and pepper them. 2. Take out core and seeds of capsicums. Slice them and add salt and pepper. 3. Peel and slice tomatoes and salt and pepper them. 4. Heat oil. First fry eggplants till soft. Remove and drain and place on a warm serving dish. 5. Then fry capsicums in the same way and, place them on top of eggplants. 6. Add yoghurt. 7. Fry tomatoes in oil and put on top. Serve hot.

11. LADIES' FINGERS WITH AUBERGINES

Ingredients	Quantity
Ladies fingers	450 gm
Olive oil	150 ml
Eggplant (large)	1 (about 225 gm)
Onions	1 (15 gm)
Tomatoes	2 large (250 gm)
Chopped parsley	1 tbsp
Salt and Pepper	

Method

1. Wash ladies fingers and cut the stems. 2. Peel and quarter tomatoes and peel and dice eggplant. 3. Chop onion and fry in olive oil till golden brown. 4. Add ladies fingers, tomatoes, eggplant, parsley, salt and pepper. Mix well. 5. Cover and cook gently for about 30 minutes.

12. TZAZIKI

Ingredients	Quantity
Tender cucumber	250 gm
Garlic	1 clove
Dry breadcrumbs	20 gm
Yoghurt	500 ml
Salt and Pepper	to taste

Method

1. Peel and grate cucumber. 2. Squeeze out juice, mix with peeled and crushed garlic. 3. Whip curd to remove lumps, add cucumber and garlic mixture and stir well. 4. Sprinkle breadcrumbs over and adjust seasoning. 5. Chill and serve.

13. CABBAGE DOLMAS

Ingredients	Quantity
Cabbage	½ kg
Beef mince	½ kg
Butter	50 gm
Pulao rice	50 gm
Parsley	1 bunch
Onions	115 gm
Salt and Pepper	to taste
Stock	500 ml
Eggs	2

Method

1. Mix minced beef with eggs, rice, chopped onions, salt and pepper. 2. Loosen cabbage leaves and remove thick vein with a knife. 3. Blanch leaves in boiling water till they become soft and pliable. 4. Put meat stuffing in centre of each cabbage leaf and fold neatly. 5. Poach in stock to which butter has been added. 6. Cook for a minimum of 20 minutes in stock. See that liquid is almost dried up when cooking ends.

14. POTATO KEPHTIDES

Ingredients	Quantity
Boiled potatoes (cold)	500 gm
Spring onions (finely chopped)	2
Tomatoes (peeled and chopped)	2 large
Refined flour	60 gm
Melted butter	15 gm
Salt and Pepper	to taste
Oil or Fat	for frying

Method

1. Sieve potatoes and mix with all the other ingredients. 2. Knead slightly and roll 2 cm (¾ inch) thick and cut in rounds about 6.25 cm (2½ inches) across. 3. Heat oil or fat till smoking hot and fry quickly.

These potato rounds may also be baked on a greased oven sheet in a hot oven till golden brown. They should be crisp outside but very soft inside.

15. HONEY PUFFS

Ingredients	Quantity
Refined flour (maida)	150 gm
Yeast	8 gm
Honey	100 ml
Lime	1
Sugar	30 gm
Cinnamon powder	2 gm
Oil	for frying

Method

1. Make a batter of flour and yeast in water and keep aside to ferment. 2. Separately make a thick syrup of sugar, lime and honey. 3. Heat oil almost to smoking point and with a spoon drop in batter bit by bit. 4. **Fry puffs till crisp and golden brown. 5. Serve hot with syrup and cinnamon powder.**

16. BAKLAVA (Turkish pastry)

Ingredients	Quantity
Pastry	
Refined flour	2 cups
Salt	1 tsp
Shortening	½ cup
Eggs (slightly beaten)	2
Water	2 tbsp
Filling	
Walnuts or Almonds (finely chopped)	1½ cups
Brown sugar	1½ cups
Melted butter	1 cup
Syrup	
Sugar	1½ cups
Water	1 cup
Lemon juice	1 tbsp

Method

1. Combine flour and salt. Cut shortening into flour until mixture has

consistency of corn meal. 2. Blend eggs and water; add to dry ingredients and mix until thoroughly dampened. 3. Turn onto wax paper; knead lightly 6 to 8 times to make a smooth ball; let it rest for half an hour. 4. Divide pastry into 5 portions; roll out each portion very thin on a lightly floured pastry cloth, into 20 × 20 cm (8 × 8 inch) squares. Place one square in bottom of 20 cm (8 inch) square pan.

Filling

Mix all ingredients together and divide into four portions. Spread quarter of filling over pastry. 2. Place second layer of pastry on top of filling. Spread another quarter of filling. 3. Continue making layers until 4 portions of pastry and all the filling have been used. Place fifth portion of pastry on top. 4. Cut Baklava diagonally across pan; then cut across to form diamonds.

Syrup

1. Combine syrup ingredients and boil for 5 minutes. Pour half the syrup over Baklava. 2. Bake at 176.6°C (approx. 350°F) for 35–40 minutes. Serve remaining syrup, cooled, over warm Baklava.

TURKEY

I. WEDDING SOUP

Ingredients	Quantity
Mutton or Lamb	450 gm
Bones–mutton or lamb	1 kg
Carrots	115 gm
Onions	115 gm
Salt	1 tbsp
Water	4 cups
Butter	100 gm
Refined flour	100 gm
Lime	½
Egg yolks	3
Melted butter	1 tbsp
Paprika	1 tbsp
Cayenne pepper	a pinch

Method

1. Put meat, bones, peeled onions, scraped carrots, salt into water. 2. Cook over medium fire in a covered pot until meat is tender (about 3 hours). 3. Strain off broth. 4. Mince cooked meat. Add it to stock and set aside. 5. Blend butter and flour in a large saucepan over low flame and

stir constantly until mixture is light brown (about 3 minutes). 6. Add meat stock gradually, stirring constantly. 7. Simmer for about 5 minutes. 8. Add lemon juice to beaten egg yolks, then gradually add about 2 ladles of hot stock. 9. Stir this mixture into soup. 10. Serve garnished with melted butter to which paprika and cayenne pepper have been added.

2. TURQUOISE (Yoghurt soup)

Ingredients	Quantity
Cucumbers	3
Salt	¼ tsp
Garlic	1 flake
Vinegar	1 tbsp
Curds (fresh)	600 ml
Olive oil	2 tbsp
Chopped mint	1 tbsp

Method

1. Peel cucumbers, quarter lengthwise and slice about 0.5 cm (or ⅛th inch) thick. 2. Place in a bowl and sprinkle with salt. 3. Rub another bowl with cut garlic and swish vinegar around in it to collect flavour. 4. Add curds. 5. Stir until mixture has consistency of thick soup adding 3 tablespoons of water if necessary. 6. Pour over cucumber and stir. 7. Pour into individual serving dishes. Sprinkle with olive oil and garnish with chopped mint.

3. BAKED FISH

Ingredients	Quantity
Large fish	1 kg
Onions	225 gm
Olive oil	½ cup
Paprika	to taste
Salt	to taste
Lime	½
Tomato purée	¼ cup
Water	1½ cups
Garlic	3 flakes
Celery	3 stalks
Carrots	450 gm
Parsley (chopped)	½ tsp

Method

1. Clean fish and cut into 2.5 cm (1 inch) slices. 2. Cut onions into rings and fry in a heavy skillet in one tbsp olive oil until light brown. 3. Add tomato paste, 1½ cups water, garlic, paprika, salt, lime juice, remaining

olive oil, chopped celery and diced carrots. 4. Cover and cook for 25 minutes. 5. Place fish in a deep baking dish and cover with sauce. 6. Bake in a fairly hot oven for 25 minutes. 7. Serve hot garnished with slices of lime and chopped parsley.

4. SHISH KEBAB

Ingredients	Quantity
Leg of lamb	1 kg
Olive oil	1 tbsp
Lemon	½
Onions	100 gm
Tomatoes	225 gm
Bay leaf	1
Capsicums	115 gm
Eggplants	225 gm

Method

1. Cut meat into 2.5 cm (1 inch) cubes. 2. Mix olive oil and lemon juice and rub into meat. 3. Place in a dish. Sprinkle with salt and pepper and cover with slices of onions and tomatoes and a bay leaf. 4. Keep in a refrigerator for 4 to 5 hours. 5. Slice eggplants and capsicums (with seeds removed). 6. Thread meat on skewers alternately with tomatoes and onions, eggplants and capsicums. 7. Broil over charcoal till done, turning regularly to ensure even cooking.

5. BRAISED KEBAB

Ingredients	Quantity
Lamb	1 kg
Small onions	12
Butter	60 gm
Tomatoes	150 gm
Salt and Pepper	to taste
Bay leaves	
Thyme	½ tsp
Water	2 tbsp

Method

1. Cut meat into small cubes and place in a heavy skillet with onions, butter, peeled tomatoes, salt, pepper, bay leaves, thyme and about 2 tbsp water. 2. Cook tightly covered over low flame for 20 minutes. 3. Increase to medium heat and continue cooking for another 2 hours.

6. MEAT WITH OKRA

Ingredients	Quantity
Lamb or Beef (diced)	450 gm
Butter	60 gm
Onions (diced)	115 gm
Lime	1
Ladies fingers	450 gm
Tomatoes (peeled and diced)	450 gm
Salt and Pepper	to taste

Method

1. Sauté meat very lightly in butter in a heavy skillet. 2. Add onions and continue cooking over medium heat for 5 minutes. 3. Add tomatoes and half-cup water. 4. Cover skillet. Reduce heat and simmer until meat is nearly tender. 5. Wash ladies fingers. Remove stem and place in rows on top of meat. 6. Add salt, pepper, lime juice and another half-cup water. 7. Cover and cook over medium heat until meat is tender (about 45 minutes).

7. DOLMAS (STUFFED VEGETABLES)

Ingredients	Quantity
Butter	4 tbsp
Water	3 cups
Stuffing:	
Minced lamb or beef (from fatty part)	450 gm
Onions (chopped)	115 gm
Uncooked rice	¼ cup
Chopped mint	1 tsp
Salt and Pepper	to taste
Tomato sauce (optional)	1 tbsp

Method

1. Place meat in a bowl. Add onions, rice, mint, salt, pepper and tomato sauce if desired. Knead well.

Stuff with: (a) Eggplants
(b) Capsicums
(c) Tomatoes
(d) Zucchini (Italian squash)
(e) Cabbage leaves.
(The stuffing is for 500 gm of vegetables.)

2. (a) Choose short, round eggplants, since they can be cooked upright in a saucepan. Cut off stems to use as covers. Peel eggplants lengthwise in strips, alternating peeled strips with unpeeled strips. Scoop out insides leaving a shell 2.5 cm (1") thick. Fill with stuffing and replace stem ends as covers.

   (b) Slice through tops of capsicums, but do not sever. Remove seeds and membranes. Fill with stuffing and close the tops.

   (c) Prepare and stuff tomatoes in the same way as capsicums.

   (d) Clean outside of zucchini and slice off one end to use as cover. Scoop out inside, leaving a shell 1.5 cm (½" thick). Stuff, replace cover, fastening it with toothpicks.

3. Place eggplant and zucchini dolmas upright at bottom of saucepan, followed by a layer of capsicum dolmas. Top with a layer of tomato dolmas. Add 2 tbsp butter and 1 cup water. Cook over medium heat for about 30–40 minutes or until vegetables are soft and meat is cooked.

4. To prepare cabbage dolmas [see (e) above] take off outer leaves of a large cabbage and parboil for 5 minutes, then drain. Put a spoonful of stuffing on each leaf and roll up. Place them in a saucepan in rows and add 2 tbsp butter and 2 cups water. Put a plate on top of the dolmas to keep them in place. Lower flame and cook over medium heat for about 35–40 minutes.

Note:

Eggplant, Capsicum, Tomato and Zucchini Dolmas can also be prepared separately. If any stuffing is left over, it can be formed into meat balls and placed between stuffed dolmas in saucepan.

8. CHICKEN à la TURE

Ingredients	Quantity
Chicken	1
Water	3 litre
Onions	150 gm
Carrots	200 gm
Parsley	1 bunch
Salt	1 tsp
Pepper	to taste
Shelled walnuts	2 cups
Paprika	1 tbsp
White bread	3 slices

Method

1. Place chicken in a pan with 3 litres water. 2. Add onions, carrots, parsley, salt and pepper. 3. Bring to a boil and skim. 4. Cover and cook for 2 hours. 5. When chicken is tender remove from pan and allow to cool. Save stock. 6. When cool, skin and bone chicken and cut into small pieces. 7. Put walnuts through a grinder twice and then add paprika. 8. Press nuts and paprika between layers of cheese cloth to get about 2 tbsp of red oil to be set aside for garnishing. 9. Soak bread in chicken stock. Squeeze dry and add to ground walnuts and paprika, mixing well. 10. Put this mixture through the grinder 3 times. Add 1 cup of chicken stock and work into a paste. 11. Divide paste into half and mix one half with chicken blending it thoroughly. 12. Spread other half of paste over chicken mixture and decorate the top with red oil. Serve cold.

9. PUMPKIN DESSERT

Ingredients	Quantity
Pumpkin	2 kg
Sugar	450 gm
Water	½ cup
Ground walnuts	½ cup

Method

1. Pare pumpkin and cut into one inch slices. 2. Place slices in a pan sprinkling sugar in between layers. Add water. 3. Cover and cook over medium heat until tender. Cool in pan then remove to a serving dish. 4. Garnish with nuts and serve.

10. TURKISH COFFEE

Ingredients	Quantity
Water	½ cup
Sugar	2 tbsp
Pulverized coffee	2 tsp

Method

This coffee is made in a cylindrical copper pot with a long handle sold in shops specializing in Mediterranean foods and called 'Jezve'.

1. Put water in 'Jezve'. Add sugar and coffee. Stir well. 2. Place over low flame and cook to a rising boil. 3. Remove from flame. Pour froth into 2 small coffee cups. 4. Bring to a boil again and remove from fire. 5. Pour enough coffee over froth to fill cups. Serve.

CHINA

SEASONING OF A CHINESE WOK

Take a reasonable quantity of assorted vegetable peelings, assorted diced vegetables including onions and fry them in a wok using a little oil. Stir continuously so that every part of the wok is rubbed well with vegetable mixture. Continue frying till mixture gives off a burning smell. At this stage pour cold water slowly and continue stirring till mixture starts boiling. Throw away this mixture and repeat the process three or four times till there is no iron smell left.

During normal use of a wok, after washing and drying the inside, smear it with oil to keep it seasoned for use the next day. Unless it is absolutely essential the outside of a wok need not be washed; this helps to make it last longer, since it is made from a comparatively thin gauge metal.

1. SWEET CORN AND CHICKEN SOUP

Ingredients	Quantity
Creamed corn	1 tin
Strong chicken stock	350 ml
Cornflour	15 gm
Celery	15 gm
Garlic	1 flake
Ginger	1 small piece
Bacon fat	1 tsp
Chicken dice (cooked)	55 gm
Eggs	2
Salt and Pepper	to taste

Method

1. Chop celery, garlic and ginger fine. Sauté in bacon fat. 2. Add stock and cook for about half an hour. Add salt and pepper. 3. Beat contents of can well. 4. Add strained stock, blended well with cornflour. 5. Beat egg slightly. Pour over boiling corn soup and stir with a fork till set. 6. Serve piping hot, with soya sauce and chillies in vinegar.

2. FRESH CORN EGG FLOWER SOUP

Ingredients	Quantity
Corn-on-the-cob (young)	4
Onions	30 gm
Small onion	1
Garlic	1 flake

Ingredients	Quantity
Ginger	1 slice
Lean pork	115 gm
Eggs	3
Oil	15 ml
Pepper	a pinch
Salt	5–10 gm
Sugar	½ tsp
Soya sauce	15 ml
Cornflour	15 gm
Boiling water	6 cups (about 1.2 litre)

Method

1. Mince pork and add cornflour, oil, sugar, pepper, soya sauce, 2 tbsp water and 5 gm of salt. 2. Using a sharp knife, scrape all corn kernels into a bowl. 3. Mince ginger, garlic and onions. 4. Heat a little oil in a pan. Fry ginger, onions, garlic and remaining salt for about a minute. 5. Add boiling water and corn kernels. 6. Cover and bring soup to a boil. Simmer for 10 minutes. 7. Add meat mixture, cover and simmer till corn and meat are cooked. 8. Take pot off fire. Remove lid. Beat eggs and stir into soup.

3. CHICKEN CLEAR SOUP

Ingredients	Quantity
Good chicken stock	1.2 litre
Boiled chicken pieces	100 gm
Salt and Pepper	to taste
Lettuce	100 gm
Soya sauce	a dash
Ajinomoto (Monosodium glutamate)	a pinch

Method

1. Heat stock and add boiled chicken pieces. 2. Season soup with salt and pepper, soya sauce and ajinomoto. Bring it to a boil. 3. Remove, garnish with finely shredded lettuce and serve hot.

4. ASPARAGUS CHICKEN SOUP

Ingredients	For 4
Raw breast of chicken (shredded)	85 gm
Chicken stock	1.2 litre
Ajinomoto (Monosodium glutamate)	a pinch
Egg	1
Canned asparagus	8

Ingredients	For 4
Salt and Pepper	to taste
Cornflour	30 gm

Method

1. Heat chicken stock, add shredded chicken and asparagus tips. 2. Add seasoning and ajinomoto. 3. Blend cornflour with a little cold water and mix with soup. 4. Bring soup to a boil. 5. Add beaten egg white and stir well. 6. When slightly thickened, remove from fire and serve hot.

5. CHICKEN NOODLE SOUP

Ingredients	Quantity
Noodles	½ pkt.
Carrots	200 gm
Spring onions	2 bunches
Salt and Pepper	to taste
Chicken stock	1.2 litre
Soya sauce	a dash
Chicken shreds	400 gm
Cabbage	200 gm
French beans	100 gm
Ajinomoto (Monosodium glutamate)	2 pinches

Method

1. Boil noodles, drain and keep aside. 2. Clean and cut all vegetables into thin long strips. 3. Heat chicken stock in a pan. Add shredded chicken and all the vegetables. 4. Add seasoning and soya sauce. 5. Put in boiled noodles and serve hot.

6. CHICKEN AND MUSHROOM SOUP

Ingredients	Quantity
Young chicken	1
Fresh mushrooms	450 gm
Galric	1 flake
Ground coriander	1 tsp
Peppercorns	1 tsp
Lard	30 gm
Chicken stock	1.2 litre
Ajinomoto (Monosodium glutamate)	1 tsp

Method

1. Cook chicken in water until tender. 2. Remove flesh and cut into small pieces. 3. Re-boil chicken bones for about 2 hours. Strain stock. 4. Prepare mushrooms. 5. Fry garlic, coriander and peppercorns in lard. 6. Add

mushrooms, chicken meat and chicken liver. 7. Add stock. Bring to a boil and simmer for 10–15 minutes. 8. Add monosodium glutamate. Stir well and serve.

7. VEGETABLE EGG CREAM SOUP

Ingredients	Quantity
Eggs	2
Hot chicken stock or Hot water	1.2 litre
Soya sauce	a little
Cornflour	30 gm
Lettuce	1 bunch
Salt and Pepper	to taste
Ajinomoto (Monosodium glutamate)	a pinch

Method

1. Heat stock or water in a pan. 2. Cut lettuce into fairly large pieces. 3. Season soup with salt, pepper and a dash of soya sauce and ajinomoto. 4. Thicken soup with cornflour blended with cold water. 5. Beat eggs. When soup begins to thicken, add eggs and keep on stirring. 6. Throw in lettuce. Remove from fire and serve immediately.

8. EGG DROP SPINACH SOUP

Ingredients	Quantity
Chicken stock	800 ml
Onions	50 gm
Garlic	3 gm
Egg	1
Vinegar	2 ml
Soya sauce	a few drops
Peppercorns	a few
Spinach	250 gm
Ginger	5 gm
Oil	10 ml
Cornflour	30 gm
Salt	to taste
Ajinomoto (Monosodium glutamate)	½ tsp

Method

1. Chop onions, ginger and garlic fine. 2. Heat oil. Add onions, ginger and garlic and sauté well. 3. Add crushed peppercorns. 4. Add stock and bring to a boil. 5. Beat egg and pour into mixture stirring all the time to form shreds. 6. Remove stalks from spinach and add to mixture. Add

vinegar, salt and ajinomoto. 7. Dissolve cornflour in water and gradually pour into soup. When soup is thick, add soya sauce. Serve hot.

9. HOT AND SOUR SOUP

Ingredients	Quantity
Chicken stock	800 ml
Shredded carrots	60 gm
Shredded capsicums	60 gm
Shredded spring onion bulbs	60 gm
Pepper	2 gm
Chili oil	10 ml
Shredded chicken (cooked)	60 gm
Salt	5 gm
Soya sauce	5 ml
Vinegar	10 ml
Cornflour	20 gm

Method

1. Bring chicken stock to a boil. 2. Add shredded vegetables and cook for 3 minutes. 3. Add shredded chicken. Add salt and soya sauce. 4. When stock begins boiling, add cornflour dissolved in water. 5. Pour a few drops of chilli oil, vinegar and pepper powder into each soup bowl. 6. Pour hot soup over and serve hot, garnished with chopped spring onion leaves.

Chilli oil

To prepare chilli oil, add very hot oil to chilli powder. Let it stand for 10 minutes and strain out clear chilli oil.

10. WONTONS

Ingredients	Quantity
Raw minced chicken or pork	225 gm
Onions (finely chopped)	50 gm
Ginger (finely chopped)	½ tsp
Salt	to taste
Refined flour	340 gm
Baking powder	½ tsp
Eggs	3
Cornflour	for rolling
Fat	for frying
Sauce	
Sugar	4 tbsp
Vinegar	2 tbsp
Tomato sauce	1 tbsp

Ingredients	Quantity
Cornflour	2 tbsp
Water	½ cup
Soya sauce	2 tbsp

Mehtod

1. Sieve flour, baking powder, and salt together. Make a well in centre. Add lightly beaten eggs. 2. Make a stiff dough using a little cold water if necessary. Sprinkle a pastry board with cornflour and knead dough gently till smooth. 3. Roll out wafer-thin and cut in 7.5 cm (3") squares. Mix minced meat with other ingredients and place a heaped tsp of mixture in middle of each square. 4. Fold crosswise and press edges together firmly, using a little water. Deep fry in smoking fat until deep brown, or boil in soup. When fried, serve with a sweet and sour sauce.

Sauce

1. Mix sugar, vinegar, tomato sauce, and water and bring to a boil. 2. Add cornflour blended with soya sauce and stir on a slow fire until sauce thickens.

11. WONTON SOUP

Ingredients	Quantity
Dough	
Refined flour (sifted)	2 cups
Salt	1 tsp
Egg (large)	1
Water	⅓ cup
Filling	
Finely cooked minced pork	500 gm
Egg (beaten)	1
Salt	½ tsp
Pepper	¼ tsp
Soup	
Chicken stock (strong)	6 cups
Lettuce or	2 bunches
Chopped green onions	2 tbsp

Noodles

1. Mix and sift flour and salt into mixing bowl. 2. Beat eggs slightly and stir into flour. 3. Add water, a little at a time, mixing until the dough is smooth and right for rolling. 4. Turn out onto a lightly floured board, and knead until smooth, turning and folding over a few times. 5. Cover

and let stand for 15–20 minutes. 6. Roll out paper thin and cut into 7.5 cm (3") squares. 7. Mix pork and remaining ingredients smoothly together with a fork. 8. Drop filled wontons, a few at a time, into 1.2 litres (approx. 1 quart) boiling salted water and cook until they float to the top (about 15 minutes), remove with a slotted spoon, and drain. 12. Place cooked wontons in bowls. Heat stock and bring to a boil. 13. Add lettuce torn into large pieces. Pour soup over wontons. Serve with soya sauce.

Variations

Cooked ground beef or shrimps can be substituted for pork filling. Finely chopped celery (½ cup) and ½ cup tightly packed spinach can be used instead of lettuce, in which case, cook for a minute or two in stock.

12. EGG FU YONG

Ingredients	Quantity
Cooked chicken, crab or lobster mean	225 gm
Tomatoes (blanched and skinned)	225 gm
Fat or Oil	for frying
Salt and Pepper	to taste
Onions	225 gm
Spring onions	2–3
Mushrooms	115 gm
Bamboo shoots	60 gm
Stock	
Cornflour	1 tbsp
Egg	1
Tomato sauce	to taste

Noodles

1. Cut chicken or shellfish into small pieces. 2. Thinly slice all vegetables in a little oil for a few minutes. 3. Add chicken or fish. Season. 4. Pour in just enough stock to cover. 5. Add soya sauce and boil for 2–3 minutes. 6. Add cornflour mixed with a little water and continue cooking until thickened. 7. Beat egg. Season and prepare an omelette. 8. Serve chicken and vegetables with omelette on top and a little tomato sauce poured over it.

13. BRINJAL IN GARLIC SAUCE

Ingredients	For 4
Brinjals	500 gm
Ginger	5 gm
Spring onions	2

Ingredients	For 4
Salt	5 gm
Soya sauce	a dash
Refined oil	to deep fry
Garlic	2 pods (30 gm)
Ajinomoto (Monosodium glutamate)	2 gm
Green chillies	2

Method

1. Peel and cut brinjals into quarters. 2. Deep fry in very hot oil till light brown. 3. Chop spring onions (white and green), ginger, green chillies and garlic. 4. Heat a little oil (30 ml) in a wok, and add chopped spring onions and ginger. Stir fry for half a minute. Put in green chillies and garlic. Stir fry for a minute. 5. Add brinjals, salt, ajinomoto and soya sauce. 6. Stir fry for half a minute and remove.

14. VEGETABLE CHOW CHOW

Ingredients	Quantity
Green peas	100 gm
Carrots	100 gm
Cauliflower	50 gm
Capsicums	100 gm
Salt and Pepper	to taste
Cornflour	20 gm
Oil	20 ml
Hot water	20 ml
Onions	100 gm
Cabbage	50 gm
Tomatoes	50 gm
French beans	50 gm
Ajinomoto (Monosodium glutamate)	2 pinches

Method

1. Cut cleaned vegetables into fairly large pieces. 2. Heat oil in a pan, and sauté all the vegetables. 3. Add about 20 ml hot water. Season with salt, pepper and ajinomoto. 4. When vegetables are cooked, thicken gravy with cornflour blended in cold water. 5. When thick remove from fire and serve hot.

15. PRAWNS IN GARLIC SAUCE

Ingredients	Quantity
Prawns (king-size)	12
Spring onions	1

Ingredients	Quantity
Ginger	1 small piece
Stock	as desired
Cornflour	50 gm
Tomato sauce	100 gm
Salt and Pepper	to taste
Garlic	6 cloves
Oil	for deep frying

Method

1. Shell and de-vein prawns. Wash well. 2. Heat oil for deep frying. Add prawns and remove after a minute. 3. Heat a little oil in a pan. Add finely crushed garlic and ginger and then add prawns and sauté for a minute. 4. Add seasoning, tomato sauce and stock. Add diced spring onions and cornflour blended in a little cold water. 5. Cook till gravy thickens. 6. Remove and serve hot.

16. FRIED PRAWNS

Ingredients	Quantity
Prawns	450 gm
Lard	60 gm
Spring onions	2
Garlic	1 flake
Ginger	2 slices
Soya sauce	2 tbsp
Vinegar	1 tsp
Sugar	1 tsp
Salt	to taste

Noodles

1. Shell prawns. Remove intestines and wash thoroughly. 2. Fry slowly in lard for 5 minutes. 3. Add all the other ingredients and cook for a another 5 minutes. Serve immediately.

17. MANDARIN FISH

Ingredients	For 4
Pomfret or Salmon (small)	1
Carrots	50 gm
French beans	50 gm
Chicken stock	30 ml
Soya sauce	2 tsp
Cornflour	100 gm
Oil	20 ml
Oil	for deep frying

Ingredients	For 4
Green peas	100 gm
Spring onions	2 bunches
Cabbage	50 gm
Tomatoes	50 gm
Salt and Pepper	to taste
Ajinomoto (Monosodium glutamate)	3 pinches
Onions	100 gm

Noodles

1. Clean fish and coat with seasoned cornflour. Deep fry and set aside.
2. Cut all vegetables into thin long strips. 3. Heat 20 ml oil in a pan and
sauté all the vegetables. 4. Add chicken stock. Add seasoning, salt,
pepper, soya sauce and monosodium glutamate. 5. When ingredients are
cooked, thicken with a little cornflour blended in cold water. 6. When
ready, remove from fire. 7. Pour over fried fish and serve hot.

18. SWEET AND SOUR FISH

Ingredients	Quantity
Fish (Salmon or Pomfret)	1 kg
Ginger	
Garlic	15 gm
Green chillies	30 gm
Vinegar	100 ml
Soya sauce	100 ml
Sugar	30 gm
Pepper	a pinch
Oil	50 ml

Noodles

1. Clean fish thoroughly, remove fins but leave head and tail. Wash well.
2. Cut gashes diagonally with a knife on both sides from head to tail.
3. Dry fish and fry in hot oil till it is brown on both sides. Remove. Drain
off most of the oil leaving a little in the pan. 4. Slice ginger, green chillies
and garlic. 5. Fry ginger, garlic and chillies. 6. Add fish, seasoning, soya
sauce and sugar and simmer on a gentle fire till fish is cooked and very
little gravy remains. 7. Add vinegar, bring to a boil and remove.

19. SWEET AND SOUR PRAWNS

Ingredients	Quantity
Shelled prawns	450 gm
Onions	225 gm

Ingredients	Quantity
Celery stems	115 gm
Egg	1
Cornflour	30 gm
Pineapple	55 gm
Tomatoes	225 gm
Vinegar	30 ml
Sugar	115 gm
Salt and Pepper	to taste
Oil	20 ml
Soya sauce	30 ml

Noodles

1. Clean prawns. Wash well. Season. 2. Prepare a thick batter with cornflour, egg and water if necessary. 3. Dip prawns in batter. Fry till crisp and cooked. Drain and leave aside. 4. Wash and cut vegetables into thick slices. 5. Remove extra oil from pan. Fry finely chopped garlic and ginger. Add tomatoes, onions and pineapple pieces. 6. Add chopped celery stems. Cook well and purée vegetables by mashing them up. Strain through a soup sieve. 7. Add soya sauce, sugar, vinegar, salt and pepper. 8. Cook till gravy is thick. 9. Pour over fried prawns.

20. SWEET AND SOUR PORK (A)

Ingredients	Quantity
Lean pork	450 gm
Onions	225 gm
Pineapple	115 gm
Tomatoes	225 gm
Vinegar	30 ml
Cornflour	55 gm
Eggs	2
Celery	115 gm
Sugar	115 gm
Oil	115 ml
Salt and Pepper	to taste
Soya sauce	50 ml

Noodles

1. Boil pork in a little water, (season it with salt and pepper), till soft, leave to cool. 2. Cut into small cubes. 3. Make a thick batter of eggs and cornflour adding a little water if necessary. 4. Dip meat into batter and deep fry in oil. Drain and leave aside. 5. Wash and cut vegetables in thick slices. 6. Remove extra oil from pan. Fry finely chopped garlic and ginger. Add tomatoes, onions and pineapple pieces. 7. Add chopped

celery. Cook well and purée vegetables. Strain through a soup sieve.
8. Add soya sauce, sugar, vinegar, salt and pepper. 9. Cook till gravy is
thick. 10. Pour over fried prawns.

SWEET AND SOUR PORK (B)

Ingredients	Quantity
Pork	450 gm
Egg	1
Refined flour	55 gm
Fat	to fry
Seasoning	to taste
Pineapple	115 gm
Celery	115 gm
Carrots	115 gm
Spring onions	115 gm
Tomato sauce	100 ml
Worcester sauce	100 ml
Soya sauce	100 ml
Chilli sauce	20 ml

Noodles

1. Clean and cut pork into small pieces. 2. Make batter with egg, flour,
seasoning and water. 3. Dip meat in batter and deep fry. 4. Mix all the
ingredients in the sauce. Bring to a boil. 5. Add meat and simmer till
cooked.

SWEET AND SOUR PORK (C)

Ingredients	Quantity
Loin of pork	500 gm
Wine or Sherry	1 tbsp
Soya sauce	2 tbsp
Refined flour	2 tbsp
Cornflour	1 tbsp
Oil	for deep frying
Vegetables	
Capsicums	3
Onions	115 gm
Carrots	115 gm
Bamboo shoots	115 gm
Oil	for frying
Pineapple	2 slices
Sauce	
Sugar	6 tbsp

Ingredients	Quantity
Soya sauce	4 tbsp
Wine or Sherry	1 tbsp
Vinegar	2 tbsp
Tomato sauce	4 tbsp
Cornflour	1 tbsp
Water	½ cup

Method

1. Cut pork into 1.5 cm (½ inch) cubes. Mix well with wine or sherry, soya sauce, flour and cornflour. 2. Deep fry in oil till golden brown and crisp. Turn out into a hot dish. 3. Heat frying pan, add 60 ml of oil and sauté quartered and seeded capsicums, quartered onions, carrots (cut into small wedges and boiled for 5–8 minutes) shredded bamboo shoots and quartered pineapple. 4. Mix all ingredients for sauce except cornflour and water, and bring to a boil. 5. Now add cornflour smoothly blended with water. Simmer, stirring constantly. Add fried pork to sautéed vegetables and mix well. Serve hot.

21. PORK FRITTERS

Ingredients	Quantity
Boiled pork	500 gm
Eggs	2
Refined flour	55 gm
Seasoning	to taste
Oil	for frying
Potatoes	450 gm

Method

1. Cut pork into thin slices. 2. Make a batter of flour and eggs adding a little water if necessary. Add seasoning. 3. Dip pork slices in batter and deep fry in hot oil. 4. Peel and cut potatoes into fingers. 5. Deep fry and serve with pork slices.

N.B. A green salad and tomato sauce may be served with pork fritters.

22. DEEP FRIED SPRING CHICKEN

Ingredients	Quantity
Spring chicken	1
Onions (chopped)	1
Sherry	½ cup
Salt	to taste
Sugar	1 tsp
Sesame oil	2 tbsp

Ingredients	Quantity
Soya sauce	½ cup
Refined flour	
Lard for frying	

Method

1. Joint chicken and cut into about a dozen pieces. 2. Mix onion, oil, soya sauce, sherry, a little salt and sugar together. Pour over chicken. Let it stand for at least an hour. 3. Remove chicken, dip pieces in flour and fry in hot fat for 5–6 minutes until golden brown. 4. Serve with a sauce made of stock flavoured with fried spring onion, garlic and chilles and thickened with cornflour. 5. Serve with noodles.

23. CHICKEN IN GARLIC SAUCE

Ingredients	Quantity
Chicken	1
Flour	60 gm
Cornflour	60 gm
Tomato sauce	100 gm
Onions	100 gm
Spring onions	1 bunch
Salt and Pepper	to taste
Chicken stock	30 ml
Oil	15 ml
Ginger	1 small piece
Garlic	6 cloves
Cornflour (for gravy)	30 gm
Ajinomoto (Monosodium glutamate)	2 pinches
Oil	for deep frying

Method

1. Debone chicken and cut into cubes. 2. Make batter using both flour and cornflour. 3. Add chicken and coat well. Drain. 4. Deep fry chicken cubes. When crisp remove. 5. Heat oil and add crushed ginger, garlic and sliced onions. Then add tomato sauce, stock and seasoning. 6. Add cornflour blended with a little cold water. 7. Cook till gravy thickens. Add fried chicken cubes and remove. Serve hot.

24. SWEET AND SOUR CHICKEN

Ingredients	For 4
Chicken	400 gm
Onions	50 gm

Ingredients	For 4
Tomato	50 gm
Capsicum	50 gm
Cucumber	50 gm
Carrots	50 gm
Sugar	200 gm
Vinegar	80 ml
Tomato sauce	150 ml
Egg	1
Cornflour	50 gm
Ajinomoto (Monosodium glutamate)	a pinch
Lemon	1
Salt and Pepper	to taste
Oil	for deep frying

Method

1. Cut boneless chicken into small pieces. 2. Add cornflour, beaten egg, pepper, salt and monosodium glutamate. Mix well. 3. Heat oil, deep fry chicken and keep aside. 4. Cut onions, tomato, capsicum, cucumber and carrots into small pieces and keep aside. 5. Make a gravy with tomato sauce, vinegar, sugar and a little water. 6. Add lemon juice and boil gravy for a few minutes. 7. Blend a little cornflour in cold water and add to gravy. Cook till thick. 8. Add chicken pieces and all the vegetables to the hot sauce and serve.

25. CHICKEN CHILI

Ingredients	For 4
Chicken	1
Soya sauce	15 ml
Chillies (shredded without seeds)	200 gm
Ginger (ground)	15 gm
Sugar	10 gm
Oil	10 ml
Seasoning	to taste
Oil	for deep frying

Method

1. Boil whole chicken with seasoning till cooked. 2. Cool chicken and cut into even pieces. Sprinkle with soya sauce, rubbing it well into chicken. 3. Heat oil and deep fry chicken. When dark brown remove. 4. Heat oil in a pan. Add shredded green chillies and ground ginger. Add fried chicken and sauté. Add a dash of soya sauce and sugar. Remove from fire and serve hot.

26. CHICKEN SHREDS WITH CHILI

Ingredients	For 4
Chicken (shredded)	500 gm
Spring onions	4 bunches
Salt and Pepper	to taste
Soya sauce	as required
Ajinomoto (Monosodium glutamate)	2 pinches
Chicken stock	30 ml
Green chillies	150 gm
Cornflour	30 gm
Sugar	5 gm
Oil	10 ml

Method

1. Shred chicken and chillies into long thin strips. Remove chilli seeds. 2. Cut spring onions into 2.5 cm pieces. 3. Heat oil in a pan and sauté shredded chicken. 4. Throw in chillies and spring onions. Add chicken stock. 5. Add seasoning (salt and pepper), sugar, soya sauce and ajinomoto. 6. Blend cornflour in a little cold water and add. 7. Bring to a boil. 8. Remove and serve hot.

27. CHICKEN PINEAPPLE

Ingredients	Quantity
Chicken	1
Pineapple cubes	1 cup
Wine	1 tbsp
Soya sauce	3 tbsp
Sugar	1 tbsp
Salt	to taste
Cornflour	1 tbsp
Ginger	2.5 cm (1 inch)
Pineapple juice	½ cup
Celery sticks (hearts)	2–3
Sesame oil	for frying
Chopped parsley	

Method

1. Deep fry whole chicken until golden brown. Place in a bowl, add sliced ginger, sugar, wine, soya sauce and salt. Steam until tender. 2. Remove bones and cut chicken into small pieces. Place on a dish and keep warm. 3. Mix pineapple juice with chicken stock. Blend in cornflour. Boil, stirring until mixture thickens. 4. Add pineapple cubes and celery and pour over chicken. Garnish with parsley.

28. FRIED CHICKEN

Ingredients	Quantity
Spring chicken	1
Wine	1 tbsp
Soya sauce	1 tbsp
cornflour	4 tbsp
Capsicums (red)	3
Capsicums (green)	5
Wine	2 tbsp
Sugar	1 tsp
Oil	to deep fry
Garlic	1 flake
Ginger	1.3 cm (½ inch) piece
Soya sauce	4 tbsp
Cornflour	1 tsp
Water	1 tbsp
Ajinomoto (Monosodium glutamate)	a pinch
Salt	to taste

Method

1. Clean and cut chicken into 5 cm (approx. 2") pieces. Sprinkle with first lot of wine, soya sauce and cornflour. 2. Heat oil and deep fry chicken till golden brown. Remove chicken to a plate. 3. Heat about 5 tbsp of oil. Add crushed garlic, sliced ginger, red capsicums cut into halves, and quartered green capsicums. 4. Fry for 2 minutes. Add deep fried chicken. Mix well and continue to fry. Add remaining wine, soya sauce, salt and monosodium glutamate. 5. Bring to a boil. Add cornflour blended with water. Stir well and serve hot.

29. BROILED CHICKEN

Ingredients	Quantity
Tender chicken	1
Mushrooms	55 gm
Kohlrabi or	
Bamboo shoots	115 gm
Minced pork	225 gm
Garlic	1 flake
Sugar	15 gm
Soya sauce	50 ml
Ginger	15 gm
Salt and Pepper	to taste
Oil	to sauté

Method

1. Clean chicken. Wash. Rub over with salt, pepper and soya sauce. Set

aside. 2. Chop mushrooms, garlic, ginger and kohlrabi. 3. Heat oil. Fry garlic and ginger. Add pork and chopped vegetables. Cook on a slow fire. When cooked, remove and cool. 4. Stuff chicken with prepared mixture. 5. Fry chicken in oil in a deep pan turning over till chicken is evenly browned. 6. Cover pan and let it cook slowly, adding water from time to time if needed.

30. HAKKA NOODLES

Ingredients	For 4
Noodles	400 gm
Cabbage	60 gm
Carrots	60 gm
Ham	60 gm
Shredded chicken	60 gm
Capsicums	60 gm
Spring onions	½ bunch
Bean sprouts	60 gm
Salt	5 gm
Soya sauce	1 tsp
Ajinomoto (Monosodium glutamate)	2 gm
Oil	30 ml

Method

1. Boil noodles till soft. 2. Shred all vegetables. 3. Shred chicken and ham. 4. Heat oil in a wok and stir fry all vegetables. 5. Add salt, ajinomoto and soya sauce. 6. Add noodles, mix well and serve immediately.

31. CHOW MEIN

Ingredients	Quantity
Noodles	200 gm
Chicken or Pork (cooked and shredded)	200 gm
Cabbage (shredded)	200 gm
Bamboo shoots	2
Eggs	2
Chicken stock	½ cup
Mushrooms	60 gm
Garlic	1 flake
Ginger	2.5 cm (1 inch) piece
Leeks	2 stalks
Soya sauce	2 tbsp
Cornflour	2 tsp
Salt	to taste
Oil	for frying

Method

1. Boil and drain noodles. Heat oil and pour in slightly beaten egg. Cook until set. Remove from pan. Cool and cut into strips. 2. Reheat pan. Add oil and fry crushed garlic, sliced leeks, shredded bamboo shoots, cabbage, mushrooms, sliced ginger and shredded meat. 3. Add stock and soya sauce blended with cornflour. Simmer until sauce thickens. 4. In another pan, fry cooked noodles in deep fat for about 5 minutes. Remove on to a hot dish. Garnish with egg strips and pour meat mixture over noodles.

32. CHINESE NOODLES

Ingredients	Quantity
Refined flour	450 gm
Eggs	3
Ripe green chilli	1
Garlic	a few flakes
Ginger	1.5 cm (½ inch) piece
Prawns (shelled)	225 gm
Pork	225 gm
Vinegar	20 ml
Soya sauce	30 ml
Beans	115 gm
Carrots	115 gm
Celery	55 gm
Oil	50 ml
Spring onions	115 gm

Method

1. Make dough with eggs and flour. Wet hands with cold water when mixing. Roll out. Cut into thin strips and dry in the sun. 2. Heat oil; fry shelled and seasoned prawns. Add vinegar and soya sauce and cook for 5 minutes. 3. Grind together chilli, garlic and ginger. Add small pieces of pork; cook till pork is nearly done. 4. Add beams, carrots, celery and spring onions cut into thin strips. Keep pan covered for about 2–3 minutes. Remove. 5. In a flat frying pan heat oil. Fry handful of boiled noodles. Turn over when brown. 6. Sprinkle over pork and vegetable mixture and serve hot.

33. STEWED NOODLES

Ingredients	Quantity
Egg noodles	100 gm
Red tomato	1
Garlic	1 flake
Green onions	½ bunch
Sugar	¼ tsp

Ingredients	Quantity
Soya sauce	1 tsp
Pepper	a dash
Cornflour	½ tsp
Oil	1 dsp
Salt	to taste
Chicken broth	600 ml
Roast pork (cut into slivers)	
Carrots	60 gm
Capsicum	1
French beans	30 gm
Ajinomoto (Monosodium glutamate)	¼ tsp

Method

1. Boil noodles in salted boiling water. Drain. Add a tsp of oil to keep them separate. 2. Heat remaining oil. Add finely chopped garlic, salt, and sliced onions. 3. Add strong chicken broth and diced and blanched tomato. Mix soya sauce with cornflour and sugar. 4. Add to pan and simmer for 10 minutes. Add monosodium glutamate, cold noodles, prepared vegetables and meat. 5. Simmer for a few minutes. Mix and remove. Serve hot.

34. CHOP SUEY

Ingredients	Quantity
Beef, Pork, Ham or Bacon	225 gm
Cabbage	340 gm
Onions	225 gm
Carrots	225 gm
Mushrooms	115 gm
French beans	115 gm
Celery	2 sticks
Bamboo shoots	60 gm
Tomatoes	2
Salt and Pepper	to taste
Oil	for frying

Method

1. Slice meat across the grain and shallow fry in oil. 2. Add a little water, cover and cook gently till tender. 3. Finely slice cabbage, onions, carrots and also slice mushrooms, bamboo shoots, beans, celery and tomatoes. 4. Put some fat or oil into a frying pan and fry all vegetables except celery and mushrooms. Season. Add 1 cup water, cover and cook stirring occasionally adding more water if necessary, until vegetables are almost tender. Now add mushrooms and celery and when these are cooked, add meat. Serve hot.

35. AMERICAN CHOP SUEY

Ingredients	Quantity
Noodles	½ packet
Chicken	300 gm (shredded)
Shrimps	300 gm
Carrots	200 gm
Salt and Pepper	to taste
Ajinomoto (Monosodium glutamte)	2 pinches
Chicken stock	10 ml
Cabbage	300 gm
Onions	100 gm
Tomato sauce	½ a small bottle
Corn starch	30 gm
Oil	10 ml
Oil	for deep frying

Method

1. Boil noodles, drain and deep fry to a crisp brown. 2. Shred chicken.
3. Shell and de-vein shrimps. 4. Cut vegetables into thin long strips.
5. Heat oil in a pan. Add shredded chicken and saute it and then add
shrimps for a few minutes. 6. Add prepared vegetables. Add chicken
stock and seasoning to taste. Add tomato sauce. Thicken with cornflour
blended with cold water. 7. When mixture becomes thick, remove from
fire and place on crisp noodles. Serve immediately.

36. CHINESE VEGETABLES (MIXED VEGETABLES)

Ingredients	Quantity
Garlic	2 flakes
Onions	100 gm
Carrots	100 gm
Cabbage	100 gm
Cauliflower	100 gm
Oil	2 tsp
Salt	
Sugar	1 tsp
Pepper powder	2 pinches
Lime juice	½ tsp
Soya sauce	1 tsp
Ajinomoto (optional)	a pinch
Cornflour	1 tbsp

Method

1. Heat oil, fry chopped garlic. 2. After a while add cut onions and cut
carrots and fry for sometime. 3. Then add cut cabbage and cauliflower.

Fry till it is half-cooked. 4. Then add lime juice, pepper powder, salt and sugar. Stir. 5. Lastly add cornflour mixed with water. Stir well. Cook for 5 minutes and remove.

37. VEGETABLE FRIED RICE

Ingredients	For 4
Rice (good quality)	400 gm
Green peas (just shelled)	50 gm
French beans	50 gm
Carrots	50 gm
Spring onions	1 bunch
Salt and Pepper	to taste
Soya sauce	15 ml
Oil	15 ml

Method

1. Prepare boiled rice and chill. 2. Dice French beans and carrots. Chop spring onions. 3. Parboil French beans and carrots. Boil green peas. 4. Heat oil in a pan and sauté green peas, French beans and carrots. 5. Add cooled boiled rice breaking up any lumps with the back of a spoon. 6. Add seasoning and soya sauce. 7. Fry rice well. Add chopped spring onions. 8. Remove and serve hot.

38. CHINESE FRIED RICE

Ingredients	For 4
Rice (good quality)	400 gm
Eggs	2
Chicken	100 gm
Shrimps	100 gm
Ham	100 gm
Soya sauce	15 ml
Oil	15 ml
Salt and Pepper	to taste
Spring onions	1 bunch

Method

1. Prepare boiled rice and chill. 2. Shred chicken and sauté till almost done. 3. Shell and de-vein shrimps. 4. Wash well and boil. 5. Add beaten eggs and make a plain omelette. 6. Heat oil in a pan. 7. Add diced or shredded chicken pieces, whole boiled shrimps and diced ham. 8. Add cooled/chilled boiled rice and with the back of a large spoon or ladle break up any lumps to separate grains and coat rice with oil. Mix in seasoning and soya sauce. Fry rice well. 9. Add chopped spring onions. 10. Remove and serve hot.

39. GARLIC SPARE RIBS

Ingredients	Quantity
Spare ribs (pork)	500 gm
Garlic	5 flakes
Ginger	2.5 cm (1 inch) piece
Ajinomoto (Monosodium glutamate)	1 tsp
Soya sauce	6 tbsp
Salt	1 tbsp
Sugar	1 tsp

Method
1. Peel and crush garlic and ginger. Mix with remaining ingredients and spread over spare ribs. Marinade for 1 hour. 2. Bake in a medium oven over a pan of boiling water till tender. Chop ribs into 7.5 cm (3 inch) lengths and separate. Serve hot.

JAPAN

I. TAMAGO SUIMONO (EGG SOUP)

Ingredients	Quantity
Eggs	4
Dried fish	115 gm
Water	1.8 litre
Soya sauce	½ tbsp
Salt	to taste
Ajinomoto (Monosodium glutamate)	¼ tsp

Method
1. Grate or grind fish fine. 2. Heat water and when it begins to boil, add fish. 3. When it boils again remove pan from fire. 4. Gradually stir in well-beaten eggs and just before serving mix in soya sauce and salt. Serve hot.

2. TEMPURA (FRIED FISH)

Ingredients	Quantity
Fish	500 gm
Refined flour	225 gm
Eggs	3
Sauce	
Fish stock	300 ml
Soya sauce	4 tbsp
Sugar	1 tbsp
Ajinomoto (Monosodium glutamate)	¼ tsp

Method

1. Fillet fish and cut into fairly large pieces. 2. Make a fairly thick batter with flour, eggs and water. 3. Dip fish in batter and deep fry in sweet oil. 4. Drain and serve hot with sauce. 5. Mix fish stock (prepared by boiling 115 gm of fish finely chopped and cooked in water for half an hour) with sugar, soya sauce and ajinomoto. Stir well and serve with fish.

N.B. Pieces of lobster, prawns, crab meat and vegetables can be cooked in the same way. Sometimes grated horseradish is mixed with soya sauce and served as the accompaniment. Tempura is always fried in front of the customer and served straight from the pan.

3. SUKI YAKI

Ingredients	Quantity
Beef, Pork or Chicken	500 gm
Onions	1
Spring onions	3
Bamboo shoots	1 tbsp
Soya sauce	1 tbsp
Fat	1 tbsp
Watercress	a little
Sugar	1 tbsp
Stock	

Method

1. Cut meat into extremely thin, small slices. Beat with a wet baton. 2. Chop spring onions, bamboo shoots and watercress and brown them in fat along with the meat. 3. Add just enough stock to moisten. Sprinkle with sugar and soya sauce. 4. Simmer on a slow fire for 15–20 minutes.

To serve: Each person has a pair of chopsticks and a bowl into which a raw egg has been broken. This is beaten up with the chopsticks. Each piece of food is then dipped in egg — the hot food cooks the egg and the egg cools the boiling food — and eaten.

BURMA

I. CHICKEN KAUSWEY

Ingredients	Quantity
Chicken	1.5 kg
Water	2–4 litre
Turmeric	1 tsp
Onions	1 kg

Ingredients	Quantity
Garlic	4 flakes
Ginger	2 slices
Salt	to taste
Chillies	4
Oil	½ cup
Coconut	1 (extract 3 cups milk)
Bengal gram powder	1 tbsp
Noodles	500 gm

Method

1. Clean and joint chicken. Rub with turmeric. 2. Cook in 2–4 litres of water adding salt to taste till tender. Remove chicken. 3. Remove skin and bones. Crack bones and add to simmering stock. 4. Pound together 400 gm of onions, garlic, ginger and chillies. Rub over chicken. 5. Heat oil in a large pan till it smokes. 6. Slice remaining onions and add to smoking oil. 7. Fry sliced onions. Add chicken and brown. 8. Add strained stock and simmer. 9. Make a paste of gram powder and 1 cup water. 10. Add to chicken and cook for 10–15 minutes. 11. Add coconut milk last. Continue cooking for a few minutes more. 12. Check for seasoning and serve hot, over boiled noodles.

Accompaniments: 4 chopped hard-boiled eggs
Green onions
Sliced raw onions
3 limes, quartered
Chilli powder

2. BALACHAUNG

Ingredients	Quantity
Dry prawns	1 cup
Oil	1 cup
Red chillies	5 or 6
Garlic	3 pods
Onions	700 gm
Ngyapyi	to taste
Salt	1 tsp

Method

1. Roast and powder prawns. 2. Grind red chillies with half the onions and garlic. 3. Slice remaining onions and garlic. 4. Heat oil. Fry sliced onions and garlic. 5. Brown and drain on paper. 6. To the same oil add prawn powder and ground onions, garlic and chillies. Fry till mixture turns brown and dry. 7. Remove from fire and add fried garlic and onions. Mix well. 8. Serve with boiled rice.

3. MOH KYA LAPPHED

Ingredients	Quantity
Onions	350 gm
Green chillies	1
Lime	¼
Sesame seeds	2 tbsp
Roasted Bengal gram	2 tbsp
Roasted lentils	2 tbsp
Garlic	2 pods
Grated copra or Fresh coconut	1 tbsp
Dry prawns	½ cup

Method

1. Slice garlic and onions fine. Fry in oil till brown. Drain and keep aside.
2. Roast and powder dry prawns. 3. Chop chillies fine. 4. Arrange each item separately in a plate, with the oil in which onions and garlic were fried in a cup in the centre.

Balachaung is eaten with the fingers, taking a little of each item in a plate and mixing with a little oil.

4. TAMARIND LETHOKA

Ingredients	Quantity
Tender tamarind leaves	a handful
Onions (sliced)	500 gm
Garlic (peeled and sliced)	10 pods
Dry prawns	1 cup
Oil	½ cup
Groundnut	2 tbsp
Red chillies	6
Salt	to taste

Method

1. Fry and drain onions and garlic. Keep aside. Powder red chillies.
2. Roast and powder prawns. 3. Keep all ingredients in a plate as for Balachaung. Mix with oil and eat.

5. LATHOK (RICE MIXTURE)

Ingredients	Quantity
Rice	1 cup
Onions	500 gm
Garlic	2 pods
Dry prawns (roasted and powdered)	½ cup
Oil	½ cup

Ingredients	Quantity
Red chillies	1
Lime	½
Cooked greens and vegetables	

Noodles

1. Boil rice. 2. Peel and slice onions and garlic and powder red chillies. 3. Fry sliced onions and garlic till brown. Drain. 4. Squeeze lime over fried onions and garlic and mix all ingredients with rice. 5. Pour in oil and cooked greens and vegetables. Mix well. 6. Serve hot.

SRI LANKA

I. IDDE APPUNG (STRING HOPPERS)

Ingredients	Quantity
Rice flour or Refined flour	450 gm
Boiling water	1 cup
Salt	to taste

Noodles

1. Roast rice flour. If refined flour is used, steam in a cloth bag over a pot of boiling water. 2. Empty into a basin. Add salt and boiling water. Mix well using a kitchen ladle. 3. Put mixture into a wet cloth. Steam in an idli steamer. This takes about 5–7 minutes. Serve with mulligatawny or Kirihoti and Seeni Sambal or Polmallung.

2. POLMALLUNG

Ingredients	Quantity
Coconut	½ (finely grated)
Onions (sliced)	1
Dry chillies	6
Turmeric	a pinch
Green chillies	3
Maldive fish (for dried fish)	1 tbsp
Cinnamon	2.5 cm (1") piece
Lime juice	½ lime
Salt	to taste

Noodles

1. Grind together red chillies and turmeric. Cut green chillies lengthwise. 2. Put all ingredients except coconut into a vessel. 3. Add half teacup water and salt and boil until ingredients are cooked. 4. Add coconut. Stir well. Cook for a couple of minutes more and remove.

3. SEENI SAMBAL

Ingredients	Quantity
Dry chillies (roasted and powdered)	60 gm
Dried prawns (roasted and powdered)	60 gm (3")
Maldive fish (pounded)	115 gm
Red onions (sliced)	115 gm
Garlic (chopped)	3 flakes
Cinnamon	5 cm (2") piece
Rampa	7.5 cm piece
Lemon grass	¼ stem
Curry leaves	1 sprig
Tamarind	60 gm
Lime (juice)	½
Sugar	2 tsp
Coconut oil	4 tbsp
Green ginger	4 slices
Ripe chillies (sliced)	2
Coconut	1 (extract 4 cups milk)

Noodles

1. Heat half the oil in a pan and fry a tablespoon of onions and a small piece each of rampa and lemon grass and a few curry leaves. 2. When onions are browned add remainder of oil. Let it get hot. 3. Put in all ingredients except tamarind, coconut milk, lime juice and sugar and fry for a few minutes stirring all the time. 4. Soak tamarind in coconut milk and extract pulp. Strain. 5. Add coconut milk mixture, and lime juice and let it simmer over a brisk fire for a few minutes. Mix in sugar. 6. Reduce heat to minimum and cook till gravy dries up. Stir frequently.

4. KIRIHOTI

Ingredients	Quantity
Coconut	1
Fenugreek (Methi)	¼ tsp
Green chillies	2
Onions	100 gm
Curry leaves	1 sprig
Lime	1
Turmeric	a pinch
Eggs	4
Cardamoms	3
Cinnamon	2.5 cm piece
Cloves	4
Salt	to taste

Noodles

1. Grate coconut. 2. Extract thick milk by sprinkling a little water (total 50 ml). 3. Add 250 ml (1 standard cup) water and prepare second extraction of coconut milk. 4. Add another 250 ml (a standard cup) of water and prepare third extraction. 5. Slice onions. 6. Add ½ cup water and turmeric. Cook till water evaporates. 7. Add third extraction of coconut milk, green chillies, fenugreek, curry leaves, cardamoms, cinnamon, cloves and salt and quartered boiled eggs. Bring to a boil. 8. Simmer for 2–3 minutes. Add second extraction and slowly bring to a boil. 9. Add first extraction of coconut milk and lime juice. Test for salt and remove.

5. MULLIGATAWNY

Ingredients	Quantity
Chicken	1 large
Cold water	900 ml
Coriander	10 gm
Fennel (grind separately)	5 gm
Tomatoes	500 gm
Onions (sliced)	30 gm
Garlic	2 flakes
Lime juice	
Turmeric	a pinch
Cumin	a pinch
Fennel	1 tsp
Ginger (sliced)	2 pieces
Cinnamon	5 cm (2") piece
Fenugreek	¼ tsp
Curry leaves	a small sprig
Fat	30 gm
Coconut milk	
Salt	to taste

Method

1. Clean and joint chicken and put into a saucepan. 2. Add water and let it simmer for half an hour. Grind together coriander, cumin, turmeric and fennel. 3. Add ground ingredients, fenugreek, half the onions, garlic, ginger, cinnamon, curry leaves, tomatoes and salt. Boil until chicken is tender. 4. Strain off stock and put back best pieces of chicken into stock. 5. Mix remaining ground fennel with coconut milk and add to stock. 6. Heat fat and fry remaining onions. 7. When nicely browned turn in the prepared stock. 8. Add lime juice and salt to taste and let it boil up once.

6. MOJU

Ingredients	Quantity
Purple brinjal	500 gm
Small onions/shallots	200 gm
Mustard	1½ tsp
Garlic	10 flakes
Ginger	one 1" piece
Molasses (Jaggery)	120 gm
Salt	to taste
Oil	
Vinegar	1 tbsp
Tamarind	

Method

1. Wash and cut brinjal into 2 cm by 1 cm pieces. Apply salt and set aside. 2. Grind together onions, mustard, garlic and ginger into a fine paste. 3. Fry brinjal in a frying pan adding just enough oil to shallow fry. 4. Melt jaggery and strain. Soak tamarind and extract pulp. 5. Add melted jaggery, tamarind pulp, and vinegar to fried brinjal. Check for seasoning. Cook till almost dry.

7. CEYLON CHICKEN CURRY

Ingredients	Quantity
Chicken	1
Garlic	5 gm
Onions	115 gm
Ginger	10 gm
Green chillies	5 gm
Turmeric	½ tsp
Lime	1
Chilli powder	1 tsp
Coriander powder	30 gm
Curry leaves	1 sprig
Coconut	1
Fat	15 gm
Salt	to taste

Method

1. Wash and joint chicken. 2. Smear well with chilli powder and salt and set aside. Chop garlic and ginger fine, slit green chillies. 3. Grate coconut and make two extractions, the first one thick and the second thin. 4. Grind coriander and turmeric to a fine paste. Heat fat. Add garlic, onions, ginger, green chillies and ground coriander and turmeric. 5. Fry for 2–3 minutes. Add chicken and fry well. 6. Add thin coconut milk and simmer till chicken is tender. 7. Add thick coconut milk, salt to taste and juice of 1 lime. 8. Simmer for 5 minutes more with lid off.

8. PRAWN BADUN

Ingredients	Quantity
Large prawns	1.5 kg
Small onion (sliced)	1 tbsp
Garlic	6 flakes
Ginger	5 gm
Cinnamon	5 cm (2") piece
Rampa	10 cm (4") piece
Lemon grass	½ stem
Curry leaves	1 sprig
Coriander	1½ tbsp
Cumin	a pinch
Fennel	1½ tsp
Fenugreek	½ tsp
Vinegar	20–30 ml
Fat	30 gm
Coconut	1
Turmeric (ground)	a little
Red chillies (roasted and ground)	10–15 gm

Method

1. Shell prawns. Remove intestines and wash well. 2. Make 2 extractions of coconut milk, the first one thick (1 cup) and the second medium (2 cups). 3. Put in all ingredients, except thick coconut milk and fat into a pan and boil gently till prawns are cooked. 4. Add thick extraction of coconut milk and simmer for 15 minutes. 5. Remove gravy. Add fat and let prawns fry well. Pour back gravy and stir for a couple of minutes.

N.B. Beef Badun and Brain Badun can be made in the same way, but adjust both amount of liquid and cooking time.

9. KALU DODOL

Ingredients	Quantity
Rice flour	500 gm
Jaggery	340 gm
Coconut milk	5 teacups (2 coconuts)
Cashewnuts	25
Cinnamon	5 cm (2" piece)
Salt	

Method

1. Put flour into a pan. Add coconut milk gradually and stir until free from lumps. 2. Add grated jaggery, cinnamon, and salt and stir over fire until mixture thickens. 3. Mix in cashewnuts cut into small pieces, a few minutes before taking dodol off fire. 4. Turn onto a flat buttered dish.

Flatten out with a piece of greased plantain leaf and cut into diamond shapes when cold.

INDONESIA

I. AJAM DALAM KELAPA (CHICKEN IN COCONUT)

Ingredients	Quantity
Coconuts	2 large or 4 small
Chicken (medium)	1
Butter	90 gm
Onions	55 gm
Capsicum	1 large (60 gm)
Tomatoes	225 gm
Garlic	4 flakes
Peppercorns	6
Refined flour for thickening	15 gm
Water	400 ml
Salt	to taste

Method

1. Saw off tops of coconut and reserve. 2. Scrape half of coconut evenly with a hand scraper. 3. Grind coconut. Add water and extract milk. 4. Blend flour in coconut milk. 5. Wash and cut chicken into small pieces. 6. Fry lightly in butter. Add finely chopped onions, tomatoes, capsicum and peppercorns. Sauté for 10 minutes. 7. Add coconut milk and cook for about 35 minutes. 8. Put mixture into coconut shell. 9. Replace the lid and seal with flour paste. 10. Place sealed coconut in a roasting pan with one inch water at the bottom. Bake at 175°C (350°F approx.) for 45 minutes–1 hour basting often with water to avoid scorching. 11. Serve on large leaves with a few bright flowers on a plate.

2. TAHITIAN CHICKEN SAUTE

Ingredients	Quantity
Chicken (broiler)	1
Salt and Pepper	to taste
Refined flour	1 tbsp
Oil	for frying
Orange juice	½ cup
Butter	1 tbsp
Ginger	2.5 cm (1" piece)
Soya sauce	1 dsp

Method

1. Clean, wash and drain chicken joints. Season with salt and pepper and set aside for 10 minutes. 2. Dredge chicken lightly with flour and fry till golden brown. 3. Place chicken in a baking pan and bake at 175°C (350°F approx.) for 30–45 minutes. 4. Mix together orange juice, crushed ginger and soya sauce. During baking, baste with this mixture frequently, glazing chicken well. Serve with fluffy rice.

3. ADOBO (CHICKEN)

Ingredients	Quantity
Chicken	1
Vinegar	½ cup
Garlic	1 flake
Salt	to taste
Black pepper	to taste
Bay leaf	½
Cooking oil	
Water	2 cups
Soya sauce	2 tbsp

Method

1. Clean chicken. Cut into pieces. Add salt, minced garlic and pepper to chicken. 2. Put into a pan and add bay leaf, vinegar, water and soya sauce. Cover and simmer until chicken is tender and liquid has almost evaporated. 3. Fry chicken in fat until brown and remove some of the excess fat from frying pan. 4. Then add remaining sauce and pour over. Serve hot or cold.

4. AJAP DJAHE (MIXED VEGETABLES)

Ingredients	Quantity
Eggs	2
Peeled fresh boiled prawns	1 cup
Sliced boiled chicken	1 cup
Cabbage	115 gm
Onions leaves	3 stalks
Celery	2 stalks
Carrots	115 gm
Cauliflower	115 gm
Ajinomoto (Monosodium glutamate)	1 tsp
Soya sauce	1 tbsp
Tomato (sliced)	½
Ground garlic	1 tsp
White pepper	1 tsp
Fried onions	1 cup
Salt	to taste

Method

1. Cut all vegetables into 2.5 cm (1") lengths and mix with ground garlic, white pepper and salt; fry in 115 gm butter for a few minutes. 2. Add boiled chicken and prawns and simmer till vegetables are cooked. 3. Beat eggs and soya sauce together and add to mixture. Take a tsp of cornflour and mix with half-cup water and then pour the paste-like mixture onto prepared chicken and prawns. 4. Add all fresh vegetables. Mix thoroughly, half-cook over slow fire. 5. Put in a long plate and serve hot. Sprinkle fried onion flakes on top.

INDIA

FOR TANDOOR SEASONING

Ingredients	Quantity
Mustard oil	1 kg
Spinach	250 gm
Salt	
Molasses	75–100 gm

Method

Mix and apply 4 times every 2 days before fixing.

KACHRI AS A TENDERISER

Dry in a Tandoor or on dry heat and powder. For every kg meat/chicken add 2 pinches. When making lamb/mutton curry, clean and cut meat, apply kachri and leave for half an hour. If too much is used, gravy gets discoloured. If kept overnight in a refrigerator or if frozen, there is a tendency for meat to break up.

I. YAKHNI SHORBA

Ingredients	Quantity
For stock	
Water	5 litre
Mutton bones	
Coriander seeds	150 gm
Ginger (roughly cut)	30 gm
Garlic pods (roughly cut)	30 gm
Onions	50 gm
Black cardamom	15 gm
Green cardamom	10 gm
Mace	5 gm

Ingredients	Quantity
Bay leaf	10 gm
Cinnamon	10 gm
Cloves	10 gm
Cream	20 ml

Method

Blanch bones. Prepare stock with above ingredients and simmer till stock is reduced to 1 litre, add salt. Finish off with warm cream.

2. TOMATO SHORBA

Ingredients	Quantity
Tomatoes	2 kg
Onions	150 gm
Ginger	50 gm
Garlic	50 gm
Bay leaf	5 gm
Cinnamon	10 gm
Cloves	10 gm
Green cardamom	5 gm
Black cardamom	5 gm
Green chillies	10 gm
Bengal gram flour	50 gm
Chickenbones	1.1 kg
Cumin (whole)	10 gm
Refined oil	10 ml
Grated coconut	70 gm
Dry red chillies (whole)	15

Method

1. Boil tomatoes in 1 litre water with onions, ginger, garlic, bay leaf, cinnamon, cloves, green cardamom, black cardamom, green chillies, chicken bones, grated coconut, and simmer for one hour. Make a roux of Bengal gram flour and mix into shorba till it thickens. Strain soup and serve with a garnish of fried whole dry red chillies on top.

3. SMOKED POMFRET (A)

Ingredients	Quantity
Fresh pomfret	1
Chinese chilli sauce	30 ml
Straw	for smoking
Ginger	30 gm
Green chillies	2
Tomato ketchup	50 ml

Ingredients	Quantity
Lime	2
Oil	125 ml
Anchovy fillets	1 small tin
Anchovy sauce	50 ml
Salt	10 gm
Fish stock	
Onions	50 gm
Pomfret bones (cleaned)	4
Carrots	30 gm
Bay leaf	1
Celery	30 gm
Parsley stalks	a few
Peppercorns	2 gm

Method

1. Clean pomfret. 2. Remove scales and fins. Fillet with skin on. 3. Wash thoroughly. 4. Marinade pomfret fillets in a mixture of oil, tomato ketchup, Chinese chilli sauce, lime juice and a little salt. 5. Keep in marinade for at least half an hour and then place pomfret fillets on top of an oiled wire-gauze before which straws are being burnt. 6. Smoke fillets on skinless side for at least 7–8 minutes and then put them back into marinade and cook for a little while. 7. Take out fillets. Make a smoked sauce with marinade adding some fish fumet. 8. Reduce sauce till it thick. 9. Garnish smoked pomfret with juliennes of green chillies and ginger.

N.B. Pomfret fillets can be cooked a little more under a salamander or a grill. This smoked pomfret can be preserved in a refrigerator and re-heated whenever required.

SMOKED POMFRET (B)

Clean and wash fish. Fillet, wash well and dry on a cloth. Season. Prepare a fire of coconut fibre which produces a fine smoke. Butter fish well on both sides and lay it on the grid iron. Cover it with the lid of a cooking pot to concentrate the smoke. In about ten minutes when fish has been smoked a rich reddish-brown on one side, turn over and smoke other side. A little anchovy sauce can be mixed with butter when buttering the fish.

4. VEGETABLE JALFRAIZI

Ingredients	Quantity
Cauliflower	100 gm
Carrots	100 gm

Ingredients	Quantity
Green peas	150 gm
Tomatoes	150 gm
Capsicums	100 gm
Onions	100 gm
Coriander seeds	2 tsp
Kashmiri chillies (without seeds)	5
Turmeric powder	½ tsp
Garlic	1 pod
Oil	50 ml
Ginger	a small piece
Mustard seeds	½ tsp
Salt	to taste
Sugar	½ tsp
Coriander leaves	a few sprigs

Method

Clean and cut vegetables. Grind coriander seeds, Kashmiri chillies, turmeric powder, ginger, garlic, mustard seeds and half the onions. Set aside. Slice remaining onions, and fry golden brown. Remove and fry ground masala and vegetables. Add fried onions, sugar, salt and a little water. Cook till vegetables are tender and gravy thickened. Garnish with coriander leaves and serve hot.

5. PANIR MAKHANI

Ingredients	Quantity
Panir	250 gm
Onions	100 gm
Cream	50 gm
Mawa	50 gm
Cashewnuts	50 gm
Poppy seeds	50 gm
Cumin seeds	10 gm
Tomatoes	100 gm
Garam masala	1 gm
Green chillies	4
Oil	100 ml
Butter	50 gm
Salt	to taste
Sugar	½ tsp
Coriander leaves	a few

Method

Cut panir into small cubes, fry it slightly in oil, drain well and set aside. Heat oil and fry chopped onions golden brown. Add ground poppy seeds, cashewnuts, cumin seeds, chopped tomatoes and garam masala. Stir well continuously till all the ingredients have blended well. Add a little water and allow to simmer. Add fried panir and cook for five minutes. Top with butter and cream and sprinkle with coriander leaves. Serve hot.

6. PALAK PANIR

Ingredients	Quantity
Spinach	500 gm
Panir (made of I litre milk)	
Galic	1 pod
Onions	250 gm
Salt	to taste
Fat or Ghee	50 gm
Cream	50 ml
Green chillies (whole)	3–4
Dry fenugreek leaves	30 gm

Method

1. Cut panir into cubes. Wash and drain spinach. Purée in a mixer. Heat fat. Add chopped onions, garlic, whole green chillies, prepared spinach and dry fenugreek leaves. Sauté till the mixture is almost dry. Add cream. Blend well. Add panir cubes.

7. MAKHANI DAL

Ingredients	Quantity
Black gram (whole)	250 gm
Kidney beans	50 gm
Onions	1
Tomato	1 large
Ginger	5 cm piece
Garlic	½ pod
Green chillies	10 gm
Red chilli powder	5 gm
Turmeric	¼ tsp
Oil	30 ml
Ghee (clarified butter)	60 gm
Cumin seeds	½ tsp
Salt	to taste
Coriander leaves	a few

Method

1. Clean and soak gram and beans separately for at least 4 hours. 2. Boil kidney beans. When half-cooked, add gram and oil and boil till both are well cooked. 3. Heat half the ghee. Add cumin seeds, sliced ginger, sliced onions and chopped garlic, and fry till golden brown. 4. Add turmeric,

chilli powder and chopped tomatoes and fry till tomatoes are cooked. 5. Add gram and beans and half the chopped coriander leaves. 6. Cook on a slow fire stirring constantly for another 20 minutes. 7. Add remaining ghee and remove from fire. 8. Garnish with remaining chopped coriander leaves.

8. KALEJI/KAPURA

Ingredients	Quantity
Liver/Kapura	500 gm
Curds	200 ml
Onions	100 gm
Fennel	3 gm
Green chillies	20 gm
Coriander leaves	50 gm
Ginger	15 gm
Garlic	10 gm
Cinnamon	2 gm
Cardamom	2 gm
Cloves	2 gm
Cumin	2 gm
Oil	to taste
Salt	to taste
Black salt	2 gm
Red colour	2 gm

Method

1. Clean liver. Cut into 4 cm (about 1½″) pieces. 2. Grind onions, coriander leaves, green chillies, garlic, ginger and fennel and mix with curds. 3. Roast cinnamon, cardamom, cloves, cumin and mix with curds and ground masala. 4. Add salt and black salt. 5. Prick liver with a fork and marinade for an hour in above mixture. 6. Put pieces of liver on a skewer. Cook on charcoal and baste with oil. Keep turning regularly to ensure even browning. Cook for 10 minutes. 7. Remove from fire. Baste again with oil and cook for another 10 minutes. Serve hot with onion salad.

9. GURDA

Ingredients	Quantity
Kidneys	500 gm
Curds	200 ml
Onions	100 gm
Fennel	3 gm
Green chillies	20 gm
Coriander leaves	50 gm
Ginger	15 gm

Ingredients	Quantity
Garlic	10 gm
Cinnamon	2 gm
Cardamom	2 gm
Cloves	2 gm
Cumin	2 gm
Oil	to taste
Salt	to taste
Black salt	2 gm
Red colour	2 gm

Method

1. Clean kidneys. Cut into 4 cm (about 1½") pieces. 2. Grind onions, coriander leaves, green chillies, garlic, ginger and fennel and mix with curds. 3. Roast cinnamon, cardamom, cloves, cumin and mix with curds and ground masala. 4. Add salt and black salt. 5. Marinade kidneys for 1 hour in above mixture. 6. Put kidneys on a skewer. Cook on charcoal and baste with oil. Keep turning regularly to ensure even browning. Cook for 10 minutes. 7. Remove from fire. Baste again with oil and cook for another 15 minutes. Serve hot with onion salad.

10. BOTI KABAB

Ingredients	Quantity
Mutton	500 gm
Curds	200 ml
Onions	100 gm
Fennel	3 gm
Green chillies	20 gm
Raw papaya	5 gm (1" piece)
Coriander leaves	50 gm
Ginger	15 gm
Garlic	10 gm
Cinnamon	2 gm
Cardamom	2 gm
Cloves	2 gm
Cumin	2 gm
Oil	to taste
Salt	to taste
Black salt	2 gm
Red colour	

Method

1. Cut mutton into 4 cm (about 1½") cubes. Beat with a steak hammer. 2. Grind onions, coriander leaves, green chillies, garlic, ginger, raw papaya and fennel and mix with curds. 3. Roast cinnamon, cardamom,

cloves, cumin and mix with curds and ground masala. 4. Add salt and black salt. 5. Marinade mutton for 1 hour in above mixture. 6. Put pieces of mutton on a skewer. Cook on charcoal and baste with oil. Keep turning regularly to ensure even browning. Cook for 20 minutes. 7. Remove from fire. Baste again with oil and cook for another 20 minutes. Serve hot with onion salad.

11. RESHMI KABAB

Ingredients	Quantity
Chicken	500 gm
Onions	100 gm
Fennel	3 gm
Green chillies	20 gm
Coriander leaves	50 gm
Eggs	2
Ginger	15 gm
Garlic	10 gm
Cinnamon	2 gm
Cardamom	2 gm
Cloves	2 gm
Cumin	2 gm
Oil	to taste
Salt	to taste
Black salt	2 gm

Method

1. De-bone and mince chicken. 2. Chop onions, coriander leaves, green chillies, garlic and ginger fine, and mix with chicken. 4. Bind with egg. Add black salt and salt. 5. Put mixture on skewer with wet hands. 6. Baste with oil and cook on charcoal for 10 minutes turning regularly to ensure even cooking. 7. Remove from fire. Baste again with oil and cook again for 10 minutes. 8. Remove from skewer and serve hot with onion salad.

12. TANGRI KABAB (A)

Ingredients	Quantity
Tandoori chicken (legs only)	10 pieces
Curds	100 gm
Salt	to taste
Pepper powder	1 tsp
Red chilli powder	2 tsp
Oil	100 ml
Red edible food colouring	
Lime	1

Method

Apply salt to chicken legs and sprinkle with lemon juice. Make small cubes of chicken, or keep them whole. Mix curds, chilli powder, pepper powder, food colouring and apply to chicken. Marinate for at least 3 hours. Put chicken legs on a skewer and roast in a tandoor or charcoal oven. Remove after five minutes. Baste meat with oil and roast again till done. Serve immediately.

TANGRI KABAB (B)

Ingredients	For I
Drumsticks (Chicken legs)	4
Plain curds	70 gm
Red chilli paste	15 gm
Ginger/Garlic paste	5 gm
Lemon	1
Salt	to taste
Garam masala powder	5 gm

Method

Clean and slit chicken legs, apply lemon juice, salt and ginger, garlic paste. Make a masala of curds, chilli paste and garam masala powder, and marinate chicken legs in it for 4–5 hours, then cook in tandoor clay oven and serve hot.

13. CHICKEN MALAI KABAB

Ingredients	For I
Boneless chicken	200 gm
Fresh cream	15 gm
Cheese	10 gm
Ginger/Garlic paste	10 gm
Garam masala powder	5 gm
White pepper powder	5 gm
Salt	to taste

Method

Cut boneless chicken breast and legs into tikka size and marinate with ginger/garlic paste, garam masala, white pepper powder and salt. Make a mixture of fresh cream and finely grated cheese and add to marinated chicken. Keep for about 4–5 hours and cook in tandoor clay oven.

14. KADAI GHOSHT

Ingredients	Quantity
Mutton	600 gm

Ingredients	Quantity
Tomatoes	150 gm
Onions	100 gm
Ginger	15 gm
Garlic (roughly ground and mixed with water)	15 gm
Peppercorns*	10 gm
Coriander*	20 gm
Chillies*	5 gm
Cumin	10 gm
Oil or Ghee	15 ml
Chopped coriander leaves	1 bunch
Green chillies (chopped)	10 gm

Method

Cut mutton into 2.5 cm pieces with bones. Sauté chopped onions, add tomatoes, ginger julienne, green chillies and garlic water in a deep frying pan (kadai). Add coarsely ground red chillies, coriander and cumin. Add salt and cook mutton covering the kadai. After mutton is cooked add coarsely ground peppercorns and oil and fry mutton with the gravy. Serve hot, garnished with chopped coriander leaves.

15. ACHAR GHOSHT

Ingredients	Quantity
Onions (chopped)	200 gm
Cumin	3 gm
Cardamom	2 gm
Cinnamon	2 gm
Cloves	2 gm
Peppercorns	2 gm
Onions seeds (Kalongi)	2 gm
Fennel (saunf)	2 gm
Tomatoes	250 gm
Cubes of mutton with bones	1 kg
Salt	to taste
Fenugreek seeds	2 gm
Cumin (whole)	2 gm
Mustard seeds	2 gm
Fat	50 gm

Method

Sauté onions in fat. Do not brown. Add cumin. Then add cardamom, cinnamon, cloves, peppercorn (whole), onion seeds and then fennel,

---

*half crushed

fenugreek and mustard seeds. Add mutton and chopped tomatoes and cook on a slow fire with a little water till mutton is cooked and gravy is thick.

16. BURANI

Ingredients	Quantity
Mutton with bones	½ kg
Onions	250 gm
Ginger	25 gm
Garlic	25 gm
Red chilli powder	15 gm
Garam masala powder	3 gm
Salt	to taste
Mint leaves	½ bunch
Fat	100 gm
Curds	¼ litre

Method

1. Slice onions and fry in hot fat till brown; add ginger/garlic paste and fry. 2. Add mutton, salt and chilli powder. Fry well and cook meat with a little water till well done. Fry till dry. 3. Tie curds in a muslin cloth and allow water to drain off. 4. Beat with a pinch of salt. 5. Arrange fried mutton on a platter. Pour beaten curds over and garnish with slices of onion and mint leaves.

17. CHICKEN MOGHLAI

Ingredients	Quantity
Chicken	1
Onions	200 gm
Ginger	10 gm
Green coriander	½ bunch
Turmeric	1 tsp
Cinnamon	3 gm
Garlic	10 gm
Red chillies (remove seeds)	15 gm
Curds	250 gm
Lime	1
Almonds or Cashewnuts	100 gm
Cardamom	3 gm
Cloves	3 gm
Bay leaves	
Fat	150 gm
Egg	1
Mawa (optional)	50 gm

Method

1. Clean, wash and cut chicken into small pieces. 2. Slice onions, brown them slightly and grind along with ginger, garlic, red chillies and turmeric. 3. Mix half the above masala with beaten curds and apply it to pieces of chicken. 4. Heat fat, add garam masala and fry remaining masala very well till it begins to separate from oil. 5. Add pieces of chicken and fry well till water from chicken also dries up. 6. Add sufficient water to cook chicken and while it is cooking, add half the chopped coriander leaves. 7. When chicken is cooked, add cashewnuts or almond paste and remove from fire. Add lime juice, mawa and before serving mix in beaten egg till it coagulates. 8. Serve hot garnished with the remaining chopped coriander leaves.

18. CHICKEN AFGHANI

Ingredients	*Quantity*
Chicken	1
Ginger	5 gm
Garlic	5 gm
Kachri	5 gm
Yellow chilli powder	5 gm
Turmeric	2 gm
Curds	200 ml
Garam masala	a pinch
Bengal gram flour	30 gm
Cumin powder	2 gm
Gravy	
Tomatoes	200 gm
Onions	200 gm
Cinnamon	3 gm
Cardamom	3 gm
Cloves	3 gm
Bay leaves	
Green coriander	½ bunch
Broken cashewnuts	150 gm
Cream	50 ml
Fat	50 ml

Method

1. Clean, skin and de-bone chicken and cut into small pieces. 2. Grind ginger and garlic; beat curds and combine together with ginger/garlic paste, kachri, yellow chilli powder, turmeric, cumin powder, garam masala powder and Bengal gram flour (besan). Mix well. Add salt. 3. Add chicken to curd mixture and set aside for about an hour. 4. Put pieces of chicken on a skewer and grill over live charcoal till chicken is half-done

and remove. 5. To prepare gravy, chop tomatoes and onions. 6. Heat fat in a pan, add whole gram masala, and chopped onions and sauté without discolouring. 7. Add tomatoes and sufficient water to form a thick gravy. Cook for about 10 minutes. Add cashewnut paste and chicken. Cook till chicken is tender. Add cream last, and serve garnished with chopped green coriander leaves.

19. CHICKEN ZAIBUNISSA

Ingredients	Quantity
Chicken	1
Cashewnuts	50 gm
Onions	150 gm
Ginger	10 gm
Garlic	10 gm
Poppy seeds	50 gm
Green chillies	10 gm
Curds	150 ml
Fat	100 gm
Cardamom	2 gm

Method

1. Joint chicken. 2. Peel and boil onions. Drain water and grind to a smooth paste. 3. Roast poppy seeds slightly. 4. Grind poppy seeds, cashewnuts, green chillies, ginger and garlic separately. 5. Heat fat. Add onions and fry on slow fire. Add ginger and garlic and fry without discolouring. Add poppy seeds and green chillies. Fry again. 6. Add chicken, fry well. Cover and cook. Add a little water if required. 7. Add curds and cashewnut paste. Fry again till dry. 8. Add a little water to make a gravy. 9. Sprinkle with cardamom powder. Mix well, remove and serve.

20. CHICKEN SHAHJAHANI

Ingredients	Quantity
Broiler chicken	1 kg
Cumin seed	10 gm
Red chillies	5
Ginger	100 gm
Garlic	10 gm
Turmeric powder	5 gm
Coriander leaves	1 bunch
Garam masala	10 gm
Vinegar	½ cup
Oil	100 ml
Cashewnuts	150 gm
Poppy seeds	100 gm

Ingredients	Quantity
Fresh cream	300 gm
Dried fruit	200 gm
Butter	50 gm
Salt	to taste

Method

Grind all the spices and set aside. Grind cashewnuts, poppy seeds and cumin seeds separately. Clean and cut chicken. Apply half the ground masala and vinegar to chicken. Set aside to marinate for at least 1 hour. Heat oil and fry chicken till tender. Add remaining masalas and cashewnut paste. Add a little water, and simmer on a low fire till done. Top with fresh cream and butter. Garnish with dry fruit and serve hot.

21. CHICKEN CURRY KASHMIRI

Ingredients	Quantity
Dressed chicken	1 kg
Ginger	5 gm
Garlic	5 gm
Turmeric	2 gm
Kashmiri chillies (remove seeds)	10 gm
Coriander	5 gm
Onions	150 gm
Whole garam masala	5 gm
Oil	30 gm
Tomatoes	60 gm
Salt	10 gm
Cashewnuts	15 gm
Raisins	15 gm

Method

1. Clean and cut chicken into small pieces. 2. Slice half the onions and grind the rest with the masala. 3. Smear masala over chicken and set it aside. 4. Heat fat, put in the whole garam masala and sliced onions and fry onions light brown. 5. Add chicken and masala and fry well. 6. Add blanched and chopped tomatoes and a little water. 7. Simmer till chicken is tender. 8. Fry dry fruit and nuts and garnish.

22. AFGHANI CHICKEN KHORMA

Ingredients	Quantity
Chicken	1
Limes	2
Onions	2 (big) or 250 gm
Ginger	2.5 cm piece
Garlic	6 cloves

Ingredients	Quantity
Coriander	1 bunch
Mint	1 bunch
Cream	½ cup
Fat	1 tbsp
Pepper powder	1 tsp
Garam masala	1 tsp
Salt	to taste

Method

Wash and joint chicken. Grind onions, ginger and garlic together. Place chicken in a vessel. Pour lime juice over it and allow to marinate. Add ground spices to chicken and set aside for a little longer. Mix together pepper, garam masala, chopped mint, coriander and salt. Spread mixture evenly over chicken. Pour in cream and fat. Cover and cook over a slow fire till chicken is tender. No water is to be added.

23. GALINHA CAFREL (CHICKEN PIRI PIRI)

Ingredients	Quantity
Chicken broiler	1
Salt	1 tsp
Garlic	1 pod
Butter or Fat	100 gm
Peppercorns	5
Sour lime	1
Small dry red chillies (Piri piri)	10

Method

Clean chicken. Make slit near stomach and remove entrails, gizzard etc. Wash chicken well, apply salt and sour lime juice and set aside. Grind together chillies, peppercorns and garlic to a fine paste and baste chicken (inside and outside). Marinate chicken for 7–8 hours. Smear chicken with butter and roast on live coals on a skewer. Keep applying butter till chicken is well roasted. Serve with salad.

N.B. Chicken can also be fried but roasted is better.

24. CHICKEN CAFREL

Ingredients	Quantity
Ginger	100 gm
Garlic	100 gm
Green chillies	150 gm
Turmeric	30 gm
Tomato sauce	250 gm
Pepper powder	5 gm

Ingredients	Quantity
Lemons	6
Rum	60 ml
Oil	50 gm
Coconut vinegar	50 ml

Method

1. Make a paste of ginger, garlic and chillies. 2. Add the rest of the ingredients and mix together. 3. Coat chicken with the above paste and set it aside for 1½ hours. 4. Cook it in an oven for 20 minutes at 250°C. 5. Remove, turn it and cook for 15–20 minutes more. 6. Cut chicken and sauté it in fat. Add rum when it is hot and cook. Garnish with sliced sautéed potatoes, onions and tomatoes cooked in the same gravy.

25. CHICKEN JAIPURI

Ingredients	Quantity
Chicken	1
Onions	250 gm
Cream	100 gm
Ginger	50 gm
Garlic	25 gm
Turmeric	5 gm
Cumin powder	2 gm
Fennel (Saunf)	5 gm
Green coriander	1 bunch
Garam masala (Cinnamon, Cardamom, Cloves, Bay leaves)	5 gm
Chilli powder	5 gm
Salt	to taste

Method

1. Clean and cut chicken into small pieces. 2. Grind together onions, ginger, garlic, turmeric, cumin powder, fennel and chilli powder to a smooth paste. 3. Apply ¼th of the masala to chicken and set aside. 4. Heat oil, add garam masala and ground masala. Fry well till oil separates. 5. Add chopped tomatoes and fry well, then add chicken with sufficient water to cook it. When chicken is cooked, add chopped green coriander and cream just before serving and serve hot.

26. TANDOORI CHICKEN

Ingredients	Quantity
Chicken	1 (1 kg)
Ginger	10 gm
Garlic	10 gm

Ingredients	Quantity
Green chillies	20 gm
Raw papaya	5 gm
Lime	1
Curds	300 ml
Chilli powder	5 gm
Kashmiri chilli powder	10 gm
Oil	15 ml
Tandoori colour	3 gm
Onions	50 gm

Method

1. Pluck, singe and skin chicken. 2. Cut slits lengthwise over breast portion and breadthwise over leg portion carefully. 3. Grind together ginger, garlic and green chillies. 4. Grind raw papaya separately. 5. Apply salt and lime juice to chicken and set it aside. 6. Beat curds thoroughly, add ground masala, ground raw papaya, chilli powder, oil and colour. 7. Smear this batter all over chicken as well as inside the slits. Set aside for 10–15 hours. 8. Thread chicken on to a thin iron rod and dip well inside a tandoor. 9. Remove after 5–7 minutes. Smear with oil and place it in the tandoor again. 10. Remove when well done. Serve hot with onion rings and pieces of lime.

27. CHICKEN TIKKA

Ingredients	Quantity
Chicken	800 gm
Curds	200 ml
Onions	100 gm
Fennel	3 gm
Cinnamon	2 gm
Cardamom	2 gm
Cloves	2 gm
Cumin	2 gm
Green chillies	20 gm
Coriander leaves	50 gm
Ginger	15 gm
Garlic	10 gm
Oil	to baste
Salt	to taste
Black salt	2 gm
Red colour	

Method

1. De-bone and cut chicken into 4 cm pieces. 2. Grind onions, coriander

leaves, green chillies, garlic, ginger and fennel and mix with curds.
3. Roast cinnamon, cardamom, cloves, cumin and mix with curds and
ground masala. 4. Add salt and black salt. 5. Marinate chicken for an
hour in above mixture. 6. Put chicken pieces on a skewer. Cook on
charcoal and baste with oil. Keep turning regularly to ensure even
browning. Cook for 10 minutes. 7. Remove from fire. Baste again with
oil and cook for another 10 minutes. Serve hot with onion salad.

28. CHARGA

Ingredients	Quantity
Chicken (remove skin and keep whole)	1

Marinade

Curds
Turmeric powder
Poppy seed paste
(Khuskhus)
White pepper powder
Egg yolks
Oil
Ginger/Garlic paste

Method

Make a marinade from the above ingredients. Make slits in chicken and
smear well with marinade. Cook chicken in a tandoor.

29. SPICY CHICKEN SAUTÉ

Ingredients	Quantity
Chicken	1 large
Onions	1 large
Ginger	5 cm piece
Garlic	1 pod
Coriander powder	2 tsp
Chilli powder	½ tsp
Cloves	6
Cinnamon	2.5 cm piece
Poppy seeds	2 tsp
Fennel (Saunf)	1 tsp
Green chillies	2
Tomato	1 large
Curds	2 tbsp
Lime juice and Salt	to taste
Oil	100 ml

Method

1. Clean and joint chicken. Slice onion. 2. In a liquidizer or blender, grind cleaned and sliced ginger, garlic, green chillies, coriander powder, chilli powder, cloves, cinnamon, slightly roasted poppy seeds and fennel. 3. Heat oil. Sauté sliced onion. Add ground spices and sauté well. 4. Add chicken and salt. Sauté for another 15 minutes. 5. Add chopped tomatoes and beaten curds. 6. Cover and cook gently till chicken is done. Add lime juice, and remove.

30. CHICKEN FARCHA

Ingredients	For 6–8
Roast chicken	1
Salt	2 gm
Green chillies	2
Onions	½
Eggs	2
Pepper	1 gm
Refined flour	15 gm
Oil	for deep frying

Method

1. Joint roast chicken in 6 or 8 pieces. 2. Prepare a batter of eggs, flour, salt, pepper, chopped onion and green chillies. 3. Dip chicken in batter and deep fry in hot oil till golden brown.

31. RANCHERS FRIED CHICKEN

Ingredients	For 4
Chicken	4 legs, 4 breasts
Eggs	3
Breadcrumbs	250 gm
Salt and Pepper	to taste
Oil	for frying
Flour	100 gm
Oriental Sauce	150 ml
French fries	400 gm

Method

1. Season flour with salt and pepper. 2. Marinade chicken in Worcester sauce, salt, pepper and mustard. 3. Roll chicken in flour until evenly coated. 4. Break eggs and beat lightly. 5. Dip chicken in egg and then coat with breadcrumbs. 6. Deep fry. 7. Serve with French Fries and Oriental Sauce.

ORIENTAL SAUCE

Ingredients	Quantity
Tomatoes (medium)	6
Green chillies	12 gm
Coriander leaves	5 gm
Salt	to taste
Oil	for cooking
Peppercorns	2
Bayleaf	1
Onion	1
Garlic	15 gm
Ginger	2 gm
Tabasco	a pinch

Method

1. Clean tomatoes, slit and keep aside. 2. Chop garlic, ginger, green chillies and coriander leaves. 3. Put water on to boil. 4. Blanch tomatoes and remove skin. Remove pulp and seed. Keep aside. 5. Heat oil in pan. Add peppercorn and bayleaf and sauté. Add chopped garlic and sauté. Add chopped onion and sauté till transparent. Add ginger, green chilli and sauté till you get an aroma. Add blanched tomato pulp. 6. Cook for 20 minutes. Check for seasoning (salt). 7. Strain sauce. Add tabasco and stir to taste. 8. Garnish chicken with julienned ginger and chopped coriander. 9. Serve hot with any fried vegetables.

32. FRIED CHICKEN

Ingredients	For 4
Salad oil	
Milk	¼ cup
All-purpose flour	1 cup
Salt	1 tsp
Pepper	¼ tsp
Broiler-fryer (cut up)	1 (1.35 kg)

Method

About 50 minutes before serving:

1. In a 12-inch (30 cm) skillet over medium-high heat, heat salad oil (filled to about 0.5 cm) until hot. 2. Meanwhile, pour milk into a pie plate. 3. On a sheet of waxed paper, combine flour, salt and pepper; dip chicken in milk, then coat well with flour mixture. 4. Carefully place chicken, skin side up, in hot oil. 5. Cook for about 5 minutes or until underside of chicken is golden; reduce heat; cook for another 5 minutes. 6. With a pancake turner, loosen chicken from pan. Turn chicken, skin side down. 7. Cook over medium-high heat for about 5 minutes or until skin-side of

chicken is golden brown; reduce heat; cook for another 5 minutes or until chicken is fork-tender. 8. Remove chicken, and place skin-side up on paper towels to drain.

33. MUSLIM BIRYANI

Ingredients	For 8
Mutton	1 kg
Basmati rice	1 kg
Onions	1 kg
Potatoes	750 gm
Garam masala (Cardamoms, Cinnamon, Cloves and Pepper)	30–50 gm
Coriander powder	3 tbsp
Red chilli powder	3 tbsp
Cumin powder	3 tbsp
Lime juice	of 4 limes
Curds	750 ml
Mint	1 bunch
Coriander leaves	1 bunch
Salt	to taste
Oil	100 ml
Milk	½ cup

Method

1. Clean and cut mutton. 2. Grind a quarter of the garam masala. 3. Wash and soak rice. 4. Slice onions and peel potatoes. 5. Soak potatoes in orange colour. 6. Heat half the oil and fry sliced onions. 7. Remove from oil and set aside. 8. Add remaining oil to frying pan and fry garam masala. 9. Add mutton and fry till moisture evaporates. 10. Add coriander powder, red chilli powder, cumin powder and ground masala. 11. Cook over slow fire. 12. Add some fried onions. When spices are well-fried, add lime juice and curds, chopped mint and coriander leaves. 13. Add potatoes and salt and cook till mutton is tender. 14. Cook rice till three-fourths done in about 1½ litres of water (absorption method) in a thick-bottomed pan. 15. In a thick-bottomed pan, put mutton and potatoes, cover with a layer of fried onions, top with rice, pour orange colour from the side. Sprinkle with milk. Place the lid on seal. Then place over a tawa and cook over slow fire. Let it cook for a another 30 minutes.

To serve: Lift from base and serve.

34. CHICKEN BIRYANI

Ingredients	Quantity
Chicken	1 kg
Pulao rice	400 gm

Ingredients	Quantity
Tomatoes	250 gm
Onions	250 gm
Garlic	50 gm
Ginger	50 gm
Green chilies	50 gm
Coriander leaves	35 gm (½ bunch)
Turmeric	2 gm
Cinnamon	3 gm
Cardamom	3 gm
Cloves	3 gm
Fat (preferably pure ghee)	150 gm
Salt	20–25 gm
Water	800 ml

Method

1. Clean and joint chicken. 2. Put into a pressure cooker with half the water, turmeric and salt. After pressure is built up, cook for 3 minutes. 3. Cool and open. (10 minutes). 4. Wash and drain rice. 5. Grind together ginger and garlic. 6. Slice onions and quarter tomatoes. 7. Heat fat. Add whole garam masala. 8. Add sliced onions and sauté. 9. Add ginger and garlic and fry for 10 minutes. 10. Add tomatoes, whole green chillies and chopped coriander leaves. Fry for another 10 minutes. 11. Add salt, add fried ingredients to chicken and add remaining water (hot). 12. Bring to a boil. Add rice and lime juice. 13. Put lid on. When steam starts escaping out put weight on and cook for 10–12 minutes over slow fire. 14. Cool slightly (10–15 minutes). Open and serve immediately.

CHETTINAD

I. NANDU MASALA (CRAB MASALA)

Ingredients	Quantity
Crabs (big)	4
Onions	150 gm
Tomatoes	100 gm
Ginger paste	2 tsp
Garlic paste	2 tsp
Tamarind	50 gm
Chilli powder	2 tbsp
Turmeric powder	1½ tsp
Fennel	2 tbsp
Black pepper	11/22 tbsp

Ingredients	Quantity
Fenugreek	1 tsp
Coconut (grated)	1
Oil	100 ml
Salt	to taste

Method

1. Joint, wash and clean crabs. Slice onions and tomatoes. In a little warm water, mix in garlic paste, ginger paste and tamarind. Mix 1½ tsp each of black pepper and fennel and powder it. 2. Heat oil in a kadai, put in whole fenugreek and fennel. Add sliced onions and sliced tomatoes, fry well, add chilli powder and turmeric powder, cook well. Add grated coconut and cook. 3. Add crabs and cook in masala. 4. Add salt, strain in tamarind mixture. 5. Cover and cook for a while, stirring occasionally until crabs are done.

2. YEERA MASALA (PRAWN MASALA)

Ingredients	Quantity
Prawns (cleaned)	2 kg
Onions	60 gm
Tomatoes	60 gm
Coconut	1
Red chillies	6 (large)
Fennel	1 tsp
Tamarind	30 gm
Garlic paste	1 tsp
Salt	to taste
Oil	50 ml

Method

1. Chop onions. Grind together grated coconut and red chillies into a fine paste. 2. Heat oil in a kadai. Add fennel and then chopped onions. Sauté well. Add quartered tomatoes and fry. 3. Mix in ground coconut. Fry till oil starts separating. 4. Add salt and garlic paste and continue frying. 5. Add prawns. Stir fry till trawns are cooked.

3. KARUVEPELLAI YERA

Ingredients	Quantity
Prawns cleaned with tail	1 kg
Ginger-garlic paste	10 gm
Chilli powder	20 gm

Ingredients	Quantity
Lime juice	2 limes
Turmeric powder	5 gm
Salt	to taste
Curry Powder	
Dried curry leaves	25 gm
Split black gram	5 gm
Split bengal gram	10 gm
Split red gram	10 gm
Cumin	3 gm
Asafoetida	3 gm
Chillies whole	5

Method

1. Clean prawns retaining tail. Devein prawns and wash in running water. 2. Marinate prawns in ginger-garlic paste, chilli powder, lime juice, salt, and turmeric powder and set aside. 3. Broil ingredients for the curry powder and powder them in a grinder. 4. Toss prawns in curry powder, and deep fry in oil. 5. Serve garnished with lime wedges, onion rings and curry leaves.

4. PORCHA MEEN (FRIED FISH)

Ingredients	Quantity
Sliced Fish	850 gm
(Bekti/fillets of pomfret)	
Chilli powder	20 gm
Turmeric	10 gm
Salt	to taste
Lime juice	3 small limes
Oil	for pan frying

Method

1. Clean, wash and dry slices of fish. Marinate with salt, lime juice, chilli powder and turmeric and set aside for 1 hour. 2. Heat oil in a shallow pan and fry fish till fully cooked.

5. MEEN VARUVAL (FISH FRIED) CHETTINAD

Ingredients	Quantity
Indian salmon	500 gm
(Rawas)	
Lime	2–3
Chilli powder (non-pungent)	10 gm

Ingredients	Quantity
Coriander powder	2 gm
Turmeric	2 gm
Ginger-garlic paste	10 gm
Salt	to taste
Oil	for frying

Method

1. Clean fish. Descale and remove sliminess using a scrubber. Rinse well. Apply lime juice and salt and set aside for 15 minutes. 2. Rub in ginger-garlic paste, chilli, coriander and turmeric powder and set aside for at least 1 hour. 3. Cook on a grid iron (tawa) in shallow fat, turning over to cook both sides.

6. MEEN KOZHAMBU

Ingredients	Quantity
Fish (black pomfret)	500 gm
Or Indian salmon (Rawas) or	
Mackerel	
Fenugreek	4 gm
Cumin	4 gm
Fennel	4 gm
Chilli powder (non-pungent)	20 gm
Coriander powder or Bedagi red	2 gm
Turmeric	2 gm
Onion (chopped)	50 gm
Shallots (sliced)	30 gm
Green chillies (whole)	2
Garlic (sliced)	20 gm
Tomatoes	100 gm
Tamarind (lime-size)	20–25 gm
Curry leaves	
Salt	to taste

Method

1. Clean fish well and wash in two or three rinses of cold water. 2. Heat oil, add fenugreek, cumin, fennel, chopped onion, sliced garlic and shallots, whole green chillies and curry leaves. Sauté till onions are well cooked. 3. Add chopped tomatoes, turmeric, chilli powder and coriander powder. Sauté for another 5 minutes. 4. Add soaked, pulped and strained tamarind and about 50 ml water. Simmer till gravy is cooked and fairly thick. 5. Add marinated fish and salt and cook till done.

7. KOZHI MULAGU VARUVAL (CHICKEN PEPPER FRY)

Ingredients	Quantity
Chicken	2 (800 gm)
Whole Madras onions (shallots)	12
Garlic	15 pods
Tomatoes	3
Red chillies	8
Black pepper	20 gm
Fennel seeds	15 gm
Cumin	10 gm
Fenugreek	10 gm
Salt	to taste
Turmeric	¼ tsp

Method

1. Clean and cut each chicken into 10 pieces. Peel garlic and Madras onions. 2. Dry roast red chillies, black pepper, and half the fennel and cumin. Pound them into a coarse powder, adding onions and garlic along with spices. 3. Heat oil in a kadai, add whole fenugreek and fennel and roughly chopped tomatoes. 4. Add chicken and fry well on high heat till it is seared. Add salt and turmeric and pounded masala and fry well. Cover and cook till done. This is a very popular and famous dish served during the festival at the temple of Chettinad.

8. CHICKEN CHETTINAD

Ingredients	Quantity
Chicken	1 kg
Grind to a paste	
Whole garam masala	5 gm
Oil	25 ml
Kalpasi (sweet sticks)	2 gm
Curry leaves	1 sprig
Ginger	10 gm
Fennel	5 gm
Cumin	3 gm
Coriander seeds	10 gm
Red chillies whole	10 gm
Poppy seeds	5 gm
Peppercorns	3 gm
Coconut	half
Shallots	50 gm
Garlic	10 gm
Cashewnuts	25 gm
Fried gram dal (pottu kadala)	15 gm

Ingredients	Quantity
Gravy	
Oil	100 ml
Bay leaf	1
Star anise	2 gm
Garam masala, whole	3 gm
Marathi mokku (Dayadphull)	2
Fennel	3 gm
Shallots	50 gm
Curry leaves	1 sprig
Ginger-garlic paste	30 gm
Tomatoes (chopped)	200 gm
Turmeric powder	a pinch
Chilli powder	5 gm
Coriander powder	10 gm
Garam masala powder	3 gm
Salt	to taste
Coriander leaves (chopped)	¼ bunch

Method

1. Saute all ingredients for grinding in oil and grind to a fine paste.
2. Clean, wash chicken and cut into small pieces. 3. Heat oil in a kadai, add bay leaf, star anise, garam masala whole, marathi mokku and fennel. Let crackle. 4. Add shallots and curry leaves. 5. Add ginger paste and chopped tomatoes. Saute well. 6. Add garam masala powder, salt and ground masala and cook till the raw flavour is gone. 7. Add chicken and cook slowly till tender. 8. Serve hot, garnished with chopped coriander leaves.

9. KOLI PORCHATHU (FRIED CHICKEN)

Ingredients	Quantity
Chicken (spring chicken)	2 (800 gm)
Madras onions (shallots)	50 gm
Coconut (grated and ground)	½
Ginger (ground)	1" piece
Garlic	30 gm
Tomatoes (medium)	4
Cinnamon sticks	2 pieces
Chilli powder	2 tbsp
Turmeric	½ tsp
Fennel	1 tsp
Salt	to taste
Oil	60 ml

Method

1. Heat oil in a kadai, put in fennel and cinnamon sticks. Add whole garlic and Madras onions. Saute for a minute and add chopped tomatoes. Fry well. 2. Add chicken and fry along with masala. Add chilli powder, turmeric and salt. Cook without adding water. 3. When the chicken is almost cooked, add ground coconut and ground ginger. Continue cooking till dry.

10. CHETTINAD KOZHI MELAGI VARAVAL (CHICKEN PEPPER FRY)

Ingredients	Quantity
Chicken	1
Shallots (small onions)	70 gm
Garlic	20 gm
Tomatoes	200 gm
Red chilli (Piriyan)	10 gm
Pepper	10–15 gm
Fennel	15 gm
Cumin	10 gm
Fenugreek	10 gm
Turmeric	½ tspn
Salt	to taste

Method

1. Roast red chillies deseeded for a milder flavour, pepper, and half the fennel and cumin in a thick-bottomed frying pan. Grind coarsely along with onion and garlic. 2. Heat oil, add remaining whole fenugreek and fennel. Fry. 3. Add chopped tomatoes and chicken. Cook on high heat to sear chicken. 4. Add salt and turmeric. Lower heat and cook covered till chicken is done adding a little water if necessary.

11. KOLI RASAMA (CHICKEN RASAM)

Ingredients	Quantity
Chicken bones	1½ kg
Split red gram	150 gm
Red chillies	5
Cumin	1½ tsp
Black pepper	2 tsp
Coriander seeds	3 tsp
Shallots	60 gm
Garlic	15 gm
Tomatoes	4
Tamarind	25 gm
Turmeric	¼ tsp

Ingredients	Quantity
Curry leaves	1 sprig
Mustard seeds	1 tsp
Asafoetida	¼ tsp
Coriander leaves	to garnish
Salt	to taste
Oil	2 tsp

Method

1. Boil 100 gm of split red gram till fully cooked. 2. Roast together cumin, black pepper, coriander seeds, 25 gm of red gram and red chillies (adding red chillies). Pound together. Put in peeled shallots and garlic and pound to a paste. 3. Prepare stock with bones and water, bring to a boil. Add whole tomatoes, and cook and mash into stock. Reduce to half. 4. Heat oil in a pan. Add mustard seeds, asafoetida and curry leaves and pour into stock. 5. Add boiled red gram, tamarind pulp, turmeric, pounded masala and salt. Bring to a boil, strain and serve garnished with chopped coriander.

12. KOLA URUNDA KOLAMBU (MUTTON KOFTA CURRY)

Ingredients	Quantity
Koftas	
Lamb (minced)	1 kg
Onions	60 gm
Green chillies	25 gm
Ginger	15 gm
Coconut	1
Cashewnuts	15 gm
Roasted bengal gram	100 gm
Fennel	15 gm
Garlic	15 gm
Cinnamon sticks	1 pc (1" size)
Cloves	4
Eggs	2
Coriander leaves	15 gm
Oil	for frying
Sauce	
Madras onions	40 gm
Tomatoes	3 (medium)
Coconut	1
Tamarind	30 gm
Fenugreek	½ tsp
Fennel	½ tsp

Ingredients	Quantity
Cinnamon sticks	2
Curry leaves	1 spring
Bay leaf	2
Chilli powder	2 tsp
Turmeric powder	½ tsp
Coriander powder	2 tsp
Garlic paste	½ tsp
Salt	to taste
Oil	100 ml

Method

1. In very little oil, roast together all the ingredients for koftas except eggs, mince and coriander leaves. 2. Fry well and add minced lamb. Sauté for just a minute, and take off the fire. Grind into a paste in a stone grinder. 3. Take out, mix in eggs, salt and chopped coriander. Form into lemon-sized koftas. 4. Lightly fry in hot oil to get a little colour. Set aside.

For the gravy

5. Grind coconut into a fine paste. Cut tomatoes in quarters. 6. Heat oil in a frying pan. Add fennel, fenugreek, cinnamon sticks, bay leaf and whole shallots. Fry well. 7. Add quartered tomatoes, tamarind pulp, turmeric, chilli powder, coriander powder and garlic paste. 8. Cook till oil seperates. Add enough water to make a medium thick gravy. Gently drop in koftas. Simmer till done.

13. KARI KOLAMBU (LAMB CURRY)

Ingredients	Quantity
Lamb (cut into small cubes)	1 kg
Tomatoes	3 (medium)
Garlic	2 pods
Madras onions	300 gm
Bay leaf	1
Fennel	1 tsp
Cinnamon sticks (I" pieces)	2
Fenugreek seeds	1 tsp
Turmeric powder	½ tsp
Chilli powder	2 tsp
Coriander powder	2 tsp
Khus khus paste	1½ tbsp
Ground coconut	1 coconut
Salt	to taste
Oil	60 ml

Method

1. Heat oil in a thick-bottomed pan. Add bay leaf, fennel, cinnamon and fenugreek seeds. Add whole peeled garlic, Madras onions and tomatoes cut into one-eights. Sauté for a while, add lamb and fry well to sear the meat. Add turmeric, chilli powder and coriander powder, and water to cover meat. 2. Simmer covered till meat is a quarter done. Add in khuskhus and ground coconut. 3. Stir well and cook till meat is done.

14. UPPU CURRY (MUTTON SALT CURRY)

Ingredients	Quantity
Mutton (cut in pieces)	1 kg
Coconut	1
Red chillies	20
Garlic	1½ pods
Madras onions	150 gm
Fennel	1 tsp
Fenugreek	1 tsp
Curry leaves	2 sprigs
Turmeric	½ tsp
Salt	to taste
Oil	150 ml

Method

1. Heat oil in a kadai, add fenugreek, fennel and curry leaves. When they crackle, add sliced Madras onions, and peeled and cut garlic. 2. Add lamb, turmeric and fry well. 3. Add salt and just enough water to cover meat. Cover and cook. 4. Add coconut into ½" cubes when meat is half-done. 5. Cook till dry, continue frying till meat is done. 6. For a bright colour, add rogan or chilli powder.

15. KARI PODIMAS (KHEEMA MASALA)

Ingredients	Quantity
Lamb (minced)	1 kg
Coconut	1
Onions	200 gm
Green chillies	60 gm
Split bengal gram	300 gm
Cinnamon	3 pieces (1" each)
Cardamom	8
Cloves	6
Bay leaf	1
Fennel	1 tbsp
Dagadphul	3

Ingredients	Quantity
Eggs	3
Salt	to taste
Oil	60 ml

Method

1. Boil bengal gram with enough water. Drain and keep the water aside.
2. Add this water to the kheema with a pinch of salt. Cook till dry.
3. Heat oil in a kadai, add whole garam masala. Put in chopped onions
and green chillies, slit in half. Sauté for 2 minutes, add a grated coconut,
sauté and then add kheema and dal. 4. Season with salt, break in eggs,
scramble and finish cooking.

16. SAMBA SAADAM

Ingredients	Quantity
Steamed rice	250 gm
green chillies	8
Cashewnuts	30 gm
Cumin	10 gm
Peppercorns	20 gm
Curry leaves	One sprig
Salt	to taste
Refined oil	5 ml

Method

1. Broil cumin and peppercorns, and pound. Heat oil in a pan. Add the
pounded cumin and peppercorns, green chillies, cashewnuts and curry
leaves. 2. Add steamed rice. Check for seasoning and serve garnished
with curry leaves.

17. KATHRIKAI KETTI KOZHAMBU (BRINJAL CURRY)

Ingredients	Quantity
Purple brinjals	250 gm
Oil	10 ml
Fennel	3 gm
Onions	120 gm
Fenugreek	2 gm
Shallots	100 gm
Green chillies (deseeded)	2
Turmeric	2 gm
Chilli powder (non-pungent)	20 gm
Coriander powder	20 gm
Tomatoes	250 gm
Tamarind pulp	15 gm

Ingredients	Quantity
Asafoetida	2 gm
Garlic	20 gm
Oil	10 ml
Salt	to taste
Curry leaves	2 sprigs

Method

1. Heat oil. Add fennel, fenugreek, cumin, chopped onion, sliced shallots and garlic. Sauté till onion is well cooked. 2. Add green chillies cut into halves (seeds removed), curry leaves, chopped tomatoes, turmeric, chilli and coriander powder. Sauté for another 5 minutes. 3. Add tamarind pulp (soaked in 300 ml water, pulped and strained), asafoetida and cubed brinjals (steeped in water to prevent discolouration) and salt. 4. Cook till the gravy is slightly thick. Check for seasoning. Remove.

18. KATRIKAI KARA KOZHUMBU

Ingredients	Quantity
Brinjals	600 gm
Sambar onions	75 gm
Garlic	25 gm
Chilli powder	50 gm
Coriander powder	25 gm
Turmeric powder	15 gm
Tamarind	50 gm
Oil	100 gm
Fenugreek	10 gm
Fennel	10 gm
Split black gram	10 gm
Curry leaves	2 sprins
Tomatoes	125 gm
Salt	to taste

Method

1. Cut brinjals lengthwise, and chop tomatoes. 2. Heat oil, sauté fenugreek seeds, black gram, fennel, curry leaves, sambar onions and garlic. When lightly browned add chilli and turmeric powder. Sprinkle a little water if necessary and add cut brinjal. Mix well. 3. When brinjal skin turns bright in colour add chopped tomatoes. 4. After a few minutes add tamarind pulp and water, as required. Check for salt. 5. Bring to a boil and simmer till brinjals are cooked.

N.B. To reduce the pungency of chilli powder, cooked dal water may be served. Serve in a dish garnished with chopped coriander and fried red chillies.

19. KATHRIKAI AVIAL

Ingredients	Quantity
Brinjal cubes fried	1 kg
Potato cubes fried	300 gm

Grind to a paste

Fried gram dal	20 gm
Cashewnuts	50 gm
Khus khus (poppy seeds)	20 gm
Garlic	30 gm
Shallots	50 gm
Coconut	½
Cumin seeds	3 gm
Aniseed	3 gm
Garam masala whole	3 gm
Green chillies	8
Ginger	15 gm
Oil	150 gm
Cinnamon	2 gm
Star Anise	2 gm
Fennel	3 gm
Onion cubes	200 gm
Garlic	25 gm
Curry leaves	1 sprig
Tomatoes (chopped)	200 gm
Turmeric powder	3 gm
Salt	to taste

Method

1. Grind to a fine paste all the ingredients specified above. 2. Heat oil in a handi, crackle cinnamon, star anise and fennel. Add onion, garlic and curry leaves and sauté well. 3. Add tomatoes and turmeric powder and cook well. 4. Add salt and ground masala and cook till the raw flavour is gone. 5. Add fried brinjal and potato cubes, bring to a boil and simmer. Serve garnished with fried curry leaves and chopped coriander leaves.

20. CAULIFLOWER PAL KOOTU

Ingredients	Quantity
Cauliflower (cut into small flowerets)	500 gm
Green gram dal	200 gm
Oil	150 gm
Cumin	5 gm
Coriander leaves	¼ bunch

Ingredients	Quantity
Curry leaves	1 spring
Split black gram	5 gm
Onion cubes	5 gm
Green chillies slit	10

Method

1. Boil cauliflower, drain and set aside. 2. Boil green gram and set aside. 3. Heat oil in a kadai add cumin and black gram. 4. When they crackle add onion cubes, green chillies and curry leaves. 5. Then add boiled cauliflower. 6. Then add ground masala and boil well till the raw flavour is gone. 7. Then add the boiled green gram and simmer till the gravy becomes thick. 8. Serve garnished with chopped coriander leaves and fried curry leaves.

21. KAIKARI PERATTAL

Ingredients	Quantity
Beetroot (boiled cubes)	200 gm
Beans (boiled cubes)	200 gm
Cauliflower (boiled flowerets)	200 gm
Potato (boiled cubes)	20 gm
To be ground to a fine paste	
Fried gram dal	20 gm
Cashewnuts	50 gm
Sonf	5 gm
Khus khus	10 gm
Garam masala whole	3 gm
Shallots	50 gm
Garlic	15 gm
Coconut	½
Gravy	
Oil	100 gm
Fennel	3 gm
Cinnamon	2 gm
Onion cubes	300 gm
Curry leaves	1 sprig
Tomatoes (chopped)	200 gm
Turmeric powder	3 gm
Chilli powder	30 gm

Method

1. Grind to a fine paste ingredients specified above. 2. Heat oil in a handi, crackle fennel and cinnamon. 3. Add onion and curry leaves and sauté

well. 4. Add tomatoes and cook well. Then add chilli powder and turmeric powder. 5. Add ground masala and cook till the raw flavour is gone. Add salt and check seasoning. 6. Toss all the vegetables so that they are evenly coated in masala. Serve garnished with fried potato cubes and chopped coriander leaves.

22. MUSHROOM KOOTU

Ingredients	Quantity
Channa dal	300 gm
Mushrooms	250 gm
Cumin	1 tsp
Split black gram	1 tsp
Chopped onions	½ cup
Curry leaves	2 sprigs
Green chillies (slit)	5
Coconut	1
Salt	to taste
Oil	75 ml

Method

Boil channa dal with enough water and 1 teaspoon oil. Grind coconut with a little water into a fine paste. Heat oil in a pan, add cumin, and black gram and fry. Add green chillies and curry leaves. Now add chopped onions and brown lightly. Add ground coconut and simmer. Meanwhile slice mushrooms and sauté till cooked. Add mushrooms to cooked coconut mixture. Pour mixture into dal, mix well, add salt, simmer for 2 minutes and take off fire.

23. PARANGIKKA PULI CURRY

Ingredients	Quantity
Red pumpkin	1 kg
Madras onions	60 gm
Garlic 20 gm	
Tomatoes	3 (medium size)
Chilli powder	2 tsp
Turmeric	½ tsp
Coriander powder	1 tsp
Tamarind	50 gm
Jaggery	25 gm
Fennel	1 tsp
Salt	to taste
Oil	50 ml

Method

Cut red pumpkin into 1½" cubes with skin. Slice onions. Prepare pulp from tamarind. Make a mixture out of pumpkin, tamarind pulp, cubed tomatoes, onions, turmeric, chilli powder, coriander powder, salt and oil. Add ½ cup water and boil. When pumpkin is half-done, add jaggery, crushed garlic and fennel. Simmer and finish cooking.

24. MANTHAKKALI KEERA (GREEN LEAFY VEGETABLE DISH)

Manthakkali is a green berry. The leaves of this plant are used for this dish. Since it has a bitter taste, a suggested alternative is spinach.

Ingredients	Quantity
Manthakkali greens	2 kg
Rice water (Mandi)	3 cups
Coconut	1
Split black gram	1 tbsp
Cumin	1 tbsp
Red Chillies	2
Madras onions (Shallots)	50 gm
Salt	to taste
Oil	50 ml

Method

Remove one extract of coconut milk. Shred the greens. Heat oil in a kadai, add cumin and split black gram. Add broken red chillies and then Madras onions. Add shredded greens. Sauté for a while and then add rice water. Cook till the greens are done. Remove from heat and add coconut extract and salt.

25. KOTHORAKKA KARAMANI PACHADI
(GOWAR SINGH AND CHOWLI BEANS "PACHADI")

Ingredients	Quantity
Gowar singh	½ kg
Chowli beans (white)	¼ kg
Madras onions (shallots)	60 gm
Tomatoes	3
Tamarind	60 gm
Split red gram	100 gm
Chilli powder	2 tsp
Turmeric	½ tsp
Coriander powder	1½ tsp
Mustard seeds	1 tsp
Split black gram	1 tsp
Curry leaves	2 sprigs

Ingredients	Quantity
Oil	150 ml
Salt	to taste

Method

Heat oil in a kadai, fry raw chowli beans, drain and pressure cook till done. In the same oil, fry gowar singh cut into ½" pieces, add a little water and cook till done, drain, and set aside. Boil split red gram in water till mashed. Make a mixture of all these and add tamarind, pulp, chilli powder, turmeric powder, coriander powder and salt. Heat little oil in a kadai, crackle mustard seeds, urad dal, curry leaves and add sliced Madras onions. Sauté well and add chopped tomatoes. Pour in bean mixture and simmer till sauce thickens.

26. GUNDU PORIAL (BABY POTATOES PORIAL)

Ingredients	Quantity
Baby potatoes	1 kg
Madras onions	60 gm
Garlic	8 cloves
Coconut	1
Cinnamon sticks	3 pieces (1" each)
Fennel	1 tbsp
Curry leaves	1 spring
Tomatoes	3 (medium)
Chilli powder	2 tbsp
Turmeric	1 tsp
Salt	to taste
Oil	70 ml

Method

Peel and cut potatoes in half. Peel and slice Madras onions. Grate and grind coconut into a paste. Cut tomatoes into cubes. Heat oil in a kadai. First add cinnamon sticks and fennel and then curry leaves. Add sliced onions and tomatoes. Put in potatoes and fry. Add chilli powder and turmeric, continue stirring, add crushed garlic, ground coconut and salt. Cover and cook, stirring occasionally. Cook till dry and potatoes are soft.

27. KIZHANGU KARVADU VARUVAL
(POTATOES FRIED LIKE FISH)

Ingredients	Quantity
Potatoes	1 kg
Lime	2
Chilli powder	2 tbsp

Ingredients	Quantity
Turmeric	1 tsp
Salt	to taste
Oil	150 ml

Method

Cut potatoes with skin lengthwise into four and cut into ¼" thick slices. Marinate with salt, turmeric, chilli powder and lime juice. Set aside for ½ hour. Heat oil in a kadai, put in potatoes and fry till cooked. Stir without breaking potatoes.

28. SENAI PORIYAL

Ingredients	Quantity
Yam (boiled cubes)	1 kg
Oil	150 gm
Red chillies (whole)	15
Mustard seeds	4 gm
Split black gram	10 gm
Curry leaves	1 sprig
Onions (chopped)	200 gm
Salt	to taste
Grated coconut	½

Method

1. Heat oil, add whole red chillies and fry well, then add mustard seeds and split black gram and let it crackle. 2. Add curry leaves, chopped onions and salt and sauté well without colouring. 3. Then add boiled senai and grated coconut and toss well. 4. Serve garnished with fried curry leaves and grated coconut.

29. KALAN MELAGU

Ingredients	Quantity
Kalan (Mushroom)	500 gm
Onions (chopped)	100 gm
Ginger/garlic paste	30 gm
Tomatoes (chopped)	80 gm
Turmeric powder	5 gm
Chilli powder	20 gm
Coriander powder	30 gm
Peppercorns (crushed)	50 gm
Salt	to taste
Refined oil	20 ml

Method

1. Heat oil in a pan, add chopped onions and sauté, then add ginger/garlic paste. 2. Add chopped tomatoes and cook well, then add turmeric, coriander and chilli powder. 3. Add blanched mushrooms to masala and cook well, then add crushed peppercorns, check for salt and finish with chopped coriander leaves.

30. PARUPPU URUNDAI KOZHAMBU

Ingredients	Quantity
For Urundai	
Split bengal gram	1 kg
Salt	to taste
Red chillies	12
Cumin	15 gm
Fennel	15 gm
Cinnamon	10 gm
Onions	100 gm
Coriander	35 gm
For kozhambu	
Oil	100 ml
Cumin	10 gm
Fennel	10 gm
Cubed onions	150 gm
Sambar onion	150
Peeled garlic	75 gm
Curry leaves	3 sprigs
Ginger, garlic paste	30 gm
Turmeric powder	20 gm
Chilli powder	70 gm
Coriander powder	70 gm
Tomatoes	200 gm
Tamarind pulp	

Method

For Urundai

Soak and grind all ingredients together. Add chopped onions and coriander leaves to the mixture and make balls. Fry the urundai in oil.

For Kozhambu

Heat oil, add cumin, fennel, sambar onion, onion cubes, peeled garlic and curry leaves. Then add ginger garlic paste, tomatoes and turmeric powder. Sauté well. Add chilli powder, coriander powder. Add tamarind pulp and a little water. Cook gravy well, put the urundai into gravy and simmer. Check for seasoning.

31. VENDAKAI MORE KOZHUMBU

Ingredients	Quantity
To be ground into paste	
Coconut grated	½
Cumin	5 gm
Split bengal gram	50 gm
Ginger	15 gm
Green chillies	15
Ladies fingers (1/3)	150 gm
Oil	100 gm
Red chillies (whole)	10
Peppercorns	10 gm
Mustard seeds	5 gm
Onions (chopped)	200 gm
Curry leaves	1 sprig
Turmeric powder	3 gm
Fresh curds	100 ml
Water	100 ml

Method

1. Grind coconut, cumin, split bengal gram, ginger and green chillies to a fine paste. 2. Heat oil, fry ladies fingers, remove and set aside. 3. To the same oil add whole red chillies, peppercorns, mustard seeds and when they crackle add chopped onions, curry leaves, turmeric powder and sauté. 4. Then add fried ladies fingers and ground masala along with water. 5. Allow the mixture to boil, then add curds mixed with 100 ml water and when this is warm remove from fire. Ensure that mixture does not boil after curds are added. 6. Serve hot garnished with chopped coriander leaves, fried curry leaves and fried red chillies.

32. VENDAKAI MANDI

Ingredients	Quantity
Oil	150 ml
Mustard seeds	3 gm
Split black gram	20 gm
Fenugreek seeds	10 gm
Turmeric powder	3 gm
Red chillies (whole)	10
Green chillies (½)	25
Onion cubes	120 gm

Ingredients	Quantity
Shallots	100 gm
Garlic whole	50 gm
Tomatoes chopped	100 gm
Rice water (first wash)	2 litre
Tamarind extract	1 litre
Salt	to taste
Curry leaves	1 sprig

Method

1. Heat oil, add mustard seeds, split black gram, fenugreek seeds, red chillies, green chillies, and turmeric powder till mustard crackles. 2. Then add onion cubes, shallots, and garlic and sauté. 3. Add chopped tomatoes and cook well. 4. Add ladies fingers and when these are half-done add rice water mixed with tamarind extract and salt and bring to a boil. 5. Reduce till thick and serve garnished with fried curry leaves.

33. PANAGAM

Ingredients	Quantity
Jaggery	100 gm
Chillies (whole)	5 gm
Dry ginger	5 gm
Lime juice	of 2 limes
Neem leaves	8
Water	500 ml

Method

1. Break jaggery into small pieces and add it to water with whole chillies, dry ginger and lime juice. 2. Chill and serve garnished with neem leaves.

34. IDLY

Ingredients	Quantity
Boiled rice	300 gm
Raw rice	100 gm
Split black gram	100 gm
Salt	to taste

Method

1. Wash all the ingredients except salt and soak in water. Grind in a grinder. Add salt and let mixture ferment. 2. Pour batter into idly moulds and steam in the steamer till done. 3. Serve chutney as an accompaniment.

35. IDIYAPPAM

Ingredients	Quantity
Rice flour (raw rice)	500 gm
Coconut oil	5 ml
Hot water	as required
Salt	to taste

Method

1. Broil rice flour in a pan. 2. Add coconut oil, salt and water and make a dough. 3. Pass dough through an Idiyappam press and steam it in a steamer.

36. DOSAI

Ingredients	Quantity
Raw rice	400 gm
Boiled rice	400 gm
Split black gram	200 gm
Split red gram	20 gm
Fenugreek	10 gm
Salt	to taste

Method

Soak and grind all ingredients except salt into a batter and ferment it for 6 hours. After fermentation add salt and little water and make a Dosai batter.

N.B. Each Dosai weight 50 gm; 1 kg batter makes 30 pieces; One portion has 2 pieces.

Accompaniments: Sambar; Chutney.

37. APPAM

Ingredients	Quantity
Raw rice	600 gm
Boiled rice	200 gm
Split black gram	100 gm
Salt	to taste
Coconut milk	150 ml
Cooking soda	5 gm

Method

Soak and grind rice and dal to a fine batter and ferment it for 8 hours. After fermentation add coconut milk and salt and make a semi-thick batter. Add water if necessary.

N.B. 2 pieces one portion (55 gm) has 2 pieces; one kg makes 32 pieces.

Accompaniments: Coconut milk – Sugar; Vegetable stew.

38. KADHAMBAM CHUTNEY

Ingredients	Quantity
Oil	5 ml
Mustard seeds	3 gm
Chillies (whole)	8
Onion cubes	50 gm
Tomato cubes	30 gm
Tamarind	5 gm
Asafoetida	3 gm
Ginger	10 gm
Salt	to taste

Method

1. Heat oil in a pan and put in mustard seeds. When they crackle, add whole chillies, onion cubes, tomato cubes, ginger, asafoetida, and sauté well. 2. Grind above ingredients in a grinder. Check for seasoning and finish.

39. THENGAI CHUTNEY

Ingredients	Quantity
Grated coconut	1
Fried bengal gram	50 gm
Tamarind	10 gm
Green chillies	5
Salt	to taste
For tempering	
Oil	3 ml
Mustard seeds	5 gm
Chillies (whole)	4
Curry leaves	

Method

1. Grind grated coconut, fried bengal gram, green chillies and tamarind together in a grinder. 2. Check salt and add tempering.

40. TOMATO CHUTNEY

Ingredients	Quantity
Tomatoes	1 kg
Refined oil	50 ml
Sesame oil	30 ml
Mustard seeds	10 gm
Curry leaves	1 sprig

Ingredients	Quantity
Chilli powder	25 gm
Salt	to taste

Method

1. Make a puree of tomatoes and set aside. 2. Heat refined oil in a kadai and add mustard seeds. 3. When they start to crackle add curry leaves and chilli powder. 4. Add tomato puree and cook well. Add salt. 5. Finish by adding sesame oil.

41. KOTHAMALI CHUTNEY

Ingredients	Quantity
Coriander leaves	2 bunches
Ginger	20 gm
Asafoetida	5 gm
Salt	to taste
Oil	5 ml
Tamarind	5 gm

Method

1. Heat oil in a pan, add the rest of the ingredients and sauté well.
2. Grind in a grinder, add salt and finish.

42. PAL KOZHUKATTAI

Ingredients	Quantity
For Kozhukattai	
Raw rice	75 gm
Water	20 ml
Coconut oil	5 ml
Salt	to taste
For Liquid	
Jaggery	250 gm
Water	350 ml
Coconut milk	100 ml

Method

1. Wash, drain and dry rice and make into a fine powder. 2. Broil rice flour till dry. 3. Sieve flour, add boiling water, coconut oil and salt and make a thick dough. 4. Make small dumplings and set aside.

For Liquid

1. Melt jaggery in water over a slow fire and strain. 2. Add coconut milk and cardamom powder after adding rice dumplins. Boil till dumplings are cooked.

THAILAND

1. TOM YOM

Ingredients	Quantity
Coconut	1
Beef (with bones)	500 gm
Curry leaves	1 sprig
Spring onion	1
Lemon grass	2.5 cm (1")
Ginger	1.5 cm (½") piece
Coriander leaves	a sprig
Green chillies	2
Lime	1

Method

1. Grate coconut. Extract thick milk and set aside. Add water and make a second extract. Add more water and make a third extract (altogether about 10 cups). 2. Clean and cut meat into small cubes. Cook in the third extract with salt and lemon grass stems, sliced ginger and curry leaves. 3. When the meat is nearly done, add second extract. Cook till meat is tender. Add chopped spring onion, coriander leaves and crushed chillies. Add first extract of coconut milk and lime juice.

N.B. Sometimes this is made with stock instead of coconut milk.

2. MOMOS

Ingredients	50 Momos
Dough	
Refined flour (maida)	500 gm
Egg	1
Salt	5 gm
Yeast	25 gm
Filling	
Mincemeat (fatty)	500 gm
Onions	250 gm
Green chillies	10 gm
Ginger	5 gm
Salt	10 gm
Soya sauce (optional)	1 tsp
Ajinomoto (optional)	¼ tsp
Oil (optional)	1 tbsp

Method

For Dough

1. Mix flour, salt and egg. 2. Add tepid water and make a soft dough, kneading vigorously for about 20 minutes. 3. Set dough aside for about 1 hour.

For Filling

1. Chop onions, green chillies and ginger. 2. Mix with mincemeat. 3. Add salt. Add soya sauce and ajinomoto (if used) and mix well.

To shape momos

1. Divide dough evenly into small balls weighing about 10 gm each and roll to about 2½" diameter. 3. Put 1 tsp of mincemeat filling into centre of each momo. Seal momo.

To steam momos

1. Boil water in bottom compartment of momo steamer, idli steamer or pressure cooker with idli steamer. 2. Grease perforated compartments and place momos keeping them least ½" apart. 3. Steam momos for 25–30 minutes. (If pressure cooker is used, do not put weight). 4. Serve steaming hot with tomato-garlic chutney.

ROMANIA

I. POULET SAUTÉ ROUMAIN

Ingredients	Quantity
Chicken (fryer or broiler)	1 (800 gm)
Parsley	1 bunch
Cream	1 cup
Fat	60 gm
Garlic shoots or Chives	1 bunch
Lime	½
Fresh curds	1 cup
Seasoning	to taste

Method

1. Clean and joint chicken. Fry lightly in hot fat. Remove. 2. Chop garlic shoots and parsley. In the same fat, fry half the parsley. Remove. 3. Add remaining parsley and chopped garlic shoots. Fry well. 4. Add cream and lime juice and chicken pieces and curd. Simmer gently till done.

2. POULET SAUTE PRINCESS

Ingredients	Quantity
Chicken (broiler or fryer)	1 (800 gm)
Fat	
Stock	
Asparagus heads	60 gm
Mushrooms	60 gm
Allemande sauce	
Chicken sauce	600 ml
Refined flour	30 gm
Butter	45 gm
Cream	1 tbsp
Nutmeg	1 pinch
Pepper	a pinch
Salt	to taste
Lime (juice)	1 tsp
Egg yolk	2

Method

1. Clean and joint chicken. Fry lightly. Remove fat. 2. Add just enough stock to cover chicken. Simmer till tender. 3. Prepare Allemande sauce. Blend with asparagus heads and mushrooms leaving a few for garnish. 4. Mix sauce with chicken. Simmer gently for a few minutes just before serving. 5. Dish out garnished with asparagus tips and mushrooms.

Allemande Sauce

1. Melt 30 gm of butter. Add flour and cook without discolouring. 2. Remove pan from fire. Add stock gradually, stirring well to prevent lumps forming. 3. Season with pepper, salt and nutmeg. Simmer for half an hour. 4. Beat egg yolks. Add cream. Add a little hot stock gradually and mix well. 5. Whisk in butter. Add to sauce. Heat without boiling. 6. Add lime juice. Remove and pass through a tammy cloth.

NEPAL

I. JOGI BHATH

Ingredients	For 6
Pulao rice	½ kg
Carrots	½ kg
Spinach	4 bunches
Onions	200 gm
Butter	100 gm

Ingredients	For 6
Bay leaf	2 gm
Cloves	2 gm
Turmeric	½ gm
Salt	to taste

Method

1. Clean, wash and drain rice. 2. Finely julienne carrots. 3. Boil spinach in water for 2 minutes. Remove and shred into 8 cm pieces. 4. Heat butter in a pan, add sliced onions, bay leaf and cloves. 5. Sauté for 2 minutes. 6. Add rice and fry till grains separate. 7. Add carrots and sauté for another 3–4 minutes. 8. Add 1 litre boiling water, salt and turmeric. 9. Reduce fire and simmer. 10. When almost all the water has been absorbed by the rice, add spinach and keep pan in an oven. 11. Finish cooking in the oven till rice is well-cooked and dry.

BAKING AND
CONFECTIONERY

SMALL CAKES

1. Vanilla Buns
2. Cream Corks
3. Mushroom Cakes
4. Coconut Buns
5. Butterfly Buns
6. Cherry Buns
7. Coburg Cakes
8. Pineapple Fans
9. Chocolate Boats
10. Praline Fingers
11. Cherry Tip Cakes
12. Madeleines
13. Coffee Jap Cakes
14. Queen Cakes (A)
    Queen Cakes (eggless) (B)
15. Cup Cakes
16. Sultana Buns
17. Rock Cakes or Buns
    (rub-in method)
18. Jam Buns (rub-in method)
19. Bran Muffins
20. Rock Buns (without eggs)
21. Orange Muffins
22. Doughnuts

ICING AND FILLINGS

23. Butter Icing (plain) (A)
    Butter Icing (B)
24. Butter Cream (rich)
25. Glacé Icing (A)
    Glacé Icing (B)
26. Royal Icing
27. Almond Paste
28. Almond Icing (for decoration)
29. Marshmallow Icing (A)
    Marshmallow Icing (B)
30. Fluffy Icing
31. American Frosting
32. Date and Nut Filling
33. Mincemeat
34. Lemon Curd
35. Confectioner's Custard
    (without eggs) (A)

Confectioner's Custard
(with egg) (B)
or Vanilla Cream
36. Cornflour Glaze

LARGE CAKES

37. Plain Sponge Cake
    (creaming method) (A)
    Sponge Cake (with milk
    powder) (B)
    Sponge Cake (fatless) (C)
38. Swiss Roll
39. Sponge Fruit Flan
40. Russian Sandwich
41. Check Cake
42. Chocolate Layer Cake
43. Low Cholesterol Chocolate
    Cake
44. Ribbon Cake
45. Lemon Cake
46. Fruit and Honey Sponge
    Cake
47. Genoese Sponge Cake (A)
    Genoese Sponge Cake (B)
48. Caramel Sandwich Cake
49. Jap Cake (one cake)
50. Madeira Cake
51. Velvet Cake
52. Fudge Cake
53. Pineapple Upside Down
    Cake
54. Walnut Sultana Cake
55. Sun Cake
56. Pound Cake (A)
    Pound Cake (B)
57. Plain Cake
58. Victoria Sandwich Cake
59. Tea Cake
60. Chocolate Cake
    (economical)
61. Chocolate Cake
62. Black Forest Cake
63. Seed Cake
    (rub-in method)

FRUIT CAKES

64. Fruit Cake (plain)
 (rub-in method)
65. Cherry Cake
66. Fruit Cake
 (creaming method) (A)
 Fruit Cake
 (creaming method) (B)
67. Rich Fruit Cake (A)
 Rich Fruit Cake (B)
 Rich Fruit Cake (C)
 Rich Fruit Cake (D)
68. Date and Walnut Cake
69. Sultana and Cherry Cake
70. Dundee Cake
71. Love Cake
72. Christmas Cake (A)
 Christmas Cake (B)
 Christmas Cake (C)
 Christmas Cake (D)
 Christmas Cake (E)
73. Christmas Cake (economical)
74. Christmas Cake
 (with semolina)
75. Christmas Cake (eggless)
76. Plum Cake
77. Wedding Cake

AMERICAN COFFEE CAKES

78. Light Coffee Cakes
79. Quick Coffee Cake
80. Gingerbread with Dates (A)
 Gingerbread (B)
81. Banana Tea Ring

PASTRIES

 Shortcrust Pastry
82. Jam Tarts
83. Lemon Curd Tarts
84. Date and Nut Turnover
85. Mock Mince Pies
86. Custard Tarts (A)
 Custard Tarts
 (with custard powder) (B)

87. Pineapple Tartlets
88. Pineapple and Cherry
 Cream Tartlets
89. Queensbury Tarts or Boats
90. Almond Tarts
91. Welsh Cheesecake
92. Apple Tarts
93. Cheesecake (A)
 Cheesecake (B)
 Cheesecake (C)
94. Swedish Slices
95. Almond Slices
96. Plate Tart
97. Deep Fruit Pie
98. Apple Pie
99. Ginger Apple Pie
100. Pumpkin Pie
101. Cheese and Aubergine Flan
102. Sardine
103. Chocolate Meringue Pie
104. Rich Walnut Pie
105. Lemon Meringue Pie
106. Custard Pie (A)
 Custard Pie (B)
107. Butterscotch Flan
108. Lime Chiffon Pie
109. Coconut Chiffon Pie
110. Egg and Cheese Flan
111. Rich Flan Pastry
112. Bakewell Tarts
113. Cheese Pastry
114. Green Pea Boats
115. Butterflies
116. Sardine Marguerites
117. Seafood Favourites
118. Cheese Biscuits
119. Cheese Straws (A)
 Cheese Straws (B)
 Cheese Straws (C)
120. Veal and Ham Pie
121. Hot Water Crust Pastry
122. Potato Sticks
123. Rough Puff Pastry
124. Jam Turnovers

128. Puff Pastry
129. Mille Feuilles
130. Chicken and Ham Pie
131. Tarte aux Crevettes
132. Chicken Vol-Au-Vent
133. Ham Bouchées
134. Cream Horns
135. Palmiers
136. Banana and Cream Puff Ring
137. Cream Slices
138. Danish Pastry (A)
     Danish Pastry (B)
139. Khara Biscuits
140. Choux Pastry
141. Éclair Swans
142. Cherry Shortbread
143. Shortbread
144. Mocha Shortcake
145. Golden Goodies
     (Coconut macaroons)
146. Nutty Pretzels
147. Melting Moments
148. Nut Rings
149. Cherry Knobs
150. Cinnamon Leaves and Crescents
151. Tricolour Biscuits
152. Pearl Cookies
153. Almond Bonbons
154. Chocolate Chip Cookies
155. Biscuit Press Cookies
156. Polka Dot Cookies
157. Peanut Butter Cookies
158. Sesame Queens
159. Swiss Tarts
160. Milan Hearts
161. Strawberry Cream Fingers
162. Chocolate Cream Fingers
163. Chocolate Whirls
164. Bachelor's Buttons
165. Butter Buttons
166. Peanut Cookies
167. Bird's Nest Cookies
168. Savoy Biscuits
169. Honey Biscuits
170. Vanilla Biscuits
171. Ginger Biscuits (A)
     Ginger Biscuits (B)
     Ginger Biscuits (C)
172. Soft Jaggery Biscuits
173. Brandy Snaps
174. Peanut Macaroons
175. Macaroons on Dry Cake
176. Coconut Macaroons (A)
     Coconut Macaroons (B)
177. Shrewsbury Biscuits (A)
     Shrewsbury Biscuits (B)

CANDY

178. Marshmallows
179. Brownies
180. Crème de Menthe
181. French Almond Rock
182. Milk Toffee
183. Chocolate Fudge
184. Fondant Peppermint Cream
185. Walnut Coffee Fudge
186. Date Fudge
187. Orange Fudge
188. Tutti Fruitti Fudge
189. Creamy Caramels
190. Walnut Fudge
191. Ginger Cream
192. Uncooked Fondant
193. Cooked Fondant
194. French Jellies
195. Gelatine Dainties
196. Crystallized Fruit
197. Chocolates
198. Moulded Chocolates (A)
     Moulded Chocolates (B)
199. Filling (A) Dark Ganache
     Filling (B) Butter Ganache
     Filling (C) Coconut Ganache
     Filling (D) Maple Ganache
200. Nougat
201. Penuche

IN CAKE MAKING IT IS MOST IMPORTANT TO ADHERE STRICTLY TO THE RECIPES

HELPFUL SUGGESTIONS

1. It is not necessary to grease tins for pastry. When greasing tins for cakes, puddings, etc. use hydrogenated fat.
2. Dried fruit should always be cleaned before it is used. It must be washed thoroughly, stems removed and spread on a cloth or over a rack covered with muslin. Never use wet fruit. A little refined flour may be mixed with the fruit before adding it to cakes. Glacé fruits should also be washed and dried.
3. To measure syrup, dip a tablespoon into boiling water, then use it quickly and the syrup will fall of the spoon easily.
4. If creamed fat and sugar tend to curdle after egg is added, add 1 tablespoon of the measured flour.
5. The hottest part of an oven is usually the top shelf. Bake large cakes in the middle of the oven, small cakes on the top shelf. Centre of oven corresponds most closely with the dial setting.
6. Fill tins only ¾ full to allow for rising. For large cakes make a slight depression in the middle so that they will rise flat.
7. To test when cake is cooked:
    (a) Sponge and sandwich cakes: Press the centre of the cake very lightly with a finger; the impression should spring back immediately. Always let cake cool slightly before removing from tin.
    (b) For large cakes such as fruit and Madeira, insert a fine skewer; it should come out clean.
8. It is necessary to pre-heat an oven for 15–20 minutes before using. Arrange shelves before heating oven. If oven door has to be opened while cakes are baking, it should be done gently as an onrush of cold air may spoil baking.

SMALL CAKES

I. VANILLA BUNS

Ingredients	For 15 buns
Butter	55 gm
Sugar	115 gm
Refined flour	115 gm
Baking powder	¼ tsp
Eggs	2
Vanilla	¼ tsp
Milk (if necessary)	

Method

1. Cream butter and sugar till light and fluffy. 2. Beat eggs and add gradually and continue beating mixture. 3. Sift together flour and baking powder and fold into creamed mixture with sufficient milk to give a dropping consistency. Add essence, mix lightly but well. 4. Half-fill some greased patty tins. 5. Bake at 195°C–205°C (375°F–400°F approx.) for 15–20 minutes till firm to the touch.

2. CREAM CORKS

Ingredients	For 15 corks
Refined flour	115 gm
Baking powder	¼ tsp
Sugar	115 gm
Butter	55 gm
Eggs	2
Vanilla	a few drops
Butter Cream	
Icing Sugar	85 gm
Butter	45 gm

Method

1. Make sponge buns using creaming method. Bake at 205°C (400°F approx.) for 15 minutes. Cool. 2. Cut out cork with 1.5 cm (½") nozzle. 3. Fill hole with cream using a star nozzle and replace cut out cake to resemble cork.

3. MUSHROOM CAKES

Ingredients	Quantity
Refined flour	115 gm
Baking powder	¼ tsp
Eggs	2
Vanilla	
Butter	55 gm
Sugar	115 gm
Chocolate Icing	
Butter	45 gm
Cocoa	1 tsp
Icing sugar	85 gm

Method

1. Make sponge buns using creaming method. 2. Bake at 205°C (400°F approx.) for 12–15 minutes. Cool. 3. Cut as for corks. 4. Spread with layer of chocolate icing and mark with fork. 5. Use cut out cake for stalk.

4. COCONUT BUNS

Ingredients	For 15 buns
Butter	45 gm
Egg	1
Sugar	55 gm
Baking powder	½ tsp
Refined flour	85 gm
Desiccated coconut	30 gm
Milk (a little, if necessary)	
Paper cups	15

Method

1. Sieve flour and baking powder. 2. Cream fat and sugar. 3. Beat in beaten egg. 4. Mix coconut with flour and fold into mixture using a little milk if necessary for mixing. 5. Half-fill paper cups and bake at 205°C (400°F approx.) for 15–20 minutes.

5. BUTTERFLY BUNS

Ingredients	For 15 buns
Refined flour	115 gm
Baking powder	¼ tsp
Butter	55 gm
Eggs	2
Sugar	115 gm
Vanilla	a few drops
Jam	55 gm

Method

1. Make sponge buns using creaming method. Bake at 205°C (400°F approx.) for 15 minutes. Cool. 2. Cut off top and cut it in half. 3. Spread top of bun with jam and position the two pieces cut from top to look like wings in flight.

6. CHERRY BUNS

Ingredients	Quantity
Refined flour	115 gm
Baking powder	¼ tsp
Butter	90 gm
Eggs	2
Lime juice	2 tsp
Cherries	55 gm
Icing sugar	100 gm
Sugar	115 gm

Ingredients	Quantity
Milk or Water	to mix
Paper cups	15

Method

1. Sieve flour and baking powder. 2. Cream butter and sugar till light and fluffy. 3. Beat eggs till thick, like custard, and add essence. 4. Beat in the eggs a little at a time into batter. 5. Fold in finely chopped cherries and sieved flour lightly with palette knife. 6. Add water to milk to get dropping consistency. 7. Fill paper cases two-thirds full. 8. Bake 190°C to 200°C (375°F–400°F approx.) for about 15 minutes. 9. When cold, put thick glacé icing on top and decorate by placing a half cherry in centre.

7. COBURG CAKES

Ingredients	For 15 cakes
Refined flour	170 gm
Butter	85 gm
Sugar	85 gm
Eggs	2
Soda bicarbonate	
Ginger	
Cinnamon powder	¼ tsp each
Warm water	1 tbsp
Golden syrup	1 tbsp
All spice powder	¼ tsp

Method

1. Sieve dry ingredients together. 2. Cream fat and sugar. 3. Beat eggs and add gradually, beating mixture all the time. 4. Mix warm water and golden syrup. 5. Add to mixture alternately with flour. 6. Put mixture into a well-greased and floured patty tin. Bake at 190°C (375°F approx.) for 20 minutes.

N.B. This mixture can also be baked in a lined cake tin as one cake.

8. PINEAPPLE FANS

Ingredients	Quantity
Refined flour	170 gm
Baking powder	1 tsp
Sugar	170 gm
Butter	170 gm
Eggs	3
Apricot or other yellow-coloured jam	55 gm

Ingredients	Quantity
Pineapple	6 rings
Cashewnuts (roasted and chopped)	55 gm
Butter cream:	
Icing sugar	115 gm
Butter	70 gm

Method

1. Make a sponge cake in the usual way but put in a spoonful of flour each time an egg is added to prevent curdling. 2. Pour into prepared Swiss roll tin and bake at 190°C (375°F approx.) for 25 minutes. Cool. 3. Prepare butter cream, chop 2 rings of pineapple and add to half the cream. 4. Cut cake into two and using pineapple-flavoured cream, sandwich the two pieces. 5. Spread sieved jam on top of cake. 6. Cut cake into 4 pieces widthwise. Cut each cake into 3 squares and then into 6 diagonals making 24 pieces in all. 7. Spread remaining cream, around sides of cake. Roll in roasted nuts. 8. Place a small fan of pineapple in the centre of each cake and brush with jam.

9. CHOCOLATE BOATS

Ingredients	For 12 boats
Refined flour	100 gm
Cocoa	15 gm
Baking powder	$\frac{1}{4}$ tsp
Butter	60 gm
Eggs	2
Milk	if necessary
Sugar	115 gm
Vanilla essence	a few drops
Icing:	
Icing sugar	115 gm
Butter	55 gm
Colouring and flavouring as desired.	

Method

1. Sieve flour, baking powder, and cocoa together twice. 2. Cream butter and sugar. 3. Beat eggs and add essence and beat into mixture gradually. 4. Fold in dry ingredients and milk if necessary. 5. Grease and flour boat tins well and half-fill with mixture. 6. Bake in hot oven at 190° to 205°C (375°F–400°F approx.) for 15–20 minutes. Cool. 7. Prepare icing in two colours. 8. Spread with one colour, pipe other colour with a writing nozzle.

10. PRALINE FINGERS

Sheet sponge for base. (See recipe No. 37(C)) Butter cream plain.

Ingredients	For 24 pieces
Sugar	115 gm
Water	8 tbsp
Roasted nuts	45 gm

Topping

1. Bring sugar and water to caramel stage. 2. Pour over nuts. 3. Spread on oiled surface and leave to set. 4. Break up into small pieces and mix with butter cream. 5. Sandwich and spread cake with praline and butter cream mixture. 6. Sprinkle more praline over the top and cut into fingers.

11. CHERRY TIP CAKES

Ingredients	For 18 cakes
Butter	170 gm
Sugar	170 gm
Refined flour	170 gm
Baking powder	1 tsp
Eggs	3
Glacé cherries	18
Jam	55 gm
Cake Crumbs	
Almond Icing:	
Ground almonds or cashewnuts	170 gm
Icing sugar	170 gm
Lemon juice	1 tsp
Egg	1
Vanilla	1/4 tsp
Almond essence	few drops

Method

1. Sieve flour and baking powder. 2. Cream butter and sugar. 3. Beat eggs and add gradually, beating all the time. 4. Gradually fold in sieved flour. 5. Put into a lined Swiss roll tin and bake at 190°C (375°F approx.) for 20 minutes and at 175°C (350°F approx.) for 10 minutes. 6. Allow to cool before using.

Icing

1. Grind almonds as fine as possible. 2. Mix with icing sugar. 3. Add beaten egg and lime juice. 4. Mix well by hand and work into a ball.

5. Roll out thinly on board sprinkled with a little cornflour. 6. With a flutted cutter cut to the same size as cakes.

Putting together

1. With small cutter cut out 18 round cakes from sponge sheet. 2. Make the scraps into crumbs by drying in a moderate oven and when they are cool rubbing them through a sieve. 3. Spread sides of cakes with warmed jam and roll in cake crumbs. 4. Put a little jam on top of cakes and place a cherry in the centre. 5. Cut a cross in the centre of almond paste rounds. Place over cherry and press down so that the cherry peeps through. Serve in paper cases.

N.B. This cake should be baked the day before it is put together.

12. MADELEINES

Ingredients	For 8 cakes
Butter	115 gm
Sugar	115 gm
Refined flour	115 gm
Bakig powder	¼ tsp
Eggs	2
Dessicated coconut	55 gm
Glacé cherries	30 gm
Jam	30 gm

Method

1. Sieve flour and baking powder together. 2. Cream butter and sugar. 3. Beat eggs and add gradually, beating well all the time. 4. Fold in sieved flour lightly. 5. Grease Madeleine moulds and fill them with mixture. 6. Bake in a hot oven for 20 minutes.

Putting together

1. Trim off tops so that cakes stand firm upside down and are of even height. 2. Cool and brush tops and sides with melted jam, holding cakes on skewers. 3. Roll in coconut. Place half a cherry with a little jam on top.

13. COFFEE JAP CAKES

Ingredients	9–10 cakes
Egg whites	3
Castor sugar	170 gm
Almond essence	2 drops
Ground cashewnuts	170 gm

Ingredients	9–10 cakes
Filling:	
Icing sugar	115 gm
Butter	55 gm
Coffee essence	
Icing:	
Icing sugar	55 gm
Coffee essence	
Hot water	

Method

1. Whisk egg whites until stiff. Add sugar and ground cashewnuts.
2. Line Swiss roll tin with oiled paper and spread with mixture. 3. Bake in centre of slow oven gas mark 3 or 175°C electricity (350°F approx.) till it becomes golden (about 15 minutes). 4. Take out of oven and mark 18 to 20 small rounds as close to each other as possible to avoid wastage. 5. Return cake to oven and cook for about another 15 minutes. 6. Lift rounds out carefully and return trimmings to oven to brown. Cool and make into crumbs. 7. Sandwich cakes with butter cream. Coat sides and roll in crumbs. 8. Decorate top with thick glacé icing and put pieces of roasted nuts on top.

14. QUEEN CAKES (A)

Ingredients	Quantity
Refined flour	55 gm
Sugar	55 gm
Egg	1
Shortening	55 gm
Baking powder	¼ tsp
Milk	15 ml (about)
Raisins	30 gm

Method

1. Wash, pick, stone and dry raisins. 2. Sieve flour with baking powder. 3. Cream butter and sugar till light and fluffy. 4. Beat eggs and add gradually beating mixture all the time. 5. Add raisins. 6. Add flour and mix lightly using milk if necessary to get a soft dropping consistency. 7. Bake in paper cases at 205°C (400°F approx.) for 15–20 minutes.

QUEEN CAKES (eggless) (B)

Ingredients	12 cakes
Refined flour	170 gm
Baking powder	3 level tsp

Ingredients	12 cakes
Salt	a pinch
Margarine	70 gm
Sugar	55 gm
Golden syrup	1 level tsp
Milk and Water	295 ml
Sultanas	30 gm

Method

1. Cream margarine and sugar together. 2. Add syrup and salt and beat well again. 3. Sieve baking powder and flour together and add to creamed mixture with milk and water. 4. Stir in cleaned and dried sultanas. 5. Put mixture into greased patty tins. 6. Bake at 190°C (375°F approx.) for 20–25 minutes.

15. CUP CAKES

Ingredients	12 cakes
Butter	55 gm
Egg	1
Paper cases	
Refined flour	115 gm
Baking powder	½ tsp
Sugar	55 gm
Glacé icing	
Icing sugar	140 gm
Warm water	to mix
Pink colouring	

Method

1. Sieve flour and baking powder. 2. Cream butter and sugar. 3. Beat eggs. Add essence to egg and add gradually to cream, beating all the time. 4. Fold in flour lightly using a little milk if necessary to get a dropping consistency. 5. Divide mixture into 2 portions and colour one portion pink. 6. Put into paper cases (half full) and bake in a hot oven 205°C (400°F approx.) for 15–20 minutes; cool before decorating.

Glacé icing

1. Sieve icing sugar and mix with warm water till it coats the back of a wooden spoon thickly. Pour over pink cakes. 2. Colour remaining icing pink and pour on plain cakes.

N.B. Various colours can be used for these cakes.

16. SULTANA BUNS

Ingredients	12 buns
Flour	115 gm
Powdered sugar	115 gm
Eggs	2
Margarine	85 gm
Sultanas	40 gm
Baking powder	¼ tsp
Paper cups	12
Mixed fruit essence or	
Vanilla essence	½ tsp
Water	30 ml

Method

1. Sieve flour with baking powder. 2. Cream margarine and sugar till light and fluffy. 3. Beat eggs till thick, like custard, and add essence. 4. Beat in sultanas and sieved flour lightly with a palette knife. 6. Add water to get a dropping consistency. 7. Fill into paper cups and bake at 190°C (375°F approx.) for about 15 minutes.

17. ROCK CAKES OR BUNS (rub-in method)

Ingredients	12 buns
Refined flour	170 gm
Baking powder	1 tsp
Sultanas	30 gm
Sugar	85 gm
Candied peel	15 gm
Egg	1
Butter	85 gm
Milk	a little, if necessary

Method

1. Wash and dry sultanas. Chop candied peel. 2. Sieve flour and baking powder. 3. Rub fat into flour as for pastry. Add sugar and mix. 4. Beat egg and mix with flour, alternately with fruit, using a fork. 5. Put small heaps on a greased and floured baking sheet. The mixture must be stiff enough to stand in rock-like mounds; bake at 175°C (350°F approx.) for about 15 minutes.

18. JAM BUNS (rub-in method)

Ingredients	8–9 buns
Refined flour	115 gm
Baking powder	½ tsp
Sugar	55 gm

Ingredients	8–9 buns
Jam	45 gm
Salt	a pinch
Butter	45 gm
Milk	a little, for mixing

Method

1. Sieve together flour, salt and baking powder. 2. Rub in fat and add sugar. 3. Mix to a stiff dough with milk. 4. Turn onto a board or slab. Knead lightly and divide into 8–9 pieces. 5. Make a hole in each and fill in with a little jam. 6. Put on a greased and floured baking sheet and bake at 205°C (400°F approx.) for 15–25 minutes.

19. BRAN MUFFINS

Ingredients	Quantity
Bran	50 gm
Flour	50 gm
Baking powder	¼ tsp
Sugar (castor)	100 gm
Margarine	75 gm
Eggs	2
Orange	1 (juice)
Orange essence	¼ tsp
Paper cups	

Method

1. Sieve flour with baking powder and mix with bran. 2. Cream margarine and sugar till light and fluffy. 3. Beat eggs well and add to creamed mixture. Add essence. 4. Add flour mixture a little at a time and fold lightly. 5. Add orange juice to get a dropping consistency. 6. Spoon into muffin tins and bake at 375°F for 15 minutes. 7. Cool and put into cups.

20. ROCK BUNS (without eggs)

Ingredients	8–9 buns
Refined flour	115 gm
Salt	a pinch
Baking powder	¼ tsp
Mixed spices	¼ tsp
Butter	55 gm
Chopped candied peel	15 gm
Milk	15–30 ml
Sugar	85 gm
Sultanas	30 gm

Method

1. Sieve flour, baking powder, salt and spices together. 2. Rub in butter with finger tips. 3. Add sugar and fruit to flour mixture. 4. Add milk to form a stiff mixture. 5. Put spoonfuls onto a greased and floured baking sheet in rough piles. 6. Bake for about 15 minutes at 190°C (375°F approx.).

21. ORANGE MUFFINS

Ingredients	18 muffins
Refined flour	115 gm
Baking powder	½ tsp
Butter or Margarine	85 gm
Sugar	115 gm
Eggs	2
Milk	50 ml
Orange juice	50 ml
Orange rind (chopped fine)	1 tsp

Method

1. Cream margarine and sugar. 2. Blend in beaten egg and orange rind. 3. Sift together flour, baking powder and salt. 4. Add alternately with milk and orange juice, mixing well each time. 5. Fill greased muffin pans. 6. Bake at 205°C (400°F approx.) 15 to 20 minutes.

22. DOUGHNUTS (with baking powder)

Ingredients	10 doughnuts
Refined flour	225 gm
Baking powder	1½ tsp
Sugar	55 gm
Egg	1
Cold milk	100 ml
Vanilla or Powdered cinnamon	a few drops
Shortening	

Method

1. Sift flour and baking powder. 2. Rub in fat. 3. Beat eggs. Add milk and flavouring. 4. Mix flour with egg, milk and salt into a smooth dough. 5. Turn it onto a floured board. 6. Knead lightly and divide into 10 portions. 7. Cut into doughnuts and fry in smoking hot fat until golden brown. 8. Turn doughnuts onto a paper which has been sprinkled with sugar and cinnamon (optional).

ICING AND FILLINGS

23. BUTTER ICING (PLAIN) (A)

Ingredients	Quantity
Sifted icing sugar	115 gm
Butter	55 gm
Flavouring and Colouring	

Noodles

1. Sieve icing sugar. 2. Cream butter and add gradually to sugar beating into a light cream. 3. Add flavouring and colouring and use as required.

BUTTER ICING (B)

Ingredients	Quantity
Icing sugar	85 gm
Cocoa	30 gm
Butter	45 gm
Castor sugar	60 gm
Milk	2 tbsp
Vanilla	¼ tsp

Noodles

1. Sift sugar and cocoa into a bowl. 2. Put fat, castor sugar, and milk into a pan and warm. 3. Pour over icing sugar mixture and stir till it coats back of spoon.

24. BUTTER CREAM (rich)

Ingredients	Quantity
Sugar	115 gm
Butter	55 gm
Egg yolks	2
Water	75 ml
Flavouring/Colouring	as desired

Noodles

1. Make a syrup with sugar and water and heat to a temperature of 115°C (240°F approx.). 2. Whip egg yolks. 3. Remove syrup. Allow bubbles to subside. 4. Pour gradually into egg yolks, beating all the time. 5. Beat mixture into creamed butter gradually beating until cool.

N.B. This is suitable only for spreading and not for decoration.

25. GLACÉ ICING (A)

Whip icing sugar with warm water or warm juice till desired consistency is obtained.

GLACÉ ICING (B)

Ingredients	Quantity
Sifted icing sugar	225 gm
Water	2 tbsp
Colouring and Flavouring	as desired

Noodles

1. Put sifted icing sugar and water into a thick-bottomed pan over heat and stir until mixture is warm. Do not make icing too hot. 2. When it coats the back of spoon evenly and looks smooth and glossy, add flavouring and colouring.

26. ROYAL ICING

Ingredients	Quantity
Icing sugar	450 gm
Lime (juice)	½
Egg whites	2 (3 if small)

Noodles

1. Sieve icing sugar twice to make quite sure that there are no lumps. 2. Beat egg whites slightly. Add lime juice, then gradually add sugar beating all the time. 3. Beat until icing is of a beatable but stiff consistency. It should stand up in peaks. 4. Cover with a wet cloth and use as required immediately. 5. Use a palette knife dipped in warm water to smoothen. Let the base dry well before decorating cake.

27. ALMOND PASTE (for use under Royal Icing and to decorate Easter and simnel cakes)

Ingredients	Quantity
Icing sugar	225 gm
Ground almonds	225 gm
Cashewnuts can be used for economy	
Egg	1
Lime juice	½
Vanilla	a few drops
Almond essence (if cashewnuts are used)	

Noodles

1. Sieve sugar and put into a bowl with ground almonds. 2. Add lightly

beaten egg and remaining ingredients. 3. Stir and mix together to a stiff paste which will form into a ball. 4. Work by kneading thoroughly. Roll out using a very light dusting of cornflour to prevent sticking to roller and board. 5. Always paint cake with a little warm and sieved apricot jam before putting on paste.

28. ALMOND ICING (for decoration)

Ingredients	Quantity
Almonds	225 gm
Egg white	1
Sugar	690 gm
Water	295 ml (about)
Cream of tartar	a pinch
Almond essence	

Noodles

1. Blanch and grind almonds using a little egg white. 2. Make a sugar syrup. Clear with egg white. 3. Add cream of tartar and then boil to 113°C (235°F approx.) 4. Put in ground almonds and cook till thick. 5. Remove and grind well again.

29. MARSHMALLOW ICING (A)

Ingredients	Quantity
Egg white	1
Golden syrup	115 ml
Icing sugar	1 tbsp
Gelatine	½ tsp

Noodles

1. Whisk egg white and golden syrup over gently boiling water until thick. 2. Add dissolved gelatine. Remove from heat. Fold in sifted icing sugar, colour and essence. 3. Pour over cake and roughen. Sprinkle over with chopped nuts.

MARSHMALLOW ICING (B)

Ingredients	Quantity
Icing sugar	170 gm
Water	2 tbsp
Gelatine	1 tsp
Egg white	1
Golden syrup	1 tsp
Vanilla	a few drops

Method

1. Make a sugar syrup with water and sugar. 2. Dissolve gelatine in

warm water. 3. Add to sugar syrup and cook for a few minutes more. 4. Pour over stiffly beaten egg white. Whisk well. 5. Add golden syrup and vanilla. 6. When thick, pour over cake. 7. Decorate with nuts or crystallized cherries.

30. FLUFFY ICING

Ingredients	Quantity
Sugar	20 gm
Water	4 tbsp
Cream of tartar	a pinch
Egg white	2
Vanilla	a few drops

Method

1. Put sugar, water and cream of tartar into a thick-bottomed pan. 2. Heat slowly until sugar dissolves. 3. Bring to a boil without stirring. When temperature reaches 115°C (240°F approx.), remove. 4. Let bubbles subside. Pour syrup slowly onto stiffly beaten egg whites, beating all the time. 5. Add essence and beat until icing is cool and thick enough to spread.

31. AMERICAN FROSTING

Ingredients	Quantity
Sugar	450 gm
Water	150 ml
Egg whites	2
Essence and Colouring	as desired

Method

1. Heat sugar and water stirring until sugar dissolves completely. 2. Then bring syrup to a boil. 3. Boil without stirring to 115°C (240°F approx.). 4. Whisk egg whites till stiff. 5. Remove syrup from heat. Let it cool until bubbles subside. 6. Pour onto egg whites, beating till required consistency is reached. 7. Add essence and colouring if desired. 8. Pour over cake. Allow icing to run down and cover sides of cake.

N.B. If a swirling finish is desired, beat the mixture slightly longer and rapidly spread it over cake using a palette knife.

32. DATE AND NUT FILLING (for turnover and mock mince pies)

Ingredients	Quantity
Dates	115 gm
Sugar	30 gm
Butter	30 gm

Ingredients	Quantity
Nuts	30 gm
Mixed spices	½ tsp
Lemon rind	½ tsp
Lemon juice	1 tsp

Method

1. Wash, stone and chop dates. 2. Chop nuts and mix well. 3. Melt butter and sugar in a pan on a slow fire. 4. Add spices, rind and juice. 5. Add date and nut mixture gradually and cook for about 3 minutes stirring all the time. Let it cool before putting into pastry.

33. MINCEMEAT

Ingredients	Quantity
Apples	450 gm
Brown sugar	450 gm
Valencia raisins	450 gm
Mixed peel	225 gm
Nutmeg (grated)	1
Mixed spices	1 tsp
Rum or Sherry	150 ml
Rind and juice of orange	2
Dry ginger	1 tsp
Fat (Butter, Margarine or Suet)	
Currants	450 gm
Sultanas	225 gm
Almonds	115 gm
Rind and juice of lemon	1

Method

1. Chop apples and fat. 2. Stone raisins and chop fine. 3. Clean currants and sultanas. Chop peel. 4. Blanch and chop almonds. 5. Mix all these prepared ingredients. 6. Add spices, lemon rind and juice, rum and orange rind and juice. 7. Stir well. Let it stand overnight. Stir again. 8. Store in jars. Set aside for three weeks before using.

34. LEMON CURD

Ingredients	For 12 tarts
Sugar	115 gm
Butter	55 gm
Egg	1
Lime	1

Method

1 Grate yellow part of lime peel. 2. Melt butter and sugar. 3. Add juice and rind of lemon. 4. Remove from fire and beat in egg. 5. Return to fire and cook in a double boiler or over water until thick. 6. Cool before using.

35. CONFECTIONER'S CUSTARD (without eggs) (A)

Ingredients	Quantity
Milk	150 ml
Cornflour	15 gm
Sugar	15 gm
Butter	15 gm
Vanilla	⅛ tsp
Yellow colouring	

Method

1. Mix cornflour with a little cold milk. 2. Boil remainder of milk. 3. Remove from fire and add to blended cornflour stirring well. 4. Return to fire and cook until it thickens stirring all the time. 5. Remove from fire and whip in butter. Set aside till cool.

CONFECTIONER'S CUSTARD (with egg) (B) OR VANILLA CREAM

Ingredients	Quantity
Milk	150 ml
Sugar	15 gm
Cornflour	15 gm
Egg	1
Vanilla	a few drops

Method

1. Whisk egg and sugar till fairly thick. 2. Whisk in flour. Add hot milk. 3. Cook till thick, beating all the time. 4. Add essence and remove. Cool before using.

36. CORNFLOUR GLAZE

Ingredients	20 portions
Water	150 ml
Jam	30 gm
Lemon juice	1 tsp
Sugar	30 gm
Cornflour	15 gm
Colouring	

Method

1. Mix cornflour with a little of the water. 2. Boil remaining water with sugar, jam and juice. 3. Add to blended cornflour and cook until thick. Add colouring. 4. Cool before using.

LARGE CAKES

37. PLAIN SPONGE CAKE (creaming method) (A)

Ingredients	Quantity
Refined flour	115 gm
Baking powder	¼ tsp
Sugar	115 gm
Milk, a little if necessary	for mixing
Vanilla or other flavouring	a few drops
Butter or Margarine	60 gm
Eggs	2
Butter cream:	
Butter	85 gm
Icing sugar	170 gm
Flavouring or Cocoa	

Method

1. Sieve flour and baking powder. 2. Crush sugar if necessary. 3. Cream butter and sugar very well until light and fluffy. 4. Beat eggs. Add flavour and add to mixture gradually, beating all the time. 5. Fold in sieved flour very lightly with a little milk to get a dropping consistency. 6. Put into a prepared tin and bake at 190°C (375°F approx.) for 25 minutes. Cool. 7. Prepare butter cream by creaming together butter and sugar and use to decorate cake.

N.B. This can be used for all light buns.

SPONGE CAKE (with milk powder) (B)

Ingredients	Quantity
Refined flour	115 gm
Baking powder	¼ tsp
Sugar	115 gm
Butter	60 gm
Eggs	2
Water	1–2 tbsp
Milk powder	15 gm
Vanilla	a few drops

Method

1. Sieve flour with milk powder. 2. Cream butter and sugar. 3. Beat eggs and beat into cream. 4. Fold in sieved flour. 5. Add water and essence to get a dropping consistency. 6. Pour mixture into a lined cake tin and bake at 175°C (350°F approx.) for 20–25 minutes.

SPONGE CAKE (fatless) (C) (to be used as sheet)

Ingredients	Quantity
Eggs	4
Castor sugar	115 gm
Baking powder	½ tsp
Refined flour	115 gm
Warm water	30 ml

Method

1. Sieve flour with baking powder. 2. Beat eggs for 2–3 minutes, add sugar and place bowl over boiling water being careful not to let the water touch the bowl. 3. Beat well until thick and creamy. 4. Fold in sieved flour very lightly along with hot water. 5. Pour into prepared tins and immediately bake in a hot oven at 200°C (400°F approx.) for 10–12 minutes.

38. SWISS ROLL

Ingredients	Quantity
Eggs	2
Refined flour	85 gm
Sugar	85 gm
Vanilla	a few drops
Hot water	1 tbsp
Baking powder	¼ tsp
Jam	55 gm

Method

1. Break eggs into a bowl with sugar and place bowl over boiling water being careful not to let the water touch the bowl. 2. Whisk until stiff and creamy. 3. Sift flour and baking powder into mixture folding in flour carefully. Add hot water and fold in. 4. Pour mixture into a greased Swiss roll tin and bake at 205°C (400°F approx.) for 10–12 minutes. 5. Quickly turn on to paper dusted with sugar. 6. Remove lining paper on top. Cut off stiff edges. Spread jam and roll with help of paper. 7. Cool in paper.

N.B. This can be decorated and made into a 'Yule Log' using butter icing made with 165 gm icing sugar, 30 gm cocoa, and 85 gm butter.

39. SPONGE FRUIT FLAN

Ingredients	Quantity
Refined flour	85 gm
Bananas	2
Sugar	85 gm
Eggs	3
Vanilla	a few drops
Hot water	1–2 tbsp
Cherries	4
Bananas (sliced and sprinkled with lime juice)	2

Cornflour glaze: (jam flavoured)

Cornflour	15 gm
Sugar	30 gm
Water	150 ml
Jam	30 ml

Method

1. Beat eggs and sugar to a thick cream in a bowl over hot water. 2. Add essence and sieved flour, folding in flour with a palette knife. 3. Add 1–2 tbsp hot water. 4. Grease and flour flan tin and put mixture. 5. Bake at 230°C (450°F approx.) for about 10–12 minutes. 6. When cool lift off flan onto a plate. Arrange sliced bananas. Decorate with cherries and pour glaze over.

Glaze

1. Blend cornflour with a little cold water. 2. Boil remaining water and pour over blended cornflour, stirring well. 3. Add sugar and jam. Return to fire and cook till thick. 4. Pour over bananas, covering them completely.

40. RUSSIAN SANDWICH

Ingredients	Quantity
Eggs	2
Refined flour	55 gm
Sugar	55 gm

Filling

Milk	.150 ml
Custard powder	15 gm
Sugar	15 gm
Butter	20 gm
Vanilla	1/8 tsp
Hot water	1 tbsp
Baking powder	1/4 tsp

Ingredients	Quantity
Topping:	
Icing sugar	85 gm
Water to mix	
Cashewnuts	30 gm

Method

1. Prepare sponge using the over hot water method (see recipe No. 37(C) fatless sponge). 2. Pour into a prepared sandwich tin and bake at 200°C (400°F approx.) for 10–12 minutes. Cool. 3. Make a custard with milk, custard powder and sugar. 4. Remove from fire and beat in butter, till smooth. 5. Cut cake into two, spread custard lightly and sandwich together. 7. Chop and roast cashewnuts. 8. Pouring icing on top of cake. Decorate a 2.5 cm border round the edge with chopped, roasted nuts.

41. CHECK CAKE

Use a sponge mixture (115 gm flour). Divide the mixture into halves. Colour one pink and add a drop of raspberry essence.

Check Cake Set 1.

To get Check Pattern: 1st and 3rd layer. Put inset into place. Fill plain batter into outer and centre ring and coloured batter in middle ring. Let it set for a moment. Lift out inset.

2nd layer: Wash inset before placing it in third tin. Fill, reversing colours. Remove inset and bake as for sponge cake.

When baked turn out to cool. Sandwich together in double decker fashion with icing or jam in the right order. Cover with white or chocolate icing.

NEAPOLITAN CAKE has vertical stripes. For this make the three layers alike either from two or three differently coloured and flavoured mixtures. Sandwich as for check cake.

42. CHOCOLATE LAYER CAKE

Ingredients	Quantity
Butter	115 gm
Sugar	170 gm
Eggs	3
Refined flour	145 gm
Cocoa	30 gm
Baking powder	½ tsp
Milk	about 1 tbsp
Butter cream:	
Icing sugar	85 gm

Ingredients	Quantity
Butter	45 gm
Vanilla flavouring	
Colouring	

Method

1. Sieve flour, baking powder and cocoa. 2. Cream butter and sugar till light and fluffy. 3. Add eggs one at a time followed by 1 tbsp flour. 4. Fold in remaining flour. 5. Add milk to get a dropping consistency. 6. Put into 2 sandwich tins and bake at 175°C (350°F approx.) for 25–30 minutes. 7. When cold, fill with butter cream and decorate with remaining cream.

43. LOW CHOLESTEROL CHOCOLATE CAKE

Ingredients	Quantity
Refined flour	110 gm
Sugar	110 gm
Oil	90 ml
Eggs	2
Cocoa	2 tbsp
Chopped nuts	
Milk	to mix
Baking powder	1 tsp

Method

1. Cream together sugar and oil. Add egg yolks one at a time and mix well. 2. Sieve together flour and baking powder. 3. Dissolve cocoa in a little milk. Add flour and cocoa. Mix alternately. 4. Add chopped nuts. Fold in stiffly beaten egg whites. 5. Bake at 150°C (300°F approx.) till done.

44. RIBBON CAKE

Ingredients	Quantity
Refined flour	115 gm
Baking powder	¼ tsp
Butter	55 gm
Sugar	115 gm
Eggs	2
Green or Pink colour as desired	
Vanilla and Almond essence	

Method

1. Using the creaming method, prepare batter. 2. Divide batter into halves, add colouring and almond essence to one half and vanilla essence

to other. 3. Fill a check cake tin by piping mixture. 4. Bake in a hot oven for 20–25 minutes.

45. LEMON CAKE

Ingredients	Quantity
Refined flour	225 gm
Baking powder	2 tsp
Salt	a pinch
Butter or Margarine	115 gm
Sugar	225 gm
Eggs	2
Milk	150 ml
Lemon essence	1 tsp
For butter cream	
Icing sugar	225 gm
Butter	115 gm

Method

1. Sift flour with baking powder 3 times. 2. Cream butter and sugar till light and fluffy. 3. Beat one egg at a time and add to creamed mixture. Continue beating. 4 Fold in dry ingredients. Add essence. 5. Pour into 2 greased 25 cm (8") pans. 6. Bake at 190°C (375°F approx.) for 15–20 minutes. 7. Sandwich with jam or butter cream.

For butter cream

Cream ingredients together and use enough to sandwich cake. To the remaining cream add 55 gm butter and 225 gm icing sugar, and use this to ice and decorate cake.

Pattern		nozzle
Smooth top with No.		2
Phlox	"	11
Centre	"	2
Leaves	"	10 and 17

46. FRUIT AND HONEY SPONGE CAKE

Ingredients	Quantity
Refined flour	115 gm
Sugar	115 gm
Butter or Margarine	55 gm
Eggs	2

Ingredients	Quantity
milk, a little if necessary for mixing to dropping consistency	
Baking powder	¼ tsp
Filling	
Margarine	55 gm
Honey	2 tbsp
Vanilla	a few drops
Fruit (any, fresh or canned)	115 gm

Method

1. Make a sponge cake in the usual way (creaming method). 2. Split in half when cold. 3. Cream margarine and honey together and spread two-thirds over the bottom half of sponge cake. 4. Slice fruit and arrange most of it on top. 5. Cut other half of cake into two and arrange on top of fruit like butterfly wings. 6. Spread rest of filling down centre and decorate with remaining fruit.

47. GENOESE SPONGE CAKE (A)

Ingredients	Quantity
Butter	85 gm
Refined flour	70 gm
Cornflour	15 gm
Eggs (large)	3
Sugar	115 gm

Method

1. Clarify and cool butter. 2. Sieve flour and cornflour. 3. Put eggs and sugar into a large basin and beat over a pan of hot water till thick and creamy. 4. Remove basin from heat. 5. Sift about half the flour over surface of mixture and fold in lightly. 6. Add remaining flour in the same way alternating with cooled butter. 7. Pour into a greased and lined tin. 8. Bake at 190°C (375°F approx.) until golden brown and firm to the touch, about 30 minutes.

GENOESE SPONGE CAKE (B)

Ingredients	Quantity
Sugar	115 gm
Eggs	4
Refined flour	100 gm
Butter	85 gm

Method

Same as for Recipe A.

48. CARAMEL SANDWICH CAKE

Ingredients	Quantity
Butter	115 gm
Sugar	115 gm
Sugar for caramel	55 gm
Hot milk	150 ml
Eggs	2
Refined flour	170 gm
Baking powder	½ tsp
Apricot jam	
Icing sugar, a little for topping	

Method

1. Cream fat and 115 gm sugar. 2. Separate eggs and beat in yolks. 3. Make caramel with 55 gm sugar and add hot milk till well mixed. 4. When caramel mixture is lukewarm add it gradually to creamed ingredients. 5. Stir in sieved dry ingredients and mix well adding more milk if required to get a dropping consistency. 6. Fold in stiffly beaten egg whites and put mixture into 2 prepared sandwich tins. 7. Bake in a moderately hot oven at 175°C (345°F approx.) for 30 minutes. 8. When cool, sandwich with apricot jam filling and sprinkle with icing sugar.

49. JAP CAKE (one cake)

Ingredients	Quantity
Almonds or Cashewnuts	170 gm
Sugar	170 gm
Egg whites	4
Almond essence	¼ tsp
Salt	a pinch

For filling of rich butter cream

Egg yolks	2
Butter	55 gm
Coffee essence	a few drops
Walnuts	55 gm
Cocoa	2 tsp
Water	75 ml
Sugar	115 gm
Vanilla flavour	¼ tsp
Icing sugar	45 gm

Method

1. Line and oil three 18 cm (7" approx.) sponge cake tins. 2. Grind nuts, mix with sugar. 3. Beat egg white till stiff. Add flavouring and salt. 4. Fold in sugar and nut mixture. 5. Divide evenly among 3 tins. 6. Bake at gas mark 3 or 175°C (350°F approx.) electricity for 30 minutes. 7. Remove paper. Turn upside down on bottom of tin and return to oven for 10 minutes. Cool. 8. Melt sugar for filling in warm water and bring to a boil. Boil to a syrup. 9. Pour gradually into beaten egg yolks and beat to a stiff cream until cool. 10. Cream butter and coffee essence and add gradually to egg mixture beating all the time. 11. Spread cream liberally between the 3 cakes, sandwich them together and press down. 12. Add sieved icing sugar to remainder of cream and coat cake and decorate. Chopped walnuts can be used on sides.

50. MADEIRA CAKE

Ingredients	Quantity
Refined flour	170 gm
Baking powder	½ tsp
Eggs	3
Milk for mixing	50 ml
Grated lemon rind	½ tsp
Sugar	115 gm
Butter	115 gm
Lemon essence	2 drops
Citron peel (optional)	

Method

1. Sieve dry ingredients and add grated lemon rind. 2. Cream butter and sugar. 3. Beat in eggs a little at a time. 4. Add sieved dry ingredients to creamed mixture alternately with a little milk and essence. Bake for 1–1½ hours at 175°C (350°F approx.) or gas mark 4.

N.B. Place a slice of peel on top before baking.

51. VELVET CAKE

Ingredients	Quantity
Refined flour	225 gm
Butter	115 gm
Castor sugar	225 gm
Cream of tartar	1 tsp
Soda bicarbonate	½ tsp
Vanilla	a few drops
Cold water	120 ml

Method

1. Sieve flour and cream of tartar 3 times. 2. Mix soda in cold water.
3. Cream butter and sugar till light and fluffy. 4. Add water and soda.
5. Beat eggs separately and gradually add to mixture beating all the
time. 6. Fold in flour gradually. Add vanilla. 7. Pour into a greased and
floured pan. 8. Bake at 175°C–190°C (350°–375°F approx.) for about 30
minutes. Turn onto a cake cooler.

52. FUDGE CAKE

Ingredients	Quantity
Butter	85 gm
Sugar	225 gm
Vanilla	1 tsp
Eggs (small)	2
Milk (sour)	220 ml
Cocoa	40 gm
Hot water	85 ml
Refined flour	200 gm
Soda	¼ tsp
Salt	a pinch

Method

1. Cream butter, sugar and vanilla together till light and fluffy. 2. Add
beaten eggs. Beat well. 3. Mix cocoa in hot water and add alternately
with sour milk. Mix well. 4. Sift together flour, soda and salt and add to
mixture. Mix well. 5. Bake 25–30 minutes at 175°C (350°F approx.).

53. PINEAPPLE UPSIDE DOWN CAKE

Ingredients	Quantity
Topping:	
Butter	55 gm
Brown sugar	55 gm
Sliced pineapple	1 tin
Glacé cherries	55 gm
Shelled walnuts	3
Cake:	
Refined flour	200 gm
Baking powder	1 tsp
Salt	a pinch
Ground cinnamon	½ tsp
Margarine	115 gm
Castor sugar	140 gm
Eggs	2
Milk	5 tbsp

Method

1. Cream butter and brown sugar together. 2. Spread on bottom of 22 cm × 18 cm (9" × 7") tin. 3. Arrange well-drained pineapple slices on this and fill centers with glace cherries.

Cake

1. Sift flour, baking powder, salt and cinnamon. 2. Cream fat and sugar until light and fluffy. 3. Gradually add beaten eggs to creamed mixture. 4. Fold in sieved flour alternately with milk. 5. Pour into prepared tin to cover fruit topping. 6. Bake at 205°C (400°F approx.) or gas 5 for about 40 minutes. 7. Let it cool for 5 minutes and then turn out on a wire rack. 8. Put halved walnuts between slices of pineapple.

54. WALNUT SULTANA CAKE

Ingredients	Quantity
Butter or Margarine	½ cup
Castor sugar	1 cup
Vanilla	½ tsp
Egg	1
Cocoa	2 dsp
Walnuts	½ cup
Sultanas	½ cup
Refined flour	1 cups
Baking powder	1 tsp
Salt	a pinch
Milk	1 cup
Soda bicarbonate	1 level tsp

Method

1. Sieve together flour, salt and baking powder. 2. Cream butter/margarine with sugar and vanilla till light and fluffy. Add well beaten egg. 3. Stir in cocoa blended with a little milk, chopped walnuts and sultanas. Fold in sifted flour alternately with remaining milk in which soda bicarbonate has been dissolved. 4. Turn into greased tin. Bake at 190°C (375°F approx.) for 45–50 minutes. 5. When cold, decorate with chocolate icing and sprinkle over with chopped walnuts.

N.B. Raisins or dates can be used instead of sultanas.

55. SUN CAKE

Ingredients	Quantity
Cornflour	375 gm
Eggs	10
Butter	375 gm
Sugar	375 gm

Method

1. Cream butter. Add cornflour gradually. 2. Whisk eggs and sugar over hot water till quite thick. 3. Add eggs and sugar gradually to cornflour and butter. 4. Bake at 175°C–190°C (350°–375°F approx.) for about 25 minutes. 5. Remove and sprinkle with icing sugar.

56. POUND CAKE (A)

Ingredients	Quantity
Refined flour	450 gm
Sugar (soft)	450 gm
Butter	450 gm
Eggs	450 gm (10–12)
Baking powder	1 tsp
Vanilla	2 tsp

Method

1. Cream butter and sugar till light and fluffy. 2. Add egg yolks and flavouring and beat mixture well. 3. Sieve flour with baking powder. 4. Whisk egg whites to a stiff froth. 5. Alternately add flour and egg whites to creamed mixture and blend lightly. 6. Pour mixture into a lined cake tin and bake at 150°C (300°F approx.) for about 1–2 hours.

POUND CAKE (B)

Ingredients	Quantity
Refined flour	400 gm
Salt	½ tsp
Baking powder	1 tsp
Butter	450 gm
Sugar	600 gm
Eggs	8
Milk	240 ml
Vanilla	
Brandy or	2 tbsp
Rose water	8 drops

Method

1. Sift flour with salt and baking powder. 2. Cream butter and sugar till light and fluffy. 3. Add beaten eggs one at a time. Continue beating. 4. Add flour mixture alternately with milk flavoured with essence and brandy. Blend lightly. 5. Bake in two 10.45 cm × 20.5 cm (4" × 8") loaf tins (lined) at 150°C (300°F approx.) for 1½–2 hours.

57. PLAIN CAKE

Ingredients	Quantity
Refined flour	225 gm
Salt	a pinch
Baking powder	3½ tsp
Margarine	85 gm
Sugar	85 gm
Egg	1
Milk and Water	120 ml
Vanilla	a few drops

Method

1. Sieve flour, baking powder and salt together. 2. Rub in margarine and add sugar. 3. Mix to a dropping consistency with egg and liquid. 4. Add essence and mix well. Put into a greased 18 cm (7") cake tin and bake at 205°C (400°F approx.) for 45 minutes–1 hour.

58. VICTORIA SANDWICH CAKE

Ingredients	Quantity
Refined flour	180 gm
Baking powder	1 level tsp
Sugar	180 gm
Butter or Margarine	180 gm
Salt	a pinch
Eggs	3
Milk	2 tbsp (approx.)
Jam	50 gm
Vanilla	1 tsp

Method

1. Cream margarine and sugar till light and fluffy. 2. Add salt and essence beating well. 3. Beat eggs well and gradually add to creamed mixture. Continue beating. 4. Sift flour and baking powder and fold into mixture using milk for moistening. 5. Divide mixture into 2 greased 18 cm sandwich tins and bake at 190°C (375°F approx.) for 20–30 minutes. Cool and sandwich together with jam.

59. TEA CAKE

Ingredients	Quantity
Butter	180 gm
Castor sugar	180 gm
Grated lemon rind	½ tsp
Grated orange rind	½ tsp
Vanilla	

Ingredients	Quantity
Eggs	3
Refined flour	225 gm
Baking powder	½ tsp
Salt	a pinch
Milk	5 tbsp

Method

1. Soften butter with vanilla, lemon and orange rind. 2. Gradually beat in sugar and continue beating until soft, white and fluffy. 3. Add eggs one at a time, beating well each time. 4. Sift flour, baking powder and salt. Fold into mixture alternately with milk. 5. Turn into well-greased tin. Bake for 50–60 minutes in a moderate oven 190°C (375°F approx.). Let cake stand in tin a few minutes before turning out.

60. CHOCOLATE CAKE (economical)

Ingredients	Quantity
Refined flour	170 gm
Baking powder	1 tsp
Cocoa	2 tbsp
Salt	¼ tsp
Margarine	55 gm
Sugar	85 gm
Eggs	2
Golden syrup	1 tbsp
Vanilla essence	a few
Soda bicarbonate	1 tsp
Milk and water	150 ml (approx.)
Chocolate Cream Icing	
Sugar	45 gm
Margarine	45 gm
Essence	1 tsp
Soya flour	2 tbsp
Cocoa	1 tbsp
Hot water	1 tbsp

Method

1. Sieve together flour, baking powder, cocoa and salt. 2. Dissolve soda in milk. 3. Cream butter and sugar thoroughly and beat in syrup and essence. 4. Fold in dry ingredients with sufficient milk and water to get a soft consistency. 5. Spread evenly in two well-greased 18 cm (7" approx.) sandwich tins and bake at 195°C (375°F approx.) for 20–25 minutes. 6. Let cake cool in tin for a minute or two. 7. Turn out, sandwich together with some chocolate cream icing and spread remaining icing on top using a fork to form a pattern.

Chocolate Cream Icing

1. Cream sugar and margarine well. 2. Add soya flour, cocoa and hot water gradually and continue beating till icing is smooth and light coloured.

61. CHOCOLATE CAKE

Ingredients	Quantity
Flour	250 gm
Cocoa powder	40 gm
Powdered sugar	225 gm
Eggs	3
Margarine	100 gm
Soda bicarbonate	1 tsp (level)
Milk	150 ml
Vanilla essence	½ tsp

Method

1. Sieve flour, soda and cocoa powder twice. 2. Cream fat and sugar until light and fluffy. 3. Beat eggs until stiff and gradually beat them into creamed mixture. Add vanilla essence. 4. Fold in sieved flour lightly and add milk to get a dropping consistency. 5. Put batter into a lined 18 cm cake mould. 6. Bake at 325°F for 45 minutes.

62. BLACK FOREST CAKE

Ingredients	Quantity
Refined flour	60 gm
Cocoa powder	60 gm
Baking powder	¼ tsp
Soda bicarbonate	a pinch
Sugar	120 gm
Eggs	4
Melted butter	120 gm
Vanilla	2 droups
For Decoration	
Whipped cream (fresh)	200 gm
Chocolate (grated)	15 gm
Cashewnuts or Walnuts	

Method

1. Line and grease two 18 cm (7") cake tins. 2. Sieve flour, cocoa, soda and baking powder together twice. 3. Beat eggs and sugar over hot water to custard consistency. 4. Lightly fold in sieved flour and melted butter, adding a little water to get a pouring consistency. 5. Put mixture in tins and bake at 205°C (400°F approx.) for about 20 minutes. 6. Cool and

sandwich together with fresh cream and put a thick layer of cream on top. Finish with chopped nuts on sides and grated chocolate on top.

63. SEED CAKE (rub-in method)

Ingredients	Quantity
Refined flour	170 gm
Butter	85 gm
Egg (large)	1
Caraway seeds	10 gm
Salt	a pinch
Baking powder	¾ tsp
Vanilla	¼ tsp
Sugar	85 gm
Milk	for mixing

Method

1. Sieve flour, salt and baking powder together. 2. Rub in fat. 3. Add seeds and sugar. 4. Mix well to distribute seeds. 5. Add beaten egg, essence and a little milk to get a dropping consistency. 6. Bake in a moderate oven 175°C (350°F approx.) for about 45 minutes.

FRUIT CAKES

64. FRUIT CAKE (plain) (rub-in method)

Ingredients	Quantity
Refined flour	170 gm
Baking powder	¾ tsp
Mixed spice	½ tsp
Egg (large)	1
Milk	30 ml
Shortening	85 gm
Sugar	85 gm
Sultanas	45 gm
Candied peel	45 gm

Method

1. Clean sultanas and chop candied peel. 2. Sieve flour, baking powder and mixed spice. 3. Rub fat into flour. Add sugar and mix. 4. Add fruit, well-beaten egg and milk to get a dropping consistency. 5. Put into a lined tin and bake at 175°C (350°F approx.) for about 45 minutes.

65. CHERRY CAKE

Ingredients	Quantity
Refined flour	115 gm
Baking powder	½ tsp
Salt	a pinch
Butter	85 gm
Sugar	85 gm
Glacé cherries	55 gm
Eggs	2
Milk	1 tbsp
Vanilla	a few drops

Method

1. Grease and line a cake tin. 2. Wash and cut cherries into quarters. 3. Sieve flour, baking powder and salt. Add cherries. 4. Cream fat and sugar thoroughly and beat in well-beaten eggs gradually. 5. Lightly fold in flour mixture together with a little milk to get a dropping consistency and blend mixture well. 6. Put into prepared tin and bake in a moderate oven 175°C (350°F approx.) or gas 3–4 for about 45 minutes until firm and golden brown.

66. FRUIT CAKE (creaming method) (A)

Ingredients	Quantity
Refined flour	130 gm
Mixed spice	½ tsp
Baking powder	¼ tsp
Butter	85 gm
Sugar	85 gm
Sugar for caramel	30 gm
Salt	a pinch
Cherries	30 gm
Sultanas	85 gm
Currants	45 gm
Candied peel	30 gm
Cashewnuts	45 gm
Eggs	2
Milk	30 ml

Method

1. Line a tin. 2. Wash, pick and dry fruit. Chop cashewnuts and candied peel. Cut cherries. 3. Sieve flour, baking powder and spice. 4. Cream butter and sugar till light and fluffy. 5. Beat eggs and add to mixture gradually. 6. Add fruit and flour gradually with milk to which caramel has

been added to get a stiff dropping consistency. 7. Put into prepared tin and bake at 160°C (325°F approx.) for 1–1½ hours.

FRUIT CAKE (creaming method) **(B)**

Ingredients	Quantity
Refined flour	225 gm
Baking powder	3 tsp
Salt	1 pinch
Mixed spice	½ tsp
Cinnamon powder	¼ tsp
Grated nutmeg	⅛ tsp
Margarine	115 gm
Sugar	55 gm
Treacle or Golden Syrup	1 tbsp
Marmalade	1 tbsp
Sultanas	
Currants and Dates	340 gm
Milk and Water	6 tbsp
Eggs	2

Method

1. Prepare fruit, wash and dry sultanas and currants and stone dates. 2. Sieve together flour, baking powder and salt and spices. 3. Cream margarine and sugar till light and fluffy. 4. Add syrup or treacle and marmalade. Beat well. 5. Add well-beaten eggs. Continue beating. 6. Fold in flour alternately with liquid and fruit. 7. Pour into a lined cake tin and bake at 150°C (300°F approx.) for 2 hours.

67. RICH FRUIT CAKE (A)

Ingredients	Quantity
Currants	115 gm
Candied peel	30 gm
Cherries	30 gm
Cashewnuts	55 gm
Sultanas	170 gm
Butter	100 gm
Eggs	2
Refined flour	115 gm
Sugar	100 gm
Sugar for caramel	30 gm
Mixed spice	1 tsp
Lime rind	1 lime
Lime juice	1 tsp

Method

1. Clean fruit, chop nuts and candied peel. 2. Grate lemon rind and squeeze juice. 3. Sieve flour and spice. 4. Cream butter and sugar. 5. Add in beaten eggs gradually. 6. Caramelize sugar and add to mixture with 1 tablespoon flour and beat well. 7. Mix fruit, nuts and juice. 8. Add to creamed mixture and stir in lemon rind. 9. Fold in flour. Put into lined tin and bake at 175°C (350°F approx.) or gas mark 3 for half an hour. 10. Lower temperature to 149°C (300°F approx.) or gas mark 2 and bake till done.

RICH FRUIT CAKE (B)

Ingredients	Quantity
Refined flour	225 gm
Baking powder	¼ tsp
Salt	a pinch
Allspice	½ tsp
Butter	170 gm
Sugar	225 gm
Currants	115 gm
Sultanas	115 gm
Cherries	55 gm
Cashewnuts	30 gm
Candied peel	30 gm
Eggs	4
Milk	30 ml

Method

1. Prepare fruit. Chop nuts and candied peel. 2. Cream butter and sugar. 3. Sieve flour with baking powder, salt and spice. 4. Beat and add one egg at a time with 1 tablespoon flour, beating mixture all the time. 5. Add prepared fruit and nuts. 6. Fold in rest of flour with milk. 7. Put into a lined tin and bake 149°C (300°F approx.) for about 3 hours.

RICH FRUIT CAKE (C)

Ingredients	Quantity
Butter	225 gm
Refined flour	225 gm
Sultanas	225 gm
Lemon peel	15 gm
Eggs	3
Orange peel	15 gm
Raisins	225 gm
Cashewnuts	15 gm
Brown sugar	225 gm

Ingredients	Quantity
Cinnamon	½ tsp
Ginger powder	½ tsp
Brandy	½ wine glass

Method

1. Cream butter and sugar together. Add flour slowly, alternately with prepared fruit, nuts, peel and spice. 2. Add beaten eggs and mix well. Add brandy. 3. Bake at 150°C (300°F approx.) for 1 hour. Reduce temperature to 120°C (250°F approx.) and bake for 1–1½ hours more.

RICH FRUIT CAKE (D)

Ingredients	25 pieces	600 pieces
Refined flour	225 gm	5.4 kg
Sugar	225 gm	5.4 kg
Margarine	170 gm	4 kg
Eggs	4	96
Black raisins	200 gm	4.8 kg
Sultanas	50 gm	1.2 kg
Cashewnuts	50 gm	1.2 kg
Candied peel	50 gm	1.2 kg
Baking powder	½ tsp	9 tsp
Limes	1	24

Method

1. Prepare fruit. Chop nuts and candied peel. Cut cherries. 2. Cream butter and sugar. 3. Sieve flour with baking powder. 4. Beat and add eggs one at a time with 1 tablespoon flour, beating mixture all the time. 5. Add prepared fruit and nuts. 6. Fold in rest of flour. 7. Put into a lined tin and bake at 150°C (300°F approx.) till done.

68. DATE AND WALNUT CAKE

Ingredients	Quantity
Dates	450 gm
Soda bicarbonate	1 tsp
Water (warm)	200 ml
Soft sugar	225 gm
Butter	170 gm
Refined flour	225 gm
Eggs	4
Walnuts (chopped)	115 gm
Baking powder	1½ tsp
Vanilla	2 tsp

Method

1. Wash, stone, chop and soak dates in water mixed with soda bicarbonate, overnight. 2. Chop walnuts. 3. Sieve flour with baking powder. 4. Cream butter and sugar till light and fluffy. 5. Beat eggs separately and add gradually to mixture, beating well. Add essence. 6. Fold in flour alternating with dates. 7. Put into lined tin and bake at 150°C (300°F approx.) for about 45 minutes.

69. SULTANA AND CHERRY CAKE

Ingredients	Quantity
Sultanas	340 gm
Glacé cherries	250 gm
Butter	115 gm
Castor sugar	115 gm
Eggs (large)	3
Refined flour	180 gm
Salt	a pinch
I round cake tin	
15.5 cm (6") diameter	
Greaseproof paper for lining the tin	
A little melted fat or Cooking oil	

Method

1. Wash sultanas, unless they have already been cleaned. Washing is also a good idea if sultanas have been stored and are a little dry. To do this, put them into a colander and immerse them in a bowl full of cold water. Lift them out and let cold water drain off, then spread them on trays lined with two thicknesses of absorbent kitchen paper. 2. Cover sultanas with absorbent paper and dab off water; then leave them to dry overnight, loosely covered with paper. 3. Wash cherries the same way. This is necessary to remove the stickiness which is apt to make cherries sink in a cake. Dab them dry with absorbent kitchen paper and leave them to dry overnight. 4. Warm the mixing bowl slightly; this speeds creaming as it stops butter clinging to sides of bowl. Butter should be at room temperature when it is put into the bowl with castor sugar. 5. Using a flat beater, cream butter and sugar slowly until they are mixed, then increase to about three-quarter speed. When the mixture is light in colour and texture, stop mixer and raise beater. 6. Break an egg into a cup to make sure it is fresh, then add it to mixture. Lower beater and beat egg into creamed sugar and butter at about three-quarter speed. Add the other eggs in the same way. 7. While mixer is on, line a cake tin. To do this, place it on a double piece of greaseproof paper, draw around it with a pencil, and cut out the two rounds just inside the penciled line. 8. Cut a double strip of greaseproof paper 5 cm (2") deeper

than the tin and long enough to go around the inside. Make a 2.5 cm (1") wide fold along the length of the strip, and cut diagonal snips into the fold, 2.5 cm (1") apart. 9. Brush inside of tin with melted fat or cooking oil, and fit one paper round into base of tin. Brush it with melted fat or oil, then fit the strip round inside of tin with the snipped edge fitting snugly around the base. Finally, lay the second paper round in place and brush the whole lining with melted fat or cooking oil. 10. Halve the cherries and mix them with sultanas. Sift flour with salt on to fruit, and mix. 11. When all the eggs have been beaten into mixture remove beater, scraping off all the mixture. Take the bowl and place it on a folded cloth to prevent it slipping. Add all the fruit and mix it thoroughly into the mixture with a large metal spoon. Make sure the spoon scrapes the bowl each time you mix so that all the ingredients are really well combined. 12. Turn the mixture into the prepared tin, scraping the bowl clean with a plastic or rubber spatula. Smooth over the surface of the mixture and then hollow out the centre fairly deeply. 13. Put the cake on a baking tray and into the centre of a moderate oven, about gas mark 3 or 150°C (325°F approx.) for 2 hours. 14. The cake is ready when a thin, warmed skewer pressed into the centre comes out clean. Leave the cake in the tin until it is cold, then carefully slip it out and peel off greaseproof paper.

For long storage

Take cake out of tin while it is still warm and remove greaseproof paper. Turn cake upside down and sprinkle about 2 tablespoonfuls of brandy (half a miniature bottle) over the top. Wrap cake in foil and store it in a cool, dry place; the keeping mellows the fruit and adds to the flavour.

70. DUNDEE CAKE

Ingredients	Quantity
Sultanas	170 gm
Currants	85 gm
Candied peel	85 gm
Chopped cashewnuts	55 gm
Almonds	30 gm
Refined flour	225 gm
Salt	a pinch
Baking powder	½ tsp
Butter	170 gm
Castor sugar	170 gm
Eggs	3
Milk	60 ml

Method

1. Prepare fruit and slice peel fine. 2. Chop the nuts. 3. Blanch and skin almonds for topping. 4. Sieve flour with baking powder and salt. 5. Cream together fat and sugar. 6. Beat in eggs one by one with 1 tablespoon of flour. 7. Fold in remaining flour alternately with mixed fruit and nuts. 8. Add milk to get a stiff dropping consistency. 9. Put batter into prepared 20.5 cm (8") tins and place halved blanched almonds on top. 10. Bake at 175°C (350°F approx.) for 1–2 hours.

71. LOVE CAKE

Ingredients	Quantity
Semolina	375 gm
Soft sugar	115 gm
Butter	180 gm
Cashewnuts	375 gm
Egg yolks	12
Egg whites	3
Rose water	15 ml
Honey	45 ml
Nutmeg (grated)	1
Lemon rind	
Powdered cinnamon	
Vanilla	2 tsp

Method

1. Soften butter with semolina and set aside in a warm oven for a few minutes. It should not be oily. Butter should be well soaked into semolina. 2. Cream egg yolks with soft sugar until very light. 3. Add all the spices and essence, add semolina–butter mixture. 4. Add cashewnuts minced or finely chopped. 5. Pour into a cake tin lined with 2 layers of paper and bake at 150°C (300°F approx.) until done. If a nice crust is desired, sprinkle a thin layer of icing sugar.

72. CHRISTMAS CAKE (A)

Ingredients	Quantity
Refined flour	170 gm
Butter	140 gm
Castor sugar	140 gm
Currants	140 gm
Sultanas	140 gm
Valencia raisins	140 gm
Cherries	115 gm
Mixed peel	85 gm
Lemon rind	1

Ingredients	Quantity
Black treacle	1 dsp
Eggs	4
Mixed spice	½ tsp

Method

1. Prepare fruit. 2. Cream butter and sugar till light and fluffy. 3. Add eggs gradually and beat well. 4. Stir in flour. 5. Add fruit, treacle, lemon rind and spice. 6. Put into a 18 cm (7") cake tin lined with paper. 7. Cook in a moderate oven at 150°–160°C (300°–325°F approx.) for about 3 hours. 8. Keep in airtight tin 6–8 weeks before using.

CHRISTMAS CAKE (B)

Ingredients	Quantity
Butter or Margarine	140 gm
Sugar	140 gm
Refined flour	200 gm
Candied peel	55 gm
Cherries	55 gm
Cashewnuts	55 gm
Eggs	4
Salt	a pinch
Raisins (stoned)	115 gm
Currants	115 gm
Sultanas	115 gm
Vanilla	½ tsp
Black treacle	1 tsp
Baking powder	½ tsp
Mixed spice	½ tsp

Method

1. Clean and prepare fruit and mix with 1 tablespoon flour and baking powder. 2. Cream butter and sugar. 3. Beat eggs in carefully. 4. Mix in flour, salt, treacle, fruits, chopped nuts and vanilla essence. Put into a lined cake tin and bake at 160°C (325°F approx.) for 2½–3 hours.

N.B. This cake can be topped with almond paste and decorated with royal icing.

CHRISTMAS CAKE (C)

Ingredients	Quantity
Margarine	115 gm
Sugar	85 gm
Golden syrup or	
Treacle	3 tbsp

Ingredients	Quantity
Mixed spice	1 tsp
Cinnamon powder	1 tsp
Eggs (large)	3
Refined flour	225 gm
Soda bicarbonate	½ level tsp
Salt	a pinch
Mixed dried fruit	450 gm
Cold tea	3 tbsp

Method

1. Cream margarine and sugar till light and fluffy. 2. Beat in treacle or syrup. 3. Sieve flour, soda, salt and spices together and add alternately with beaten eggs to creamed mixture. 4. Add fruit and mix in the tea. 5. Turn mixture into a 18 cm (7") tin lined with greased paper. 6. Bake at 150°C (300°F approx.) for 2 hours.

CHRISTMAS CAKE (D)

Ingredients	Quantity
Semolina	750 gm
Soft sugar	900 gm
Pumpkin preserve	250 gm
Brandy, Rosewater and Bee's honey	a wine glassful of each
Ginger preserve	450 gm
Chow chow preserve	450 gm
Candied peel (mixed)	250 gm
Egg yolks	15–17
Egg whites	10
Cashewnuts	900 gm
Butter	450 gm
Raisins	450 gm
Sultanas	750 gm
Cherries (if available)	250 gm
Cardamoms	1 tsp
Cinnamon	of
Cloves (powdered)	1 each
Nutmeg (grated)	
Almond paste	
Royal icing	

Method

1. First prepare fruit. Stone and cut raisins in three or four pieces, wash and stem sultanas, cut pumpkin, ginger and chow chow preserves into small pieces, shred candied peel fine and skin and chop cashewnuts.

2. Mix the different kinds of fruit with essence and spices and set aside for a few days. 3. Chop butter over warmed semolina and set in the sun or in a warm oven until butter is soft and can be mixed into semolina. 4. The butter should be well soaked into the semolina but should not be melted into oil. 5. Cream egg yolks and soft sugar until very light, add semolina–butter mixture. 6. Mix well, add fruits mixed very well and add sufficient egg whites beaten to a stiff dropping consistency. 7. Put into flat trays, lined with 4–6 layers of paper and one sheet of oil paper, oiled. Bake at 135°C (275°F approx.) for first hour and at 120°C (250°F approx.) until the cake is done.

CHRISTMAS CAKE (E)

Ingredients	Quantity
Refined flour	340 gm
Semolina	115 gm
Powdered sugar	450 gm
Butter	570 gm
Eggs	12
Mixed spice	1 tsp
Baking powder	1 tbsp (level)
Raisins	45 gm*
Almonds or Cashewnuts	225 gm*
Mixed peel	225 gm*
Petch or Mixed fruit	225 gm*
Currants	115 gm*
Ginger (preserve)	30 gm*
Cherries	15 gm*

Method

1. Mix 115 gm butter and sieved semolina and set aside for 3–4 hours. 2. Cream remaining butter and sugar. Separate eggs adding yolks one at a time. (Sieve together flour, mixed spices and baking powder three times). 3. When mixture (butter, sugar, eggs) is creamed well and has a light and fluffy texture, add semolina. Set aside for a couple of hours. 4. Then add flour and rest of ingredients. 5. Add a little burnt sugar and vanilla essence. 6. Lastly add stiffly beaten egg whites. 7. Bake at 135°C (275°F approx.) – 150°C (300°F approx.) and bake till firm.

73. CHRISTMAS CAKE (economical)

Ingredients	Quantity
Refined flour	225 gm
Margarine	85 gm

*Soak in brandy 3 days in advance

Ingredients	Quantity
Brown sugar	85 gm
Currants	115 gm
Valencia raisins	115 gm
Candied peel	30 gm
Milk	150 ml
Salt	¼ tsp
Mixed spice	¼ tsp
Black treacle	1 tsp
Soda bicarbonate	¼ tsp
Milk	1 tbsp
Vinegar	1 tbsp

Method

1. Rub fat into flour. 2. Add salt, spice, peel cut up fine and prepared fruit. 3. Mix to a soft dough with milk and treacle. 4. Dissolve soda in 1 tablespoon milk. 5. Add vinegar and stir at once into mixture. 6. Put into a greased tin and bake in a moderate oven at 190°C (375°F approx.) for 1½–2 hours.

74. CHRISTMAS CAKE (with semolina)

Ingredients	Quantity
Semolina	450 gm
Refined flour	55 gm
Soft sugar	900 gm
Butter	450 gm
Sultanas	450 gm
Currants	225 gm
Pumpkin preserve	225 gm
Egg yolks	25
Rosewater	
Honey	1 wine glassful of each
Brandy	
Ginger preserve	225 gm
Chow chow preserve	225 gm
Candied peel (mixed)	225 gm
Raisins	450 gm
Egg whites	8–10
Cashewnuts	225 gm
Nutmeg (grated)	½
Cinnamon	½ tsp
Cardamoms (powdered)	each
Cloves (powdered)	¼ tsp
Almond paste	
Royal icing	

Method

1. Prepare fruit and mix with flour. 2. Cream butter and sugar till light and fluffy. 3. Add beaten egg yolks. Keep beating. 4. Mix in semolina gradually, then add fruit, chopped nuts and spices. 5. Add brandy, rose water and honey. 6. Fold in stiffly beaten egg whites. 7. Pour mixture into a lined tin and bake at 160°C (325°F approx.) for 4–5 hours. 8. When cake begins to brown cover it with a double fold of paper to prevent it burning on top. 9. When ready, remove. Let it stand for a few minutes. Turn out and allow to cool. 10. Keep in an airtight tin for at least a week. 11. Cover cake with almond paste then coat with royal icing. 12. Allow to dry before decorating.

75. CHRISTMAS CAKE (eggless)

Ingredients	Quantity
Refined flour	225 gm
Salt	½ tsp
Grated nutmeg	¼
Margarine	115 gm
Sugar	55 gm
Grated rind	½ lemon
Glacé cherries	30 gm
Golden syrup	1 tbsp
Baking powder	2 tsp
Soda bicarbonate	1 tsp
Mixed fruit including candied peel	680 gm
Treacle	1 tbsp
Milk and Water	295 ml
Vinegar	1 tbsp

Method

1. Sift flour, salt, baking powder, soda and nutmeg together. 2. Rub in margarine. 3. Mix in sugar, lemon rind, and prepared fruit. 4. Make a well in the centre. Add syrup and treacle and enough milk and water to get a fairly soft consistency. 5. Stir in vinegar and pour into a greased 20 cm cake tin. 6. Bake at 150°C (300°F approx.) for 2 hours.

76. PLUM CAKE

Ingredients	Quantity
Semolina	675 gm
Eggs	18
Clarified butter	340 gm
Candied peel or	55 gm
Skin of 1 orange	
Sugar	900 gm

Ingredients	Quantity
Raisins	450 gm
Sultanas	225 gm
Currants	225 gm
Cashewnuts	225 gm
Cake seeds	1 tsp
Nutmeg	1
Salt	a pinch
Flour	30 gm
Butter	30 gm

Method

1. Beat egg yolks with powdered sugar till light and creamy. 2. Add clarified butter alternately with semolina. 3. Add prepared fruit gradually and blend well. 4. Beat the egg whites stiff, fold into mixture while adding cake seeds and grated nutmeg. 5. Fold in flour and butter. 6. Pour into prepared tins and bake at 160°C (325°F approx.) for about 2 hours.

77. WEDDING CAKE

(800 pieces–2½" × ½" × ¾"/60 cm × 1 cm × 1½ cm)

Ingredients	Quantity
Semolina	1.35 kg
Butter	1.8 kg
Sultanas	2.75 kg
Raisins	1.8 kg
Soft sugar	3.4 kg
Ginger preserve syrup	1.8 kg
Pumpkin preserve	2.75 kg
Nutmeg	a pinch
Cloves (powder)	a small pinch
Cardamom	a pinch
Rose essence	½ tsp
Almond essence	½ tsp
Candied peel	0.90 kg
Cherries	1.35 kg
Pineapple jam	0.90 kg
Chow chow with syrup	1.8 kg
Cashewnuts	2.25 kg
Golden syrup	1 tin medium size (450 gm)
Eggs	75 (65 if large)
Almond Icing:	
Cashewnuts	1.8–2.25 kg

Ingredients	Quantity
Icing sugar	1.8–2.25 kg
Almond essence	2 tsp

Method

1. Chop all fruit or put through a mincer. Mix spices and set aside for a few days if possible. 2. Mix semolina and butter and keep in the sun. Mix well. 3. Cream egg yolks and sugar till light and creamy. 4. Add semolina and butter mixture and beat well. 5. Add fruit. Mix well. 6. Fold in a third to half the egg whites stiffy beaten. 7. Bake in a slow oven for 4–5 hours. Cool.

Almond Icing

1. Grind cashewnuts and mix with icing sugar. Add egg white with essence to bind. 2. Roll out and use to top cake.

AMERICAN COFFEE CAKES

78. LIGHT COFFEE CAKES

These are served at a midmorning coffee-break or at tea time.

Ingredients	Quantity
Egg	1
Sugar	115 gm
Refined flour	140 gm
Baking powder	1 tsp
Salt	½ tsp
Milk	about 75 ml
Lemon essence	¼ tsp
Melted butter	3 tbsp
Vanilla	½ tsp

Method

1. Beat egg and sugar together till light and creamy. 2. Sift flour with baking powder and salt and add to creamed mixture. 3. Blend in milk and melted butter. 4. Add essence. 5. Pour into greased 18 cm × 25.5 cm (about 7" × 10") rectangular pan and bake at 175°C (about 850°F) for 25 minutes. 6. Cut into squares and serve.

For Plum Cake

Cover surface of batter densely with stoned cooked prunes or fresh plums. Sprinkle over with 75 ml juice and 55 gm sugar mixed with a teaspoonful of cinnamon before baking.

For Apple Cake

Cover with a thick layer of thinly-sliced apples and sprinkle with 55 gm mixed brown and white sugar and a pinch of cinnamon or a few chopped walnuts.

79. QUICK COFFEE CAKE

Ingredients	Quantity
Sugar	225 gm
Refined flour	225 gm
Baking powder	2 tsp
Salt	¼ tsp
Butter	55 gm
Egg	1
Milk	150 ml
Sugar for sprinkling	3 tsp
Cinnamon	1½ tsp

Method

1. Mix flour, sugar, baking powder and salt. 2. Rub in butter. 3. Mix into a batter with egg and milk. 4. Pour into a greased rectangular pan measuring 18 cm 5. Sprinkle with 3 tsp sugar mixed with 1 tsp cinnamon. 6. Bake at 195°C (375°F approx.) for about 20 minutes.

Plum or Apple Kuchen

Arrange fruit on top of batter. Sprinkle with brown sugar and pour over an egg beaten with 75 ml milk or cream.

Streusel Coffee Cake

Mix 85 gm brown sugar, 2 tbsp flour, 2 tsp cinnamon, 115 gm melted butter and 55 gm chopped walnuts and sprinkle on batter before baking.

80. GINGERBREAD WITH DATES (A)

Ingredients	Quantity
Refined flour	225 gm
Sugar	100 gm
Bicarbonate of soda	½ tsp
Baking powder	1¼ tsp
Salt	1 tsp
Ginger powder	1½ tsp
Shortening	70 gm
Molasses	150 gm
Water	½ cup
Egg	1
Dates (pitted and sliced thin)	170 gm

Method

1. Sift together flour, sugar, soda bicarb, baking powder, ginger powder and salt. 2. Add shortening, molasses and half the water. Beat well. 3. Add remaining water and unbeaten egg. Beat well. 4. Stir in dates. 5. Put batter into a greased, floured 20.5 cm (about 8") square pan. 6. Bake at 195°C (375°F approx.) for 30–35 minutes. 7. Serve warm, topped with whipped cream.

GINGERBREAD (Damp) (B)

Ingredients	Quantity
Refined flour	285 gm
Margarine	170 gm
Brown sugar	170 gm
Bicarbonate of soda	½ tsp
Eggs	2
Warm milk	a little
Nuts (Almonds or Cashews)	85 gm
Sultanas	170 gm
Treacle and Syrup	120 ml
Ginger powder	1½ tsp
Cinnamon powder	1½ tsp

Method

1. Cream margarine and sugar. 2. Add eggs gradually and beat well. 3. Add dry ingredients and syrup and treacle adding a little milk if necessary. 4. Bake at 176°C (350°F approx.) for about 2 hours.

81. BANANA TEA RING

Ingredients	Quantity
Margarine	75 gm
Sugar	50 gm
Brown sugar	100 gm
Eggs (slightly beaten)	2
Vanilla	1 tsp
Refined flour	220 gm
Baking powder	1 tsp
Bicarbonate of soda	¼ tsp
Salt	¼ tsp
Mashed ripe bananas	200 gm
Buttermilk	60 ml
Chopped nuts (Peanuts and Cashewnuts)	50 gm

Ingredients	Quantity
Glaze	
Milk	2 tbsp
Icing sugar	160 gm
Vanilla	
Salt	a pinch

Method

1. Cream margarine and sugar. 2. Blend in eggs and vanilla. 3. Sift together flour, baking powder, soda, and salt and add alternately with mashed bananas and buttermilk, mixing well each time. 4. Stir in nuts. 5. Pour into a greased 23 cm (about 9") ring mould. 6. Bake in a moderate oven at 175°C (350°F approx.) for 30–35 minutes. Cool for 5 minutes. 7. Turn out of pan and glaze. Sprinkle with chopped nuts.

Glaze

Blend milk with sugar, mixing well. Stir in vanilla and salt.

PASTRIES

SHORTCRUST PASTRY

There are certain rules to remember when making Shortcrust Pastry.

The first and most important is that *all the ingredients and the utensils should be as cool as possible.* This keeps the fat hard, for if it becomes at all warm it will become very oily and thus make it difficult to rub into the flour; the result will be that the mixture will become heavy instead of being light and airy.

The second important point is *that only a minimum amount of water should be added*—only just enough to make the pastry of a rollable consistency. Too much liquid invariably makes pastry tough.

The third point is that *the oven must be hot for the first few minutes of baking*, because the heat bursts the grains of flour which will absorb the melting fat. If the oven is too cool, the fat will ooze out of the pastry before there is sufficient heat for the grains to burst.

SHORTCRUST PASTRY

Ingredients	Quantity
Flour	115 gm
Margarine	60 gm
Salt	a pinch
Cold water	to mix

Method

Sieve flour with salt to aerate flour and lighten pastry Using finger-tips, rub in (fat) margarine very lightly, to breadcrumb texture. Mix in enough cold water (preferably iced in hot climates) to gently bind mixture and form it into a smooth ball. Use as desired. Shortcrust pastry is baked at 425°F or 218–220°C.

82. JAM TARTS

Ingredients	Quantity
Refined flour	115 gm
Fat	60 gm
Baking powder	¼ tsp
Cold water	for mixing
Sugar (optional)	5 gm
Jam	55 gm

Method

1. Sieve flour and baking powder. 2. Rub in fat lightly with finger tips until it resemble breadcrumbs. 3. Add sugar if it is being used and mix. 4. Mix with cold water to a dough and then roll on a floured slab or board and cut as required. 5. Line patty tins with rolled-out dough and fill two-thirds with jam. 6. Bake in a hot oven at 205°C (about 400°F) for 15 minutes.

83. LEMON CURD TARTS

Follow recipe for jam tarts but bake pastry blind, pricking centers before baking. Fill three-quarters with lemon curd.

84. DATE AND NUT TURNOVER

Shortcrust pastry with 115 gm refined flour.

1. Roll out pastry and cut into 6.5 cm (2½") squares. 2. Put in 2 teaspoonsfuls of date and nut filling. 3. Wet sides of pastry with water. 4. Turn over diagonally and seal. 5. Brush over with sugar and water or beaten egg and bake at 195°C (375°F) for 25 minutes. 6. Sprinkle over with castor sugar.

85. MOCK MINCE PIES

Follow method for mince pie using shortcrust pastry. Fill with date and nut filling.

86. CUSTARD TARTS (A)

Shortcrust pastry with 115 gm flour.

Ingredients	Quantity
Filling:	
Milk	300 ml
Egg (large)	1
Sugar	115 gm
Nutmeg	1 pinch

Method

1. Roll out pastry. Cut with large cutter and line patty tins. Prick.
2. Make custard mixture with beaten eggs, sugar and milk. 3. Fill pastry three-quarters with custard. Sprinkle top with grated nutmeg. 4. Bake at 195°C (about 375°F) for 20–25 minutes.

CUSTARD TARTS (with custard powder) (B)

Shortcrust pastry with 115 gm of refined flour.

Ingredients	Quantity
Filling:	
Milk	150 ml
Custard powder	115 gm
Sugar	30 gm
Buter	15 gm

Method

1. Proceed as for custard tarts. 2. Make a thick custard with custard powder, milk and sugar. 3. Remove from fire and beat in butter. 4. Fill pastry cases and bake at 195°C (about 375°F) for 15–20 minutes.

87. PINEAPPLE TARTLETS

Ingredients	10
Pastry:	
Refined flour	55 gm
Butter	30 gm
Sugar	30 gm
Cornflour	55 gm
Milk	2 tsp
Egg yolk	½
Filling:	
Any yellow jam	30 gm
Biscuit crumbs	45 gm

Ingredients	10
Egg	1 white and ½ yolk
Pineapple slices	55 gm
Pineapple juice	1 tsp
Angelica	a few pieces
Butter	55 gm
Sugar	30 gm

Method

1. Sieve flour and cornflour. Rub in butter and add sugar. 2.Separate white and yolk of eggs. 3. Beat half the yolk and mix with 2 teaspoons milk. 4. Add milk and egg to dough. Mix well. 5. Roll out and cut to fit 10 patty.tins. 6. Leave to stand until filling is ready.

Filling

7. Crush biscuit crumbs. 8. Cream butter and sugar till light and fluffy. Add pineapple juice. 9. Whisk rest of yolk and white of egg. Stir into biscuit crumbs. 10. Add to creamed mixture to get a dropping consistency. 11. Put a little filling into each pastry case and bake in a hot oven, 205°C (about 400°F) for 15 minutes. 12. Remove from tins and allow to cool. 13. Drain pineapple slices. Split if too thick and cut into 4 wedges for each tart. 14. Brush some hot jam on each tart. 15. Arrange pineapple wedges and brush over with jam. 16. Garnish centre of each tart with small pieces of angelica.

88. PINEAPPLE AND CHERRY CREAM TARTLETS

Ingredients	For 10
Shortcrust pastry:	
Refined flour	115 gm
Baking powder	¼ tsp
Butter	60 gm
Sugar	5 gm
Mock cream	3 tbsp
Chopped glace cherries	30 gm
Cold water	for mixing
Mock cream	
Cornflour	15 gm
Sugar	15 gm
Chopped pineapple	1 tbsp
Butter	30 gm
Milk	15 ml
Vanilla	a few drops

Method

1. Prepare shortcrust pastry in the usual way. 2. Roll out and cut with round pastry cutter. 3. Line greased patty tins. Prick and bake blind. 4. Blend cornflour and sugar with a little milk. 5. Boil rest of milk and pour over blended cornflour, stirring well. 6. Return to fire and cook until thick. 7. Remove from fire. Add butter and whip until cold. 8. Fold in chopped pineapple and cherries lightly into the mock cream. (If you overmix, the cherries will give out colour and spoil the appearance of the tarts). 9. Pile mixture into cases and top with half a cherry.

89. QUEENSBURY TARTS OR BOATS

Ingredients	Quantity
Refined flour	115 gm
Butter	60 gm
Baking powder	¼ tsp
Sugar	1 tsp
Cold water	for mixing
Filling:	
Sugar	55 gm
Butter	55 gm
Refined flour	55 gm
Cherries	30 gm
Egg	1
Glacé Icing:	
Icing sugar	85 gm
Water	to mix

Method

1. Make shortcrust pastry. Roll out. Cut pastry with pastry cutter and put into greased patty tins.

Filling

1. Prepare a cake mixture using the creaming method. 2. Add cherries before folding in flour. 3. Put mixture in pastry cases and bake at 175°C (about 350°F) for 20 minutes. 4. Cool and top with glacé icing.

90. ALMOND TARTS

Ingredients	Quantity
Shortcrust pastry:	
Refined flour	115 gm
Butter	60 gm
Water	for mixing
Sugar a little, if desired	

Ingredients	Quantity
Filling:	
Sugar	55 gm
Ground almonds	115 gm
Butter	55 gm
Egg	1
Lime juice	¼ tsp
Jam	15 gm

Method

1. Make shortcrust pastry. Roll and line patty tins. 2. Mix sugar and almonds. Add melted butter and beaten egg. Add lime juice. 3. Smear pastry with jam and put a little almond mixture on top. 4. Bake at 195°C (about 375°F) till done.

91. WELSH CHEESECAKE

Ingredients	10 Cakes
Shortcrust pastry:	
Refined flour	115 gm
Baking powder	¼ tsp
Fat	60 gm
Sugar	5 gm
Cold water	for mixing
Filling:	
Refined flour	55 gm
Butter	55 gm
Egg	1
Sugar	55 gm
Jam	45 gm

Method

1. Make pastry in the usual way. 2. Roll out and cut out 10 rounds using large cutter. 3. Line greased patty tins with pastry. 4. Put ½ tsp jam in the centre of each. 5. Cream butter and sugar. Beat egg and add gradually to the mixture, beating all the time. 6. Fold in sieved flour lightly. 6. Place mixture on top of jam and bake in a hot oven for about 25 minutes. 8. Sprinkle a little icing sugar on top as decoration.

92. APPLE TARTS

Ingredients	10 pieces
Pastry:	
Flour	115 gm

Ingredients	10 pieces
Butter	60 gm
Sugar	30 gm
Cold water	for mixing
Filling:	
Fresh apple	1
Butter	30 gm
Sugar	30 gm
Cardamom (powdered)	a pinch
Cinnamon (crushed)	a pinch

Method

1. Sieve flour. 2. Rub in butter lightly with fingertips until it resembles breadcrumbs. 3. Add sugar. 4. Mix with cold water to a dough and then roll on a floured board. 5. Cut with medium cutter and line patty tins. 6. Fill three-quarters with apple filling. Sprinkle top with powdered cinnamon. 7. Bake at 375°F to 400°F for 20–25 minutes.

Filling

1. Peel and core apple and chop into fine pieces. 2. Melt butter in a saucepan. Add sugar, chopped apple, powdered cinnamon, crushed cardamom and cook for 5–6 minutes.

93. CHEESECAKE (A)

Ingredients	Quantity
Shortcrust Pastry:	
Refined flour	115 gm
Sour milk	590 ml (about 1 pint)
Currants	60 gm
Butter	30 gm
Egg	1
Sugar	45 gm
Almond essence	a few drops
Grated lemon rind	a little
Grated nutmeg	a little

Method

1. Boil sour milk until it separates into curds and whey. 2. Strain off curds, press well with a spoon. Let it cool. 3. Stir butter, eggs and sugar in a saucepan over a low heat until thick. Do not boil. 4. Add curds with currants, spice, almond essence and lemon rind. 5. Line patty tins with shortcrust pastry. 6. Fill with mixture and bake in a hot oven for about 10 minutes.

CHEESECAKE (B)

Ingredients	For 12
Crumb mixture:	
Melted butter	3 tbsp
Cream cracker crumbs	¾ cup
Sugar	2 tbsp
Cinnamon and Nutmeg	¼ tsp each
Filling:	
Gelatine	60 gm
Sugar (divided)	1 cup
Eggs (separated)	2
Milk	1 cup
Lemon rind (grated)	1 tsp
Lemon juice	1 tbsp
Salt	⅛ tsp
Vanilla	1 tsp
Creamed cottage cheese	3 cups (750 gm)
Heavy cream (whipped)	1 cup

Method

1. Combine ingredients of crumb mixture. Press cupful of mixture into 20 cm (8" approx.) or 23 cm (about 9") pan. Leave rest of crumbs for topping.

Filling

1. Combine gelatine, ¾ cup sugar, and salt in a large saucepan. 2. Beat egg yolks and milk together. 3. Stir in gelatine mixture. Place over low heat and stir constantly until gelatine dissolves and mixture thickens slightly (3–5 minutes). 4. Remove from heat, stir in lemon rind, lemon juice and vanilla. 5. Cool, stirring occasionally, till mixture mounds slightly when dropped from spoon. 6. Sieve or beat cottage cheese till smooth. Stir into gelatine mixture. 7. Beat egg whites stiff. Gradually add remaining ¼ cup sugar and beat till very stiff. 8. Fold into gelatine mixture; fold in whipped cream. 9. Turn into prepared pan; sprinkle rest of crumb mixture. Chill until firm (2–3 hours).

CHEESECAKE (C)

Ingredients	Quantity
For Pastry:	
Refined flour	150 gm
Baking powder	¼ tsp
Ice cold water	1 tbsp
Butter	80 gm

Ingredients	Quantity
Filling:	
Milk	1 litre
Lime	½ no.
Butter	75 gm
Almond essence	¼ tsp
Egg	1
Powdered sugar	30 gm
Sultanas	100 gm
Lime	½

For Pastry

1. Sieve flour with baking powder. 2. Cut butter into small pieces and rub into flour using fingertips, to breadcrumb consistency. 3. Add cold water and make dough using a palette knife. 4. Cut with a medium pastry cutter and line 12 patty cups.

For Filling

1. Boil milk, add lime juice to it, make cottage cheese and drain it thoroughly. 2. Melt butter and blend with powdered sugar. 3. Add beaten egg little by little and beat well. 4. Mix cottage cheese and sultanas into mixture and fill in pastries. 5. Bake at 176°C (350°F) for 25–30 minutes or till golden brown.

94. SWEDISH SLICES (sweet shortcrust pastry)

Ingredients	Quantity
Refined flour	115 gm
Fat	60 gm
Sugar	45 gm
Cold water	to mix
Egg yolk	1
Jam	45 gm
Filling:	
Sugar	55 gm
Butter	55 gm
Refined flour	115 gm
Vanilla	a few drops

Method

1. Make short-crust pastry in the usual way. 2. Roll out into a rectangle 25 cm × 6 cm (about 10″ × 2½″). 3. Place on a greased baking sheet. 4. Prepare filling—cream butter and sugar. 5. Add beaten egg alternately with sieved flour and beat to a soft consistency. Do not over-beat. 6. Add

flavouring. 7. Using star nozzle pipe three lines down pastry. 8. Prick pastry and bake in a hot oven for 20 minutes. 9. Allow to cool a little in baking tray. 10. Spread jam between lines of piping and cut into 10 slices. 11. Carefully lift slices from tray.

95. ALMOND SLICES

Ingredients	12 fingers
Refined flour	115 gm
Margarine	45 gm
Castor sugar	30 gm
Egg yolk	1
Mixture:	
Castor sugar	115 gm
Cold water	2 tsp
Almonds (blanch and shred)	55 gm
Egg white	1
Jam	a little

Method

1. Rub fat into flour. 2. Add sugar and egg yolk. 3. Knead till smooth adding water if necessary. 4. Roll paste into a strip 30 cm by 7 cm (about 12" × 3"). 5. Turn up edges and decorate. 6. Spread bottom with jam. Cover with mixture. 7. Bake at 195°C (about 375°F) for 25–30 minutes. 8. Remove from oven and when cold cut into fingers.

Mixture

1. Put egg white, sugar and shredded almonds into a pan. 2. Cook stirring all the time until it begins to thicken slightly and leaves the side of pan.

N.B. The mixture must not be made until pastry is ready.

96. PLATE TART
(shortcrust pastry for 18 cm aluminium plate)

Ingredients	Quantity
Shortcrust pastry with 115 gms. of flour	
Jam	55 gm

Method

1. Roll out pastry 0.35 cm (about 1/8") thick and line plate. 2. Cut out edges with a sharp knife and decorate edges. 3. Roll out scraps again for strips. 4. Spread jam on tarts and decorate with strips. 5. Bake at 195°C· (about 375°F) for about 15 minutes.

N.B. Care should be taken to prevent burning during baking.

97. DEEP FRUIT PIE (with shortcrust pastry)

Ingredients	Quantity
Shortcrust pastry with 115 gm flour	
Mixed fruit (Orange, Banana, Chikkoo, etc.)	450 gm
Jam	55 gm
Granulated or Brown sugar	85 gm
Water	a little if necessary

Method

1. Prepare fruit. Put half of it into a pie dish. 2. Add sugar and rest of fruit with a little water. 3. Turn pastry on to a board and roll into desired shape. 4. Cut to size. 5. Wet edge of pie dish and put on a strip of pastry all round. 6. Damp strip and cover the fruit with pastry. Trim and decorate. 7. Cook at 195°C (about 375°F) for about half an hour. Sprinkle with castor sugar. 8. Lift pastry from the sides to let steam escape or cut a hole in the centre of pastry before baking.

N.B. Fruits such as guava, plums, apples, etc. should be stewed first and cooled before using.

98. APPLE PIE

Ingredients	Quantity
Pastry:	
Refined flour	115 gm
Butter	85 gm
Salt	a pinch
Iced water	45–50 ml
Filling:	
Tart apples	450 gm
Sugar	225 gm
Refined flour	10 gm
Nutmeg	a pinch
Butter	20 gm

Method

1. Rub fat into flour. 2. Add water gradually to form a stiff dough. Mix well. 3. Chill for 10 minutes in refrigerator. 4. Roll out thinly. Cut two rounds, one for lining and the other for top crust to fit a 18 cm pie tin.

Filling

1. Arrange apples in pie tin that has been lined with pastry. 2. Sprinkle sugar, flour and nutmeg over apples. 3. Add melted butter. 4. Cover with pastry, brush top with milk, make one or two cuts to allow steam to escape. 5. Bake at 220°C (about 425°F) for 15 minutes. 6. Lower temperature to 175°C (about 350°F) and bake for 30 minutes more or until apples are done.

99. GINGER APPLE PIE

Ingredients	Quantity
Apples	1 kg
Arrowroot	1 tbsp
Brown sugar	⅔ cups (150 gm)
Crystallised ginger	2 tbsp
Butter	1 tbsp
Refined flour	115 gm
Butter	85 gm
Salt	a pinch
Baking powder	a pinch
Iced water	45–50 ml

Method

1. Prepare pastry: rub fat into flour. Add water gradually to form a stiff dough. Mix well. 2. Chill for 10 minutes. Roll out thinly. Cut two rounds, one for lining and other for top crust, to fit pie tin. 3. Peel and slice apples. Mix arrowroot with a little water and cook over slow heat till it starts thickening. Stir in sugar, apples and chopped ginger. 4. Line the pie tin. Fill with fruit. Dot with butter. Top with pastry. Bake at 205°C (about 400°F) for 40 minutes. Serve hot.

100. PUMPKIN PIE

Ingredients	Quantity
Eggs (slightly beaten)	2
Pumpkin (cooked and mashed)	2 cups
Salt	½ tsp
Cinnamon	1 tsp
Brown sugar	170 gm
Ginger	½ tsp
Top milk	1½ cups
Cloves	¼ tsp
Unbaked pastry shell	23 cm (about 9")
Pastry:	
Refined flour	1½ cup (165 gm)

Ingredients	Quantity
Shortening	½ cup (112 gm)
Cold water	5–6 tbsp

Method

1. Mix ingredients in order given. 2. Pour into pastry shell. Bake at 220°C (about 425°F) for 15 minutes. 4. Reduce heat to 175°C (about 350°F) and continue baking for 45 minutes. 5. Serve with whipped cream and chopped nuts.

101. CHEESE AND AUBERGINE FLAN

Ingredients	Quantity
Aubergines (eggplants)	1 large or 2 small
Flan case	1
Cheese sauce	300 ml
Grated cheese	30 gm

Method

1. Slice eggplant and fry in a little oil till tender. 2. Arrange at bottom of flan case; cover with sauce and then put another layer of eggplant, and finally cover with a thin layer of sauce and sprinkle with cheese. 3. Brown in a hot oven for 10–15 minutes and serve at once.

102. SARDINE, TOMATO AND EGG FLAN

Ingredients	Quantity
Refined flour	85 gm
Margarine	60 gm
Salt and Cayenne pepper	a pinch
Cold water	1½–2 dsp
Finely grated cheese	60 gm
Filling:	
Sardines	8
Tomatoes	2 or 3
Hard-boiled eggs	2
Salt and Pepper	to taste
Lemon juice	to taste
Salad cream	a little

Method

1. Rub margarine into flour, add finely grated cheese and mix. 2. Add a pinch of salt and cayenne pepper and stir in cold water to make a stiff paste. 3. Form this into a smooth dough and roll it out to a round large enough to line a 16 cm (approx. 6") flan ring. 4. Place ring on an

upturned baking sheet, lift pastry into ring and line it evenly, moulding it into base of tin and sides of ring. 5. Trim edge by running rolling pin firmly across top of ring, first in one direction and then in the other. 6. Line ring with a round of greased paper and weight it with some dry beans or rice. Chill well before baking. 7. Put flan into a hot oven to bake until pastry is set and beginning to brown, then reduce heat and finish baking. This will take about 20 minutes. 8. When pastry is almost ready, remove paper lining and weight and return pastry to oven for a few minutes with heat turned off, or very low to dry off base of flan. 9. When pastry is ready, lift flan ring and leave pastry until cold, then put it on to plate or dish on which it is to be served.

Filling

1. Skin and slice tomatoes and cut hard- boiled eggs into slices. 2. Open sardines, remove backbones, then close them up again and trim off tails. 3. Arrange a layer of hard-boiled egg slices at bottom of flan, season it with salt and pepper, and dab it with a little salad cream. 4. Add a layer of sliced tomatoes, season these with just salt and pepper, and arrange sardines on top. 5. Sprinkle sardines with lemon juice, and place a slice of hardboiled egg in the centre. 6. Garnish with wedges of tomatoes and arrange some parsley around.

103. CHOCOLATE MERINGUE PIE

Ingredients	10 portions
Shortcrust Pastry:	
Refined flour	170 gm
Baking powder	¼ tsp
Butter	85 gm
Sugar	5 gm
Cold water	for mixing
Filling:	
Cornflour	30 gm
Cocoa	15 gm
Water and Milk	250 ml
Egg yolks	2
Sugar	55 gm
Butter	15 gm
Meringue:	
Egg whites	2
Sugar	30 gm

Method

1. Prepare shortcrust pastry in the usual way. 2. Line a greased flan tin, prick centre and bake blind.

Filling

1. Blend cornflour and cocoa with a little water and milk. 2. Boil rest and stir into blended mixture. 3. Cook for 3 minutes. 4. Allow to cool. Stir in sugar and egg yolks. 5. Pour mixture into flan case. 6. Whisk egg whites stiffly. Fold in sugar, saving a little. 7. Pile on top of chocolate mixture. 8. Sprinkle with remaining sugar and return to a slow oven for about 30 minutes.

104. RICH WALNUT PIE

Ingredients	Quantity
Shortcrust Pastry:	
Refined flour	170 gm
Shortening	85 gm
Baking powder	1/4 tsp
Salt	a pinch
Cold water	for mixing
Filling:	
Brown sugar	45 gm
Granulated sugar	55 gm
Eggs	2
Maple syrup	30 gm
Milk	60 gm
Chopped walnuts	55 gm
Vanilla	few drops
Butter	55 gm
Salt	a pinch

Method

1. Make shortcrust pastry in the usual way. Line a greased flan tin and decorate edges.

Filling

1. Blend brown sugar and butter in a pan over hot water. 2. Add granulated sugar and mix well. Remove from fire. 3. Gradually add slightly beaten eggs mixed with milk and keep beating. 4. Add salt and maple syrup and mix well. 5. Return to fire and cook over boiling water until mixture thickens. 6. Remove from fire. Stir in chopped walnuts (keeping a few whole for decoration). Add vanilla. Cool. 7. Fill flan tin and bake at 175°C (about 350°F) for about 1 hour. 8. Five minutes before removing sprinkle remaining walnuts over.

105. LEMON MERINGUE PIE

Ingredients	Quantity
Pastry:	
Refined flour	170 gm
Baking powder	¼ tsp
Fat	85 gm
Cold water	for mixing
Sugar	1 tsp
Filling:	
Eggs	2
Sugar	100 gm
Line rind and juice	2
or Lemon rind and juice	2
Cornflour	30 gm
Milk or	
Milk and water	145–150 ml

Method

1. Make a pastry as for shortcrust pastry. 2. Line a flan tin. Prick centre. 3. Bake at 205°C (about 400°F) for about 20–25 minutes. 4. Cool. 5. Blend a little cold milk with cornflour, and 85 gm of sugar. 6. Boil remaining milk. Add to blended mixture. Stir well. 7. Return to fire and cook till it is thick. 8. Add lime juice and rind. Remove from fire and cool slightly. 9. Add beaten egg yolk and mix well. 10. Pour mixture into pastry case. 11. Whisk egg whites stiff. Fold in 15 gm of sugar. 12. Pile on top of pie. See that egg whites completely cover custard and meet edge of pastry. 13. Bake in a slow oven until meringue is crisp and has a pale biscuit colour.

106. CUSTARD PIE (A)

Ingredients	Quantity
Shortcrust Pastry:	
Refined flour	170 gm
Baking powder	¼ tsp
Shortening	85 gm
Cold water	for mixing
Sugar	5 gm
Filling:	
Eggs	2
Sugar	30 gm
Milk	300 ml
Vanilla	a few drops
Nutmeg (grated)	a pinch

Method

1. Make pastry in the usual way. 2. Line a greased flan tin. Decorate edges. 3. Prick centre and bake at 205°C (about 400°F) for 15 minutes. 4. Beat eggs well. Add sugar, a few drops of vanilla and milk. 5. Strain on to pastry, sprinkle with nutmeg and bake at 160°C (about 325°F) for about 40 minutes.

CUSTARD PIE (B)

Ingredients	Quantity
Eggs (slightly beaten)	4
Sugar	½ cup
Salt	¼ tsp
Vanilla extract	1 tsp
Almond essence	½ tsp
Milk (scalded)	2½ cups
Ground nutmeg (optional)	
Pastry shell*	23 cm (about 9")

Method

1. Place a lightly greased 23 cm (about 9") pie pan on a rack about 1.5 cm (about ½") high) in a shallow baking pan. Pour in and surround pie pan with enough hot water to come to about half the depth of pie pan. 2. Prepare custard mixture in a wide-mouthed bowl. Blend eggs, sugar salt, and essences. Slowly pour milk into egg mixture stirring constantly. 3. Pour custard mixture into pie pan. Bake in a slow oven at 160°C (about 325°F) 25–30 minutes or until a knife inserted halfway between outside edge and centre comes out clean. 4. Remove promptly from oven and water and set on a rack to cool. Do not combine custard and pie shell until both are cooled. 5. Pass a knife around edge between custard and pan. Lay a piece of foil or moisture proof paper over custard, still in pie pan. Place a rack over foil or paper. Hold rack and pie pan securely and invert. Remove pie pan. 6. Place baked shell inside of pie pan. Hold pie shell and pan together and lay over custard. Hold pie pan and rack securely and invert. This brings the custard right side up in pie shell. 7. Remove foil or moisture-proof paper. If desired, sprinkle nutmeg over surface. It is best to cut pie into serving pieces just before serving or a bit earlier.

---

*Pastry shell can be baked on the outside of pie pan. Cool before placing shell inside pie pan for filling. A decorative edge can be made.

If pastry bulges away from pan during first 4-5 minutes of baking, prick more holes in bulging areas.

107. BUTTERSCOTCH FLAN

Ingredients	10 portions
Refined flour	170 gm
Baking powder	¼ tsp
Butter	85 gm
Sugar	5 gm
Egg (small)	1
Cold water	for mixing
Filling:	
Moist sugar	100 gm
Refined flour	55 gm
Water	4 tbsp
Milk	150 ml
Butter	55 gm
Egg yolk	1
Vanilla	a few drops
Meringue:	
Egg white	1
Sugar	15 gm

Method

1. Make pastry as for shortcrust but add sugar and egg. 2. Roll out and line greased flan tin. Decorate edges.

Filling

1. Mix sugar and flour. Blend with water. 2. Heat milk and butter and pour over mixture. 3. Cook till it thickens slightly. 4. Cool slightly and add egg yolks and vanilla. 5. Pour into prepared flan. 6. Bake in a hot oven at 200°C (about 400°F) for 25 minutes. 7. Whisk whites stiff. Beat in half the sugar. 8. Fold in remaining sugar and pile on top of flan. 9. Place in a slow oven at 121°C (about 250°F) for about 30 minutes till set.

108. LIME CHIFFON PIE

Ingredients	Quantity
Filling:	
Sugar	200 gm
Gelatine (unflavoured)	1 pkt. (12 gm about)
Water	200 ml
Lime	3
Egg yolks	4
Grated rind	1 tbsp
Egg whites	4
Cream of tartar	½ tsp

Ingredients	Quantity
Pastry:	
Refined flour	170 gm
Butter	115 gm
Egg	1

Method

1. Make a pastry as for shortcrust using egg to make it richer. 2. Line two 18 cm (about 7") sandwich cake tins. 3. Bake blind at 195°C (about 375°F) for about 25 minutes. Prick centre before baking. 4. Blend half the sugar, gelatine water, lime juice and slightly beaten egg yolk together thoroughly in a saucepan. 5. Cook over low heat stirring constantly until mixture comes to a boil. 6. Remove from fire and stir in grated lime rind. 7. Place pan in cold water and cool until mixture mounds slightly when dropped from a spoon. 8. Beat egg whites with cream of tartar until frothy. 9. Gradually beat in remaining sugar a little at a time and continue beating until stiff and glossy. 10. Fold lime mixture into meringue and pile into cooled pastry shell. 11. Chill for several hours until set.

109. COCONUT CHIFFON PIE

Ingredients	Quantity
Gelatine	1 pkt. (about 12 gm)
Sugar	100 gm
Salt	1/3 tsp
Eggs	3
Milk	430 ml
Vanilla	1 tsp
Coconut (fry)	50 gm
Pastry:	
Refined flour	170 gm
Butter	115 gm
Egg	1
Apricot jam	50 ml

Method

1. Mix half the sugar, gelatine and salt together thoroughly over a double boiler. 2. Beat egg yolks and milk together. 3. Add to gelatine mixture. Cook over boiling water stirring constantly until gelatine is thoroughly dissolved (about 8 minutes). 4. Remove from heat. Add 1 teaspoon vanilla and chill until mixture mounds slightly. 5. Stir in shredded coconut. 6. Beat egg whites stiff. Beat in remaining sugar. 7. Fold in gelatine

mixture. 8. Pour into baked pie shells. Chill until firm. 9. Serve with whipped cream.

Pastry

1. Make pastry as for shortcrust using egg to make it richer. 3. Bake blink at 195°C (375°F approx.) for about 25 minutes. Prick centre before baking. 4. Spread heated jam on pastry after baking.

N.B. The same basic gelatine mixture can be used to make cherry chiffon pie, pistachio chiffon pie or chocolate chiffon pie by using different flavours and colouring. Omit jam on pastry.

For Cherry: Use 50 gm glacé cherries and pink colour.
For Pistachio: Use 50 gm pistachios, green colour and vanilla flavour.
For Chocolate: Use 50 gm cooking chocolate broken into small pieces.

110. EGG AND CHEESE FLAN

Shortcrust pastry with 225 gm flour.

Ingredients	Quantity
Filling:	
Eggs	3
Grated cheese	85 gm
Salt	1 tsp
Pepper	a pinch
Tomatoes	225 gm
Mushrooms	55 gm

Method

1. Roll out pastry and line a shallow rectangular tin like a Swiss roll tin. 2. Decorate edge by crimping. 3. Beat eggs, add cheese and seasoning. Add half the cooked mushrooms. 4. Spread mixture over pastry case. 5. Roll out any scraps of leftover pastry. 6. Cut into strips and place diagonally over filling. 7. Place tomato slices and mushrooms over filling between alternate rows of pastry strips. 8. Bake at 195°C (about 375°F) for about 25 minutes.

111. RICH FLAN PASTRY

Ingredients	Quantity
Refined flour	115 gm
Salt	¼ tsp
Butter	85 gm
Egg yolk	1
Castor sugar	1 tsp

Method

1. Sieve flour with salt. 2. Rub in fat as for shortcrust. 3. Add sugar.
4. Mix yolk of egg with a little water. 5. Add to mixture. Mix till smooth
and roll to the size and thickness required.

N.B. For a savoury dish omit sugar.

112. BAKEWELL TARTS

Ingredients	Quantity
Pastry:	
Butter	85 gm
Egg yolk and water	for mixing
Filling:	
Butter or Margarine	85 gm
Castor sugar	85 gm
Eggs	2
Cake crumbs	85 gm
Almonds or Cashewnuts	55 gm
Jam	1 tbsp
Almond essence (if cashewnuts are used)	a little

Method

1. Cream margarine and sugar. 2. Add eggs and beat well. Add cake
crumbs and nuts (ground). 3. Make pastry as for shortcrust using egg
and water to mix. 4. Roll out pastry and line an 18 cm (about 7")
sandwich cake tin. Trim. 5. Roll out trimmings. Cut into strips and
dampen. 6. Lay strips inside edge of cake tin. Press lightly and pinch
edges. 7. Spread jam on pastry then put in mixture. 8. Bake at 175°C
(about 350°F) for about 1 hour 45 minutes. Dredge with castor sugar.
Serve hot or cold. This can be made on a tin plate in which case only
half the mixture will be required.

113. CHEESE PASTRY

Ingredients	Quantity
Refined flour	115 gm
Butter	55 gm
Grated cheese	55 gm
Egg yolk	1
Cold water	for mixing
Salt and Pepper	to taste

Method

1. Sift flour, salt and pepper together. 2. Rub in fat. Add grated cheese.

3. Beat egg yolk, mix with water and add to make a stiff dough. 4. Roll out as desired.

114. GREEN PEA BOATS

Ingredients	Quantity
Pastry as in recipe No. 113	
Filling:	
Green peas	450 gm
Butter	30 gm
Tomato chutney	
Red radish	2
Seasoning	to taste

Method

1. Roll out pastry into boats, prick and bake at 195°C (about 375°F).
2. When cool take out of tin. 3. Spread ½ tsp chutney in each boat.
4. Boil peas. Make a purée. Add butter and seasoning. 5. Pipe pea purée over chutney. Cut out slices of radish and use as sails.

115. BUTTERFLIES

Ingredients
Some pea purée
Tomato slices
Cheese pastry

Method

1. For each butterfly make 2 round discs of pastry. Cut one smaller than the other. Prick all over and bake. 2. When baked, remove and cool.
3. Spread a thin layer of butter on bigger disc. 4. Cut tomato slices into halves. 5. Place slices on the buttered pastry leaving a margin in the centre. 6. Pipe a row of pea purée down centre. 7. Cut smaller disc into 2 and arrange to form butterfly wings.

116. SARDINE MARGUERITES

Ingredients	Quantity
Sardines	1 tin
Butter	55 gm
Egg (hard-boiled)	1
Cheese pastry	

Method

1. Prepare pastry discs as for Butterflies, using a medium-sized cutter.
2. Skin and bone sardines; cream with butter. 3. Spread on discs. 4. Cut petals of egg white and arrange. 5. Sprinkle centre with sieved egg yolk.

117. SEAFOOD FAVOURITES

Ingredients	Quantity
Prawns	
White sauce	
Hard-boiled egg	
Anchovy sauce	
Butter	15 gm
Cheese pastry	

Method

1. Line patty tins with pastry and make pastry stars for decoration and bake blind. Make a white sauce, add chopped hard-boiled egg and chopped cooked prawns. Cool. Pile into cases, put a pastry star on top of each and decorate with piped butter flavoured with anchovy sauce.

118. CHEESE BISCUITS

Ingredients	Quantity
Cheese	55 gm
Refined flour	170 gm
Milk	60 ml
Baking powder	(a pinch) 2–3 gm
Butter	30 gm
Salt	a pinch
Mustard	a pinch

Method

1. Sieve flour, salt and baking powder. Add mustard. 2. Rub in butter and add grated cheese. 3. Make dough adding milk gradually till dough leaves the vessel clean. 4. Roll out thick and cut into shapes. 5. Place in a greased tin and bake at 195°C (about 375°F) for 15 minutes.

119. CHEESE STRAWS (A)

Ingredients	Quantity
Butter	55 gm
Cheese	55 gm
Refined flour	85 gm
Salt	¼ tsp
Pepper	a small pinch
Cayenne pepper	a pinch

Method

1. Rub cheese through a wire sieve. 2. Partly cream fat. Add cheese and seasoned flour. 3. Make a paste and allow to stand for at least half an

hour. 4. Roll out 0.5 cm thick on a slightly flour board. 5. Cut into strips and twist. 6. Place on a baking sheet. Cook in a moderate oven for about 15 minutes.

CHEESE STRAWS (B)

Ingredients	Quantity
Butter	55 gm
Cheese	55 gm
Refined flour	115 gm
Mustard	¼ tsp
Salt	¼ tsp
Cayenne pepper	a pinch
Egg yolk	1
Worcester sauce	a few drops

Method

1. Sieve flour with seasoning and salt. 2. Rub butter into the flour. 3. Add grated cheese. Mix well. 4. Add egg yolks and Worcester sauce. 5. Roll out 0.5 cm thick. Cut into strips and bake at 195°C (about 375°F) for 10–15 minutes.

CHEESE STRAWS (flaky pastry method) (C)

Ingredients	Quantity
Refined flour	225 gm
Lime juice	1 tsp
Margarine	170 gm
Salt	½ tsp
Ice cold water	150 ml
Chilli powder	½ tsp
Cheese	30 gm
Pepper powder	¼ tsp

Method

1. Make a soft dough with flour, salt, lime juice and ice cold water. 2. Keep dough covered with a wet cloth for 30 minutes. 3. Roll dough into a rectangle 30 cm × 20 cm and spread a third of the margarine on two-thirds of rolled dough. 4. Fold into three, folding the empty portion first. 5. Refrigerate for 15 minutes. Repeat process three times more, twice with fat and once without, giving it 15 minutes rest after each rolling. 6. Roll into 0.5 cm thickness and sprinkle grated cheese and all seasonings and fold into two. 7. Roll again to 0.5 cm thickness, cut into strips, twist them and put on a baking sheet, sprinkled with water.

8. Bake at 230°C (about 450°F) for 15 minutes and at 175°C (about 350°F) for a another 15 minutes.

120. VEAL AND HAM PIE

Ingredients	Quantity
Crust pastry (hot water)	500 gm
Veal	375 gm
Salt and Pepper	to taste
Eggs (hard-boiled)	2
Ham	125 gm
Chopped parsley	½ tsp
Lemon	1
Jelly stock	100 gm
Onions	100 gm
Beaten egg	for glazing

Method

1. Make a pastry case. Remove skin and bone from veal and cut into small pieces. 2. Add chopped ham, chopped parsley, grated lemon rind and a good squeeze of lime juice. 3. Season with salt and pepper and add chopped eggs. Moisten with stock or cold water. 4. Fill pastry cases and follow method 7 to 12 of recipe 117.

121. HOT WATER CRUST PASTRY

Ingredients	Quantity
Refined flour	450 gm
Salt	1 tsp
Lard or Butter	115 gm
Water	600 ml
Egg	to glaze
Savoury filling	450 gm

Method

1. Put fat and water into a pan and bring to a boil. 2. Pour into centre of sieved flour and salt. 3. Quickly make into a dough with a wooden spoon. 4. Turn onto a slightly floured board and knead until paste is smooth and free from cracks and keep pastry warm in a bowl covered with a cloth. 5. Mould a part of paste by hand to form a pie case. It becomes firm when cold and keeps it shape. 6. Fill with savoury filling. 7. Make a lid from another portion of pastry and place on top of filling. 8. Dampen edges of pastry and pinch firmly together. 9. Using kitchen scissors, cut the sealed pie edge at 1.5 cm intervals all round and bend in alternate pieces of pastry, for turret edging. 10. Make a hole in the

centre to allow steam to escape. 11. Glaze pie with beaten egg. 12. Pin a doubled thickness of greaseproof paper round the outside. 13. Bake at 230°C (about 450°F) till pastry is lightly browned and set. 14. Reduce heat and bake for about 40 minutes.

N.B. Hot water crust pastry may be used for lining small or large cake tins to make pies of various shapes.

Large pies need a longer cooking time. Veal and ham, pork or game require about 2 hours.

122. POTATO STICKS

Ingredients	Quantity
Potatoes	85 gm
Refined flour	85 gm
Butter	85 gm
Egg	1
Poppy seeds	a little

Method

1. Peel potatoes. Cook in simmering salted water till done. 2. Drain. Dry on fire. Mash with fork or sieve free of lumps. 3. Put into a warmed basin with warm but not oiled butter and mix into a dough with flour. Cool and roll into a rectangle 2 cm (about ¾″) thick. 4. Paint with beaten egg and cut into strips 16 cm (about 6″) long. 5. Sprinkle over with poppy seeds. 6. Bake in a hot oven at 205°C (about 400°F) for 15–20 minutes or until crisp and brown.

123. ROUGH PUFF PASTRY

Ingredients	Quantity
Refined flour	225 gm
Butter	150–170 gm
Squeeze of lemon juice	
Cold water	for mixing

Method

1. Sift flour and salt together into a bowl. 2. Add fat cut into small cubes (Do not rub in). 3. Mix with lemon juice and sufficient cold water to make a stiff dough. 4. Turn onto a lightly floured board and roll into a rectangle keeping edges straight. 5. Fold bottom third of pastry up and top third down. Seal edges lightly with a rolling pin. 6. Set aside for 15 minutes in a cool place. 7. Turn pastry so that folded edge is to your right. Repeat rolling, folding and turning process three or four times. 8. Roll

out and use as required. Bake at 250°C (about 475°F) for about
15–20 minutes.

124. JAM TURNOVERS

Ingredients	Quantity
Jam	a little
Rough puff pastry	
Sugar	a little

Method

1. Roll out rough puff pastry about 0.3 cm thick. 2. Cut into squares.
Spread one half with jam to within about 1.5 cm of edge of pastry.
3. Brush with water. 4. Fold over and seal edges tightly. 5. Flake edges
with a knife and scallop them boldly. 6. Brush with water and sprinkle
with sugar. 7. Bake at 205°C (about 475°F) for 15–20 minutes. Serve
with or without sauce.

125., MINCE PIES

Mince pies are a must during the Christmas season. They can be made
with shortcrust or rough puff pastry.

Method

1. Cut thinly-rolled pastry into rounds to fit patty tins with an equal
number of slightly smaller rounds for tops. 2. Put about 2 teaspoonfuls
of mincemeat into each and brush edges with water. 3. Put tops on and
seal. Flake edges against back of forefinger, using a sharp knife. 4. Make
a hole in the top of each pie with a knife or scissors. Brush over with
milk or beaten egg and bake in a hot oven at 230°C–250°C (450°F–475°F
approx.) for 25–30 minutes. 5. Dredge tops of the mince pies lightly with
a little icing sugar. Serve hot or cold as desired.

126. FLAKY PASTRY

Ingredients	15 portions
Refined flour	225 gm
Salt	½ tsp
Lemon juice	1 tsp
Margarine	170 gm
Ice cold water	for mixing
Rice flour	for dusting
Filling	as desired
Egg for coating	1

Method

1. Sieve flour with salt. 2. Add water and lemon juice and knead into a smooth, soft dough. 3. Keep dough covered under a wet cloth for at least 20–25 minutes. 4. Divide margarine into 3 parts. 5. Roll dough into a rectangle. 6. Put one part of margarine in flakes on 2/3 of the rectangle leaving 1.5 cm edge all around as shown in diagram. 7. Fold into three, folding in empty portion first. 8. Repeat process twice more to use up all the margarine and once without putting in margarine. 9. Rest the pastry wrapped in greaseproof paper in a cool place (preferably in a refrigerator) for at least 45 minutes. 10. Roll, cut and place pastry on a *watered* baking sheet. Brush with egg yolk before baking. 11. Bake first at 230°C (about 450°F) for about 10 minutes. Take out. Cool. 12. Bake again for about 15 minutes at 150°C (about 300°F).

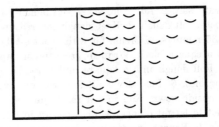

127. EGGLESS CAKES (with flaky pastry)

Ingredients	8 cakes
Flaky pastry	170 gm
(Make pastry in the usual way)	
Filling:	
Butter	30 gm
Currants	115 gm
Chopped candied peel	30 gm
Grated nutmeg or Allspice	⅛ tsp
Sugar	30 gm

Method for Filling

Melt butter, add currants, peel, spices and sugar. Cool.

Cakes

1. Roll out pastry 2 cm (about ¾″) thick. 2. Cut into large rounds with plain pastry cutter. 3. Place a spoonful of filling on each round. 4. Dampen edge of pastry and draw together to enclose filling. 5. Turn smooth side up. Mark a cross with three cuts to show filling. 6. Flatten pastry with a rolling pin so that currants just show. 7. Place on a

prepared baking sheet. 8. Brush with egg white and sprinkle with sugar.
9. Bake as for flaky pastry.

128. PUFF PASTRY

Ingredients	30 portions
Refined flour	450 gm
Lemon juice	2 tsp
Margarine	450 gm
Ice cold water	
Salt	1 tsp
Filling	as desired
Eggs for coating	2

Method

1. Sieve flour with salt. 2. Add cold water and lemon juice to flour and
knead to a smooth, soft dough. 3. Keep dough covered under a wet cloth
for at least 30–35 minutes. 4. Cream fat with about a tablespoon of flour
and make into a square block. Wrap in greaseproof paper and cool in
refrigerator. 5. Roll dough into a square and place block of fat in the
centre (See diagram). 6. Fold down all four corners overlapping each
other. 7. Turn upside down. Roll into a rectangle and fold into three,
being careful not to let fat escape. 8. Rest pastry in refrigerator for at
least 15 minutes. 9. Repeat process four times more, resting pastry for
15 minutes after each rolling. 10. Let it rest for one hour after the final
rolling. 11. Roll, cut and put on watered tray. 12. Brush with egg and
bake at 232.2°C (about 450°F) for 15 minutes and then bake at 140°C
(about 300°F) for about 15–20 minutes.

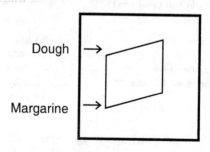

Dough →

Margarine →

129. MILLE FEUILLES (THOUSAND LEAVES)

Ingredients	25 portions
Pastry:	
Refined flour	450 gm
Salt	1 tsp

Ingredients	25 portions
Lemon juice	2 tsp
Ice cold water	for mixing
Margarine	450 gm
Filling	
Milk	300 ml
Sugar	20 gm
Cornflour	2 tsp
Butter	55 gm
Egg yolks	2
Vanilla	a few drops
Decoration:	
Icing sugar	225 gm
Colour	as required
Vanilla essence	

Method for Custard

1. Blend cornflour and milk. Add sugar and cook on a slow fire till quite thick. 2. Remove from fire and beat in egg yolks stirring all the time. 3. Cook again till custard is very thick. 4. Add vanilla and beat in butter. 5. Use when cool.

Method for Glacé Icing

1. Mix icing sugar and hot water to a thick consistency. 2. Add essence and pour over pastry. 3. Decorate with different coloured lines cutting across one another. The lines must merge into original icing.

Method for Pastry

1. Sieve flour with salt. 2. Add cold water and lemon juice and knead to a smooth, soft dough. 3. Keep dough covered under a wet cloth for at least 30–35 minutes. 4. Cream margarine with a little flour and shape into a square block. Wrap in greaseproof paper and cool in

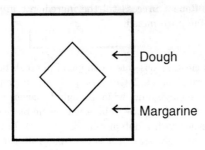

refrigerator. 5. Roll dough into a square and put cold margarine in the centre of the dough thus. 6. Fold all four corners overlapping one another. 7. Turn upside down and roll into a rectangle and fold into four. 8. Rest pastry in refrigerator for at least 15 minutes. 9. Repeat process 5 times more, resting pastry for 15 minutes after each rolling. 10. After final rolling let it rest for one hour at least. 11. Roll out 0.8 cm (about ⅓") thick and cut into 25 square or rectangular pieces. 12. Bake on a watered tray at 230°C (about 450°F) for about 15 minutes. 13. Cool and bake again at 150°C (about 300°F) for about 15 minutes. 14. When cool, slit it in the centre and spread a thick layer of confectioner's custard. 15. Turn upside down and decorate top with glacé feather icing.

130. CHICKEN AND HAM PIE

Puff pastry with 225 gm of flour and a little beaten egg

Ingredients	Quantity
Filling:	
Chicken (boiled and boned)	450 gm
Onions (minced)	55 gm
Ham (cooked)	170 gm
Eggs (hard-boiled)	2
Lime	½
Parsley (finely chopped)	3 tsp
Pepper	a pinch
Salt	to taste
Stock	75 ml
Pie dish with capacity of 600 ml liquid	

Method

1. Cut chicken into cubes; sprinkle with parsley, minced onion, grated lemon rind, salt and pepper. 2. Put a layer of chicken at bottom of pie dish. 3. Cover with a layer of sliced egg and over this put a layer of chopped ham. 4. Repeat process till the ingredients are used up. Pour over stock and lime juice mixed.

Pie

1. Roll pastry as close as possible to shape of pie dish but about 3.5 cm (about 1½") larger all round. 2. Cut a strip about 1.5 cm (about ½") wide from pastry long enough and wide enough to cover rim of pie dish. 3. Brush around rim with a little milk or water and place strip in position sealing ends together with a dab of milk or water. 4. Lift pastry lid over pie to see if it is the right size. If it is too small roll it out a little larger but do not stretch. (If stretched it will shrink while cooking and fall away

from edge of pie dish.) 5. When pastry is of right size, brush strip of pastry with a little milk or water to make the lid stick to it. 6. Put pastry lid on top of pie and press lightly onto pastry around edges. 7. Surplus pastry should be trimmed off with a sharp knife The knife should be sloped so that pastry will overlap pie dish a little as pastry shrinks a bit during cooking. 8. Next make cuts in edge of the pastry with a floured knife. This process is called 'knocking up' the edge. Keep first finger of left hand firmly just inside edge of pastry pushing pastry slightly forward as you knock up edge. This process helps heat to penetrate quickly into pastry when it goes into the oven. 9. Press edge of pastry well forward with left thumb at the same time push it back with back of knife. Hold knife upright so that fluting will be straight up and down. Flutes should be 2.5 cm (about 1") apart. 10. Make a rather large hole in centre of pastry. Brush top with beaten egg. Roll out a scrap of pastry to make a strip about 7.5 cm (about 3") long and 2.5 cm (about 1") wide; cut to make a fringe and place around hole. Cut leaves from scraps, arrange over pie and glaze with beaten egg. 11. Bake at 210°C (about 425°F) or gas 6 or 7 for 25 minutes. Reduce the heat to 195°C (about 375°F) or gas 4 or 5 and bake for another 30 minutes. Finally reduce heat to 160°C (about 325°F) or gas 2 or 3 and bake for 45 minutes (total time 1 hour 35 minutes) Serve pie hot or cold.

131. TARTE AUX CREVETTES

Puff pastry made with 225 gm flour and a little beaten egg

Ingredients	Quantity
Filling:	
Margarine	55 gm
Mushroom stalks	225 gm
Refined flour	45 gm
Milk	600 ml
Carrots	15 gm
Onions	10 gm
Bay leaf	1
Peppercorns	4
Parsley	2 sprigs
Salt	to taste
Shrimps	225 gm
Mushrooms	55 gm
Egg	1

Method

1. Roll pastry very evenly into a rectangle 30 cm (about 12") long and

18 cm (about 7") wide. 2. Trim sides so that they are absolutely straight. 3. Cut centre out of pastry leaving a 2 cm (about ¾") wide border all round. 4. Lift out centre. Lay it beside border. 5. Roll centre rectangle as nearly as possible to size of border. 6. Place rectangle in a baking tray. 7. Brush over with beaten egg. Lift border on to base and trim edge carefully. 8. Knock up (see previous recipe) sides of pastry around the outside and inside of border. 9. Prick base with a fork and brush border with beaten egg being very careful not to brush knocked up sides which would prevent the pastry rising up evenly; set aside in a cool place for half an hour. 10. Bake the tarte at 220°C (about 425°F) or gas 7 or 8 for 10 minutes. Reduce heat to 205°C (about 400°F) or gas 5 or 6 for another 10 minutes and then to 175°C (about 350°F) or gas 3 or 4 for 10 minutes more. Finally reduce heat to 160°C (about 325°F) or gas 2 or 3 and bake for 10–15 minutes longer. (Puff pastry should be well baked. Although it may appear ready after about the first twenty minutes it will be uncooked in the centre.) 11. Cool tarte on a wire tray.

Filling

1. Wash mushrooms and stalks in cold salted water. Put mushrooms aside for garnish. 2. Melt margarine. Add chopped stalks and fry them lightly for a few minutes. 3. Boil milk slowly with sliced onion, carrots and parsley to pick up flavours. 4. Remove pan of mushroom stalks from fire. Stir in flour. Add strained milk. Beat to make it smooth. 5. Return to fire and cook over gentle heat stirring all the time. 6. Clean and wash shrimps (remove intestines) and boil in salted water. 7. Keep aside a few shrimps for garnish and mix rest with sauce. 8. Sauté mushrooms in very little margarine. 9. Hard-boil eggs and slice. 10. Heat prepared tarte in a hot oven for a few minutes. 11. Pour sauce into centre, garnish top with hot sliced hard-boiled eggs and sautéed mushrooms and shrimps. Heap remaining shrimps in centre and sprinkle chopped parsley over.

132. CHICKEN VOL-AU-VENT

Puff pastry using 225 gm flour and beaten egg.

Ingredients	Quantity
Filling:	
Refined flour	15 gm
Butter	15 gm
Milk	300 ml
Salt	a pinch
Pepper	a pinch
Diced cooked chicken	170 gm

Ingredients	Quantity
Mushrooms	30 gm
Parsley	to garnish

Method

1. Prepare pastry (see puff pastry recipe). 2. Roll it out about 2.5 cm thick and cut through using a large round cutter or a round saucer. (Try not to cut more than 1.5 cm (about ½") from edge of pastry). 3. With a small cutter or knife make a circle inside larger one to form a lid. Cut about half way through pastry. 4. 'Knock up' the edge of pastry and brush top with beaten egg. 5. Bake at 220°C (about 425°F) or gas 7 or 8 for 7 minutes. Lower heat to 175°C (about 350°F) or gas 6 for a further 10–15 minutes. 6. When cooked remove lid and take out any soft pastry inside. Return to oven for 2–3 minutes to dry the insides. 7. Put in heated filling. Garnish with parsley and serve at once.

N.B. Vol-au-vents can be served cold in which case a cold filling is used, but any type of filling may be used.

Filling

1. Prepare a medium consistency white sauce using flour, butter and milk. Add seasoning. 2. Add chopped cooked mushrooms and diced chicken.

133. HAM BOUCHÉES

Puff pastry using 225 gm flour and a little beaten egg.

Ingredients	Quantity
Filling:	
Stock	15 ml
Margarine	30 gm
Milk	150 ml
Refined flour	30 gm
Ham (lean)	85 gm
Salt and Pepper	
Two round cutters, 5.7 cm (2½" approx.)	
and 2.5 cm (1″ approx.) in diameter.	

Method

Pastry

1. Roll pastry into a rectangle just large enough for eight rounds to be cut with larger cutter. 2. Flour cutter and as far as possible, cut from the centre of pastry. (If rounds are cut from too near edge, pastry may

rise unevenly.) 3. Place rounds on a baking tray and 'knock up' edges. Brush top of each bouchée with beaten egg. 4. Using smaller cutter mark centre of each. The cutter need only just break the surface. Leave bouchées in a cool place for 20 minutes. 5. Bake at 220°C (about 425°F) or gas 7 or 8 for 7 minutes. Then lower heat to 205°C (about 400°F) or gas 6 for a further 5–10 minutes. 6. Scoop the bouchées and any moist pastry from centre of bouchées with a teaspoon handle. 7. Leave lids in a warm place and return bouchées to oven for 2–3 minutes to dry the insides. 8. Fill with prepared filling and put the lids on. 9. Put them back on baking tray and into a hot oven for just a few minutes to heat through thoroughly.

Filling

1. Melt margarine. Remove from fire and stir in flour. 2. Add stock and milk. Beat till smooth. 3. Return to fire and bring sauce to a boil slowly, stirring all the time. 4. Season with salt and pepper and allow to simmer for 2–3 minutes. 5. Stir in chopped ham.

N.B. Any savoury filling can be used for bouchées. Kidneys, mushrooms and Espagnole sauce make an appetizing filling.

134. CREAM HORNS

Ingredients	Quantity
Puff pastry (Scraps can be used)	170 gm
	(weighted after making)
Cream	150 ml
Apricot jam	50 gm
Egg white	1
Cream horn tins	6

Method

1. Roll out pastry into a rectangle 20 cm (about 8") long, 14 cm (about 5") wide and 0.25 cm (about ⅛") thick. 2. Flour a sharp knife and cut pastry into six strips 2 cm (¾" approx.) wide. 3. Wrap a strip around each tin starting at the pointed end and being careful not to let pastry go over rim of tin. 4. Leave horns in a cool place for half an hour. 5. Put them on a baking tray which has been rinsed with cold water. 6. Bake them at 205°C (about 400°F) or gas 5 or 6 for 10–15 minutes until they are light golden brown. 7. Remove tins and cool pastry horns on a wire tray. 8. When cold put a little sieved apricot jam into the point of each. 9. Dilute rest of sieved jam with a few drops of water to a brushing consistency. 10. Whip cream until it holds its shape. 11. Whip egg white stiff and fold in cream. 12. Put cream into a forcing bag with a

star nozzle. 13. Pipe it into horns. Brush surface of pastry with apricot glaze.

135. PALMIERS

Ingredients	Quantity
Puff pastry (Scraps may be used)	115 gm (weight after making)
Castor sugar	

Method

1. Put pastry on a board well-dusted with castor sugar. 2. Roll into 35 cm (about 14") square. 3. Dust surface with sugar. 4. Loosely roll up one side of the pastry to the centre. 5. Then roll other side to centre in the same way. 6. Fold one roll over the other and press them rather firmly together. 7. Cut palmiers from strip making each little piece 0.7 cm (about ¼") wide. 8. Toss them in castor sugar to coat one side and place them on a lightly greased baking sheet, sugared side up. 9. Bake at 205°C (about 400°F) or gas 5 or 6 for 8–10 minutes, until tops are lightly golden. 10. Take them out of oven and turn them over, then return them to oven and brown other side (2–3 minutes). 11. Cool palmiers on a wire tray.

136. BANANA AND CREAM PUFF RING

Ingredients	Quantity
Puff pastry (Scraps may be used)	285 gm (weight after making)
Castor sugar	1 level tsp
Bananas	2
Strawberry jam	for spreading
Cream	150 ml
Egg white	1
Two cutters 8.3 cm (about 3¼") and 3.8 cm (about 1½") in diameter.	

Method

1. Roll out pastry paper-thin and cut out 21 rounds with larger cutter. (The scraps will have to be re-rolled to get 21 rounds). 2. From centre of each of these rounds cut a round with smaller cutter. 3. Collect centre rounds and put them in piles of three. 4. Stack each pile neatly. Then roll out each pile into a round the same size as ring. (There should be 7 of these and they make the bases for puff ring.) 5. Put rings and bases on a baking tray which has been rinsed with cold water. 6. Prick them

all over and leave them in a cool place for 20 minutes. 7. Bake at 205°C (about 400°F) or gas 5 or 6 for 7 minutes. Lower heat to 195°C (about 375°F) or gas 4 to 5 and bake for a further 3–5 minutes. Cool pastry on a wire tray. 8. Whip cream until it holds its shape. Fold in stiffly beaten egg white. 9. Spread one of the bases liberally with jam and put one ring on base. 10. Put cream into a forcing bag with a star nozzle. Pipe a circle of cream on ring. 11. Put another ring over this and spread jam over it. 12. Put top ring in place. 13. Repeat same process with all the puffs. 14. Mash bananas with castor sugar. Divide this mixture between puff rings and put an equal amount into the centre of each. 15. Fill up the centre with cream and pipe whorls on top of the puffs.

137. CREAM SLICES

Ingredients	Quantity
Puff pastry	170 gm
	(weight after making)
Beaten eggs	
Jam	
Vanilla flavoured mock cream or	
Confectioner's custard or Cream	
White glacé icing	

Method

1. Roll out pastry 0.7 thick and 10 cm wide. 2. Cut into pieces about 4 cm wide. Brush over with beaten eggs. 3. Bake as for puff pastry. 4. When cold, sandwich 2–3 together with jam and vanilla flavoured mock cream, cream or custard. 5. Top with white glacé icing.

138. DANISH PASTRY (A)

Ingredients	33–35 pastries
Refined flour	45 gm
Salt	1 tsp
Egg	1
Egg for brushing	1
Sugar (powdered)	4 tbsp
Milk	300 ml
Margarine	310+30 gm
Dry yeast	15 gm
For Sugar Syrup	
Sugar	30 gm
Water	60 ml

Method

1. Mix yeast in lukewarm milk and keep aside. 2. Sieve flour, sugar and salt. 3. Rub 30 gm margarine into flour. 4. Add yeast to flour and knead to a smooth and fairly soft dough which should be just soft enough to be workable.) 5. Roll dough into a rectangle. 6. Divide 310 gm margarine into three equal portions. 7. Spread one portion of creamed margarine on ¾ of rectangle. 8. Fold (empty portion first) into three. 9. Repeat process till all the margarine is folded in. 10. Rest pastry for about 15 minutes.

11. Roll and shape as required. (The following shapes are suggested). 12. After shaping put pastry on a very lightly greased baking sheet and rest for about 20 minutes in warm place. 13. Put in a filling if required (such as custard etc.) 14. Brush with beaten egg. 15. Bake at 220°C (about 425°F) for about 15–20 minutes. 16. Brush with sugar syrup and bake at 220°C (about 400°F) about 7–8 minutes more. 17. Cool before serving. 18. Different types of filling can be used after baking, such as fresh cream, custard etc.

DANISH PASTRY (B)

Ingredients	Quantity
(1)	
Dried yeast	30 gm
Water	200 ml
Bread flour	40 gm
(2)	
Milk powder	50 gm
Castor sugar	100 gm
Salt	10 gm
Whole egg	120 gm
Water (variable)	240 ml
(3)	
Bread flour	960 gm
Margarine	50 gm
(4)	
Margarine	600 gm

Method

1.Mix yeast in water and keep aside for about 10 minutes. 2. Stir in flour

(1) TWIST

(2) SQUARES

(3) CINNAMON ROLLS

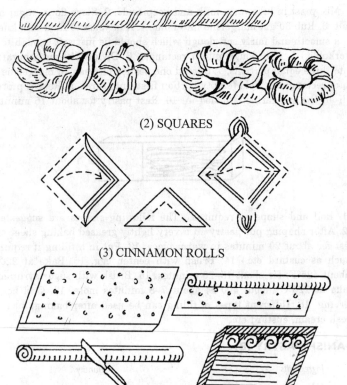

(4) BUTTERFLY BUNS

(5) CRESCENTS

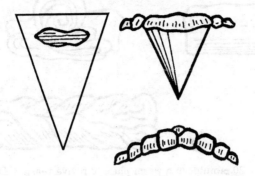

(6) CROWNS

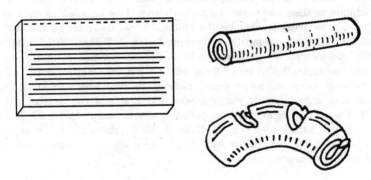

(7) PINEAPPLE SLICES

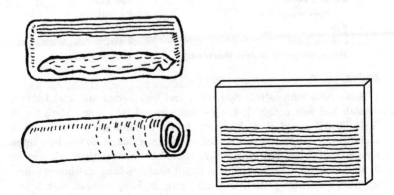

(8) SLIPS

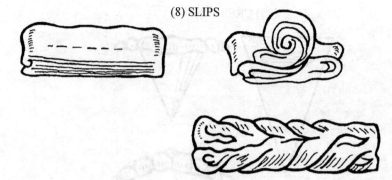

and set aside for 20 minutes in a warm place to revive yeast. 3. Dissolve milk powder, castor sugar and salt in water and add egg. 4. Sieve flour and rub in 50 gm margarine. 5. Add yeast ferment and milk solution to flour and make a dough. (It should be kneaded as little as possible to avoid toughening the gluten). 6. Set aside for 15 minutes, under slightly damp muslin, to prevent drying. 7. Roll out dough into a 0.35 cm (about ⅛") thick rectangle. 8. Spread creamed margarine all over rectangle. 9. Cut into 7.5 cm (about 3") strips lengthwise and roll one strip on top of another (spool method). 10. Rest pastry for about 20 minutes under slightly damp muslin. 11. Roll and cut as required. 12. Place on a slightly greased tray to prove for about 15–20 minutes. 13. Brush with beaten egg. 14. Bake at 205°C (about 400°F) for about 10–15 minutes. 15. Brush with thick sugar syrup 2 minutes before removing from oven.

139. KHARA BISCUITS

Ingredients	60 portions
Refined flour	450 gm
Ice cold water	for mixing
Salt	1–2 tsp
Lemon juice	2 tsp
Margarine or Grainless shortening	280–340 gm

Method

1. Sieve flour with salt. 2. Add water and lemon juice and knead into a smooth and soft dough. 3. Keep dough covered with a wet cloth for at least 20–25 minutes. 4. Roll out dough as thin as possible into a rectangle. 5. Cream fat and spread evenly over dough. 6. Cut into three pieces lengthwise. The centre piece should be broader than side pieces. 7. Pull and roll side pieces into a pencil shape, rolling one inside other. 8. Place on centre portion and roll again. 9. Keep covered with a wet

cloth for at least 45–50 minutes. 10. Roll and cut into desired shape and place biscuits on a watered tray. 11. Wet them thoroughly for baking. 12. Bake at 230°C (about 450°F) for about 15 minutes. Cool and bake again at 150°C (about 300°F) for about 15 minutes.

140. CHOUX PASTRY

Ingredients	24 eclairs
Refined flour	115 gm
Butter	55 gm
Eggs	4
Water	300 ml
Icing	
Icing sugar	115 gm
Cocoa	30 gm
Water	1 tbsp

Filling: **Fresh whipped cream, or confectioner's custard.**

Method

1. Put butter and water into a thick pan and bring to a boil. 2. Remove from fire and add sieved flour all at onc. 3. Return to fire and cook, beating all the time until mixture leaves sides of pan. Remove and cool slightly. 4. Beat eggs and add to mixture gradually, beating all the time. The mixture should be smooth and soft but firm enough to pipe. 5. Pipe through a 1.5 cm (about ½") nozzle into fingers about 5 cm (about 2") long on a greased baking tray. 6. Bake in a moderately hot oven at 175°C–195°C (about 350°F–375°F) for 30–35 minutes. 7. When ready, do not remove from oven immediately but let stand in oven with door open for about 10 minutes. This is to prevent the shrinking that takes place if the pastry is removed suddenly from heat. 8. Cool and fill as required with cream or confectioner's custard and dip the tops in chocolate glacé icing.

Icing

1. Sieve icing sugar. Mix water and cocoa and cook. Add sugar to form a stiff glacé icing.

N.B. Cooking chocolate can be melted over hot water and used instead of icing.

141. ÉCLAIR SWANS (choux pastry)

Ingredients	Quantity
Mock Cream:	
Cornflour	2 tsp
Castor sugar	30 gm

Ingredients	Quantity
Vanilla	a few drops
Milk	150 ml
Margarine	45 gm
Choux pastry	

Method for Mock Cream

1. Make a thick sauce with cornflour and milk and set aside to cool.
2. Cream butter and sugar and whisk in cornflour mixture a little at a time. Flavour with vanilla essence.

Method for Swan

1. Using a forcing bag and a plain wide nozzle, pipe rounds of choux pastry to form body of swan. 2. Using a smaller nozzle make rounds for the tail feathers and "S" shape for heads and necks. 3. Bake in a moderately hot oven at 220°C (about 425°F) for 15–20 minutes until golden brown. Slit to allow steam to escape. 4. Cut off the rounded top of large buns and divide each top in half to form wings. 5. Fill body with mock cream. Stick on wings and tail feathers with cream. Stick neck onto body. 6. Use currants for eyes and browned almonds for beaks.

142. CHERRY SHORTBREAD

Ingredients	Quantity
Refined flour	115 gm
Sugar	30 gm
Cherries	30 gm
Butter	100 gm

Method

1. Chop cherries. Sieve flour. 2. Rub butter lightly into flour. 3. Add sugar and chopped cherries. 4. Knead lightly to a dough. 5. Roll out 0.35 cm (about ⅛") thick on a floured board. Prick and cut with a medium cutter. 6. Bake at 175°C (about 350°F) for about 15–20 minutes.

143. SHORTBREAD

Ingredients	10 fingers
Refined flour	130 gm
Butter	90 gm
Sugar	55 gm
Salt	a pinch

Method

1. Sieve flour and salt together. 2. Add sugar. Rub in butter by hand.

3. **Knead** into a smooth dough. 4. Roll out onto a floured board and cut into fingers 2 cm (about ¾") thick. 5. Score with back of fork. 6. Bake in a slow oven at 120°C (about 250°F) for 30 minutes.

144. MOCHA SHORTCAKE

Ingredients	Quantity
Shortcake	
Refined flour	285 gm
Salt	a pinch
Margarine or	
Butter	285 gm
Castor sugar	30 gm
Cocoa	45 gm
Butter	150 gm
Chopped walnuts	55 gm
Filling:	
Icing sugar	225 gm
Nescafé or	2 tsp
any Instant coffee	1½ tsp
Caramel Top	
Oil	1 tsp
Granulated sugar	85 gm
Water	120 ml

Method

1. Make shortcake in usual way. 2. Divide dough into 3 portions. 3. Roll and cut out three 18 cm (about 7") rounds and bake on a floured baking sheet. 4. Do not remove from the baking sheet till nearly cold since these are rather delicate. 5. Make a cream icing with all ingredients except nuts. 6. Sandwich icing between layers of cake, cover sides with icing and roll in chopped nuts.

Caramel Top:

1. Put granulated sugar and water into a thick-bottomed pan **and melt** slowly, then boil rapidly till it turns golden brown. Remove. Allow bubbles to subside. 2. Pour on top of cake using an oiled **knife** to guide it to the edges. Oil knife again and mark caramel into slices before it sets completely. 3. When caramel is set, pipe around edge of cake with remaining mocha cream using a star nozzle.

145. GOLDEN GOODIES (Coconut macaroons)

Ingredients	Quantity
Butter	60 gm
Soft brown sugar	120 gm
Egg	1
Coconut	60 gm
Vanilla	1 tsp
Plain flour	90 gm
Baking powder	1 level tsp
Salt	a pinch

Method

1. Melt butter and sugar. Cool. 2. Beat egg. Add essence. Mix. 3. Stir coconut into mixture. 4. Sift flour with baking powder and salt into pan and mix. 5. Place teaspoonfuls into a baking tray. 6. Place a ¼ cherry on top. 7. Space well. 8. Bake at gas 4 or 175°C (350°F) for 10 minutes.

146. NUTTY PRETZELS

Ingredients	5
Refined flour	115 gm
Butter	55 gm
Sugar	55 gm
Chopped nuts	30 gm
Salt	a pinch
Icing sugar (optional)	55 gm
Egg	1

Method

1. Sieve flour and salt together. 2. Rub in butter. Add sugar and mix with beaten egg yolk. 3. Knead mixture until smooth and roll out 0.7 cm (about ¼") thick. 4. Cut into strips 0.7 cm (about ¼") wide and 23 cm (about 9") long. Roll these by hand into pencil shapes and tie into a fancy knot. 5. Brush over with egg white. 6. Sprinkle with chopped nuts and bake in hot oven at 205°C (about 400°F) for 15 to 20 minutes. 7. Make a thin icing with sieved icing sugar and warm water and dip pretzel tops whilst still warm. 8. The coating should be almost transparent. Cool before serving.

147. MELTING MOMENTS

Ingredients	Quantity
Butter	115 gm
Sugar	85 gm
Egg	½

Ingredients	Quantity
Refined flour	140 gm
Baking powder	¼ tsp
Cornflakes	55 gm
Vanilla	

Method

1. Cream fat and sugar till light and fluffy. 2. Add beaten egg and vanilla essence. Beat well. 3. Work in flour and mix to a smooth dough. 4. Wet hands and divide dough into small portions. Shape into balls. 5. Roll in crushed cornflakes and put onto a greased and floured baking sheet. 6. Bake in a moderate oven at 175°C (about 350°F) or gas 4 for 15–20 minutes.

148. NUT RINGS

Ingredients	Quantity
Refined flour	115 gm
Butter	55 gm
Sugar	55 gm
Egg	1
Milk if necessary	for mixing
Cashewnuts	45 gm
Almond essence	a drop

Method

1. Sieve flour and rub in butter. Add crushed sugar. 2. Beat egg yolk. Add milk and essence. 3. Mix egg and milk with flour mixture and knead to a smooth dough. 4. Roll out and cut with a medium cutter. Then cut out centre with a 1.5 cm (about ½″) meringue nozzle. 5. Brush ring with egg white and cover with chopped nuts. 6. Bake in a moderately hot oven at 175°C (about 350°–375°F) for 15–20 minutes.

149. CHERRY KNOBS

Ingredients	Quantity
Refined flour	225 gm
Egg	1
Butter	115 gm
Sugar	55 gm
Chopped cashewnuts	55 gm
Grated lemon rind	½ tsp
Milk for mixing	1 tbsp
Glacé cherries	30 gm

Method

1. Sift flour. 2. Cream fat and sugar. 3. Beat egg yolk and rind into fat mixture until light and fluffy. 4. Add milk and flour alternately until dough is soft but not sticky. Knead well. 5. Divide into walnut-sized portions. 6. Form into balls and dip in slightly beaten egg white. 7. Roll in chopped nuts. 8. Press half a cherry into centre of each knob. 9. Put onto prepared baking tray and bake at 175°C (about 350°F) for 20–25 minutes.

150. CINNAMON LEAVES and CRESCENTS

Ingredients	Quantity
Refined four	115 gm
Butter	55 gm
Sugar	55 gm
Milk (approx.)	30 ml
Egg yolk	1
Filling:	
Sugar	2 tsp
Cinnamon powder	1 tsp

Method

1. Sift flour. Rub in fat. 2. Add sugar and mix well with milk into a smooth dough. 3. Roll out into a rectangle. Paint half with milk, sprinkle sugar and cinnamon and fold over other half. 4. Roll again. Prick and cut into leaves and crescents. 5. Vein leaves and paint with egg yolk. Bake at 175°C (about 350°F) for 15 minutes.

151. TRICOLOUR BISCUITS

Ingredients	Quantity
Biscuit Base:	
Refined flour	170 gm
Butter	85 gm
Baking powder	¼ tsp
Sugar	85 gm
Vanilla	
Milk	145–150 ml
Filling:	
Yellow jam	115 gm
Red and green colouring	

Method

1. Sift flour and baking powder. 2. Cream butter and sugar till light and

fluffy. 3. Add essence to milk. 4. Work in flour by hand using as much milk as necessary to make a pliable dough. 5. Roll out and cut out an even number of biscuits using a medium cutter. 6. On half the number cut out three holes on each with 1.5 cm (about 1.2") savoy nozzle. 7. Bake at 195°C (about 375°F) for about 15 minutes. 8. Sandwich a plain biscuit with a perforated one using a thin layer of jam. 9. Sprinkle over with icing sugar and fill each hole with different coloured jam: yellow, green and red.

152. PEARL COOKIES

Ingredients	Quantity
Butter	55 gm
Sugar	55 gm
Egg (small)	1
Refined flour	170 gm
Baking powder	½ tsp
Chopped dates	85 gm
Chopped walnuts	30 gm
Cornflakes	30 gm
Glacé cherries	6

Method

1. Sift flour and baking powder. 2. Cream fat and sugar well. 3. Add beaten egg and salt and fold in flour alternately with chopped nuts and dates. 4. Roll into knobs, and then roll knobs in crushed cornflakes. 5. Place half a cherry in the centres and bake on a greased and floured baking tray at 195°C (about 375°F) for 20 minutes.

153. ALMOND BONBONS

Ingredients	Quantity
Butter	115 gm
Sugar	85 gm
Refined flour	140 gm
Vanilla	¼ tsp
Egg (small)	1
Soda bicarbonate	½ tsp
Almond essence	¼ tsp
Cream of tartar	½ tsp
Almonds	30 gm

Method

1. Sift flour, soda, and cream of tartar. 2. Cream butter and sugar till light and fluffy. 3. Mix flavours with beaten egg and add to creamed

mixture. 4. Add sifted dry ingredients and mix well. 5. Chill for an hour. 6. Form into small balls. Flatten slightly and place half a blanched almond in centres. 7. Bake at 195°C (about 375°F) for 10–15 minutes.

154. CHOCOLATE CHIP COOKIES

Ingredients	Quantity
Refined flour	170 gm
Salt	¼ tsp
Brown sugar	85 gm
Egg	1
Butter	85 gm
Granulated sugar	85 gm
Vanilla	
Block chocolate (sweet)	115 gm

Method

1. Sift flour and salt. 2. Cream fat and sugar and beat in egg and a few drops of essence. 3. Add dry ingredients and chocolate cut into small pieces. 4. Put teaspoonfuls into a greased baking tin and bake at 175°C (about 350°F) for about 10 minutes.

155. BISCUIT PRESS COOKIES

Ingredients	Quantity
Margarine	115 gm
Castor sugar	115 gm
Refined flour	225 gm
Egg	1
Vanilla	a few drops

Method

1. Cream fat and sugar till light and fluffy. 2. Add flour and egg with a few drops of vanilla a little at a time until mixture is like a soft shortbread mixture. 3. Put it into a biscuit forcing syringe and pipe it on to a greased baking tray. 4. Bake at 205°C (about 400°F) for 15–20 minutes.

N.B. Chocolate press cookies can be made by substituting 30 gm cocoa for 30 gm flour.

156. POLKA DOT COOKIES

Ingredients	4 dozen
Margarine	115 gm
Sugar	50 gm

Ingredients	4 dozen
Brown sugar	100 gm
Egg (slightly beaten)	1
Refined flour	220 gm
Baking powder	1 tsp
Soda bicarbonate	¼ tsp
Salt	¼ tsp
Milk	60 ml
Semi-sweet chocolate	170 gm
Walnuts (shelled)	55 gm
Cherries	55 gm

Method

1. Cream margarine and sugar. 2. Blend in egg and vanilla. 3. Sift flour with baking powder, soda and salt. 4. Add to creamed mixture alternately with milk, mixing well each time. 5. Stir in chocolate bits, cherries and nuts. 6. Put rounded teaspoons of dough on greased baking sheets. 7. Bake at 195°C (about 375°F) for 10–12 minutes.

157. PEANUT BUTTER COOKIES

Ingredients	5 dozen
Margarine	170 gm
Sugar	50 gm
Brown sugar	150 gm
Egg (slightly beaten)	1
Peanut butter	200 gm
Vanilla	1 tsp
Refined flour	140 gm
Soda bicarbonate	½ tsp
Salt	½ tsp

Method

1. Cream margarine and sugar. 2. Blend in egg, peanut butter and vanilla. 3. Sift flour with soda and salt and add to creamed mixture. 4. Form rounded teaspoonfuls of dough into balls. 5. Roll in sugar and place on ungreased baking sheets. 6. Bake in a moderate oven 195°C (about 375°F) 10–12 minutes.

158. SESAME QUEENS

Ingredients	2 dozen
Margarine	100 gm
Sugar	100 gm
Egg (slightly beaten)	1

Ingredients	2 dozen
Almond essence	¼ tsp
Lemon rind	½ tsp
Refined flour	140 gm
Salt	a pinch
Sesame (Til) seeds	

Method

1. Cream margarine and sugar. 2. Blend in egg. Add almond essence and lemon rind. 3. Add flour sifted with salt. Mix well and chill. 4. Form rounded teaspoonfuls of dough into balls and roll in sesame seeds. 5. Place on greased baking sheets and flatten slightly. 6. Bake at 205°C (about 400°F) 10–12 minutes.

159. SWISS TARTS

Ingredients	7 tarts
Refined flour	115 gm
Sugar	30 gm
Butter	115 gm
Vanilla or Lime rind	a little
Jam	55 gm
Paper cases	7

Method

1. Cream fat and sugar till light and fluffy. 2. Add essence or lemon rind. 3. Beat in half the flour mixing well. 4. Beat in remainder of flour and beat until mixture is well-blended but not over beaten. 5. Using a star nozzle, pipe mixture into paper cases with a spiral motion, leaving a hole in the centre. 6. Bake in a moderate oven at 160°C (about 325°F) for 20–30 minutes. Cool. 7. Fill depressions in the centre with jam.

160. MILAN HEARTS

Ingredients	Quantity
Refined flour	130 gm
Butter	65 gm
Sugar	65 gm
Egg	1
Large cutters 10; small cutters 30	

Method

1. Sieve flour, crush sugar. 2. Rub butter into flour. Add sugar and mix well. 3. Add beaten egg and knead into a dough. 4. Roll out evenly to 0.18 cm (about ¹⁄₁₆") thickness. 5. Cut with heart-shaped cutters.

6. Brush over very carefully with egg mixed with caramelized sugar so that the egg does not run down sides of biscuits. 7. Bake at 175°C (about 350°F) for 15 minutes.

N.B. If desired these biscuits can be flavoured with almonds.

161. STRAWBERRY CREAM FINGERS

Ingredients	12 pairs
Refined flour	170 gm
Sugar	85 gm
Butter	85 gm
Egg	1
Strawberry essence	a few drops
Milk for mixing	if necessary
Pink colouring	
Cream:	
Icing sugar	85 gm
Butter	45 gm
Colouring and Flavouring	

Method

1. Sieve flour. 2. Cream butter and sugar till light and fluffy. 3. Beat egg and beat it in with cream. Add colouring and flavouring. 4. Beat flour gradually into mixture. 5. Pipe through a star nozzle into finger shapes. 6. Bake at 195°C (about 375°F) for 10–15 minutes; cool. 7. Sandwich fingers in pairs with butter cream.

Butter Cream

1. Sieve icing sugar twice. 2. Cream butter and add icing sugar. 3. Add essence and cream well.

162. CHOCOLATE CREAM FINGERS

Ingredients	12 pairs
Refined flour	140 gm
Cocoa	30 gm
Butter	85 gm
Sugar	85 gm
Egg	1
Vanilla essence	a few drops
Milk	a little if necessary
Butter Cream:	
Icing sugar	85 gm
Butter	45 gm

Ingredients	12 pairs
Vanilla	a few drops
Cocoa (optional)	5 gm

Method

1. Sieve flour and cocoa twice. 2. Cream butter and sugar till light and fluffy. 3. Add slightly beaten egg and vanilla essence and beat well. 4. Add flour and cocoa mixture gradually beating all the time to a smooth paste. 5. Pipe into 5 cm (about 2") fingers with a large star nozzle on to a greased and floured baking tray. 6. Bake in a moderate oven at 175°C (about 350°F) for 20 minutes. Cool. 7. Sandwich fingers in pairs with butter cream.

163. CHOCOLATE WHIRLS

Same recipe as above but pipe in whorls, using a star nozzle. Sandwich with chocolate butter cream.

164. BACHELOR'S BUTTONS

Ingredients	Quantity
Butter	55 gm
Sugar	55 gm
Sugar for coating	15 gm
Egg	1
Refined flour	140 gm

Method

1. Cream fat and sugar and beat in part of the egg. 2. Add flour working in as much egg as required to bind creamed mixture. Mixture should be stiff. 3. Form into balls. Roll in sugar and bake in a moderately hot oven at 195°C (about 375°F) until golden brown.

165. BUTTER BUTTONS

Ingredients	Quantity
Refined flour	115 gm
Icing sugar	30 gm
Butter	115 gm
Vanilla	a few drops

Method

1. Set oven at 175°C (about 350°F). 2. Grease and flour a baking sheet. 3. Cream butter and sugar till light and fluffy. 4. Mix in flour beating well. 5. Using a large star nozzle pipe, on to the baking sheet keeping stars a little apart. 6. Bake for 15–20 minutes at 175°C (about 350°F). 7. Cool.

166. PEANUT COOKIES

Ingredients	14
Refined flour	140 gm
Salt	¼ tsp
Baking powder	1 tsp
Milk	for mixing
Butter	85 gm
Sugar	85 gm
Egg	1
Skinned and chopped peanuts	115 mg.

Method

1. Sieve flour, salt and baking powder together. 2. Cream fat and sugar. 3. Add egg and three-quarters of the nuts. 4. Mix with a little milk and put teaspoonfuls on a greased baking tin. 5. Top with remaining nuts and bake in a moderate oven at 175°C (about 350°F) for 15–20 minutes.

167. BIRD'S NEST COOKIES

Ingredients	Quantity
Refined flour	85 gm
Butter	45 gm
Baking powder	¼ tsp
For piping:	
Refined flour	55 gm
Icing sugar	15 gm
Sugar	30 gm
Milk	½ tbsp
Butter	55 gm
Chopped nuts	15 gm
Jam	30 gm
Vanilla	a few drops

Method

1. Sieve flour and baking powder. 2. Cream butter and sugar and mix in flour, adding milk gradually. 3. Knead lightly into a smooth dough. 4. Roll out and cut with a medium-sized cutter. 5. Place on prepared baking tins.

For Piping

1. Cream butter and sugar. Add essence. 2. Beat in flour to a smooth cream. 3. Pipe mixture with a 0.7 cm (¼" approx.) star nozzle around edges of biscuits. 4. Sprinkle a few nuts on piping. 5. Bake at 175°C (about 350°F) for about 15 minutes. 6. Cool and fill centres with jam.

168. SAVOY BISCUITS

Ingredients	Quantity
Flour	50 gm
Sugar	40 gm
Margarine	30 gm
Egg white	1

Method

1. Cream fat and sugar till light and fluffy. 2. Fold in flour. 3. Add stiffly beaten egg white and mix lightly. 4. Put into a piping bag with a savoy nozzle. 5. Pipe out into 5 cm length strips. 6. Tap tray on table to flatten piped mixture. 7. Bake at 175°C for 15 minutes.

169. HONEY BISCUITS

Ingredients	16
Sweet Shortcrust Pastry:	
Flour	150 gm
Sugar	70 gm
Butter	75 gm
Apricot jam	50 gm
Sugar	125 gm
Cashewnuts or Walnuts (cut into flakes)	125
Honey	30 gm
Liquid glucose	1 tbsp
Fresh cream	50 gm
Butter	75 gm

Method

1. Prepare sweet shortcrust pastry by the creaming method and line a Swiss roll tray (23 cm × 28 cm). Brush with apricot jam. 2. Melt butter in a thick-bottomed pan and add sugar, fresh cream, honey, liquid glucose and cook on a slow fire or in a double boiler for 7 minutes. 3. Remove and stir in flaked nuts. 4. Spread mixture evenly on pastry and bake at 175°C for 40 minutes. 5. Cool and cut into 16 even rectangular pieces.

170. VANILLA BISCUITS

Ingredients	Quantity
Eggs	12
Clarified butter	340 gm
Ammonium carbonate	1 Re.wt. (12 gm)
Sugar	910 gm
Cashewnuts	455 gm

Ingredients	Quantity
Salt	1 tsp
Flour	1.8 kg
Vanilla	1½ tsp

Method

1. Beat together eggs and sugar till light and fluffy. 2. Add clarified butter, ammonium carbonate and chopped nuts. 3. Add flour and knead into a dough. 4. Roll out, cut into desired shapes. Bake at 175°C (about 350°F) for 15–20 minutes.

N.B. A mixture of pure clarified butter and hydrogenated fat may be used.

171. GINGER BISCUITS (A)

Ingredients	Quantity
Eggs	12
Sugar	910 gm
Clarified butter	340 gm
Salt	1 tsp
Ginger powder	115 gm
Refined flour	1.8 kg
Ammonium carbonate	12 gm

Method

1. Beat together eggs and sugar till creamy. 2. Add ginger powder, clarified butter and salt and ammonium carbonate. Mix well. 3. Gradually fold in flour to form a dough. 4. Roll out, cut into shapes and bake at 175°C (about 350°F) for about 7–10 minutes.

GINGER BISCUITS (B)

Ingredients	Quantity
Whole wheat flour (Atta)	680 gm
Clarified butter	115 gm
Ginger powder	34–40 gm
Jaggery or Molasses	680 gm
Soda bicarbonate	15 gm
Water	170 ml

Method

1. Dissolve jaggery in water. Heat gently. Remove. 2. Add clarified butter, fold in flour sieved with soda bicarbonate. 3. Roll out, cut into desired shapes and bake at 175°C (about 350°F) for about 7–10 minutes. (Cool dough before rolling.)

GINGER BISCUITS (C)

Ingredients	Quantity
Molasses or Jaggery	910 gm
Butter	455 gm
Refined flour	1.35 kg
Dry ginger	55 gm
Egg yolks	2
Soda bicarbonate	3 tbsp
Salt	1 tsp

Method

1. Put 2 cups of water into a pan and melt molasses; strain and cook to form a thick syrup (it should form soft balls when poured into water). 2. Add butter and melt on a slow fire. Remove. 3. Mix soda, salt, ginger powder and egg yolks in syrup. 4. Add flour and knead. 5. Roll out and cut into desired shapes. 6. Brush top with egg white and sprinkle with sugar. Bake at 175°C (about 350°F) for about 7–10 minutes. (Cool dough before rolling.)

172. SOFT JAGGERY BISCUITS

Ingredients	Quantity
Refined flour	6 cups
Salt	1 tsp
Sugar	1 cup
Jaggery	1½ cups
Baking soda	2 tsp
Oil	¾ cup
Warm water	¾ cup
Vanilla	1½ tsp
Dry ginger	1 tsp

Method

1. Sift together flour, baking soda, salt and ginger powder. 2. Combine sugar, jaggery, oil, warm water and vanilla in a large bowl. Beat until well blended. 3. Gradually add sifted dry ingredients, mixing to form a soft dough. Chill for about 1 hour. 4. Roll out dough 0.7 cm (about ¼") thick on a lightly floured board. Cut with a 6.5 cm (about 2½") cutter. 5. Bake on greased baking trays at 195°C (about 375°F) for 10–12 minutes. Cool. 6. Store in air-tight tins. Put in a slice of fresh bread to keep biscuits soft and moist.

173. BRANDY SNAPS

Ingredients	20
Butter	55 gm
Sugar	55 gm
Golden syrup	20 gm
Refined flour	55 gm
Ginger powder	½ tsp
Grated lemon rind	¼ tsp

Method

1. Melt fat, sugar and syrup in a pan. 2. Remove from heat and add other ingredients. Mix well. 3. Drop teaspoonfuls onto a greased baking tray 5 cm (about 2") apart. 4. Bake in a moderate oven at 175°C (about 350°F) until golden brown all over. 5. Remove tray from oven and stand on a stove or in a warm place to prevent biscuits getting hard. 6. Remove biscuits with a palette knife and roll around handle of a wooden spoon while they are still hot. 7. Leave on a cooling rack to cool. 8. Fill with desired cream. These biscuits should be eaten at once.

N.B. Put into airtight tins unfilled if they are to be stored for a few days.

174. PEANUT MACAROONS

Ingredients	Quantity
Salt	a pinch
Peanuts	85 gm
Brown sugar	85 gm
Egg whites	2
Vanilla	½ tsp

Method

1. Toast peanuts in oven for a few minutes. 2. Skin, chop and sprinkle with salt. 3. Beat egg whites to a stiff forth. Add flavouring. Add sugar gradually and continue beating. 4. Fold in nuts. 5. Put teaspoonfuls of mixture 2.5 cm apart on a greased and floured tin and bake in a slow oven at 150°C (about 300°F) till firm and light brown in colour.

175. MACAROONS ON DRY CAKE

Ingredients	10 cakes
For Cakes:	
Refined flour	115 gm
Shortening	55 gm

Ingredients	10 cakes
Sugar	55 gm
Milk	for mixing
For Macaroons:	
Egg whites	2
Brown sugar	85 gm
Peanuts	85 gm
Vanilla	a few drops
Salt	a pinch

Method

1. Sieve flour. 2. Cream butter and sugar. 3. Mix in flour, kneading slightly and adding milk if required. 4. Wrap in greaseproof paper and place in a refrigerator to cool. 5. Roll out and cut with a medium-sized cutter. 6. Bake for 5 minutes at 175°C (about 350°F). 7. Remove and cool on a wire tray.

Macaroons

1. Roast, skin and chop nuts, and sprinkle with salt. 2. Beat egg whites stiff. 3. Beat in sugar gradually. Add flavouring. 4. Fold in nuts. 5. Put spoonfuls on tops of dry cakes. 6. Bake at 135°C (about 275°F) for 20–25 minutes.

176. COCONUT MACAROONS (A)

Ingredients	8 pieces
Egg whites	2
Granulated sugar	90 gm
Dessicated coconut	90 gm
Vanilla essence	¼ tsp

Method

1. Put egg white into a clean thick-bottomed brass pan. 2. Add sugar and cook on a slow fire till sugar dissolves. 3. Remove. Stir in desiccated coconut and add essence. 4. Put mixture into a piping bag and using through a 1.5 cm savoy nozzle, pipe 8 even-sized roundels onto a greased and floured baking tray. 5. Bake at 175°C (about 350°F) for 35 minutes.

COCONUT MACAROONS (B)

Ingredients	8
Egg whites	2
Granulated sugar	90 gm

Ingredients	8
Vanilla essence	¼ tsp
Dessicated coconut	90 gm

Method

1. Beat egg whites to a stiff froth. Add flavouring. 2. Add sugar gradually and continue beating. Fold in dessicated coconut and remaining sugar. 3. Place teaspoonfuls of mixture about 2.5 cm apart on a greased and floured baking tray. 4. Bake in a slow oven at 150°C (about 300°F) till firm and light brown in colour.

177. SHREWSBURY BISCUITS (A)

Ingredients	20
Flour	175 gm
Powdered sugar	85 gm
Butter	100 gm
Baking powder	¼ tsp
Cinnamon powder	a pinch
Milk	1 tbsp

Method

1. Sieve flour with baking powder. 2. Cream butter and sugar and mix with flour; add cinnamon powder. 3. Add one tablespoon of milk and make a dough. 4. Roll out 0.3 cm thick and cut with biscuit cutter. 5. Place onto a lightly greased baking sheet and bake at 175°C for 10–15 minutes.

SHREWSBURY BISCUITS (B)

Ingredients	32
Refined flour	225 gm
Butter	115 gm
Sugar	115 gm
Grated lemon rind	2 tsp
Egg	1

Method

1. Cream butter and sugar very thoroughly. 2. Add well-beaten egg gradually and beat well. 3. Add sieved flour and lemon rind and mix into a stiff dough. 4. Turn on to a floured slab. Knead lightly and roll out thinly. 5. Cut into desired rounds with pastry cutter. 6. Place on a prepared baking sheet and bake in a moderate oven for about 15 minutes.

CANDY

TIPS ON MAKING PERFECT CANDY

Equipment

1. Choose the right cooking pan. It should be large enough to let the candy boil freely without running over, and heavy enough to prevent candy sticking to the bottom. 2. Measure ingredients accurately using standard measuring cups and spoons. Use a wooden spoon; it never gets too hot to handle.

To Test Candy

1. A candy thermometer is a good buy because it takes the guess-work out of testing the readiness of candy. Before dipping into candy, place thermometer bulb in lukewarm water and gradually heat to boiling point to check the temperature. To get an accurate reading of candy temperature, the thermometer bulb should be well covered with the candy mixture; but it should not rest on the bottom of the pan. Clean thermometer by placing it in warm water to dissolve any hardened candy. 2. Without a thermometer, follow the cold-water test. Do this by dropping, from a spoon, a few drops of boiling syrup into a cup of cold water. Shape into a ball with fingers. Use fresh water for each test.

Cold-water Test: Temperature

Soft ball	112.2°C (234°F)	Shapes into ball, but flattens out.
Firm ball	117.7°C (244°F)	Holds shape until pressed.
Hard ball	121.1°C (250°F)	Hard, firm ball.
Soft crack	129.4°C (265°F)	Separates into threads, but is not brittle.
Hard crack	143.3°C (290°F)	Separates into hard and brittle threads.

Be sure to remove candy from the fire as you test for readiness since even a few moments of extra cooking may cause overcooking.

Storing Candy

1. Keep creamy-type candy such as fudge or fondant fresh for several weeks by wrapping in waxed paper, cellophone, plastic wrap, or aluminium foil and then storing in tightly covered containers. Candy keeps best when stored in a cool dry place. 2. Wrap "chewy" candy such as caramels, individually in waxed paper or aluminium foil to prevent them becoming sticky. Store in the same way as fudge. 3. Wrap rolled candy in waxed paper, cellophane, plastic wrap, or aluminium foil and store in a refrigerator; slice off pieces as needed.

178. MARSHMALLOWS

Ingredients	Quantity
Sugar	450 gm
Davis gelatine	30 gm
Water	300 ml
Colouring and Flavouring	
Icing sugar and	
Cornflour for rolling	115 gm
Vanilla	1 tsp
Raspberry and Almond essences	

Method

1. Soak gelatine in cold water for 5 minutes in a thick-bottomed pan. 2. Cook on a slow fire. 3. When gelatine has dissolved, add sugar. 4. Cook to the right consistency (when dropped from spoon it should drop in one gelatinous string). 5. Remove from fire. Add one tsp vanilla. 6. Beat with a spring beater or in a food mixer till creamy and thick. 7. Separate into 3 portions. Add pink colouring and raspberry essence to one portion and almond essence and green colour to the second. Pour in layers into a deep Swiss roll tin previously sprinkled over with icing sugar and cornflour, keeping plain white portion in between. 8. Smooth top and leave to set at room temperature (3–4 hrs). 9. Cut into squares and roll in icing sugar mixed with cornflour. Put into airtight containers.

N.B. Success in making marshmallows depends on the amount of beating.

179. BROWNIES

Ingredients	20 pieces
Refined flour	115 gm
Granulated sugar	225 gm
Margarine	115 gm
Eggs	3
Cocoa	25 gm
Walnuts	115 gm
Baking powder	½ tsp (level)
Vanilla essence	¼ tsp

Method

1. Sieve flour and baking powder. 2. Melt fat (margarine) and gradually add cocoa to fat until well-blended. 3. Remove from heat and stir in vanilla essence. 4. Whisk eggs and sugar over hot steam into a thick mixture. 5. Add cooled cocoa mixture. 6. Fold in sieved flour and 85 gm chopped walnuts. 7. Pour batter into 23 cm × 18 cm lined cake mould and bake at 190°C for 25–30 minutes. 8. Cool and spread chocolate fudge

icing on top. 9. Cut into 20 rectangular pieces and decorate each piece with a shelled walnut.

Chocolate Fudge Icing:

Ingredients	Quantity
Cocoa	25 gm
Icing sugar	100–150 gm
Butter	75 gm
Milk	30 ml

Method

1. Melt butter in a pan. 2. Cool and add sifted cocoa and icing sugar alternately. 3. Add cold milk to get a butter cream consistency.

180. CRÈME DE MENTHE

Ingredients	Quantity
Gelatine	30 gm
Sugar	450 gm
Water	300 ml
Oil of peppermint	for flavouring
Green colouring	
Sieved icing sugar	30 gm

Method

1. Dissolve gelatine in half the water. 2. Put sugar into a thick-bottomed pan with remaining water and dissolve gently over low heat. 3. On no account should the syrup be allowed to boil till all the sugar has dissolved. It can be stirred with a metal spoon. 4. Once sugar has dissolved stop stirring. Syrup should not be stirred once it comes to a boil. 5. When syrup is boiling add melted gelatine and boil mixture slowly for 20 minutes. 6. Take pan off heat and allow mixture to cool slightly. 7. Add green colouring and peppermint flavouring. 8. Pour mixture into a greased tin and leave to cool and set. 9. When crème de menthe is cold take it out of tin. 10. Toss in sieved icing sugar and cut into squares. 11. Put into dark coloured cases and store in tins.

N.B. These sweets are at their best after 12 hours when the icing sugar coating becomes firm.

181. FRENCH ALMOND ROCK

Ingredients	Quantity
Almonds	115 gm
Water	225 ml

Ingredients	Quantity
Sugar	450 gm
Cream of tartar	a pinch

Method

1. Blanch almonds. 2. Dry them in the sun. 3. Lightly oil a 15 cm (6")
square tin and cover the base with blanched almonds. 4. Put sugar and
water into a fairly large thick-bottomed pan. 5. Dissolve sugar slowly
over gentle heat. 6. Using a metal spoon to stir it, be careful to dissolve
every single grain of sugar, before sugar comes to boil. 7. As soon as
sugar has dissolved thoroughly take spoon out of pan and bring syrup to
a boil, adding cream of tartar. 8. Boil syrup rapidly until it starts to
change colour. 9. Watch it carefully as it boils. When it becomes a light
caramel colour take it off the heat and pour it slowly over almonds.
10. Leave almond rock to become quite cold and set. 11. Turn slab of rock
out of tin and break it into pieces.

N.B. Walnuts may be used instead of almonds in which case they should
be toasted first.

182. MILK TOFFEE

Ingredients	Quantity
Sweetened condensed milk	1 tin
Water	½ tin
Sugar	225 gm
Butter	30 gm
Nuts	55 gm

Method

1. Cook milk, water and sugar together to a toffee consistency 115°C
(about 240°F). 2. Add butter, pour on to a buttered slab. 3. Roll out
evenly, mark into squares and cut when cold.

N.B. 1 tbsp of liquid glucose can be added with milk, water and sugar
to get a smooth texture.

183. CHOCOLATE FUDGE

Ingredients	Quantity
Granulated sugar	450 gm
Fresh milk	300 ml
Cocoa	30 gm
Liquid glucose	30 ml (1 tsp)
Butter	55 gm

Ingredients	Quantity
Vanilla	½ tsp
Cream of tartar	a pinch

Method

1. Put sugar, milk, cocoa, glucose and butter into a thick-bottomed pan. 2. Heat gently until all the sugar dissolves completely. 3. Bring to a boil and cook until temperature reaches 155°C (about 240°F) or soft ball consistency. 4. Remove pan from heat and leave to stand until all bubbles subside (about 5 minutes). 5. Add vanilla and beat with a wooden spoon until mixture is thick and creamy. 6. Pour into a buttered tin. When cool mark into squares; cut into pieces when cold.

184. FONDANT PEPPERMINT CREAM

Ingredients	Quantity
Icing sugar	225 gm
Egg white	1
Oil of peppermint	
Green colour	

Method

1. Sift icing sugar. 2. Beat egg white lightly. Beat in icing sugar gradually. Add essence and colour. 3. Knead by hand. Roll out and cut with fancy cutters. 4. Dry on a sugared tray.

185. WALNUT COFFEE FUDGE

Ingredients	Quantity
Granulated sugar	450 gm
Liquid glucose	30 ml (1 tbsp)
Butter	30 gm
Milk	300 ml
Coffee essence	2 tbsp
Roughly chopped walnuts	115 gm
Vanilla	1 tsp

Method

1. Put all the ingredients except the nuts and vanilla essence into a pan and heat gently till all the sugar is completely dissolved. 2. Bring to a boil and heat until temperature reaches 115°C (about 240°F) or soft ball consistency. Stir all the time. 3. Remove pan from heat. Add nuts, reserving some for decoration, and essence. 4. Beat well till mixture is thick and creamy. 5. Pour into a greased tin. Mark into squares and place a piece of walnut on top of each square. 6. Cut into pieces when cold.

186. DATE FUDGE

Ingredients	Quantity
Sugar	395 gm
Butter	55 gm
Milk	150 ml
Water	150 ml
Soda bicarbonate	a pinch
Vanilla	a few drops
Finely chopped dates	85 gm

Method

1. Put the sugar, butter, milk, water and soda into a thick-bottomed pan. 2. Heat gently till sugar dissolves completely. 3. Bring to a boil and cook until temperature reaches 115°C (about 240°F). 4. Remove from heat. Add essence and dates. 5. Beat mixture till it becomes thick and creamy. 6. Pour into a greased tin. Mark into squares. Break when cold.

Variations

Raisin Fudge: Replace dates with 85 gm chopped seeded raisins.
Ginger Fudge: Replace dates with 55 gm finely chopped preserved ginger.

187. ORANGE FUDGE

Ingredients	Quantity
Sugar	395 gm
Milk	150 ml
Water	90 ml
Soda bicarbonate	a pinch
Butter	55 gm
Orange rind	2 tsp
Orange juice	2 tsp

Method

1. Put sugar, milk, water and soda into a thick-bottomed pan. 2. Cook over gentle heat till sugar dissolves completely. 3. Add butter, grated rind and orange juice. 4. Bring to a boil and cook till temperature reaches 114.4°C (about 238°F), stirring gently. 5. Remove from heat. Let bubbles subside and beat until mixture is thick and creamy. 6. Pour into an oiled tin. When nearly cold cut into squares.

188. TUTTI FRUITTI FUDGE

Ingredients	Quantity
Golden syrup	115 gm
Butter	30 gm
Condensed milk	5 tbsp

Ingredients	Quantity
Water	2 tbsp
Chocolate	30 gm
Sugar	170 gm
Vanilla	2–3 drops
Prunes, Dates (chopped and stoned)	170 gm

Method

1. Put the syrup, butter, milk, water and chocolate into a pan. 2. Heat to boiling point and boil for 2 minutes. 3. Remove from heat. 4. Add sugar and dissolve it slowly. 5. As soon as sugar is dissolved bring mixture to a boil rapidly and continue to boil without stirring, to a temperature of 115°C (about 240°F). 6. Remove from heat and add essence and fruit. 7. Beat until creamy and turn out at once into greased tins. 8. Cut into squares when cold.

189. CREAMY CARAMELS

Ingredients	Quantity
Sweetened condensed milk	1 tin
Brown sugar	225 gm
Butter	115 gm
Golden syrup	2 tbsp

Method

1. Put all the ingredients into a saucepan. 2. Stir over low heat until mixture becomes dark brown and leaves sides of pan. 3. Pour into a greased tin. When cool mark into squares. 4. Cut when cold.

190. WALNUT FUDGE

Ingredients	Quantity
Brown sugar	395 gm
Milk	235 ml
Butter	55 gm
Glucose (liquid)	1 tbsp
Chopped nuts	60 gm

Method

1. Put all the ingredients except walnuts into a saucepan. 2. Stir gently over medium heat until mixture boils. 3. Boil to 115°C (about 240°F) or to soft ball stage. 4. Remove from heat. When bubbles subside, beat until thick. 5. Fold in walnuts and beat till stiff. 6. Turn out into a greased tin. When almost set mark into squares. Cut with a sharp knife.

191. GINGER CREAM

Ingredients	Quantity
Sugar	400 gm
Milk	150 ml
Water	90 ml
Soda bicarbonate	a pinch
Glucose (liquid)	1 tsp
Chopped crystallized ginger	85 gm
Yellow food colour	

Method

1. Put sugar, milk and glucose into a pan over heat. 2. Stir occasionally until sugar dissolves. 3. Boil to 113.3°C (about 236°F) or to soft ball stage. 4. Remove from heat. 5. Allow to stand until slightly cooled. 6. Beat until it begins to thicken. 7. Fold in ginger and yellow food colour. 8. Beat again till stiff. 9. Press into greased tin. 10. When quite cold and set, cut into squares.

N.B. Cherry creams may be made in the same way using chopped glacé cherries, and pink food colour.

192. UNCOOKED FONDANT

Ingredients	Quantity
Icing sugar	250 gm
Egg white	1
Liquid glucose	55 ml
Vanilla	½ tsp
Food colour	

Method

1. Sift icing sugar. Make a well in centre. 2. Add egg white, (broken up with a fork but not beaten) melted glucose and flavouring. 3. Work icing sugar in from the sides until all ingredients are mixed into a stiff mass. 4. Turn on to a board dusted with icing sugar. 5. Knead until mixture has absorbed sufficient icing sugar to hold its shape. 6. Add dabs of colour and knead until evenly-coloured.

193. COOKED FONDANT

Ingredients	Quantity
Sugar	450 gm
Water	150 ml
Glucose	1 dsp
Vanilla	½ tsp
Squeeze of lemon juice or any flavouring, and food colour.	

Method

1. Put sugar, water and glucose into a pan over low heat. 2. Stir occasionally till sugar dissolves completely. 3. Bring to a boil. Do not stir again. Place lid on saucepan and leave for 2 minutes. 4. Remove lid. Boil to 115°C (240°F approx.) or soft ball stage. 5. Pour into a basin. Allow to cool. Beat until thick. 6. Knead well by hand. Colour and flavour as desired, kneading until evenly coloured.

Fruit Rolls: Mix 1 tablespoon chopped dates with 1 chopped fig, 1 tablespoon chopped raisins, 5 or 6 chopped cherries. Roll pieces of fondant (coloured and flavoured) into thin strips. Place fruit mixture on one half, roll up and shape into a 2.5 cm (about 1") roll. Cut into 1.5 cm (about ½") slices.

Walnut Creams: Colour and flavour fondant as desired. Shape pieces into small rounds, press a walnut half onto each side.

Almond Creams: Method same as for walnut creams, flavour fondant with almond essence using whole blanched almonds.

Prune Creams: Remove stones from large, soft prunes. Fill with a small piece of coloured and flavoured fondant.

Date Creams: Method same as for prune creams.

194. FRENCH JELLIES

Ingredients	Quantity
Gelatine	55 gm
Sugar	900 gm
Cold water	900 ml (3 glasses)
Lemon juice or any fruit juice for flavouring.	

Method

1. Soften gelatine in 300 ml (1 glass) of water. 2. Add balance of water and sugar. 3. Bring to a boil. 4. Cook steadily for 20 minutes. 5. Allow to become cold. Colour and flavour as desired. 6. Pour into square tins rinsed with cold water. 7. When set turn out on to greased paper dusted with castor sugar. Cut into squares. Dust with castor sugar.

195. GELATINE DAINTIES

Ingredients	Quantity
Gelatine	45 gm (4 pkts.)
Sugar	600 gm
Salt	¼ tsp
Water	590 ml
Cinnamon extract and Red food colour	
Oil of peppermint and Green food colour	
Sugar	30 gm

Method

1. Mix salt, gelatine and sugar in a thick-bottomed pan. 2. Add water and heat over gentle heat till gelatine is dissolved. 3. Bring to a boil and simmer for 15 minutes. 4. Remove from heat. Divide into two equal parts. 5. Add 1 tsp cinnamon extract and red colour to one part and ½ tsp oil of peppermint and green colour to the other. 6. Rinse two 20 cm × 10 cm (8" × 4") pans in cold water. Pour candy mixture into pans till they are about three quarters full. 7. Put in a cool place (not a refrigerator) and let it stand overnight. 8. When ready to use loosen candy round edges of pans with sharp wet knife. 9. Turn out on to a board lightly covered with sugar. Cut into cubes and roll in sugar.

196. CRYSTALLIZED FRUIT

Ingredients	Quantity
Ash pumpkin	450 gm
Sugar	450 gm
Water	300 ml
Lime (calcium)	5 gm
Food colour and Flavouring	

Method

1. Peel core and cut pumpkin into 2.5 cm cubes. Weigh. 2. Prick cubes with a fork and soak them in water mixed with calcium. Stand for 2–3 hrs. 3. Drain and dry in the sun for 1 hour. 4. Make a sugar syrup with sugar and water (3-string consistency). 5. Add pumpkin cubes and cook till pumpkins are transparent. 6. Remove from heat and set aside overnight. 7. Reheat over boiling water. Add colour and flavouring. 8. Remove with fork and roll in granulated sugar.

N.B. Cubes can be made in a variety of colours and flavourings.

197. CHOCOLATES

Ingredients	Quantity
Walnuts	200 gm
Cashewnuts	250 gm
Icing sugar	400 gm
Dates	100 gm
Cherries	100 gm
Chocolate	565 gm or 5 bars
	(3 sweet, 2 bitter)
Biscuits	50 gm
Orange peel	50 gm
Vanilla	2 tsp
Egg whites	4

Method

1. Grind walnut and cashewnut bits. Mix with icing sugar, egg whites and vanilla. Knead till all ingredients are mixed and form into a ball. 2. Break slabs of chocolate and melt them in a double boiler over hot water and mix well. 3. When chocolate has melted, change hot water for tap water and let it cool completely, beating vigorously. 4. Take a walnut-sized bites of mixture and roll them into different shapes putting dates, cherries etc. as centres and dip them into melted chocolate with a dipping fork. 5. Place on trays lined with tissue paper and freeze on ice or in a refrigerator. When dry, wrap in fancy paper.

198. MOULDED CHOCOLATE (A)

Ingredients	Quantity
Semi sweet chocolate	500 gm
Cocoa butter	50 gm

Method

1. Melt semi-sweet chocolate in a double boiler at 31°C to melt and temper the chocolate. 2. Tempered chocolate is half-filled into a readymade chocolate mould. Put in desired filling. After 5–10 minutes, fill moulds with tempered chocolate. 3. Set in a refrigerator for about 1 hour. Unmould and wrap in multi-coloured or patterned silver foil. These chocolates should be stored in dehumidified containers or refrigerators.

N.B. If a darker colour is desired, cocoa mass can be added while chocolate is being melted or tempered.

MOULDED CHOCOLATE (B)

Ingredients	Quantity
Semi sweet chocolate	500 gm
Cocoa butter	50 gm

Method

1. Melt chocolate in a double boiler till quite warm. 2. Remove from heat and mix in melted cocoa butter till it reaches room temperature. 2. Half-fill readymade moulds. Turn around and tap to allow melted chocolate to set in. Allow to set till it starts becoming hard. 3. Add fillings like chocolate truffle, mint syrup, mixed nuts, fondant, etc. Fill moulds with remaining melted and tempered chocolate. 4. Allow to set in a refrigerator (cool) for about 10–15 minutes. Wrap in multic- coloured silver foil.

N.B. Roasted and chopped nuts like almond, cashewnuts, etc. can be added to chocolate-cocoa butter mixture and spoonfuls dropped on butterpaper. These should then be allowed to cool in a refrigerator till they become hard. They are then wrapped in chocolate paper and stored for future use in a cool place.

199. FILLING (A) DARK GANACHE

Ingredients	Quantity
Dark chocolate	1500 gm
Cream	700 ml
Liquid glucose	300 ml
Liquer (Cointreau, Grand Marnier, Rum or Brandy)	180 ml

Method

1. Chop chocolate into small pieces. 2. In a double boiler, boil cream liquid glucose, stirring well. 3. Pour over chocolate and whisk well until chocolate melts. Cool by stirring. When cool, add liquer. Whisk again till well-blended.

FILLING (B) BUTTER GANACHE

Ingredients	Quantity
Dark chocolate	1500 gm
Unsalted butter	500 gm
Fondant	500 gm
Liquer (Malibu)	180 ml

Method

1. Melt chocolate in a double boiler. 2. Cream butter and fondant. Add (tempered) melted chocolate. Whisk to blend. Cool slightly and add liquer. Blend well. 3. Leave to sit. When it becomes of piping consistency, fill piping bag with desired nozzle and pipe to desired shape on butterpaper. Allow to set. 4. These chocolate can be dipped in tempered chocolate (recipe A), and coated with chocolate flakes.

FILLING (C) COCONUT GANACHE

Ingredients	Quantity
White chocolate	1800 gm
Cream	700 gm
Liquid glucose	300 ml
Coconut milk (powder)	70 gm
Liquer (Malibu)	180 ml
Dessicated coconut	

Method

1. Boil cream, liquid glucose and coconut milk powder, stirring well. 2. Add to finely chopped white chocolate. Whisk until chocolate melts. Cool. Add liquer and mix well. Allow to cool and set till it is of piping consistency. 3. Fill piping bag with desired nozzle and pipe on butter

paper into pieces. A thin coating of tempered white chocolate is poured over. 4. As it sets, each piece is rolled in dessicated coconut.

FILLING (D) MAPLE GANACHE

Ingredients	Quantity
Dark chocolate	200 gm
Maple syrup	500 ml
Cream	500 ml
Whisky	100 ml

Method

1. Boil maple syrup and cream. 2. Pour onto chopped dark chocolate. Whisk till it melts. 3. When it cools, add whisky and whisk well. 4. Shape into rounds. When chocolates set coat lightly with tempered dark chocolate and finish with cocoa powder.

200. NOUGAT

Ingredients	Quantity
Cashewnuts	115 gm
Sugar	225 gm

Method

1. Melt sugar in a dry saucepan stirring all the time with a wooden spoon till it melts into a golden coloured syrup. Immediately add cashewnuts and remove from heat on to a greased marble slab and cut into pieces before it cools.

201. PENUCHE

Ingredients	25 pieces
Ground sugar	1 cup
Condensed milk	1 tin
Water	½ cup
Butter	2 tbsp
Finely chopped nuts	½ cup
Vanilla	1 tsp

Method

1. Cook sugar, condensed milk and water together till sugar dissolves. 2. Cook until mixture reaches soft ball stage (122.2°C or about 234°F) stirring continuously. 3. Remove from heat. Add vanilla, butter and chopped nuts. 4. Beat until mixture is thick and creamy and starts to lose it shine. 5. Quickly spread it in a 20 cm (about 8") buttered square pan. 6. Cool and cut into squares.

BREAD MAKING

BREAD MAKING

1. Bread Rolls (no-time dough)
2. Bread Rolls (straight method)
3. Covering for Bread Rolls
4. Toddy Buns
5. Savoury Picnic Rolls
6. Cinnamon Rolls
7. Yeast Rolls (with eggs)
8. Bread (straight dough method)
9. Bread (normal straight method)
10. Bread (100% sponge method)
11. Bread (70% sponge method)
12. Bread (soaker and dough method)
13. Bread (wholemeal no-time dough method)
14. Bread (no-time dough method)
15. Bread (hot dough method)
16. Bread (with milk powder)
17. Enriched White Bread
    Enriched White Bread (with dry milk)
18. Bread (with soya flour)
19. Cheese Loaf Sandwich
20. French Bread
21. Christmas Bread
22. Wholewheat Bread (100%)
23. Garlic Bread
24. Garlic and Cheese Bread
25. Kulcha
26. Sweet Dough (lean) Sweet Dough (rich)
27. Milk Bread
28. Yeast Doughnuts
29. Sally Lunn
30. Chelsea Buns (A)
    Chelsea Buns (B)
31. Meringues
32. Nutty Meringues
33. Nankhatai
34. Surti Nankhatai
35. Tea Scones
36. Drop Scones
37. Banana Drop Scones
38. Pikelets
39. Date and Walnut Bread
40. Banana Bread

Characteristics of a good loaf

1. *Shape:* well-proportioned with an evenly-rounded top.
2. *Crust:* uniformly brown but with a slightly darker top; about 0.35 cm (about ⅓") thick; tender and smooth; not split or bulging.
3. *Volume:* light in weight in proportion to size.
4. *Texture:* tender elastic crumbs, free from dryness or doughiness.
5. *Grain:* small cells evenly distributed; thin cell walls.
6. *Colour of crumbs:* depends on ingredients used. Free from dark streaks.
7. *Flavour:* Free from sourness or bitterness.
8. *Aroma:* must be free of musty, foreign or sharp odours.

Faults in Bread and their Causes

Poorly Shaped Loaf 1. Inexperience in handling. 2. Too much flour or not enough flour. 3. Dough too light before baking. 4. Oven not hot enough or heat uneven.

Coarse Grain 1. Dough not kneaded enough. 2. Allowed to rise too much before baking. 3. Oven temperature too low.

Streaks 1. Dough allowed to dry on top during rising period. 2. Dough not kneaded enough. 3. Dry flour folded into loaves during shaping. 4. Dough too heavily greased on top during rising.

Crumbly 1. Too much flour. 2. Not enough kneading. 3. Allowed to rise too much before baking.

Crust Splitting on Top or Sides 1. Oven too hot or oven heat uneven. 2. Loaves placed too closely together during baking.

Soggy or Heavy 1. Too much flour. 2. Insufficient rising or baking. 3. Poor yeast or poor flour.

Off-Flavour 1. Old yeast. 2. Dough allowed to rise for too long. 3. Too high temperature during rising. 4. Too slow or incomplete baking. 5. Insufficient scalding of milk.

Important Steps

Scald fluid milk Milk, even though pasteurized, needs to be scalded. The bacteria left in the milk will grow during the rising of the dough and may cause bread to become off-flavour. The best scalding temperature for milk is 85°C–90.5°C (about 185°F–195°F). Scalding milk at this temperature range kills all the bacteria and the bread will have a better volume and texture than if the milk were scalded at a lower temperature.

Add yeast when milk mixture is lukewarm Yeast consists of tiny plants which are killed by liquid that is too warm. Therefore, add the softened yeast only when the milk mixture is at 35°C (about 95°F) or lower. If you have no thermometer, put a drop of milk on the inside of your wrist; if it feels neither warm nor cold, it is lukewarm.

Rest period By letting the dough rest for about 10 minutes before kneading, the dough tightens and requires less flour. Before shaping the dough into loaves or rolls, allow it to rest another 10 minutes for easier handling.

Kneading Thorough kneading mixes the flour and other ingredients. It develops the gluten which helps to hold in the gas formed by yeast.

Rising period The rising period may determine the quality of your bread. Allow the dough to rise at between 24°C and 29.4°C (about 75°F and 85°F). At temperatures lower than 24°C (about 75°F) rising will be prolonged. At temperatures above 29.4°C (about 85°F) an off-flavour may develop.

Good bread can be made when you allow the dough to rise only once before it is shaped. A finer textured bread may result with a second rising.

Baking temperature Baking sets the gluten and stops gas forming. The best temperature for baking bread in a metal pan is 205°C (about 400°F). More thiamine (vitamin B1) is preserved at this temperature than at temperatures above or below 205°C (about 400°F).

Bread is done when it shrinks from the pan or sounds hollow when you tap the top of the loaf with your hand. Remove it from the pan immediately. To prevent steaming of the crust, place the loaf on a cooling rack or across the top of a pan so air can circulate freely around it.

Storage of bread Allow the bread to cool thoroughly; then place it in a clean, well-aired, covered container.

Ingredients

Flour Generally, refined flour is used to make bread. It contains enough gluten to make the framework for the loaf. Bread flour, which contains stronger gluten, makes excellent bread. Wholemeal flour can also be used to make certain kinds of bread.

Sugar Sugar furnishes food for the yeast and aids in browning the loaf.

Salt Salt improves flavour and texture. It controls yeast action so dough does not rise too quickly. Too much salt slows down rising.

Yeast Yeast is the leavening agent in the bread. When the tiny yeast plants feed on sugar, they produce carbon dioxide gas which makes the dough rise.

Yeast comes in two forms, compressed and granular. The compressed yeast cakes are moist and must be kept under refrigeration or frozen. Granular yeast will keep longer if stored in a refrigerator.

Fat Fat used in bread could be lard, a hydrogenated fat, butter, margarine, or cooking oil. The fat used in bread increases tenderness and volume, improves texture, flavour, and keeping quality; it also contributes to the golden-brown colour of the crust.

Liquid Liquid used for making bread could be milk or water. Different kinds of milk, such as fluid milk, buttermilk, evaporated milk, or dry milk, may be used. Milk in any form increases the food value of the bread and improves its keeping quality. Bread made with water has a nutty flavour and a crisper crust than bread made with milk. Water in which potatoes are cooked can also be used.

Other ingredients Other ingredients that could be used in bread are eggs, fruit, nuts and spices.

I. BREAD ROLLS (no-time dough)

Ingredients	16
Refined flour	450 gm
Sugar	1 tsp
Fat	30 gm
Lukewarm water	300 ml
Salt	1 tsp
Dry yeast	2¼ tsp (7½–10 gm)

Method

1. Mix yeast in 170 ml lukewarm water and keep aside. 2. Dissolve salt and sugar in remaining water and mix roughly with sieved flour. 3. Add yeast ferment and mix to a smooth, soft dough. 4. Knead in creamed fat and divide dough into 16 portions. 5. Make round balls and shape them. 6. Place rolls on a greased baking sheet and keep under a wet cloth until they are double in size. (about 45 minutes). 7. Sprinkle a little water on rolls before baking. 8. Bake at 230°C (about 450°F0 for about 10–15 minutes. 9. Remove and brush over with melted fat.

2. BREAD ROLLS (straight method)

Ingredients	Quantity
Refined flour	450 gm
Salt	1 tsp
Dry yeast	1 tsp (5 gm)
Sugar	1 tsp
Fat	30 gm
Lukewarm water	300 ml (about)

Method

1. Mix yeast in 120 ml lukewarm water and keep aside. 2. Dissolve salt and sugar in remaining water. 3. Mix roughly with sieved flour. 4. Add yeast ferment and knead to a smooth, soft dough. 5. Cream fat and knead .into dough. 6. Keep dough in a warm place for 1½ hrs. 7. Punch dough and keep again for 55 minutes. 8. Divide dough into 16 portions. 9. Make round balls and shape them. 10. Place them on a greased tray under a

wet cloth. 11. Sprinkle water on rolls before baking. 12. Bake at 230°C (about 450°F) for about 10–15 minutes.

3. COVERING for BREAD ROLLS

Ingredients	Quantity
Refined flour	285 gm
Sugar	170 gm
Butter	115 gm
Vanilla	a few drops
Water (about)	120 ml
Yellow food colour	

Method

1. Cream butter and sugar. 2. Beat in colour and water. 3. Knead in sifted flour. 4. Divide into 50 portions. Flatten each portion in the palm of the hand leaving the centre thicker. 5. Keep a round ball of bread roll dough in the centre and gently cover with prepared covering. 6. Mark and sprinkle sugar. 7. Leave for final proving. 8. Bake at 230°C (about 450°F) for about 10 minutes.

4. TODDY BUNS

Ingredients	Quantity
Refined flour	450 gm
Toddy	200 ml
Fat	30 gm
Salt	a pinch
Sugar	30 gm
Egg	1
Fat for frying	300 gm

Method

1. Sieve flour and salt. Add toddy and beaten eggs. 2. Add sugar and melted (30 gm) fat and knead well. 3. Keep aside for 1 hour to prove. Knead again and divide dough into 25 small balls. 4. Round them out and place in a greased and floured tray. Keep aside again for 1 hour (till it doubles in size). 5. Fry in hot smoking fat. (These buns go well with any meat dish.)

N.B. If toddy is not available, add 1 tsp of yeast to 200 ml lukewarm water and make in the same way. Toddy however, gives a unique flavour and taste.

5. SAVOURY PICNIC ROLLS

Ingredients	Quantity
Refined flour	450 gm
Sugar	1 tsp
Salt	1 tsp
Fat	30 gm
Active dry yeast	
for straight dough	1 tsp
for no-time dough	2¼ tsp
Lukewarm water	295–300 ml (about)
For Filling:	
Green peas	120 gm
Onions	60 gm
Potatoes	120 gm
Green chillies	1
Ginger	a small piece
Lime juice	½ lime
Salt	to taste
Turmeric	a pinch
Chilli powder	1 tsp

Method

1. Follow method for straight dough or no-time dough as desired. 2 After making round balls, flatten them leaving them thicker in the centre. 3. Put in filling and fold. Shape to form a round ball again. 4. Turn upside down and place on a greased tray. 5. Continue as for bread rolls.

6. CINNAMON ROLLS

Ingredients	Quantity
Refined flour	450 gm
Sugar	30 gm
Brown sugar	30 gm
Salt	1 tsp
Powdered cinnamon	20 gm
Fat	30 gm
Yeast	2¼ tsp
Coating:	
Powdered sugar	100 gm
Milk	½ cup

Method

1. Proceed as for no-time dough till fat is added. 2. Roll dough into a rectangle 1 cm (about ⅓") thick. 3. Spread melted butter on it.

4. Sprinkle with brown sugar and cinnamon mixed. 5. Roll as for Swiss Roll. 6. Cut into 2 cm ($^3/_4$" approx.) thick slices. 7. Place (cut surface down) on well-greased baking sheets. 8. Leave to prove in a warm place under a wet cloth until it doubles in size (about 45 minutes). 9. Bake at 205°C–220°C (about 400°F–425°F) for 15–20 minutes. 10. After removing from oven, coat with powdered sugar mixed with milk.

Bread Sticks

1. Prepare dough as for bread rolls. 2. Prove and roll into thin sticks. 3. Dry prove again for about 30 minutes. 4. Brush with water and bake at 175°C (about 350°F) for about 20 minutes.

7. YEAST ROLLS (with egg)

Ingredients	Quantity
Milk	600 ml
Dry yeast	15 gm
Water	60 ml
Sugar	50 gm
Salt	1 tbsp
Fat	75 gm
Egg (large)	1
Refined flour	770–880 gm
	(7–8 cups)

Method

1. Scald milk at 87.8°C (about 190°F). 2. Mix yeast in lukewarm water. Set aside for 5–10 minutes. 3. Measure sugar, salt, and fat into a mixing bowl. 4. Add hot milk and stir until sugar and salt have dissolve and fat melts. 5. When milk mixture is lukewarm, add yeast ferment. 6. Add egg and beat until well-mixed. 7. Add about half the flour and beat vigorously with a wooden spoon. 8. Add more flour, ½ cup at a time, to make dough stiff enough to knead easily. *Caution:* Keep dough soft rather than too stiff. 9. Turn dough out on to a floured board cover it with wax paper to prevent it drying and allow it to rest 10 minutes. Clean dough from sides of mixing bowl and grease bowl. 10. Knead dough until it is smooth and satiny—about 5–10 minutes or until it springs back when you press it with your finger. 11. Shape dough into a ball and place it in greased bowl. Grease surface of dough lightly with melted fat or oil; cover and leave to rise at 29°C (about 85°F) or a few degrees lower, until dough doubles in bulk or retains the imprint of your finger when you press it. 12. Punch down dough, or turn it under, to remove all gas bubbles. 13. Shape into rolls and place on greased baking sheets or pans. Let

YEAST ROLLS (WITH EGGS AND DRIED MILK)

1. Soften yeast in 1 cup (235 ml) lukewarm water, 35°C (about 95°F) for 5–10 minutes. 2. Measure sugar, salt, and fat into a mixing bowl. 3. Add 1¼ (300 ml) cup hot water and stir until sugar and salt dissolve and fat melts. 4. When mixture is lukewarm, 35°C (about 35°F) add softened yeast. 5. Sift ½ cup dry milk with about half the flour. Follow steps 6 to 14 of Yeast Roll recipe.

PARKER HOUSE ROLLS

Roll some of the dough to a 0.7 cm (about ¼") thickness; cut out rounds with a 6.5 cm (about 2½") biscuit cutter. Cover them with wax paper and let them rest for 15 minutes. Then make a deep crease just off-centre on each round. Grease one part with melted shortening and fold larger part over smaller, the crease serving as a hinge. Place about 2.5 cm (about 1") apart in a greased pan. Let it rise until double in bulk. Bake in a hot oven at 205°C (about 400°F approx.) for 12–15 minutes.

BREAD PAN ROLLS

Roll part of the dough 1 cm (⅓" approx.) thick; cut with a 6.5 cm (about 2½") biscuit cutter. Form each cut piece into a ball by drawing the edges under and pinching them together. Dip each ball of dough into melted fat or oil and place them close together in a greased pan. Let it rise until double in bulk. Bake in a hot oven at 205°C (about 400°F) for 12–15 minutes.

SWEDISH TEA RING

Roll one-third of the dough into an oblong 23 cm by 46 cm (about 9" by 18") and 7 cm (¼" approx.) thick. Spread rolled dough with 1 tablespoon melted butter and a mixture of 3 tablespoons brown sugar and ¼ teaspoon cinnamon. Add ⅓ cup currants, nuts or raisins. Roll dough lengthwise, Swiss roll fashion, sealing edge firmly. Place sealed edge down on a greased baking sheet. Shape into a ring and seal ends together by pinching dough. Using scissors, cut through the ring to within 1.5 cm (about ½") of inner edge, in slices 2.5 cm (about 1") wide. Twist each slice slightly on its side. Brush with melted butter and cover with wax paper: let it rise until double in bulk, and bake at 195°C (about 365°F) for about 25 minutes.

WALNUT ROLLS

Into each cup of deep patty tins put 2 teaspoons brown sugar, ½ teaspoon melted butter, ¼ teaspoon water, and 4–5 pieces of walnut. Roll out half the dough into an oblong 23 cm by 40 cm (about 9" by 18") and 0.7 cm (about ¼") thick. Brush with melted butter and sprinkle with ¾ cup brown sugar. Roll the dough with a string. Place cut side down in the patty tins. Let them rise until double in bulk. Bake at 195°C (about 375°F) for about 20 minutes.

CRESCENTS

Roll half the dough into a circular shape about 30 cm (122 approx.) in diameter and 0.7 cm (about ¼") thick. Cut into 12 pie-shaped pieces. Brush with melted butter. Beginning at the outer edge, roll up each section with the point underneath. Place on a greased baking sheet, cover with wax paper, and let them rise until double in bulk. Bake at 205°C (about 400°C) for about 15 minutes.

KNOTS

Roll out half the dough into a rectangle shape about 0.35 cm (about ⅓") thick. Cut into 3.8 cm (about 1½") wide strips. For various knots cut the strips in 16 cm to 25 cm (about 6" to 10") lengths. Roll each strip between your palms or on a board to make it round. Tie shorter strips in single knots and longer ones in double knots. Place on greased pans and let them rise until double in bulk. Bake at 205°C (about 400°F) for 12–15 minutes.

8. BREAD (straight dough method)

Ingredients	Quantity
Refined flour	1.5 kg
Dried yeast or	15 gm
Compressed yeast	30 gm
Sugar	30 gm
Salt	30 gm
Fat	30 gm

Water up to 55% of flour or more depending on quality of flour

Method

1. Mix yeast in 300 ml lukewarm water and keep aside. Add a teaspoon of sugar if yeast is weak. 2. Dissolve salt and sugar in remaining water and strain (water up to 55%). 3. Sieve flour. 4. Mix water in which salt and sugar have been dissolved, with flour roughly. 5. Add yeast mixture to flour and knead to a smooth, soft dough adding more water if necessary. 6. Cream fat and knead into dough. 7. Keep dough in dry prover 27°C (about 82°F approx.) for 1½ hours. 8. Punch dough and again keep in dry prover for 55 minutes more at 27°C (about 82°F approx.) 9. Divide and scale dough and form into balls. 10. Keep these balls under a dry cloth at room temperature for about 15–20 minutes.

11. Roll and mould either by machine or by hand. 12. Pan in greased bread tins. 13. Keep tins in a wet prover at 35°C (about 95°F) or under a wet cloth for about 1 hour or till it fills the tin. 14. Spray water on surface of bread before putting it into oven. 15. Inject steam into oven or put a pan with hot water inside. 16. Bake bread at 205°C (about 400°F) for 30–35 minutes. 17. Remove and brush over with oil.

N.B. If a dry prover is not available allow dough to ferment till it doubles in volume.

9. BREAD (normal straight method)

Ingredients	Quantity
Refined flour	1.5 kg
Dry yeast	15 gm
Sugar	30 gm
Salt	20 gm
Shortening	30 gm
Water upto 55% of flour or more depending on quality of flour (Add 7 parts in the beginning and one part after 3 hours)	

Method

1. Mix yeast and 1 tsp sugar in 180 ml of water and keep it aside until it starts working. 2. Sieve flour. 3. Dissolve salt and sugar in 600 ml water and mix that water into the flour roughly. 4. Add yeast ferment and knead. 5. Cream shortening and add to mixture. Knead to a smooth dough. 6. Keep dough in a dry prover at 27°C (about 82°F) for 3 hours. 7. Divide dough into small pieces and add remaining water. Knead and keep in dry prover for another 55 minutes at 27°C (about 82°F). 8. Divide, roll and keep under a cloth for 15 minutes. 9. Roll, mould and pan dough. 10. Wet prove, at 35°C (about 95°F) for 55 minutes or keep under a wet cloth. 11. Spray water on bread before putting it into oven. 12. Inject steam into oven or put a pan with hot water inside. 13. Bake at 205°C (about 400°F) for 30 minutes. 14. Remove and brush over with oil.

10. BREAD (100% sponge method)

Ingredients	Quantity
Sponge:	
Refined flour	1.5 kg
Dry yeast	15 gm
Shortening	30 gm
Water	750 ml

Ingredients	Quantity
Dough:	
Water	150 ml
Salt	30 gm
Sugar	30 gm

N.B. Water up to 55% of flour or more depending on quality of flour. Proportion 5:1.

Method

1. Mix yeast in 180 ml lukewarm water; add 1 teaspoon sugar and keep aside till it starts working (about 20–25 minutes). 2. Sieve flour, add remaining water and mix roughly. 3. Add yeast ferment and knead well. 4. Add shortening and knead well till smooth. 5. Keep in a dry prover for 3 hours at 27°C (about 82°F). 6. Dissolve salt and sugar in remaining 150 ml of lukewarm water. 7. Break sponge. 8. Add solution sponge and knead to a smooth dough. 9. Keep in dry prover for 30–40 minutes at 27°C (about 82°F). 10. Divide and keep for 15 minutes. 11. Roll, pan and keep in a wet prover for 55 minutes. 12. Inject steam into oven or put a pan with hot water in oven. 13. Bake at 205°C (about 400°F) for 30 minutes. 14. Brush with oil after baking.

I I. **BREAD** (70% sponge method)

Ingredients	Quantity
Sponge:	
Refined flour	1 kg
Dry yeast	15 gm
Water	600 ml
Dough:	
Refined flour	450 gm
Salt	30 gm
Sugar	30 gm
Shortening	30 gm
Water	300–350 ml
Water upto 55% of flour and more	
depending on quality of flour.	
Proportion:	
Sponge to dough 2:1	

Method

1. Mix yeast sugar and warm water and keep aside until it starts working. 2. Sieve flour for the sponge. Add water and knead roughly.

3. Add yeast ferment and knead to a smooth dough. 4. Keep sponge in a dry prover for 3 hours at 27°C (about 82°F). 5. Dissolve salt and sugar in water and add with 450 gm flour to sponge. Knead. 6. Add shortening and knead to a smooth, soft dough. 7. Keep dough in dry prover at 27°C (about 82°F) for 30 minutes. 8. Divide and roll and keep under cover for 15 minutes. 9. Roll, mould and pan and keep in a wet prover at 35°C (about 95°F) or under a wet cloth for 55 minutes. 10. Spray bread with water. 11. Inject steam into oven or put a pan of hot water in oven. 12. Bake at 205°C (about 400°F) for 30 minutes. 13. Brush over with oil.

12. BREAD (soaker and dough method)

Ingredients	Quantity
Soaker:	
Refined flour	1.25 kg
Salt	30 gm
Sugar	30 gm
Shortening	30 gm
Water	600 ml
Dough:	
Refined flour	150 gm
Yeast	30 gm
Water	300 ml

Water upto 55% of flour and more
depending on quality of flour.

Proportion:

Soaker to dough 2:1

Method

1. Dissolve salt and sugar in lukewarm water. 2. Add to flour. Mix roughly. 3. Add shortening and knead well (mixture will not be very smooth). 4. Keep in a dry prover for 3 hours. 5. Mix yeast in remaining water. 6. Add yeast mixture and remaining flour to dough. Knead well. 7. Leave in a dry prover at 27°C (about 82°F) for 1½ hours. 8. Divide and scale dough and form into balls. 9. Keep these balls at room temperature for about 15–20 minutes. 10. Roll, mould and pan. 11. Keep pan in a wet prover at 35°C (about 95°F) or under a wet cloth for about 1 hour or till it fills the tin. 12. Spray bread with water before putting it into the oven. 13. Inject steam into oven or put a pan of hot water inside. 14. Bake 205°C (about 400°F approx.) for 30–35 minutes. 15. Remove and brush over with oil.

N.B. This method is not very suitable for high speed mechanical mixers since the swelling power of gluten tends to develop irregularly and threads get broken. It is also inclined to be a good breeding ground for bacteria since the yeast is used later. In ordinary cases yeast fights bacteria during fermentation and overcomes them. The most suitable type of wheat for this method is Punjab wheat. In this type the gluten content is high but of an inferior quality.

13. BREAD (wholemeal no-time dough method)

Ingredients	Quantity
Wholemeal flour	1.5 kg
Dry yeast	38 gm
Sugar	30 gm
Fat	30 gm
Salt	30 gm
Lukewarm water	1–1.2 litre

Method

1. Mix yeast in 170 ml lukewarm water and keep aside. 2. Dissolve salt and sugar in remaining water and mix roughly. 3. Mix in yeast ferment and knead to a smooth and soft dough. 4. Cream fat and knead into dough. 5. Divide and form into round balls. 6. Roll, mould and pan dough. 7. Keep pan under a wet cloth in a warm place until the bread rises (about 30–45 minutes). 8. Lightly spray bread with water. 9. Bake at 205°C (about 400°F) for about 30 minutes. 10. Brush with fat after baking.

14. BREAD (no-time dough method)

Ingredients	Quantity
Refined flour	1.5 kg
Dry yeast	38 gm
Sugar	30 gm
Salt	30 gm
Fat	30 gm
Lukewarm water	1–1.2 litre

Method

Same as for wholemeal bread.

15. BREAD (hot dough method)

Ingredients	Quantity
Refined flour	11.5 kg
Yeast	30 gm
Salt	150 gm
Lukewarm water	6–7 litre

Method

1. Mix yeast in lukewarm water and keep aside. 2. Sieve flour. 3. Mix remaining water roughly with sieved flour. 4. Add yeast ferment and make a dough. The dough should be smooth and soft. 5. Keep dough at 30°C (about 88°F) for about 2 hours. 6. Punch and again keep dough at 30°C (about 88°F) for about 1 hour. 7. Cut, weigh and make round balls and keep for 15 minutes at 30°C (about 88°F). 8. Roll, mould and pan dough. 9. Keep in a wet prover at 45°C (about 110°F) for about 45–55 minutes. 10. Spray bread with water before baking. 11. Bake at 205°C (about 400°F) for about 30 minutes. 12. Brush with fat after baking.

16. BREAD (with milk powder)

Ingredients	Quantity
Refined flour	1.5 kg
Yeast	15 gm
Sugar	125 gm
Salt	30 gm
Fat	100 gm
Milk powder	150 gm
Lukewarm water	1 litre (about)

Method

1. Mix yeast with 170 ml lukewarm water and keep aside. 2. Dissolve salt and sugar in remaining water and strain. 3. Sieve flour with milk powder twice. 4. Mix salt and sugar solution with flour roughly. 5. Add yeast ferment and knead to a smooth, soft dough. 6. Cream fat and knead into dough. 7. Keep dough in a dry prover at 27°C (about 82°F) for 1½ hours. 8. Punch dough and keep again in dry prover for 55 minutes. 9. Scale and divide dough (5 sandwich loaves or 4 open loaves), make round balls and let them stand at room temperature for 15 minutes. 10. Roll out, mould and pan dough. 11. Keep pan covered with a wet cloth in a warm place for 50 minutes or until the dough rises enough. 12. Spray bread with water and bake at 205°C (about 400°F) for about 30 minutes. (Sandwich loaf at 220°C (about 425°F) for about 35–40 minutes.) 13. Brush with melted fat after baking.

17. ENRICHED WHITE BREAD

Ingredients	Quantity
Milk	475 ml (2 cups)
Active dry yeast	15 gm
Lukewarm water	60 ml
Sugar	2 tbsp

Ingredients	Quantity
Salt	2 tsp
Fat	2 tbsp
Refined flour (sifted)	660 gm (6 cups)

Method

1. Scald milk at 87.8°C (about 190°F). Use a dairy or candy thermometer to test temperatures of milk and other ingredients. 2. Soften yeast in lukewarm water at 35°C (about 95°F) for 5–10 minutes. 3. Measure sugar, salt, and fat into a mixing bowl. 4. Add hot milk and stir until sugar and salt have dissolved and fat has melted. 5. When milk mixture is lukewarm, 35°C (about 95°F), add softened yeast. Test with a thermometer or with a drop of liquid on your wrist. If the mixture feels neither cold nor warm, it is lukewarm. 6. Add about half the flour to mixture and beat vigorously with a wooden spoon (at least 75 strokes). 7. Add more flour, ½ cup at a time, to make a dough stiff enough to knead easily. *Caution:* Keep dough softer rather than stiffer. 8. Turn dough out on to a floured board, cover it with wax paper to prevent drying and allow it to rest for 10 minutes. Clean dough from sides of mixing bowl and grease bowl. 9. Knead dough until it is smooth and satiny— about 10 minutes or until it springs back when pressed with a finger. To knead, fold the dough over and with the lower part of your palms, push dough with two or three rocking motions; turn dough one-quarter way around on board, fold it over again, and repeat kneading process until dough is smooth and satiny. 10. Shape it into a ball and place it in greased bowl. Grease surface of dough lightly with melted fat or oil; insert a thermometer into dough, cover with wax paper, and let it rise out of a draft until it doubles in bulk or retains an imprint when pressed with a finger. Dough temperature should be between 24°C and 29.4°C (about 75–85°F). If the room is cold, place dough in an unheated oven with a large pan of warm water on the shelf underneath it, or in a cupboard with a pan of warm water on the same shelf. The rising time will be about 1½–2 hours. 11. Punch down dough, or turn it under to remove all gas bubbles. The dough can be allowed to rise a second time, but a satisfactory product can be made when bread rises just once. 12. Divide dough into two equal portions and let it rest, covered, for about 10 minutes. This rest period makes dough easier to handle. 13. Shape dough into loaves by rolling each portion of dough into a rectangle about 38 cm (about 152) long and 23 cm (about 9") wide. 14. Fold one-third of rolled dough lengthwise; on the folded edge press firmly from the centre toward the ends to remove any trapped air. Now fold the other third of the long side over and seal in the same way as the first fold. 15. Overlap the ends of the folded dough so that the loaf is slightly shorter than the bread pan. Press out any trapped air.

16. Again fold dough lengthwise in thirds and seal well. Place it in the greased baking pan with the sealed edge down. 17. Brush the top lightly with melted fat or oil; cover with wax paper and allow to rise at 29°C (about 85°F), or a few degrees lower, until double in bulk. 18. Bake pound loaves for 30–35 minutes in a moderately hot oven at 205°C (about 400°F) if you use a metal pan. For loaves larger than a pound, bake for 10 minutes longer. 19. The bread is done when it shrinks from the pan or if the loaf sounds hollow when you tap it with your fingers. 20. Remove loaves from pans immediately and place them on a cooling rack. 21. When loaves are thoroughly cold, place them in a clean, well-aired covered container.

ENRICHED WHITE BREAD (with dry milk)

Ingredients	Quantity
Dry yeast	15 gm
Lukewarm water	475 ml (2 cups)
Salt	2 tsp
Sugar	2 tbsp
Fat	2 tbsp
Hot water	235 ml
Dry milk (nonfat)	55–114 gm (½–1 cup)
Refined flour	660 gm (6 cups)

Method

1. Soften yeast in lukewarm water at 35°C (about 95°F) for 5–10 minutes. 2. Measure sugar, salt and fat into mixing bowl; add hot water and stir until sugar and salt have dissolved and fat has melted. 3. When sugar-fat mixture is lukewarm at 35°C (about 95°F), add softened yeast. 4. Sift ½ cup dry milk with about half the flour into liquid mixture. For a more nutritious loaf, use 1 cup dry milk. Beat vigorously with wooden spoon (at least 75 strokes). 5. Add more flour, ½ cup at a time, to make a dough stiff enough to knead easily. *Caution:* Make the dough soft rather than too stiff. 6. Turn dough out on to a floured board and allow it to rest for 10 minutes; cover it with wax paper to prevent it drying. Clean dough from sides of mixing bowl and grease bowl. 7. Knead dough until it is smooth and satiny—about 10 minutes or until it springs back when pressed it with a finger. To knead, fold dough and with the lower part of your palms, push it with two or three rocking motions; turn dough one-quarter way around on the board, fold it over again, and repeat the kneading until dough is smooth and satiny. 8. Now follow steps 10 through 21, of previous recipe.

18. BREAD (with soya flour)

Ingredients	Quantity
Active dry yeast	15 gm
Lukewarm water	235 ml (1 cup)
Sugar	4 tsp
Salt	1 tbsp
Fat	4 tsp
Hot water	235 ml (1 cup)
Sifted wholemeal flour	550–600 gm
	(5 to 5½ cups)
Sifted full-fat soya flour	6 tbsp
Nonfat dry milk	55 gm

Method

1. Mix yeast with 235 ml (1 cup) lukewarm water and let it stand for 5–10 minutes. 2. Measure sugar, salt and fat into a mixing bowl. 3. Add 235 ml (1 cup) hot water and stir until sugar and salt have dissolved and fat has melted. 4. Combine about half the flour with soya flour and nonfat dry milk. Now follow steps 6 through 21 of Enriched White Bread.

19. CHEESE LOAF SANDWICH

Ingredients	Quantity
Refined flour	1 cup
Baking powder	½ tsp
Salt	¼ tsp
Cayenne pepper	a pinch
Butter	1 dsp
Grated cheese	½ cup
Sugar	½ tsp
Egg	1
Milk	1

Thin, well-drained slices of a firm tomato.
Celery salt or garlic salt and pepper.

Method

1. Sift flour and baking powder, salt and cayenne. 2. Rub in shortening. Add sugar and cheese. 3. Mix to a soft dough with beaten egg and milk. (Egg may be omitted and more milk used instead.) 4. Turn mixture into a greased loaf tin. Bake in a moderate oven at 205°C (about 400°F) for 25–30 minutes. 5. Turn on to a cake cooler. When quite cold, cut into thin slices. Spread lightly with butter. 6. Top with tomato slices sprinkled with celery or garlic salt.

20. FRENCH BREAD

Ingredients	Quantity
Dry yeast	15 gm
Water (warm)	118 ml
Salt	1 tbsp
Lukewarm water	475 ml
Sifted refined flour	770–825 gm
Cornflour	110 gm
Egg white	1

Method

1. Soften active dry yeast in 118 ml (½ cup) warm water. 2. Dissolve salt in 475 ml (2 cups) lukewarm water. 3. Mix with 220 gm (2 cups) flour. 4. Blend in softened yeast and then stir in 440 to 495 gm (4 to 4½ cups) flour and make a soft dough. 5. Turn out on a lightly floured board, cover and let it rest for 10 minutes. 6. Knead for 5–8 minutes till smooth and elastic, working in the remaining 110 gm (1 cup) flour. 7. Place in a lightly greased bowl turning once to grease surface. 8. Cover. Let it rise in a warm place or in a dry prover at 30°C (about 86°F) till it doubles (about 1 hours). 9. Punch down. Let it rise till it doubles again (about 1 hour). Punch down. 10. Turn out on a lightly floured surface and divide into 2 portions. 11. Cover. Let it rest for 10 minutes. 12. Roll each portion into a 38 cm × 30 cm (about 15" × 12") rectangle. 13. Roll up tightly beginning with the long side, sealing well as your roll. Taper ends if desired. 14. Place each loaf diagonally seam side down on a greased baking sheet, that has been sprinkled with cornflour. 15. With a sharp knife gash the top diagonally every 6.5 cm (about 2½") and about 0.35 cm to 0.7 cm (about ⅛" to ¼") deep. 16. Beat egg whites till just foamy and add 1 tbsp water. 17. Brush this mixture over tops and sides of loaves. 18. Cover with a damp cloth but do not let it touch loaves. (Drape cloth over inverted tall glass). 19. Allow to rise till it doubles (1 hrs.). 20. Bake in a moderate oven at 195°C (about 375°F) till light brown (about 20 minutes). 21. Brush again with egg white mixture. 22. Continue baking for about 20 minutes more till nicely brown and done. Cool.

N.B. Increase all ingredients except yeast by half to make 3 loaves.

21. CHRISTMAS BREAD

Ingredients	Quantity
Milk	425 ml
Sugar	135 gm
Salt	2 tsp
Fat	110 gm

Ingredients	Quantity
Yeast	15 gm
Water	60 ml
Eggs	2
Sifted refined flour	660 gm (6 cups)
Grated lemon rind	1½ tsp
Candied peel	184 gm
Sultanas	140 gm
Cashewnuts	115 gm

Method

1. Scald milk at 87.8°C (about 190°F). 2. Mix yeast in lukewarm water at 35°C (about 95°F) for 5–10 minutes. 3. Measure sugar, salt and fat into a mixing bowl. 4. Add hot milk and stir until sugar and salt have dissolved and fat has melted. 5. When milk mixture is lukewarm (if no thermometer is available put a drop on the wrist. If it feels neither warm nor cold it is lukewarm) add yeast. 6. Add beaten eggs. 7. Add 330 gm (3 cups) flour and beat vigorously (75 strokes). 8. Add lemon rind, fruit and nuts. 9. Add more flour, 55 gm (½ cup) at a time to make a dough stiff enough to knead easily. (Make the dough soft rather than too stiff). 10. Turn dough out on to a floured board cover it with wax paper to prevent it drying and allow it to rest for 10 minutes. Clean dough from sides of bowl and grease bowl. 11. Knead dough until it is smooth and satiny (about 10 minutes) or until it springs back when pressed with the fingers. 12. Shape dough into a ball and place it in greased bowl. Grease surface of dough lightly with melted fat or oil. 13. Keep in a dry prover at 30°C (about 86°F) for about 1½–2 hours. (Dough should double in bulk or retain an imprint when pressed with a finger.) 14. Punch dough. 15. Divide it into 3 or 4 equal portions. 16. Make each portion into a roll 38 cm to 46 cm (about 152 to 182) long. Seal edges and pan. 17. When loaves are double in bulk, bake for 30–40 minutes at 195°C (about 375°F). 18. Remove on to racks. While still warm ice with confectioner's icing.

Confectioner's icing (for Christmas Bread)

Ingredients	Quantity
Icing sugar	255 gm
Milk	2 tbsp
Vanilla	1 tsp

Method

1. Stir sugar into milk; add vanilla. 2. Spread on bread rolls as soon as they are placed on cooling racks. Place wax paper under the bread or rolls to catch any drip.

22. WHOLEWHEAT BREAD (100%)

Ingredients	Quantity
Milk	425 ml
Dry yeast	15 gm
Lukewarm water	60 ml
Honey or Molasses	85 gm
Salt	1 tbsp
Fat	55 gm
Wholewheat flour	600 gm

Method

1. Scald milk at 87.8°C (about 190°F). 2. Mix yeast in lukewarm water at 35°C (about 95°F) for 5–10 minutes. 3. Measure honey, salt and fat into a mixing bowl. 4. Add hot milk and stir until sugar and salt have dissolved and fat melted. 5. When milk mixture is lukewarm add yeast ferment. 6. Add 330 gm (3 cups) wholewheat flour and beat well (75 strokes). 7. Add remaining wholewheat flour, ½ cup at a time until dough is stiff. The rest of the flour can be used on the board during kneading. 8. Follow steps 8 through 21 of Enriched White Bread.

23. GARLIC BREAD

Crush a clove of garlic with ½ a level teaspoon salt and 55 gm butter. Slice a French loaf from end to end at 1.5 cm (about 2) intervals without cutting right through. Spread garlic flavoured butter between slices and over outside of loaf. Wrap in aluminium foil and place in a hot oven for 5–10 minutes till crust is crisp. Serve while still warm.

24. GARLIC AND CHEESE BREAD

Ingredients	Quantity
Flour	500 gm
Sugar	10 gm
Salt	10 gm
Yeast (compressed)	10 gm
Fat	10 gm
Water	300 ml
Garlic	2 pods
Cheese	60 gm

Method

1. Mix yeast in 150 ml lukewarm water and keep aside. 2. Dissolve salt and sugar in remaining water. 3. Sieve flour. Mix the water in which salt and sugar have been dissolved roughly with flour. 4. Add yeast mixture to flour and knead to a smooth, soft dough adding more water

if necessary. 5. Cream fat and knead into dough. 6. Keep dough aside for 1½ hr. to ferment. 7. Punch dough and add crushed garlic and grated cheese. 8. Mix well and let it rest for 10–15 minutes. 9. Mould dough and pan in a greased bread tin. 10. Keep tin in a wet prover for 45 minutes. 11. Spray water on bread before putting it into oven. 12. Bake at 200°C (about 400°F) for 30–35 minutes. 13. Remove and brush over with oil.

25. KULCHA

Ingredients	Quantity
Refined flour	450 gm
Eggs	2
Yeast	1 tsp
Curds	115 gm
Water	to mix
Salt	1½ tsp

Method

1. Mix yeast with water and keep aside. 2. Mix salt with curds and knead in sieved flour. 3. Add yeast ferment and beaten egg and knead to a smooth and hard dough. 4. Keep dough aside for 1 hour, punch, and keep for another hour. 5. Divide dough into 5 pieces, make round balls and keep aside again for 10 minutes. 6. Roll, leaving a mound in the centre and place on a tray. 7. Keep in a wet prover for about 35 minutes. 8. Mark with a knife and brush with beaten egg before baking. 9. Bake at 204°C (about 400°F) for about 15 minutes. 10. Brush with fat and bake for about 3 minutes more.

26. SWEET DOUGH (lean)

Ingredients	Quantity
Yeast	30 gm
Refined flour	1 kg
Sugar	100 gm
Salt	20 gm
Shortening	110 gm
Skimmed milk powder	60 gm
Grated lemon rind	½ tsp

Method

1. Mix yeast with 300 ml lukewarm water and set aside. Cream well. 2. Sift skimmed milk powder with flour. 3. Dissolve salt and sugar in 300 ml lukewarm water. Strain. Add grated lemon rind. 4. Mix sugar and salt solution roughly with flour and skimmed milk powder. 5. Add yeast ferment roughly. 6. Add 120 ml more lukewarm water and knead

well. (Dough should be wetter than for bread). 7. Cream fat well and gradually mix it with dough, kneading till dough is smooth. 8. Dust with flour and shape into a smooth ball. 9. Grease a bowl. Put in dough. Turn over to see that both sides of dough are greased. Set aside to prove for about 1 hour till it doubles in bulk. 10. Remove it to a slab dusted with flour (the dough should be soft and on the wet side). 11. Cut into portions and shape as desired. 12. Bake at 250°C (about 450°F) till done. Baking time will vary with size of product. The smaller ones take approximately 10–12 minutes and the larger ones about 20 minutes. 13. Remove. Brush over with milk and sugar.

(i) BRIOCHE FANCY

Cut out a portion of dough. Roll. Divide into even lemon-sized pieces. Roll three quarters of each portion into a round ball. Place in a greased fluted deep patty tin or a Brioche tin. Flatten small portion. Fill with fruit and nut filling. Form it into a small ball and place it on top of bigger ball.

(ii) CINNAMON TWISTS

Cut out some dough. Roll out into a rectangle. Smear with melted butter and sprinkle with brown sugar and cinnamon. Fold once. Seal edges. Cut into strips and twist.

(iii) BUNS WITH FILLING

Cut out some dough. Roll. Divide into even pieces. Flatten and fill each piece with fruit and nuts. Pinch edges together and form into a ball.

SWEET DOUGH (rich)

Ingredients	Quantity
Yeast	60 gm
Refined flour	1 kg
Water (lukewarm)	450 ml

Ingredients	Quantity
Sugar	180 gm
Butter	180 gm
Salt	20 gm
Skim milk powder	60 gm
Eggs	6
Water	15 ml (about)

Method

1. Mix yeast in 445 ml lukewarm water. Set aside till it starts working.
2. Add eggs to yeast ferment and beat well. 3. Dissolve salt in 150 ml
lukewarm water. 4. Sift flour and skim milk. 5. Cream butter and sugar.
Add flour and salt solution. Mix roughly. 6. Add egg and yeast ferment.
7. Knead to a smooth, soft dough. 8. Put into a greased bowl. Turn over
to see that both sides of dough are greased. 9. Set aside to prove at 28°C
(about 82°F) for about 1 hour till it doubles in bulk. 10. Remove on to a
slab dusted with flour (the dough should be soft and on the wet side).
11. Cut into portions and shape as desired. 12. Bake at 230°C (about 450°F)
till done. Baking time will vary with size of product. The small ones take
approximately 10–20 minutes and the large ones about 20 minutes.
13. Remove. Brush over with milk and sugar.

(i) SWEET DOUGH ALMOND TEA LOAF

Grease an 18 cm (about 7") sandwich tin or an aluminium plate. Decorate
the base with almonds and cherries. Sprinkle sugar. Roll out enough
dough to fit into tin. Press over design. Leave to ferment.

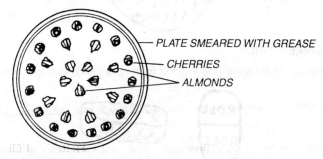

PLATE SMEARED WITH GREASE
CHERRIES
ALMONDS

(ii) SWEET DOUGH SWEDISH TEA RING

Roll out some dough into an oblong 23 cm. × 46 cm (about 9" × 18").
Spread with melted butter and fruit and nut mixture. Roll dough
lengthwise like a Swiss roll, sealing edge firmly. Place sealed edge down
on a greased baking sheet. Shape into a ring and seal ends together by
pinching edges. Using scissors cut through ring to within 1.5 cm (½"

approx.) of the inner edge in slices 1 inch wide. Twist each slightly on its side. Let it rise until it doubles.

(iii) FLOWER BUN

Roll out an oblong. Smear over with melted butter and cinnamon and sugar or butter, nutmeg, cream and finely chopped cherries and almonds. Fold into narrow strips, one strip at a time. Cut strip. Cut into small pieces with scissors. Arrange in a greased sandwich tin to form a floral design, starting from the outer ring to the centre. The folded end should always be on the outer ring.

(iv) SWEET TAIL

Proceed as for Swedish ring but roll from either end. Cut with scissors.

(v) PANETONE

Knead well with fruit and nuts and a little melted butter. Shape as for French bread.

(vi) FRUIT AND NUT FILLING FOR SWEET DOUGH

Ingredients	Quantity
Glacé cherries	450 gm
Angelica	225 gm
Sultanas	225 gm
Cashewnuts	225 gm

Method

Chop fine and mix. Use as required.

27. MILK BREAD

Ingredients	Quantity
Refined flour	300 gm
Water	500 gm
Milk	300 gm
Fresh yeast	30 gm
Sugar	10 gm

Method

1. Dissolve yeast in lukewarm water with sugar. 2. When it rises, mix it with flour and warm milk and set it aside to rise.

Part 2

Ingredients	Quantity
Refined flour	1 kg
Sugar	200 gm
Fat	30 gm
Salt	30 gm
Water	250 gm

Method

1. Dissolve salt and sugar in slightly warm water. 2. Sieve flour and add ferment (Part I). Knead thoroughly, adding salt and sugar water to make a soft dough. 3. Then add fat and let it stand for 1–2 hours to rise. 4. Then knock it down again and then mould it into 2 loaves of bread in greased tins and bake for 1 hour in a moderate oven (350°F).

28. YEAST DOUGHNUTS

Ingredients	Quantity
Yeast	1 tsp
Sugar	1 tsp
Warm milk	120 ml

Ingredients	Quantity
Refined flour	225 gm
Egg	1
Jam	50 gm
Butter	50 gm

Method

1. Mix yeast with warm milk and 1 tsp of sugar; stand for half an hour. Add beaten egg. 2. Warm sieved flour and salt in a basin and rub in fat. 3. Pour ferment into centre of flour and mix to a soft dough. 4. Beat well with wooden spoon and leave to rise till dough doubles in bulk. 5. Knead lightly. Divide into even portions. Roll out lightly. 6. Put some jam in each and press edges together. 7. Leave doughnuts to prove until they are well-risen. 8. Fry a few at a time in smoking hot fat or oil. (about 5 minutes). 9. Drain and toss in castor sugar.

29. SALLY LUNN

Ingredients	Quantity
Refined flour	175 gm
Butter	30 gm
Milk	120 ml
Egg	1
Dried yeast	½ tsp
Salt	¼ tsp
Sugar	1 tsp
Sultanas	50 gm

Method

1. Mix yeast with warm milk and leave to ferment. 2. Sift flour into a warm basin. 3. Make a well in the centre and add melted butter. 4. Beat egg. Add salt and mix with ferment. 5. Add ferment, butter and flour mixture and beat well with a spoon or by hand to a soft consistency. 6. Put into a greased and flour cake tin. 7. Allow to rise for 1 hour. 8. Bake at 220°C to 232°C (about 425°F to 450°F) for 15–20 minutes. 9. Glaze with milk and sugar a minute before removing from oven. 10. Serve cold, sliced thickly and well buttered.

30. CHELSEA BUNS (A)

Ingredients	Quantity
Refined flour	225 gm
Butter	50 gm
Currants	50 gm
Dried yeast	1 tsp

Ingredients	Quantity
Sugar	15 gm
Milk	150 ml

Method

1. Sift flour and salt into a warm basin and keep warm. 2. Mix yeast with warm milk and 1 teaspoon sugar. 3. Rub butter into flour saving about 15 gm for brushing over. 4. Mix flour with ferment and beat well by hand. 5. Put into a warm basin and leave to rise until it doubles in bulk. 6. Turn out on to a board and knead lightly. 7. Roll into a rectangle. 8. Brush with melted butter. Sprinkle with sugar and washed and dried fruit. 9. Roll up as for Swiss roll. 10. With a sharp knife cut roll into 2.5 cm (about 1") pieces. 11. Place, close together cut side up on a baking tin. 12. Prove for about 20 minutes. 13. Bake at 230°C (about 450°F) for 15–20 minutes. 14. When cold, ice with glacé icing.

CHELSEA BUNS (B)

Ingredients	Quantity
Refined flour	225 gm
Currants or Sultanas	75 gm
Sugar	50 gm
Dried yeast	1 tsp
Milk	150 ml
Butter	50 gm
Egg	1

Method

1. Sift flour and salt into a warm basin and keep warm. 2. Clean fruit and mix with 2 dsp sugar. 3. Mix yeast with 1 teaspoon sugar, warm milk and one-third of the flour and set aside to sponge. 4. Rub 30 gm of fat into rest of flour and add remaining sugar. 5. Gradually beat in egg and then the sponge mixture. 6. Beat thoroughly by hand and keep in a warm place to rise until it doubles in bulk. 7. Knead lightly and roll out into a rectangle. 8. Brush with rest of melted butter. 9. Sprinkle fruit and sugar and roll as for a Swiss roll. 10. With a sharp knife cut 2.5 cm (about 1") thick slices and place them close together cut side up in a greased tin. 11. Prove for about 20 minutes. 12. Bake at 230°C (about 450°F) for 15–20 minutes until well-risen and golden. 13. When buns are almost cooked brush them over with sugar glaze.

Glaze: Dissolve 50 gm sugar in about 3 tbsp water. Boil for 3–4 minutes into a syrup.

31. MERINGUES

Ingredients	Quantity
Egg whites	3
Castor sugar	175 gm
Salt	a pinch
Filling	as required

Method

1. The egg whites must be very fresh. Put egg whites with salt into a basin. 2. Whisk until froth can be lifted out in a mass and will stand up on the whisk. 3. Then remove whisk and gradually fold in sugar using a metal spoon. Stir as little as possible. 4. Have a couple of baking tins turned upside down. Cover with white paper and brush over with a little olive oil. 5. For shaping the meringues have two dessertspoons and a knife standing in a jug of cold water. 6. Take up a spoonful of mixture in one spoon, smooth it out with the other spoon and lay it on prepared tin. 7. Mixture can be put into a forcing bag fitted with a plain nozzle and piped into pyramid whirls. 8. Repeat process. 9. When all meringues are ready dredge them with sugar and bake in a cool oven at 120°C to 133°C (about 250°F–275°F) for 3–4 hours or even longer. They should not be brown but firm and crisp right through. 10. When baked remove from oven and remove them from the tins by slipping a knife underneath. If the paper adheres dampen it slightly and it will soon peel off.

Filling

Any flavoured cream or frozen ice cream may be used to fill meringues. For Meringue à la Chantilly, fill with pure cream which has been whipped lightly until stiff, sweetened with fine sugar and flavoured with vanilla. Meringues should not be filled until about to be served. Small pieces of fruit may be mixed with the cream.

N.B. To get coloured meringues tint them pink, green or other pastel shades by adding one or two drops of food colour with the sugar. For chocolate meringues include 1 teaspoon cocoa with each egg white sieving it with sugar before folding it into egg whites.

32. NUTTY MERINGUES

Ingredients	Quantity
Egg whites	2
Castor sugar	125 gm
Chopped nuts	125 gm
Butter cream	

Method

1. Whisk egg whites and half the sugar until very stiff. 2. Fold in remaining sugar and most of the nuts. 3. Place mixture in spoonfuls on a very lightly oiled paper and sprinkle with a few finely chopped nuts. 4. Bake in a cool oven at 95°C (about 200°F) for several hours until crisp and dry. 5. When the meringues are cold sandwich them in pairs with buttercream.

33. NANKHATAI

Ingredients	20 small portions or 15 large
Refined flour	150 gm
Sugar	125 gm
Hydrogenated fat or	
Clarified butter	100 gm
Ammonium bicarbonate	⅛ tsp
Soda bicarbonate	each
Curds	1 tsp
Cardamoms	10
Pistachos	10 gm

Method

1. Cream fat and sugar. 2. Beat in curds. 3. Sift flour with ammonium and soda bicarbonates. 4. Add to creamed mixture and knead well with cardamom powder. 5. Divide into 20 portions. 6. Form into smooth round balls and place on a greased tray. 7. Decorate with sliced pistachio nuts. 8. Rest mixture for 1–2 hours. 9. Bake at 120°C (about 250°F) for about 25 minutes.

34. SURTI NANKHATAI

Ingredients	20 portions
Refined flour	150 gm
Soda bicarbonate	⅛ tsp
Hydrogenated fat	100 gm
Sugar	125 gm
Ammonium bicarbonate	⅛ tsp
Cardamoms	5
Pistachios	10 gm
Curds	1 tsp

Method

1. Cream fat and sugar. 2. Beat in curds. 3. Beat in soda and ammonium bicarbonates. 4. Beat in cardamom powder. 5. Knead in sieved flour. 6. Divide into small walnut-sized balls and place on a greased tray.

7. Decorate with chopped pistachio nuts and rest nankhatai at least half an hour to 1 hour before baking. 8. Bake at 120°C (about 250°F) for about 25 minutes.

35. TEA SCONES

Ingredients	8 pieces
Refined flour	225 gm
Baking powder	1 tsp
Salt	a pinch
Butter	50 gm
Sultanas	50 gm
Milk to mix	150 ml

Method

1. Sieve flour, baking powder and salt. 2. Rub in fat. Add washed sultanas. Mix well. 3. Make a well in the centre and using a fork stir in enough milk to make a light spongy dough. 4. Turn on to a floured board. Knead lightly to remove any cracks. 5. Roll out lightly to 2.5 cm (about 1") thickness. 6. Cut with a plain pastry cutter or into triangles. 7. Place on a greased floured baking sheet and glaze with beaten egg or a little milk. 8. Bake near the top of a hot oven at 230°C (about 450°F) for 10 minutes until well-risen and neatly browned. 9. Cool slightly and serve split and buttered.

N.B. Sour milk may be used instead of fresh milk.

36. DROP SCONES

Ingredients	Quantity
Refined flour	125 gm
Soda bicarb	¼ tsp
Cream of tartar	½ tsp
Salt	a pinch
Sugar	½ tbsp
Egg	1
Milk and Water	150 ml

Method

1. Sieve flour, soda, cream of tartar and salt and mix in sugar. 2. Mix to a smooth batter with egg and milk and beat well. 3. Heat a lightly greased griddle, hotplate or frying pan. 4. Drop spoonfuls of batter on to hot griddle and cook until the surface is full of bubbles and the underside golden brown. 5. Turn and cook other side. 6. If the scones are to be served cold, cool between folds of a tea cloth.

N.B. To ensure a good round shape drop mixture from tip of spoon holding it upright over griddle. If mixture is poured from side of spoon the scone will not be well-shaped.

37. BANANA DROP SCONES

Ingredients	Quantity
Refined flour	1 cup
Sour curds	¼ cup
Warm water	as required
Sugar	2 tbsp
Bananas	2

Method

1. Mix flour, curds, warm water and sugar into a thick batter. 2. Set aside till batter becomes very spongy. 3. Melt a little butter in a frying pan. 4. Make a small circle 5 cm (about 2") diameter of batter. 5. Top with sliced bananas slices and cover with more batter. 6. When properly browned on one side, turn over and brown other side. 7. Serve with honey.

38. PIKELETS

Ingredients	Quantity
Refined flour	1 cup
Baking powder	½ tsp
Salt	2 pinches
Grated Lemon and Orange rind	1 tsp each
Sugar	1 tbsp
Egg	1
Milk	½ cup

Method

1. Sift baking powder, flour and salt. Add rind and sugar. 2. Stir in beaten egg and milk. Mix into a smooth batter. 3. Drop spoonfuls on to a hot greased griddle iron or heavy frying pan. 4. Cook over steady medium heat until lightly browned underneath and set on top. 5. Turn carefully and brown other side. Lift on to clean kitchen paper. Before cooking next batch, grease griddle thoroughly. Allow to cool. 6. Spread lightly with butter before serving.

39. DATE AND WALNUT BREAD

Ingredients	Quantity
Date	225 gm
Soda bicarb	1 tsp
Salt	a pinch

Ingredients	Quantity
Butter	30 gm
Egg	1
Sugar	175 gm
Boiling water	15 ml
Refined flour	225 gm
Baking powder	1 tsp
Walnuts (shelled and chopped)	50 gm

Method

1. Clean, chop and soak dates in water and soda bicarbonate overnight.
2. Cream butter and sugar, beat in egg. 3. Add sieved flour and baking powder alternately with dates. 4. Add chopped walnuts. 5. Put mixture in a well-greased bread tin and bake in slow oven at 150°C (about 300°F) for 2 hours.

40. BANANA BREAD

Ingredients	Quantity
Butter	125 gm
Sugar	225 gm
Eggs	2
Bananas	2
Chopped walnuts	50 gm
Refined flour	225 gm
Soda bicarbonate	½ tsp
Salt	¼ tsp

Method

1. Cream butter and sugar. 2. Beat eggs well and add gradually to creamed mixture. 3. Add mashed bananas. 4. Sieve flour with soda and salt. 5. Fold flour into mixture. Add chopped nuts. 6. Pour into a greased and floured loaf tin, and bake at 160°C (about 325°F) or gas mark 3 for 1 hour.

N.B. If dry bananas are being used, chop bananas fine and soak in 30 ml water. Add a pinch of soda bicarbonate and then cook mixture for 5–10 minutes until all the moisture has been absorbed by bananas.

SANDWICHES AND LIGHT SAVOURIES

SANDWICHES AND LIGHT SAVOURIES

1. Savoury Butters
2. Cucumber and Salmon Sandwiches
3. Asparagus Sandwiches
4. Beef Sandwiches
5. Beetroot Sandwiches
6. Cheese Sandwiches
7. Cheese and Chilli Sandwiches
8. Cheese and Egg Sandwiches
9. Chicken and Ham Sandwiches
10. Cucumber Sandwiches
11. Egg Sandwiches
12. Egg and Lettuce Sandwiches
13. Ham Sandwiches
14. Harlequin Sandwiches
15. Lettuce Sandwiches
16. Mutton Sandwiches
17. Potted Meat Sandwiches
18. Prawn and Egg Sandwiches
19. Prawn Sandwiches
20. Salmon Sandwiches
21. Sardine Sandwiches (A) Sardine Sandwiches (B)
22. Sardine and Egg Sandwiches
23. Tomato Sandwiches
24. Carrot Sandwiches
25. Celery Sandwiches
26. Banana Joy
27. True Love
28. Kidney Sandwiches
29. Mint Chutney Sandwiches
30. Coriander Leaf Chutney Sandwiches
31. Clown Sandwiches
32. Donkey Sandwiches
33. Sandwich Loaf
34. Closed Sandwiches
35. Checkerboard Sandwiches
36. Ribbon Sandwiches
37. Rolled Sandwiches
38. Pinwheel Sandwiches
39. Cornucopia Sandwiches
40. Open-faced Sandwiches
41. Sandwich Plates
42. Ribbon Sandwiches
43. Suggested Spreads
44. Cheese Toast (grilled)
45. Tomato Cheese Toast
46. Welsh Rarebit (A) Welsh Rarebit (B)
47. Cheese Bouchées
48. Liver Puffs
49. Egg Pasties
50. Sardine Rolls
51. Sardine-stuffed Eggs
52. Shrimp Rarebit
53. Ham Croûtes
54. Bacon and Banana Toast
55. Savoury Meat Toast
56. Pyramid Egg on Toast
57. Cheese Toast
58. Potato and Cheese Balls
59. Potato and Sausage Rolls
60. Swiss Patties
61. Bacon Puffs
62. Cheese Splits
63. Egg Pakoras
64. Savoury Minced Meat Balls
65. Jack Baskets
66. Sombrero Snack
67. Onion Scramble

SANDWICHES

Few foods are as convenient to serve as sandwiches and since sandwiches are so popular today it is useful to know some guiding principles to provide variety and to fit the sandwich to the occasion.

Originally the term sandwich was applied to thin slices of meat placed between slices of bread and butter. Sandwiches were first introduced around the eighteenth century.

Day-old, bread is generally used for sandwiches, but fresh bread is more tasty although it is more difficult to cut. For rolled sandwiches however, the bread has to be very fresh.

A sandwich may be one of many things — it can be a delicious bit of nonsense that makes you ask for more, it can be prim and proper or staunch and hearty, or it can be an empty promise. This reminds me: have sufficient filling for each sandwich. The label should not be the only means of identification.

The type of sandwich you make will vary with the purpose for which it is used. Rapid industrialization and the faster temp of work plus the fact that many people live in the suburbs and work in the city, has meant that the use of a quickly-prepared sandwich as a meal in itself is becoming not just increasingly popular but more or less imperative. Sandwich meals are easy to prepare, not messy and can easily be a balanced meal provided a little thought and care are given to preparation. To avoid monotony variety should be stressed. Hamburgers, cheeseburgers, kabab sandwiches, hot dogs and varieties of toasted sandwiches are a few of the types that can be made when sandwiches have to serve as a complete meal. A glass of cold milk and some fruit served with these sandwiches make them as good nutritionally as the best meals. Whether the crust should be taken off or left on will again depend on the purpose. Generally the heartier the meal for which the sandwich is used, the more the reason for keeping the crust on. Relishes and pickles such as cocktail onions, pickled gherkins, cucumber etc. increase the appeal of sandwiches. They can be chopped up with the filling or sliced and put on the filling or used as garnish. Sandwiches of this type are also used for picnic baskets—sandwiches are really a godsend to a picniker—for fishing trips, for parties and for luncheon clubs, etc. Sandwiches are also popular with teenagers, youngsters, for tea parties, for barbecues and for afternoon teas at home, and to serve with drinks. Vary the pattern with the occasion.

A more delicate type of sandwich is served at a tea party. Cut the bread into very thin slices whether they are for open sandwiches or otherwise. The sandwichesshould be delicate-looking and attractive as should be the fillings used. Fillings should be mostly pastes of cream cheese, shrimp, crabmeat, salmon, chutney, peanut butter etc. For visual appeal cut bread with fancy cutters. Vary the bread as well as the filling—white bread, brown bread, rye bread rolls, etc.

When cutting bread, pile up the slices in the order in which they are cut. This is to get even and neat-looking sandwiches even if the cutting is not perfect, as very often happens when the bread is cut by hand. Use a thin long sharp knife and stand the knife in a jug of hot water. This helps to make cutting easier. Remember to butter both slices of bread in a sandwich. Fillings are usually spread only on one side. Here again variety can be provided by changing the butter—soften the butter before spreading by beating—never by melting.

When more than one variety of sandwich is needed, see that one variety is a salad sandwich such as tomato, cucumber, lettuce; another cream cheese, meat paste or fish; a third, chutney or peanut butter, beetroot paste or carrot paste. Sharp contrasts should be provided not only in types of bread but also in the fillings. This also applies to Neapolitan or Harlequin sandwiches. When making beef, mutton or chicken sandwiches never let the meat be too dry. For beef and mutton sandwiches slightly underdone rather than overdone should be the rule.

Arrangements

Variety can be provided by changing the way in which bread is cut and also by changing the arrangement. The type of filling and the method of serving the sandwich will determine the way it is to be cut. The following diagrams are illustrations of how to cut and serve sandwiches. In open spaces, place garnishes, relishes, a salad or a serving of soup. A pretty doily of lace or paper may be put on the plate. This adds to visual appeal. Cane baskets or trays could also be used as containers for display. When different types of sandwiches are served at a reception or party they should have sign flags or labels.

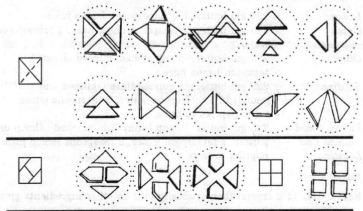

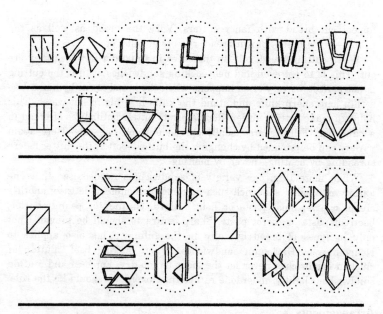

Keeping Sandwiches

After cutting, wrap in waxed paper or aluminium foil, or in bags made of transparent plastic. Do this also when displaying them on your counter. Keep the lots containing identical fillings together and label each batch. Keep sandwiches in a cool place till required but do not refrigerate. A napkin wrung in cold water and wrapped around each batch prevents drying out.

I. SAVOURY BUTTERS

Lemon	225 gm butter, 1¾ tablespoons lemon juice.
Onion	225 gm butter, 2 teaspoons onion juice, 1 tablespoon water.
Olive	225 gm butter, ¼ cup stoned, minced olives, 1 teaspoon lemon juice.
Sardine	225 gm butter, ⅓ cup sardines (skinned and pounded), 1 tablespoon water, 2 teaspoons lemon juice, paprika to taste.
Tunny, Smoked Salmon and Lobster	225 gm butter, ⅓ cup tunny fish, smoked salmon or lobster, 1 tablespoon water, 2 teaspoons lemon juice, paprika to taste.

Method

Beat butter to a cream, then gradually beat in other ingredients given in a recipe. Season to taste. Use savoury butter instead of ordinary butter in the following way:

Lemon: With fish sandwiches, especially those made of crab, lobster and all smoked fish.
Onion: With any cold meat sandwiches.
Olive: With fish, chicken or game sandwiches.
Sardine: With cress, watercress, or tomato sandwiches.
Tunny, Smoked Salmon and Lobster: With cucumber or cress sandwiches.

2. CUCUMBER AND SALMON SANDWICHES

Ingredients	Quantity
Flaked and boiled salmon	1 cup
Chopped lettuce	2 tbsp
Salt and Pepper	to taste
Chopped cucumber	½ cup
Salad dressing	
White or brown bread	

Method

Mix salmon, cucumber and lettuce, with just enough dressing to keep mixture together. Season to taste. Spread on thin slices of bread thinly buttered. Cover with shredded lettuce and buttered bread. Cut into fancy shapes.

3. ASPARAGUS SANDWICHES

Ingredients

Asparagus tips
Bread and Butter

Method

Cut asparagus tips into 5 cm (2" approx.) lengths and either split them in two or use them whole. Place each piece on a thin slice of well-buttered bread and then roll up.

N.B. If desired, sprinkle a little grated cheese over asparagus.

4. BEEF SANDWICHES

Ingredients

Cold roast beef
Bread
Prepared mustard
Butter

Method

Spread butter on some slices of bread, first mixing butter with little prepared mustard . Lay thin slices of roast beef between two slices of bread, press well together, trim, and cut into neat sandwiches.

N.B. Cold mutton, chicken, corned beef, etc. can be made into sandwiches in the same way.

5. BEETROOT SANDWICHES

Ingredients

Boiled beetroot
Grated cheese
Salt and Pepper
Butter
Prepared mustard
White or brown bread

Method

Spread some slices of white or brown bread with butter mixed with a little prepared mustard. On half the slices put a layer of thinly sliced beetroot and sprinkle over with grated cheese, salt and pepper. Cover with the remaining slices of bread and press well together. Then trim and cut into shapes.

6. CHEESE SANDWICHES

Ingredients	Quantity
Grated cheese	3 tbsp
Butter	1 tbsp
Prepared mustard	1 tbsp
Bread	

Method

Mix cheese, butter and mustard, and spread between slices of bread and butter. Press lightly together, trim and cut into fingers.

N.B. Any kind of plain biscuit can be used instead of bread and butter, and instead of grated cheese, slices of cheese may be used.

7. CHEESE AND CHILLI SANDWICHES

Ingredients

Grated cheese
Capsicum
Bread and Butter

Method

Spread butter on some slices of bread, sprinkle grated cheese and a little finely chopped capsicum over half of them, cover with remaining slices, press together, trim and cut into shape.

N.B. If capsicum is not available tips of tender green chillies may be used.

8. CHEESE AND EGG SANDWICHES

Ingredients	*Quantity*
Egg (hard-boiled)	1
Grated cheese	2 tbsp
Butter	1 tbsp
Sugar (optional)	½ tsp
Salt and Pepper	to taste
Prepared mustard	
Bread	

Method

Chop hard-boiled egg, mix it with cheese and butter and season with salt, pepper and mustard. Half a teaspoon of sugar may be added, if desired. Spread a thickish layer of this mixture between two thin slices of bread. Press together, trim and cut into triangles.

9. CHICKEN AND HAM SANDWICHES

Ingredients

Roast chicken
Butter
Boiled ham
Prepared mustard
Bread

Method

Cut some cold chicken and cold ham into very thin slices. Spread butter on thin slices of bread, mixed with a little prepared mustard. Place a slice of chicken and a slice of ham between each sandwich slices of bread, press well together, trim and cut in shapes.

10. CUCUMBER SANDWICHES

Ingredients

Cucumber
Bread and Butter (preferably whole meal bread)
Prepared mustard
Salt and Pepper

Method

Slice cucumber thin, and put slices into salt water, let them remain for a few minutes, then drain well and season with salt and pepper. Lay sliced cucumber between slices of bread and butter; spread mustard lightly on them, press together, trim and cut into neat shapes.

11. EGG SANDWICHES

Ingredients	Quantity
Eggs	2
Butter	30 gm
Pepper	Salt
Bread and Butter	

Method

Bread the eggs into a basin, beat and season with salt and pepper. Melt butter in a saucepan, add beaten egg and stir over a fire until eggs just begin to set and the mixture is thick and creamy. Turn out on a plate and allow to cool. Spread a thickish layer of this between two slices of bread and butter, trim neatly and cut in shapes.

N.B. A slice of cucumber or tomato placed between improves these sandwiches immensely.

12. EGG AND LETTUCE SANDWICHES

Ingredients	Quantity
Hard-boiled eggs	2
Lettuce	
Bread and Butter	
Salt and Pepper	to taste

Method

Shell eggs, slice them thin and season with salt and pepper. Take the inside of a lettuce, wash and dry it lightly in a towel and cut it into fine shreds. Prepare the slices of bread and butter, place the egg on half the slices, put a little shredded lettuce on top, and cover with the remaining slices of bread. Press together, trim and cut into shapes.

N.B. Watercress may be used instead of lettuce.

13. HAM SANDWICHES

Ingredients	Quantity
Cooked ham	
Prepared mustard	1 tsp

Ingredients	Quantity
Butter	1 tsp
Bread	

Method

Mix butter and mustard, and spread it on thin slices of bread. Lay thin slices of ham between slices of bread, press well together and cut into triangles.

14. HARLEQUIN SANDWICHES

Ingredients

Bread and Butter

Different fillings

Method

Spread butter on slices of bread and then put them together in 5 or 6 layers spreading each with a different filling, such as—cream, cheese, chopped beetroot (boiled), shredded lettuce, chopped hard-boiled egg, salmon paste, sliced cucumber, etc. Press well together and wrap in a damp cloth. When ready to serve, cut into fingers.

15. LETTUCE SANDWICHES

Ingredients	Quantity
Hard-boiled egg yolks	3
Chilli vinegar	
Butter	1 dsp
Crisp lettuce	
Salt	to taste
Bread	

Method

Mash egg yolks, season with salt and a little chilli vinegar and mix with butter into a paste and spread on thin slices of bread. Place a crisp, fresh lettuce leaf between two slices of prepared bread. Press together and cut into shape with a sharp knife.

16. MUTTON SANDWICHES

Ingredients

Cold roast mutton

Butter

Prepared mustard

Bread

Method

Spread mixed little prepared mustard with a butter on some slices of bread. Lay thin slices of roast mutton between two slices of bread, press well together and cut into neat sandwiches.

17. POTTED MEAT SANDWICHES

Potted meats that are sold in tins and jars are very convenient for making sandwiches. Spread the paste thinly between sandwiches of buttered bread, press lightly together and cut into any fancy shape.

N.B. A little butter and mustard mixed with the paste improves the sandwich.

18. PRAWN AND EGG SANDWICHES

Ingredients	Quantity
Boiled prawns	a few
Hard-boiled eggs	2
Dry chillies (powdered)	a pinch
Lime juice	a squeeze
Bread and Butter	

Method

Chop prawns and add chopped eggs. Season to taste, add the butter and mix well. Spread this paste between slices of bread and butter, press together, and cut into triangular shapes.

19. PRAWN SANDWICHES

Ingredients	Quantity
Chopped prawns	3
Mayonnaise sauce	
Anchovy essence	few drops
Pickled gherkins	
Salt and Pepper	to taste
Bread and Butter	

Method

Chop or cut some boiled prawns into small pieces. Put them into a basin and moisten with mayonnaise sauce. Season with salt and pepper and add a few drops of anchovy essence. Butter some thin slices of bread, spread prawn mixture on half of them with the, sprinkle over with a few chopped gherkins and cover with remaining slices of bread. Press together, trim and cut into shapes.

20. SALMON SANDWICHES

Ingredients	Quantity
Salmon	2 tbsp
Seasoning	to taste

Ingredients	Quantity
Butter	1 dsp
Bread and Butter	

Method

Remove any skin and bones from salmon, put it into a small bowl and break it up with a fork. Season to taste, add butter and mix well. Put this paste on thin slices of bread and butter. Place a fresh, crisp lettuce leaf between two slices of prepared bread, press together, trim and cut into fingers.

21. SARDINE SANDWICHES (A)

Ingredients

Sardines
Butter
Mustard
Salt
Powdered dry chillies
Lime juice or Vinegar
Bread and Butter

Method

Skin and bone sardines and mix them into a paste with a little butter; add mustard, salt, a pinch of powdered dry chillies and a squeeze of lime juice or a little vinegar. Spread this paste between thin slices of bread and butter, trim neatly and cut in shapes.

N.B. A thin slice of cucumber may be placed between, if desired.

SARDINE SANDWICHES (B)

Ingredients	Quantity
Sardines (boned)	3 tbsp
Butter	1 dsp
Pepper	to taste
Bread and Butter	

Method

Skin and bone sardines and mix them into a paste with the butter, and season with pepper. Spread paste between slices of buttered bread, press together and cut into neat sandwiches.

22. SARDINE AND EGG SANDWICHES

Ingredients	Quantity
Sardines	6

Ingredients	Quantity
Hard-boiled egg	1
Butter	1 tbsp
Salt and Pepper	to taste
Brown bread and Butter	

Method

Skin and debone sardines and mix into a paste with butter. Add egg yolk and season to taste with salt and pepper. Butter some slices of brown bread, spread sardine mixture on half of them, sprinkle with finely chopped egg white and cover with remaining bread. Press together, trim and cut into shapes.

23. TOMATO SANDWICHES

Ingredients	Quantity
Tomatoes	1 or 2
Vinegar	1 tsp
Salad oil	2 tsp
Powdered dry chillies	a pinch
Salt and Pepper	to taste
Bread and Butter	to taste

Method

Choose good, ripe tomatoes, put them into a basin, pour boiling water over them and leave for a few minutes. Then lift them out and remove skin. Put tomatoes into a bowl, add vinegar, salad oil, powdered chillies, salt and pepper and mash everything together. Spread this paste between thin slices of bread and butter, press lightly and cut into fingers.

24. CARROT SANDWICHES

Grate and mix some young raw carrots with white sugar, olive oil, vinegar and pepper. Spread between slices of white bread and butter.

25. CELERY SANDWICHES

Grate some fresh celery. Mix with a little grated cheese and spread between slices of white bread and butter.

26. BANANA JOY

Madeira cake, not too new, forms the base of this sandwich. Cut into slices about 7.6 cm (about 3") square. Spread bottom slice with strawberry jam. Mash some very ripe bananas and mix with whipped cream. Spread this thickly over the layer of jam and cover with plain slice of cake. Decorate with a circle of banana and half a glacé cherry.

27. TRUE LOVE

Wash a sheep's heart and stew until tender. Chop meat fine and spread while hot on a slice of buttered toast. Season and cover with another buttered toast. Pack this layer with some good veal stuffing, cover with a third piece of toast and serve.

28. KIDNEY SANDWICHES

Mince some cold cooked kidney. Sprinkle with mushrooms and ketchup and spread between slices of either brown or white bread and butter.

29. MINT CHUTNEY SANDWICHES

Ingredients	Quantity
Mint	60 gm
Green chillies	2
Onions	40 gm
Pomegranate seeds	20 gm
Salt	Sugar
Bread and Butter	

Method

Grind together mint, green chillies, onion, pomegranate seeds, and add salt and sugar to taste. Spread mint chutney between buttered slices of bread. Trim and cut into desired shapes.

30. CORIANDER LEAF CHUTNEY SANDWICHES

Ingredients	Quantity
Bread and Butter	
Green chillies	2
Coriander leaves	1 bunch
Coconut	¼ (50 gm)
Onions	15 gm
Lime juice	½ tsp
Salt	to taste

Method

Chop coriander leaves. Remove hard stems and stalks. Grind into a smooth paste with onions, coconut, green chillies and salt. Add lime juice to taste. Spread paste between thin slices of bread and butter. Trim neatly and cut into desired shapes.

31. CLOWN SANDWICHES

Cut 10.5 cm (about 4") circles from 4 slices of white bread, 9 cm (about 3½") circles from 4 slices of wholemeal bread and 6.3 cm (about 2½") circles from 4 slices of white bread. Spread peanut butter on brown circles and place spread side down on the large white circles. Spread peanut butter on small circles and place spread side down on the brown circles. Cut stuffed olives into slices to make 8 olive eyes and place them on the small white bread circles. Use ripe olive slices as eyebrows; triangular-shaped pieces of green pepper as noses; half-moons of pimento as mouths. For the clowns' collars, pipe softened cream cheese through a pastry tube. For the hats, use yellow cheese spread formed into triangles, topping them off with parsley tassles. Makes 4 sandwiches.

32. DONKEY SANDWICHES

Cut crusts off 6 slices wholemeal bread and 2 slices white bread. With a donkey cookie cutter or a pattern, cut out a donkey from 2 slices white bread and 2 slices brown bread. Fit white bread donkeys into cut-out spaces in brown bread. Spread 4 slices of brown bread with cream cheese and jam. Place donkey slices on top of brown slices. Decorate each donkey with ripe olive slices as ears and ripe olive slice as tail. Use tiny slices of pimento as mouth and a silver ball as an eye. Make donkey's hooves and saddle from finely chopped parsley. Makes 4 sandwiches.

33. SANDWICH LOAF

Take a day-old uncut loaf of white sandwich bread and slice it horizontally, making seven or eight long even slices 1.5 cm (about ½") thick. Remove crusts. Spread one slice with creamed butter and cover it with chutney. Cover with the next slice. Butter top and spread a layer of creamed cheese, spread next slice with mashed-up cooked beetroot, and the next with hard-boiled egg yolks mashed-up with mayonnaise. Repeat process. Stake slices neatly. Cover top and sides of loaf with soft creamed potatoes mixed with cream cheese or only cream cheese. Garnish with rosettes of cream cheese tinted with 2–3 drops of pink or green food colour and hard-boiled egg whites. Decorate with slices of cucumber and prawns. Chill and serve on a bed of salad.

N.B. Chicken and mayonnaise, shrimp, salmon, devilled eggs, sardines, liver, mint chutney or salads can be used as fillings. Creamed cottage cheese can be used to cover using red radish and devilled prawns to decorate.

34. CLOSED SANDWICHES

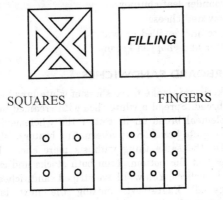

SQUARES   FINGERS

Butter untrimmed slices. Mark divisions on one slice and cut out. Put filling on second slice. If insets are to be put into openings (pimento, green, pepper, parsley, etc.) the filling need not be colourful. If a coloured filling is used, leave insets so that filling shows through. Suggested fillings.:

Egg salad — pimento inset.
Ham and pickle relish.
Olives and (hard-boiled) egg white.
Cream cheese and cocktail onions.
Chicken salad.

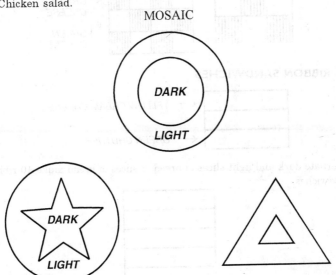

MOSAIC

Liver, bacon and onion.
Mint or coriander leaf chutney.
Date chutney and cheese.
Tomato paste and devilled prawns.
Peanut butter and chopped bacon.

35. CHECKERBOARD SANDWICHES

To make checkerboards, take three slices of white bread and three slices of wholemeal bread. Spread a white slice with creamed butter and place a slice of wholemeal bread on it. Butter the wholemeal slice and add another slice of white bread. Keep alternating buttered slices till the six are stacked. Do the same thing with six more slices, but start with wholemeal bread at the bottom. Trim both stacks and cut each pile in 1.3 cm (about ½") slices. You will have striped sandwiches. Butter them. lay the strips all East–West, putting the next layer of strips North–South. Chill. Slice them against or across the stripe. Sandwiches can be spread with savoury butter or coloured cream cheese instead of plain butter, different coloured jam, or mint, coriander leaf or date chutney, or fish and shrimp pastes with anchovy essence. The fillings must be very smooth. Caution—fillings must not be put on too heavily. Can also be rolled into a cornucopia.

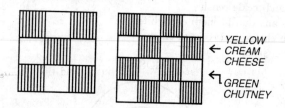

← YELLOW CREAM CHEESE

← GREEN CHUTNEY

36. RIBBON SANDWICHES

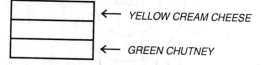

← YELLOW CREAM CHEESE

← GREEN CHUTNEY

Alternate dark and light slices of bread. 3 slices of bread make 10 ribbon sandwiches.

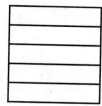

37. ROLLED SANDWICHES

Cheese filling — plain or roasted

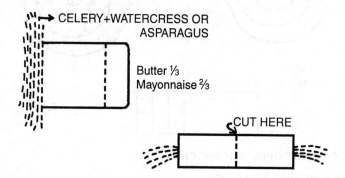

38. PINWHEEL SANDWICHES

Use unsliced bread. Cut sandwich loaf in half. Cut each half into slices lengthwise. Trim crust. Spread slices with butter and then filling. Roll firmly lengthwise. Seal edge with butter. Slice down through the roll. Each half loaf makes 6 rolls—each roll 6 sandwich cuts—72 sandwiches per loaf.

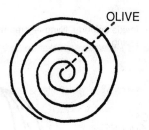

1. Spread pimento cheese and with cream cheese and olives on ⅓ or ½ of slice.
2. Spread any desired filling and roll stuffed olive-ends cut off and placed close together in centre. The slice of olive will be in the centre of the roll.

3. Spread light coloured filling. Place 3 strips of green pepper or pimento and roll.
4. Lay green pepper and pimento strips at intervals all along a slice. Roll.

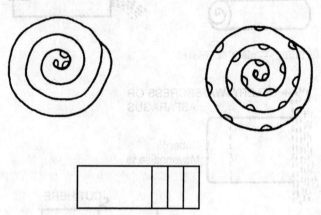

39. CORNUCOPIA SANDWICHES

Slice bread thin. Trim crusts.

1. Spread flavoured butter, roll into a cornucopia shape and seal with butter. Fill with a thin rolled slice of ham or with chopped meat and celery or fish and celery filling with a parsley garnish.
2. Spread white or green chutney, roll with a center of tomato or green pepper strip.

40. OPEN-FACED SANDWICHES

Inside colourful filling — cream cheese piping.

PIPING OF
CREAM CHEESE

STRIP OF TOMATO

THIN SLICE
OF SARDINE

CREAM CHEESE

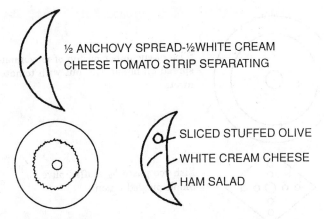

½ ANCHOVY SPREAD-½WHITE CREAM
CHEESE TOMATO STRIP SEPARATING

SLICED STUFFED OLIVE

WHITE CREAM CHEESE

HAM SALAD

Rounds of breads—with colourful tops and cream cheese piped around.
1. Thin slice of tomato cut with the same cutter used to cut bread. Chopped parsley dusted on edge of cream cheese.
2. Beet and horseradish—piping of egg yolk.
3. Raspberry or currant jam and cream cheese.

Round of bread with seasoned egg yolk spread with overlapping slices of ripe olives—centre piping of egg yolk.

Pale green chutney on bread—rounds made of slices of beef or ham, spread with cottage cheese and sliced like a jam roll. Parsley trim.

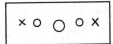

Fish and tomato paste, thin slices of pickled onion. Rosettes of red radish.

Spread on diamond-shaped bread—green pepper strip for stems—carrot flowers with a tiny white centre, small flowers cut from red chilli skin or candied cherry.

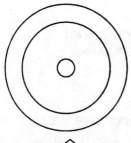

Slice of cucumber on top of mayonnaise spread on bread. Cut out with tomato inset.

Fish roe paste ½ stuffed olive. Small pickled onion.

Strip of salted herring or any filling. ½ slice stuffed olive.

Shrimp
Star of cream cheese
Cream cheese and horseradish

Yellow egg yolk
Red chilli skin
Strip of green pepper

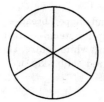

Brown bread sliced 1.05 cm. (about ⅜") thick—cut in sixths and put together with white cottage cheese.

41. SANDWICH PLATES

Use flat glass or silver or flat wooden trays. Dark blue glass is especially attractive.

Tray 1.

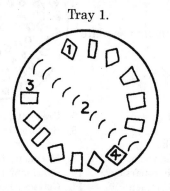

1. Cornucopias with yellow cream cheese and pimento garnish.
2. Pinwheels overlapping and alternating—white with pale green and white with pale blue-pimento centre.
3. Finger sandwiches—blue cream cheese with slices of onion.
4. Finger sandwiches—pale green cream cheese with ham and cottage cheese rounds.

Tray 2.
On silver tray

1. Rolled celery and watercress on alternate dark and white bread.
2. Triangles of wholemeal bread with cheese filling.
3. Rounds of chutney sandwiches.
4. Crescents with yellow backgrounds, pimento strips and white cream cheese piping.

Tray 3.
On dark blue glass plate

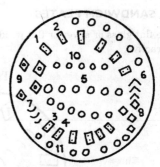

1. Rolled ham and cheese
   sandwiches.
2. Ribbon sandwiches.
3. Open finger sandwiches.
4. Finger sandwiches–parsley
   in centre cutout, pimento in
   both ends.
5. Tomato open-face sandwiches
   with parsley dusted edges.
6. Overlapping checker-boards.

7. Crescents, open.
8. Buttered rounds of bread
   with slices of salami on top.
9. Mosaic in diamonds.
10. Overlapping pinwheels.
11. Cottage cheese balls rolled in
    chopped parsley and dusted
    with paprika and watercress
    between.

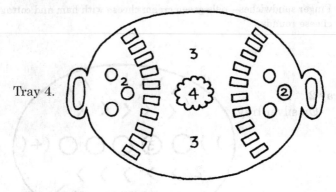

Tray 4.

1. Rows of ribbon sandwiches.
2. Open-faced, watercress between.
3. Open-faced, pinwheels, mosaics—all round.
4. Watercress with radishes.

Tray 5.

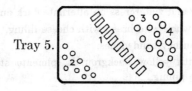

1. Ribbon sandwiches
2. Open-faced sandwiches
3. Pinwheels
4. Watercress and Cheeseball.

42. RIBBON SANDWICHES

Ingredients

White bread
Wholemeal bread
Cheese
Chives
Fish paste
Tomatoes
Lettuce
Butter

Method

Slice bread. Trim crusts. Butter. Thinly grate cheese. Mix with chopped chives, and cream well. Spread mixture on a slice of bread, cover with a slice of wholemeal bread. Spread a layer of fish paste mixed with finely chopped pieces of tomatoes. Top with a slice of white bread, cover firmly with greaseproof paper. When ready to serve cut into strips lengthwise. Place sandwiches wide side up on a serving plate and garnish with shredded lettuce.

43. SUGGESTED SPREADS

Orange butter. 125 gm butter, 2 tsp orange juice, ½ tsp grated orange rind.

Honey butter. 125 gm butter, 350 gm honey. For blending, butter and honey must be slightly warm. Beat well.

Date butter. 125 gm butter, 100 gm chopped pitted dates and a dash of lime juice.

Curry butter. 125 gm butter, 1 tsp curry powder, ½ tsp salt and a few drops of onion juice.

Mustard. 125 gm butter, 1 tsp mustard.

Avocado. 125 gm butter, ¼ cup mustard, avocado, a little minced onion, a dash of lime juice.

Celery and Cheese. 125 gm butter, 125 gm cheese, 2 tsp cream, ½ tsp mustard, and 75 gm chopped celery heart.

Horseradish. 125 gm butter, 2 tbsp grated radish and salt.

Sardines. 125 gm butter, 1 tin sardines, dash of lime juice, ½ tsp Worcester sauce, and a pinch of mustard.

Chicken. 225 gm cooked chopped chicken, 50 gm celery, ⅓ cup mayonnaise, 2 tbsp chopped olives.

Chicken and Green pepper. Replace olives with finely chopped green pepper. The seeds must be removed and the green pepper rinsed several times in cold water. Salt to taste.

Chicken and Ham. 125 gm cooked chopped chicken, 125 gm ham, 75 gm celery, ⅓ cup mayonnaise, 2 tbsp grated radish, ½ tsp lime juice, salt to taste.

Corned beef and Lettuce. 125 gm corned beef, 55 gm finely shredded lettuce, a few pieces of pickled cucumber, salt to taste.

Ham. 125 gm chopped cooked ham, ¼ cup salad dressing, 2 tsp minced onion, dash of salt, pepper to taste.

Bacon and Peanut butter. 2. rashers chopped grilled bacon, ½ cup peanut butter.

Peanut butter and Egg. 2 chopped hard-boiled eggs, 30 gm chopped celery, 2 tsp finely chopped onion, ½ cup peanut butter.

Carrots and Peanut. 125 gm grated raw carrot, 55 gm finely chopped roasted peanuts, 1 tbsp chopped pickled vegetables, ¼ cup. mayonnaise.

Egg and Bacon. 2 chopped hard-boiled eggs, 55 gm grilled chopped bacon, 3 tbsp salad dressing.

Ham and Egg. 55 gm devilled ham, 2 chopped hard-boiled eggs, 2 tbsp mayonnaise. ½ tsp mustard.

Shrimp and Egg. 125 gm chopped cooked shrimp, 2 chopped hard- boiled eggs, ¼ cup mayonnaise, and 30 gm chopped red radish.

Date and Fig. Combine ⅓ cup (about 60 gm) minced dates, and ⅓ cup minced dried figs with 2 tbsp chopped nuts, 2 tbsp castor sugar and 2 tbsp orange juice.

44. CHEESE TOAST (grilled)

1. Keep a slice of buttered toast ready.
2. Spread a good layer of chopped or grated cheese.
3. Place under a hot grill until cheese melts and is lightly browned on top (2–3 minutes).

N.B. Short quick cooking is essential.

45. TOMATO CHEESE TOAST

Ingredients	Quantity
Cheese	100 gm
Thick milk or	
Evaporated milk	½ cup
Tomato purée	1 cup
Onions	15 gm
Cayenne pepper	a small pinch

Ingredients	Quantity
Buttered toast	
or Cream crackers	
Cornflour (optional)	1 tsp

Method

1. In a double boiler, melt cheese (grated) in milk. 2. Add tomato purée and finely chopped onion. Add cayenne pepper and test for seasoning. Cook till thick. 3. If desired, a teaspoon of cornflour can be mixed with the tomato purée. Serve hot on hot buttered toast or on cream crackers.

46. WELSH RAREBIT (A)

Ingredients	Quantity
Grated cheese	50 gm
Vinegar	1 tsp
Milk	1 tbsp
Dry mustard	½ tsp
Margarine	15 gm
Salt, Pepper and Cayenne pepper	a pinch each

Method

1. Mix dry ingredients together. 2. Mix to a paste with milk. 3. Add vinegar and mix well. 4. Spread on buttered toast. 5. Place under a hot grill and cook until golden brown on top (2–3 minutes).

WELSH RAREBIT (B)

Ingredients	Quantity
Cheese	75 gm
Margarine	50 gm
Egg	1
Worcester sauce	1 tsp

Method

1. Melt margarine. 2. Add cheese, beaten egg and sauce and mix well. 3. Cook very lightly over gentle heat for 2–3 minutes. 4. Spread mixture on a slice of toast. 5. Place under a hot grill until golden brown on top (about 2–3 minutes). 6. Short quick cooking is essential. Longer cooking will make the cheese hard and tough.

47. CHEESE BOUCHÉES

Ingredients	Quantity
Cheese	125 gm
Refined flour	75 gm

Ingredients	Quantity
Eggs	2
Salt and Pepper	to taste
Oil	for frying

Method

1. Sieve flour with salt and pepper. 2. Add finely grated cheese. 3. Stir in well beaten egg yolks, and mix well. 4. Stand mixture for at least half an hour. 5. Heat oil. 6. While oil is heating fold in stiffly beaten egg whites lightly but thoroughly. 7. Drop teaspoonfuls of the mixture into hot oil. 8. Drain on absorbent paper and serve on a warmed dish on a folded napkin.

N.B. Do not allow the bouchees to fry too long or they will become tough.

48. LIVER PUFFS

Ingredients	Quantity
Shortcrust pastry	175 gm
Cooked liver	125 gm
Streaky bacon (cooked)	4 rashers
Breadcrumbs (fresh)	30 gm
Onions (finely chopped)	30 gm
Thick brown gravy	1 tsp
Beaten egg for brushing pastry	

Method

1. Roll out pastry. Cut into rounds with biggest pastry cutter. 2. Mince liver and bacon. Mix with breadcrumbs, onion and gravy. 3. Place a little on each round of pastry. 4. Brush edges with beaten egg. Fold over and seal edges well together. Crimp edges to make them attractive. 5. Glaze with beaten egg and bake for 30 minutes in a moderately hot oven (200°C or about 425°F) until brown and crisp.

49. EGG PASTIES

Ingredients	Quantity
Shortcrust pastry	175 gm
Hard-boiled eggs	4
Melted butter	15 gm
Parsley (chopped)	1 dsp
Nutmeg	a pinch
Thyme (chopped)	1 tsp
Lime rind (grated)	½ tsp
Salt and Pepper	to taste
Grated cheese	50 gm

Method

1. Mix parsley, thyme, lime rind, nutmeg, salt and pepper. 2. Cut hard-boiled eggs into halves. 3. Brush with melted butter and roll in parsley mixture. 4. Roll out pastry thin and cut into ovals. 5. Place an egg half on an oval. Dampen edges and place another oval on top. Press edges together to seal well. 6. Place on a greased baking tray. Sprinkle with grated cheese and bake for 20–30 minutes in a moderately hot oven (220°C or about 425°F) until brown and crisp.

50. SARDINE ROLLS

Ingredients	Quantity
Puff pastry or Shortcrust pastry	175 gm
Worcester sauce	1 tsp
Salt and Pepper	to taste
Sardines	1 tin
Fresh breadcrumbs	30 gm
Lemon juice or Vinegar	a dash
Beaten egg	

Method

1. Roll out pastry into a strip about 13 cm (about 5") wide. 2. Mash sardines, after removing backbones. 3. Add salt, pepper, a little of the oil, breadcrumbs, Worcester sauce and lemon juice or vinegar. 4. Spread along the pastry. Dampen edges with egg. Fold over. Seal well. 5. Cut into even-sized pieces. Glaze with remaining egg. 6. Place on greased tray and cook in a hot oven at 250°C (about 475°F) for 20 minutes if puff pastry is used, or at 220°C (about 425°F) for 20 minutes if shortcrust pastry is used.

51. SARDINE-STUFFED EGGS

Ingredients	Quantity
Eggs	6
Sardines	1 tin (about 100 gm)
Mayonnaise sauce	½ cup
Onions (finely chopped)	1 tsp
Green chilli (finely chopped or a pinch of chilli powder)	1
Lime juice	1 tsp
Salt	to taste

Method

1. Hard-boil eggs, crack and cool immediately. (this is to prevent a blue rim forming around egg yolk.) 2. Shell and cut into halves. Remove the

616 | MODERN COOKERY FOR TEACHING AND THE TRADE / II

yolk. 3. Drain sardines. 4. Mash yolks and sardines with the rest of ingredients. 5. Refill whites, and serve on a bed of lettuce.

52. SHRIMP RAREBIT

Ingredients	Quantity
Fresh cleaned shrimps	225 gm
Eggs	3
Butter	30 gm
Top of milk	2 tbsp
Salt and Pepper	to taste
Buttered toast	4 slices
Cayenne pepper	a pinch
Chopped parsley	

Method

1. Boil cleaned shrimps. Cut each into two. 2. Melt butter. Add top of milk and seasoning. 3. Beat eggs and stir in. 4. Add shrimps and cook until creamy and thick. 5. Spread thickly on hot buttered toast and sprinkle with chopped parsley and cayenne pepper. Serve at once.

53. HAM CROÛTES

Ingredients	Quantity
Cooked ham	25 gm
Butter or Margarine	30 gm
Hard-boiled eggs	2
Buttered toast	4 slices
Chopped parsley	
Salt and Pepper	to taste

Method

1. Shell and chop eggs and keep them hot. 2. Melt margarine in a saucepan. When hot add chopped ham, seasoning and parsley. Heat through. 3. Spread thickly on hot buttered toast and top with chopped eggs. Serve at once.

54. BACON AND BANANA TOAST

Ingredients	Quantity
Buttered toast	4 slices
Bacon	4 rashers
Bananas	2
Refined flour	a little
Salt and Pepper	to taste

Method

1. Peel and slice bananas lengthwise (4 pieces). 2. Make toast and fry bacon. Keep hot. 3. Season bananas with salt and pepper. 4. Dip in flour and fry in bacon fat. 5. Place a bacon rasher on each piece of toast. Lay bananas on top and serve very hot.

55. SAVOURY MEAT TOAST

Ingredients	Quantity
Cooked meat	225 gm
Breadcrumbs	60 gm
Thick brown gravy or Tomato sauce	75 ml
Curry powder	1 tsp
Salt and Pepper	to taste
Buttered toast	4 slices

Method

1. Mince cold meat, removing any fat or gristle. 2. Put into a saucepan with all the other ingredients except toast and heat through. 3. Spread thickly on hot buttered toast and serve at once.

56. PYRAMID EGG ON TOAST

Ingredients	Quantity
Eggs	4
Round toast	4
Grilled tomatoes	2
Thick white sauce	150 ml
Grated cheese	60 gm
Seasoning	

Method

1. Hard-boil eggs. Cool quickly in cold water. Shell. 2. Cut a small slice off base of each egg so that it can stand firmly. 3. Place grilled slices of tomato on toast and season. 4. Stand eggs in centre of each round. 5. Stir in two-thirds of the cheese into sauce. 6. Coat each egg with sauce. 7. Sprinkle remaining cheese on top. 8. Brown quickly in a moderately hot oven at 220°C (about 425°F)

57. CHEESE TOAST

Ingredients	Quantity
Grated Kalimpong or sharp cheese	50 gm
Worcester sauce	½ tsp
Mustard	1 tsp

Ingredients	Quantity
Refined flour/Cornflour	1 tbsp
Egg (optional)	1
Cayenne pepper or Chili powder	to taste
Milk or Water	1 dsp
Bread	
Fat	for frying

Method

1. Mix all ingredients. Spread on slices of bread. 2. Cut into rectangles or triangles. 3. Deep fry and serve piping hot.

N.B. For variations, use ground garlic or ginger, chopped coriander leaves or green chillies and/or tomato sauce instead of milk and water.

58. POTATO AND CHEESE BALLS

Ingredients	Quantity
Potatoes	450 gm
Butter	15 gm
Grated cheese	125 gm
Salt and Pepper	to taste
Mustard	a pinch
Egg yolks	2
Refined flour	a little
Fat	for frying

Method

1. Boil peeled potatoes in salted water. 2. Drain and dry over fire. 3. Mash very smoothly adding butter, grated cheese and seasoning. 4. Bind with beaten egg yolk. 5. Cool and roll mixture into balls. 6. Roll lightly in flour and fry in hot fat till golden brown. 7. Serve sprinkled over with more cheese on a hot dish.

59. POTATO AND SAUSAGE ROLLS

Ingredients	Quantity
Sausages	225 gm
Mashed potatoes	450 gm
Egg yolks	2
Refined flour	1 dsp
Eggs	2
Breadcrumbs	60 gm
Fat	for frying

Method

1. Prepare mashed potatoes. Bind with egg and allow to cool. 2. Grill or fry sausages. 3. Cut lengthwise and then across each sausage. 4. Cover these pieces with mashed potatoes and coat with flour. 5. Roll each in egg and breadcrumbs and fry in hot fat till golden brown.

60. SWISS PATTIES

Ingredients	Quantity
Tomatoes (large and firm)	3 (350–450 gm)
Hard-boiled egg	1
Grated cheese	60 gm
Stale bread	4 slices
Milk	a little
Margarine	30 gm
Breadcrumbs	15 gm
Salt, Pepper and Mustard	to taste

Method

1. Shell and chop hard-boiled egg. 2. Remove crusts from bread and dip quickly in and out of milk. 3. Brush over with melted margarine. 4. Toss in breadcrumbs and brown in a moderately hot oven 220°C (about 425°F). 5. Arrange some tomato slices on each piece 6. Sprinkle a little chopped egg over. 7. Season with salt, pepper and mustard. 8. Sprinkle cheese on top and return to oven to brown cheese and lightly cool.

61. BACON PUFFS

Ingredients	Quantity
Refined flour	30 gm
Baking powder	⅛ tsp
Egg	1
Salt and Pepper	to taste
Milk	to mix
Cooked bacon	2 rashers
Fat	for frying

Method

1. Sieve flour and seasoning into a basin. 2. Separate white and yolk of egg. 3. Drop yolk into sieved flour and mix to a stiffish batter with milk. 4. Add chopped bacon. 5. Whisk egg white stiffly. 6. Fold lightly into batter. 7. Drop spoonfuls into hot fat. 8. When golden brown, turn and brown other side. Drain on absorbent paper and serve hot.

62. CHEESE SPLITS

Ingredients	Quantity
Refined flour	225 gm
Baking powder	1½ tsp
Salt	¼ tsp
Mustard	¼ tsp
Margarine	60 gm
Grated cheese	75 gm
Milk	150 ml
Filling	
Any hot savoury filling–	
Fish, Meat, Egg or Vegetable.	

Method

1. Sieve flour, baking powder; salt and mustard into a bowl. 2. Rub in margarine very lightly. 3. Add grated cheese and mix with milk into a rather slack dough. 4. Turn out on to a floured board. Lightly knead to get rid of cracks. 5. Roll or pat it out 0.7 cm (about ¼") thick. 6. Cut out into rounds with a 6.5 cm (about 2½") plain cutter. 7. Place on a greased tray and cook for 15 minutes in a hot oven at 249°C (475°F approx.) 8. Split while hot and put in hot savoury filling.

63. EGG PAKORAS

Ingredients	Quantity
Hard-boiled egg	4
Chilli powder	1.4 tsp
Water	50 ml
Bengal gram flour	50 gm
Salt	to taste
Soda bicarbonate	a pinch
Oil	to fry

Method

1. Cool eggs in cold water quickly. 2. Shell and cut into quarters. 3. Prepare batter with gram flour, water, salt and chilli powder and soda. Beat well to a smooth consistency. 4. Dip pieces of egg into batter and deep fry till golden brown on allround. 5. Drain on absorbent paper and serve hot with tomato sauce or green chutney.

64. SAVOURY MINCED MEAT BALLS

Ingredients	36
Minced meat	225 gm
Onions	200 gm

Ingredients	36
Ginger	5 gm
Salt	to taste
Tomatoes	125 gm
Soda bicarbonate	1 tsp
Lime	1
Green chillies	3
Bengal gram flour	225 gm
Fat	to fry
Water	200 ml

Method

1. Boil minced meat in just enough water to cook it till tender but dry.
2. Grind green chillies and ginger into a fine paste. 3. Mix minced meat, ground ingredients, salt, finely chopped onions, gram flour, lime juice, chopped tomatoes and enough water to form a thick batter. Beat well until smooth and light. 4. Stand for 15 minutes. Add soda. Mix well. 5. Heat fat. Fry tablespoonfuls of mixture till golden brown allround. 6. Drain on absorbent paper and serve hot.

65. JACK BASKETS

Take well-matured jack bulbs, clean well, cut off a piece from tip, remove seed and serrate edge. Level it so that the bulb can stand. Heat oil in a deep frying pan. Add jack bulbs and fry till crisp. Drain. Fill with minced meat or vegetables or the following filling:

Ingredients	Quantity
Hard-boiled eggs	4
Butter	1 tbsp
Grated cheese	30 gm
Green chillies (finely chopped)	a few
Ham	15 gm
Mayonnaise	
Salt and Pepper	to taste
Celery stems	

Method

1. Sieve 2 hard-boiled egg yolks. Add 1 tbsp butter, grated cheese, finely chopped green chillies (with seeds removed) and set aside. 2. Chop ham, 2 hard-boiled eggs and mix with a little mayonnaise, mustard, salt and pepper. 3. Fill jack bulbs. Pipe flowers over with first egg yolk mixture. Form handles with celery stems.

66. SOMBRERO SNACK

Ingredients	4
Onions	225 gm
Butter	60 gm
Marmite or	
Bovril	1 tsp
Bread	4 slices
Butter for toast	30 gm
Processed cheese	4 slices

Method

1. Peel and slice onions. Fry lightly in melted fat until golden brown and tender. 2. Toast bread. Butter while still hot. Spread with Marmite or Bovril. 3. Top each slice with cooked onion. Cover with slices of cheese. 4. Put under a medium grill until cheese melts and turns golden brown.

67. ONION SCRAMBLE

Ingredients	4
Bread or	4 slices
Crumpets	4
Butter	
Scramble:	
Onions	200 gm
Butter	30 gm
Eggs	4
Milk	2 tbsp
Salt, Pepper and Paprika	to taste

Method

1. Toast bread or crumpets. Butter well and set aside. 2. Peel and chop onions. Melt butter. Add onions and stir well. Cover and cook gently for 5 minutes. 3. Beat eggs with milk, adding salt and pepper to taste. 4. Add eggs and stir until thickened but not dry. 5. Spread scrambled egg on toasts, sprinkle with a little paprika and serve immediately.

PICKLES, PRESERVES, CHUTNEYS AND BEVERAGES

PICKLES

1. Gujarati Pickle
2. Whole Mango Pickle
3. Maharashtra Pickle
4. Marwari Pickle (A)
   Marwari Pickle (B)
   Marwari Picle (C)
5. Punjabi Pickle (A)
   Punjabi Pickle (B)
6. Avakkai (A)
   Avakkai (B)
   Avakkai (C)
   Avakkai (D)
7. Ginger Mango Pickle
8. Garlic Mango Pickle
9. Mango Magaya
10. Mango Mustard Pickle
11. Mysore Mango Pickle
12. Madras Mangai Oorkai
13. Dried Mango Pickle
14. Adamanga (A)
    Adamanga (B)
15. Kanni Manga
16. Kadukumanga
17. Mango Kasoondi (A)
    Mango Kasoondi (B)
    Mango Kasoondi (C)
18. Mango Relish
19. Lime Pickle (A)
    Lime Pickle (B)
    Lime Pickle (C)
    Lime Pickle (D)
    Lime Pickle (E)
20. Lime Pickle (sweet) (A)
    Lime Pickle (sweet) (B)
21. Lime Pickle (white) (A)
    Lime Pickle (white) (B)
22. Limes In Vinegar
23. Lime Pickle with Mustard
24. Lime Pickle
    (Maharashtrian)
25. Lime Pickle in Juice
26. Lime Chilli Pickle
27. Karinellika
28. Vadukapuli Naranga
29. Hot Brinjal Pickle (A)
    Hot Brinjal Pickle (B)
30. Piccalilli (A)
    Piccalilli (B)
    Piccalilli (C)
31. Carrot Pickle (A)
    Carrot Pickle (B)
    Carrot Pickle (C)
32. Cucumber Pickle
33. Brinjal and Chilli Pickle
34. Bitter Gourd Pickle
35. Mixed Vegetable Pickle (A)
    Mixed Vegetable Pickle (B)
36. Pickle Cauliflower
37. Pickled Onion (A)
    Pickled Onion (B)
    Pickled Onion (C)
38. Pickled Red Cabbage
39. Chow Chow
40. Green Chilli Pickle (A)
    Green Chilli Pickle (B)
41. Capsicum Pickle (A)
    Capsicum Pickle (B)
    Capsicum Pickle (C)
42. Preserved Chillies
43. Papaya Chillies
44. Game Pickle
45. Meat or Game Pickle
46. Mutton Pickle
47. Pickled Beef
48. Salted Meat
49. Chicken Pickle
50. Malabar Fish Pickle
51. Prawn or Fish Pickle
52. Prawn Pickle (Malayalee)
53. Watermelon pickle

54. Carrot Kanji
55. Dudhi Kanji
56. Potato Kanji
57. Bhalla Kanji

FRESH CHUTNEYS
58. Green Chilli Chutney
59. Channa Dal Chutney
60. Moong Dal Chutney
61. Dal Chutney
62. Coconut and Moong Dal Chutney
63. Curry Leaf Chutney
64. Copra Chutney
65. Mango Chutney (A)
    Mango Chutney (B)
    Mango Chutney (C)
66. Coconut Chutney (A)
    Coconut Chutney (B)
    Coconut Chutney (C)
67. Coconut Chutney for Idlis
68. Dried Coconut Chutney
69. Parippu Podi
70. Groundnut Chutney (A)
    Groundnut Chutney (B)
71. Onion Chutney
72. Garlic Chutney (A)
    Garlic Chutney (B)
73. Dudhi Peel Chutney
74. Mint Chutney (A)
    Mint Chutney (B)
75. Hara Dhania Chutney (A)
    Hara Dhania Chutney (B)
76. Green Chutney
77. Thuvayyel
78. Bitter Gourd Chutney
79. Khajur Chutney
80. Banana Chutney
81. Prawn Paste
82. Sweet and Sour Chutney

83. Mango Chutney (A)
    Mango Chutney (B)
    Mango Chutney (C)
    Mango Chutney (D)
    Mango Chutney (E)
84. Sweet Mango Chutney
85. Kashmiri Chutney (mango)
86. Kharek Chutney
87. Lime and Date Chutney
88. Mint Chutney
89. Raw Papaya Chutney
90. Cocum Chutney
91. Date Chutney
92. Date and Carrot Chutney
93. Dried Apricot Chutney
94. Apple Chutney (A)
    Apple Chutney (B)
95. Green Tomato Chutney
96. Tomato Chutney (A)
    Tomato Chutney (B)
    Tomato Chutney (C)
    Tomato Chutney (D)
97. Tamarind Chutney
98. Woodapple Chutney
99. Pineapple Chutney
100. Dry Coconut Chutney (Idichuppumuluku)
101. Tomato Sauce
102. Chilli Sauce (A)
     Chilli Sauce (B)
103. Tomato Ketchup (mild)
104. Tomato Ketchup (spiced)

JAM AND JELLY MAKING
105. Banana Jam
106. Pineapple Jam
107. Grapefruit and Lime Marmalade
108. Orange Marmalade

109. Guava Jelly (A)
    Guava Jelly (B)
110. Guava Cheese
111. Roselle Jelly
112. Apple Murabba
113. Candied Peels

BEVERAGES
114. Orange Wine
115. Raisin Wine
116. Pea Pod Wine
117. Pineapple Wine
118. Ginger Wine
119. Grape Wine
120. Iced Tea
121. Iced Coffee (plain)
122. Iced Coffee with Condensed Milk
123. Iced Coffee with Cream
124. Fruit Punch (A)
    Fruit Punch (B)
125. Fruit Fizz
126. Ginger Punch
127. Fruit Punch with Whipped Cream
128. Tea Punch
129. Woodapple Punch
130. Pineapple Punch
131. Orchata
132. Orange or Lemon Squash
133. Ginger Beer
134. Gingo
135. Orange Milk Shake
136. Pineapple Milk Shake
137. Mango Fool
138. Banana Milk Shake
139. Malted Mocha Frost
140. Cucumber and Tomato Frost
141. Lassi
142. Ice Cream Fizz
143. Orange or Lemon Sherbet
144. Grapefruit Cocktail
145. Melon Cocktail
146. Melon Cooler
147. Pineapple Cocktail
148. Mixed Fruit Drink
149. Pineappleade
150. Lime Syrup
151. Lime-Ginger Squash
152. Sarasaparilla Syrup
153. Grape Squash
154. Lime Squash
155. Mango Squash
156. Orange Squash
157. Pineapple Squash
158. Sparkling Lemonade
159. Orange and Grapefruit Squash
160. Mint Julep
161. Apple Drink
162. Jeera Pani
163. Sambharam
164. Tomato Bisque Cocktail
165. Tamarind Drink
166. Sugarcane Vinegar
167. Alaska Special
168. Kollu Vellam
169. Panakam

MANGO PICKLES

Introduction

Select hard mangoes without any marks or bruises. Cut them into small square pieces so that there is no waste in serving. No water should come in contact with these pickles, so you must wipe the mangoes and your hands must be absolutely dry. Always use a wooden or stainless steel spoon for stirring the spices. Even the vessel in which the oil is boiled and the plate in which the ingredients are mixed together must be of stainless steel. To ensure that pickles have a longer shelf-life, heat the salt before grinding.

I. GUJARATI PICKLE

Ingredients	Quantity
Raw mangoes (small)	50
Fenugreek	125 gm
Mustard seeds (skins removed)	100 gm
Salt	1.35 kg
Turmeric	700 gm
Asafoetida	2 tsp
Sesame oil	1 litre
Chilli powder	700 gm

Method

1. Slit mangoes into four. 2. Remove seeds and fibres. 3. Stuff them with a mixture of salt and turmeric powder. Put them into a glass jar and store for 48 hours. 4. Remove and dry for 4–5 hours, on a clean cloth. 5. Mix all remaining ingredients, except oil, asafoetida and a tsp of mustard. 6. Heat half the oil. Add asafoetida and 1 tsp mustard. When the seeds crackle remove and pour over mixed spices. Mix well. 7. Stuff mangoes with spices. Mix well. 8. Pack in a clean glass jar. Set aside for three days. 9. Heat remaining oil. Cool and pour into a jar.

2. WHOLE MANGO PICKLE

Ingredients	Quantity
Raw mangoes (medium-sized)	1.35 kg
Dry ginger powder	4 tsp
Mustard seeds (skins removed)	125 gm
Fennel	125 gm
Fenugreek	50 gm
Chilli powder	50 gm
Asafoetida	1 tsp
Peas	115 gm

Ingredients	Quantity
Whole red chillies	30 gm
Mustard oil	700 ml

Method

1. Powder spices (except whole red chillies). 2. Mix with enough mustard oil to form a thick paste. 3. Slit mangoes into four. Stuff them with prepared spices. Stuff one whole red chilli and 8–10 peas into each mango. 4. Pack in a glass jar. 5. After 2–3 days pour the remaining oil over, so that mangoes are steeped in oil.

3. MAHARASHTRA PICKLE

Ingredients	Quantity
Raw mangoes (medium-sized)	18
Salt	700 gm
Chilli powder	225 gm
Turmeric powder	4 tbsp
Mustard seeds (skins removed)	3 tbsp
Asafoetida	1 tbsp
Fenugreek powder	4 tbsp
Garlic	40 gm
Sesame oil	680 ml

Method

1. Cut mangoes into small pieces. 2. In a plate mix all the spices except garlic and asafoetida. 3. Heat half the oil. Add asafoetida and garlic flakes. Remove and pour over mixed spices. Mix well. 4. When spices cool, add mangoes. 5. Store in a covered glass jar. Set aside for 4 days. 6. Heat remaining oil, cool and pour into jar. Cover and keep for a fortnight before using.

4. MARWARI PICKLE (A)

Ingredients	Quantity
Raw mangoes (medium-sized)	15
Mustard seeds (skins removed)	3 tbsp
Fennel	125 gm
Turmeric powder	2½ tbsp
Asafoetida	1 tsp
Whole dry chillies	125 gm
Salt	225 gm
Mustard oil	700 ml

Method

1. Clean chillies, remove seeds and sun dry. 2. Roast fennel. 3. Grind

both coarsely. 4. Cut mangoes into small pieces. 5. Mix all the ingredients and mango pieces with the oil and store in a glass jar. 6. Pickle will be ready for use after about 20 days.

MARWARI PICKLE (B)

Ingredients	Quantity
Raw mangoes (medium-sized)	15
Chilli powder	4 tbsp
Turmeric powder	1 tbsp
Coriander	3 tbsp
Salt	225 gm
Cumin	½ tsp
Asafoetida	½ tsp
Onions seeds	3 tsp
Oil	60 ml
Sugar	115 gm

Method

1. Peel and grate mangoes. 2. Squeeze out water. 3. Mix all ingredients with mangoes and oil. 4. Pack into a glass jar. 5. Cover mouth of jar with a piece of muslin tied round. 6. Keep jar in the sun for about a month. 7. At night, cover it with a lid.

MARWARI PICLE (C) (Chilli pickle)

Slit green chillies and keep them to dry on a muslin cloth. Fry fennel, onion seeds, white mustard, and asafoetida in oil. Add salt. Stuff green chillies with above mixture and put them into a glass container. Pour lime juice over. Keep jar in the sun for about 10 days. Use as required.

5. PUNJABI PICKE (A)

Ingredients	Quantity
Raw mangoes (medium-sized)	25
Mustard seeds	450 gm
Fenugreek	225 gm
Fennel	225 gm
Chilli powder	225 gm
Turmeric powder	125 gm
Salt	550 gm
Peppercorns	125 gm
Mustard oil	2 litre

Method

1. Roast fennel. Powder fennel and peppercorns coarsely. 2. Powder mustard and fenugreek seeds fine. 3. Cut mangoes into small pieces. 4. Mix all ingredients including mangoes with oil. 5. Store in a glass jar.

PUNJABI PICKLE (B)

Ingredients	Quantity
Mangoes	1 kg
Salt	¼ kg
Fennel	60 gm
Black pepper	60 gm
Mustard seeds	10 gm
Fenugreek	60 gm
Onions seeds	60 gm
Turmeric	60 gm
Mustard oil	1 litre

Method

1. Roast fennel. Powder fennel and peppercorns coarsely. 2. Powder mustard and fenugreek seeds fine. 3. Cut mangoes into small pieces. 4. Mix all ingredients including mangoes with oil. 5. Store in a glass jar.

ANDHRA PICKLES

6. AVAKKAI (A)

Ingredients	Quantity
Mangoes (medium-sized)	50
Salt	1 kg
Mustard seeds	1 kg
Red chillies	750 gm
Turmeric	125 gm
Fenugreek	100 gm
Whole Bengal gram	100 gm
Sesame oil	1 litre

Method

1. Cut mangoes into four with seeds. Remove kernel. 2. Sun dry and powder mustard, chillies, turmeric and fenugreek separately. Mix with salt immediately. 3. Mix all ingredients together. 4. Pack in a glass or earthenware jar. 5. Keep tightly covered for a week. 6. Mix well and use. (If necessary add a little more oil).

AVAKKAI (B)

Ingredients	Quantity
Raw mangoes	100
Sesame oil	1.4 litre
Red chillies	1 kg
Salt	2 kg
Mustard seeds	1.5 kg
Garlic	250 gm
Fenugreek	100 gm

Method

1. Cut mangoes into four with seeds. Remove kernel. 2. Sun dry and powder mustard, chillies, turmeric and fenugreek separately. Mix with salt immediately. 3. Mix all ingredients together including peeled garlic flakes. 4. Pack in a glass or earthenware jar. 5. Keep tightly covered for a week. 6. Mix well and use. (If necessary add a little more oil).

AVAKKAI (C)

Ingredients	Quantity
Mangoes	50
Red chilli	1 kg
Salt	1 kg
Fenugreek	250 gm
Asafoetida	10 gm
Sesame oil	1.3 litre
Turmeric powder	1 tsp

Method

1. Cut mangoes into four with seeds. Remove kernel. 2. Sun dry and powder mustard, chillies, turmeric and fenugreek separately. Mix with salt immediately. 3. Mix all ingredients together. 4. Pack in a glass or earthenware jar. 5. Keep tightly covered for a week. 6. Mix well and use. (If necessary add a little more oil).

AVAKKAI (D)

Ingredients	Quantity
Raw mangoes	4
Mustard seeds	125 gm
Red chillies	125 gm
Sesame oil	½ litre
Turmeric	30 gm

Method

1. Pick and sun dry mustard seeds, red chillies and turmeric well. 2. Grind them into dry powder separately. 3. Wash mangoes and wipe them dry. 4. Cut them into cubes, retaining seed. 5. Add all the ingredients and store in an air-tight container for a week. 6. Mix well and use. (If necessary add a little more oil).

7. GINGER MANGO PICKLE

Ingredients	Quantity
Raw mangoes	50
Fresh ginger	350 gm
Red chillies	1.75 kg
Mustard seeds	2 kg
Salt	2.25 kg
Fenugreek seeds	225 gm
Whole Bengal gram	225 gm
Sesame oil	2 litre

Method

1. Cut mangoes into four with seeds. Remove kernel. 2. Sun dry and powder mustard, chillies, turmeric and fenugreek separately. Mix with salt immediately. 3. Mix all ingredients together with peeled sliced ginger and whole Bengal gram. 4. Pack in a glass or earthenware jar. 5. Keep tightly covered for a week. 6. Mix well and use. (If necessary add a little more oil.)

8. GARLIC MANGO PICKLE

Ingredients	Quantity
Raw mangoes	50
Garlic	700 gm
Fenugreek	225 gm
Whole Bengal gram	225 gm
Sesame oil	3 litre
Salt	2.25 kg
Red chillies	2 kg
Mustard seeds	2.25 kg

Method

1. Cut mangoes into four with seeds. Remove kernel. 2. Sun dry and powder mustard, chilies, turmeric and fenugreek separately. Mix with salt immediately. 3. Mix all ingredients together. Add peeled and sliced garlic. 4. Pack in a glass or earthenware jar. 5. Keep tightly covered for a week. 6. Mix well and use. (If necessary add a little more oil.)

9. MANGO MAGAYA

Ingredients	Quantity
Dry mango pieces	1 kg
Salt	175 gm
Red chillies	175 gm
Oil	175 ml
Whole Bengal gram	2 tbsp
Red chillies	10
Curry leaves	2 sprigs
Mustard seeds	60 gm
Garlic	30 gm
Turmeric powder	1 tbsp
Fenugreek seeds (powder)	1 tbsp
Fenugreek seeds	1 tbsp

Method

Same as for recipe No. 6 Avakkai (A). Add peeled garlic and whole
Bengal gram. Heat oil. Add fenugreek seeds. Cool and mix with
remaining ingredients.

10. MANGO MUSTARD PICKLE

Ingredients	Quantity
Mangoes	450 gm
Mustard seeds	75 gm
Salt	30 gm
Red chillies	6–10
Mustard oil	300 ml

Method

1. Wash and cut mangoes into pieces. 2. Grind mustard seeds and red
chillies. 3. Add salt and mix well with mango pieces, add half the
mustard oil. 4. Pack into a jar. Add remaining mustard oil. 5. Sun for
2–3 days.

11. MYSORE MANGO PICKLE

Ingredients	Quantity
Raw mangoes (big)	50
Salt	½ kg
Mustard seeds	225 gm
Red chillies	½ kg
Sesame oil	½ litre
Asafoetida	10 gm

Method

1. Cut mangoes into four with seeds. Remove kernel. Mix with salt. Set aside for 3–4 days. 2. Sun dry, and powder mustard and red chillies coarsely. 3. Heat oil and then set it aside to cool. 4. Mix oil, powdered spices and mangoes. 5. Heat a little oil separately. Add asafoetida. Pour over mangoes.

12. MADRAS MANGAI OORKAI

Ingredients	Quantity
Green mangoes	25
Red chillies	150 gm
Salt	150 gm
Mustard seeds	15 gm
Asafoetida	10 gm
Fenugreek	10 gm
Sesame oil	150 ml
Turmeric powder	1½ tsp

Method

1. Same as for recipe No. 6, Avakkai (A).

13. DRIED MANGO PICKLE

Ingredients	Quantity
Dried mangoes	40
Sugar	225 gm
Onions (small)	225 gm
Salt	225 gm
Garlic	225 gm
Green chillies	225 gm
Ginger	225 gm
Sultanas	125 gm
Vinegar	500 ml

Method

1. Peel and slice mangoes. Salt and dry. 2. Peel and slice onions. Chop garlic and ginger. Pound chillies. 3. Mix all ingredients together. Fill in dry jars. 4. Boil vinegar. Pour it over dry ingredients. Cool and cover. 5. Keep in the sun for one month.

14. ADAMANGA (Malayalee mango pickle) (A)

Ingredients	Quantity
Raw mangoes (small sour variety)	100
Salt	2 kg (approx.)

Ingredients	Quantity
Fenugreek	350 gm
Red chillies	700 gm
Turmeric	125 gm
Mustard seeds (without skin)	1 kg
Garlic	600 gm
Sesame oil	2 litre

Method

1. Cut mangoes into quarters without separating. Remove white kernel of seeds but not hard covering. 2. Mix with salt and set aside for 2 days. 3. Roast and powder fenugreek seeds. 4. Remove seeds from chillies. Sun dry and powder. 5. Peel garlic. 6. Grind all the spices using salt solution that has drained out from mangoes. 7. Mix with sesame oil and stuff mangoes. 8. Pack in jars and pour remaining oil over. 9. Cover well and set aside for 2 weeks before using.

ADAMANGA (B)

Ingredients	Quantity
Mangoes (big)	4
Red chillies	100 gm
Salt	25 gm
Turmeric	2.5 cm (about 1")
Fenugreek	1 tsp
Garlic	3 pods
Mustard seeds (skins removed)	2 tbsp (heaped)
Sesame oil	180 ml (1 cup)

Method

1. Slice mangoes. Apply salt and set aside for 3 days, shaking pot 2–3 times a day. 2. Roast chillies, turmeric and fenugreek separately (see that fenugreek is not roasted too much). Powder. 3. Add powdered spices, ground garlic, mustard and some oil to mangoes. Mix well. 4. Bottle and pour oil on top to cover mixture.

15. KANNI MANGA

Ingredients	Quantity
Raw mangoes	200
Spices and Oil as for Adamanga	

Method

As for recipe No. 14 Adamanga but keep mangoes whole. Pack in jars with spices.

16. KADUKUMANGA

Ingredients	Quantity
Mangoes (cut into small pieces with skin)	1 kg
Red chillies	125 gm
Turmeric	5 gm
Water	
Fenugreek	10 gm
Mustard seeds	10 gm
Salt	125 gm
Coconut oil or Sesame oil	60 ml

Method

1. Roast and powder red chillies, turmeric and fenugreek seeds. 2. Heat oil. Put in mustard seeds. When they crackle remove pan from fire. 3. Add powdered spices, salt and water. 4. Return to the fire and bring to a boil. 5. Remove and when liquid cools, add mango pieces.

N.B. This is best eaten fresh. It does not last for more than a fortnight.

17. MANGO KASOONDI (A)

Ingredients	Quantity
Mangoes	25
Mustard oil	500 ml
Cumin	60 gm
Ginger	60 gm
Vinegar	500 ml
Mustard seeds	60 gm
Fenugreek	60 gm
Garlic	60 gm
Sugar	350 gm
Red chillies	30 gm

Method

1. Grind fenugreek, cumin, red chillies and mustard seeds in vinegar. 2. Slice garlic and ginger. 3. Heat mustard oil. Fry ground spices. Add sugar, mangoes and remaining vinegar. 4. Cook till as thick as a curry.

MANGO KASOONDI (B)

Ingredients	Quantity
Mangoes	1 kg
Vinegar	450 ml
Salt	2½ tbsp
Sweet oil	150 ml

Ingredients	Quantity
Sugar	2 tbsp
Curry leaves	2 sprigs
To be ground into paste	
Red chillies	15 gm
Mustard seeds	1 tsp
Turmeric	1 tsp
Peppercorn	6
Dry ginger	1 tsp
Cumin	1½ dsp
Garlic	1 pod

Method

1. Cut mangoes into eight pieces. Sprinkle over with 1½ tbsp salt. 2. Put into a glass jar – cover with a cloth and keep in the sun for 4 days. 3. Grind spices to a smooth paste using a little vinegar. 4. Heat oil. Add curry leaves. Put in ground spices and fry for about 15 minutes, stirring occasionally. 5. Add mango slices and salt water. 6. Add sugar, remaining salt and simmer for about 10 minutes. 7. Add remaining vinegar and cook till well blended.

MANGO KASOONDI (C)

Ingredients	Quantity
Green mangoes	2.8 kg
Vinegar	325 ml
Mustard oil	325 ml
Turmeric powder	85 gm
Chilli powder	60 gm
Mustard seeds	60 gm
Salt	to taste
Sugar	2 tbsp
Garlic	1 pod (15 gm)
Ginger	30 gm

Method

1. Wash, peel and slice mangoes thin. 2. Mix turmeric and chilli powder with mangoes. 3. Grind garlic, ginger and mustard in a little vinegar. 4. Mix all ingredients. Pack into jars and keep in the sun for a week. Use as required.

18. MANGO RELISH

Ingredients	Quantity
Sour country mangoes	3
Salt	30–50 gm

Ingredients	Quantity
Fenugreek	5 gm
Sesame oil	60 ml
Red chillies	15
Asafoetida	5 gm

Method

1. Peel and chop mangoes into very small pieces. Heat oil and add mangoes. 2. Cook till moisture evaporates. Remove and put into a pickle jar. 3. Sun dry chillies, fenugreek, salt and asafoetida and powder them fine. Sprinkle over mangoes. Mix well. Set aside for 3 days. Use as required.

LIME AND OTHER VEGETABLE PICKLES

19. LIME PICKLE (A)

Ingredients	Quantity
Limes	25
Chilli powder	225 gm
Turmeric powder	30 gm
Salt	225 gm
Sesame oil	1.25 litre
Coarsely powdered	
Asafoetida	2 tsp

Method

1. Wash and dry limes. 2. Slit them into four halfway down. 3. Fry asafoetida powder in a little oil. 4. Mix turmeric, chilli powder, asafoetida and salt. 5. Stuff the spices into limes and leave them in an earthen jar for one day. 6. Heat oil in a deep frying pan to smoking point, cool and pour over limes. 7. The pickle will be ready in 15 days.

LIME PICKLE (B)

Ingredients	Quantity
Limes	50
Chilli powder	450 gm
Fenugreek (coarsely powdered)	30 gm
Ginger	125 gm
Garlic	125 gm
Green chillies	125 gm
Salt	1 kg
Vinegar	600 ml

Method

1. Bring a pan of water to a boil. 2. Put in limes. Remove. Drain and wipe. 3. Cut limes into four three-quarters down. 4. Slice ginger. Slit green chillies and peel garlic. 5. Mix salt, chilli powder and fenugreek powder. 6. Stuff limes with spices. Place in a glass jar alternating with garlic, ginger and green chillies. 7. Pour vinegar over to cover. Seal and set aside for 10–15 days before using.

LIME PICKLE (C)

Ingredients	Quantity
Limes	25
Red chillies	125 gm
Mustard seeds	225 gm
Garlic	125 gm
Turmeric	60 gm
Vinegar	2.35 litre
Sesame oil	600 ml
Green chillies	12

Method

1. Cut limes into four. Sprinkle with salt and set aside for 1 day. 2. Keep in the sun for 2 days. 3. Grind chillies, mustard and turmeric with vinegar. 4. Heat oil. Add curry leaves and green chillies. 5. Add ground spices. Fry for 5 minutes. 6. Add limes and peeled garlic and remaining vinegar. 7. Bring to a boil and boil for about 10 minutes. 8. Remove, cool and bottle.

LIME PICKLE (D)

Ingredients	Quantity
Limes	30
Fenugreek powder	125 gm
Ginger	125 gm
Water	
Sweet oil	120 ml
Green chillies	225 gm
Salt	125 gm
Chilli powder	30 gm

Method

1. Boil water in a big pan. 2. Remove from fire as water starts boiling. 3. Add limes, cover and leave for 3 minutes. 4. Remove lid and let limes remain in water for half an hour. 5. Remove and dry limes. 6. Slit each lime into four halfway down. 7. Peel and slice ginger. Slit half the green

chillies. 8. Mix ginger and slit green chillies with chilli powder, fenugreek powder and salt. 9. Stuff limes, pack into an earthen jar; sprinkle remaining mixture over limes and put remaining whole chillies on top. 10. Heat oil and allow to cool. When oil is cold pour over limes. 11. Cover mouth of jar with a piece of muslin and keep pickle in the sun for a week. Seal well.

LIME PICKLE (E)

Ingredients	Quantity
Limes	10
Salt	5 dsp
Chilli powder	2 dsp
Turmeric	½ dsp
Lime juice	10–12 limes
Oil	2 tsp
Asafoetida (roughly ground)	½ dsp
Fenugreek seeds	1 tsp
For chillies	
Green chillies	¼ kg
Salt	1 dsp
Chilli powder	½ dsp

Method

1. Wash, wipe, dry and cut limes into 8 pieces each. 2. Fry asafoetida and fenugreek seeds and grind roughly. 3. Mix them with salt, chilli powder, turmeric. 4. Mix powdered spices with limes and put into a jar. (Put a little powder in the bottom of the jar first). 5. Squeeze other limes and pour juice on top till the limes are soaked. 6. Stir after 3–4 days. The pickle will mature in 14 days.

To prepare chillies

7. Slit green chillies. 8. Mix salt and chilli powder. 9. Stuff into slit green chill'es and add to limes.

20. LIME PICKLE (Sweet) (A)

Ingredients	Quantity
Limes	1 kg
Jaggery	1 kg
Salt	1 tbsp
Chilli powder	2 tbsp

Method

1. Wash and dry limes. Cut each into eight pieces. 2. Mix them with salt

and chilli powder. 3. In a stainless steel pan put limes and jaggery in alternate layers. 4. Keep pan on fire. 5. Bring to a boil and continue boiling for 10 minutes. 6. Remove from fire, cool and bottle.

LIME PICKLE (Sweet) (B)

Ingredients	Quantity
Limes	25
Red chillies	5 gm
Mustard seeds	30 gm
Green chillies	10 gm
Turmeric	30 gm
Asafoetida	5 gm
Salt	150 gm
Sugar	1.35 kg
Fenugreek	5 gm
Vinegar	4 dsp
Sesame oil	200 ml

Method

1. Cut each lime into eight. Mix half the salt and turmeric together and mix with cut limes. Set aside for 24 hours. 2. Heat a little sesame oil. Fry asafoetida, fenugreek, turmeric, green chillies and half the mustard. 3. Grind with vinegar and mix with limes. 4. Add salt and sugar and mix thoroughly. 5. Heat remaining oil. Add mustard and when it crackles, remove. 6. Cool for 10 minutes. Add red chillies broken into two. When quite cold pour over limes.

21. LIME PICKLE (White) (A)

Ingredients	Quantity
Limes	25
garlic	60 gm
Green chillies	115 gm
Ginger	115 gm
Salt	115 gm
White vinegar	250 ml
Sesame oil	50 ml
Mustard seeds	2 tsp

Method

1. Wash and cut limes into quarters. 2. Slit green chillies, peel and slice garlic and ginger. 3. Heat oil. Add mustard seeds. When they crackle add prepared spices. Fry for about 5 minutes. Add lime and fry for 2–3 minutes. 4. Remove, add vinegar and salt and bottle. Use after a week.

LIME PICKLE (White) (B)

Ingredients	Quantity
Limes	6
Salt	½ cup
Green chillies	10
Ginger	60 gm
"Karonda" (Carissa carandas)	60 gm

Method

1. Soak "karonda" in brine for 2–3 days. 2. Squeeze juice of three limes. 3. Wash, wipe and cut other limes into quarters. 4. Wash and wipe green chillies. Peel and slice ginger. 5. Put all ingredients into a jar. Sun for 7 to 10 days.

22. LIMES IN VINEGAR

Ingredients	Quantity
Limes	50
Lime juice	12 limes
Salt	1.7 kg
Vinegar	350 ml

Method

1. Boil water in a large pan. Remove, add limes. Keep covered for 3 minutes. 2. Remove lid and let limes stand in hot water for half an hour. Remove and wipe dry. 3. Pack into a glass jar. 4. Add lime juice, salt and vinegar. 5. Cover mouth of jar with a muslin cloth and sun for 2 months. 6. At night remove muslin cover and put on lid.

23. LIME PICKLE WITH MUSTARD

Ingredients	Quantity
Limes	15
Salt	150 gm
Fenugreek	30 gm
Lime juice	10 limes
Turmeric (whole)	30 gm
Asafoetida	10 gm
Mustard seeds	75 gm

Method

1. Wash and dry limes. Cut into small pieces. 2. Rub over with salt and store in a stainless steel pan or glass jar for three days. 3. Remove and drain. 4. Roast turmeric, fenugreek seeds and asafoetida separately and powder them. 5. Dry and powder mustard. Mix all powdered spices. 6. Add lime pieces and mix well. 7. Pack into a glass jar, pour salt liquid and lime juice over. 8. Stir well and cover jar.

24. LIME PICKLE (Maharashtrian)

Ingredients	Quantity
Limes	30
Salt	125 gm (approx.)
Chilli powder	50 gm
Fenugreek powder	40 gm
Sweet oil	350 ml

Method

1. Boil water in a pan. Remove from fire. Add limes. Cover and keep for 3 minutes. 2. Remove lid and let limes stand in hot water for half an hour. 3. Remove limes. Wipe dry. 4. Heat oil. When it starts smoking reduce heat and add limes. Fry till they become pale brown. 5. Slit each lime into 2 halfway down. 6. Mix chilli powder, fenugreek powder and salt. Add hot oil. 7. Stuff limes with mixed spices. 8. Pack into a glass or earthenware jar. Cover well. 9. Pickle should be ready to use in 10 days.

25. LIME PICKLE IN JUICE

Ingredients	Quantity
Limes	35
Chilli powder	225 gm
Salt	1.35 kg
Turmeric	60 gm
Fenugreek powder	60 gm
Asafoetida	30 gm
Lime juice	25 limes

Method

1. Wash limes; dry them. 2. Cut each lime into eight pieces. 3. Mix all the ingredients, except lime juice, and cut limes. 4. Wash and dry a big glass jar. 5. Heat asafoetida on live coals. Hold jar, mouth down over the fumes of asafoetida. 6. Remove; put in a layer of salt. Add mixed ingredients; cover and keep for 2 days. 7. Open jar and add lime juice. Mix well. Use as required. 8. Open jar at least once a fortnight and mix contents well with a wooden spoon.

26. LIME CHILLI PICKLE

Ingredients	Quantity
Limes	4 kg
Salt	900–1000 gm
Asafoetida	50 gm
Chilli powder	200 gm

Ingredients	Quantity
Fenugreek	50 gm
Mustard seeds (skin removed)	50 gm
Green chillies	½–1 kg

Method

1. Weigh and wash limes and chillies and wipe dry. Cut limes into 8 pieces and slit chillies lengthwise. 2. Mix all other ingredients separately in a bowl. Put a layer of limes in a jar, and add a layer of salt and spice mixture. 3. Repeat the same process, taking care to have a layer of the mixture at the top. 4. Press whole mass gently, close lid and tie a muslin cloth over the mouth of jar. 5. Store in a well-ventilated place for 4–6 weeks before using. (The pickle can be kept in the sun for a week to hasten ripening.)

N.B. For added shelf-life, add 2 gm of sodium benzoate.

27. KARINELLIKA

Ingredients	Quantity
Amla (Indian goosebeery)	2 kg
Red chillies	100 gm
Red onions (small)	225 gm
Garlic	50 gm
Pepper	2 tbsp
Green chillies or "Kanthari"	100 gm
Mustard seeds	1 tsp
Pepper stems (tender)	20
Ginger	2.5 cm (about 1")
Salt	125 gm
Water	1 litre
Sesame oil	60 ml
Curry leaves	1 sprig

Method

1. Wash gooseberries. Peel garlic, onion, ginger, etc. Slice ginger. Mix with broken red chillies and all the other ingredients. 2. Cover with water. Mix well and put into an earthenware fireproof pot. Cover by tying banana leaves tied over month of pot. Boil for half an hour. 3. Remove and set aside. Re-heat on a slow fire every day for about 10–15 minutes. 4. Repeat for a week and ensure that by the end of the week the water has completely evaporated. 5. Heat oil. Add 1 tsp mustard seeds, 1 sprig curry leaves and 2 tbsp pepper. When mustard seeds crackle, add amla. Mix well and bottle.

28. VADUKAPULI NARANGA

Ingredients	Quantity
Vadukapali narenga	1
Red chillies	100 gm
Turmeric	1" piece
Fenugreek	1 tsp
Salt	100 gm
Garlic	50 gm
Ginger	15 gm
Green chillies	30 gm

Method

1. Wash, dry and cut narenga into 12 pieces. Roast and powder spices.
2. Peel and slice ginger and garlic. 3. Mix narenga, spices, garlic and
ginger. 4. Bottle and set aside for 3-days. 5. Fill bottle with vinegar
(boiled and cooled).

29. HOT BRINJAL PICKLE (A)

Ingredients	Quantity
Brinjals	2 kg
Gingelly oil	1.5–2 kg
Green chillies	150
Vinegar	1.2 litre
Ginger	150 gm
Garlic	100 gm
Cumin	75 gm
Mustard	50 gm
Turmeric powder	20 gm
Red chilli powder	175 gm
Curry leaves	3 bunches
Mogadi root (optional)	50 bunches
Salt	155–200 gm
Fenugreek (roasted and powdered)	5 gm
Asafoetida (roasted and powdered)	6 gm
Mustard (whole)	45 gm
Fenugreek seeds (whole)	50 gm

Method

1. Weigh, wash and remove stalks of brinjals. 2. Cut brinjals into circular
pieces .60 cm thick or 3.75 cm long and 0.60 cm thick strips. Immerse
cut brinjals in salt water to prevent browning. 3. Heat oil and fry on
medium heat till they are light brown and crisp. Set aside fried brinjal.
4. Clean garlic and ginger. Grind garlic, ginger, cumin and mustard
using 120 ml vinegar. Mix this masala with chilli and turmeric powder

using 800 ml vinegar. 5. Remove stalks from green chillies, wash them along with curry leaves and set aside. 6. Roast fenugreek and asafoetida, grind each into powder separately and set aside. 7. Heat oil, and add fenugreek and mustard seeds. When they crackle add masala mixture and remaining vinegar. Boil the mass for 5–10 minutes on a slow flame. Add whole green chillies and curry leaves to boiling masala mixture. Add red colour if necessary, drop by drop. 8. Add salt and magadi root (cleaned and cut). 9. Sprinkle roasted fenugreek and asafoetida powder onto masala mixture and mix well. Add fried brinjal to masala mixture and boil for 1–2 minutes. Remove pan from fire, add sodium benzoate* dissolved in a little water and leave pickle to cool. 10. Add more salt if necessary.

Bottling: Bottle the Brinjal Pickle in the same way as Hot Lime Pickle.

HOT BRINJAL PICKLE (B)

Ingredients	Quantity
Brinjals	1 kg
Oil	250 ml
Garlic	15 gm
Ginger (fresh)	10 gm
Green chillies	40 gm
Chilli powder	40 gm
Turmeric powder	20 gm
Mustard (whole)	20 gm
Fenugreek (whole)	15 gm
Sugar	50 gm
Cumin seeds	10 gm
Table salt	35 gm
White vinegar	150 ml

Method

1. Wash and dry brinjals, remove stalks and cut into halves lengthwise. Slice each half into thin slices. Heat oil and fry till light brown, remove, add salt and sugar and set aside. 2. Grind green chillies, garlic and ginger to a paste, using white vinegar. 3. Pound fenugreek, cumin and mustard into coarse powder. 4. Fry paste in remaining oil for 2–3 minutes, add pounded dry masala and finally fried brinjal. Mix well on slow fire, add red chilli powder at the end and remove from fire. Leave overnight. 5. Fill in jars, close tightly, use after 4–5 days.

---

*For longer shelf-life add 1 gm of sodium benzoate.

30. PICCALILLI (A)

Ingredients	Quantity
Cauliflower	450 gm
Cucumber	225 gm
Vegetable marrow	225 gm
Vinegar	1.20 litre
Sugar	115 gm
Whole allspice	30 gm
Ground ginger	15 gm
Mustard powder	30 gm
Turmeric	15 gm
Refined flour	30 gm
Salt	to taste

Method

1. Prepare vegetables. Sprinkle over with salt and leave overnight. 2. Boil whole allspice in most of the vinegar in a covered pan for a few minutes. 3. Mix other spices and remaining vinegar into a smooth paste. 4. Add strained spiced vinegar. 5. Boil drained and rinsed vegetables in this liquid for about 15 minutes. 6. Thicken sauce with flour blended with a little cold water. Bottle and seal.

PICCALILLI (B)

Ingredients	Quantity
Cabbage	225 gm
Cauliflower	225 gm
French beans (tender)	450 gm
Small onions	450 gm
Green tomatoes	450 gm
Cucumber	125 gm
Vinegar	2.35 litre
Garlic	1 flake
Cloves	6
Ginger	60 gm
Red chillies	60 gm
Peppercorns	30 gm
Turmeric	15 gm
Mustard	30 gm
Salt	to taste

Method

1. Prepare vegetables. Spread on a flat dish. Sprinkle over with salt and set aside for 48 hours. 2. Drain vegetables and pack into a large jar. 3. Boil spices (except turmeric and mustard) with vinegar. 4. Mix

turmeric and mustard with a little cold vinegar. 5. Drain vinegar. When cool pour vinegar over prepared vegetables.

PICCALILLI (C)

Ingredients	Quantity
Green tomatoes	1 kg
Red peppers	2
Capsicums	2
White onions	225 gm
Cabbage	225 gm
Salt	cup
Vinegar	3 cups
Brown sugar	450 gm
Mixed pickle spices	30 gm
(Red chillies, Peppercorns, Aniseed, Cloves, Garlic, Allspice)	

Method

1. Chop vegetables and onions. Mix with salt and let stand overnight. 2. Drain and press out excess moisture using clean cloth. 3. Tie spices in a muslin bag, put into vinegar mixed with sugar and bring to a boil. 4. Add vegetables. Simmer for about 30 minutes. 5. Remove spice bag. Pack into clean, hot, sterile jars. Fill to top and seal tightly.

31. CARROT PICKLE (A)

Ingredients	Quantity
Carrots	225 gm
Red chillies	6–8
Mustard seeds	2 tbsp
Fennel	1 tbsp
Mustard oil	300 ml (½ bottle)
Salt	to taste

Method

1. Wash, scrape and cut carrots into thin long strips, cover with salt. 2. Coarsely pound mustard seeds, fennel and red chillies. 3. Add to carrots with part of the oil. 4. Pour remaining oil over and keep in the sun for 2–4 days.

CARROT PICKLE (B)

Ingredients	Quantity
Carrots	1 kg
Salt	4 tbsp

Ingredients	Quantity
Vinegar	1½ cup
Salad oil	½ cup
Spices:	
Kashmiri or Sankeshwari chillies	12
Turmeric	5 cm piece (about 2")
Garlic	8 flakes
Ginger	7.5 cm piece (about 3")
Cloves	6

Method

1. Peel carrots and cut into thin strips. 2. Sprinkle salt and cover with a muslin cloth. Leave for 24 hours in a cool place and drain. 3. Grind spices together, with 1 cup vinegar. 4. Fry spices in oil. Add ½ cup more vinegar and carrots. Bring to a boil and remove. 5. Allow to cool. Fill jar and seal.

CARROT PICKLE (C)

Ingredients	Quantity
Carrots	1 kg
Dried apricots	100 gm
Dried dates	100 gm
Currants	100 gm
Jaggery	1 kg
Chilli powder	100 gm
Turmeric powder	1 tsp
Vinegar (of sugarcane)	1 bottle
Mustard seeds	50 gm
Ginger	50 gm
Garlic flakes	50 gm
Peppercorns	1 tsp

Method

1. Scrape and wash carrots. Cut off green portion at top, and grate carrots. 2. Mix in some salt and turmeric powder. Squeeze out juice and dry carrots thoroughly by putting out in the sun for 2–3 days. 3. Meanwhile, wash dried apricots and dried dates in a little vinegar. Soak overnight in some vinegar to which salt has been added. 4. Next day, cut dried dates into long strips. Wash currants in a little vinegar. 5. Cut ginger and garlic into long, thin strips. Finely grind mustard seeds with a little vinegar. 6. Dissolve jaggery in half a bottle of vinegar over gentle heat. Let it cool thoroughly. Strain through a piece of muslin.

7. Mix prepared ingredients with salt. Pour into a clean jar. The pickle will be ready to use in 7 days.

N.B. This pickle is very tasty. No Parsi feast is considered complete without it.

32. CUCUMBER PICKLE

Ingredients	Quantity
Cucumber (even-sized, small, white skinned)	1 kg
Salt	125 gm
Dry chillies	6
Peppercorns	12
Onions (sliced)	115 gm
Garlic (sliced)	15 gm
Asafoetida	¼ tsp
Fennel leaves	¼ bunch
Alum	¼ tsp
Vinegar	60 ml
Bread slices	

Method

1. Clean cucumber with a damp cloth. Remove stems. Prick all over with a fork. 2. Arrange cucumber and spices in layers of alum and salt, ending with a layer of spices. Pour vinegar. 3. Cover with bread slices. After 4 days remove bread slices. Add more salt if desired. Use after 8 days.

33. BRINJAL and CHILLI PICKLE

Ingredients	Quantity
Medium-sized brinjals	450 gm (4)
Mustard seeds	20 gm
Coriander seeds	15 gm
Cumin	5 gm
Turmeric	1 tsp
Ginger	5 gm
Garlic	5 gm
Green chillies	100 gm
Red chillies	10 gm
Cinnamon	1 small piece
Vinegar	300 ml
Coconut oil	60 ml
Curry leaves	2 sprigs
Salt	to taste

Method

1. Wash and cut brinjals into pieces lengthwise. 2. Rub over with turmeric and salt and set aside. 3. Grind red chillies, mustard, coriander and cumin, ginger and garlic using vinegar. 4. Heat oil. Fry brinjals. Remove. Fry green chillies. Remove. 5. Mix fried ingredients, ground ingredients, vinegar and salt, cinnamon and curry leaves. Mix well and bottle.

34. BITTER GOURD PICKLE

Ingredients	Quantity
Bitter gourd (fresh, white variety)	250 gm
Vinegar	150–200 ml (1 cup)
Mustard seeds	1 tsp
Green chillies	5
Ginger (sliced)	2 dsp
Garlic (sliced)	3 dsp
Salt	to taste
Fenugreek	1 tsp
Sesame oil	60 ml

Method

1. Slit bitter gourd into half. Remove seeds. Cut into 0.70 cm × 2 cm (about ¼" × ¾") slices. 2. Apply salt and set aside for half an hour. 3. Heat oil. Add mustard seeds and fenugreek. Add garlic. Sauté. 4. Then add ginger and green chillies cut into 3 or 4 pieces each. 5. Sauté well. Squeeze out bitter gourd; add to sautéed spices. 6. Stir for a minute. Add vinegar and salt. 7. Bring to a boil and remove. Cool and bottle.

35. MIXED VEGETABLE PICKLE (A)

Ingredients	Quantity
Carrots	225 gm
Cauliflower	225 gm
Chilli powder	30 gm
Turmeric	¼ tsp
Garlic	1 pod
Green chillies	10
Ginger	15 gm
Vinegar	300 ml (about)
Salad oil	60 ml
Salt	½ cup

Method

1. Wash, scrape and cut carrots into slices. Break cauliflower into flowerets. Sprinkle over with salt and set aside for 48 hours. 2. Peel and slice garlic and ginger. Slit green chillies. 3. Heat oil. Add garlic, ginger and green chillies. 4. Fry for 1 minute. Remove pan from fire. Add chilli powder and turmeric. Stir well. 5. Add vinegar and salt. Bring to a boil. Remove, cool and add prepared vegetables.

MIXED VEGETABLE PICKLE (B)

Ingredients	Quantity
Cauliflower	1 kg
Carrots	½ kg
Turnip	250 gm
Fresh peas	500 gm
French beans	250 gm
Green chillies	100 gm
(Total dressed weight of all vegetables should be I kg)	
Table salt	200 gm
Turmeric powder	15 gm
White vinegar	400 ml
Mustard dal or powder	50 gm
Fenugreek dal or powder	20 gm
Red chilli powder	30–50 gm
Asafoetida powder	10 gm
Refined oil (groundnut)	200 ml

Method

1. Wash all vegetables thoroughly and dry in shade. 2. Dress each vegetable and cut into suitable pieces. 3. Mix all vegetables, weigh and add salt-turmeric mixture. 4. Mix well and keep in a jar or stainless steel vessel. 5. Cover with muslin cloth for 4–5 days (mix every day). 6. Pour in white vinegar after 4–5 days. Mix well and leave for curing in the same jar or vessel for 5–6 days with occasional mixing (once in 2 days). 7. After 5–6 days of curing, add fried spice mixture and store for 10–12 days before using. 8. Heat oil (not to smoking point). Add asafoetida, fenugreek and mustard. Switch off burner. 9. Cool for 5–6 minutes and then put in red chilli powder. 10. Mix well. Cool to room temperature and mix well with pickled vegetables.

36. PICKLED CAULIFLOWER

1. Select a fresh cauliflower. Remove outer leaves. Break flowerets into small pieces. 2. Wash in salt and water. Place into a large basin, cover

with brine (450 gm salt to 4.7 litre water) and leave for 24 hours. 3. Rinse in cold water. Drain well and put into in jars. Pour pickling vinegar over.

Pickling Vinegar

Ingredients	Quantity
Peppercorns	60 gm
Mace	3 blades
Bruised ginger	60 gm
Mustard seeds	85 gm
Garlic	2 flakes
White radish	1

Method

1. Boil all ingredients in 300 ml vinegar for 5 minutes. Strain through muslin and use.

37. PICKLED ONION (A)

Select small, even-sized onions. Place (with skin) in brine (450 gm salt to 4.7 litre water) and leave for 12 hours. Peel, put into fresh brine for another 24–36 hours. Remove from brine, wash thoroughly in cold water, drain well. Pack onions into jars. Cover with cold pickling vinegar. Seal and keep for 3–4 months before using.

PICKLED ONION (B)

Select even-shaped small white onions. Sun dry mustard seeds for 1 hour. Crush and remove skin. Mix with onions and put into a jar with salt and enough water to cover onions. Add a tsp of chilli powder if desired. Pickle will be ready to use in 2–3 days.

PICKLED ONION (C)

Method

Mix small white onions, whole red chillies, white vinegar, salt, beetroot slices. Set aside for 3–5 days and use as required.

38. PICKLED RED CABBAGE

Ingredients	Quantity
Red cabbage	5.5 kg
Salt	350 gm

Method

Quarter cabbage. Remove outer leaves and centre stalk, and cut them into fine strips. Place in a large bowl, sprinkle plenty of salt over layers and leave until next day. Drain off all moisture. Cover with cold spiced vinegar.

Spiced Vinegar

Ingredients	Quantity
Vinegar	300 ml
Mace	20 gm
Red chillies (whole)	50 gm
Cloves	10 gm
Cinnamon	10 gm
Peppercorns	30 gm
Ginger	30 gm

Method

1. Tie spices in muslin. Place in a pan with vinegar. 2. Heat with lid on, bringing slowly to boiling point. Remove from fire and leave for 2 hours. Remove muslin bag and use cold.

39. CHOW CHOW

Ingredients	Quantity
Onions (small)	2 kg
Gherkins (young tindli)	3 kg
Vinegar	600 ml
Refined flour	125 gm
Turmeric	30 gm
Cauliflower	2 kg
Capsicum	1 kg
Mustard seeds	125 gm
Sugar	200 gm
Salt	

Method

Prepare vegetables and soak overnight in brine. Drain and cook in fresh brine till tender. Strain again. Boil vinegar. Add a paste made with mustard, sugar, turmeric and a little cold vinegar. Stir until mixture thickens. Add vegetables and cook for 10 minutes.

40. GREEN CHILLI PICKLE (A)

Ingredients	Quantity
Limes	500 gm
Green chillies	1 kg

Ingredients	Quantity
Turmeric powder	1 tbsp
Freshly powdered mustard	2 tbsp
Salt	3 tbsp
Sesame oil	2 tbsp

Method

1. Slit green chillies down the middle. 2. Mix coarsely powdered mustard, turmeric, salt and oil. 3. Stuff spices in green chillies. Place them in an earthen jar. 4. Next day pour juice of the limes over chillies. 5. Store for a week and use.

GREEN CHILLI PICKLE (B)

Ingredients	Quantity
Green chillies	125 gm
Tamarind	50 gm
Jaggery	450 gm
Salt	100 gm
Mustard seeds	1 tbsp
Fenugreek	1 tbsp
Asafoetida	1 tsp
Sweet oil	30 ml

Method

1. Slit chillies. Soak tamarind. 2. In a little oil fry mustard and fenugreek seeds; powder. 3. Mix with tamarind pulp and jaggery; stuff chillies. 4. Heat remaining oil. Add asafoetida and fry. Add chillies; cook for 5 minutes. Remove, cool and bottle.

41. CAPSICUM PICKLE (A)

Ingredients	Quantity
Capsicums	2 kg
Cumin (roasted and powdered)	60 gm
Yellow mustard (powdered)	60 gm
Ginger	125 gm
Garlic	125 gm
Turmeric	1 tbsp
Salt	200 gm
Brown sugar	200 gm
Vinegar	1 litre (1½ bottles)
Mustard oil	1 litre

Method

1. Grind all spices in a little vinegar. 2. Fry well in mustard oil. 3. Slit and stuff capsicum. 4. Pack into a glass jar. 5. Add sugar and remaining vinegar and oil.

CAPSICUM PICKLE (B)

Ingredients	Quantity
Capsicums	2 kg
Mustard oil	500 ml
Red chillies	50 gm
Garlic	30 gm
Mustard seeds	10 gm
Vinegar	320 ml (½ bottle)
Ginger	30 gm
Cinnamon	
Cloves	15 gm
Peppercorns	a few
Fennel	5 gm
Garlic	15 gm
Salt	225 gm

Method

1. Clean capsicums. Rub salt and keep in sun for 8–10 hours. 2. Grind spices in vinegar. Heat a little oil, fry spices. Allow to cool and mix with capsicums. 3. Heat remaining oil. Add garlic and fry till golden brown. Remove and cool, pour over pickle. 4. Bottle and use after 3–4 days.

CAPSICUM PICKLE (C)

Ingredients	Quantity
Capsicums	2 kg (or 20 large)
Vinegar	650 ml (1 bottle)
Whole red chillies	15 gm
Peppercorns	a few
Ginger ·	55 gm
Garlic	55 gm
Sugar	30 gm
Mustard powder	15 gm
Salt	225 gm

Method

1. Clean capsicums. Wash well. 2. Rub salt and keep in the sun for 6–10 hours. 3. Boil vinegar with crushed ginger, garlic, red chillies, sugar and

peppercorns for about 10 minutes. 4. Remove, cool and pour over capsicums. 5. Add mustard powder. Store in a glass jar.

42. PRESERVED CHILLIES

Wash green chillies. Dry and salt them and sun for a day. For every kg of chillies add 750 gm of thick curds. Mix well. Dry in the sun for several days, till all moisture has evaporated. Tin or bottle and when required fry in oil and use.

43. PAPAYA CHILLIES

Ingredients	Quantity
Raw papaya (after peeling and seeding)	1 kg
Sugar	1 kg
Water	1 litre
Vinegar	200 ml
Salt	50 gm
Citric acid	a pinch
Grind together	
Chilli powder	15 gm
Ginger (fresh)	15 gm
Garlic	16 gm
Onions	50 gm

Method

1. Wash, peel, seed and slice raw papaya. 2. Boil fruit to soften. 3. Drain off water. Add sugar to water. When sugar has dissolved, add pinch of citric acid and strain. 4. Return to pan and boil to 2 string consistency. 5. Add vinegar and ground spices (tied loosely in a muslin bag), and salt. Boil for 5 minutes. Remove bag. Add fruit. 6. Pour into jars when cool. Cover and keep airtight.

N.B. This pickle improves if kept for a few weeks before using.

44. GAME PICKLE

Ingredients	Quantity
Meat (with bones)	5 kg
Red chillies	125 gm
Garlic	30 gm
Ginger	30 gm
Peppercorns	30 gm
Cumin	10 gm
Cloves	
Cinnamon	5 gm

Ingredients	Quantity
Vinegar	2 bottles (1.3 litre)
Salad oil	½ bottle (320 ml)
Salt	225 gm

Method

1. Wash meat with vinegar. Wipe dry. 2. Smear with pepper and salt.
3. Roast using salad oil. Cool and cut into cubes. 4. Grind spices using
vinegar. 5. Fry spices using left over fat from roasting pan. 6. Add
remaining vinegar and salt. Cook for a few minutes. 7. Add meat.
Remove from fire, cool and bottle. 8. Seal with a little melted wax.

45. MEAT OR GAME PICKLE

Ingredients	Quantity
Meat or Game (without bones)	1 kg
Salt	60 gm
Turmeric	10 gm
Spices for pickle:	
Red chillies	10 gm
Turmeric	2 tsp
Cumin	2 tsp (10 gm)
Grated ginger	4 tsp (20 gm)
Garlic (chopped)	10 gm
Vinegar	650 ml
Mustard	10 gm (2 tsp)

Method

1. Cut meat into large cubes. Prick all over. Rub with salt and turmeric.
2. Spread on a flat plate in layers. 3. Cover with another plate. Place
weights on top. Leave for a day. 4. Wash meat in vinegar. Wipe dry.
5. Grind spices, using vinegar. 6. Pack in a jar in alternate layers of meat
and spices. 7. Pour vinegar over to cover. Close lid tightly. 8. Shake jar
every day for a week to mix well. This pickle will be ready in a week.
9. When required heat some oil. Fry meat adding some of the gravy.

N.B. Pieces of game, after being smeared with turmeric and salt, have
to be strung on thread and sun-dried before pickling.

46. MUTTON PICKLE

Ingredients	Quantity
Mutton	1 kg
Coriander seeds	½ tsp
Mustard seeds	1 tsp

Ingredients	Quantity
Cumin	2 tbsp
Turmeric	1 tsp
Dry coconut (copra)	½
Salt	1 tsp
Chilli powder	1 tsp
Lime juice	3 large limes (or 6 small)
Garlic (sliced lengthwise)	2 large
Green chillied (cut lengthwise)	10–12
Ginger (sliced lengthwise)	1"
Oil	150 ml
Fenugreek	½ tsp

Method

1. Fry coriander, cumin, fenugreek and mustard in a little oil till brown.
2. Fry grated copra in a little oil and grind with above. 3. Then fry ginger, garlic and green chillies in a little oil and mix with above ground masala. 4. Add turmeric, chilli powder and salt. Mix well and set aside. 5. Cook mutton in a little water till done. 6. In a little oil, put in cooked mutton and cook till all the water evaporates. 7. To dry meat, add prepared masala and mix well over fire. 8. Add freshly squeezed lime juice and keep stirring on very slow fire till meat is dry. 9. Remove from fire and store in a vessel.

47. PICKLED BEEF

Ingredients	Quantity
Cleaned beef (rump/sirloin)	2 kg
Salt	100 gm
Brown sugar/Molasses	100 gm
Limes/Lemons	3 large
Saltpetre	50 gm

Method

1. Mix all ingredients in a large thick-bottomed stainless steel pan. Juice limes/lemons, seeds and all. 2. Marinate meat in the mixture. Rub with lemon/lime leaving rinds on meat. 3. Rub twice a day for 10 days, pricking occasionally with a fork. Take out the brine. 4. Boil on a slow fire or roast till done. Cool and cut slices as required and use for making sandwiches. 5. Use butter beaten with mustard and finely chopped garlic as sandwich spread.

48. SALTED MEAT

Ingredients	Quantity
Beef	5kg
Salt	180–200 gm
Brown sugar	100 gm
Limes	1½

Method

1. Brown salt and pepper. Remove. Powder fine. Juice limes. Add the salt, pepper and brown sugar. 2. Clean meat with a damp cloth rinsed in vinegary water. Add lime juice and salt to meat. Prick meat twice. Dry with a fork and put back into lime juice mixture. Keep in a refrigerator. Repeat process for 5 days. 3. Using a thick-bottomed pan cook the meat at simmering point without adding any liquid. When tender remove. 4. Drain out liquid and leave to cool.

49. CHICKEN PICKLE

Ingredients	Quantity
Chicken	1 kg
Turmeric	30 gm
Garlic	30 gm
Red chillies	125 gm
Fenugreek	15 gm
Mustard seeds	30 gm
Ginger	55 gm
Vinegar	120 ml
Mustard oil	500 ml (approx.)
Salt	125 gm

Method

1. Cut chicken into small pieces. 2. Fry in mustard oil. 3. Grind all the spices separately in vinegar. 4. Take some of the mustard oil and fry turmeric, ginger, garlic, red chillies. 5. Add salt, mustard and fenugreek. Fry for 2–3 minutes. 6. Add fried chicken. Fry for another 2–3 minutes. Cool. 7. Add remaining mustard oil that has been previously heated and cooled.

50. MALABAR FISH PICKLE

Ingredients	Quantity
Seer or any other good fish	450 gm
Vinegar	160 ml
Chilli powder	10–15 gm
Ginger	5 gm

Ingredients	Quantity
Mustard seeds	1 tbsp
Green chillies	4
Garlic	30 gm (2 pods)
Poppy seeds	1 tbsp
Salt	to taste
Sesame oil	30 ml
Curry leaves	

Method

1. Cut fish into slices and wash well. 2. Fry fish well and set aside.
3. Grind chilli powder and poppy seeds in vinegar. 4. Cut garlic, ginger
and green chillies. 5. Mix ground spices, garlic, ginger and green chillies
and salt with vinegar. 6. Heat sesame oil and add mustard seeds and
curry leaves. 7. Pour vinegar mixture into oil and bring it to a boil.
Remove from fire. 8. When cool put in fried fish.

51. PRAWN OR FISH PICKLE

Ingredients	Quantity
Prawn or Fish	1 kg
Turmeric	30 gm
Garlic	30 gm
Mustard seeds	30 gm
Red chillies	15 gm
Ginger	55 gm
Fenugreek	15 gm
Vinegar	100–120 ml
Salt	115 gm
Mustard oil	450 ml
Limes	2

Method

1. Clean fish or prawns. 2. Apply a little salt, turmeric and fresh lime.
3. Fry in mustard oil. 4. Grind all the spices separately with vinegar.
5. Heat 120 ml mustard oil. Fry spices. Add salt, mustard and fenugreek.
Fry for 2–3 minutes. 6. Add fried prawns. Cool. 7. Add remaining
mustard oil that has been previously heated and cooled.

52. PRAWN PICKLE (Malayalee)

Ingredients	Quantity
Prawns (medium to large with shells)	1 kg
Salt	10 gm
Garlic	30 gm

Ingredients	Quantity
Chilli powder	30 gm
Green chillies	15 gm
Ginger	10 gm
Red chillies	2 gm
Peppercorns	5
Turmeric	½ tsp
Salt	30–40 gm
Salad oil	120 ml
Vinegar (white)	200 ml
Mustard seeds	5 gm

Method

1. Shell prawns. Remove intestines; wash and drain on cloth. 2. Grind together whole red chillies, peppercorns, turmeric and salt using a little vinegar. 3. Smear ground paste on prawns. 4. Heat some of the salad oil and shallow fry prawns till cooked. 5. Peel and slice garlic and ginger and slit green chillies. 6. Heat remaining oil. Add mustard seeds and curry leaves. 7. Add green chillies, garlic and ginger and fry lightly. 8. Remove pan from fire. Add chilli powder. 9. Stir well. Add vinegar and salt. Return to fire and bring to a boil. 10. Remove from fire. Cool and add prawns.

53. WATERMELON PICKLE

Ingredients	Quantity
Thick watermelon rind	2 kg
Peppercorns (whole)	2 tbsp
Lime water, made with cold water and lime (calcium oxide)	1 tbsp
Cloves	10
Cinnamon	5 cm (about 2") piece
Red chillies	10
Vinegar	1 litre
Water	1 litre
Sugar	2 kg

Method

1. Select thick rind from a firm, but not over-ripe melon. To prepare, trim off green skin and pink flesh. Weigh 2 kg of remaining portion and cut into 2.5 cm (about 1") pieces. 2. Soak for 1 hour in lime water. Drain, cover with fresh water and cook for 1 hour or until tender. Add more water as needed. Drain. 3. Put all the spices (except red chillies) in a

muslin bag. Tie. Bring to a boil the spices, vinegar, water and sugar.
4. Add watermelon rind and boil gently for 2 hours. Remove from fire.
5. Add whole chillies and let stand overnight. Remove spice bag. 6. Boil
for 1 minute and pack into sterilized jars. Fill jars to the top with hot
syrup and seal tightly.

54. CARROT KANJI

Ingredients	Quantity
Carrots (preferably black variety)	1 kg
Salt	50–100 gm
Water	3 litre
Mustard seeds	100 gm
Chilli powder	30 gm
Beetroot	125 gm (1)

Method

1. Wash carrots. Cut into four. 2. Crush mustard. Peel and slice beetroot.
3. Mix all ingredients together and put into an earthen pot. Cover tightly
and set aside for 4 days. Use as required.

55. DUDHI KANJI (Bottle gourd kanji)

Substitute dudhi for carrots and omit beetroot. Method and other
ingredients same as for Carrots Kanji.

56. POTATO KANJI

Substitute potatoes for carrots; omit beetroot. Use old potatoes and
parboil after removing skin. Method and other ingredients same as for
Carrots Kanji.

57. BHALLA KANJI

Ingredients	Quantity
Water	3 litre
Black gram	½ kg
Mustard seeds	100 gm
Salt	50–100 gm (to taste)
Chilli powder	30 gm
Asafoetida	a pinch
Potato (small)	1
Bhalla:	
Split black gram	½ kg
Asafoetida	a pinch
Salt	to taste

Ingredients	Quantity
Soda bicarbonate	a pinch
Lime	1
Oil	for frying
Green chillies	5
Ginger	60 gm
Onion	

Method

Peel and parboil potato. Add remaining ingredients. Mix well and set aside for 3 days. Add fried bhalla and keep for 1–2 days.

Bhalla

1. Soak dal for 5–6 hours. 2. Grind to a smooth and fluffy paste. 3. Add grated ginger, finely chopped green chillies, minced onion, salt, soda bicarbonate and asafoetida. 4. Add 1 tsp heated oil and 1 tsp lime juice. 5. Set aside for 1–2 hours. 6. Shape like small dahibaras and deep fry.

FRESH CHUTNEYS

58. GREEN CHILLI CHUTNEY

Ingredients	Quantity
Green chillies	50 gm (about 10)
Salt	1½ tsp
Cumin	1 tsp
Asafoetida	½ tsp
Tamarind	5 gm
Coriander leaves	½ bunch

Method

1. Clean all ingredients. Wash thoroughly. 2. Grind to a smooth paste.

59. CHANNA DAL CHUTNEY

Ingredients	Quantity
Split bengal gram	30 gm (about 2 tbsp)
Red chillies	3
Salt	1½ tsp
Asafoetida	½ tsp
Cumin	½ tsp
Oil	2 tsp
Curry leaves	1 sprig
Green chilli	1
Mustard seeds	1 tsp

Ingredients	Quantity
Curds	85 gm (½ cup)
Pepper	½ tsp

Method

1. Heat oil in a frying pan. Separately fry gram, red chillies and cumin. 2. Grind together with salt, asafoetida and pepper. Mix curds. 3. Heat remaining oil. Fry mustard seeds, chopped green chilli and curry leaves. 4. Pour into curd mixture. Mix well.

60. MOONG DAL CHUTNEY

Ingredients	Quantity
Split green gram	30 gm
Red chillies	3
Asafoetida	½ tsp
Salt	1 tsp
Oil	2 tsp

Method

1. Soak gram for a couple of hours. 2. Heat oil. Fry gram. Remove. 3. Fry chillies and mustard. 4. Grind all ingredients together.

61. DAL CHUTNEY

Ingredients	Quantity
Split black gram	125 gm
Split bengal gram	125 gm
Coconut	225 gm (1)
Green chillies	20 gm
Tamarind	10 gm
Coriander leaves	½ bunch
Curry leaves	1 sprig
Salt	to taste
Oil	½ tsp

Method

1. Heat oil. Fry black gram and bengal gram with curry leaves. Grate coconut. 3. Grind all ingredients together into a smooth paste, adding a little water if necessary.

62. COCONUT AND MOONG DAL CHUTNEY

Ingredients	Quantity
Coconut (fresh)	125 gm
Salt	to taste

Ingredients	Quantity
Tamarind	10 gm
Split green gram	3 gm
Red chilli	1
For Tempering:	
Oil	2 tsp
Mustard seeds	½ tsp
Curry leaves	1 sprig

Method

1. Fry chillies and gram. 2. Grind all ingredients. 3. Temper.

63. CURRY LEAF CHUTNEY

Ingredients	Quantity
Curry leaves	1 bunch
Red chillies	3
Salt	1½ tsp
Dry coconut	30 gm
Tamarind	5 gm
Oil	1 tsp

Method

1. Pick leaves and wash and dry. 2. Heat oil. Fry curry leaves. Remove. Add sliced dry coconut and red chillies. 3. Grind all ingredients together into a smooth paste.

64. COPRA CHUTNEY

Ingredients	Quantity
Dry coconut	½
Red chillies	4
Turmeric	a small piece
Salt	1½ tsp

Method

1. Grate coconut. Roast on a hot iron frying pan. 2. Remove. Roast chillies and turmeric. 3. Grind all ingredients together coarsely.

65. MANGO CHUTNEY (A)

Ingredients	Quantity
Green mango (large)	2
Green chillies	4
Salt	1½ tsp

Ingredients	Quantity
Asafoetida	a pinch
Cumin	½ tsp
Ginger	2.5 cm piece (about 1")

Method

1. Peel and slice mango. 2. Grind all ingredients together.

MANGO CHUTNEY (B)

Ingredients	Quantity
Raw green mango	1
Onions	100 gm
Coconut (fresh, grated)	15 gm
Garlic	3 flakes
Ginger	1.3 cm (about ½")
Green chillies	2
Salt	to taste
Cumin	a pinch

Method

1. Peel and slice mangoes. 2. Grind all ingredients together.

MANGO CHUTNEY (C)

Ingredients	Quantity
Raw green mango	1
Onions	1
Ginger	1.3 cm (about ½")
Green chillies	3
Coconut	½ (125 gm)
Salt	to taste

Method

1. Take out a thick extraction of coconut milk. 2. Slice all other ingredients fine. Add coconut milk and salt. Mix well.

66. COCONUT CHUTNEY (A)

Ingredients	Quantity
Coconut	1
Red chillies	5 gm
Ginger	10 gm
Onions	125 gm
Tamarind	10 gm

Method

1. Grate coconut and grind all ingredients together. If desired this mixture can be tempered with mustard seeds and curry leaves with a little water added for moistening.

COCONUT CHUTNEY (B)

Ingredients	Quantity
Fresh, grated coconut	125 gm (half)
Dry chillies	10 gm
Lentils	30 gm
Mustard seeds	½ tsp
Salt	to taste
Curds	120 ml
Oil	1 tsp

Method

1. Soak lentils in water for half an hour. Drain. 2. Grate coconut. 3. Heat oil. Add mustard seeds. As they crackle add dal. Fry till golden. Add chillies and grated coconut. 4. Fry for about 2 minutes. 5. Remove and grind into a smooth paste with salt. 6. Add curds to ground ingredients and mix well.

COCONUT CHUTNEY (C)

Ingredients	Quantity
Fresh coconut (large)	1 (225–275 gm)
Onions	125 gm
Tamarind	10–15 gm
Green chillies	10 gm
Red chillies	5 gm
Asafoetida	a pinch
Mustard seeds	1 tbsp
Split black gram	1 tsp
Sesame oil	1 tbsp
Salt	to taste

Method

1. Grate coconut and slice onions. 2. Heat oil and fry mustard, gram, chillies and asafoetida. 3. Grind fried ingredients with coconut, tamarind and onion into a thick paste. Add a little water if necessary.

67. COCONUT CHUTNEY for IDLIS

Ingredients	Quantity
Coconut (large)	1 (225–275 gm)
Buttermilk	1 tbsp

Ingredients	Quantity
Mustard seeds	½ tsp
Tamarind	10 gm
Green chillies	15 gm
Asafoetida	5 gm
Sesame oil	1 tbsp
Salt	to taste

Method

1. Grate coconut. 2. Grind together coconut, chillies, asafoetida and tamarind. 3. Add buttermilk to thin down paste. Add salt. 4. Heat oil. Fry mustard seeds. Pour over chutney and mix well.

68. DRIED COCONUT CHUTNEY

Ingredients	Quantity
Dried coconut	1
Red chillies	10 gm
Oil	10 ml
Tamarind	5 gm
Split bengal gram	45 gm
Curry leaves	4 sprigs
Salt	to taste

Method

1. Grate coconut. 2. Roast on a tawa or griddle until dry and browned. 3. Fry gram in oil. 4. Roast red chillies and curry leaves till dry and crisp. 5. Pound all ingredients including tamarind and salt together in a mortar to a fine powder. 6. Serve as a dry chutney.

69. PARIPPU PODI (dry dal chutney for idli, dosa, etc.)

Ingredients	Quantity
Split black gram (urad dal)	½ cup
Red chillies	5
Asafoetida	½ tsp
Split bengal gram (Channa dal)	¼ cup
Salt	to taste

Method

1. Separately roast (without using oil) urad dal, channa dal, red chillies and asafoetida. Powder fine. Add salt and bottle. When needed mix with oil as desired and serve with Idli, Dosa, etc.

70. GROUNDNUT CHUTNEY (A)

Ingredients	Quantity
Groundnuts	125 gm
Dry coconut	15 gm
White sesame seeds	2 tsp
Tamarind	5 gm
Cumin	½ tsp
Mustard seeds	½ tsp
Asafoetida	½ tsp
Green chillies	7
Jaggery	a small piece
Salt	to taste (about 1½ tsp)
Oil	1 tbsp

Method

1. Roast groundnuts and remove skin. 2. Roast sesame seeds. 3. Hold dry coconut over fire with a pair of tongs for a few minutes. 4. Grind together groundnut, coconut, chillies, jaggery, sesame seeds, tamarind and salt. 5. Heat oil; add asafoetida, cumin and mustard. When they crackle pour over prepared chutney and mix well.

GROUNDNUT CHUTNEY (B)

Ingredients	For 4	For 100
Roasted peanuts	50 gm	2.8 kg
Salt	to taste	100 gm
Red chillies	2	60 gm
Ginger (chopped)	5 gm	85 gm
Lime juice	2 drops	6 limes

Method

1. Grind all ingredients together. 2. Chillies must be roasted before being ground.

71. ONION CHUTNEY

Ingredients	Quantity
Red chillies	5 gm
Onions	500 gm
Tamarind	marble-sized
Asafoetida	a pinch
Salt	to taste
Sesame oil	1 tbsp
Mustard seeds	1 tsp
Split black gram	1 tsp

Method

1. Slice onion. 2. Heat oil. Fry mustard seeds and gram until they crackle. 3. Add asafoetida and red chillies and fry crisp. Remove. 4. In remaining oil, fry onions till crisp and brown. 5. Grind spices with tamarind. Add onion and salt with a little water and grind into a thick paste.

72. GARLIC CHUTNEY (A)

Ingredients	Quantity
Curry leaves	1 sprig
Coconut	(½) 125 gm
Red chillies	10 gm
Garlic	15 gm
Lime (juice)	to taste
Sesame oil	1½ tbsp
Salt	to taste

Method

1. Peel garlic; grate coconut. 2. Grind garlic and chillies. Add coconut and grind. 3. Add lime juice and salt. 4. Heat oil. Fry curry leaves and add to chutney.

GARLIC CHUTNEY (B)

Ingredients	Quantity
Garlic	50 gm
Dry coconut	½
Salt	1 tsp
Tamarind	5 gm
Chilli powder	2 tsp
Turmeric	¼ tsp
Sugar	1 tsp

Method

1. Grate coconut and pound coarsely with all the other ingredients (this chutney will keep for a week.)

73. DUDHI PEEL CHUTNEY

Ingredients	Quantity
Bottle gourd peel	50 gm
Sesame seeds	15 gm
Dry coconut	15 gm
Green chillies	5 gm
Salt	to taste

Ingredients	Quantity
Oil	1 dsp
Mustard seeds	¼ tsp
Asafoetida	a pinch

Method

1. Wash bottle gourd. Peel thick. 2. Fry in oil, mustard, asafoetida, chopped green chillies, sliced coconut, sesame seeds and peel. When crisp, remove. 3. Grind into a fine paste using little water.

74. MINT CHUTNEY (A)

Ingredients	For 4	For 100
Mint	¼ bunch	8 bunches
Pomegranate seeds or Tamarind	10 gm	250 gm
Green chillies	5 gm	125 gm
Onions	30 gm	700 gm
Salt	to taste	80–100 gm
Sugar	a pinch	1 tsp

Method

1. Wash mint. Remove coarse stems. 2. Peel and chop onions. 3. Grind all ingredients together.

MINT CHUTNEY (B)

Ingredients	Quantity
Mint	1 large bunch
Spring onions or	6
Onions	125 gm
Green chillies (small)	10 gm (4)
Green mango (small)	1
Salt	to taste
Sugar	½ tsp

Method

1. Wash mint leaves thoroughly. 2. Slice onion and chop mango. 3. Grind all ingredients together into a smooth paste.

75. HARA DHANIA CHUTNEY (A)

Ingredients	Quantity
Coriander leaves	1 bunch
Green chillies	10 gm (2)

Ingredients	Quantity
Garlic	4 flakes
Cumin	½ tsp
Peppercorns	2
Lime (juice)	1
Peanuts	10 gm
Salt	to taste

Method

1. Wash and pluck coriander leaves. 2. Peel garlic. 3. Grind all ingredients together into a smooth paste.

HARA DHANIA CHUTNEY (B)

Ingredients	Quantity
Coriander leaves	1 bunch
Green chillies	15 gm (6)
Coconut	125 gm (½)
Garlic	3 flakes
Cumin	1 tsp
Lime	½
Onions	125 gm
Sugar	1 tsp
Salt	to taste

Method

1. Wash and pluck coriander leaves. 2. Grate coconut. Slice onions. 3. Grind all ingredients together into a fine paste. 4. Add lime juice. Mix well.

76. GREEN CHUTNEY

Ingredients	For 4	For 100
Coriander leaves	30 gm	700 gm
Coconut	50 gm	1.35 kg
Tamarind	5 gm	125 gm
Green chillies	5 gm	125 gm
Onions	30 gm	750 gm
Salt	to taste	100 gm
Ginger	a small piece	50 gm

Method

Grind all ingredients together.

77. THUVAYYEL

Ingredients	Quantity
Groundnuts	75 gm
Ginger	5 gm
Coriander leaves	5 gm
Salt	5–7 gm
Green chillies	10 gm
Curry leaves	a few
Tamarind	5 gm

Method

1. Boil groundnuts in just enough water to cook them dry. 2. Grind with all the other ingredients into a smooth paste. Serve as an accompaniment.

78. BITTER GOURD CHUTNEY

Ingredients	Quantity
Bitter gourd	1 cup
Red onions (Madras)	½ cup
Green chillies (finely chopped)	6
Curry leaves	a sprig
Tamarind	size of a lime
Ginger (finely chopped)	½ tsp
Concentrated salt water	½ cup
Coconut oil (or Refined oil)	60 ml

Method

1. Put finely chopped bitter gourd into some salt water and knead it several times. 2. Collect pieces of gourd and squeeze out salt water by hand. 3. Put gourd into a vessel along with finely chopped onions, green chillies, ginger and curry leaves. 4. Make a tamarind pulp solution with ¼ cup concentrated salt water and tamarind and add it to other ingredients. Mix well. 5. Add oil and mix again. 6. Take two 30.5 cm (about 12") pieces of aluminium foil. Put the mixture into one of the pieces and make it into a small flat packet. 7. Fold this packet again in the other piece of foil and tie it two or three times with string. 8. Bake the packet for 5 hours in hot ashes from which glowing cinders have been removed. 9. Put a few cinders over ash to keep ash warm. 10. After 5 hours take the packet out, unfold and when cool bottle in clean bottles.

N.B. The packet can be placed under a grill and turned over several times till done. Traditionally, banana leaves are used instead of aluminium foil.

79. KHAJUR CHUTNEY

Ingredients	Quantity
Dates	225 gm
Salt	1½ tsp
Chilli powder	1 tsp
Cumin	½ tsp
Green chillies	2
Coriander powder	½ tsp
Coriander leaves	¼ bunch
Tamarind	10 gm (approx.)
Sugar	10 gm
Asafoetida	a pinch
Ginger	1.3 cm piece (about ½")
Oil	1 tsp

Method

1. Stone dates. Wash and grind with green chillies, ginger and cumin.
2. Add chilli powder, coriander powder and tamarind pulp. 3. Wash and chop coriander leaves and add them to the prepared ingredients with salt and sugar. 4. Heat oil. Add asafoetida. When hot, pour over chutney.

80. BANANA CHUTNEY

Ingredients	Quantity
Dried dates	6–7
Ripe bananas	3
Coconut	½ (125 gm)
Onions	1 (125 gm)
Mint	1 sprig
Green chillies	2
Mustard seeds	a pinch
Lime juice	½

Method

1. Stone dates and soak in boiling water until soft. 2. Peel bananas. 3. Grind all the ingredients into a fine paste. 4. Add lime juice and blend well.

81. PRAWN PASTE

Ingredients	Quantity
Dry prawns	30 gm (about a handful)
Turmeric	a pinch
Coriander powder	¼ tsp
Red chillies	2

Ingredients	Quantity
Coconut	125 gm (½)
Bengal gram (roasted)	1 tbsp
Cumin	a pinch
Tamarind	5–10 gm
Salt	to taste

Method

1. Clean and roast prawns. 2. Pound prawns into a powder. 3. Grind powder with all the other ingredients into a fine paste.

82. SWEET and SOUR CHUTNEY

Ingredients	Quantity
Tamarind	30 gm
Ginger	2.5 cm (about 1") piece
Red chillies	4
Sugar	1–2 tsp
Salt	to taste
Lime	2

Method

1. Soak tamarind in enough water to extract pulp. 2. Grind remaining ingredients and mix with tamarind. 3. Add lime juice.

83. MANGO CHUTNEY (A)

Ingredients	Quantity
Green mangoes (fresh, medium-sized)	6
Sugar	350 gm
Ginger (chopped)	30 gm
Garlic	1 pod
Red chillies	3 to 6
Chopped almonds	60 gm
Raisins	125 gm
Salt	to taste
Vinegar	300 ml (about ½ bottle)

Method

1. Peel, slice and cut mangoes into small pieces lengthwise. 2. Sprinkle a little salt on them and set aside. 3. Grind chillies and vinegar into a fine paste. 4. Heat vinegar in a stainless steel pan. 5. Add sugar. Keep stirring. 6. When sugar melts add mangoes. Cook for 5 minutes on a slow fire. 7. Add peeled garlic and chopped ginger. Mix well. 8. Add chilli paste. 9. Stir well and cook for 10 minutes. 10. Add almonds, cleaned

raisins, salt and more sugar if desired. 11. Cook for 5 minutes. 12. Cool and bottle. (This chutney will keep for a year.)

MANGO CHUTNEY (B)

Ingredients	Quantity
Green mangoes	450 gm
Sultanas	125 gm
Red chillies	5–10 gm
Mustard seeds	30 gm
Sugar	450 gm
Garlic	30 gm
Ginger	30 gm
Vinegar	320 ml

Method

1. Peel and slice mangoes, sprinkle them with salt and sun dry for a day. 2. Then bruise the slices. 3. Wash sultanas and remove stalks. 4. Grind chillies, mustard, garlic and ginger with vinegar. 5. Dissolve sugar in remaining vinegar, add salt and ground ingredients and boil until the syrup is very thick. 6. Then add mangoes and boil for 10 minutes more. 7. Allow chutney to cool and then mix in sultanas.

MANGO CHUTNEY (C)

Ingredients	Quantity
Raw mangoes (large)	7
Sugar	1.35 kg
Ginger	125 gm
Garlic	125 gm
Almonds	125 gm
Raisins	125 gm
Chilli powder	50 gm
Salt	125 gm
Vinegar	120 ml
Brandy (optional)	2 tbsp

Method

1. Peel and slice mangoes into thin pieces. 2. Clean and cut ginger, garlic and blanched almonds into slices. 3. Clean raisins and wash in a little vinegar. 4. In a wide stainless steel pan boil mangoes and sugar, adding a little water. 5. When sugar melts add other ingredients gradually till mixture develops a jam-like consistency. 6. Add vinegar and brandy. Stir for 5 minutes more. 7. Remove from fire. Cool and bottle.

N.B. This chutney will keep for a year. Reduce chilli powder to 30 gm if less pungency is desired.

MANGO CHUTNEY (D)

Ingredients	Quantity
Peeled and sliced mangoes	225 gm (about 2 cups)
Sugar	300 gm
Almonds	10–15
Raisins	15 gm
Salt	30 gm
Chilli powder	2 gm

Method

1. Wash and peel mangoes. 2. Blanch almonds and cut into slices lengthwise. 3. Wash and clean raisins. 4. Put mangoes, sugar, salt and chilli powder into a saucepan and cook on a gentle fire till mangoes are soft and cooked. 5. Add almonds and raisins. 6. Allow to simmer gently for a few minutes more. 7. Remove. Cool and bottle in sterilized jars.

MANGO CHUTNEY (E)

Ingredients	Quantity
Peeled mango slices	1 kg
Sugar	1 kg
Salt	70 gm
Cardamom	5 gm
Cinnamon	5 gm
Cumin	10 gm
Cloves	2 gm
Garlic	5 gm
Red chillies	5 gm
Vinegar	150 ml
Onions	30 gm
Ginger	25 gm
Water	¼ litre

Method

1. Choose slightly under-ripe mangoes and peel and slice them. Add very little water and cook mangoes. Add sugar and salt. 2. Tie all the masalas in a cloth bag or muslin cloth and drop into mangoes. 3. Cook to a jam-like consistency. Add vinegar and cook for 5 minutes more. 4. Remove spice bag and squeeze extract into chutney. Put into sterilized jars.

84. SWEET MANGO CHUTNEY

Ingredients	Quantity
Mangoes	2 kg
Vinegar	about 3 bottles
Sugar	1 kg
Red chillies	125 gm
Garlic	125 gm
Ginger	125 gm
Salt	125 gm
Raisins	500 gm
Sultanas	500 gm
Mustard seeds	1 tbsp

Method

1. Pare and cut mangoes into thin slices and simmer in 2 bottles vinegar.
2. Boil sugar in remaining vinegar. Grind chillies (after removing seeds), garlic and ginger and salt into a fine paste using vinegar. 3. Stone raisins, clean sultanas. When mangoes are cooked, add ground ingredients, prepared dry fruit, sugar syrup and cleaned mustard. 4. Simmer for 5 minutes. Remove when thick. Cool and bottle.

85. KASHMIRI CHUTNEY (Mango)

Ingredients	Quantity
Mangoes (peel and grind)	10 kg
Mustard (yellow)	200 gm (ground dry)
Red chillies (ground)	400 gm
Garlic	200 gm
Ginger	400 gm
Sugar	800 gm
Salt	400 gm
Vinegar	3 bottles (about 2 litre)
Mustard oil	60 ml

Method

1. Boil vinegar with sugar. Cool. 2. Grind all spices and mangoes using vinegar. 3. Mix all ingredients together. 4. Heat oil. Cool and pour over mixture. 5. Bottle and use as required.

86. KHAREK CHUTNEY

Ingredients	Quantity
Dried dates	30 gm
Dried mango slices	30 gm
Oil	1 tsp

Ingredients	Quantity
Mustard seeds	⅛th tsp
Red chilli (whole)	1
Chopped coriander leaves	a few
Chilli powder	½ tsp
Turmeric	¼ tsp
Salt	½ tsp
Sugar	55 gm

Method

1. Stone and soak dates and mango slices in about 150 ml of water for a few hours. 2. Heat oil. Add mustard seeds and whole red chilli. 3. When mustard seeds crackle add dates along with liquid, mango slices and spices. 4. Cook for 10–15 minutes. 5. Mash up all ingredients and mix well.

8₇. LIME and DATE CHUTNEY

Ingredients	Quantity
Limes	25
Chilli powder	125 gm
Jaggery	700 gm
Cumin	1 tbsp
Garlic	125 gm
Dried dates	350 gm
Salt	200 gm
Vinegar	1 bottle (750 ml)

Method

1. Wash limes. Cut into four, sprinkle over with salt. 2. Pack in a glass jar. Cover tightly and set aside for 3 days. 3. Remove limes from jar and sun dry for 4–5 days. 4. Mince finely in a mincing machine. 5. Stone dates and mince. 6. Grind cumin, garlic and jaggery. 7. Mix all the ingredients with vinegar. 8. Put into air-tight jars. Set aside for 15 days before using.

88. MINT CHUTNEY

Ingredients	Quantity
Green mint leaves	125 gm
Red chillies	15 gm
Ginger	30 gm
Salt	60 gm
Raisins	85 gm
Sugar	125 gm
Onions	15 gm
Vinegar	350 ml

Method

1. Grind mint leaves, chillies, ginger, raisins, onion and garlic with vinegar. 2. Heat remaining vinegar to boiling point. 3. Put ground ingredients into a jar. Add salt and sugar. 4. Pour over hot vinegar. Cork and set aside for 2 weeks before using.

89. RAW PAPAYA CHUTNEY

Ingredients	Quantity
Raw papaya	450 gm
Sultanas	85 gm
Sugar	225 gm
Garlic	5 gm
Ginger	15 gm
Chilli powder	15 gm
Vinegar	375 ml (½ bottle)

Method

1. Peel and slice papaya. 2. Slice ginger and garlic. 3. Clean and wash sultanas in a little vinegar. 4. In a stainless steel pan mix sugar and vinegar and put on fire. 5. When sugar dissolves add chilli powder, ginger, garlic, papaya and salt. 6. Cook on a slow fire without covering pan. Keep stirring. 7. After 10–15 minutes add sultanas. 8. Cook till liquid is thick. 9. Remove, cool and bottle.

90. COCUM CHUTNEY

Ingredients	Quantity
Cocum	125 gm
Salt	to taste
Jaggery	30 gm
Sugar	3 tbsp
Red chillies	5
Vinegar	4 tbsp
Garlic	3 flakes
Ginger	2.5 cm (about 1")

Method

1. Wash cocum with hot water. 2. Grind with chillies. 3. Slice ginger and garlic. 4. Mix vinegar, sugar, jaggery, ground ingredients, ginger, garlic and salt. 5. Cook on a slow fire stirring all the time. 6. When thick, remove.

91. DATE CHUTNEY

Ingredients	For 4	For 100
Dates	50 gm	1.56 kg

Ingredients	For 4	For 100
Sugar	20 gm	500 gm
Red chillies	2	60 gm
Ginger	5 gm	125 gm
Garlic	5 gm	125 gm
Vinegar	60 ml	1.5 litre
Salt	to taste	100 gm

Method

1. Remove seeds from chillies and soak in vinegar. 2. Stone and grind dates. 3. Grind chillies, garlic, and ginger using a little vinegar. 4. Make a syrup of remaining vinegar and sugar. 5. Add ground spices and salt. Boil till syrup is thick. 6. Cool and add ground dates.

92. DATE and CARROT CHUTNEY

Ingredients	Quantity
Vinegar	1 bottle (750 ml)
Brown sugar	1 kg
Carrots (chopped)	¾ kg
Dates (minced)	½ kg
Raisins (optional)	¼ kg
Onions	¼ kg
Salt	100 gm
Ginger (shredded)	a small piece
Cinnamon	a stick
Chilli powder	1 tsp
Coriander powder	1 tsp
Cloves	3–4

Method

1. Scrape and chop carrots into 1.3 cm (about ¼") long, thin strips.
2. Remove seeds from dates and mince or crush. Chop onions fine.
3. Mince raisins (after picking stalks). Powder all spices (or grind).
4. Cook carrots in about 2 cup water. Add onions, dates, raisins, salt, brown sugar, ginger and powdered spices and cook to a jam-like consistency. 5. Add vinegar and cook a little longer. Pour into bottles while hot. Cool, cork and label.

93. DRIED APRICOT CHUTNEY

Ingredients	Quantity
Dried apricots	250 gm
Sugar	250 gm

Ingredients	Quantity
Dry chillies	10 gm
Garlic	10 gm
Ginger	10 gm
Vinegar	150 ml
Salt	to taste

Method

1. Wash apricots well and put them into a basin with cold water to cover, and let them soak overnight. 2. Remove seeds and put apricots and water in which they were soaked into a saucepan and simmer slowly until fruit is tender, mashing fruit with a spoon. 3. Remove seeds from chillies and grind with garlic and vinegar. 4. Put remaining vinegar into a saucepan, add sugar, ground ingredients and salt and stir over fire until ingredients are cooked. 5. Then add stewed apricots and boil till it has the consistency of good chutney.

94. APPLE CHUTNEY (A)

Ingredients	Quantity
Cooking apples	2 kg
Raisins	500 gm
Sultanas	1 kg
Brown sugar	1.8 kg
Salt	225 gm
Ginger	125 gm
Garlic	30 gm
Chilli powder	15 gm
Mustard seeds	125 gm
Vinegar	1.2 litre

Method

1. Peel, core and cut apples into slices lengthwise. Clean and pick raisins, stoning and slicing large ones. 2. Peel and cut ginger and garlic, and pound them to a pulp in a mortar. Pick mustard seeds. 3. Boil sugar, and half the vinegar, into a thick syrup. 4. Lay cut apples in a dish, cover them with about half the salt, and let them stand 15–16 hours, or all night. 5. When apples have stood long enough, boil them in the remaining half bottle of vinegar till tender, but do not mash them. 6. Let the apples get cold; then add syrup (cold) and all the other ingredients, including the remaining salt. Cork securely, and let the chutney stand for 5–6 weeks before using.

APPLE CHUTNEY (B)

Ingredients	Quantity
Cooking apples (weighed after peeling and coring)	1.35 kg
Malt vinegar	1 litre
Onions	180 gm
Raisins (cleaned and stoned)	250 gm
Brown sugar	250 gm
Salt	1 level tbsp
Ginger	30 gm
Red chillies	3

Method

1. Mince apples, onions and raisins. If it is easier you may grate the apples, but you must mince or very finely chop raisins and onions. 2. Bruise the ginger with a weight so that the flavour comes out and tie it in a piece of muslin with the chillies. 3. Put it into a pan with the minced ingredients, salt and vinegar and simmer them together for about an hour until they are well combined and reduced; then stir in the sugar. 4. When this has dissolved, boil the chutney for a further 30–45 minutes until it is rather thick and the liquid has evaporated. The watery look on the surface should disappear during cooking. 5. Remove the bag of spices. 6. Fill cleaned warmed jars with the chutney to within 13 cm (about ½") of the rim. If jam jars are used then fill them well up to the neck. 7. Cover them with a round of greaseproof paper and cover the jars with polythene for storing.

95. GREEN TOMATO CHUTNEY

Ingredients	Quantity
Green tomatoes	450 gm
Sugar	450 gm
Red chillies	15 gm
Mustard seeds	30 gm
Garlic	15 gm
Ginger	15 gm
Vinegar	320 ml
Salt	

Method

1. Slice tomatoes, sprinkle them with salt and leave until the next day. 2. Grind chillies, mustard, garlic and ginger with vinegar. 3. Boil the prepared tomatoes in remaining vinegar until soft. 4. Add sugar, ground ingredients and salt, and boil gently until you get the right consistency for chutney.

96. TOMATO CHUTNEY (A)

Ingredients	Quantity
Ripe tomatoes	450 gm
Sugar	450 gm
Red chillies	10 gm
Garlic	15 gm
Ginger	15 gm
Vinegar	160 ml
Salt	

Method

1. Grind chillies, garlic and ginger with vinegar. 2. Scald tomatoes and remove their skins. 3. Cut them into slices, add remaining vinegar and boil until soft. 4. Add sugar, ground ingredients and salt, and boil gently till the right consistency for chutney.

N.B. Remove seeds from red chillies if a less pungent chutney is desired.

TOMATO CHUTNEY (B)

Ingredients	Quantity
Tomatoes	4
Mustard seeds	a pinch
Split black gram	1 tsp
Chilli powder	a small pinch
Sugar	1 tbsp
Fat	1 tsp
Onions	½
Turmeric	a small pinch
Salt	to taste

Method

1. Blanch tomatoes and slice. Slice onion. Put tomatoes, onion, salt, sugar, chilli powder, turmeric and 2 tbsp water into a bowl. 2. Heat a thick-bottomed pan. Add fat. When hot, add mustard seeds and split black gram. Fry well. 3. Now add tomato mixture and cook over a slow fire till mixture becomes thick. Stir occasionally to prevent sticking and burning.

TOMATO CHUTNEY (C)

Ingredients	Quantity
Ripe tomatoes	2 kg
Cooking apples (weighed before peeling)	500 gm

Ingredients	Quantity
Onions	350 gm
Ground ginger	1 tsp
Ground cloves	1 tsp
Cayenne pepper	½ tsp
Salt	15 gm
Mustard seeds	15 gm
Vinegar	30 ml
Brown sugar	350 gm

Method

1. It is best to peel tomatoes in about four batches. Pour boiling water over them, leave them for a few seconds until skin slips off easily, then pour off hot water and replace it with cold water. 2. Peel tomatoes and cut them into quarters. 3. Peel and roughly chop cooking apples and onion. 4. Put tomatoes, cooking apples, onion, ginger, ground cloves, cayenne pepper, and salt into a pan. 5. Add mustard seeds tied in a small piece of muslin. 6. Stir in half the vinegar and simmer the mixture steadily but slowly for about 1 hour. 7. Meanwhile, dissolve sugar in rest of vinegar over gentle heat and add it to the cooking chutney. 8. Boil the chutney more rapidly, without a lid, until it is quite thick. 9. Put chutney into jars and when it is cold, cover jars with polythene.

TOMATO CHUTNEY (D)

Ingredients	Quantity
Bhutanese chillies	3
(Kashmiri chillies can be used)	
Red tomatoes (medium-sized)	2
Garlic	a few flakes
Salt	to taste

Method

1. Soak broken chillies in hot water. 2. Grind chillies, salt and garlic. 3. Roast tomatoes. Peel and mash. Mix with ground chillies etc.

N.B. To be served with Momos.

97. TAMARIND CHUTNEY

Ingredients	Quantity
Tamarind	450 gm
Sugar	700 gm
Sultanas	225 gm
Red chillies	30 gm

Ingredients	Quantity
Mustard seeds	30 gm
Garlic	30 gm
Ginger	30 gm
Vinegar	650 ml
Salt	to taste

Method

1. Squeeze tamarind well in vinegar and strain it through a coarse cloth. 2. Wash sultanas and remove stalks. 3. Grind chillies, mustard, garlic and ginger with vinegar. 4. Make a syrup of sugar and remaining vinegar, add ground ingredients and salt and bring to a boil. 5. Add tamarind and boil till chutney has good consistency. 6. Let it cool and then mix in the sultanas.

98. WOODAPPLE CHUTNEY

Ingredients	Quantity
Woodapple	450 gm
Sugar	450 gm
Sultanas	125 gm
Red chilllies	15 gm
Garlic	30 gm
Ginger	30 gm
Vinegar	650 ml
Salt	to taste

Method

1. Break shell of wood apple and scoop out the inside with a spoon and weigh it. 2. Squeeze the fruit well in vinegar, using about half the vinegar, and strain it through a coarse cloth. 3. Wash sultanas and remove stalks. 4. Grind chillies, garlic and ginger with vinegar. 5. Make a syrup of sugar and remaining vinegar; add ground ingredients and salt and bring to a boil. 6. Add woodapple and boil till it has good consistency for chutney. 7. Let it cool and then mix in sultanas.

99. PINEAPPLE CHUTNEY

Ingredients	Quantity
Medium-sized ripe pineapple	1
Sugar	175 gm
Red chillies	5 gm
Garlic	10 gm
Ginger	10 gm

Ingredients	Quantity
Vinegar	150 ml
Salt	to taste

Method

1. Pare pineapple and dice it very small. 2. Grind chillies, mustard, garlic and ginger with vinegar. 3. Add all the ingredients to pineapple and boil until it is well cooked and the chutney has a good consistency.

100. DRY COCONUT CHUTNEY (Idichuppumuluku)

Ingredients	Quantity
Coconut	1
Red onions	12
Ginger	2.5 cm (about 1") piece
Curry leaves	a few sprigs
Coriander seeds	1 tsp
Red chillies	10 gm
Tamarind	10 gm
Salt	to taste

Method

1. Grate coconut. In a pan roast grated coconut, sliced ginger, sliced onions and curry leaves. 2. Roast and powder red chillies and coriander seeds. 3. Pound tamarind with red chillies and coriander powder. 4. Add coconut mixture gradually and pound coarsely. Mix well and put into airtight containers.

N.B. This can be stored for few months.

101. TOMATO SAUCE

Ingredients	Quantity
Tomatoes (ripe, red)	10 kg
Ginger	125 gm
Garlic	125 gm
Red chillies	50 gm
Sugar	125 gm
Salt	50 gm
Vinegar	1½ bottle (975 ml)

Method

1. Cut up tomatoes and cook without water. 2. Mash and strain. 3. Grind all spices using vinegar. 4. Mix with tomatoes. Add remaining vinegar and sugar. 5. Boil again till thick. Remove and cool. 6. Bottle when cold and use as required.

102. CHILLI SAUCE (A)

Ingredients	Quantity
Ripe large tomatoes	25 (4 kg)
Red capsicum (seeds removed)	350 gm
Black pepper	2 tsp
Cider vinegar	600 ml
Brown sugar	225 gm
Celery	100 gm
Onions	800 gm
Garlic	3 flakes
Allspice	2 tbsp
Mustard	1 tsp
Cayenne	½ tsp

Method

1. Blanch and peel tomatoes. 2. Cut into pieces. Take out seeds and drain any removable liquid. 3. Put pulp into a large pan and cook rapidly until soft and mushy. 4. Remove clear liquid as it comes to the top while cooking. 5. Remove seeds from pepper. Chop finely with celery and onions. 6. When tomatoes are thick, add vegetables and remaining ingredients. (Put allspice in a muslin bag). 7. Boil for about 1½ hours. (Remove spice bag after the first 30 minutes). 8. Stir occasionally. Test for seasoning. 9. When it reaches a good thick consistency pour into hot sterilized bottles and seal.

CHILLI SAUCE (B)

Ingredients	Quantity
Green mangoes (large)	3
Red tomatoes	225 gm
Salt	125 gm
Garlic	50 gm
Onions	125 gm
Dry ginger powder	100 gm
Vinegar	3.5 litre
Red chillies	125 gm
Raisins	225 gm
Sugar	225 gm

Method

1. Peel and slice mangoes. Cut up tomatoes. 2. Roughly powder chillies. 3. Seed raisins. Grind garlic; slice onions. 4. Put all ingredients into a pan. Stir till boiling. 5. Cook gently for 2 hours. 6. Pass through a coarse sieve. Put into sterilized bottles and cork tightly.

103. TOMATO KETCHUP (Mild)

Ingredients	Quantity
Tomatoes	5.5 kg
Onions (sliced)	200 gm
Vinegar	250 ml
Whole cloves	1 tbsp
Sugar	150 gm
Salt	2½ tsp
Paprika	1 tsp
or Chilli powder	½ tsp
Pepper	½ tsp

Method

1.Wash and slice tomatoes. Boil until soft and pulpy. 2. Put sliced onions in a pan. Barely cover with water and cook till tender. 3. Pass tomatoes and onion through a sieve and boil until reduced to half. 4. Put vinegar, and cloves tied in a muslin bag into a stainless steel or enamel pan. 5. Simmer for 30 minutes. Bring to a boil, cover and remove from heat. 6. Add sugar, salt, paprika, pepper and vinegar with spice bag removed, to tomato mixture. 7. Boil together for another 10 minutes or until desired consistency is obtained. 8. Pour into hot sterilized jars or bottles and seal.

N.B. If ketchup is to be preserved for a long period sodium benzoate in the proportion of 50 gm per 45 kg (about 1.6 oz per 100 lb) should be added.

104. TOMATO KETCHUP (Spiced)

Ingredients	Quantity
Ripe red tomatoes	3.6 kg
Cloves (whole)	1½ tsp
Red chillies	5
Garlic (optional)	2 flakes
	(to be ground with chillies)
Cinnamon sticks (broken)	1½ tsp
White vinegar	150 ml
Onions (chopped)	1 tbsp
Sugar	200 gm (about 1 cup)
Salt	4 tsp

Method

1. Grind red chillies into a paste. 2. Add cloves and cinnamon to vinegar. Cover and bring to a boil. 3. Allow vinegar to stand for a whole day to

let it absorb the spices. 4. Blanch tomatoes. Place in a large vessel. Add onion and chilli paste. 5. Keep on fire and cook for 15 minutes stirring occasionally. 6. Pass tomatoes through a coarse sieve. Add sugar to the pulp. 7. Heat till boiling and then simmer briskly till reduced to half (about 45–50 minutes). 8. Strain spiced vinegar into mixture. Add salt and simmer till quite thick, stirring frequently. 9. Fill into hot sterilized bottles and seal.

N.B. If tomato ketchup has to be kept for a long period, sodium benzoate in the proportion of 50 gm to 45 kg (about 1.6 oz per 100 lb.) minimum should be used.

JAM AND JELLY MAKING

Rub the base of the preserving pan with a little butter to prevent jam sticking. Put prepared fruit into a pan with water (if any is needed) and lemon juice if necessary. Simmer fruit until it is tender and skin is soft. The time taken varies with different fruit, but fruit must be tender before sugar is added as it tends to harden later. Fruit used for jelly making should have a good pectin content.

It is best to warm sugar slightly. Add it slowly and allow it to dissolve before bringing jam back to boil. Boil it rapidly; it should bubble all over the surface. Stir frequently with a long-handled wooden spoon until setting point is reached.

Skim any froth and allow jam to cool slightly. Ladle jam into clean, warmed jars, filling them well. Put filled jars on a tray covered with folded newspaper. Wipe any drips off sides of jars while they are still warm; leave jam to cool.

When the jam is cold, seal jars with jam-pot covers or cut out squares of polythene and tie them tightly over jars.

Test for Setting

Draw the pan off the heat, put a little bit of jam on to a plate and cool it off quickly. Draw a metal spoon across it and, if the jam wrinkles, it has reached setting point.

When you are experienced in jam-making, a quicker way to test it is to hold the wooden spoon sideways well above the pan. The jam should slip slowly off the spoon in long, clinging drops.

Points about a Preserving Pan

A large preserving pan is not necessary for small amounts of jam, though it is required for larger quantities.

It is important to remember that jam will boil up to three or four times its original bulk and that it must boil really fast. If you have no preserving pan, use your strongest aluminium saucepan, because when jam reaches a high temperature it burns easily in a thin pan or in one made of enamel.

Bottling all Kinds of Fruit

Always use the freshest and highest quality fruit for bottling; fruit straight from the garden is best of all. It is wisest to bottle fruit at the height of the season because it is at its cheapest and has the best flavour and texture. Fruit should be just ripe — never overripe. Gooseberries are the exception. They should fully grown but still hard and green.

Jars

Jars for bottling have either glass or metal lids and screwbands or rubber rings which fit under the caps: these should never be kept on from one season to the next in case they deteriorate. Leave them on in a screw-topped jar until bottling time comes. Soak them in hot water for a few minutes before using.

Metal covers with a ring of plastic round the inside can be bought to fit one and two pound jars. If you use these, be sure to follow the manufacturer's instructions carefully. One pound jars are especially useful for small households.

Syrup

The flavour and colour of fruit is infinitely better if it is bottled in syrup rather than in water.

If you are going to bottle a quantity of fruit make a fairly large amount of syrup. Syrup which is not to be used immediately will keep in sealed jars for a week or so.

The proportion of sugar and water for the syrup can be varied according to taste, but the norm is 225 gm of sugar to every 600 ml (pint) water. A heavier syrup (450 gm of sugar to every 600 ml of water) is better for some fruit, such as peaches or pears. This heavier syrup tends to make the fruit rise in the jars but it does not in any way harm the flavour and the fruit will often sink again during storage.

Put sugar into a saucepan with water and stirring occasionally, heat it slowly until sugar dissolves. Bring syrup to a boil quickly and allow it to boil for two minutes. It is used either boiling or cold, according to the method of sterilization.

Brine for Tomatoes

For every 600 ml of water use 1 rounded teaspoonful of sugar and one rounded teaspoonful of salt. Prepare it in the same way as sugar syrup.

Preparation of the Fruit

This applies to all methods of sterilization. Select the fruit carefully and remove any that is over-ripe. Cut out any bruised parts. Wash the fruit only if necessary.

Filling the Jars

Wash the jars and their tops. Sterilize the tops by pouring boiling water over them. To sterilize a jar, hold the opening over the spout of a kettle and let the steam circulate round the inside for a few seconds. Leave the jar damp; then the fruit will slip easily inside.

Grade the fruit for size so that more or less the same sized fruit goes into each jar. Using the handle of a wooden spoon to pack the fruit eases the fruit in without bruising it. Pack it gently under the shoulder of the jar as this helps to prevent it rising while sterilizing. Fill jar with fruit to within half an inch of the top.

Pressure Cooker Method of Sterilisation

This is a very quick method if you have a pressure cooker large enough for bottling fruit. Follow the manufacturer's instructions about bottling fruit carefully. Remember to fill a jar with boiling syrup only up to the shoulders or it may overflow while sterilizing and be wasted. Wide jars are a little more awkward for this method as they take up more space and fewer can be fitted into the cooker.

The Oven Method

This is very successful for all soft fruit, though it is perhaps not quite so successful for pears, peaches, and apples, as these tend to discolour at the top of the jar.

After the fruit has been packed into jars, without liquid, cover each jar with a glass lid or patty tin. (The rubber rings and bands are put on after sterilizing.) Stand jars on bars of oven shelf, not too close together so that the air can circulate. Put them into the centre of a slow oven, not higher than 120° (about 250°F). Leave fruit until it is just cooked; this is when the juice begins to flow from it. Soft fruit such as raspberries, gooseberries, strawberries, loganberries and rhubarb will take about 1 hour, while currants and stone fruit such as plums, greengages, damsons, cherries, peaches, and apricots will take about 1½ hours. Pears and tomatoes will take 2 hours.

Some fruit shrinks slightly, so use fruit from one of the jars to fill up the others. Once this is done, the jars should be returned to the oven for ten minutes to get hot again.

Meanwhile have the syrup boiling in a pan with the lid on to prevent evaporation. Take a jar out of the oven and stand it on a wooden board or folded newspaper to prevent it cracking. Place a rubber in position and fill the jar to the neck with syrup. Slip a knife down the sides of the jar to burst air bubbles, then fill up the jar. Put on the lid, then screwband or clip. If a band is used, screw it on as tightly as possible.

When filling jars, always using boiling syrup. Let the jars stand on a wooden board or folded newspaper overnight.

The Second Oven Method

Pack the jars with fruit then fill them up to one and quarter inches from the top. Screw on the tops. Unscrew them a half turn, to allow for expansion. Stand the jars in a tray of hot water and put them into the centre of a slow oven 135°–140° (about 275°–300°F) for 1 hour for soft fruit, 1¼ hours for stoned fruit, and 1 hour twenty minutes for pears or tomatoes. Lift the jars out of the oven, screw the bands as tightly as possible, and leave them overnight.

The Water Method

Any heat-resistant container that holds enough water to cover jars completely can be used. A fish-kettle, a preserving-pan, or even a bucket can be used, or special sterilizers can be bought. The base of the container must be covered with a thick layer of newspaper or some slats of wood so that the jars do not come into contact with direct heat.

When the fruit has been packed into jars, fill them with cold syrup. Release any air by slipping a knife down the side of the jar when it is nearly full. Fill the jars to the brim; put on rings and tops, then clips or screwbands. If you use screw- bands, twist them as tightly as possible, then unscrew them half a turn to allow for expansion. Stand the jars on the protected base of the container; then immerse them in cold water. Make sure that the jars do not touch the sides of the container or each other.

Heat the containers slowly until the water reaches simmering point about 74° (about 165°F). This should take about 1½ hours. If you do not have a thermometer, you can know the temperature is correct when small bubbles appear on the surface of the water. It is slow heating which kills bacteria. If the fruit is heated too quickly sterilizing may not be successful or the fruit may tend to rise from the bottom of the jars. Keep the temperature at 74° (about 165°F) for 10 minutes then lift out the jars one at a time onto a wooden board or a newspaper. Screw each band really tight as the jar is lifted out. Leave the jars overnight before testing them to make sure that they have been sealed.

N.B. Pears and tomatoes need to be heated to 88° (about 190°F) and should be kept at that temperature for half an hour.

105. BANANA JAM

Ingredients	Quantity
Bananas (Yellow, sour variety)	50
Cloves	50
Sugar	450 gm
Limes	2

Method

1. Peel bananas. Put into a stainless steel pan with cloves and water just level with dry ingredients. 2. Cook till bananas are well cooked. 3. Remove cloves. Mash bananas. Strain through a coarsely woven cloth or through a fine stainless steel sieve. 4. Add sugar and cook to jam-consistency. 5. Add lime juice. Remove from fire. Cool and bottle.

N.B. To test jam pour a spoonful into a saucer. Pass the handle of a spoon through it. If surface wrinkles it is ready.

106. PINEAPPLE JAM

Ingredients
Pineapple
Sugar
Lime

Method

1. Cut pineapple into small pieces and cook till done. Mash and strain. 2. Weigh it and take an equal amount of sugar. (If pineapple is sweet, the proportion is 1 : ¾). 3. Cook to jam-consistency. Add lime juice and remove.

N.B. A few fine pieces of pineapple can be added, if desired to the liquid.

107. GRAPEFRUIT AND LIME MARMALADE

Ingredients	Quantity
Grapefruit	2
Sweet limes	3
Sour limes	4
Water	2.5 litre (about 4½ pts.)
Sugar	2.27 kg

Method

1. Wash and dry fruit. 2. Cut into segments. 3. Skin fruit and put into a large glass or china bowl. Reserve pips and skin. 4. Remove all white pith from peel, shred into thin strips and add to fruit segments. 5. Put pips into a muslin bag. Tie and place in bowl. 6. Add 2.25 litre (4 points) of water. Cover and leave overnight. 7. Next day simmer all the fruit in a strong pan (covered) for about 2 hours. By this time the liquid should have been reduced to half. 8. Remove bag of pips after squeezing out juice. 9. Add remaining water and sugar. Stir till sugar dissolves. 10. Bring to a boil and boil fast for about 20 minutes or till it jells. 11. Stand for 10 minutes. Pour into warmed glass jars. Cool, cover with waxed paper and seal.

108. ORANGE MARMALADE

Ingredients	Quantity
Punjab oranges	1 kg
Limes	3
Water	2.5 litre
Sugar	1.75 kg

Method

Same as for Grapefruit and Lime marmalade.

109. GUAVA JELLY (A)

Ingredients	Quantity
Guavas (with stem and blemished portions removed)	1 kg
Water	1–1¼ litre
Citric acid	7.5 gm/kg sugar added

Method

1. Select fresh guavas at their optimum stage of maturity. 2. Wash thoroughly several times with drinking water. 3. Remove stems and blemished portions. 4. Cut into thin slices. 5. Add measured quantity of

water to prepared guavas. 6. Cook in stainless steel or aluminium vessel for about 20–30 minutes. 7. After 20 minutes of cooking do the pectin test given below:

(a) Take a teaspoonful of the clear extract in a test tube and cool it.
(b) When the extract is completely cooled, add double the quantity of methylated spirit to it and let it stand for two minutes.
(c) Pour out onto a plate.

(1) If there is one jelly-like lump   'A' Grade pectin
(2) If two or three jelly-like lumps   'B' Grade pectin
(3) If numerous jelly-like lumps   'C' Grade pectin

8. If 'B' or 'C' grade pectin means that the jelly must be cooked a little more. 9. Strain the juice through a piece of muslin. Do not squeeze the cloth. 10. Bring to a boil and add sugar.

N.B. (a) If 'A' Grade pectin—one cup sugar to one cup juice
(b) If 'B' Grade pectin—¾ cup sugar to one cup juice
(c) If 'C' Grade pectin—¼–½ cup sugar to one cup juice.

11. Dissolve the sugar and boil. 12. Strain it through a muslin cloth to remove impurities. 13. Cook the strained juice till the end point is reached i.e. when a temperature of 105° (about 221°F) is reached (at sea level) or when it drips in the form of vapour. 14. When end point is reached, add weighed amount of citric acid and immediately remove from fire. 15. Remove scum and fill it into previously sterilized dried bottles. 16. When cooled, seal bottles air-tight by pouring boiling hot paraffin wax on surface of cooled bottles.

GUAVA JELLY (B)

Select ripe guavas, wash and cut them into small pieces. Weigh and add water 1½ times the weight of guavas (i.e. for every kg guavas add 1½ litre water). Cook for ½ hour and strain through a muslin cloth. (This extract is called "pectin extract"). Pass the pectin extract through a thick cloth or jelly bag to make it clear. The pectin extract can also be kept overnight and the clear extract collected by pouring without disturbing the sediment.

Ingredients	Quantity
Pectin extract	1 litre
Sugar	1 kg
Citric acid	8 gm
(or juice of 4 limes)	

Method

1. Dissolve sugar in pectin extract by heating. Let it boil. Strain immediately through a muslin cloth. 2. Cook till jelly starts "setting". Setting can be determined by dipping a wooden spoon into the jelly and

then taking out the spoon and allowing the jelly sticking to the spoon to drip slowly. 3. If it has set, it will drop slowly and fall in shape. If it is yet to set, if will fall in a stream of drops. 4. When the jelly has started setting, add citric acid or lime juice. Fill white hot into sterilized bottles. 5. Wax bottles after cooling and put on lids.

110. GUAVA CHEESE (made out of the pulp of Guava Jelly)

Ingredients

Guava pulp
Lime juice
Red colouring

Method

1. Pass pulp through a stainless steel sieve, being careful to remove all seeds. 2. Allow 1 tablespoon of lime juice and 700 gms. sugar to 700 gms. pulp. 3. Put pulp into a strong pan and warm it slightly; add sugar gradually and cook slowly, stirring constantly till it reaches jam-consistency. 4. Colour red and mix well. 5. Cool and put into sterile jars and when quite cold, seal. Use as jam.

111. ROSELLE JELLY

Ingredients	*Quantity*
Roselle juice	300 ml
Sugar	225 gm
Lime (juice)	1

Method

1. Wash calyxes. 2. Add an equal quantity of water. Boil for half an hour. 3. Strain through a jelly bag or muslin cloth without squeezing pulp. 4. Measure strained juice. 5. Bring to a boil and add sugar (¾ of the total quantity of juice). 6. Boil again till sugar dissolves and strain while hot. 7. Cook quickly until jelly drops in sheets from spoon. 8. When jelly reaches desired consistency add lime juice. Remove foam from top and pour into previously sterilized dry bottles. Do not cover until jelly is cold. 9. When jelly is cold, pour some hot paraffin wax over to seal. Screw on lids.

N.B. If the juice is not sour enough add more lime juice about 5 minutes before removing from fire. This jelly can be used instead of red currant jelly.

112. APPLE MURABBA

Select small ripe firm apples. Weigh, wash and remove skin and core with a coring knife. Keep dipped in water. With a pricking knife, prick all over the apples uniformly but do not break the apples (if the pricking is not uniform the apples will float in the murabba).

Ingredients	Quantity
Apples	1 kg
Sugar	1 kg
Water	1½ litre
Citric acid (or juice of 2 limes)	4 gm

Method

1. Prepare sugar syrup by boiling sugar and water. Strain syrup through a fine muslin cloth. 2. Put apples in syrup and bring to a boil. Remove from fire and cool overnight. 3. Next day (a) take out apples (b) strain syrup (c) add apples and boil for 20–30 minutes. Cool overnight. 4. Repeat same process till syrup is quite thick.

Test: (Put a drop of the syrup in a saucer of water; it should form a bead). Takes about 4–6 days. 5. Add lime juice or citric acid (prevents sugar crystallization). Allow it to cool. 6. The following ingredients can be added: saffron for colour, pepper for taste and cardamom for flavour. Fill into bottles and put lids on. Store in a cool dark place.

113. CANDIED PEEL

Ingredients	Quantity
Peel	1 kg
Sugar	1½ kg
Water	800 ml
Citric acid	3 gm
Sodium benzoate	8 gm

Method

1. Select good quality peel and remove fibres and pips without damaging rind. 2. Boil some water and add soda bicarbonate at the rate of 20 gm per litre and remove from fire. 3. Put peel into this water and keep immersed by keeping a plate or thali with a weight on it. 4. Remove peel after 15 minutes. Rinse in cold water. 5. Put into a pan and add sufficient water to cover and cook till the soft (Peel will become firm after absorbing sugar syrup). 6. Prepare a syrup with sugar and water. Add citric acid, boil and strain. 7. Put peel into syrup and concentrate gradually as for glazed cherries. 8. Add preservative and remove from syrup and dry in the shade.

BEVERAGES

114. ORANGE WINE

Ingredients	Quantity
Oranges	8
Water (boiling)	3.5 litre
Ginger	small piece
Sugar	225 gm to 1.15 litre liquid

Method

1. Wipe oranges and peel removing pith and pips. 2. Place in a bowl with a small piece of bruised ginger. Cover and leave for a week, stirring every day. 3. Strain slowly through fine cloth (do not push liquid through). 4. Measure sugar in the proportion of 225 gm sugar to 1.15 litre liquid and stir well. 5. When dissolved, bottle and cover with plastic for a fortnight. Then cork up. Set aside for 3 months before using.

115. RAISIN WINE

Ingredients	Quantity
Raisins	450 gm
Sugar	225 gm
Water	875 ml

Method

1. Wash and soak raisins for 24 hrs. 2. Squeeze to pulp. 3. Add sugar and leave for 48 hrs. 4. Strain and bottle.

116. PEA POD WINE

Ingredients	Quantity
Pea pods	1.5 kg
Water	4.7 litre
Sugar	1.6 kg
Lemon rind	2 lemons
Bread	1 slice
Brewer's yeast	15 gm
Isinglass	15 gm

Method

1. Put pea pods into a large pan. 2. Pour water over and bring to a boil. Add lemon rind; continue boiling until pods are tender and yellowish. 3. Strain liquor over sugar. 4. When nearly cold float a piece of toast spread over with brewer's yeast on the wine. Let it stand for 24 hours. 5. Remove scum. 6. Bottle and set aside for four months. 7. Take out

some wine and dissolve isinglass in it. 8. Pour it back. Cover tightly and leave undisturbed for 2 months.

117. PINEAPPLE WINE

Ingredients	Quantity
Peel of I medium-sized pineapple	
Water	3 cups
Sugar	3 cups
Baker's yeast	1 pinch
Egg white	1

Method

1. Soak peel in water. Add sugar, baker's yeast and beaten egg white. Leave for three days. Strain and bottle. The wine will be ready after ten days.

118. GINGER WINE

Ingredients	Quantity
Sugar	1.35 kg
Water	3½ bottles
Bruised ginger	60 gm
Limes (large)	3–4
Seedless raisins	60 gm
Baker's yeast	½ tsp

Method

1. Scrape off pith from lemon rinds but do not chop into small pieces. Put lemon rind and ginger in water in which sugar has been dissolved. Boil for 30–45 minutes. Remove from fire. Cool and when lukewarm add lime juice. Put seedless raisins and yeast into a jar. Pour syrup over. Stir the wine every day for 10 days. Then strain it and bottle.

119. GRAPE WINE

Ingredients	7 bottles
Grapes	1 kg
Sugar	2 kg
Dry yeast	2 tsp
Egg white	1
Wheat	a handful
Water	5 bottles

Method

1. Wash and dry grapes. Crush grapes and add 1 kg sugar and other

ingredients. 2. Keep for 21 days stirring on alternate days. 3. Add remaining sugar out of which 1 cup should be browned. 4. Strain, decant and bottle.

120. ICED TEA

Ingredients	6 glasses
Cold weak tea	¼ litre
Lemon	2 slices
Orange	2 slices
Sugar	to taste
Ice cubes	4

Method

1. Mix tea and slices of orange and lemon. Sweeten to taste. 2. Add ice cubes, serve in glasses.

121. ICED COFFEE (Plain)

Ingredients	Quantity
Milk	600 ml
Strong coffee	600 ml (2 glasses)
Sugar	55–85 gm
Vanilla	a few drops

Method

Mix all ingredients. Cover and chill.

122. ICED COFFEE WITH CONDENSED MILK

1. For 10 bottles, use 225 gm coffee, 450 gm sugar and 2 tins condensed milk. 2. As water boils put in coffee (in muslin bags). Let it boil for 5 minutes. Remove from fire. Take out bags. Add sugar and milk and chill.

123. ICED COFFEE WITH CREAM

Ingredients	Quantity
Strong clear hot coffee	1 litre
Milk	½ litre
Cream	½ litre
Castor sugar	175 gm
Vanilla	a few drops

Method

1. Put milk, sugar and vanilla into a stew pan. 2. Heat till it is nearly boiling then add coffee. 3. Let mixture cool. Stir in cream. 4. Chill until

it has the consistency of thick cream. 5. Beat well or shake in a cocktail shaker to make it froth and serve quickly. 6. A little castor sugar can be sprinkled on top if desired.

124. FRUIT PUNCH (A)

Ingredients	For 50
Water	300 ml
Strong tea	300 ml
Soda water	¼ litre
Fruit syrup (any kind)	60 ml
Lemon juice	300 ml
Sugar	400 gm
Orange juice	600 ml
Pineapple juice	600 ml
Diced fruit (Melon, Guavas)	100 gm
Iced water	

Method

1. Boil sugar and water for 5 minutes, add tea, fruit syrup and juices. Let it stand for 30 minutes. 2. Add iced water to make 6.85 litres of liquid. 3. Add fruit and soda water. 4. Serve in a large bowl with pieces of ice.

FRUIT PUNCH (B)

Ingredients	For 12
Cold water	¼ litre
Sugar	400 gm
Orange juice	300 ml
Lemon juice	300 ml
Pineapple juice	600 ml

Method

1. Boil sugar and water for 10 minutes. 2. Add juices. Chill. 3. Dilute with iced water.

125. FRUIT FIZZ

Ingredients	For 27
Cold tea	600 ml
Oranges	2
Limes	2
Pineapple (small)	1
Sugar	175 gm

Method

1. Make tea. Add sugar and strain. Cool. 2. Extract juice from oranges, limes and pineapple. 3. Add ginger ale. 4. Chill and serve.

126. GINGER PUNCH

Ingredients	For 10
Ginger root	225 gm
Cold water	¼ litre
Lemon juice	145 ml
Sugar	200 gm
Orange juice	145 ml

Method

1. Chop ginger; add to water and sugar. 2. Boil for 15 minutes. 3. Add fruit juices, cool, strain and dilute with crushed ice.

127. FRUIT PUNCH WITH WHIPPED CREAM

Ingredients	Quantity
Grape juice	600 ml
Lemon juice	60 ml
Orange juice	100 ml
Pineapple pulp	225 gm
Sugar	170 gm
Lemon rind	1
Orange rind	1
Fresh mint	4 sprigs
Salt	a pinch
Nutmeg	a pinch
Soda water	600 ml
Whipped cream	
Crushed ice	

Method

1. Mix fruit juices. 2. Rub sugar over lemon and orange rind. 3. Add mint, salt and nutmeg. Cover and let stand in a cool place for 1 hr. 4. Pour over crushed ice; add soda water and serve in tall glasses with whipped cream on top. 5. Garnish with mint leaves.

128. TEA PUNCH

Ingredients	Quantity
Cold tea	600 ml
Oranges	2
Limes	2

Ingredients	Quantity
Pineapple (small)	1
Sugar	175 gm

Method

1. To the cold tea add strained juice of oranges, limes and pineapple. Add sugar and stir till dissolved. Serve in tall glasses with a little crushed ice. A thin slice of orange or some shredded pineapple may be added.

129. WOODAPPLE PUNCH

Woodapples must be quite ripe. Break the shell and scoop out inside of fruit with a spoon. Put it into a bowl. Add a little water and squeeze fruit well. Remove seeds and strain through a coarse net. Add scraped jaggery or sugar to taste and a pinch of salt and stir well.

130. PINEAPPLE PUNCH

Ingredients	Quantity
Pineapple	1
Sweet limes	2
Limes	2
Soda	1 bottle
Sugar	225 gm

Method

1. Extract juice from fruits. Keep aside a few pieces of pineapple finely chopped and one or two segments of sweet lime. Mix all ingredients together except soda. Chill and just before serving add iced soda and let the pieces of fruit float on top.

131. ORCHATA

Ingredients	Quantity
Almonds	115 gm
Sugar	455 gm
Vanilla	½ tsp
Water	600 ml

Method

1. Blanch almonds and soak overnight. 2 Grind into a fine paste and add 300 ml water. 3. Strain through muslin and set aside. 4. Add another 300 ml water to paste and strain as before. 5. Put into a strong pan. Add sugar, dissolve, and cook over medium heat till thick and syrupy. 6. Add the first 300 ml almond milk and boil for a few minutes.

Remove. 7. Add vanilla. Cool. Bottle and keep in a cool place. Serve in the proportion of 2 tablespoons almond milk to 1 glass of iced water.

132. ORANGE OR LEMON SQUASH

Ingredients	Quantity
Grated rind and juice of oranges or lemons	6
Citric acid	55 gm
Tartaric acid	30 gm
Epsom salt	30 gm
Sugar	1.8 kg
Boiling water	1.75 litre

Method

Put all ingredients into a basin and pour 1.75 litre boiling water over. Stir till dissolved. Strain through muslin into bottles. This concentrated squash will keep for months.

133. GINGER BEER

Ingredients	Quantity
Ginger (bruised)	85 gm
Water	2 litre
Brewer's yeast	½ tbsp
Orange flower water	1 tsp
Sugar	1.35 kg
Lemon juice	300 ml
Whole peel of lemons	4
Essence of lemon	1 tsp

Method

1. Boil ginger in water for 20 minutes. 2. Add sugar, lemon juice and peel and boil again. 3. Strain very carefully. 4. Let it cool gradually; when tepid, drop in yeast and allow to become cold. 5. Add orange flower water and essence of lemon.

N.B. This ginger beer should stand for 4 days. If bottled tightly it will keep for 3–4 months.

134. GINGO

Ingredients	Quantity
Ginger (fresh)	225 gm
Lime juice	150 ml (1 cup)
Sodium benzoate	¼ tsp
Vinegar	150 ml (1 cup)
Sugar	300 gm

Method

1. Peel ginger and cut into very thin slices. 2. Wash in cold water. 3. Soak in cold water. Leave overnight. 4. Crush ginger and squeeze out juice. Strain well. Mix with other ingredients and bottle. 5. It will be ready after two days. If it is to be kept for longer periods, add sodium benzoate.

135. ORANGE MILK SHAKE

Ingredients	Quantity
Orange juice	300 ml
Grapefruit juice	150 ml
Almond essence	2 drops
Milk	600 ml
Castor sugar	50 gm
Salt	¼ tsp

Method

1. Chill fruit juice. 2. Chill milk. 3. Combine all ingredients and mix thoroughly.

136. PINEAPPLE MILK SHAKE

Ingredients	Quantity
Pineapple juice	300 ml
Milk	450 ml
Sugar syrup	to taste
Pineapple pieces	

Method

1. Whisk juice, milk and sugar syrup together. 2. Serve with pieces of pineapple on cocktail sticks or tint pale green, flavour with peppermint essence and decorate with lemon.

137. MANGO FOOL

Ingredients	Quantity
Raw mangoes	450 gm
Milk	300 ml
Sugar	30 gm

Method

1. Peel mangoes. Boil in a little warm water till soft. 2. Pass through a sieve. Cool. 3. Boil milk and sugar. Cool and add to mango pulp. 4. If thicker consistency is desired add a little custard powder to milk before boiling. Cream also can be added. Chill.

138. BANANA MILK SHAKE

Ingredients	Quantity
Ripe bananas	3
Milk	600 ml
Chocolate powder	15 gm
Vanilla	a few drops

Method

1. Mash bananas and pass through sieve (stainless steel) 2. Add chocolate powder and beat well. 3. Add milk and vanilla, mix well. Chill and serve.

139. MALTED MOCHA FROST

Ingredients	Quantity
Powdered coffee	1 tbsp
Powdered chocolate	1 tbsp
Milk	500 ml
Whipped cream	

Method

1. Make a thin paste with coffee, chocolate and boiling water. Add cold milk. Chill. Serve with whipped cream.

140. CUCUMBER AND TOMATO FROST

Ingredients	Quantity
Tomato juice	600 ml
Cucumber with peel (grated)	115 gm
Sugar	½ tsp
Salt	½ tsp
Lime juice	1 lime

Method

1. Mix all ingredients and chill. 2. Strain. 3. Serve in glasses with slice of cucumber on edge.

141. LASSI

This is made by breaking up curds and adding water and salt to taste. It is a popular summer drink. Lassi may also be served sweetened or flavoured with a little minced onion, a small piece of crushed ginger, chopped green chillies with seeds removed and curry leaves.

142. ICE CREAM FIZZ

Put a large tablespoon of vanilla ice cream into a tall glass and pour over, from a height, sufficient iced ginger ale or ginger beer or lemonade to fill the glass.

143. ORANGE OR LEMON SHERBET

Ingredients	Quantity
Oranges	3
Limes	1
Sugar	75 gm
Cochineal or red colouring	2 drops
Water	875 ml
Gelatine	1 tbsp (15 gm)
Egg whites	2

Method

1. Soak gelatine in 300 ml water for 1 hour. 2. Boil sugar in 600 ml water; add gelatine. Stir over fire till dissolved. Remove. 3. Add orange and lemon juice, and strain through a cloth. Cool. 4. Put in a freezer; when half frozen add egg whites beaten stiff. Serve in tall glasses.

Lemon sherbet can be made in the same way.

144. GRAPEFRUIT COCKTAIL

Take equal quantities of grapefruit pulp and orange pulp and add as much orange juice (sweetened to taste) as needed.

Chill and serve in cocktail glasses with cherries.

145. MELON COCKTAIL

Ingredients	Quantity
Melon	1
Sugar to taste	115 gm (approx.)
Limes	3
Gin (optional)	15 ml

Method

1. Cut off top of melon. 2. Remove seeds and pulp but retain shell. 3. With a scoop, cut marble-sized rounds of melon. Mash remaining pulp and extract juice. 4. Add sugar, lime juice and gin (optional). 5. Return to shell. Chill and serve in glasses with rims sugared.

For Sugaring Glasses

A saucer filled with castor sugar.
A saucer filled 0.7 cm (about ¼") with water.
Half a slice of lemon for each glass.

Stand a glass upside down in saucer of water so that rim is thoroughly wetted. Lift out, shake and then dip rim in sugar. Allow sugar to dry on glass and it will form quite a hard sugary edge.

Put half a slice of lemon over rim.

146. MELON COOLER

Ingredients	Quantity
Melon	1
Sugar	200 gm
Lemon (juice)	2
Water	150 ml
Sprigs of mint	

Method

1. Peel melon and cut into cubes and balls by using a small round, measuring spoon. 2. Boil water and sugar together for 5 minutes. 3. Chill and add lemon juice and pour over melon. 4. Cover and leave till very cold. Serve in small glasses garnished with sprigs of mint.

147. PINEAPPLE COCKTAIL

Peel and cut a small, ripe pineapple into cubes. Make a syrup with 255 gms. of sugar and 75 ml (½ teacup) water and pour it over a tablespoon of chopped mint. Arrange pineapple in individual glasses and strain syrup over to cover. Chill before serving.

148. MIXED FRUIT DRINK

Ingredients	For 500
Limca	64 bottles
Ginger ale	34 bottles
Gold Spot	61 bottles
Pineapple juice	17 litre
Lime juice	1 cup
Sugar	as required
Mint leaves	

Method

1. Mix all ingredients together

149. PINEAPPLEADE

Ingredients	Quantity
Pineapple	1
Lime	2

Ingredients	Quantity
Boiling water	895 ml
Sugar	to taste

Method

1. Peel and chop pineapple and add lime juice. 2. Pour boiling water over fruit. Sweeten with sugar to taste. 3. Set aside for 12 hours. Strain and serve iced.

150. LIME SYRUP (2 bottles)

Ingredients	Quantity
Limes	12
Sugar	675 gm
Water	1.20 litre (4 glasses)

Method

1. Grate outer skin of lime. 2. Add sugar and water and boil for 10 minutes. 3. Remove from fire. Add juice and strain; when cool, bottle and cork.

N.B. Care should be taken not to include any white underskin of lime as this makes the syrup bitter. This syrup can be kept in a refrigerator for about a fortnight or for about 2–3 days at room temperature. To serve, use small quantities and dilute with iced soda or iced water.

151. LIME-GINGER SQUASH

Ingredients	5 bottles
Lime juice	1 litre
Fresh ginger	250 gm
Sugar	2 kg
Water	1 litre
Preservative (Pot. metabisulphite)	2.5 gm
Orange-red colour	10 drops (optional)
Bottles	5 (650 ml)

Method

1. Extract lime juice. Strain to remove seeds. 2. Wash, peel and finely chop ginger; crush it with lime juice into paste in a liquidizer and mix this paste with remaining lime juice and keep for 1–2 hours. 3. Prepare sugar syrup with water, bring to a boil and add 2 tsp of lime juice to clarify; filter through cloth and cool to room temperature. 4. Mix syrup with lime-ginger juice, stir well. Strain through strainer to remove coarse ginger. 5. Add preservative (dissolved in cold water earlier). Mix well. Add colour if desired, mix well. Fill into dry sterile bottles with 1.25–2 cm

head space; cork airtight, check for leakage. 6. Wash, wipe, dry and label.
7. Store for 10–15 days before using.

152. SARSAPARILLA SYRUP

Ingredients	4 bottles
Sarsaparilla	100 gm
Water	1 litre (4 glasses)
Sugar	3 kg
Citric acid	30 gm
Lime juice	½ litre
Sodium benzoate	2–3 gm

Method

1. Add sarsaparilla to 1 litre boiling water. 2. Remove from fire and soak
overnight. 3. Next day, bring mixture to a boil and let it soak for another
2–3 hours. 4. Remove roots, filter through a thick muslin cloth and
measure quantity of liquid (approx. 800 ml). 5. To this, add sugar and
make syrup of two-thread consistency. Let cool. 6. Add citric acid, lime
juice and benzoate to syrup and bottle.

153. GRAPE SQUASH

Ingredients	For 4 bottles (750 ml each)
Grape juice	1 litre
Sugar	1.3 kg
Citric acid	30 gm
Water	0.6 litre
Preservative (sodium benzoate)	3 gm
Quantity of squash obtained	3 litre

Method

As for Lime-Ginger Squash.

154. LIME SQUASH

Ingredients	For 5 bottles (800 ml each)
Lime juice	1 litre
Sugar	1.7 kg
Water	1.3 litre
Quantity of squash obtained	4 litre
Preservative (Potassium-metabisulphite)	2.5 gm
Lemon colour	as required

Method

As for Lime-Ginger Squash.

155. MANGO SQUASH

Ingredients	For 4 bottles (750 ml each)
Mango juice	1 litre
Sugar	1.3 kg
Citric acid	40 gm
Water	0.9 litre
Preservative (Potassium metabisulphite)	2 gm
Mango colour and flavour	as required
Quantity of squash obtained	3 litre

Method

As for Lime-Ginger Squash.

156. ORANGE SQUASH

Ingredients	For 4 bottles (750 ml each)
Orange juice	1 litre
Sugar	1.25 kg
Citric acid	30 gm
Water	0.8 litre
Preservative (Potassium metabisulphite)	2 gms.
Orange colour and flavour	as required
Quantity of squash obtained	3 litre

Method

As for Lime-Ginger Squash.

157. PINEAPPLE SQUASH

Ingredients	For 5½ bottles (750 ml each)
Pineapple juice	1 litre
Sugar	1.8 kg
Citric acid	40 gm
Water	1.1 litre
Preservative (Potassium metabisulphite)	2.5 gms.
Pineapple colour and flavour	as required
Quantity of squash obtained	4 litre

Method

As for Lime-Ginger Squash.

158. SPARKLING LEMONADE

Ingredients	Quantity
Lemons (large)	6
Sugar	280 gm
Cold water	¾ litre

Method

1. Slice lemons. Remove pips. 2. Sprinkle over with sugar. Allow to stand for 15 minutes. 3. Add cold water. Stir well and leave for 1 hour, then strain.

To make lemonade sparkle, put a pinch of bicarbonate of soda into each glass, just before serving.

159. ORANGE AND GRAPEFRUIT SQUASH

Mix equal quantities of orange and grapefruit juice. Half-fill glasses and top up with ginger ale. Add pieces of orange and grapefruit.

160. MINT JULEP

Ingredients	For 12 glasses
Lemon squash	300 ml
Water	300 ml
Mint leaves	1 bunch
Ginger ale	1.75 litre

Method

1. Mix lemon squash and water. 2. Add washed mint leaves. 3. Just before serving, add ginger ale.

161. APPLE DRINK

Ingredients	Quantity
Apples	3
Water	875 ml
Sugar	30 gm
Lemon (thinly peeled rind)	½
Lemon juice	a few drops

Method

1. Wipe apples with damp cloth. 2. Slice thinly without peeling or coring. 3. Put into a jug with lemon rind and sugar. 4. Pour boiling water over. Cover jug to trap steam and let it stand till cold.

162. JEERA PANI

Ingredients	Quantity
Mint leaves	50 gm
Cold water	2 litre
Cooking salt	15 gm
Cumin	2 tsp
Cloves	4
Fennel	15 gm
Black pepper	15 gm
Black salt	15 gm
Dry mango powder	125 gm
Ginger	1 piece

Method

1. Wash mint leaves. 2. Grind cumin, fennel, cloves and ginger. 3. Soak dry mango powder for half an hour and sieve pulp. 4. Powder salt and dissolve in cold water. 5. Mix ground spices with mango pulp and salt water. 6. Strain and keep in an earthen pot.

163. SAMBHARAM

Ingredients	Quantity
Buttermilk (thin)	16 cups
Ginger	5 cm (about 2") piece
Green chillies	12–16
Garlic	2 pods
Small red onions	100 gm
Cumin	1 dsp
Turmeric	1 dsp
Lemon leaf and Curry leaves	
Salt	to taste

Method

1. Remove all fat from buttermilk. 2. Add salt, lemon leaf and curry leaves. 3. Crush together ginger, green chillies, garlic with skin on, onions, turmeric and cumin. 4. Tie in a muslin bag and let flavours seep into buttermilk. 5. Set aside for an hour or so and serve as a drink.

164. TOMATO BISQUE COCKTAIL

Season equal parts of chilled tomato juice and buttermilk with salt, pepper and a dash of Worcester sauce. Shake well and top with finely chopped onion leaves (small variety).

165. TAMARIND DRINK

Ingredients	Quantity
Fresh tamarind	225 gm
Water	2.35 litre
Sugar	675 gm

Method

1. Soak tamarind in water for half an hour. 2. Squeeze, remove seeds and strain. 3. Boil for 20 minutes. Add sugar and boil for another 30 minutes. 4. Strain and bottle. Dilute with iced or aerated water and serve.

166. SUGARCANE VINEGAR

Ingredients	Quantity
Fresh sugarcane juice	5 litre with fibrous residue
China jar	1

Method

Store sugarcane juice with fibrous residue in china jar covered with a sieve. Keep for 2 days. One 3rd day, put screw cap on china jar. Leave it in a dark corner. After about 4 months strain vinegar through a muslin cloth. This will make three bottles of clear vinegar and 2 to 3 bottles of vinegar with a little scum on it. The best time for making this vinegar is April–May.

167. ALASKA SPECIAL

To 1 glass of fizzy mineral water add 1 tsp of sweetened condensed milk. Mix thoroughly.

N.B. Ginger beer is especially suited to this recipe.

168. KOLLU VELLAM

Ingredients	Quantity
Horse gram	2 tbsp
Dry ginger	1 small piece
Peppercorns	6–12

Method

1. Crush ingredients coarsely. 2. Add 3 cups water. 3. Boil. Keep for 3 hours. Strain. 4. Serve warm.

169. PANAKAM

Ingredients	Quantity
Molasses (Gur, Vellam)	100 gm
Water	400 ml
Cardamoms	2
Salt	a small pinch
Dry ginger powder	1 tsp (4 gm)
Lime	½
or Tamarind	10 gm

Method

1. Dissolve enough molasses in water to make it sweet. Strain. 2. Add salt, dry ginger powder and crushed cardamoms and if desired, a little lime juice.

N.B. Fresh ripe tamarind can be soaked in water and strained and added instead of lime juice.

PRESERVING PICKLES

When pickling ensure that fruit and spices, after washing, are dried thoroughly and there are no traces of water whatsoever.

Sterilize containers by placing them in a pan, covering them with cold water and heating to boiling point. Remove containers while they are still hot and place them upside down on a clean surface to dry.

Cover pickles with a film of oil to prevent mould forming or ensure that the liquid fully covers solids in the case of brine pickles.

One gram of sodium benzoate may be added per kilogram of total pickle if desired, as a reliable preservative. The chemical should be added to the spices and blended thoroughly. If spices are to be fried, add them after they have been fried and cooled.

SAUCES

SAUCES

SAUCES

I. MEATLESS SAUCE

Ingredients	Quantity
Oil	60 ml
Garlic	1 flake
Onions	1
Capsicum	1
Tomatoes	125 gm
Water	2 cups
Worcester sauce	1 tbsp
Chilli powder	½ tsp
Salt	to taste

Method

1. Heat oil in a pan. 2. Add chopped garlic, onion and capsicum.
3. Blanch tomatoes and add to rest of ingredients. 4. Add water,
Worcester sauce, chilli powder and salt and simmer for 1 hour. 5. Serve
over boiled macaroni.

N.B. Grated cheese sprinkled over the dish improves it immensely.

2. QUICK SAUCE

Ingredients	Quantity
Fat	30 gm
Onions	1
Capsicum	1
Tomatoes	225 gm
Water	125 ml
Salt	

Method

1. Heat fat in a pan. 2. Add chopped onion and capsicum. Sauté. 3. Add
blanched tomatoes, water and salt. Simmer for 10 minutes. 4. Serve over
boiled macaroni.

N.B. Garnish with chopped hard-boiled eggs to improve the dish.

3. CURRY SAUCE

Ingredients	Quantity
Fat	60 gm
Refined flour	50 gm
Vegetable stock	2 cups
Salt	1 tsp

Ingredients	Quantity
Curry powder	2 tsp
Onions	1
Lime (juice)	1

Method

1. Heat fat. Stir in flour and when well-blended add vegetable stock. 2. Stir over a low fire until smooth and thick. 3. Add chopped onion, curry powder and lime juice. Simmer for 10 minutes. Serve with boiled macaroni.

N.B. A green salad accompaniment is ideal for this the dish.

MISCELLANEOUS

MISCELLANEOUS

1. Satpura Parathas
2. Moghlai Parathas
3. Potato Kachories
4. Pesarattu
5. Balushai
6. Kulfi
7. Carrots Kheer
8. Lentil Mulligatawny Soup

I. SATPURA PARATHAS

Ingredients	For 8
Wholemeal flour	500 gm
Salt	to taste
Water to make a soft dough	
Fat for dough	125 gm
Fat to brush over after baking	

Method

1. Sift flour. Add salt. 2. Make a soft dough with water. Set aside for one hour. Knead well. 3. Divide into 8 portions. Form into balls. 4. Roll into rounds 8 cm (about 7") in diameter. 5. Smear with melted fat. Roll into the pencil-shape. 6. Apply fat over. 7. Press lightly vertically. Set aside for 15 minutes. 8. Roll out to 0.7 cm (about ¼") thick rounds. 9. Bake on a dry griddle over slow fire. Place over live coal or over a gas flame to finish the cooking. Smear over immediately with fat. 10. Toss lightly between palms of hands and separate flakes. Divide into 4 or 5 pieces and serve hot.

2. MOGHLAI PARATHAS

Ingredients	For 8
Refined flour	500 gm
Salt	to taste
Water to make a soft dough	
Melted fat (for dough)	125 gm
Fat	for frying

Method

1. Sift flour. Add salt. Make a soft dough with water. Knead well. Set aside covered for one hour. 2. Divide into 8 portions. Form into balls and set aside for another 15 minutes. 3. Roll into a round 18 cm (about 7") in diameter. Smear over with melted fat. 4. Make a cut from centre to

the edge. 5. Roll from one end of the cut side to the other end to form a cone. 6. Press cone between palms. Roll out into 0.7 cm (about ¼″) thick rounds. 7. Deep fry till golden brown. Remove and drain on absorbent paper. Serve hot.

3. POTATO KACHORIES

Ingredients	For 6
Potatoes	225 gm
Onions	30 gm
Green peas	50 gm
Sugar	a pinch
Lemon juice	⅛ tsp (a few drops)
Sultanas	15 gm
Turmeric	a pinch
Chilli powder	a pinch
Salt	to taste
Coriander leaves	¼ tsp
Fat	20 gm
Flour	to roll
Fat	for frying

Method

1. Peel and boil potatoes, remove water and dry (on fire). 2. Mash potatoes into a smooth paste. 3. Chop onion and fry in fat; add turmeric, chilli powder, boiled peas, salt, lemon juice, sugar, coriander leaves and sultanas. 4. Divide potatoes into 6 portions and put in filling, making round balls. 5. Roll these balls in flour. 6. Fry in deep fat and serve hot.

4. PESARATTU (GREEN DOSA)

Ingredients	For 25
Green gram	500 gm
Coriander leaves	50 gm
Onions	150 gm
Ginger	50 gm
Green chillies	50 gm
Salt	30 gm
Oil	to shallow fry
Cumin (optional)	10 gm
Water	800 ml

Method

1. Soak green gram overnight; grind coarsely with salt. 2. Add finely chopped coriander, onions, ginger, green chillies and cumin. 3. Add sufficient water to make the batter of such a consistency as to spread

easily on griddle. Mix thoroughly. 4. Spread batter over hot griddle and cook in shallow fat. Turn over dosa and cook other side. 5. Serve hot with pickle or chutney.

N.B. If dosas are preferred sour, the batter can be kept for 12 hours. The dosas can be made with either soaked green gram or green gram flour. If a dark colour is not desired, split green gram can be used either partly or fully. Dosas can be made with thick batter like Uthappam or with thin batter like Masala Dosa.

5. BALUSHAI

Ingredients	Quantity
Refined flour	125 gm
Soda bicarbonate	a pinch
Hydrogenated vegetable fat	50 gm
For Syrup:	
Sugar	125 gm
Water	30 gm
Curds	15 gm
Salt	a pinch
Cold water	2 tbsp
Cardamoms	4
Lime juice	½ tsp
Pistachios	4

Method

1. Sieve flour and rub in fat. 2. Beat curds with soda bicarbonate, salt and water. 3. Mix in flour to make a soft and smooth dough. 4. Divide mixture into 8 balls. Make a depression in centre of each, with thumb and fore finger; the pressed portion should be very thin. 5. Heat fat and remove from fire. 6. Put balushais in fat and shake frying pan. (This is to allow the balushais to rise and avoid browning on the under-side). 7. Prick balushais with sticks as soon as they come up. 8. Return frying pan to fire. Cook on a slow fire till balushais are light brown. 9. Drain and dip them in one-string sugar syrup. 10. Decorate with chopped pistachios.

6. KULFI

Ingredients	Quantity
Milk	1 litre
Sugar	125 gm

Ingredients	Quantity
Saffron	a large pinch
Pistachio nuts	20
Almonds	20
Cardamoms	4
Whole dried fresh milk	125 gm
Rose syrup	for flavouring

Method

1. Boil milk on very low heat, and by stirring occasionally, bring it to a thick creamy consistency (the richer the consistency desired, the more the milk can be reduced by boiling). 2. Add whole dried fresh milk, pistachios, almonds, cardamoms and crushed saffron. Boil for another five minutes and remove from heat. Cool. 3. When mixture is cold pour into kulfi cups, screw caps on tight and place cups in the freezing chamber of a refrigerator or in a freezer cabinet for an hour. 4. Take out cups and roll each briskly into your hands pressing a little. Remove screw cap and squeeze out kulfi into a dish. Cut each kulfi into four pieces. Sprinkle with a small quantity of rose syrup for flavouring.

7. CARROT KHEER

Ingredients	Quantity
Carrots	250 gm
Milk	600 ml
Sugar	50 gm
Almonds	30 gm
Cream	30 ml
Saffron	¼ tsp
Water	150 ml
Silver paper	2

Method

1. Wash, scrape and grate carrots. 2. Put into a pan with water. 3. Cover pan and cook over slow heat till carrots are half cooked and water absorbed. 4. Remove. 5. Add milk, sugar and ground blanched almonds (keep aside a few for garnishing) to carrots. 6. Cook gently stirring all the time. 7. Soak saffron in a dessertspoon of warm water. Mix well. 8. When carrots are cooked and mixture thick, add saffron. 9. Remove from fire and allow to cool (preferably over ice or in a refrigerator). 10. When cold stir in cream. 11. Pour into a glass bowl. Garnish with silver paper and sliced almonds.

8. LENTIL MULLIGATAWNY SOUP

Ingredients	Quantity
Tomatoes	225 gm
Cinnamon	small piece
Lentils	50 gm
Carrots	125 gm
Turnips	30 gm
Curry leaves	1 sprig
Oil	15 ml
Garlic	2 flakes
Onions	15 gm
Ginger	a small piece
Vegetable stock	600 ml
Coconut	1
Lime	1
Coriander	10 gm each
Cumin	(roasted and
Fennel	powdered)
Turmeric	a pinch
Fenugreek	a pinch
Rice (raw)	10 gm

Method

1. Wash lentils. Cover with cold vegetable stock or water. Allow to simmer till cooked. 2. Add washed and prepared vegetables, coriander, fennel and cumin powder, turmeric, fenugreek, half the onions, garlic, ginger, cinnamon, curry leaves, tomatoes and salt. Simmer till vegetables are tender. 3. Strain and pass vegetables through a sieve saving a few pieces for garnish. 4. Extract thick coconut milk from coconut and add to stock. 5. Heat fat in a pan. Add remaining sliced onion and fry till crisp. 6. Add soup, lime juice and more salt if necessary. Remove and serve hot, garnished with boiled rice and pieces of vegetables.

APPENDIX

Oven Temperature

	Electricity		Gas Regulo
	°F	°C	
Cool oven	225–250	107–121	1–9
Very slow oven	250–275	121–135	½–1
Slow oven	275–300	135–149	1–2
Very moderate oven	300–350	149–177	2–3
Moderate oven	375	190	4
Moderate hot oven	400	204	5
Hot oven	425–450	218–233	6–7
Very hot oven	475–500	246–260	8–9

General temperature ranges

	°F	°C	
Very Hot oven	450–475	232–246	For bread, pastries, searing of meat
Grilling heat at source	450 and up	232	Grilling meat, fish, bacon
Hot oven	400–425	204–208	
Moderate oven	350–375	177–190	
Shallow frying/deep frying and griddling	300–375	149–190	
Slow oven	300–325	149–163	
Steam range	228–250	109–128	
Water: boiling point at sea level	212	100	
Flour and cornflour thickened	203	95	
Simmering, poaching, stewing, braising, good for dissolving gelatine holding coffee and chocolate	185–195	85–91	
Maximum for egg custard, Hollandaise sauce	185	85	
Final rinse in dishwashing machine (10 seconds)	180	82	
Well-cooked meat, medium-cooked meat (internal temp.)	160	71	

	°F	°C
Eggs: yolks coagulate at 76°C; whites at 74°C	156	69
Thermotainers: most food for serving	150	65
Hot fudges and other sauces; rare meat	140	60
Danger range in which food bacteria thrive if in moist non-acid food materials	45–120	7.5–49
Holding most fruits, vegetables and dairy products	40	5
Meat storage (short-term)	34–36	0
Water freezer	32	0
Holding ice-cream	8–12	−22.5
Holding frozen foods	0 to 20	−29 to −18
Holding frozen foods	0 to −20	−29 to −18

GLOSSARY OF SOME EUROPEAN TERMS IN THE BOOK

N.B. Unless otherwise indicated, the words explained are French. Abbreviations in square brackets: G. = German; Sp. = Spanish; It. = Italian; D. = Dutch; P. = Portuguese

Abricot(s) : Apricot(s)

Affelsinen : Oranges [G.]

Agneau : Lamb

Ail : Garlic

Alcachofas de Jerusalem :
Jerusalem Artichokes [Sp.]

Allemande : German style

Amande (s) : Almond(s)

Ananas : Pineapple

Anchois : Anchovies

Anges à Cheval : Angels on
Horseback

Anglaise : English style

Apfel : Apple [G.]

Arlesienne : as served in Arles

Arroz : Rice [Sp.]

Artichauts : Artichokes

Asperges : Asparagus

Aubergines : Brinjals

Barquette(s) : (Literally) Little
boat(s)

Berenjenas : Brinjals [Sp.]

Beurre : Butter

Blanc (he)(s): White

Blumenkohl : Cauliflower [G.]

Boeuf : beef

Bordelaise : as served in Bordeaux

Branche, en : whole (as applied
to spinach leaves, broccoli
spears, etc.)

Bretonne : Breton style

Brochette, en : on a skewer

Cadgeree : Kedgeree, dish of fish
and rice

Camarones : Prawns [Sp.]

Cacciatore : Huntsman [It.]

Canard : Duck

Caneton : Duckling

Carotte(s) : Carrot(s)

Céleri : Celery

Cervelle : Brain

Champignon(s) : Mushroom(s)

Chasseur : Hunter

Chou-fleur : Cauliflower

Choucroute : Sauerkraut (pickled
cabbage)

Choux : Cabbages; also a type of
pastry

Choux de Bruxelles : Brussels
sprouts

Chuletas : Chops [Sp.]

Concombre(s) : Cucumber(s)

Consommé : Clear soup

Coq : Cockerel

Coquetel : Cocktail

Cordero : Lamb [Sp.]

Côté : Side

Côtelette(s) : Cutlets

Courge : Baby vegetable marrow

Crabe : Crab

Crème : Cream; also applied to a
thick type of soup

Crevettes : Shrimps or prawns

Danoise : Danish style

Diable : Devilled

Dinde : Turkey (the fowl)
Dieppoise : as served in Dieppe

Ecarlate : Scarlet
Egyptienne : Egyptian style
En : in the manner of
Épinards : Spinach
Espagnol(e) : Spanish style
Estilo : Style [Sp.]
Estouffade : Brown stock

Farce : Stuffing
Farci(e) (s) : Stuffed
Fausse tortue : mock turtle
Flamande : Flemish style
Foie : Liver
Foie gras : Goose liver
Foie de Veau : Calves' liver
Foie de Volaille : Chicken liver
Fondantes : (literally) Melting
Frais : Fresh
Frappé (e) : Half-frozen
Fromage : Cheese
Frita (s) : Fried (fem.) [Sp.]
Frito (s) : Fried (masc.) [Sp.]
Fritto : Fried [It.]
Fumé(e) (s) : Smoked

Galantine : A jelly made with
   boned cold meat
Garnie(e) (s) : Decorated
Gâteau : A rich cake
Gêlée : Jelly
Gestoofde : Stuffed [D.]
Gibier : Game
Gigot : Leg of lamb or mutton
Gratin, au : Cooked with grated
   cheese
Grecque : as served in Greece
Grillé(e) (s) : Grilled

Harengs : Herrings
Haricots Blancs : Dried haricot
   beans

Haricots verts : French beans
Hollandaise : Dutch style
Homard : Lobster
Hongroise : Hungarian style
Huile : Oil
Huîtres : Oysters

Indienne : Indian style

Jambon : Ham
Jus : Juice

Kartoffel : Potato [G.]
Komkommers : Cucumbers [D.]

Laitances : Soft fish roe
Langue : Tongue
Légumes : Vegetables
Lentilles : Lentils
Lyonnaise : As served in Lyons

Madrilène : As served in Madrid
Maïs : Maize, sweet corn
Mangue(s) : Mango (es)
Maquereau : Mackerel
Marseillaise : As served in
   Marseilles
Menthe : Mint
Mexicain(e) (s) : Mexican
Milanaise : As served in Milan
Mouton : Mutton

Napolitain : As served in Naples
Navets : Turnips
Niçoise : As served in Nice
Noir(e) (s) : Black

Oeufs : Eggs
Oie : Goose
Oignons : Onions
Okra : Ladies' fingers
Ovos : Eggs [P.]
Orientale : Oriental style

Pailles : Straws
Pamplemousse : Grapefruit
Parisienne : Parisian style
Pato : Duck [Sp. &P.]
Paysanne : Peasant style
Pêche(s) : Peach (es)
Petits Pois : Peas
Pimento : Capsicum
Pôché(e) (s) : Poached
Pôelé : Roasted in butter
Pôeling : Roasting in butter
Poire(s) : Pear(s)
Poireaux : Leeks
Poisson : Fish
Poitrine d'Oie : Breast of goose
Polonaise : Polish style
Pommes : Apples; (loosely)
    potatoes
Pommes de Terre : potatoes
Porc : Pork
Portugaise : Portuguese style
Potage : Soup
Pouding de Noël : Christmas
    pudding
Poularde : Large, fully grown fowl
Poulet : Chicken
Pré : Field

Quartiers : Quarters
Queue de Bœuf : Oxtail

Ragout : Stew
Reine : Queen
Riz : Rice
Rognons : Kidneys

Rôti(e) (s) : Roasted
Russe : Russian

Sagou : Sago
Salade : Salad
Salsa : Sauce [Sp. & It.]
Saucisson : Sausage
Saumon : Salmon
Soupe : Soup
Suppe : Soup [G.]

Tasse : Cup
Thon : Tuna; tunny
Tocino : Pork [Sp.]
Tomate : Tomato
Topinambours : Jerusalem
    artichokes
Tortue : Turtle
Turque : Turkish style

Varié(e) (s) : Varied
Veau : Veal
Velouté : Soup
Vert : Green
Viande : Meat
Viennoise : As served in Vienna
Vin : Wine
Vischkoekjes : Fish cakes [D.]
Volaille : Fowl

Wiener Schnitzel : Veal escalope
    [G.]

Zuppa : Soup [It.]

INDEX

INDEX

Achar Ghosht, 385–86
Adamanga (Malayalee Mango Pickle)
  (A), 635–36; (B), 636
Adobo (Chicken), 375
Affelsinenbiscuitort Ungefult (Orange
  Cake), 281
Afghani Chicken Khorma, 389–90
Aigo Menager (Provençale Soup), 54–55
Ajam Dalam Kelapa (Chicken in
  Coconut), 374
Ajap Djahe (Mixed Vegetables), 375–76
Alaska Special, 717
Alcachofas de Jerusalem al Gratin, 290
Alesondigas (Meat Balls), 312–13
Allemande Sauce, 117
Allumettes aux Anchois aux Farces de
  Poisson, 4
Almond Bonbons, 527–28
Almond Icing (for decoration), 444
Almond Paste (for use under royal
  icing and to decorate easter and
  simnel cakes), 443–44
Almond Slices, 489
Almond Tarts, 484–85
Amaretti, 296–97
American Chop Suey, 363
American Coffee Cakes, 428, 477
American Frosting, 445
Ananas Royale, 226–27
Andhra Pickles, 626
Anges à Cheval, 252
Apfelstrudel (Apple Strudel), 281–82;
  Filling, 282
Appam, 418
Apple Chutney (A), 684; (B), 685
Apple Crisp, 329
Apple Drink, 715
Apple Kissel, 307–08
Apple Murabba, 699–700
Apple Pie, 490–91
Apple Soufflé, 308
Apple Tarts, 485–86
Armenian Soup, 302
Arroz Estilo Barcelones (Rice
  Barcelona Style), 289
Artichauts à la Grecque, 4
Artichauts en Branche, 187
Asparagus Chicken Soup, 344–45

Asparagus Sandwiches, 593
Asperges, 187–88
Aubergines à l'Egyptienne, 188
Aubergines Frites, 188
Aubergines à la Provençale, 188–89
Aubergines à la Turque, 189
Aubergine Sauce, 332
Aubergines with Peppers, 334
Avakkai (A), 631; (B), 632; (C), 632;
  (D), 632–33

Baba au Rhum, 237
Bachelor's Buttons, 532
Bacon and Banana Toast, 616–17
Bacon Puffs, 619
Baked Cheese Fondue, 169
Baked Fish, 315
Baked Fish in Sour Cream Sauce, 303
Baked Fish, 338–39
Bakewell Tarts, 500
Baklava (Turkish pastry), 336–37
Balachaung, 367
Ballotines de Volaille Printanière, 163
Balushai, 727
Banana and Cream Puff Ring, 515–16
Banana Bread, 586
Banana Chocolate Sundae, 235
Banana Chutney, 676
Banana Drop Scones, 585
Banana Jam, 696
Banana Joy, 600–601
Banana Milk Shake, 709
Banana Tea Ring, 479–80
Barquettes, 4
Barquettes de Crevettes, 256
Bavarois d'Abricot, 245
Bavarois à la Crème, 222
Bavarois Diplomate, 222
Bavarois aux Fruits, 225–26
Beef Sandwiches, 593–94
Beef Stroganoff, 305
Beetroot and Horseradish Sauce, 300
Beetroot Sandwiches, 594
Beignets d'Ananas à la Favorite,
  248–49
Beignets de Fromage, 261–61
Berenjenas Salteadas (Aubergines
  Sautés), 290

Beurre à Bercy (Bercy Butter), 100
Beverages, 696
Bhalla Kanji, 659
Bird's Nest Cookies, 533
Biscuits à la Duchesse, 259
Biscuits Au Fromage, 259
Biscuit Press Cookies, 528
Bitter Gourd Chutney, 675
Bitter Gourd Pickle, 652
Black Forest Cake, 462–63
Blanquette de Veau à l'Ancienne, 107
Blanquette de Veau aux Céleris, 109
Blumenkohl Salat (Cauliflower Salad), 280–81
Bœuf Wellington, 103
Bordelaise Sauce, 120
Boston Baked Beans , 328
Boti Kabab, 382–83
Bouchée Indienne, 255
Bouillabaisse (Provençale Fish Soup), 271–72
Braised Kebab, 339
Braised Wild Duck, 181
Bran Muffins, 440
Brandy Snaps, 537
Bread Pan Rolls, 562
Bread (hot dough method), 567–68
Bread (no-time dough method), 567
Bread (normal straight method), 564
Bread (70% sponge method), 565–66
Bread (100% sponge method), 564–65
Bread (soaker and dough method), 566–67
Bread (straight dough method), 563–64
Bread (wholemeal no-time dough method), 567
Bread (with milk powder), 568
Bread (with soya flour), 571
Bread Making, 555–58
Bread Rolls (no-time dough), 558
Bread Rolls (straight method), 558–59
Brinjal and Chilli Pickle, 651–52
Brinjal in Garlic Sauce, 349–50
Brioche Fancy, 574
Broccoli, 189
Broiled Chicken, 359–60
Brownies, 541–42
Buns with Filling, 574
Burani, 386
Butter Buttons, 532
Butter Cream (rich), 442
Butter Icing (plain) (A), 442; (B), 442
Butterflies, 501
Butterfly Buns, 432
Butterscotch Flan, 497

Cabbage Dolmas, 335
Cadgeree de Saumon, 78
Cakes, helpful suggetions for making, 430
Camarones Fritos (Fried Prawns), 286
Canapés, 4
Canapés aux Anchois, 4
Canapés au Caviar, 4
Canapé Charlemagne, 255
Canapés aux Crevettes, 4
Canapés Danoise, 4
Canapé Diane, 258
Canapés Homard, 4
Canapé Laitances, 257
Canapés Langue Écarlate, 4
Canapé Quo Vadis, 258
Canapé Yorkaise, 256
Canard Rôti à L'anglaise, 165
Candied Peel, 700
Candy, Tips on Making, 540
Caneton Braisé aux Navets, 166
Caneton Braisé à l'Orange, 166–67
Caneton aux Olives, 166
Caneton aux Petits Pois, 167
Caneton Poêle à la Menthe, 165–66
Canneloni, 210
Capilotade de Volaille, 159
Capsicum Pickle (A), 656–57; (B), 657; (C), 657–58
Caramel Sandwich Cake, 455
Caramel Toffee, 244
Carolines Diverse, 7
Carottes au Beurre ou Glacées, 189–90
Carottes à la Crème, 190
Carrot Kanji, 664
Carrot Kheer, 728
Carrot Pickle (A), 649; (B), 649–50; (C), 650–51
Carrot Pudding, 329
Carrot Sandwiches, 600
Caucasian Salad, 300–01
Caucasian Shashlik , 306
Cauliflower Pal Kootu, 409–10
Caviar with Eggs, 298
Caviar, 9
Céleri Bonne Femme (A), 13; (B), 13
Céleri Bonne Femme, 5
Céleri Braisé, 190–91
Céleri Rave, 5
Celery, 15
Celery Sandwiches, 600
Cervelle au Beurre Noir, 110
Cervelle au Beurre Noisette, 110–11
Cervelle à la Maréchale, 111
Cervelle à la Poulette, 111
Cervelle à la Robert, 7
Ceylon Chicken Curry, 372

Chakhokhbily (Caucasian Chicken Dish), 306
Champignons Grillés, 191
Channa Dal Chutney, 665–66
Charcutière Sauce, 124
Charga, 393
Charlotte d'Orange, 219
Charlotte Russe, 218
Châteaubriand, 99
Chaudfroid de Poulet, 161–62
Check Cake, 451
Checkerboard Sandwiches, 604
Cheese Biscuits, 502
Cheese Bouchées, 613–14
Cheese and Aubergine Flan, 492
Cheese and Bacon Frittata, 129
Cheese and Chilli Sandwiches, 594–95
Cheese and Egg Sandwiches, 595
Cheese Loaf Sandwich, 571
Cheese Pastry, 500–501
Cheese Sandwiches, 594
Cheese Splits, 620
Cheese Straws (A), 502–03; (B), 503; (C), 503–04
Cheese Toast, 617–18
Cheese Toast (grilled), 612
Cheesecake (A), 486; (B), 487; (C), 487–88
Chelsea Buns (A), 580–81; (B), 581
Cherry Buns, 432–33
Cherry Cake, 464
Cherry Knobs, 525–26
Cherry Shortbread, 522
Cherry Tip Cakes, 435–36
Chettinad Kozhi Melagi Varaval (Chicken Pepper Fry), 403
Chicken a Portuguesa, 320
Chicken Afghani, 387–88
Chicken Biryani, 396–97
Chicken Cafrel, 390–91
Chicken Chettinad, 401–02
Chicken Chili, 357
Chicken Clear Soup, 344
Chicken Curry Kashmiri, 389
Chicken Farcha, 394
Chicken in Garlic Sauce, 356
Chicken Gumbo Soup (A), 323; (B), 323–24
Chicken and Ham Pie, 510–11
Chicken and Ham Sandwiches, 595
Chicken Jaipuri, 391
Chicken Kauswey, 366–67
Chicken Liver Tartlets, 292
Chicken Malai Kabab, 384
Chicken Moghlai, 386–87
Chicken and Mushroom Soup, 345–46
Chicken Noodle Soup, 345

Chicken Pickle, 661
Chicken Pilaff, 333–34
Chicken Pineapple, 358
Chicken Risotto, 295
Chicken Salad, 313
Chicken as Served in Rome, 296
Chicken Shahjahani, 388–89
Chicken Shreds with Chili, 358
Chicken Tartlets, 291
Chicken Tikka, 392–93
Chicken à la Ture, 341–42
Chicken Vol-au-Vent, 512–13
Chicken Zaibunissa, 388
Chilli Sauce (A), 690; (B), 690
Chinese Fried Rice, 364
Chinese Noodles, 361
Chinese Vegetables (Mixed Vegetables), 363–64
Chocolate Boats, 434
Chocolate Cake (economical), 461–62
Chocolate Cake, 462
Chocolate Chiffon Pudding, 318
Chocolate Chip Cookies, 528
Chocolate Cream Fingers, 531–32
Chocolate Creams, 291
Chocolate Fudge, 543–44
Chocolate Layer Cake, 451–52
Chocolate Meringue Pie, 493–94
Chocolate Sauce, 235
Chocolate Whirls, 532
Chocolates, 549–50
Chop Suey, 362
Chou-Fleur, 193
Chou-Fleur à la Crème, 191–92
Chou-Fleur au Gratin, 192
Chou-Fleur à la Milanaise, 192
Chou-Fleur à la Polonaise, 193
Choux Braisé, 191
Choux de Bruxelles à l'Anglaise, 193
Choux de Bruxelles au Beurre, 194
Choux de Bruxelles Sautés, 193
Choux Fleurs, 5
Choux Pastry, 521
Chow Chow, 655
Chow Mein, 360–61
Christmas Bread, 572–73
Christmas Cake (A), 470–71; (B), 471; (C), 471–72; (D), 472–73; (E), 473
Christmas Cake (economical), 473–74
Christmas Cake (eggless), 475
Christmas Cake (with semolina), 474–75
Chuletas de Cordero Vilareal (Lamb Chops), 287
Chuletas de Tocino con Salsa de Tomate (Pork Chops with Tomato Sauce), 286–87

Churros (Fried Batter), 291
Cinnamon Leaves and Crescents, 526
Cinnamon Rolls, 560–61
Cinnamon Twists, 574
Clarified Consommé, 20–21
Closed Sandwiches, 603–04
Clown Sandwiches, 602
Coburg Cakes, 433
Coconut and Moong Dal Chutney,
    666–67
Coconut Buns, 432
Coconut Chiffon Pie, 498–99
Coconut Chutney (A), 668–69; (B), 669;
    (C), 669
Coconut Chutney for Idlis, 669–70
Coconut Macaroons (A), 538; (B),
    538–39
Cocum Chutney, 682
Coffee Jap Cakes, 436–37
Compote de Fruits, 8
Concombres, 14
Concombres à la Crème, 195
Concombres à la Danoise, 7
Concombres Farcis, 7
Confectioner's Custard (without eggs)
    (A), 447; (B) (with egg) or Vanilla
    Cream, 447
Consommé Ailerons, 31
Consommé Alexandra, 26
Consommé Allemande, 31
Consommé Ambassadrice, 24
Consommé Andalouse, 28
Consommé Anglaise, 32
Consommé à la Balzac, 32
Consommé avec Bœuf, 21
Consommé Bouquetière, 28–29
Consommé Bretonne, 32
Consommé Brunoise, 24
Consommé à la Carmen, 23
Consommé Célestine, 21–22
Consommé Clermont, 32–33
Consommé à la Fermiere, 29
Consommé Florentine, 27
Consommé Girondine, 34
Consommé Grimaldi, 27–28
Consommé à l'Indienne, 29–30
Consommé à l'Italienne, 24
Consommé Jacqueline, 22
Consommé à la Jardinière, 23
Consommé à la Julienne, 22
Consommé Madrilène (cold), 33
Consommé Marie Louise, 24
Consommé à la Milanaise, 34
Consommé Montmorency, 35
Consommé Niçoise, 25
Consommé Orientale, 33
Consommé Parisienne, 30

Consommé Paysanne, 33
Consommé Printanier, 30–31
Consommé aux Profiteroles, 25–26
Consommé Réjane, 30
Consommé Royale, 23
Consommé Sagou, 25
Consommé Tapioca, 25
Consommé en Tasse, 33
Consommé Vermicelli, 25
Consommé Vert Pré, 35
Cooked Fondant, 547–48
Copra Chutney, 667
Coq au Vin, 144–45
Coquetel de Crabe, Homard, Crevettes,
    10–11
Coquetel Florida, 8
Coquetel de Fruits, 8
Coquetel de Melon, 10
Coquetel d'Orange, 8
Coquetel de Pamplemousse, 8
Coriander Leaf Chutney Sandwiches,
    601
Cornflour Glaze, 447–48
Cornucopia Sandwiches, 606
Côte de Porc à la Charcutière, 124
Côte de Porc à la Flamande, 124
Côte de Porc Hongroise, 125
Côtelettes d'Agneau à l'Ambassadrice,
    116
Côtelettes d'Agneau à la Réforme,
    114–15
Côtelettes de Mouton à la Villeroi, 117
Côtelettes à la Murillo, 118
Côtelettes à la Provencale, 118
Coupe Jacques, 235
Courge Farcie, 194
Courge Provençale, 194–95
Courge, 194
Covering for Bread Rolls, 559
Crab in Egg Sauce, 304–05
Crabe en Coquille, 11, 97
Cream Corks, 431
Cream Horns, 514–15
Cream Slices, 516
Creamy Caramels, 546
Crème d'Asperges, 35–36
Crème Brûlée, 245–46
Crème de Céleri, 36
Crème de Champignons (A), 36–37;
    (B), 37
Crème de Concombres, 37–38
Crème Crécy, 38
Crème Dubarry, 38–39
Crème d'Épinards (Crème Florentine),
    39
Crème Garibaldi, 224–25
Crème de Haricots Blancs, 42–43

Crème de Maïs (Créme Washington), 39–40
Crème de Menthe, 542
Crème Mosaique, 223–24
Crème Portugaise, 42
Crème St. Germain, 40
Crème de Volaille (A) (Crème à la Reine), 40–41; (B), 41
Crème de Volaille Princesse, 41–42
Crèmes Beatrice, 259–60
Crêpes Georgette, 248
Crêpes Suzette, 277
Crescents, 563
Crevettes, 12
Croquettes d'Œuf, 63–64
Croque Monsieur, 256
Croquettes de Pommes de Terre à la Dauphine, 204
Croûte Baron, 253
Croûte Radjah, 257
Croûtes au Jambon à la Ménagère, 270–71
Crystallized Fruit, 549
Cucumber and Salmon Sandwiches, 593
Cucumber and Tomato Frost, 709
Cucumber Pickle, 651
Cucumber Sandwiches, 595–96
Cucumber with Smetana, 300
Cup Cakes, 438
Curry Leaf Chutney, 667
Curry Sauce, 721–22
Custard Pie (A), 495–96; (B), 496
Custard Tarts (A), 482; (B) (with custard powder), 482
Cuts of Chicken, 131–32
Cuts of Fish, 76
Cuts of Vegetables, 186

Dal Chutney, 666
Danish Parsley Chicken, 317–18
Danish Pastry (A), 516–17; (B), 517–20
Darne de Saumon Poché, 77
Date and Carrot Chutney, 683
Date Chutney, 682–83
Date Fudge, 545
Date and Nut Filling (for turnover and mock mince pies), 445–46
Date and Nut Turnover, 481
Date and Walnut Bread, 585–86
Date and Walnut Cake, 467–68
Deep Fried Spring Chicken, 355–56
Deep Fruit Pie, 490
Devil Mixture, 134
Devilled Crab, 325
Diables à Cheval, 253
Dinde Rôtie, 167–68

Dolmas (Stuffed Vegetables), 340–41
Donkey Sandwiches, 602
Dosai, 418
Doughnuts (with baking powder), 441
Dried Apricot Chutney, 683–84
Dried Coconut Chutney, 670
Dried Mango Pickle, 635
Drop Scones, 584–85
Dry Coconut Chutney (Idichuppumuluku), 689
Dry Duxelle, 84–85
Duchesses Nantua, 7
Dudhi Kanji (Bottle Gourd Kanji), 664
Dudhi Peel Chutney, 672–73
Dundee Cake, 469–70

Éclair Swans (Choux Pastry), 521–22
Egg and Cheese Flan, 499
Egg Drop Spinach Soup, 346–47
Egg Fu Yong, 349
Egg and Lettuce Sandwiches, 596
Egg Pakoras, 620
Egg Pasties, 614–15
Egg Sandwiches, 596
Egg Sauce, 304–05
Eggless Cakes (with flaky pastry), 507–08
Enriched White Bread, 568–70
Enriched White Bread (with dry milk), 570
Entrecôte (Sirloin Steaks), 102
Entrecôte Minute (Minute Steaks), 102
Entrées and Relevés, 98
Entremets, 215
Épinards en Branches, 195
Épinards à la Crème, 196
Épinards au Gratin, 196
Épinards en Purée, 196
Escalope de Veau, 105
Escalope de Veau Napolitaine, 105–06
Escudella Catalina, 282–83

Filet de Pomfret au Sauce Verte (Pomfret Fillet in Green Sauce), 91–92
Filet de Pomfret ou Sole aux Aubergines, 82
Filet de Pomfret ou Sole Bercy, 85–86
Filet de Pomfret Bretonne, 82
Filet de Pomfret ou Sole Cubat, 83
Filet de Sole ou Pomfret Dorée, 81
Filet de Pomfret ou Sole Dugléré, 82
Filet de Pomfret ou Sole Hongroise, 86
Filet de Pomfret Meunière Andalouse, 80–81

Filet de Pomfret ou Sole Meunière à l'Orange, 82
Filet de Pomfret ou Sole Mexicaine, 86–87
Filet de Pomfret ou Sole Miramar, 87–88
Filet de Pomfret ou Sole Mornay, 80
Filet de Pomfret ou Sole Newburg, 88
Filet de Pomfret ou Sole Orientale, 88–89
Filet de Pomfret ou Sole en Pilau à la Levantine, 89
Filet de Pomfret ou Sole Pompadour, 89
Filet de Pomfret ou Sole Provençale, 83–84
Filet de Pomfret ou Sole Verdi, 90
Filet de Pomfret ou Sole Veronique (A), 90; (B), 91
Filet de Pomfret ou Sole Walewska, 91
Finare Lammragu (Fine Lamb Stew), 316–17
Fio de Ovos, 321
Fisch in Pikanter Sauce (Fish with Piquant Sauce), 278–79
Filling (A) Dark Ganache, 551
Filling (B) Butter Ganache, 551
Filling (C) Coconut Ganache, 551–52
Filling (D) Maple Ganache, 552
Fish Balls with Spinach, 279
Fish Belle Meunière, 81
Fish Fillets with Mushrooms and Vegetables, 314–15
Flaky Pastry, 506–07
Flan d'Ananas, 247–48
Flan de Jambon Soubise, 125–26
Flensjes, 310
Flower Bun, 576
Fluffy Icing, 445
Foie Gras, 9
Foie de Veau à l'Anglaise, 110
Fondant Peppermint Cream, 544
Fondue Bourguignonne, 170
Fondue Without Wine, 169
Fondues, 168
For Tandoor Seasoning, 376
Forshmak, 298–99
French Almond Rock, 542–43
French Beans with Mushrooms, 307
French Bread, 572
French Jellies, 548
Fresh Chutneys, 660
Fresh Corn Egg Flower Soup, 343–44
Fricadelles, 109–10
Fricassee de Volaille, 154–55
Fried Chicken, 327–28
Fried Chicken, 359

Fried Chicken, 395–96
Fried Prawns, 351
Frittos de Volaille, 160
Frivolités, 5
Fruit Cake (creaming method) (A), 464–65; (B), 465
Fruit Cake (plain) (rub-in method), 463
Fruit Cake (rich), 465–66
Fruit Fizz, 704–05
Fruit and Honey Sponge Cake, 453–54
Fruit and Nut Filling for Sweet Dough, 577
Fruit Punch (A), 704; (B), 704
Fruit Punch with Whipped Cream, 705
Fudge Cake, 457

Galantine de Poulet, 162–63
Galinha Cafrel (Chicken Piri Piri), 390
Game, 171–73; gravy for, 172; to keep, 171; marinade for, 173; selection of, 171; taint in, prevention of, 172; taint in, removal of, 172; time chart for cooking, 184–85
Game Birds, 174–75
Game Hot-Pot, 183–84
Game Pickle, 658–59
Garlic and Cheese Bread, 574–75
Garlic Bread, 574
Garlic Chutney (A), 672; (B), 672
Garlic Mango Pickle, 633
Garlic Spare Ribs, 365
Gâteau d'Abricot, 228–29
Gâteau d'Ananas, 230
Gâteau de Chocolat, 230–31
Gâteau à la Florentine, 229–30
Gazpacho (A), 283; (B), 283–84
Gâteau de Pêches, 228
Gelatine Dainties, 548–49
Gelée à la Mandarine, 216
Genoese Sponge Cake (A), 454; (B), 454–55
Gestoofde Komkommers, 310
Gibier, 171
Gigot à la Boulangére, 113
Gigot de Mouton Braisé, 112–13
Gigot à la Soubise, 113–14
Gigot d'Agneau Rôti, 111–12
Gigot de Mouton Farci à L'Ail au Sauce Herbes, 114
Gigot Rôti à l'Ail (Leg of Lamb with Garlic), 275
Ginger Apple Pie, 491
Ginger Beer, 707
Ginger Biscuits (A), 535; (B), 535; (C), 536
Ginger Cream, 547

Ginger Fruit Cocktail, 322–23
Ginger Mango Pickle, 633
Ginger Punch, 705
Ginger Wine, 702
Gingerbread with Dates (A), 478–79;
 (B), 479
Gingo, 707–08
Glacé Icing (A), 443; (B), 443
Gnocchi (dumpling), 213
Gnocchi Romane, 213
Golden Goodies, 524
Goulash de Bœuf à la Hongroise, 105
Goulash de Poulet (A), 156; (B)
 (Chicken Goulash), 156–57
Grape Squash, 713
Grape Wine, 702–03
Grapefruit and Lime Marmalade, 697
Grapefruit Cocktail, 710
Grapefruit with Shrimps, 311
Gratin de Pommes de Terre à la
 Dauphinoise, 205
Greek Béchamel, 332
Green Chilli Chutney, 665
Green Chilli Pickle (A), 655–56; (B),
 656
Green Chutney, 674
Green Pea Boats, 501
Green Tomato Chutney, 685
Grilled Venison Steaks, 182
Groundnut Chutney (A), 671; (B), 671
Grouse (sautéed, vincent style), 175–76
Guava Cheese (made out of the pulp
 of Guava Jelly), 699
Guava Jelly (A), 697–98; (B), 698–99
Gujarati Pickle, 628
Gulyas Soupe, 55–56
Gundu Porial (Baby Potatoes Porial),
 413
Gurda, 381–82

Hakka Noodles, 360
Ham Bouchées, 513–14
Ham Croûtes, 616
Ham Pasties, 307
Ham Sandwiches, 596–97
Hara Dhania Chutney (A), 673–74;
 (B), 674
Harengs Dieppoise, 16–17
Harengs Dieppoise, 5
Haricot Bean Soup, 292
Haricots Blancs, 196–97
Haricots Verts, 5
Harlequin Sandwiches, 597
Homard à la Diable, 274–75
Homard à la Newburg (A), 94–95; (B),
 95

Homard à la Thermidor, 94
Honey Biscuits, 534
Honey Puffs, 336
Hors d'Œvres, 3
Hot and Sour Soup, 347
Hot Brinjal Pickle (A), 646–47; (B), 647
Hot Water Crust Pastry, 504–05
How to Pot Roast, 178–79
Huîtres, 5
Hunter's Steak, 182
Hutspot (Hotchpotch), 309–10

Ice Cream Fizz, 709–10
Iced Coffee (plain), 703
Iced Coffee with Condensed Milk, 703
Iced Coffee with Cream, 703–04
Iced Tea, 703
Idde Appung (String Hoppers), 369
Idiyappam, 418
Idly, 417

Jack Baskets, 621
Jam Buns (rub-in method), 439–40
Jam and Jelly Making, 687
Jam Tarts, 481
Jam Turnovers, 506
Jap Cake, 455–56
Jeera Pani, 716
Jellied Crab Consommé, 26–27
Jogi Bhath, 423–24
Jus de Tomate, 10
Jus-lié, 135

Kachri, 376
Kadai Ghosht, 384–85
Kadhambam Chutney, 419
Kadukumanga, 637
Kaikari Perattal, 410–11
Kalan Melagu, 414–15
Kaldolmar, 316
Kaleji/Kapura, 381
Kalu Dodol, 373–74
Kanni Manga, 636
Kari Kolambu (Lamb Curry), 405–06
Kari Podimas (Kheema Masala),
 406–07
Karinellika, 645
Kartoffel Suppe (Cream of Potato
 Soup), 277–78
Karuvepellai Yera, 398–99
Kashmiri Chutney (Mango), 680
Kathrikai Avial, 409
Kathrikai Ketti Kozhambu (Brinjal
 Curry), 407–08
Katrikai Kara Kozhumbu, 408

Khajur Chutney, 676
Khara Biscuits, 520–21
Kharek Chutney, 680–81
Kidney Sandwiches, 601
Kirihoti, 370–71
Kizhangu Karvadu Varuval (Potatoes
    Fried Like Fish), 413–14
Knots, 563
Kola Urunda Kolambu (Mutton Kofta
    Curry), 404–05
Koli Porchathu (Fried Chicken), 402–03
Koli Rasama (Chicken Rasam), 403–04
Kollu Vellam, 717
Konigsberger Klops, 279–80
Kothamali Chutney, 420
Kothorakka Karamani Pachadi (Gowar
    Singh and Chowli Beans
    "Pachadi"), 412–13
Kozhi Mulagu Varuval (Chicken
    Pepper Fry), 401
Kromeskies, 123
Kulcha, 575
Kulfi, 727–28

Ladies' Fingers with Aubergines, 334
Laitances Méphisto, 257
Lamb Kebab, 331
Lamb and Vegetable Soup, 313–14
Languouste, to cook and clean, 93–94
Languouste à la Parisienne, 96–97
Langue de Mouton Choucroute, 122
Large Cakes, 427
Lassi, 709
Lathok (Rice Mixture), 368–69
Lazy Shchy, 301–02
Légumes et Pâtés Alimentaires, 185
Lemon Cake, 453
Lemon Curd, 446–47
Lemon Curd Tarts, 481
Lemon Meringue Pie, 495
Lemon Soufflé, 239
Lentil Mulligatawny Soup, 729
Les Huîtres, 9
Lettuce Sandwiches, 597
Light Coffee Cakes, 477–78
Lime Chiffon Pie, 497–98
Lime Chilli Pickle, 644–45
Lime and Date Chutney, 681
Lime and Other Vegetable Pickles, 634
Lime Pickle (A), 639; (B), 639–40; (C),
    640; (D), 640–41; (E), 641
Lime Pickle (Maharashtrian), 644
Lime Pickle (Sweet) (A), 641–42; (B),
    642
Lime Pickle (White) (A), 642; (B), 643
Lime Pickle in Juice, 644

Lime Pickle with Mustard, 643
Lime Squash, 713
Lime Syrup, 712
Lime-ginger Squash, 712–13
Limes in Vinegar, 643
Liver Puffs, 614
Lobster à la King, 325–26
Lobster a Portuguesa, 319–20
Love Cake, 470
Low Cholesterol Chocolate Cake, 452

Macaroni à l'Italienne, 211
Macaroni à la Napolitaine, 211–12
Macaroons on Dry Cake, 537–38
Macédoine de Fruits, 227
Macédoine de Légumes, 200
Mackerel for the Smorgasbord, 311
Madeira Cake, 456
Madeleines, 436
Madras Mangai Oorkai, 635
Madras Shepherd's Pie, 127
Maharashtra Pickle, 629
Maïs, 16, 197
Makhani Dal, 380–81
Makrel in Ragoût (Mackerel Stew), 278
Malabar Fish Pickle, 661–62
Malakoff Cake, 308
Malted Mocha Frost, 709
Mandarin Fish, 351–52
Mango Chutney (A), 667–68; (B), 668;
    (C), 668
Mango Chutney (A), 677–78; (B), 678;
    (C), 678–79; (D), 679; (E), 679
Mango Fool, 708
Mango Kasoondi (A), 637; (B), 637–38;
    (C), 638
Mango Magaya, 634
Mango Mustard Pickle, 634
Mango Pickles, 628
Mango Relish, 638–39
Mango Squash, 714
Mangue Bavarois (A) (tinned
    Mangoes), 226; (B), 226
Mangue Cardinal, 232–33
Manthakkali Keera (Green Leafy
    Vegetable Dish), 412
Maquereau Grillé, 93
Maquereau au Beurre Noir, 273–74
Marshmallow Icing (A), 444; (B),
    444–45
Marshmallows, 541
Marwari Pickle (A), 629–30; (B), 630;
    (C) (chilli pickle), 630

Mayonnaise de Crabe; Mayonnaise de Homard; Mayonnaise de Crevettes, 12
Mayonnaise de Homard, 95–96
Mayonnaise de Volaille, 160–61
Meat Balls For Smorgasbord, 312
Meat or Game Pickle, 659
Meat with Okra, 340
Meatless Sauce, 721
Medallion de Saumon, 79
Meen Kozhambu, 400
Meen Varuval (Fish Fried) Chettinad, 399–400
Melba Sauce, 234
Melon Cantaloupe, 5
Melon Cocktail, 5, 710–11
Melon Cooler, 711
Melon Frappé, 10
Melting Moments, 524–25
Meringues, 582
Milan Hearts, 530–31
Milk Bread, 579
Milk Toffee, 543
Mille Feuilles (Thousand Leaves), 508–09
Mince Pies, 506
Mincemeat, 446
Mint Chutney, 681–82
Mint Chutney (A), 673; (B), 673
Mint Chutney Sandwiches, 601
Mint Julep, 710
Mixed Fruit Drink, 711
Mixed Vegetable Pickle (A), 652–53; (B), 653
Mocha Shortcake, 523
Mock Cream, 217–18
Mock Mince Pies, 481
Moghlai Parathas, 725–26
Moh Kya Lapphed, 368
Moju, 372
Momos, 421–22
Moong Dal Chutney, 666
Moulded Chocolate (A), 550; (B), 550
Moussaka à la Grecque, 331–32
Mousse au Citron, 220
Mousse aux Fruits, 219–20
Mousseline Sauce, 238
Mulligatawny, 371
Mushroom Cakes, 431
Mushroom Kootu, 411
Muslim Biryani, 396
Mutton Pickle, 659–60
Mutton Sandwiches, 597–98
Mysore Mango Pickle, 634–35

Nandu Masala (Crab Masala), 397–98

Nankhatai, 583
New Orleans Shrimp, 326–27
Noodles with Tuna Sauce, 293
Norwegian Biscuits, 318–19
Nougat, 552
Nouilles Vertes, 215
Nut Rings, 525
Nutty Bretzels, 524
Nutty Meringues, 582–83

Oeufs Aurore, 63
Oeufs Bercy, 57
Oeufs Brouillés aux Champignons, 68
Oeufs Brouillés Chasseur, 68
Oeufs Brouillés aux Crevettes, 68
Oeufs Brouillés aux Fromage, 69
Oeufs Brouillés Grandmère, 69
Oeufs Brouillés à la Portugaise, 69
Oeufs Chasseur, 57–58
Oeufs en Cocotte avec Crème, 65–66
Oeufs en Cocotte au Jus, 66
Oeufs en Cocotte à la Lorraine, 66–67
Oeufs en Cocotte à la Maraîchère, 67
Oeufs en Cocotte à la Reine, 66
Oeufs en Cocotte à la Soubise, 67
Oeufs à la Bretonne, 273
Oeufs à la Coque Chimay, 62–63
Oeufs à la Coque en Rissole, 64
Oeufs Diable (A), 17; (B), 17
Oeufs Farcis, 16
Oeufs Farcis aux Sardines (Eggs with Sardine Stuffing), 270
Oeufs Farcis et Garnis, 5
Oeufs Florentine, 58
Oeufs Frits à la Bordelaise, 70
Oeufs Frits à la Portugaise, 70
Oeufs Frits à la Provençale, 71
Oeufs Isoline, 58–59
Oeufs Lully, 59
Oeufs Mayonnaise, 12
Oeufs à la Mimosa, 273
Oeufs Noyés, 272–73
Oeufs Omer Pach, 59–60
Oeufs Parmentier, 60
Oeufs Pochés à la Clamart, 60
Oeufs Pochés Colbert, 60–61
Oeufs Pochés Maintenon, 61
Oeufs Pochés Mornay, 62
Oeufs Pochés Mirelle, 61
Oeufs Poché d'Orsay, 62
Oeufs à la Tripe, 64–65
Oeufs à la Tripe Bourgeoise, 65
Oie Rôtie, 167
Oignons Braisés, 198
Oignons Frits à la Française, 197
Oignons Sautés, 197

Okra Soup, 324–25
Olives Farcies, 6
Omelette aux Asperges, 74
Omelette aux Champignons, 71
Omelette à la Clamart, 72
Omelette aux Epinards, 72
Omelette à la Fermière, 72
Omelette aux Foies de Volaille, 73
Omelette à la Lyonnaise, 73
Omelette Parmentier, 73
Omelette à la Provençale, 74
Omelette aux Rognons, 74
Omelette Surprise (baked Alaska),
    235–36
Onion Chutney, 671–72
Onion Scramble, 622
Open-faced Sandwiches, 606–08
Orange and Grapefruit Squash, 715
Orange Fudge, 545
Orange or Lemon Squash, 707
Orange Marmalade, 697
Orange Milk Shake, 708
Orange Muffins, 441
Orange or Lemon Sherbet, 710
Orange Squash, 714
Orange Wine, 701
Orchata, 706–07
Oriental Sauce, 395
Osso Bucco, 297
Ovos Duros a Portuguesa (Portuguese
    Hard-Boiled Eggs), 319

Paella à la Valencina, 288–89
Pains de Fruits, 216–17
Pal Kozhukattai, 420
Palak Panir, 380
Palmiers, 515
Pamplemousse, 8
Panagam, 417
Panakam, 718
Panetone, 576
Panir Makhani, 379–80
Papaya avec Noix et Crème, 227–28
Papaya Chillies, 658
Parang.kka Puli Curry, 411–12
Parippu Podi (dry dal chutney for idli,
    dosda, etc.), 670
Parker House Rolls, 562
Partridge (boiled with celery sauce),
    176
Partridge (braised), 177
Partridge (roast), 177–78
Paruppu Urundai Kozhambu, 415–16
Pastel de Tortillas Especial, 284
Pâté de Foie, 9–10
Pâté de Pommes, 247

Pâté Maison, 104
Pato Alcaparrada (Duck with Caper
    Sauce), 289–90
Pea Pod Wine, 700–701
Peanut Butter Cookies, 529
Peanut Cookies, 533
Peanut Macaroons, 537
Pearl Cookies, 527
Pêche Melba, 234
Pelota, 286
Penuche, 552
Pesarattu (Green Dosa), 726–27
Petite Marmite, 271
Petits Pois à la Flamande, 198–99
Petits Pois à la Française, 198
Piccalilli (A), 648; (B), 648–49; (C), 649
Piccate Milanaise, 108
Piccatta de Bœuf (Beef Piccatta),
    108–09
Pickled Beef, 660
Pickled Cauliflower, 653–54
Pickled Game, 184
Pickled Onion (A), 654; (B), 654; (C),
    654
Pickled Red Cabbage, 654–55
Pikelets, 585
Pimentos Farcis, 199
Pineapple and Cherry Cream Tartlets,
    483–84
Pineapple Chutney, 688–89
Pineapple Cocktail, 711
Pineapple Fans, 433–34
Pineapple Jam, 696
Pineapple Milk Shake, 708
Pineapple Punch, 706
Pineapple Squash, 714
Pineapple Tartlets, 482–83
Pineapple Upside Down Cake, 457–58
Pineapple Wine, 702
Pineappleade, 711–12
Pinwheel Sandwiches, 605–06
Pizza, 295–96
Plain Cake, 460
Plain Sponge Cake (creaming Method)
    (A), 448; (B) (with milk powder),
    448–49; (C) (fatless) (to be used as
    sheet), 449
Plate Tart, 489
Plum Cake, 475–76
Poêling, 145
Poireaux Braisés, 199–200
Poireaux à la Grecque, 6
Poires au Fromage Blanc, 18
Poires Condé, 232
Poires à la Florentine, 231
Poires à la Portugaise, 231–32
Poisson au Vin Blanc, 92–93

Poitrines d'Oies Fumées, 6
Pokhlyobka (Russian Country Soup),
   301
Polka Dot Cookies, 528–29
Polmallung, 369
Pomfret ou Sole Bonne Femme, 85
Pomfret ou Sole Dieppoise, 85
Pomfret ou Sole Grillée, 82–83
Pomfret ou Sole Saint Germain, 83
Pomfret Wiesbaden, 93
Pommes Allumettes, 201
Pommes Bataille, 202
Pommes Bonne Femme, 246–47
Pommes Boulangère, 202
Pommes Brioche, 203
Pommes Charlotte, 246
Pommes Château, 203
Pommes Chateâu, 209
Pommes Chips, 203
Pommes Croquettes, 204
Pommes Fondantes, 205
Pommes Gaufrettes, 205
Pommes Pailles, 207
Pommes Persillées, 201
Pommes à la Royale, 233
Pommes de Terre Anna, 201–02
Pommes de Terre Lorette, 206
Pommes de Terre à la Maître d'Hôtel,
   206
Pommes de Terre Marquise, 206
Pommes de Terre à la Menthe, 206–07
Pommes de Terre Noisette, 207
Pommes de Terre Robert, 207–08
Pommes de Terre à la Saint
   Florentine, 208
Pommes de Terre Soufflés, 208
Porcha Meen (Fried Fish), 399
Pork Fritters, 355
Potage aux Amandes, 48
Potage Ambassadeurs, 47
Potage à la Bonne Femme, 48
Potage Ciboulette, 47
Potage Fausse Tortue, 48–49
Potage à la Hollandaise, 49
Potage Longchamps, 47
Potage Marigny, 48
Potage Minestrone, 50
Potage à la Queue de Bœuf, 50–51
Potato Croquettes, 297–98
Potato Kachories, 726
Potato Kanji, 664–65
Potato Kephtides, 335–36
Potato Sticks, 505
Potato and Cheese Balls, 618
Potato and Sausage Rolls, 618–19
Potted Meat Sandwiches, 598
Pouding d'Ananas, 225

Pouding Cabinet, 238–39
Pouding Diplomate, 223
Pouding de Maïs (Corn Pudding),
   200–201
Pouding de Noël (A), 250–51
Pouding Mousseline, 238
Pouding de Noël (B), 251–52
Pouding Saxon, 239
Pouding Soufflé au Chocolat, 240
Pouding à la Viennoise, 239–40
Poularde Andalouse, 145–46
Poularde au Céleri, 146–47
Poularde Chipolata, 147–48
Poularde Demidoff, 148
Poularde Diva, 148–49
Poularde Edouard VII, 149–50
Poularde en Estouffade, 150
Poularde à la Fermière, 150
Poularde à la Grecque, 150–51
Poularde à l'Indienne, 151
Poularde Mireille, 151–52
Poularde Polignac, 153
Poularde au Riz, 152
Poularde Stanley, 152–53
Poulet en Casserole, 155–56
Poulet en Casserole Campanini avec
   Nouilles, 157–58
Poulet de Grains à la Bergère, 163–64
Poulet de Grains à la Limousine, 164
Poulet Grillé, 134
Poulet Grillé Diable, 134
Poulet à la Navaressa, 275–76
Poulet Poché au Riz (Sauce Suprême),
   153–54
Poulet à la Provençale (Chicken with
   Garlic), 276
Poulet à le Rex, 158–59
Poulet Rôti, 132
Poulet Rôti à l'Anglaise, 133
Poulet Rôti Farci aux Fines Herbs, 133
Poulet Rôti au Lard, 132
Poulet Sauté, 135
Poulet Sauté Cacciatore, 144
Poulet Sauté aux Champignons, 136
Poulet Sauté Chasseur, 136
Poulet Sauté à l'Egyptienne, 136–37
Poulet Sauté à l'Espagnole, 137
Poulet Sauté à la Fermière, 137–38
Poulet Sauté Forestière, 138
Poulet Sauté Gabrielle, 138–39
Poulet Sauté Hongroise, 139
Poulet Sauté à l'Indienne, 139–40
Poulet Sauté Lyonnaise, 140
Poulet Sauté Marengo, 140–41
Poulet Sauté Marseillaise, 141–42
Poulet Sauté Maryland, 141
Poulet Sauté Mexicaine, 142

Poulet Sauté Mireille, 142–43
Poulet Sauté Parmentier, 143
Poulet Sauté Portugaise, 143–44
Poulet Sauté Princess, 423
Poulet Sauté Roumain, 422
Poultry and Game Birds, 173–74
Pound Cake (A), 459; (B), 459
Praline Fingers, 435
Prawn Badun, 373
Prawn and Egg Sandwiches, 598
Prawn or Fish Pickle, 662–63
Prawn Paste, 676–77
Prawn Pickle (Malayalee), 662–63
Prawn Risotto, 294–95
Prawn Sandwiches, 598
Prawn/Shrimp Créole, 326
Prawn/Shrimp Gumbo, 324
Prawns in Garlic Sauce, 350–51
Preserved Chillies, 658
Preserving Pickles, 718
Provençale Sauce, 84
Psari Plaku (Baked Fish), 330–31
Psarosoupa (Greek Fish Soup), 330
Pudim de Noses, 320–21
Puff Pastry, 508
Pumpkin Dessert, 342
Pumpkin Pie, 491–92
Punjabi Picke (A), 630–31; (B), 631
Purée de Carottes, 43
Purée de Céleri Rave, 43–44
Purée Dubarry, 47
Purée de Lentlles (Purée de Conti), 44
Purée de Parmentier, 44–45
Purée de Pois aux Croûtons, 46
Purée de Pois Frais à la Menthe, 46–47
Purée de Pois Frais (Purée de Pois
    Saint Germain), 46
Purée de Tomates (Purée Portugaise),
    45
Pyramid Egg on Toast, 617

Quail, 182–83
Queen Cakes (A), 437; (B) (eggless),
    437–38
Queensbury Tarts or Boats, 484
Quenelles, 27
Queue de Bœuf Lié, 51
Quiche Lorraine, 126–27
Quick Coffee Cake, 478
Quick Sauce, 721

Rabbits, to keep, 172–73
Radish (red), 16
Raisin Wine, 701
Ranchers Fried Chicken, 394–95
Ravioli Paste, 209–10

Ravioli à l'Italienne, 210–11
Raw Papaya Chutney, 682
Red Pumpkin, 328
Reshmi Kabab, 383
Ribbon Cake, 452–53
Ribbon Sandwiches, 604, 611
Rich Flan Pastry, 499–500
Rich Fruit Cake (A), 465–66; (B), 466;
    (C), 466–67; (D), 467
Rich Walnut Pie, 494
Roast Grouse, 179
Roast Haunch of Venison, 181
Roast Quail, 179–80
Roast Snipe, 180
Roasted Spare Ribs, 317
Rock Buns (without eggs), 440–41
Rock Cakes or Buns (rub-in method),
    439
Rognons à la Brochette, 121
Rogons Brochette à l'Espagnole, 121–22
Rognons à la Diable (A), 254; (B), 254
Rognons Norvegienne, 254–55
Rognons Sautés Bercy, 118–19
Rognons Sautés Bordelaise, 119–20
Rognons Sautés Chasseur, 120
Rognons Sautés Hongroise, 120
Rognons Sautés à l'Indienne, 121
Rognons Sautés à la Turbigo, 122
Rolled Sandwiches, 605
Roselle Jelly, 699
Rôti de Porc à ma Façon, 275
Rotie à la Lucille, 7
Rough Puff Pastry, 505–06
Royal Icing, 443
Rum Savarin, 249–50
Rum Syrup, 237
Russian Sandwich, 450–51

Salade Russe, 13
Salade de Betterave, 14
Salade de Concombres, 15
Salade de Haricots Verts, 16
Salade de Homard, 96
Salade de Poisson, 13–14
Salade de Pommes de Terre, 12
Salade de Saumon, 79–80
Salade de Thon, 17
Salade de Tomate et Concombres, 15
Salade de Tomate, 15
Salade de Viande, 14
Sally Lunn, 580
Salmis of Pheasant, 178
Salmon Sandwiches, 598–99
Salmon à la Alicantina, 285
Salted Meat, 661
Salted ox Tongue, 123

Samba Saadam, 407
Sambharam, 716
Sandwich Loaf, 602
Sandwich Plates, 609–11
Sardinas Fritas (Fresh Fried
    Sardines), 285
Sardine and Egg Sandwiches, 599–600
Sardine Marguerites, 501
Sardine Rolls, 615
Sardine Sandwiches (A), 599; (B), 599
Sardine-Stuffed Eggs, 615–16
Sardine, Tomato and Egg Flan, 492–93
Sardines en Croûtes, 257
Sardines à la Diable, 253–54
Sardines à l'Huile, 11
Sarsaparilla Syrup, 713
Satpura Parathas, 725
Sauce (Espagnole and Réforme), 115
Saucisson, 7
Saumon à la Bretonne, 274
Saumon Fumé, 6, 9
Saumon Grillé, 77
Saumon à la Meunière, 78
Saumon Mayonnaise, 77
Saumon Poché, 76
Saumon Royale, 78–79
Saurbraten, 321–22
Savouries (Bonnes Bouches), 252
Savoury Butters, 592–93
Savoury Meat Toast, 617
Savoury Minced Meat Balls, 620–21
Savoury Picnic Rolls, 560
Savoy Biscuits, 534
Scrambled Egg Crêpes, 260–61
Seafood Favourites, 502
Seasoning of a Chinese Wok, 343
Seed Cake (rub-in method), 463
Seeni Sambal, 370
Selle d'Agneau Rôti, 112
Senai Poriyal, 414
Sesame Queens, 529–30
Shellfish Cocktail Sauce, 11
Shish Kebab, 339
Shortbread, 522–23
Shortcrust Pastry, 480–81
Shrewsbury Biscuits (A), 539; (B), 539
Shrimp Rarebit, 615
Simple Roast Wild Duck, 180–81
Small Cakes, 430
Smoked Pomfret (A), 377–78; (B), 378
Soft Jaggery Biscuits, 536
Sombrero Snack, 622
Soufflé d'Ananas (A), 240–41
Soufflé à l'Ananas (B), 241
Soufflé au Caramel, 244
Soufflé au Chocolat (A), 242; (B),
    242–44

Soufflé au Chocolat Praline, 221
Soufflé au Fromage, 262
Soufflé à l'Indienne, 239
Soufflé à la Milanaise, 220–21
Soufflé aux Lichis, 241–42
Soufflé de Pommes de Terre, 208–09
Soufflés au Jambon, 125
Soupa Avgolemono (Chicken, Egg and
    Lemon Soup), 329–30
Soupe Cockie Leekie, 56
Soupe aux Gombos au Okra, 53–54
Soupe à l'Oignon à la Française, 54
Soupe Vichyssoise, 55
Sour Cream Sauce, 303
Spaghetti à la Créole, 212–13
Spaghetti with Meat Balls, 294
Spaghetti avec Sauce Barbaque, 214
Spaghetti avec Sauce Champignons et
    Fromage, 214–15
Spaghetti Tetrazzini Armando, 212
Spanish Rice Omelette, 288
Spanish Rice, 287
Sparkling Lemonade, 715
Spicy Chicken Sauté, 393–94
Spinach and Mushroom Quiche, 127–28
Spinazie Soep (Spinach Soup), 309
Sponge Fruit Flan, 450
Spring Soup, 314
Steak and Kidney Pie, 102–03
Stewed Noodles, 361–62
Stewed Steak and Onions, 102
Strawberry Cocktail, 323
Strawberry Cream Fingers, 531
Stuben Kuecken, 280
Studen (Calf's Foot Jelly), 299–300
Stuffed Fish, 303–04
Stuffed Heart, 129–30
Stuffed Meat Loaf, 305–06
Sugarcane Vinegar, 717
Suggested Spreads, 611–12
Suki Yaki, 366
Sultana and Cherry Cake, 468–69
Sultana Buns, 439
Sun Cake, 458–59
Suprême de Volaille à la Kiev, 158
Surti Nankhatai, 583–84
Swedish Slices (sweet shortcrust
    pastry), 488–89
Swedish Tea Ring, 562
Sweet and Sour Chicken, 356–57
Sweet and Sour Chutney, 677
Sweet and Sour Fish, 352
Sweet and Sour Pork (A), 353–54; (B),
    354; (C), 354–55
Sweet and Sour Prawns, 352–53
Sweet Corn and Chicken Soup, 343
Sweet Dough (rich), 576–77

Sweet Dough (lean), 575–76
Sweet Dough Almond Tea Loaf, 575
Sweet Dough Swedish Tea Ring, 575
Sweet Mango Chutney, 680
Sweet Tail, 576
Swiss Cheese Fondue, 168–69
Swiss Patties, 619
Swiss Roll, 449
Swiss Tarts, 530

Tahitian Chicken Sauté, 374–75
Tamago Suimono (Egg Soup), 365
Tamarind Chutney, 687–88
Tamarind Drink, 717
Tamarind Lethoka, 368
Tandoori Chicken, 391–92
Tangerine au Blancmange, 233
Tangerine Chartreuse, 217
Tangri Kabab (A), 383–84; (B), 384
Tarte aux Crevettes, 511–12
Tartelettes au Fromage, 258–59
Tartelettes de Thon, 6
Tea Cake, 460–61
Tea Punch, 705–06
Tea Scones, 584
Tempura (Fried Fish), 365–66
Tenderloin, 103–04
Thengai Chutney, 419
Thon, 11
Thon à l'Huile, 6
Thon à la Marinette, 6
Thuvayyel, 675
Times to Allow for Cooking Poultry
    and Game by Various Methods,
    184–85
Tips on Making Perfect Candy, 540
To Cook and Clean Lobster or
    Langoustes, 93–94
To Preserve Your Pickles, 718
Toddy Buns, 559
Tom Yom, 421
Tomate, 15
Tomates aux Crevettes (Tomatoes with
    Shrimps), 270
Tomates à la Monégasque, 6
Tomates au Naturel, 6
Tomates en Quartiers, 6–7
Tomato Bisque Cocktail, 716
Tomato Cheese Toast, 612–13
Tomato Chutney (A), 686; (B), 686;
    (C), 686–87; (D), 687
Tomato Chutney, 419–20
Tomato Juice Cocktail, 322
Tomato Ketchup (mild), 691
Tomato Ketchup (spiced), 691–92
Tomato Sandwiches, 600

Tomato Sauce, 689
Tomato Shorba, 377
Tomatoes with Sardine Stuffing, 320
Topinambours à la Crème, 187
Tortillas, 284–85
Tournedos Arlésienne, 99
Tournedos Béarnaise, 99–100
Tournedos Bercy, 100
Tournedos Chasseur, 100–101
Tournedos Forestière, 101
Tournedos à la Mexicaine, 101
Tournedos Parmentier, 101–02
Tournedos, 99
Tricolour Biscuits, 526–27
Trifle Alaska, 236–37
True Love, 601
Tuna and Chilli Fondue, 170
Tuna Puffs, 327
Turkish Coffee, 342
Turquoise (Yoghurt Soup), 338
Tutti Fruitti Fudge, 545–46
Tzaziki, 335

Uncooked Fondant, 547
Uppu Curry (Mutton Salt Curry), 406

Vadukapuli Naranga, 646
Vanilla Biscuits, 534–35
Vanilla Buns, 430–31
Vanilla Glacé, 234
Variantes, 8–9
Variation of Charlotte Russe, 218
Veal and Ham Pie, 504
Vegetable Chow Chow, 350
Vegetable Egg Cream Soup, 346
Vegetable Fried Rice, 364
Vegetable Jalfraizi, 378–79
Vegetable Quiche, 128–29
Velouté d'Artois, 52
Velouté aux Concombres (Velouté
    Danoise), 51–52
Velouté Dame Blanche, 52–53
Velouté Marie Louise, 53
Velouté Marie Stuart, 53
Velouté Sauce, 52
Velvet Cake, 456–57
Vendakai Mandi, 416–17
Vendakai More Kozhumbu, 416
Venison, 173, 181; to keep, 172;
    seasoning for and selection of, 173
Victoria Sandwich Cake, 460
Vischkoekjes (Fish Cakes), 309
Vol-au-Vent de Volaille, 161
Volailles, 131

Waffles, 261
Waldorf Salad, 328
Walnut Coffee Fudge, 544
Walnut Fudge, 546
Walnut Rolls, 562–63
Walnut Sultana Cake, 458
Watermelon Pickle, 663–64
Wedding Cake, 476–77
Wedding Soup, 337–38
Welsh Cheesecake, 485
Welsh Rarebit (A), 613; (B), 613
White Coleslaw, 313
White Consommé, 19–20
Whole Mango Pickle, 628–29
Whole Wheat Bread (100%), 574
Wiener Schnitzel (A), 106; (B), 106–07
Wild Duck, hanging of, preparation of,
    174
Wonton Soup, 348–49

Wontons, 347–48
Woodapple Chutney, 688
Woodapple Punch, 706

Yakhni Shorba, 376–77
Yeast Doughnuts, 579–80
Yeast Rolls (with egg), 561–62
Yeast Rolls (with eggs and dried milk),
    562
Yeera Masala (Prawn Masala), 398
Youvarlakia with Avgo Lemono Sauce,
    333

Zabaglione, 298
Zuppa Paradiso, 292
Zuppa Pavese (Chicken Soup with
    Poached Eggs), 292–93